THE MACARTHUR NEW TESTAMENT COMMENTARY

MATTHEW 1-7

John MacArthur, Jr.

MOODY PRESS/CHICAGO

© 1985 by
THE MOODY BIBLE INSTITUTE
OF CHICAGO

Unless noted otherwise, all Scripture quotations in this book are from *The New American Standard Bible,* © 1960, 1962, 1963, 1968, 1971, 1972, 1973, 1975, and 1977 by The Lockman Foundation, and are used by permission.

Library of Congress Cataloging in Publication Data

MacArthur, John F.
  Matthew 1-7.

  (The MacArthur New Testament commentary)
  Bibliography: p.
  Includes indexes.
  1. Bible. N.T. Matthew—Commentaries. I. Title.
II. Series: MacArthur, John F. MacArthur New
Testament commentary.
BS2575.3.M24 1985   226'.2077   85-15225
ISBN 0-8024-0755-2

234567 Printing/RR/Year 89 88 87 86 85

Printed in the United States of America

To Fred Barshaw,
diligent colaborer and
loyal personal friend

Contents

Preface

It continues to be a rewarding divine communion for me to preach expositionally through the New Testament. My goal is always to have deep fellowship with the Lord in the understanding of His Word, and out of that experience to explain to His people what a passage means. In the words of Nehemiah 8:8, I strive "to give the sense" of it so they may truly hear God speak and, in so doing, may respond to Him.

Obviously, God's people need to understand Him, which demands knowing His Word of truth (2 Tim. 2:15) and allowing that Word to dwell in us richly (Col. 3:16). The dominant thrust of my ministry, therefore, is to help make God's living Word alive to His people. It is a refreshing adventure.

This New Testament commentary series reflects this objective of explaining and applying Scripture. Some commentaries are primarily linguistic, others are mostly theological, and some are mainly homiletical. This one is basically explanatory, or expository. It is not linguistically technical, but deals with linguistics when this seems helpful to proper interpretation. It is not theologically expansive, but focuses on the major doctrines in each text and on how they relate to the whole of Scripture. It is not primarily homiletical, though each unit of thought is generally treated as one chapter, with a clear outline and logical flow of thought. Most truths are illustrated and applied with other Scripture. After establishing the context of a passage, I have tried to follow closely the writer's development and reasoning.

My prayer is that each reader will fully understand what the Holy Spirit is saying through this part of His Word, so that His revelation may lodge in the minds of believers and bring greater obedience and faithfulness—to the glory of our great God.

Introduction

The central personality of Old Testament prophecy is the coming great King who will rule in God's promised kingdom. Over and over we are told of a special individual who has the righteousness, the wisdom, the power, the authority, and the right to reign not only over Israel but over the entire earth.

This coming great King will have the power to bruise Satan's head (Gen. 3:15), take back man's dominion that was lost through sin, and establish at last a kingdom on earth that will extend into eternity. From Him the "scepter shall not depart from Judah, nor the ruler's staff from between his feet" (Gen. 49:10). That could not be said of any Old Testament king, and could only apply to the coming great King. The host of other predictions that refer to a reign described by such terms as everlasting, eternal, and forever obviously could not apply to a merely human king.

The words of the Lord spoken to David through Nathan had to refer to other than David himself: "And your house and your kingdom shall endure before Me forever; your throne shall be established forever" (2 Sam. 7:16). David's kingdom was shattered and divided as soon as his successor, Solomon, died—and as yet has never been reestablished.

Yet in Psalm 2 God tells us, "But as for Me, I have installed My King upon Zion, My holy mountain. I will surely tell of the decree of the Lord: He said to Me, 'Thou art My Son, today I have begotten Thee. Ask of Me, and I will surely give the nations as Thine inheritance, and the very ends of the earth as Thy possession'" (vv. 6-8). David calls the coming One "the King of glory" and "the Lord of hosts" (Ps. 24:10). The coming King is spoken of in similar ways in Psalms 45, 72, 110, and others.

The prophets speak of the great King as both human and divine. Isaiah tells us that He would be born of a virgin (7:14) and that He would be despised, forsaken, stricken, pierced through, crushed, chastened, scourged, oppressed, and afflicted (53:3-7). Daniel speaks of Him as "One like a Son of Man" (7:13). Yet Isaiah also tells us that "the government will rest on His shoulders; and His name will be called Wonderful Counselor, Mighty God, Eternal Father, Prince of Peace. There will be no end to the increase of His government or of peace" (9:6-7) and that He will be called "Immanuel," which means "God with us" (Isa. 7:14; Matt. 1:23). Through Micah, the Lord promised Bethlehem: "From you One will go forth for Me to be ruler in Israel. His goings forth are from long ago, from the days of eternity" (5:2). Zephaniah tells his people that when this King comes He will be "the King of Israel, the Lord" in their midst (3:15). Zechariah tells us that He will "be just and endowed with salvation" (9:9) and that when He reigns, every family on earth will be able to "go up to Jerusalem to worship the King, the Lord of hosts" (14:17). The coming great King would be the Man-God.

None of those ancient writers comprehended the full nature of the One of whom they prophesied. "As to this salvation," Peter tells us, "the prophets who prophesied of the grace that would come to you made careful search and inquiry, seeking to know what person or time the Spirit of Christ [that is, Messiah] within them was indicating as He predicted the sufferings of Christ and the glories to follow" (1 Pet. 1:10-11).

The full identity and nature of the predicted King are initially presented and explained in the gospels, of which Matthew is the first. Like a divine spotlight they focus on Jesus and, through one event after another, show Him to be the only One who fulfills all the requirements of those prophesies. By the same token all impostors are unmasked by their inability to fit the predictions.

The whole New Testament acknowledges Jesus as the promised great King. In its twenty-seven books the term *basileia* (kingdom) is used one hundred forty-four times in referring to the reign of Jesus Christ; *basileus* (king) is used directly of Jesus at least thirty-five times; and *basileuō* (to reign) is used of Him some ten times.

AUTHORSHIP

At the time Christ was born, Israel had been under Roman domination for some sixty years. One of the worst aspects of Roman oppression was the system of taxation, which was methodical, relentless, and ruthless. Two basic taxes were levied—the toll tax, which was comparable to the modern income tax, and the ground tax, a property and land tax.

Roman senators and various other high-ranking officials would buy from the central government at public auction the right of collecting the toll taxes in a given country, province, or region at a fixed rate for a period of five years. Whatever was collected above that amount was kept as profit. Those who held such taxing rights were called *publicani*. The *publicani* would hire others, usually citizens of the country being taxed, to do the actual collecting.

Those collectors had somewhat the same arrangement with the *publicani* that the *publicani* had with Rome. Whatever they managed to collect above the amount demanded by the *publicani* they kept as their own profit. Both the *publicani* and the tax-gatherers, therefore, had strong motivation to exact and collect as much tax as possible—knowing they were backed by the full authority, including the military authority, of Rome.

The tax-gatherers (Greek *telōnēs*) quite naturally were hated by their own people, not only as extortioners but as traitors. In Israel they were ranked with the lowest of human society—sinners, prostitutes, and Gentiles (Matt. 9:10-11; 18:17; 21:31-32; Mark 2:15-16; Luke 5:30; etc.).

Matthew, who was also called Levi, was a tax-gatherer when Jesus called him to be one of the twelve disciples (Matt. 9:9; Mark 2:14). We have little idea as to what sort of person Matthew was before Jesus called him. It is doubtful that he was very religious, because tax-gatherers were ostracized, practically if not officially, from many synagogues and sometimes even from the Temple. It was no doubt partly for that reason that Matthew so quickly responded to Jesus' invitation and that so many other tax-gatherers were attracted to Him (Matt. 9:9-10; 11:19; Luke 15:1). It was rare that they were accepted and befriended by a fellow Jew, especially by a rabbi, or teacher, such as Jesus.

Matthew was particularly modest in writing his gospel account. He always refers to himself in the third person and nowhere speaks of himself as the author. We know of his authorship because his name is attached to all early copies of the manuscripts and because the early church Fathers unanimously attest him to be the book's author.

It is obvious from the text itself that Matthew wrote this gospel before the destruction of Jerusalem and the Temple in A.D. 70. Apart from that general dating, it is impossible to be dogmatic as to a specific year.

MESSAGE

The first four books of the New Testament report the same gospel account, but from four distinct perspectives. They give the same message with differing but perfectly harmonious emphases. Matthew presents Jesus as the sovereign, whereas Mark presents Him in the extreme opposite role as servant. Luke presents Him as the Son of Man, whereas John presents Him as the Son of God. The same Jesus is shown to be both sovereign God and servant Man.

In presenting the sovereignty of Jesus, Matthew begins his gospel with the genealogy of the Lord—going back to Abraham, the father of the Hebrew people, through King David, Israel's model king. In presenting Jesus' servanthood, Mark gives no genealogy at all, because a servant's lineage is irrelevant. In presenting

Jesus as the Son of Man, Luke traces His genealogy back to the first man, Adam. In presenting Jesus as the divine Son of God, John gives no human genealogy or birth and childhood narratives. He opens his gospel by giving, as it were, Jesus' divine genealogy: "In the beginning was the Word, and the Word was with God, and the Word was God" (John 1:1).

The message of the book of Matthew centers on the theme of Jesus' kingship. Just as virtually every paragraph of the gospel of John points to something of Christ's deity, so virtually every paragraph of Matthew points to something of His kingship.

Matthew presents the Messiah King who is *revealed,* the King who is *rejected,* and the King who will *return.* Jesus is painted in royal colors in this gospel as in none of the others. His ancestry is traced from the royal line of Israel; his birth is dreaded by a jealous earthly king; the magi bring the infant Jesus royal gifts from the east; and John the Baptist heralds the King and proclaims that His kingdom is at hand. Even the temptations in the wilderness climax with Satan offering Jesus the kingdoms of this world. The Sermon on the Mount is the manifesto of the King, the miracles are His royal credentials, and many of the parables portray the mysteries of His kingdom. Jesus identifies Himself with the king's son in a parable and makes a royal entry into Jerusalem. While facing the cross He predicts His future reign, and He claims dominion over the angels in heaven. His last words are that all authority has been given to Him in both heaven and earth (28:18).

Yet Matthew also focuses most uniquely on the rejection of Jesus as King. In no other gospel are the attacks against Jesus' character and Jesus' claims so bitter and vile as those reported in Matthew. The shadow of rejection is never lifted from Matthew's story. Before Jesus was born, His mother, Mary, was in danger of being rejected by Joseph. Soon after He was born, Herod threatened His life, and His parents had to flee with Him to Egypt. His herald, John the Baptist, was put in a dungeon and eventually beheaded. During His earthly ministry Jesus had no place to lay His head, no place to call home. In Matthew's gospel no penitent thief acknowledges Jesus' Lordship, and no friend or loved one is seen at the foot of the cross—only the mockers and scorners. Even the women are pictured at a distance (27:55-56), and in His death Jesus cries out, "My God, My God, why hast Thou forsaken Me?" (27:46). Only a Gentile centurion speaks a favorable word about the crucified One: "Truly this was the Son of God!" (27:54). When some of the soldiers who had stood guard over the tomb reported its being empty, the Jewish authorities paid them to say that Jesus' body was stolen by His disciples (28:11-15).

Yet Jesus is also shown as the King who ultimately will return to judge and to rule. All the earth one day "will see the Son of Man coming on the clouds of the sky with power and great glory" (24:30), His coming will be "at an hour when you do not think He will" (v. 44), and He will come in glory and in judgment (25:31-33).

No reader can fully immerse himself in this gospel without emerging with a compelling sense of both the eternal majesty of the Lord Jesus Christ and the strong power that sin and Satan held over the apostate Israel that rejected Christ.

No gospel is more instructive to those who are the Lord's disciples and who are called to represent Him in the world. The lessons on discipleship are life-changing for the committed reader, as they were for the eleven who were Jesus' first followers. Thus, with all its great themes of majesty and glory, rejection and apostasy, the book of Matthew lacks no practicality. Woven through all that is the constant thread of revealed instruction for those who are His representatives among men.

Outline

The King's ancestry—His genealogy (1:1-17)
The King's arrival—His virgin birth (1:18-25)
The King's adoration—the worship of the magi (2:1-12)
The King's anticipation—the fulfilled prophecies of His coming (2:13-23)
The King's announcer—John the Baptist (3:1-12)
The King's affirmation—His baptism; His sonship affirmed by the Father (3:13-17)
The King's advantage—His defeat of Satan (4:1-11)
The King's activity—His ministry and miracles (4:12-25)
The King's address—His manifesto: The Sermon on the Mount (5-7)
 Righteousness and happiness (5:1-12)
 Righteousness and discipleship (5:13-16)
 Righteousness and the Scriptures (5:17-20)
 Righteousness and morality (5:21-48)
 Righteousness and practical religion (6:1-18)
 Righteousness and mundane things (6:19-34)
 Righteousness and human relations (7:1-12)
 Righteousness and salvation (7:13-29)

The Gracious King (1:1-17)

The book of the genealogy of Jesus Christ, the son of David, the son of Abraham.

 To Abraham was born Isaac; and to Isaac, Jacob; and to Jacob, Judah and his brothers; and to Judah were born Perez and Zerah by Tamar; and to Perez was born Hezron; and to Hezron, Ram; and to Ram was born Amminadab; and to Amminadab, Nahshon; and to Nahshon, Salmon; and to Salmon was born Boaz by Rahab; and to Boaz was born Obed by Ruth; and to Obed, Jesse; and to Jesse was born David the king. And to David was born Solomon by her who had been the wife of Uriah; and to Solomon was born Rehoboam; and to Rehoboam, Abijah; and to Abijah, Asa; and to Asa was born Jehoshaphat; and to Jehoshaphat, Joram; and to Joram, Uzziah; and to Uzziah was born Jotham; and to Jotham, Ahaz; and to Ahaz, Hezekiah; and to Hezekiah was born Manasseh; and to Manasseh, Amon; and to Amon, Josiah; and to Josiah were born Jeconiah and his brothers, at the time of the deportation to Babylon.

 And after the deportation to Babylon, to Jeconiah was born Shealtiel; and to Shealtiel, Zerubbabel; and to Zerubbabel was born Abiud; and to Abiud, Eliakim; and to Eliakim, Azor; and to Azor was born Zadok; and to Zadok, Achim; and to Achim, Eliud; and to Eliud was born Eleazar; and to Eleazar, Matthan; and to Matthan, Jacob; and to Jacob was born Joseph the husband of Mary, by whom was born Jesus, who is called Christ.

Therefore all the generations from Abraham to David are fourteen generations; and from David to the deportation to Babylon fourteen generations; and from the deportation to Babylon to the time of Christ fourteen generations. (1:1-17)

As discussed in the introduction, one of Matthew's major purposes in his gospel, and the primary purpose of chapters 1 and 2, is to establish Jesus' right to Israel's kingship. To any honest observer, and certainly to Jews who knew and believed their own Scriptures, these two chapters vindicate Jesus' claim before Pilate: "You say correctly that I am a king. For this I have been born, and for this I have come into the world" (John 18:37).

Consistent with that purpose of revealing Jesus to be the Christ (Messiah) and the King of the Jews, Matthew begins his gospel by showing Jesus' lineage from the royal line of Israel. If Jesus is to be heralded and proclaimed king there must be proof that He comes from the recognized royal family.

Messiah's royal line began with David. Through the prophet Nathan, God promised that it would be David's descendants through whom He would bring the great King who would ultimately reign over Israel and establish His eternal kingdom (2 Sam. 7:12-16). The promise was not fulfilled in Solomon, David's son who succeeded him, or in any other king who ruled in Israel or Judah; and the people waited for another one to be born of David's line to fulfill the prophecy. At the time Jesus was born the Jews were still anticipating the arrival of the promised monarch and the restored glory of the kingdom.

The Jews' concern for pedigrees, however, existed long before they had a king. After they entered Canaan under Joshua and conquered the region God had promised to them, the land was carefully and precisely divided into territories for each tribe—except the priestly tribe of Levi, for whom special cities were designated. In order to know where to live, each Israelite family had to determine accurately the tribe to which it belonged (see Num. 26; 34-35). And in order to qualify for priestly function, a Levite had to prove his descent from Levi. After the return from exile in Babylon, certain "sons of the priests" were not allowed to serve in the priesthood because "their ancestral registration . . . could not be located" (Ezra 2:61-62).

The transfer of property also required accurate knowledge of the family tree (see, e.g., Ruth 3-4). Even under Roman rule, the census of Jews in Palestine was based on tribe—as can be seen from the fact that Joseph and Mary were required to register in "Bethlehem, because he [Joseph] was of the house and family of David" (Luke 2:4). We learn from the Jewish historian Josephus that in New Testament times many Jewish families maintained detailed and highly valued ancestral files. Before his conversion, the apostle Paul had been greatly concerned about his lineage from "the tribe of Benjamin" (see Rom. 11:1; 2 Cor. 11:22; Phil. 3:5). For Jews, tribal identification and line of descent were all-important.

It is both interesting and significant that since the destruction of the Temple in A.D. 70 no genealogies exist that can trace the ancestry of any Jew now living. The primary significance of that fact is that, for those Jews who still look for the Messiah, his lineage to David could never be established. Jesus Christ is the last verifiable claimant to the throne of David, and therefore to the messianic line.

Matthew's genealogy presents a descending line, from **Abraham** through **David**, through **Joseph**, to **Jesus, who is called Christ**. Luke's genealogy presents an ascending line, starting from Jesus and going back through David, Abraham, and even to "Adam, the son of God" (Luke 3:23-38). Luke's record is apparently traced from Mary's side, the Eli of Luke 3:23 probably being Joseph's father-in-law (often referred to as a father) and therefore Mary's natural father. Matthew's intent is to validate Jesus' royal claim by showing His legal descent from David through Joseph, who was Jesus' legal, though not natural, father. Luke's intent is to trace Jesus' actual royal blood ancestry through his mother, thereby establishing His racial lineage from David. Matthew follows the royal line through David and Solomon, David's son and successor to the throne. Luke follows the royal line through Nathan, another son of David. Jesus was therefore the blood descendant of David through Mary and the legal descendant of David through Joseph. Genealogically, Jesus was perfectly qualified to take the throne of David.

It is essential to note that in His virgin birth Jesus not only was divinely conceived but through that miracle was protected from regal disqualification because of Joseph's being a descendant of **Jeconiah** (v. 12). Because of that king's wickedness, God had declared of Jeconiah (also called Jehoiachin or Coniah) that, though he was in David's line, "no man of his descendants will prosper, sitting on the throne of David or ruling again in Judah" (Jer. 22:30). That curse would have precluded Jesus' right to kingship had He been the natural son of Joseph, who was in Jeconiah's line. Jesus' legal descent from David, which was always traced through the father, came through Jeconiah to Joseph. But His blood descent, *and His human right to rule,* came through Mary, who was not in Jeconiah's lineage. Thus the curse on Jeconiah's offspring was circumvented, while still maintaining the royal privilege.

The book of the genealogy of Jesus Christ, the son of David, the son of Abraham. (1:1)

Biblos (**book**) can also refer to a record or account, as is the case here. Matthew is giving a brief record of **the genealogy** (*genesis,* "beginning, origin") **of Jesus Christ. Jesus** is from the Greek equivalent of Jeshua, or Jehoshua, which means "Jehovah (Yahweh) saves." It was the name the angel told Joseph to give to the Son who had been miraculously conceived in his betrothed, Mary, because this One who would soon be born would indeed "save His people from their sins" (Matt. 1:21). *Christos* (**Christ**) is the Greek form of the Hebrew *māshîaḥ* (Eng., messiah), which means "anointed one." Israel's prophets, priests, and kings were anointed, and Jesus was anointed as all three. He was *the* Anointed One, *the* Messiah, whom the Jews had long expected to come as their great deliverer and monarch.

Yet because of their unbelief and misunderstanding of Scripture, many Jews refused to recognize Jesus as the Christ, the Messiah. Some rejected Him for the very reason that His parents *were* known to them. When He went back to His hometown of Nazareth He "began teaching them in their synagogue, so that they became astonished, and said, 'Where did this man get this wisdom, and these miraculous powers? Is not this the carpenter's son? Is not His mother called Mary, and His brothers, James and Joseph and Simon and Judas? And His sisters, are they not all with us?'" (Matt. 13:54-56). On another occasion, others in Jerusalem said of Jesus, "The rulers do not really know that this is the Christ, do they? However, we know where this man is from; but whenever the Christ may come, no one knows where He is from" (John 7:26-27). A short while later, "Some of the multitude therefore, when they heard these words, were saying, 'This certainly is the Prophet.' Others were saying, 'This is the Christ.' Still others were saying, 'Surely the Christ is not going to come from Galilee, is He?'" (John 7:40-41). Still others, better taught in the Scriptures but unaware of Jesus' lineage and birthplace, said, "Has not the Scripture said that the Christ comes from the offspring of David, and from Bethlehem, the village where David was?" (v. 42).

The genealogy establishes the Messiah's royal lineage. Matthew's intent is not to have the reader digress into a study of each person listed, but is to show that all of these persons point to the royalty of Christ.

THE GRACIOUS KING

Even so, from Matthew's genealogy we learn more than Jesus' lineage. We also see beautiful reflections of God's grace. Jesus was sent by a God of grace to be a King of grace. He would not be a King of law and of iron force, but a King of grace. His royal credentials testify of royal grace. And the people He chose to be His ancestors reveal the wonder of grace, and give hope to all sinners.

The graciousness of this King and of the God who sent Him can be seen in the genealogy in four places and ways. We will look at these in logical, rather than chronological, order.

THE GRACE OF GOD SEEN IN THE CHOICE OF ONE WOMAN

And to Jacob was born Joseph the husband of Mary, by whom was born Jesus, who is called Christ. (1:16)

God showed His grace to Mary by choosing her to be the mother of Jesus. Although descended from the royal line of David, Mary was an ordinary, unknown young woman. Contrary to claims of her own immaculate conception (her being conceived miraculously in her own mother's womb), Mary was just as much a sinner as all other human beings ever born. She was likely much better, morally and spiritually, than most people of her time, but she was not sinless. She was deeply devout and faithful to the Lord, as she demonstrated by her humble and submissive response to the angel's announcement (Luke 1:38).

Mary needed a Savior, as she herself acknowledged at the very beginning of her song of praise, often called the Magnificat: "My soul exalts the Lord, and my spirit has rejoiced in God my Savior. For He has had regard for the humble state of His bondslave" (Luke 1:46-48). The notions of her being co-redemptrix and co-mediator with Christ are wholly unscriptural and were never a part of early church doctrine. Those heretical ideas came into the church several centuries later, through accommodations to pagan myths that originated in the Babylonian mystery religions.

Nimrod, a grandson of Ham, one of Noah's three sons, founded the great cities of Babel (Babylon), Erech, Accad, Calneh, and Nineveh (Gen. 10:10-11). It was at Babel that the first organized system of idolatry began with the tower built there. Nimrod's wife, Semiramis, became the first high priestess of idolatry, and Babylon became the fountainhead of all evil systems of religion. In the last days, "the great harlot" will have written on her forehead, "BABYLON THE GREAT, THE MOTHER OF HARLOTS AND OF THE ABOMINATIONS OF THE EARTH" (Rev. 17:5). When Babylon was destroyed, the pagan high priest at that time fled to Pergamum (or Pergamos; called "where Satan's throne is" in Rev. 2:13) and then to Rome. By the fourth century A.D. much of the polytheistic paganism of Rome had found its way into the church. It was from that source that the ideas of Lent, of Mary's immaculate conception, and of her being the "queen of heaven" originated. In the pagan legends, Semiramis was miraculously conceived by a sunbeam, and her son, Tammuz, was killed and was raised from the dead after forty days of fasting by his mother (the origin of Lent). The same basic legends were found in counterpart religions throughout the ancient world. Semiramis was known variously as Ashtoreth, Isis, Aphrodite, Venus, and Ishtar. Tammuz was known as Baal, Osiris, Eros, and Cupid.

Those pagan systems had infected Israel centuries before the coming of Christ. It was to Ishtar, "the queen of heaven," that the wicked and rebellious Israelite exiles in Egypt insisted on turning (Jer. 44:17-19; cf. 7:18). While exiled in Babylon with his fellow Jews, Ezekiel had a vision from the Lord about the "abominations" some Israelites were committing even in the Temple at Jerusalem— practices that included "weeping for Tammuz" (Ezek. 8:13-14). Here we see some of the origins of the mother-child cult, which has drawn Mary into its grasp.

The Bible knows nothing of Mary's grace except that which she received from the Lord. She was the recipient, never the dispenser, of grace. The literal translation of "favored one" (Luke 1:28) is "one endued with grace." Just as all the rest of fallen mankind, Mary needed God's grace and salvation. That is why she "rejoiced in God [her] Savior" (Luke 1:47). She received a special measure of the Lord's grace by being chosen to be the mother of Jesus; but she was never a source of grace. God's grace chose a sinful woman to have the unequaled privilege of giving birth to the Messiah.

THE GRACE OF GOD SEEN IN THE DESCENDANTS OF TWO MEN

The book of the genealogy of Jesus Christ, the son of David, the son of Abraham. (1:1)

Both **David** and **Abraham** were sinners, yet by God's grace they were ancestors of the Messiah, the **Christ**.

David sinned terribly in committing adultery with Bathsheba and then compounded the sin by having her husband, Uriah, killed so that he could marry her. As a warrior he had slaughtered countless men, and for that reason was not allowed to build the Temple (1 Chron. 22:8). David was a classic example of a poor father, who failed to discipline his children, one of whom (Absalom) even tried to usurp the throne from his own father by armed rebellion.

Abraham, though a man of great faith, twice lied about his wife, Sarah. Out of fear for his life and lack of trust in God, he told two different pagan kings that she was his sister (Gen. 12:11-19; 20:1-18). In so doing he brought shame on Sarah, on himself, and on the God in whom he believed and whom he claimed to serve.

Yet God made Abraham the father of His chosen people, Israel, from whom the Messiah would arise; and He made David father of the royal line from whom the Messiah would descend. Jesus was the Son of David by royal descent and Son of Abraham by racial descent.

God's grace also extended to the intervening descendants of those two men. Isaac was the son of promise, and a type of the sacrificial Savior, being himself willingly offered to God (Gen. 22:1-13). God gave the name of Isaac's son, Jacob, (later renamed Israel) to His chosen people. Jacob's sons (Judah and his brothers) became heads of the tribes of Israel. All of those men were sinful and at times were weak and unfaithful. But God was continually faithful to them, and His grace was always with them, even in times of rebuke and discipline.

Solomon, David's son and successor to the throne, was peaceful and wise, but also in many ways foolish. He sowed seeds of both domestic and spiritual corruption by marrying hundreds of wives—most of them from pagan countries throughout the world of that time. They turned Solomon's heart, and the hearts of many other Israelites, away from the Lord (1 Kings 11:1-8). The unity of Israel was broken, and the kingdom soon became divided. But the royal line remained unbroken, and God's promise to David eventually was fulfilled. God's grace prevailed.

A careful look at the descendants both of Abraham and of David (vv. 2-16) reveals people who were often characterized by unfaithfulness, immorality, idolatry, and apostasy. But God's dealing with them was always characterized by grace. **Jesus Christ, the son of David, the son of Abraham,** was sent to overcome the failures of both those men and of all their descendants, and to accomplish what they could never have accomplished. The King of grace came through the line of two sinful men.

THE GRACE OF GOD SEEN IN THE HISTORY OF THREE ERAS

Therefore all the generations from Abraham to David are fourteen generations; and from David to the deportation to Babylon fourteen generations; and from the deportation to Babylon to the time of Christ fourteen generations. (1:17)

From Matthew's summary of the genealogy we see God's grace at work in three periods, or eras, of Israel's history.

The first period, **from Abraham to David,** was that of the patriarchs, and of Moses, Joshua, and the judges. It was a period of wandering, of enslavement in a foreign land, of deliverance, of covenant-making and law-giving, and of conquest and victory.

The second period, **from David to the deportation to Babylon,** was that of the monarchy, when Israel, having insisted on having human kings like all the nations around them, discovered that those kings more often led them away from God and into trouble than to God and into peace and prosperity. That was a period of almost uninterrupted decline, degeneracy, apostasy, and tragedy. There was defeat, conquest, exile, and the destruction of Jerusalem and its Temple. Only in David, Jehoshaphat, Hezekiah, and Josiah do we see much evidence of godliness.

The third period, **from the deportation to Babylon to the time of Christ,** was that of captivity, exile, frustration, and of marking time. Most of the men Matthew mentions in this period—from Shealtiel to Jacob the father of Joseph— are unknown to us apart from this list. It is a period shrouded largely in darkness and characterized largely by inconsequence. It was Israel's Dark Ages.

Nevertheless, God's grace was at work on behalf of His people through all three periods. The national genealogy of Jesus is one of mingled glory and pathos, heroism and disgrace, renown and obscurity. Israel rises, falls, stagnates, and finally rejects and crucifies the Messiah that God sent *to* them. But God, in His infinite grace, yet sent His Messiah *through* them.

THE GRACE OF GOD SEEN IN THE INCLUSION OF FOUR OUTCASTS

and to Judah were born Perez and Zerah by Tamar; and to Perez was born Hezron; and to Hezron, Ram; and to Ram was born Amminadab; and to Amminadab, Nahshon; and to Nahshon, Salmon; and to Salmon was born Boaz by Rahab; and to Boaz was born Obed by Ruth; and to Obed, Jesse; and to Jesse was born David the king. And to David was born Solomon by her who had been the wife of Uriah. (1:3-6)

Matthew's genealogy also shows us the work of God's grace in His choosing four former outcasts, each of them women (the only women listed until the mention of Mary), through whom the Messiah and great King would descend. These women are exceptional illustrations of God's grace and are included for that reason in the genealogy that otherwise is all men.

The first outcast was **Tamar**, the Canaanite daughter-in-law of **Judah**. God had taken the lives of her husband, Er, and of his next oldest brother, Onan, because of their wickedness. Judah then took the young, childless widow into his own household, promising that his third son, Shelah, would become her husband and raise up children in his brother's name when he grew up. After Judah failed to keep that promise, Tamar disguised herself as a prostitute and tricked him into having sexual relations with her. From that illicit union were born twin sons, **Perez and Zerah**. The sordid story is found in Genesis 38. As we learn from the genealogy, **Tamar** and **Perez** joined **Judah** in the messianic line. Despite prostitution and incest, God's grace fell on all three of those undeserving persons, including a desperate and deceptive Gentile harlot.

The second outcast also was a woman and a Gentile. She, too, was guilty of prostitution, but for her, unlike Tamar, it was a profession. **Rahab**, an inhabitant of Jericho, protected the two Israelite men Joshua sent to spy out the city. She lied to the messengers of the king of Jericho in order to save the spies; but because of her fear of Him and her kind act toward His people, God spared her life and the lives of her family when Jericho was besieged and destroyed (Josh. 2:1-21; 6:22-25). God's grace not only spared her life but brought her into the messianic line, as the wife of **Salmon** and the mother of the godly **Boaz**, who was David's great-grandfather.

The third outcast was **Ruth**, the wife of **Boaz**. Like Tamar and Rahab, **Ruth** was a Gentile. After her first husband, an Israelite, had died, she returned to Israel with her mother-in-law, Naomi. Ruth was a godly, loving, and sensitive woman who had accepted the Lord as her own God. Her people, the pagan Moabites, were the product of the incestuous relations of Lot with his two unmarried daughters. In order to preserve the family line, because they had no husbands or brothers, each of the daughters got their father drunk and caused him to unknowingly have sexual relations with them. The son produced by Lot's union with his oldest daughter was Moab, father of a people who became one of Israel's most implacable enemies. Mahlon, the Israelite man who married **Ruth**, did so in violation of the Mosaic law (Deut. 7:3; cf. 23:3; Ezra 9:2; Neh. 13:23) and many Jewish writers say his early death, and that of his brother, were a divine judgment on their disobedience. Though she was a Moabite and former pagan, with no right to marry an Israelite, God's grace not only brought **Ruth** into the family of Israel, but later, through Boaz, into the royal line. She became the grandmother of Israel's great King David.

The fourth outcast was Bathsheba. She is not identified in the genealogy by name, but is mentioned simply as the wife of **David** and the former **wife of Uriah**. As already mentioned, David committed adultery with her, had her husband sent to the battlefront to be killed, and then took her as his own wife. The son produced by the adultery died in infancy, but the next son born to them was **Solomon** (2 Sam. 11:1-27; 12:14, 24), successor to David's throne and continuer of the messianic line.

By God's grace, Bathsheba became the wife of David, the mother of Solomon, and an ancestor of the Messiah.

The genealogy of Jesus Christ is immeasurably more than a list of ancient names; it is even more than a list of Jesus' human forebears. It is a beautiful testimony to God's grace and to the ministry of His Son, Jesus Christ, the friend of sinners, who "did not come to call the righteous, but sinners" (Matt. 9:13). If He has called sinners by grace to be His forefathers, should we be surprised when He calls them by grace to be His descendants? The King presented here is truly the King of grace!

The Virgin Birth (1:18-25)

2

Now the birth of Jesus Christ was as follows. When His mother Mary had been betrothed to Joseph, before they came together she was found to be with child by the Holy Spirit. And Joseph her husband, being a righteous man, and not wanting to disgrace her, desired to put her away secretly. But when he had considered this, behold, an angel of the Lord appeared to him in a dream, saying, "Joseph, son of David, do not be afraid to take Mary as your wife; for that which has been conceived in her is of the Holy Spirit. And she will bear a Son; and you shall call His name Jesus, for it is He who will save His people from their sins." Now all this took place that what was spoken by the Lord through the prophet might be fulfilled, saying "Behold, the virgin shall be with child, and shall bear a Son, and they shall call His name Immanuel," which translated means, "God with us." And Joseph arose from his sleep, and did as the angel of the Lord commanded him, and took her as his wife, and kept her a virgin until she gave birth to a Son; and he called His name Jesus. (1:18-25)

Biblical history records some amazing and spectacular births. The birth of Isaac to a previously barren woman nearly one hundred years old, who was laughing at the thought of having a child, was a miraculous event. The womb of

Manoah's barren wife was opened and she gave birth to Samson, who was to turn a lion inside out, kill a thousand men, and pull down a pagan temple. The birth of Samuel, the prophet and anointer of kings, to the barren Hannah, whose womb the Lord had shut, revealed divine providential power. Elizabeth was barren, but through the power of God she gave birth to John the Baptist, of whom Jesus said there had yet been no one greater "among those born of women" (Matt. 11:11). But the virgin birth of the Lord Jesus surpasses all of those.

Fantasy and mythology have counterfeited the virgin birth of Jesus Christ with a proliferation of false accounts intended to minimize His utterly unique birth.

For example, the Romans believed that Zeus impregnated Semele without contact and that she conceived Dionysus, lord of the earth. The Babylonians believed that Tammuz (see Ezek. 8:14) was conceived in the priestess Semiramis by a sunbeam. In an ancient Sumerian/Accadian story inscribed on a wall, Tukulti II (890-884 B.C.) told how the gods created him in the womb of his mother. It was even claimed that the goddess of procreation superintended the conception of King Sennacherib (705-681 B.C.). At the conception of Buddha, his mother supposedly saw a great white elephant enter her belly. Hinduism has claimed that the divine Vishnu, after reincarnations as a fish, tortoise, boar, and lion, descended into the womb of Devaki and was born as her son Krishna. There is even a legend that Alexander the Great was virgin born by the power of Zeus through a snake that impregnated his mother, Olympias. Satan has set up many more such myths to counterfeit the birth of Christ in order to make it seem either common or legendary.

Modern science even speaks of parthenogenesis, which comes from a Greek term meaning "virgin born." In the world of honey bees, unfertilized eggs develop into drones, or males. Artificial parthenogenesis has been successful with unfertilized eggs of silkworms. The eggs of sea urchins and marine worms have begun to develop when placed in various salt solutions. In 1939 and 1940, rabbits were produced (all female) through chemical and temperature influences on ova. Nothing like that has ever come close to accounting for human beings; all such parthenogenesis is impossible within the human race. Science, like mythology, has no explanation for the virgin birth of Christ. He was neither merely the son of a previously barren woman nor a freak of nature. By the clear testimony of Scripture, He was conceived by God and born of a virgin.

Nevertheless, religious polls taken over the past several generations reveal the impact of liberal theology in a marked and continuing decline in the percentage of professed Christians who believe in the virgin birth, and therefore in the deity, of Jesus Christ. One wonders why they want to be identified with a person who, if their judgment of Him were correct, had to have been either deceived or deceptive—since all four gospels explicitly teach that Jesus considered Himself to be more than a man. It is clear from the rest of the New Testament as well as from historical records that Jesus, His disciples, and all of the early church held Him to be none other than the divine Son of God. Even His enemies knew He claimed such identity (John 5:18-47).

A popular religious personality said in an interview a few years ago that he could not in print or in public deny the virgin birth of Christ, but that neither could he preach it or teach it. "When I have something I can't comprehend," he explained, "I just don't deal with it." But to ignore the virgin birth is to ignore Christ's deity. And to ignore His deity is tantamount to denying it. Real incarnation demands a real virgin birth.

But such unbelief should not surprise us. Unbelief has been man's greatest problem since the Fall and has always been man's majority view. But "What then?" Paul asks. "If some did not believe, their unbelief will not nullify the faithfulness of God, will it? May it never be! Rather, let God be found true, though every man be found a liar" (Rom. 3:3-4). Every faithful prophet, preacher, or teacher at some time has asked with Isaiah and Paul, "Lord, who has believed our report?" (Rom. 10:16; cf. Isa. 53:1). But popular opinion, even within the church, has not always been a reliable source of truth. When men pick and choose which parts of God's Word to believe and follow, they set themselves above His Word and therefore above Him (cf. Ps. 138:2).

Matthew's purpose in writing his gospel account was partly apologetic—not in the sense of making an apology for the gospel but in the more traditional sense of explaining and defending it against its many attacks and misrepresentations. Jesus' humanity was often maligned and His deity often denied. Possibly during His earthly ministry, and certainly after His death and resurrection, it is likely Jesus was slandered by the accusation that He was the illegitimate son of Mary by some unknown man, perhaps a Roman soldier garrisoned in Galilee. It was Jesus' claim of deity, however, that most incensed the Jewish leaders and brought them to demand His death. "For this cause therefore the Jews were seeking all the more to kill Him, because He not only was breaking the Sabbath, but also was calling God His own Father, making Himself equal with God" (John 5:18).

It is surely no accident, therefore, that the beginning of Matthew's gospel, at the outset of the New Testament, is devoted to establishing both the regal humanity and the deity of Jesus Christ. Apart from Jesus' being both human and divine, there is no gospel. The incarnation of Jesus Christ is the central fact of Christianity. The whole superstructure of Christian theology is built on it. The essence and the power of the gospel is that God became man and that, by being both wholly God and wholly man, He was able to reconcile men to God. Jesus' virgin birth, His substitutionary atoning death, resurrection, ascension, and return are all integral aspects of His deity. They stand or fall together. If any of those teachings—all clearly taught in the New Testament—is rejected, the entire gospel is rejected. None makes sense, or could have any significance or power, apart from the others. If those things were not true, even Jesus' moral teachings would be suspect, because if He misrepresented who He was by preposterously claiming equality with God, how could anything else He said be trusted? Or if the gospel writers misrepresented who He was, why should we trust their word about anything else He said or did?

Jesus once asked the Pharisees a question about Himself that men have been asking in every generation since then: "What do you think about the Christ, whose son is He?" (Matt. 22:42). That is the question Matthew answers in the first chapter of this gospel. Jesus is the human Son of man and the divine Son of God.

As we have seen, the first seventeen verses give Jesus' human lineage—his royal descent from Abraham through David and through Joseph, His legal human father. The Jewish leaders of New Testament times acknowledged that the Messiah would be of the royal line of David; but, for the most part, they agreed on little more than that concerning Him.

History informs us that even the conservative Pharisees did not generally believe that the Messiah would be divine. Had Jesus not claimed to be more than the son of David, He may have begun to convince some of the Jewish leaders of His messiahship. Once He claimed to be God, however, they rejected Him immediately. Many people still today are willing to recognize Him as a great teacher, a model of high moral character, and even a prophet from God. Were He no more than those things, however, He could not have conquered sin or death or Satan. In short, He could not have saved the world. He would also have been guilty of grossly misrepresenting Himself.

It is interesting that certain condescending interpreters of the New Testament acknowledge that Matthew and other writers sincerely believed and taught that Jesus was conceived by the Holy Spirit, that He had no human father. But, they claim, those men were uneducated and captive to the usual superstitions and myths of their times. They simply picked up on the many virgin birth legends that were common in the ancient world and adapted them to the gospel story.

It is true that pagan religions of that day, such as those of Semiramis and Tammuz, had myths of various kinds involving miraculous conceptions. But the immoral and repulsive character of those stories cannot be compared to the gospel accounts. Such stories are Satan's vile counterfeits of God's pure truth. Because the virgin birth of Jesus Christ is crucial to the gospel, it is a truth that false, satanic systems of religion will deny, counterfeit, or misrepresent.

Matthew's account of Jesus' divine conception is straightforward and simple. It is given as history, but as history that could only be known by God's revelation and accomplished by divine miracle. It is essential to the incarnation.

After establishing Jesus' human lineage from David, Matthew proceeds to show His divine "lineage." That is the purpose of verses 18-25, which reveal five distinct truths about the virgin birth of Christ. We see the virgin birth conceived, confronted, clarified, connected, and consummated.

THE VIRGIN BIRTH

Now the birth of Jesus Christ was as follows. When His mother Mary had

been betrothed to Joseph, before they came together she was found to be with child by the Holy Spirit. (1:18)

Though it does not by itself prove divine authorship, the very fact that the account of Jesus' divine conception is given in but one verse strongly suggests that the story was not man-made. It is simply not characteristic of human nature to try to describe something so absolutely momentous and marvelous in such a brief space. Our inclination would be to expand, elaborate, and try to give every detail possible. Matthew continues to give additional information related to the virgin birth, but the *fact* of it is given in one sentence—the first sentence of verse 18 being merely introduction. Seventeen verses are given to listing Jesus' human genealogy, but only part of one verse to His divine genealogy. In His divinity He "descended" from God by a miraculous and never-repeated act of the Holy Spirit; yet the Holy Spirit does nothing more than authoritatively state the fact. A human fabrication would call for much more convincing material.

Birth is from the same Greek root as "genealogy" in verse 1, indicating that Matthew is here giving a parallel account of Jesus' ancestry—this time from His Father's side.

We have little information about **Mary.** It is likely that she was a native of Nazareth and that she came from a relatively poor family. From John 19:25 we learn that she had a sister who also was named Mary, a not uncommon practice in that day. From Luke 3 we receive her Davidic lineage. If, as many believe, the Eli (or Heli) of Luke 3:23 was Joseph's father-in-law (Matthew gives Joseph's father as Jacob, 1:16), then Eli was Mary's father. We know that Elizabeth, the wife of Zacharias, was Mary's "relative" (Luke 1:36), probably her cousin. Those are the only relatives, besides her husband and children, of whom the New Testament speaks.

Mary was a godly woman who was sensitive and submissive to the Lord's will. After the angel Gabriel's announcement that she would be the mother of "the Son of God," Mary said, "Behold, the bondslave of the Lord; be it done to me according to your word" (Luke 1:26-38). Mary was also believing. She wondered how she could conceive: "How can this be, since I am a virgin?" (Luke 1:34). But she never questioned that the angel was sent from God or that what he said was true. Elizabeth, "filled with the Holy Spirit," testified of Mary, "And blessed is she who believed that there would be a fulfillment of what had been spoken to her by the Lord" (v. 45). Mary's humble reverence, thankfulness, and love for God is seen in her magnificent Magnificat, as Luke 1:46-55 is often called. It begins, "My soul exalts the Lord, and my spirit has rejoiced in God my Savior. . . . For the Mighty One has done great things for me; and holy is His name" (vv. 47, 49).

We know even less of **Joseph** than of Mary. His father's name was Jacob (Matt. 1:16) and he was a craftsman, a construction worker (*tektōn*), probably a carpenter (Matt. 13:55). Most importantly, he was a "righteous man" (1:19), an Old Testament saint.

It is possible that both Joseph and Mary were quite young when they were **betrothed**. Girls were often betrothed as young as twelve or thirteen, and boys when they were several years older than that.

By Jewish custom, a betrothal signified more than an engagement in the modern sense. A Hebrew marriage involved two stages, the *kiddushin* (betrothal) and the *huppah* (marriage ceremony). The marriage was almost always arranged by the families of the bride and groom, often without consulting them. A contract was made and was sealed by payment of the *mohar,* the dowry or bride price, which was paid by the groom or his family to the bride's father. The *mohar* served to compensate the father for wedding expenses and to provide a type of insurance for the bride in the event the groom became dissatisfied and divorced her. The contract was considered binding as soon as it was made, and the man and woman were considered legally married, even though the marriage ceremony (*huppah*) and consummation often did not occur until as much as a year later. The betrothal period served as a time of probation and testing of fidelity. During that period the bride and groom usually had little, if any, social contact with each other.

Joseph and Mary had experienced no sexual contact with each other, as the phrase **before they came together** indicates. Sexual purity is highly regarded in Scripture, in both testaments. God places great value on sexual abstinence outside of marriage and sexual fidelity within marriage. Mary's virginity was an important evidence of her godliness. Her reason for questioning Gabriel's announcement of her conception was the fact that she knew she was a virgin (Luke 1:34). This testimony protects from accusation that Jesus was born of some other man.

But Mary's virginity protected a great deal more than her own moral character, reputation, and the legitimacy of Jesus' birth. It protected the nature of the divine Son of God. The child is never called the son of Joseph; Joseph is never called Jesus' father, and Joseph is not mentioned in Mary's song of praise (Luke 1:46-55). Had Jesus been conceived by the act of a man, whether Joseph or anyone else, He could not have been divine and could not have been the Savior. His own claims about Himself would have been lies, and His resurrection and ascension would have been hoaxes. And mankind would forever remain lost and damned.

Obviously Jesus' conception by the Holy Spirit is a great mystery. Even had He wanted to do so, how could God have explained to us, in terms we could comprehend, how such a blending of the divine and human could have been accomplished? We could no more fathom such a thing than we can fathom God's creating the universe from nothing, His being one God in three Persons, or His giving an entirely new spiritual nature to those who trust in His Son. Understanding of such things will have to await heaven, when we see our Lord "face to face" and "know fully just as [we] have been fully known" (1 Cor. 13:12). We accept it by faith.

The virgin birth should not have surprised those Jews who knew and believed the Old Testament. Because of a misinterpretation of the phrase "A woman shall encompass a man" in Jeremiah 31:22, many rabbis believed the Messiah would have an unusual birth. They said, "Messiah is to have no earthly father," and "the birth of Messiah shall be like the dew of the Lord, as drops upon the grass without the action of man." But even that poor interpretation of an obscure text (an interpretation also held by some of the church Fathers) assumed a unique birth for the Messiah.

Not only had Isaiah indicated such a birth (7:14), but even in Genesis we get a glimpse of it. God spoke to the serpent of the enmity that would henceforth exist between "your seed and her [Eve's] seed" (Gen. 3:15). In a technical sense the seed belongs to the man, and Mary's impregnation by the Holy Spirit is the only instance in human history that a woman had a seed within her that did not come from a man. The promise to Abraham concerned "his seed," a common way of referring to offspring. This unique reference to "her seed" looks beyond Adam and Eve to Mary and to Jesus Christ. The two seeds of Genesis 3:15 can be seen in a simple sense as collective; that is, they may refer to all those who are part of Satan's progeny and to all those who a part of Eve's. That view sees the war between the two as raging for all time, with the people of righteousness eventually gaining victory over the people of evil. But "seed" also can be singular, in that it refers to one great, final, glorious product of a woman, who will be the Lord Himself—born without male seed. In that sense the prediction is messianic. It may be that the prophecy looks to both the collective and the individual meanings.

Paul is very clear when he tells us that "When the fulness of the time came, God sent forth His Son, born of a woman" (Gal. 4:4). There is no human father in that verse. Jesus had to have one human parent or He could not have been human, and thereby a partaker of our flesh. But He also had to have divine parentage or He could not have made a sinless and perfect sacrifice on our behalf.

THE VIRGIN BIRTH CONFRONTED

And Joseph her husband, being a righteous man, and not wanting to disgrace her, desired to put her away secretly. But when he had considered this, behold, an angel of the Lord appeared to him in a dream, saying, "Joseph, son of David, do not be afraid to take Mary as your wife; for that which has been conceived in her is of the Holy Spirit." (1:19-20)

As already mentioned, although Joseph and Mary were only betrothed at this time (v. 18), he was considered her **husband** and she was considered his **wife**. For the very reason that he was **a righteous man**, Joseph had a double problem, at least in his own mind. First, because of his righteous moral standards, he knew that he should not go through with the marriage because of Mary's pregnancy. He knew that he was not the father and assumed, quite naturally, that Mary had had relations with another man. But second, because of his righteous love and kindness, he could not bear the thought of shaming her publicly (a common practice of his day in regard to such an offense), much less of demanding her death, as provided by the law (Deut. 22:23-24). There is no evidence that Joseph felt anger, resentment, or bitterness. He had been shamed (if what he assumed had been true), but his concern was not for his own shame but for Mary's. He was **not wanting to disgrace her** by public exposure of her supposed sin. Because he loved her so deeply he determined simply **to put her away secretly.**

Apoluō means literally **to put . . . away,** as translated here, but was the common term used for divorce. Joseph's plan was to divorce her **secretly,** though before long everyone would have guessed it when the marriage never materialized. But for a while, at least, she would be protected, and she would live.

While he **considered this,** however, **an angel of the Lord appeared to him in a dream** and allayed his fears. "**Joseph, son of David, do not be afraid** [stop being afraid] **to take Mary as your wife; for that which has been conceived in her is of the Holy Spirit.**" This verse emphasizes the supernatural character of the whole event. To reinforce the encouraging words, as well as to verify Jesus' royal lineage, the angel addressed Joseph as **son of David.** Even though He was not the real son of Joseph, Jesus was his legal son. His Father, in actuality, was God, who conceived Him by the Holy Spirit. But His royal right in the Davidic line came by Joseph.

The phrase **that which has been conceived in her is of the Holy Spirit** is profound. In those words is the ultimate testimony to the virgin birth. It is the testimony of the holy angel from the Lord God Himself.

One critic has waved his fist at God and called Him an unholy liar with these words: "There was nothing peculiar about the birth of Jesus. He was not God incarnate and no virgin mother bore him. The church in its ancient zeal fathered a myth and became bound to it as a dogma." But the testimony of Scripture stands.

THE VIRGIN BIRTH CLARIFIED

"And she will bear a Son; and you shall call His name Jesus, for it is He who will save His people from their sins" (1:21)

As if to reinforce the truth of Jesus' divine conception, the angel tells Joseph that **she will bear a Son.** Joseph would act as Jesus' earthly father, but he would only be a foster father. Luke's genealogy of Jesus through Mary's line accurately says He was "*supposedly* the son of Joseph" (3:23, emphasis added).

Joseph was told to name the **Son . . . Jesus,** just as Zacharias was told to name his son John (Luke 1:13). We are not told the purpose or significance of John's name, but that of **Jesus** was made clear even before His birth. **Jesus** is a form of the Hebrew Joshua, Jeshua, or Jehoshua, the basic meaning of which is "Jehovah (Yahweh) will save." All other men who had those names testified by their names to the Lord's salvation. But *this* One who would be born to Mary not only would testify of God's salvation, but would Himself be that salvation. By His own work **He** would **save His people from their sins.**

THE VIRGIN BIRTH CONNECTED

Now all this took place that what was spoken by the Lord through the prophet might be fulfilled, saying, "Behold, the virgin shall be with child, and shall bear a Son, and they shall call His name Immanuel," which translated means, "God with us." (1:22-23)

At this point Matthew explains that Jesus' virgin birth was predicted by God in the Old Testament. The Lord clearly identifies the birth of Christ as a fulfillment of prophecy. **All this** refers to the facts about the divine birth of Jesus Christ. And the great miracle of His birth was the fulfillment of **what was spoken by the Lord through the prophet.** That phrase gives a simple, straightforward definition of biblical inspiration as the Word of the Lord coming through human instruments. God does the **saying;** the human instrument is only a means to bring the divine Word to men. Based on these words of the Lord given through Matthew, the Old Testament text of Isaiah must be interpreted as predicting the virgin birth of Jesus Christ.

Matthew repeatedly uses the phrase **might be fulfilled** (2:15, 17, 23; 8:17; 12:17; 13:35; 21:4; 26:54; etc.) to indicate ways in which Jesus, and events related to His earthly ministry, were fulfillments of Old Testament prophecy. The basic truths and happenings of the New Testament were culminations, completions, or fulfillments of revelation God had already made—though often the revelation had been in veiled and partial form.

The scene in Isaiah 7 is the reign of King Ahaz in Judah. Though son of the great Uzziah, he was the most wicked king ever. He filled Jerusalem with idols, reinstated the worship of Molech, and burned his own son as a sacrifice to that god. Rezin, king of Syria (Aram), and Pekah, king of Israel (also called Samaria at that time), decided to remove Ahaz and replace him with a king who would do their bidding. In the face of such a threat to the people of Israel and to the royal line of David, Ahaz, instead of turning to God for help, secretly surrendered his kingdom and people to Tiglath-pileser, the evil king of the Assyrians. It was at that time that God sent Isaiah to face Ahaz and show him the unfaithful stupidity of seeking refuge in the Assyrians instead of in God. But Ahaz ignored Isaiah's plea and did all he could to confirm the relationship with Assyria. He even plundered and sent to Tiglath-pileser the gold and silver from the Temple.

Isaiah came a second time to Ahaz and reported that God would deliver the people from the two enemy kings. When Ahaz again refused to listen, Isaiah responded with the remarkable messianic prophecy of 7:14.

How did a prediction of the virgin birth of Messiah fit that ancient scene? Isaiah was telling the wicked king that no one would destroy the people of God or the royal line of David. When the prophet said, "The Lord shall give you a sign," he used a plural *you,* indicating that Isaiah was also speaking to the entire nation, telling them that God would not allow Rezin and Pekah, or anyone else, to destroy them and the line of David (cf. Gen. 49:10; 2 Sam. 7:13). Even though the people came into the hands of Tiglath-pileser, who destroyed the northern kingdom and overran Judah on four occasions, God preserved them just as He promised.

Isaiah also refers to another child who would be born; and before that child (Maher-shalal-hash-baz) would be old enough to "eat curds and honey" or "know enough to refuse evil and choose good," the lands of Rezin and Pekah would be forsaken (7:15-16). Sure enough, before the child born to Isaiah's wife was three years old those two kings were dead. Just as that ancient prophecy of a child came to pass, so did the prophecy of the virgin birth of the Lord Jesus Christ. Both were signs that God would not ultimately forsake His people. The greatest sign was that **Immanuel, which translated means, "God with us,"** would come.

In Isaiah 7:14, the verse here quoted by Matthew, the prophet used the Hebrew word *'almâ*. Old Testament usage of *'almâ* favors the translation "virgin." The word first appears in Genesis 24:43, in connection with Rebekah, the future bride of Isaac. The King James Version reads, "Behold I stand by the well of water; and it shall come to pass, that when the virgin cometh forth to draw water." In verse 16 of the same chapter Rebekah is described as a "damsel" (*na'ǎrâ*) and a "virgin" (*beṭûlâ*). It should be concluded that *'almâ* is never used to refer to a married woman. The word occurs five other times in Scripture (Ex. 2:8; Ps. 68:25; Prov. 30:19; Song of Sol. 1:3; 6:8), and in each case contains the idea of a virgin. Until recent times, it was always translated as such by both Jewish and Christian scholars.

The most famous medieval Jewish interpreter, Rashi (1040-1105), who was an opponent of Christianity, made the following comment: "'Behold the *'almâ* shall conceive and bear a son and shall call his name Immanuel' means that our Creator shall be with us. And this is the sign: The one who will conceive is a girl (*na'ǎrâ*) who never in her life has had intercourse with any man. Upon this one shall the Holy Spirit have power." It should be noted that in modern Hebrew the word *virgin* is either *'almâ* or *beṭûlâ*. Why did not Isaiah use *beṭûlâ?* Because it is sometimes used in the Old Testament of a married woman who is not a virgin (Deut. 22:19; Joel 1:8).

'Almâ can mean "virgin," and that is how the Jewish translators of the Septuagint (Greek Old Testament) translated the word in Isaiah 7:14 (by the Greek *parthenos,* "virgin")—several hundred years before the birth of Christ. The "sign" of which Isaiah spoke was given specifically to King Ahaz, who feared that the royal line of Judah might be destroyed by Syria and Israel. The prophet assured the king that God would protect that line. The birth of a son and the death of the kings would be the signs guaranteeing His protection and preservation. And in the future there would be a greater birth, the virgin birth of God incarnate, to assure the covenant with God's people.

Matthew did not give the term *'almâ* a Christian "twist," but used it with the same meaning with which all Jews of that time used it. In any case, his teaching of the virgin birth does not hinge on that word. It is made incontestably clear by the preceding statemments that Jesus' conception was "by the Holy Spirit" (vv. 18, 20).

The **name** of the **Son** born to a virgin would be **Immanuel, which translated means, "God with us."** That **name** was used more as a title or description than as a proper name. In His incarnation Jesus was, in the most literal sense, **God with us.**

The fact that a **virgin shall be with child** is marvelous—a pregnant virgin! Equally marvelous is that she **shall call His name Immanuel.**

The Old Testament repeatedly promises that God is present with His people, to secure their destiny in His covenant. The Tabernacle and Temple were intended to be symbols of that divine presence. The term for tabernacle is *mishkān,* which comes from *shākan,* meaning to dwell, rest, or abide. From that root the term *shekinah* has also come, referring to the presence of God's glory. The child born was to be the Shekinah, the true Tabernacle of God (cf. John 1:14). Isaiah was the instrument through which the Word of the Lord announced that God would dwell among men in visible flesh and blood incarnation—more intimate and personal than the Tabernacle or Temple in which Israel had worshiped.

THE VIRGIN BIRTH CONSUMMATED

And Joseph arose from his sleep, and did as the angel of the Lord commanded him, and took her as his wife, and kept her a virgin until she gave birth to a Son; and he called His name Jesus. (1:24-25)

That **Joseph arose from his sleep** indicates that the revelatory dream had come to him while he slept (cf. v. 20). Such unique, direct communication from God was used on other occasions to reveal Scripture (see Gen. 20:3; 31:10-11; Num. 12:6; 1 Kings 3:5; Job 33:14-16). It should be noted that all six New Testament occurrences of *onar* ("to dream") are in Matthew and concern the Lord Jesus Christ (see 1:20; 2:12-13, 19, 22; 27:19).

We know nothing of Joseph's reaction, except that he immediately obeyed, doing **as the angel of the Lord commanded him.** We can imagine how great his feelings of amazement, relief, and gratitude must have been. Not only would he be able to take his beloved Mary as his wife with honor and righteousness, but he would be given care of God's own Son while He was growing up.

That fact alone would indicate the depth of Joseph's godliness. It is inconceivable that God would entrust His Son into a family where the father was not totally committed and faithful to Him.

We know nothing else of Joseph's life except his taking the infant Jesus to the Temple for dedication (Luke 2:22-33), his taking Mary and Jesus into Egypt to protect Him from Herod's bloody edict and the return (Matt. 2:13-23), and his taking his family to the Passover in Jerusalem when Jesus was twelve

(Luke 2:42-52). We have no idea when Joseph died, but it could have been well before Jesus began His public ministry. Obviously it was before Jesus' crucifixion, because from the cross Jesus gave his mother into the care of John (John 19:26).

Apparently the marriage ceremony, when Joseph **took her as his wife**, was held soon after the angel's announcement. But he **kept her a virgin until she gave birth to a Son**. Matthew makes it clear that she remained a virgin **until she gave birth**, implying that normal marital relations began after that time. The fact that Jesus' brothers and sisters are spoken of numerous times in the gospels (Matt. 12:46; 13:55-56; Mark 6:3; etc.) prove that Mary did not remain a virgin perpetually, as some claim.

As a final act of obedience to God's instruction through the angel, Joseph **called His name Jesus**, indicating that He was to be the Savior (cf. v. 21).

The supernatural birth of Jesus is the only way to account for the life that He lived. A skeptic who denied the virgin birth once asked a Christian, "If I told you that child over there was born without a human father, would you believe me?" The believer replied, "Yes, if he lived as Jesus lived." The greatest outward evidence of Jesus' supernatural birth and deity is His life.

Fools and Wise Men
(2:1-12)

Now after Jesus was born in Bethlehem of Judea in the days of Herod the king, behold, magi from the east arrived in Jerusalem, saying, "Where is He who has been born King of the Jews? For we saw His star in the east, and have come to worship Him." And when Herod the king heard it, he was troubled, and all Jerusalem with him. And gathering together all the chief priests and scribes of the people, he began to inquire of them where the Christ was to be born. And they said to him, "In Bethlehem of Judea, for so it has been written by the prophet, 'And you, Bethlehem, land of Judah, are by no means least among the leaders of Judah; for out of you shall come forth a Ruler, who will shepherd My people Israel.'"

Then Herod secretly called the magi, and ascertained from them the time the star appeared. And he sent them to Bethlehem, and said, "Go, and make careful search for the Child; and when you have found Him, report to me, that I too may come and worship Him." And having heard the king, they went their way; and lo, the star, which they had seen in the east, went on before them, until it came and stood over where the Child was. And when they saw the star, they rejoiced exceedingly with great joy. And they came into the house and saw the Child with Mary His mother; and they fell down and worshiped Him; and opening their treasures they presented to Him gifts of gold and frankincense and myrrh. And having been warned by God in a

dream not to return to Herod, they departed for their own country by another way. (2:1-12)

Continuing his thrust to establish Jesus' right to Israel's true and final kingship, in chapter 2 Matthew gives three additional evidences of Jesus of Nazareth's legitimate, unique, and absolute royal right to the throne of David. In chapter 1 we saw the evidence of Jesus' royal genealogy and of His virgin birth. In the present chapter we first see the testimony of the magi, who came to give homage and gifts to the infant Jesus, "He who has been born King of the Jews" (2:2). The powerful oriental kingmakers from Persia traveled a great distance to recognize and honor a King in whose coronation they had no part, a King far greater than any they had ever, or would ever, set on a throne.

The next evidence of Christ's kingship is shown in a negative, or reverse, way, through the antagonism and hatred of Herod. Herod's devious scheme to discover and destroy this unknown baby shows his fear that the magi's declaration about the Child could be correct, and gives unintended testimony to Jesus' true royalty. Herod knew that he himself was a usurper to the throne on which he sat only by virtue of Rome—who herself ruled Judah only by the "right" of military force. Herod was an Edomite, not a Jew, and had no legitimate claim to be the Jew's king. He therefore feared and hated even the suggestion of a rival claimant. But even the hatred of the false king gave indirect testimony to the identity of the true King.

The third evidence of Christ's kingship given in chapter 2 is presented through four fulfilled messianic prophecies. Some three hundred thirty Old Testament predictions concern Jesus Christ. In chapter 2 Matthew points out four of those prophecies that were fulfilled during Jesus' infancy. There is no reasonable possibility that even those four—much less all three hundred thirty—could have been fulfilled accidentally in the life of a single individual. That fact in itself is overwhelming evidence of God's sovereign control of history and of the utter reliability of His Word.

Matthew uses the four prophecies as a literary framework around which he presents the events recorded in this chapter. Each of the predictions is directly related to a geographical location closely related to Jesus' birth and early childhood. The four locations are Bethlehem, Egypt, Ramah, and Nazareth.

The present passage—built around the prediction of Jesus' birth in Bethlehem—focuses on the coming of the magi to worship Jesus, the One they somehow knew had **been born King of the Jews.** Within this story we also see the reaction of Herod and of the chief priests and scribes to that same news. In this brief text we see examples of the three basic responses that men made to Jesus when He was on earth, the same three responses that men throughout history have made to the Lord. Some, like Herod, are hostile to Him; some, like the chief priests and scribes, are indifferent to Him; and some, like the magi, worship Him.

THE ARRIVAL OF THE MAGI

Now after Jesus was born in Bethlehem of Judea in the days of Herod the king, behold, magi from the east arrived in Jerusalem, saying, "Where is He who has been born King of the Jews? For we saw His star in the east, and have come to worship Him." (2:1-2)

The events described in this passage probably occurred several months **after Jesus was born**. We see from 2:11 that Jesus' family was now staying in a house rather than the stable where He was born (Luke 2:7). Jesus, therefore, would already have been circumcised, and Mary would have completed her period of purification (Luke 2:21-27). The fact that she offered "a pair of turtledoves, or two young pigeons" (Luke 2:24) instead of the normal lamb (Lev. 12:6-8) indicates that the family was poor. Had this offering been made after the magi with their expensive gifts (Matt. 2:11) had already visited Jesus, the lamb could easily have been afforded and would have been required.

BETHLEHEM OF JUDEA

As it still is today, **Bethlehem** was then a small town five or six miles south of Jerusalem, in the fertile hill country of **Judea** (Judah). It is cradled between two ridges and was located along the main ancient highway from Jerusalem to Egypt. It was once called Ephrath, or Ephrathah, and is referred to by that name several times in the Old Testament (Gen. 35:16; Ruth 4:11; Ps. 132:6; Mic. 5:2). The town came to be called **Bethlehem** after the conquest of Canaan under Joshua, its new name meaning "house of bread."

It was at Bethlehem that Jacob buried Rachel (Gen. 35:19), the traditional site of whose tomb is still shown to tourists today. It was also here that Ruth met and married Boaz (Ruth 1:22; 2:4) and that their illustrious grandson, David, grew up and tended sheep (1 Sam. 17:12, 15). By the time of Jesus' birth, it had long been called "the city of David" (Luke 2:4, 11). The prophet Micah specifically promised that the Messiah would come from this small village (5:2).

HEROD THE KING

This **Herod**, known as "the Great," is the first of several Herods mentioned in the New Testament. Julius Caesar had appointed his father, Antipater, to be procurator, or governor, of Judea under the Roman occupation. Antipater then managed to have his son Herod appointed prefect of Galilee. In that office Herod was successful in quelling the Jewish guerilla bands who continued to fight against their foreign rulers. After fleeing to Egypt when the Parthians invaded Palestine, Herod then went to Rome and in 40 B.C. was declared by Octavian and Antony (with the concurrence of the Roman senate) to be the king of the Jews. He invaded

Palestine the next year and, after several years of fighting, drove out the Parthians and established his kingdom.

Because he was not Jewish, but Idumean (Edomite), Herod married Mariamne, heiress to the Jewish Hasmonean house, in order to make himself more acceptable to the Jews he now ruled. He was a clever and capable warrior, orator, and diplomat. In times of severe economic hardship he gave back some tax money collected from the people. During the great famine of 25 B.C. he melted down various gold objects in the palace to buy food for the poor. He built theaters, race tracks, and other structures to provide entertainment for the people, and in 19 B.C. he began the reconstruction of the Temple in Jerusalem. He revived Samaria and built the beautiful port city of Caesarea in honor of his benefactor Caesar Augustus (Octavian's title). He embellished the cities of Beirut, Damascus, Tyre, Sidon, and Rhodes, and even made contributions to rebuilding work in Athens. He built the remarkable and almost impregnable fortress of Masada, where in A.D. 73 nearly a thousand Jewish defenders committed suicide rather than be captured by the Roman general Flavius Silva.

But Herod was also cruel and merciless. He was incredibly jealous, suspicious, and afraid for his position and power. Fearing his potential threat, he had the high priest Aristobulus, who was his wife Mariamne's brother, drowned— after which he provided a magnificent funeral where he pretended to weep. He then had Mariamne herself killed, and then her mother and two of his own sons. Five days before his death (about a year after Jesus was born) he had a third son executed. One of the greatest evidences of his bloodthirstiness and insane cruelty was having the most distinguished citizens of Jerusalem arrested and imprisoned shortly before his death. Because he knew no one would mourn his own death, he gave orders for those prisoners to be executed the moment he died—in order to guarantee that there would be mourning in Jerusalem. That barbaric act was exceeded in cruelty only by his slaughter of "all the male children who were in Bethlehem and in all its environs, from two years old and under" (Matt. 2:16) in hopes of killing any threat to his throne from the One the magi said had **been born King of the Jews.**

MAGI FROM THE EAST

Few biblical stories are as well known, yet so clouded by myth and tradition, as that of the **magi,** or wise men, mentioned by Matthew. During the Middle Ages legend developed that they were kings, that they were three in number, and that their names were Casper, Balthazar, and Melchior. Because they were thought to represent the three sons of Noah, one of them is often pictured as an Ethiopian. A twelfth-century bishop of Cologne even claimed to have found their skulls.

The only legitimate facts we know about these particular **magi** are the few given by Matthew in the first twelve verses of chapter 2. We are not told their number, their names, their means of transportation to Palestine, or the specific country or countries from which they came. The fact that they came from **the east** would have been assumed by most people in New Testament times, because the magi were primarily known as the priestly-political class of the Parthians—who lived to the east of Palestine.

The magi first appear in history in the seventh century B.C. as a tribe within the Median nation in eastern Mesopotamia. Many historians consider them to have been Semites, which if so, made them—with the Jews and Arabs—descendants of Noah's son Shem. It may also be that, like Abraham, the magi came from ancient Ur in Chaldea. The name magi soon came to be associated solely with the hereditary priesthood within that tribe. The magi became skilled in astronomy and astrology (which, in that day, were closely associated) and had a sacrificial system that somewhat resembled the one God gave to Israel through Moses. They were involved in various occult practices, including sorcery, and were especially noted for their ability to interpret dreams. It is from their name that our words *magic* and *magician* are derived.

A principle element of magian worship was fire, and on their primary altar burned a perpetual flame, which they claimed descended from heaven. The magi were monotheistic, believing in the existence of only one god. Because of their monotheism, it was easy for the magi to adapt to the teaching of the sixth-century B.C. Persian religious leader named Zoroaster, who believed in a single god, Ahura Mazda, and a cosmic struggle between good and evil. Darius the Great established Zoroastrianism as the state religion of Persia.

Because of their combined knowledge of science, agriculture, mathematics, history, and the occult, their religious and political influence continued to grow until they became the most prominent and powerful group of advisors in the Medo-Persian and subsequently the Babylonian empire. It is not strange, therefore, that they often were referred to as "wise men." It may be that "the law of the Medes and Persians" (see Dan. 6:8, 12, 15; Esther 1:19) was founded on the teachings of these magi. Historians tell us that no Persian was ever able to become king without mastering the scientific and religious disciplines of the magi and then being approved and crowned by them, and that this group also largely controlled judicial appointments (cf. Esther 1:13). Nergal-sar-ezer the Rab-mag, chief of the Babylonian magi, was with Nebuchadnezzar when he attacked and conquered Judah (Jer. 39:3).

We learn from the book of Daniel that the magi were among the highest-ranking officials in Babylon. Because the Lord gave Daniel the interpretation of Nebuchadnezzar's dream—which none of the other court seers was able to do—Daniel was appointed as "ruler over the whole province of Babylon and chief prefect over all the wise men of Babylon" (Dan. 2:48). Because of his great wisdom and because he had successfully pleaded for the lives of the wise men who had failed to interpret the king's dream (Dan. 2:24), Daniel came to be highly regarded among the magi. The plot against Daniel that caused him to be thrown into the lions' den was fomented by the jealous satraps and the other commissioners, not the magi (Dan. 6:4-9).

Because of Daniel's high position and great respect among them, it seems certain that the magi learned much from that prophet about the one true God, the God of Israel, and about His will and plans for His people through the coming glorious King. Because many Jews remained in Babylon after the Exile and intermarried with the people of the east, it is likely that Jewish messianic influence remained strong in that region even until New Testament times.

During both the Greek and Roman empires the magi's power and influence continued in the eastern provinces, particularly in Parthia. As mentioned above, it was the Parthians that Herod, in behalf of Rome, drove out of Palestine between 39 and 37 B.C., when his kingship of Judea began. Some magi—many of them probably outcasts or false practitioners—lived in various parts of the Roman Empire, including Palestine. Among them was Simon of Samaria (Acts 8:9), whom tradition and history have come to refer to as Simon Magus because of his "practicing magic" (Greek, *mageuō*, derived from the Babylonian *magus*, singular of *magi*). The Jewish false prophet Bar-Jesus was also a sorcerer, or "magician" (Greek, *magos*). These magicians were despised by both Romans and Jews. Philo, a first-century B.C. Jewish philosopher from Alexandria, called them vipers and scorpions.

The **magi from the east** (the word literally means "from the rising" of the sun, and refers to the orient) who came to see Jesus were of a completely different sort. Not only were they true magi, but they surely had been strongly influenced by Judaism, quite possibly even by some of the prophetic writings, especially that of Daniel. They appear to be among the many God-fearing Gentiles who lived at the time of Christ, a number of whom—such as Cornelius and Lydia (Acts 10:1-2; 16:14)—are mentioned in the New Testament.

When these magi, however many there were, **arrived in Jerusalem**, they began asking, **"Where is He who has been born King of the Jews?"** The Greek construction (**saying** is a present participle emphasizing continual action) suggests that they went around the city questioning whomever they met. Because they, as foreigners, knew of the monumental birth, they apparently assumed that anyone in Judea, and certainly in Jerusalem, would know of this special baby's whereabouts. They must have been more than a little shocked to discover that no one seemed to know what they were talking about.

During that time there was widespread expectation of the coming of a great king, a great deliverer. The Roman historian Suetonius, speaking of the time around the birth of Christ, wrote, "There had spread over all the Orient an old and established belief that it was fated at that time for men coming from Judea to rule the world." Another Roman historian, Tacitus, wrote that "there was a firm persuasion that at this very time the east was to grow powerful and rulers coming from Judea were to acquire a universal empire." The Jewish historian Josephus reports in his *Jewish Wars* that at about the time of Christ's birth the Jews believed that one from their country would soon become ruler of the habitable earth.

As seen in the writings of the Roman poet Virgil (70-19 B.C.), Rome was expecting its own golden age. Augustus Caesar, Herod's benefactor, had for some time been hailed as the savior of the world. Many magi could be found in the great cities of the west, including Athens and Rome, and were frequently consulted by Roman rulers. The Romans were looking for a coming great age, wise men from the east had long influenced the west with their ideas and traditions, and—though the particulars varied considerably—there was a growing feeling that from somewhere a great and unprecedented world leader was about to arise.

We are not told *how* the God of revelation caused the magi to know that the **King of the Jews** had been born, only that He gave them the sign of **His** [the One called **King**] **star in the east**. Almost as much speculation has been made about the identity of that **star** as about the identity of the men who saw it. Some suggest that it was Jupiter, the "king of the planets." Others claim that it was the conjunction of Jupiter and Saturn, forming the sign of the fish—which was used as a symbol for Christianity in the early church during the Roman persecutions. Still others claim that it was a low-hanging meteor, an erratic comet, or simply an inner vision of the star of destiny in the hearts of mankind.

Since the Bible does not identify or explain the star, we cannot be dogmatic, but it may have been the glory of the Lord—the same glory that shone around the shepherds when Jesus' birth was announced to them by the angel (Luke 2:9). Throughout the Old Testament we are told of God's glory being manifested as light, God radiating His presence (Shekinah) in the form of ineffable light. The Lord guided the children of Israel through the wilderness by "a pillar of cloud by day . . . and in a pillar of fire by night" (Ex. 13:21). When Moses went up on Mount Sinai, "to the eyes of the sons of Israel the appearance of the glory of the Lord was like a consuming fire on the mountaintop" (Ex. 24:17). On a later occasion, after Moses had inscribed the Ten Commandments on stone tablets, His face still glowed with the light of God's glory when he returned to the people (Ex. 34:30).

When Jesus was transfigured before Peter, James, and John, "His face shone like the sun, and His garments became as white as light" (Matt. 17:2). On the Damascus road, just before Jesus spoke to him, Saul of Tarsus was surrounded by "a light from heaven" (Acts 9:3), which he later explained was "brighter than the sun" (26:13). In John's first vision on the Island of Patmos, he saw Christ's face "like the sun shining in its strength" (Rev. 1:16). In his vision of the New Jerusalem, the future heavenly dwelling of all believers, he reports that "the city has no need of the sun or of the moon to shine upon it, for the glory of God has illumined it, and its lamp is the Lamb" (Rev. 21:23).

Both the Hebrew (*kôkāb*) and the Greek (*astēr*) words for star were also used figuratively to represent any great brilliance or radiance. Very early in the Old Testament the Messiah is spoken of as a "star [that] shall come forth from Jacob" (Num. 24:17), and at the end of the New Testament He refers to Himself as "the bright morning star" (Rev. 22:16). It was surely the glory of God, blazing as if it were an extremely bright star—visible only to the eyes for whom it was intended to be seen—that appeared to the magi in the east and later guided them to Bethlehem. It was a brilliant manifestation of "the sign of the Son of Man" (see Matt. 24:29-30; Rev. 1:7). The Shekinah glory of God stood over Bethlehem just as, centuries before, it had stood over the Tabernacle in the wilderness. And just as the pillar of cloud gave light to Israel but darkness to Egypt (Ex. 14:20), only the eyes of the magi were opened to see God's great light over Bethlehem.

That the magi were not *following* the star is clear from the fact that they had to inquire about where Jesus was born. They **saw His star in the east**, but there is no evidence that it continued to shine or that it led them to Jerusalem. It was not until they were told of the prophesied birthplace of the Messiah (2:5-6) that the star reappeared and then guided them not only to Bethlehem but to the exact place "where the Child was" (v. 9).

These travelers from the east had come to Palestine with but one purpose: to find the One **born King of the Jews** and **worship Him**. The word **worship** is full of meaning, expressing the idea of falling down, prostrating oneself, and kissing the feet or the hem of the garment of the one honored. That truth in itself shows that they were true seekers after God, because when He spoke to them, in whatever way it was, they heard and responded. Despite their paganism, quasi-science, and superstition they recognized God's voice when He spoke. Though having had limited spiritual light, they immediately recognized God's light when it shone on them. They had genuinely seeking hearts, hearts that the Lord promises will never fail to find Him (Jer. 29:13).

On a plane trip several years ago I was hoping that whoever sat next to me would take a nap and not want to talk, so that I could get some urgent work done. The Lord obviously had other plans, because as soon as the man next to me saw I was studying he asked if I were a teacher. I replied that I was not a classroom teacher but that I did teach the Bible. His next question was, "Can you tell me how to have a personal relationship with Jesus Christ?" After I explained the way of salvation, he received Christ. He was looking for God's light and, like the magi, when he saw it he knew it.

THE AGITATION OF HEROD

And when Herod the king heard it, he was troubled, and all Jerusalem with him. And gathering together all the chief priests and scribes of the people, he began to inquire of them where the Christ was to be born. And they said to him, "In Bethlehem of Judea, for so it has been written by the prophet, 'And you, Bethlehem, land of Judah, are by no means least among the leaders of Judah; for out of you shall come forth a Ruler, who will shepherd My people Israel.'"
Then Herod secretly called the magi, and ascertained from them the time the star appeared. And he sent them to Bethlehem, and said, "Go, and make careful search for the Child; and when you have found Him, report to me, that I too may come and worship Him." (2:3-8)

The response of **Herod** was exactly the opposite of that of the magi.

Whereas the magi rejoiced at hearing of Jesus' birth, **when Herod the king heard it, he was troubled**. The king's anxiety is not hard to understand. In the first place, he was sitting on a political and religious powder keg. He had driven the Parthians out of Palestine but had to continue fighting the bands of Jewish zealots who wanted their country to be free from Roman occupation and domination. Especially in light of his intense jealousy and paranoia, any mention of another king of the Jews sent him into a frenzy of fear and anger.

The fact that the magi themselves were probably Parthians, or closely associated with the Parthians, gave Herod special cause for concern. Because the magi at this time were still powerful in the east, it is likely that they traveled with a large contingent of soldiers and servants—causing their presence in Jerusalem to seem even more threatening to Herod. Because of their wealth, prestige, and power, they had the appearance and demeanor of royalty—which is why they have long been traditionally pictured and sung about as kings from the Orient. The magi were not simple mystics and, as mentioned above, their number could have been considerably more than three. To Herod, the appearance of this impressive company portended a renewed political threat from the east. And though He was by now some seventy years old, he wanted to maintain his position and power to the end, and did not want to spend his last years in warfare.

The ruling body in the Parthian-Persian empire at this time was much like the Roman senate. They were the king-makers in an almost absolute way, and were composed entirely of magi. They had become discontent with the weak king that presently ruled them and were looking for someone more capable to lead them in a campaign against Rome. Caesar Augustus was old and feeble, and since the retirement of Tiberius the Roman army had had no commander in chief. The time was propitious for the east to make its move against Rome.

That **all Jerusalem with him** was also troubled may indicate that their concern, like Herod's, was political and military. Perhaps they too viewed the magi as the precursors of another conquest by the Parthians, who had sent this forward body ahead to discover and perhaps even crown some new king that would rule Palestine in Parthia's behalf—much in the same way that Herod ruled it in Rome's behalf. The fact that the magi came to worship the newborn king would not have indicated to Herod or the others in Jerusalem that the mission of the magi was purely religious. The magi had long been known as much for their politics as for their religion, and the practice of worshiping the king or emperor was then common in both the east and the west.

It is more likely, however, that the concern of the populace was not directly about the magi but about Herod's reaction to them. By bitter experience they knew that Herod's agitation usually meant maniacal bloodshed. He did not bother to identify his enemies carefully. Anyone even suspected of doing him harm or of threatening his position or power was in considerable danger. In his sweeping carnage many totally innocent people were often destroyed. The people's fear for their own safety was well founded. Although Herod's maliciousness was not vented against Jerusalem, it would shortly be vented against Bethlehem, her small neighbor to the south, when the enraged king ordered the slaughter of all the infant male children there (Matt. 2:16). Herod feared for the throne, which was not really his, and Jerusalem knew what Herod's fear meant. It meant rebellion, bloodshed, and terrible suffering.

Herod's first response to the news of the magi was to gather **together all the chief priests and scribes of the people** and **to inquire of them where the Christ was to be born**. Obviously Herod connected the King of the Jews with the Messiah, the **Christ**. Though Herod was not himself a Jew he knew Jewish beliefs and customs rather well. The current messianic expectations of most Jews at that time was more for a political and military deliverer than a spiritual savior—an expectation apparently shared by Jesus' own disciples (Acts 1:6).

THE CHIEF PRIESTS

All Jewish **priests** were of the priestly tribe of Levi and, even more particularly, descendants of Aaron, the first high priest. In some ways the priests were like the magi, having considerable political as well as religious power.

First among the **chief priests** was the high priest. According to Old Testament law, there was to be but one high priest at a time, who served for life and whose special and unique duty it was to enter the Holy of Holies once a year on the Day of Atonement and offer sacrifice for all the people. But by the time of Christ the office had become subject to political favoritism and even purchase. High priests were appointed and removed at the whim of various rulers. Consequently, there were often several living at one time. And, though the ones who had been removed from office lost their high priestly function, they usually kept the title, as well as considerable prestige and power (see Luke 3:2). The ruling high priest also presided over the Sanhedrin, a type of combined senate and supreme court, made up of seventy of the key Jewish religious leaders.

Another of the **chief priests** was the captain of the Temple, who was appointed by and responsible to the high priest. Among his powers, approved by the Romans, was that of arrest and imprisonment. He therefore was allowed to have a rather large contingent of soldiers, all Jewish, at his disposal, who acted as the Temple police. He ranked second to the high priest in authority.

The others included among the chief priests were not a particular category but were composed of various other leading, influential priests, including the leaders of the daily and weekly course of priests, the Temple treasurer, and other Temple overseers and officials. Together with the high priests and the captain of the Temple, they formed the priestly aristocracy often referred to loosely as the **chief priests**. For the most part, these chief priests were Sadducees, whereas the normal priests were Pharisees. By New Testament times they had become little more than a group of corrupt, religiously oriented politicians. From the time of Jesus' birth to His crucifixion they are shown by the gospel writers to have been in opposition to the true revelation and work of the Lord.

SCRIBES

The **scribes** were primarily Pharisees, authorities on Jewish law, scriptural and traditional, who were often referred to as lawyers. They had considerable prestige among Jews, and were recognized as the key scholars of religious Judaism. They were conservative theologically, held a literalistic view of Scripture, and were generally legalistic and strict in regard to both ceremonial and moral law. Those of the scribes who were Sadducees were liberal in their interpretation of Scripture, not believing in such things as the resurrection and angels (Acts 23:8). Whether conservative or liberal, however, the scribes of Jesus' day were alike in their opposition to Him.

Herod called together all of those Jewish religious leaders, who were both politicians and theologians, in order **to inquire of them where the Christ was to be born** (the imperfect tense of **inquire** suggests a constant asking). Although they proved that they knew where His birth was predicted to be (common knowledge among the Jews, John 7:42), they showed no belief or special interest in the announcement of the magi that they had seen the star given as a sign of that birth.

In any case, the **chief priests and scribes** told Herod what he wanted to know, referring him to the specific passage (Mic. 5:2) where the birthplace is predicted. Out of **Bethlehem** would **come forth a Ruler**. The last phrase, **Who will shepherd My people Israel**, is not from Micah, but does express the emphasis of One who would rule. Either the Jews said this or Matthew added the words as his own comment to indicate the kind of **Ruler** the **Christ** would be. Though the popular idea of a shepherd is that of kind, tender care (Ps. 23), the Scripture emphasis is also on authority and strong, even stern, leadership. The combination of a **Ruler** (*hēgemōn*) who will **shepherd** (*poimainō*) shows that the shepherding function is more than tender care. It is sovereign dominance. Nowhere is that made more clear than by the use of the verb *poimainō* in Revelation 2:27; 12:5; and 19:15. In each of those verses the verb is justifiably translated "rule"—and "with a rod of iron" at that. Its appearance in Revelation 7:17, as well as its use in John 21:16; Acts 20:28; and 1 Peter 5:2, could warrant a similar rendering. The point is that the statement here in Matthew is a consistent elucidation of the idea of a shepherd's being a **Ruler**, and thus fits the intent of Micah's prediction. Unlike Herod, Jesus not only would be a legitimate King of the Jews, but would also be the final and perfect **Ruler** of **Israel**.

Even the unbelieving, politicized, self-serving Jewish leaders recognized that God's Word clearly spoke of a literal, personal Messiah—a historical figure, born in Bethlehem in Judea, come to rule Israel. They did not accept Him when He was born or when He preached and taught or when He suffered and died; they were, in fact, His supreme enemies. Yet they acknowledged that the One predicted to come would be sent by the Lord to rule the Lord's people. Contrary to what many, perhaps most, unbelieving Jews today think, those ancient teachers of Israel knew that the coming Messiah, **the Christ**, would be more than a godly attitude or the personified perfection of the Jewish kingdom. The Messiah would be a real man born among men, sent to rule men. Those chief priests and scribes had a far from perfect idea of what Christ would be like and of what He would do, but they had more than enough knowledge to have enabled them to recognize Him when He came and to know that they, like the magi, should worship Him. They knew, but they did not believe. Consequently, a few years later their initial indifference to Jesus would turn to rejection and persecution. These who now ignored Him would soon become His hateful, venomous murderers.

The magi had much less knowledge of the true God than did the Jewish leaders, but what they knew of Him they believed and followed. The Jewish leaders had the letter of God's Word, which, by itself, kills because it judges and condemns those who know it but do not know and accept the One who has given it. The Gentile magi, on the other hand, had little of the letter of God's Word but were remarkably responsive to God's Spirit, who "gives life" (2 Cor. 3:6).

We see in this account the three typical responses to Jesus Christ that men have made throughout history. Some, like Herod, are immediately hateful, wanting to know nothing of God's way except how to attack and, if possible, destroy it. Others, like the chief priests and scribes, pay little if any attention to God and His way. They are those over whom Jeremiah heartbrokenly lamented, "Is it nothing to all you who pass this way?" (Lam. 1:12). What they know of God they do not accept or obey. At most, He is given lip service. Eventually, of course, this second group inevitably joins the first—because indifference to God is simply hatred that is concealed and rejection that is delayed.

Others, however, like the magi from the east, accept the Lord when He comes to them. They may have little of His light initially, but because they know it is *His* light, they believe, obey, and worship—and live.

After Herod received the information he wanted from the Jewish leaders, he **secretly called the magi, and ascertained the time the star appeared.** His concern was for the **time** of the star's appearance, not its meaning or significance. It was enough for him to know only that the sign pointed to the birth of someone who could be a threat to his own power and position. The time of the star's appearance would indicate the age of the child who had been born.

Herod then instructed the magi to proceed with their mission and then report their findings to him as they returned home. He hypocritically gave them a good-sounding reason for wanting to know the exact location and identity of the **Child**—in order that **I too may come and worship Him.** His ultimate purpose, of course, was made clear by what he actually did. When the magi, again obedient to the Lord's leading (2:12), did not report to Herod, he ordered his soldiers to slaughter every male child in and around Bethlehem that was under two years of age (v. 16), in order to guarantee, he thought, the destruction of his rival newborn "King."

THE ADORATION BY THE MAGI

And having heard the king, they went their way; and lo, the star, which they

had seen in the east, went on before them, until it came and stood over where the Child was. And when they saw the star, they rejoiced exceedingly with great joy. And they came into the house and saw the Child with Mary His mother; and they fell down and worshiped Him; and opening their treasures they presented to Him gifts of gold and frankincense and myrrh. And having been warned by God in a dream not to return to Herod, they departed for their own country by another way. (2:9-12)

We are not told what, if anything, the magi told Herod. They had no way of knowing his wicked intent. They proceeded to Bethlehem, not because of Herod's instruction, but because at last they knew where to find the One they had come to worship. The Lord gave them even more specific help, leading them directly to Jesus. **The star, which they had seen in the east, went on before them, until it came and stood over where the Child was.** That the star was not a physical heavenly body is again evident from the fact that it was able to stand directly over the house where Jesus and His family now lived—which for obvious reasons could not be possible for an actual star (cf. Ex. 40:34-38; Ezek. 10:4).

The magi were overwhelmed that the special star reappeared to them. It seems almost as if Matthew was at a loss for words to describe their ecstasy: **And when they saw the star, they rejoiced exceedingly with great joy.** The original text piles up superlatives to emphasize the extent of exhilaration they felt, thus indicating to us their uniquely strong interest in this great event.

Joseph and his family were no longer in the stable but had found a **house** in which to live until the Lord told them where to go and what to do next. It was there that the magi found the One for whom they had so diligently searched, and at last **they fell down and worshiped Him.** In His wonderful grace God had led them to His Son and allowed them to see Him face to face. Charles Wesley captured the experience in his beautiful Christmas hymn: "Veiled in flesh the Godhead see; hail the incarnate deity; pleased as man with men to dwell, Jesus our Immanuel!"

Matthew is careful to say that the magi **worshiped Him,** that is, **the Child,** not His **mother.** They knew better than Cornelius, who attempted to worship the apostle Peter (Acts 10:25), and the crowd at Lystra who tried to offer sacrifices to Paul and Barnabas (Acts 14:11-13). No doubt the magi were delighted to meet both Mary and Joseph, who had been so specially favored by God to be entrusted with caring for His own Son while He grew to manhood. But they worshiped only Jesus. Only He was God, and only He was worthy of adoration.

It was also **to Him** that **they presented** their **gifts of gold and frankincense and myrrh.** Their giving was not so much an addition to their worship as an element of it. The gifts were an expression of worship, given out of the overflow of adoring and grateful hearts.

Right worship is always, and must be, the only basis for right giving and right learning and right service. Giving that is generous but done apart from a loving relationship with God is empty giving. Learning that is orthodox and biblical but is learned apart from knowing and depending on the Source of truth, is empty knowledge, like that of the chief priests and scribes. Service that is demanding and sacrificial but done in the power of the flesh or for the praise of men is empty service.

Throughout history **gold** has been considered the most precious of metals and the universal symbol of material value and wealth. It was used extensively in the construction of the Temple (see 1 Kings 6-7, 9; 2 Chron. 2-4). It was also a symbol of nobility and royalty (see Gen. 41:4; 1 Kings 10:1-13; etc.). Matthew continually presents Christ as the King, and here we see the King of the Jews, the King of kings, appropriately being presented with royal gifts of gold.

The Savior of the world is also the true King of the world, and He will not be Savior of those who will not accept Him as sovereign Lord. As wonderful as Jesus' saviorhood was to them, the early Christians' first known creed was "Jesus is Lord," acknowledging His rule.

The great British admiral Lord Nelson was known for treating vanquished opponents with courtesy and kindness. After one naval victory a defeated officer strode confidently across the quarterdeck of Nelson's ship and offered the admiral his hand. With his own hand remaining at his side, Nelson replied, "Your sword first, sir, and then your hand." Before we can be Christ's friends, we must be His subjects. He must be our Lord before He can be our elder Brother.

Frankincense was a costly, beautiful-smelling incense that was used only for the most special of occasions. It was used in the grain offerings at the Tabernacle and Temple (Lev. 2:2, 15-16), in certain royal processions (Song of Sol. 3:6-7), and sometimes at weddings if it could be afforded.

Origen, the great church Father, suggested that frankincense was the incense of deity. In the Old Testament it was stored in a special chamber in front of the Temple and was sprinkled on certain offerings as a symbol of the people's desire to please the Lord.

Myrrh was also a perfume, not quite so expensive as frankincense but nevertheless valuable. Some interpreters suggest that myrrh represents the gift for a mortal, emphasizing Jesus' humanity. This perfume is mentioned often in Scripture, beginning in Genesis (37:25; 43:11). Mixed with wine it was also used as an anesthetic (Mark 15:23), and mixed with other spices it was used in preparation of bodies for burial, even Jesus' body (John 19:39).

Those were the magi's gifts to Jesus. **Gold** for His royalty, **frankincense** for His deity, and **myrrh** for His humanity.

We do not know what was done with the gifts, but it seems reasonable that they were used to finance the trip to Egypt and to help support the family while there (see Matt. 2:13-15).

With their mission of worship and adoration completed, the magi left Bethlehem. But **having been warned by God in a dream not to return to Herod, they departed for their own country by another way.** No doubt they expected to hear at a later date the details of the life and accession to the throne of the Child born in Bethlehem.

The warning by God suggests that He was directly communicating with these men, and that their role in the whole event was by divine design. In fact, it may have been the same method, **a dream**, by which He originally brought them to Jerusalem in search of the King. The use of dreams as a means of divine communication is seen in Genesis 28:12; 31:11; Numbers 12:6; 1 Kings 3:5; and Job 33:14-16. Even the birth of Christ was accompanied by other special revelatory dreams (Matt. 1:20-23; 2:13, 19-20, 22).

So the magi avoided **Herod** and traveled a homeward route that would allow them to escape his notice—a feat that was not simple, due to the nature and size of their entourage.

Scripture records nothing else about these unusual visitors from the east, but blessed and grateful as they were, they surely must have witnessed of the Messiah in **their own country**. Because they were among the kingmakers of Parthia, it is likely that the news of Jesus became as well known in the courts of the east as it one day would become in the palace of Caesar (Phil. 1:13; cf. 4:22).

The King Fulfills Prophecy (2:13-23)

4

Now when they had departed, behold, an angel of the Lord appeared to Joseph in a dream, saying, "Arise and take the Child and His mother, and flee to Egypt, and remain there until I tell you; for Herod is going to search for the Child to destroy Him." And he arose and took the Child and His mother by night, and departed for Egypt; and was there until the death of Herod, that what was spoken by the Lord through the prophet might be fulfilled, saying, "Out of Egypt did I call My Son."

Then when Herod saw that he had been tricked by the magi, he became very enraged, and sent and slew all the male children who were in Bethlehem and in all its environs, from two years old and under, according to the time which he had ascertained from the magi. Then that which was spoken through Jeremiah the prophet was fulfilled, saying, "A voice was heard in Ramah, weeping and great mourning, Rachel weeping for her children; and she refused to be comforted, because they were no more."

But when Herod was dead, behold, an angel of the Lord appeared in a dream to Joseph in Egypt, saying, "Arise and take the Child and His mother, and go into the land of Israel; for those who sought the Child's life are dead." And he arose and took the Child and His mother, and came into the land of Israel. But when he heard that Archelaus was reigning over Judea in place of his father Herod, he was afraid to go there. And being warned by God in a dream, he departed for the regions of Galilee, and came and resided in a city called Nazareth, that what was spoken through the prophets might be fulfilled, "He shall be called a Nazarene." (2:13-23)

The first of the four Old Testament passages around which Matthew presents the events of chapter 2 is that of the Messiah's being born in Bethlehem (2:6; cf. Mic. 5:2), which has been discussed in relation to the coming of the magi. The other three are given in the present text. One refers to the escape to Egypt, another to the slaughter at Ramah, and the other to the return to Nazareth.

THE ESCAPE TO EGYPT

Now when they had departed, behold, an angel of the Lord appeared to Joseph in a dream, saying, "Arise and take the Child and His mother, and flee to Egypt, and remain there until I tell you; for Herod is going to search for the Child to destroy Him." And he arose and took the Child and His mother by night, and departed for Egypt; and was there until the death of Herod, that what was spoken by the Lord through the prophet might be fulfilled, saying, "Out of Egypt did I call My Son." (2:13-15)

The coming of the magi no doubt was a time of great encouragement and assurance to Joseph and Mary, confirming the wondrous words of the angels to them (Matt. 1:20-23; Luke 1:26-38), to Zacharias (Luke 1:11-20), and to the shepherds (Luke 2:8-14). It also confirmed the testimonies of Elizabeth (Luke 1:39-45) and of Simeon and Anna (Luke 2:25-38) about the Child to whom Mary gave birth. Even these wise men from far-off Parthia had been told the news by God and came to worship Jesus and give Him gifts.

But the rejoicing was short-lived. No sooner had the magi **departed** than **an angel of the Lord appeared to Joseph in a dream**, giving him a warning from God. This news was not of joy and hope, but of danger and urgency. **Arise and take the Child and His mother, and flee to Egypt, and remain there until I tell you; for Herod is going to search for the Child to destroy Him.** Just as the magi had been warned by God to disobey Herod (v. 12), Joseph was now warned by God to flee the evil, murderous king.

From *pheugō* (to **flee**) we get our word *fugitive,* one who escapes from something or someone. The word is here in the present imperative, indicating the beginning of action that is to be continued. Joseph and his family were immediately to begin fleeing, and were not to stop until they were safely within **Egypt** and beyond the reach of Herod. The distance from Bethlehem to the border of Egypt was about 75 miles, and another 100 miles or so would have been required to get to a place of safety in that country. Traveling with a baby made the trip both slower and more difficult.

Egypt was a natural asylum for the young Jewish family. During the period of Greek rule of the Mediterranean world, which occurred during the intertestamental period, Alexander the Great established a sanctuary for Jews in Alexandria, the Egyptian city he named for himself. Throughout the Roman rule that followed, that city was still considered a special place of safety and opportunity for Jews. The Jewish philosopher and historian Philo, himself a prominent resident of Alexandria, reported that by A.D. 40, a few years after the death of Christ, the city's population included at least one million Jews. In the third century B.C. a group of Jewish scholars in Alexandria had produced the Septuagint, a translation of the Old Testament from Hebrew into Greek. The Septuagint was used by much of the early church, and it was from that version of the Old Testament that many New Testament writers quote.

As mentioned in the previous chapter, it seems reasonable that Joseph used the valuable gifts of the magi (the gold, frankincense, and myrrh) to pay for the trip to Egypt and the stay there, where the Lord instructed Joseph to keep his family **until I tell you.**

Obviously God could have protected His Son in many other ways and in many other places, even in Bethlehem or Jerusalem, under Herod's very nose. He could have blinded Herod's soldiers, destroyed them by an angel, or simply have miraculously hidden the family. But God chose to protect Him by the very ordinary and unmiraculous means of flight to a foreign country. The commands to go to Egypt and then to leave were given supernaturally, but the trip itself and the stay there were, as far as we are told, marked by no special divine intervention or provision. The family was not instantly transported to Egypt, but had to make the long, tiresome journey on their own, just as hundreds of other Jewish families had done during the previous several centuries. To decrease the chance of being noticed, Joseph took the common precaution of leaving **by night**, probably telling no one of his plans.

We know nothing of the stay in Egypt except the bare fact that Jesus and His family were there. Countless speculations have been made about the sojourn. Some ancient writers, supposing perhaps to enhance and improve on the biblical account, manufactured stories of the baby Jesus healing a demon-possessed child by placing His swaddling clothes on the afflicted child's head, of causing robbers to flee into the desert, and of causing idols to disintegrate as He walked by them. Others, such as the second-century pagan philosopher Celsus, sought to discredit Jesus by claiming that He spent His childhood and early manhood in Egypt learning the occultic practices for which that country had long been famous. Like many Jewish opponents of Christianity during his day, Celsus maintained that Jesus then returned to Palestine to impress the people with miracles and deceive them into thinking He was the Messiah.

It is likely that the stay in Egypt **until the death of Herod** lasted no more than a few months. It is now that we are told the primary reason for the family's going to Egypt: **that what was spoken by the Lord through the prophet might be fulfilled, saying, "Out of Egypt did I call My Son."** The Old Testament writers were the Lord's spokesmen. Just as they had no way of knowing, apart from divine revelation, that the Messiah would be born in Bethlehem, they had no other way of knowing that He would live awhile in Egypt. The flight to Egypt was one more piece of divine evidence that Jesus was God's Son, the promised Messiah.

Seven centuries earlier God had told Hosea that "out of Egypt I called My son" (Hos. 11:1). Herod's threat was no surprise to the Lord, who, long before Herod was born, had made plans to foil that wicked king's plans against the true King. The reference to "My son" in the book of Hosea is to the nation Israel. It was a historical statement about what God had done in delivering His people from bondage under Pharaoh, calling them out from Egypt under the leadership of Moses. Why, then, did Matthew interpret as predictive an event that occurred perhaps 700 years before Hosea and an additional 700 years before Matthew quoted Hosea?

The setting of the book of Hosea is failure, decadence, and spiritual tragedy. Through the unfaithfulness of his own wife, Gomer, Hosea vividly portrays the unfaithfulness of Israel to the Lord. Gomer was a physical prostitute, and Israel was a spiritual prostitute. God's chosen people had chased after false gods as unashamedly as Gomer had chased after her lovers. Though Hosea's heart was grieved and broken, he continued to love his wife and sought to win her back. She wound up in a brothel, having lost all sense of decency and shame. The Lord then commanded Hosea to redeem her: "Go again, love a woman who is loved by her husband, yet an adulteress, even as the Lord loves the sons of Israel, though they turn to other gods" (Hos. 3:1). The prophet then bought Gomer's freedom "for fifteen shekels of silver and a homer and a half of barley" (v. 2). He brought her home, gave her back her place of honor as his wife, and continued to love her as he had before. She was his wife, and he maintained his covenant. Hosea 11:3-4 tells how God taught the Israelites, carried them, healed them, led them, loved them, eased their burdens, and fed them. He called them from Egypt in order to be faithful to them, in spite of their unfaithfulness to Him.

Despite everything, God promised to bring Israel back to Himself. Israel would suffer His rebuke and His judgment, but one day that people would return to their God, because He had called Israel to be His son. Thus God reminded His people of His great and long-lasting love for them. "When Israel was a youth I loved him, and out of Egypt I called My son" (Hos. 11:1). He would not go back on that calling. When Matthew quotes the last part of that verse from Hosea, he applies it to Christ. Though Hosea was not knowingly predicting that the Messiah would also one day be brought out of Egypt, Matthew shows that Jesus' return from Egypt was *pictured* by Israel's calling from that same country many centuries earlier. The Exodus, therefore, was a type of Jesus' return from Egypt with Joseph and Mary. As God had once brought the people of Israel out of Egypt to be His chosen nation, He now had brought out His greater Son to be the Messiah.

A type is a nonverbal prediction, an Old Testament person or event that illustrates some aspect of the person and work of the Lord Jesus Christ in the future but does not specifically describe it; the writer has no way to see the future antitype. God's nonverbal predictions are as true and vivid as His verbal ones. But we cannot legitimately call a person or event a true Old Testament type except as the Bible itself tells us of it. The only certain Old Testament types are those given as such in the New Testament. No type is in itself visibly a type; such reality awaits the New Testament identification. When the New Testament uses something in the Old as a prefigurement of something that has occurred or will occur later, we can safely refer to the Old Testament something as a type. Ignoring such limits results in the freedom to allegorize, spiritualize, and typify the Old Testament by whimsy. Because types are veiled revelation, divine testimony to their identity must be given by the Holy Spirit in the New Testament text. Therefore, because of the specific association that Matthew gives here, we know that the Exodus of Israel from Egypt is a type of Jesus' return from Egypt as a young child.

In a still deeper sense Jesus came out of Egypt with Israel under Moses. As Matthew has already shown, Jesus descended from Abraham and from the royal line of David. Had Israel perished in Egypt, or in the wilderness, or in any other way, the Messiah could not Himself have come out of Egypt or even have been born.

THE SLAUGHTER AT RAMAH

Then when Herod saw that he had been tricked by the magi, he became very enraged, and sent and slew all the male children who were in Bethlehem and in all its environs, from two years old and under, according to the time which he had ascertained from the magi. Then that which was spoken through Jeremiah the prophet was fulfilled, saying, "A voice was heard in Ramah, weeping and great mourning, Rachel weeping for her children; and she refused to be comforted, because they were no more." (2:16-18)

The third fulfilled prophecy that Matthew mentions in chapter 2 is that of Herod's brutal slaughter in Bethlehem. After Joseph had secretly taken Jesus and His mother to the safety of Egypt, the malevolent Herod, enraged by the magi's failure to report back to him (see 2:7-8), committed one of the bloodiest acts of his career, and certainly the cruelest.

The Greek word *empaizō* generally carried the idea of mocking, and is so translated in the King James Version of this passage. The root meaning is "to play like a child," especially in the sense of making sport of or jesting. It is used to describe the accusations and taunts of Jesus' enemies against Him (Matt. 20:19; 27:41; Mark 15:20; Luke 22:63; 23:11; etc.). But the idea in Matthew 2:16 is better rendered as **tricked**. Either meaning, however, refers to Herod's perception of the motives of the **magi**, not their true intention. It was not their purpose to trick or mock the king but simply to obey God's command "not to return to Herod" (v. 12). The king, of course, knew nothing of God's warning and saw only that the wise men did not do as he had instructed.

Herod's hatred of the newborn contender to his throne began when he first heard the news of His birth. The purpose of having the magi report back to him was to learn the exact information needed to discover and destroy the Child—not to worship Him, as he had deceitfully told the magi (2:8). The magi's going home by another way, and so avoiding Herod, added infuriation to hatred, so that **he became very enraged.**

Thumoō (to be **enraged**) is a strong word, made still stronger by *lian* (**very,** or better, exceedingly). The Greek is in the passive voice, indicating that Herod had lost control of his passion and now was completely controlled by it. His senses, and what little judgment he may have had, were blinded. He did not bother to consider that, because the magi did not return to him, they probably had guessed his wicked intent and that, if so, they would surely have warned the family. The family, in turn, would have long fled Bethlehem and probably the country. In light of Herod's perverted mind, however, he possibly would have taken the same cruel action— out of the same senseless rage and frustration—even had he known that the primary object of his hatred had escaped. If he was not able to guarantee killing Jesus by killing the other babies, he would kill them in place of Jesus.

In any case Herod's rage was vented in the desperate and heartless slaughter of **all the male children who were in Bethlehem and in all its environs, from two years old and under.** He went up to the age of **two** because of **the time which he had ascertained from the magi.** Jesus was probably no older than six months at this time, but even if that had been the age Herod determined from the magi's information (2:7), it is likely he would have taken no chances. Killing all the male babies up to age two was a small precaution in his evil thinking, in case the magi had miscalculated or deceived him.

Herod's crime was made even more vile and heinous by the fact that he knew that the Child he sought to destroy was the Messiah, the Christ. He questioned the chief priests and scribes specifically about "where the Christ was to be born" (2:4). He arrogantly and stupidly set himself against God's very Anointed (cf. 1 Cor. 16:22).

It seems as if, from the earliest part of his message, Matthew wanted to portray the rejection of the Messiah by those from among whom He came and in whose behalf He first came (Acts 3:26; Rom. 1:16). The chief priests and the scribes, along with the many other Jews in Jerusalem who must have heard or known about the magi's message of the one "who has been born King of the Jews," showed no interest at all in finding Him, much less in worshiping Him (see Matt. 2:2-5). Though Herod was not himself a Jew and had no right to a Jewish throne, he nevertheless declared himself to be the king of the Jews and made a pretense of concern for Jewish religious and economic interests. In an illegitimate and perverted way, therefore, Herod's rejection of Christ both reflected and represented the Jews' rejection of Him.

The slaughter in Bethlehem was the beginning of the tragedy and bloodshed that would result from Israel's rejection of her Savior and true King. Those innocent and precious babies of Bethlehem were the first casualties in the now-intensified warfare between the kingdoms of this world and the kingdom of God's Christ, God's Anointed. Within two generations from that time (in A.D. 70)

Jerusalem would see its Temple destroyed and over a million of its people massacred by the troops of Titus. Yet that destruction will pale in comparison with that of the Antichrist—a ruler immeasurably more wicked and powerful than Herod—when in the Great Tribulation he will shed more of Israel's blood than will ever have been shed before (Dan. 12:1; Matt. 24:21-22). All of that bloodshed is over the conflict with the Messiah.

The least of Herod's intentions was to fulfill prophecy, but that is what his slaughter did. **Then that which was spoken through Jeremiah the prophet was fulfilled.** Herod's beastly act is recorded only by Matthew, yet it was predicted in a text given to the prophet Jeremiah. The term **fulfilled** (from *plēroō*, "to fill up") marks this out as completing an Old Testament prediction. This prophecy, like that of Jesus' return from Egypt, was in the form of a type, which, as we have seen above, is a nonverbal prediction revealed in the New Testament. In the passage (Jer. 31:15) from which Matthew here quotes, Jeremiah was speaking of the great sorrow that would soon be experienced in Israel when most of her people would be carried captive to Babylon. **Ramah,** a town about five miles north of Jerusalem, was on the border of the northern (Israel) and southern (Judah) kingdoms. It was also the place where Jewish captives were assembled for deportation to Babylon (Jer. 40:1). **Rachel,** the wife of Jacob-Israel, was the mother of Joseph, whose two sons, Ephraim and Manasseh, became progenitors of the two half-tribes that bore their names. Ephraim is often used in the Old Testament as a synonym for the northern kingdom. **Rachel** was also the mother of Benjamin, whose tribe became part of the southern kingdom. She had once cried, "Give me children, or else I die" (Gen. 30:1), and now her beloved "children," her immeasurably multiplied descendants, were being taken captive to a foreign and pagan land.

Rachel weeping for her children therefore represented the lamentation of all Jewish mothers who wept over Israel's great tragedy in the days of Jeremiah, and most specifically typified and prefigured the mothers of Bethlehem weeping bitterly over the massacre of their children by Herod in His attempt to kill the Messiah. So even while Israel's Messiah was still a babe, Rachel had cause to weep again, even as the Messiah Himself would later weep over Jerusalem because of His people's rejection of Him and the afflictions they would suffer as a consequence (Luke 19:41-44).

Though Matthew does not mention it here, because he is emphasizing the tragedy of the massacre, the passage he quotes from Jeremiah continues with a beautiful word of hope and promise: "Thus says the Lord, 'Restrain your voice from weeping, and your eyes from tears; for your work shall be rewarded,' declares the Lord, 'and they shall return from the land of the enemy'" (Jer. 31:16). Within a few generations, the Lord brought His people back from Babylon, and one day He will bring all His chosen people back from captivity to Satan. "All Israel will be saved; just as it is written, 'The Deliverer will come from Zion, He will remove ungodliness from Jacob. And this is My covenant with them, when I take away their sins'" (Rom. 11:26-27; cf. Isa. 27:9; 59:20-21). But before that great and wonderful day, disobedience, rejection, and tragedy would continue in Israel. The massacre of the little ones in Bethlehem signaled the start of terrifying conflict.

THE RETURN TO NAZARETH

But when Herod was dead, behold, an angel of the Lord appeared in a dream to Joseph in Egypt, saying, "Arise and take the Child and His mother, and go into the land of Israel; for those who sought the Child's life are dead." And he arose and took the Child and His mother, and came into the land of Israel. But when he heard that Archelaus was reigning over Judea in place of his father Herod, he was afraid to go there. And being warned by God in a dream, he departed for the regions of Galilee, and came and resided in a city called Nazareth, that what was spoken through the prophets might be fulfilled, "He shall be called a Nazarene." (2:19-23)

The fourth and final prophecy that Matthew mentions in chapter 2 pertains to the journey of Jesus' family from Egypt to Nazareth.

When Herod was dead, the greatest immediate danger to Jesus was over. In his *Antiquities* Josephus reports that Herod "died of this, ulcerated entrails, putrified and maggot-filled organs, constant convulsions, foul breath, and neither physicians nor warm baths led to recovery." A rather fitting end, it seems, for such a man. Not nearly so fitting was the elaborate and costly funeral that his eldest son and successor, Archelaus, prepared in his honor—especially in light of the fact that just five days before he died, Herod, by permission from Rome, had executed another son, Antipater, because of his plots against his father.

The angel of the Lord had told Joseph to stay in Egypt "until I tell you" (2:13). Now the angel reappeared to Joseph as promised, telling him, **Arise and take the Child and His mother, and go into the land of Israel; for those who sought the Child's life are dead.** The fact that the angel spoke of **those who sought the Child's life** indicates that Herod was not alone in his plans to destroy his supposed rival. But like Herod, the other conspirators seeking the death of **the Child** were themselves now **dead.**

Joseph was not instructed to return to any particular city or region but simply to **take the Child and His mother** back **into the land of Israel.** When he arrived in southern Israel, however, and **heard that Archelaus was reigning over Judea in place of his father Herod, he was afraid to go there.** The ones who had previously sought to kill the infant Jesus were dead, but **Archelaus** posed another, more general, threat. In one of his numerous acts of brutality shortly before he died, Herod had executed two popular Jewish rabbis, Judas and Matthias, who had stirred up their disciples and other faithful Jews in Jerusalem to tear down the offensive Roman eagle that the king had arrogantly erected over the Temple gate. The following Passover an insurrection broke out, and Archelaus, reflecting his father's senseless cruelty, executed three thousand Jews, many of whom were Passover pilgrims who had no part in the revolt.

Any Jew, therefore, who lived in the territory of Archelaus was in danger. Consequently Joseph was again **warned by God in a dream**, [and] **he departed for the regions of Galilee**. That they **came and resided in a city called Nazareth** was not only because Joseph and Mary were originally from there (Luke 2:4-5) by divine providence, but **that what was spoken through the prophets might be fulfilled**. Matthew focuses on two features through all of this narrative: (1) divine revelation as indicated by angelic instruction for every move, and (2) the fulfillment of a divine plan revealed in the Old Testament.

The specific statement that the Messiah would **be called a Nazarene** does not appear in the Old Testament. Some interpreters have tried to connect **Nazarene** with the Hebrew *nēṣer* (branch) spoken of in Isaiah 11:1, but that idea is without etymological or other support, as is the idea of trying to tie the prophecy to the "shoot" of Isaiah 53:2. Because Matthew speaks of **the prophets**, plural, it seems that several prophets had made this prediction, though it is not specifically recorded in the Old Testament.

Other sayings and events unrecorded in the Old Testament are nevertheless quoted or referred to in the New. Jude tells us that "Enoch, in the seventh generation from Adam, prophesied, saying, 'Behold, the Lord came with many thousands of His holy ones, to execute judgment upon all, and to convict all the ungodly of all their ungodly deeds which they have done in an ungodly way'" (Jude 14-15). Yet no such prophecy is mentioned in Genesis or in any other part of the Old Testament. In a similar way we know of Jesus' teaching that "It is more blessed to give than to receive" only because of Paul's later reference to it (Acts 20:35). The saying is not mentioned by any of the gospel writers, including Luke, who reported the account in Acts. John tells us that he did not even attempt to record everything that Jesus said and did during His earthly ministry (John 21:25).

Matthew does not tell us which prophets predicted that the Messiah would be called a **Nazarene**, but only that more than one of them did so. The prophecy is said to be **fulfilled** when Jesus was taken to live in Nazareth, where Joseph and Mary had formerly lived. Matthew's original readers were largely Jewish, and it was probably common knowledge among them who the specific prophets were that had made the prediction. For later readers, the Holy Spirit obviously felt it was enough that we simply know that the prediction was made and that it was fulfilled as Matthew explains.

Nazareth was about 55 miles north of Jerusalem, in **the regions of Galilee**, where the Lord had directed Joseph to go. The town was in an elevated basin, about one and a half miles across, and was inhabited largely by people noted for their crude and violent ways. The term *Nazarene* had long been a term of derision, used to describe any person who was rough and rude. That is why Nathanael, who was from Cana, a few miles to the south, asked Philip, "Can any good thing come out of Nazareth?" (John 1:46). The question is especially significant coming from Nathanael, who by Jesus' own word was "an Israelite indeed, in whom is no guile!" (v. 47). Nathanael was not given to maligning his neighbors, but he was shocked that the one "of whom Moses in the Law and also the Prophets wrote" (v. 45) actually could come from such a disreputable place as Nazareth.

The early Jewish persecutors of the church apparently considered Jesus' being from Nazareth as evidence that He could *not* be the Messiah, rather than, as Matthew tells us, a sign that He *was*. Tertullus, acting as attorney for the high priest Ananias and other Jewish leaders, spoke derisively of Paul before the Roman governor Felix as "a real pest and a fellow who stirs up dissension among all the Jews throughout the world, and a ringleader of the sect of the Nazarenes" (Acts 24:5). The church Father Jerome wrote that in synagogue prayers Christians were often cursed as Nazarenes, with the petition that they would be blotted out of the Book of Life (see Ps. 69:28). Jesus' living in Nazareth not only fulfilled the unnamed prophets' prediction, but gave Him a name, Jesus the Nazarene, that would be used as a title of reproach, thus fulfilling many other prophecies that depict the Messiah as "despised and forsaken of men" (Isa. 53:3; cf. 49:7; Ps. 22:6-8; 69:20-21). The gospel writers make clear the fact that He was scorned and hated (see Matt. 12:24; 27:21-23, 63; Luke 23:4; John 5:18; 6:66; 9:22, 29).

It was therefore at lowly and despised Nazareth that the royal Son of God, along with the righteous Joseph and Mary, made His home for some thirty years.

The Greatest Man (3:1-6)

5

Now in those days John the Baptist came, preaching in the wilderness of Judea, saying, "Repent, for the kingdom of heaven is at hand." For this is the one referred to by Isaiah the prophet, saying, "The voice of one crying in the wilderness, 'Make ready the way of the Lord, make His paths straight!'" Now John himself had a garment of camel's hair, and a leather belt about his waist; and his food was locusts and wild honey. Then Jerusalem was going out to him, and all Judea, and all the district around the Jordan; and they were being baptized by him in the Jordan River, as they confessed their sins. (3:1-6)

At a conference one time a young person asked me, "What makes a person great?" I could not think of a good answer right then, but I began thinking about it. In the world's eyes, such things as being born into a famous, wealthy, or influential family bring a certain measure of greatness simply by heritage. Earning a great deal of money is another mark of the world's greatness, as are academic degrees, expertise in some field, outstanding athletic ability, artistic talent, high political or military office, and other such things.

By those criteria, however, even Jesus Christ was not great. Though He manifested surpassing wisdom and power, He was born into a quite ordinary family, His father being a simple carpenter. Even after He was grown, Jesus did not own a business, a herd of cattle or sheep, a house, or even a tent. He said, "The foxes have holes, and the birds of the air have nests; but the Son of Man has nowhere to lay His head" (Matt. 8:20). He had little, if any, formal education, no political office, no artistic accomplishments—in short, almost no marks of what the world considers greatness.

John the Baptist had even fewer of the world's marks of greatness than did Jesus. Yet Jesus called John the greatest man who had ever lived until that time: "Truly, I say to you, among those born of women there has not arisen anyone greater than John the Baptist" (Matt. 11:11). John was greater than Noah, Abraham, Isaac, Jacob, or Joseph; greater than Moses, Elijah, David, or any of the other Old Testament men of God. He was greater than any of the kings, emperors, philosophers, or military leaders of history. Yet, like Jesus, he was born into a simple, obscure family. His father, Zacharias, was one of many priests who took turns ministering in the Temple when their course, or division, was scheduled to serve. His mother, Elizabeth, was also from the priestly tribe of Levi and a descendant of the first high priest, Aaron (Luke 1:5). But there were many such descendants, most of whom had no place of special dignity or recognition.

That was John's family heritage. When he was grown, probably starting in his teen years, John the Baptist went to live in the wilderness of Judea, existing much like a hermit and forsaking even what little social and economic status he had. Yet Luke recorded of him, "for he will be great in the sight of the Lord" (1:15).

Reasons for such superlative commendation can be seen in 3:1-6, where Matthew gives a brief picture of the life and work of John the Baptist and also shows that John's ministry was yet another evidence of Jesus' kingship.

In chapter 1 Jesus' kingship is shown by his birth—by His descent from the royal line of David and by His miraculous conception. In chapter 2 His kingship is shown by the circumstances surrounding His birth—by the homage of the magi, the hatred of Herod, and God's miraculous protection of the young Jesus. Now we are shown the evidence through the herald who announced the King's arrival. The greatest man who had yet lived was primarily so because he was herald of the Messiah, the One who was greater still. His greatness was related to his calling.

In ancient times it was common for a herald to precede the arrival of the monarch, to announce his coming and to prepare for his safe and proper travel. With a coterie of servants, the herald would make sure that the roadway was as smooth and uncluttered as possible. Holes would be filled, rocks and debris would be removed, and unsightly litter would be burned or hidden. As the group traveled along and worked, the herald would proclaim the king's coming to everyone he encountered. His twofold duty was to proclaim and to prepare. That is what John's ministry did for God's great King, Jesus Christ.

In presenting the herald of Christ, Matthew shows us the man, the message, the motive, the mission, the manner, and the ministry.

THE MAN

Now in those days John the Baptist came, preaching in the wilderness of Judea, saying, (3:1)

Now in those days serves as a transition between chapters 2 and 3. It was a common literary phrase, indicating the general time in which the events being described occurred. Nearly thirty years had elapsed between Joseph's taking the young Jesus and His mother to Nazareth and the beginning of John's public ministry. Only Luke (2:39-52) tells us anything of Jesus' life during the intervening years. Apart from that brief account, Scripture is silent.

John was a common Jewish name in New Testament times and is the Greek form of the Hebrew Johanan (see 2 Kings 25:23; Jer. 40:8; etc.), which means "Jehovah, or Yahweh, is gracious." **Baptist**, or Baptizer (*baptistēs*; the Greek ending, *tēs*, signifies one who performs an act), was an epithet given him because baptizing was such an important and obvious part of his ministry.

John's father and mother "were both righteous in the sight of God, walking blamelessly in all the commandments and requirements of the Lord." But they had no children and, like Sarah before Isaac was conceived, Elizabeth was beyond normal childbearing years (Luke 1:6-7; cf. Gen. 17:17). One day as John's father was performing his priestly function in the Temple, "an angel of the Lord appeared to him, standing to the right of the altar of incense" (Luke 1:11). The angel proceeded to tell Zacharias that "Elizabeth will bear you a son, and you will give him the name John. And you will have joy and gladness, and many will rejoice at his birth. For he will be great in the sight of the Lord" (vv. 13-15). John was named by God Himself and set apart for greatness even before he was conceived!

John would "be filled with the Holy Spirit, while yet in his mother's womb. And he [would] turn back many of the sons of Israel to the Lord their God" (Luke 1:15-16). Most significantly of all, he would "go as a forerunner before Him in the spirit and power of Elijah . . . so as to make ready a people prepared for the Lord" (v. 17). John's own father, himself "filled with the Holy Spirit," declared that John "will be called the prophet of the Most High; for you [John] will go on before the Lord to prepare His ways" (vv. 67, 76). "And the child continued to grow, and to become strong in spirit, and he lived in the deserts until the day of his public appearance to Israel" (v. 80).

That was John. His conception was miraculous, he was filled with the Holy Spirit before he was born, he was great in the sight of God, and he was to be the herald of the Messiah, announcing and preparing the people for His coming. It is therefore not strange that Jesus said, "There has not arisen anyone greater than John the Baptist" (Matt. 11:11). That great man was a sovereignly designed and chosen herald for the great King.

Came is from *paraginomai*, which often was used to indicate an official arrival, such as that of the magi (Matt. 2:1), or the public appearance of a leader or teacher (Matt. 3:13). For thirty years both John and Jesus had lived in relative obscurity. Now the coming of the herald signified the coming of the King. The beginning of John's ministry signaled the beginning of Jesus' ministry (see Acts 10:37-38).

Preaching is from *kērussō,* the primary meaning of which is "to herald." It was used of the official whose duty it was to proclaim loudly and extensively the coming of the king. Matthew also uses this term with reference to Jesus and the apostles.

John knew his position and his task. He never sought or accepted honor for himself, but only for the One whose coming he proclaimed. As a child John no doubt had been told many times of the angel's announcement of his birth and his purpose, a purpose from which he never wavered, compromised, or tried to gain personal recognition or advantage. When questioned by the priests and Levites who had been sent from Jerusalem to ask his identity, John replied, "I am not the Christ" (John 1:19-20). He also denied being Elijah and "the Prophet" (v. 21; cf. Deut. 18:15). When they persisted in knowing who he was, he simply said, "I am a voice of one crying in the wilderness, 'Make straight the way of the Lord,' as Isaiah the prophet said" (v. 23).

The question about his being Elijah introduces some important truth. At every orthodox Passover ceremony even today a cup is reserved at the table for Elijah. At the circumcision of orthodox Jewish baby boys a chair is placed for Elijah. The anticipation is that, if Elijah would ever come and sit in the chair or drink from the cup, the Messiah's arrival would be imminent. That belief is based on Malachi 4:5-6, in which the prophet predicts, "Behold, I am going to send you Elijah the prophet before the coming of the great and terrible day of the Lord. And he will restore the hearts of the fathers to their children, and the hearts of the children to their fathers."

Yet, as he himself testified, John the Baptist was not the literal, resurrected Elijah most Jews of his day were expecting, or that many Jews of our own day expect. But he was indeed the Elijah that the prophet Malachi predicted would come. Luke 1:17 confirms that when it says that John "will go as a forerunner before Him in the spirit and power of Elijah."

That the Elijah who was commonly expected by the Jews was not the Elijah of God's plan was stated plainly by Jesus Himself after John the Baptist had been imprisoned and killed. "'Elijah is coming and will restore all things; but I say to you, that Elijah already came, and they did not recognize him, but did to him whatever they wished.' . . . Then the disciples understood that He had spoken to them about John the Baptist" (Matt. 17:11-13).

Because the Jews rejected John the Baptist as the true Elijah who was to come, they prevented the complete fulfillment of the prophecy as God had originally given it through Malachi. "If you care to accept it," Jesus explained about John, "he himself is Elijah, who was to come" (Matt. 11:14). But John not only was not accepted, he was ridiculed, imprisoned, and beheaded. Because he was not received by the great body of God's chosen people, he was not able to be the Elijah and there is therefore an Elijah yet to come. Some interpreters believe he will be one of the two witnesses of Revelation 11, but we cannot be certain. In any case, John the Baptist was rejected as the coming Elijah. And just as the herald was rejected, so was the King he heralded. John was beheaded, and Jesus was crucified. Israel therefore was set aside, and the kingdom was postponed.

Everything about John the Baptist was unique and amazing—his sudden public appearance, his life-style, his message, his baptizing, and his humility. He was born to a mother who was barren. He was a priest by heritage but became a prophet. He forsook his earthly father's ministry for the sake of his heavenly Father's. After spending most of his life in the desert, at the right moment God spoke to his heart, and he began to thunder out the message God had given him in that desert—to announce the coming of the King.

John's primary place of ministry, like his primary place of training, was **in the wilderness of Judea.** By the world's standards and procedures, the coming of a king, or of a great person of any sort, is proclaimed and prepared for with great expense, pomp, and fanfare. Even the announcer dresses in the best suits, stays in the best hotels, contacts only the best people, and makes preparations for the monarch to visit only the best places. But that was not God's plan for the heralding of His Son. John the Baptist was born of obscure parents, dressed strangely even for his day, and carried on his ministry mostly in out-of-the-way and unattractive places.

All of that, however, was not incidental or circumstantial. It was symbolic of John's ministry to call the people away from the corrupt and dead religious system of their day—away from ritualism, worldliness, hypocrisy, and superficiality. John called them away from Jerusalem and Jericho, away from the cities into the **wilderness**—where most people would not bother to go if they were not serious seekers. John brought them away, where they were freer to listen, think, and ponder, without the distractions and the misleading leaders they were so accustomed to following. In such a seemingly desolate place, they could begin to see the greatness of this man of God and the even greater greatness of the One whose coming he announced.

THE MESSAGE

The message John proclaimed was simple, so simple it could easily be summarized in one word: **repent** (3:2a; cf. Acts 13:24; 19:4). The Greek word (*metanoeō*) behind **repent** means more than regret or sorrow (cf. Heb. 12:17); it means to turn around, to change direction, to change the mind and will. It does not denote just any change, but always a change from the wrong to the right, away from sin and to righteousness. In his outstanding commentary on Matthew, John A. Broadus observes that "wherever this Greek word is used in the New Testament the reference is to changing the mind and the purpose from sin to holiness." Repentance involves sorrow for sin, but sorrow that leads to a change of thinking, desire, and conduct of life. "The sorrow that is according to the will of God," Paul says, "produces a repentance without regret, leading to salvation" (2 Cor. 7:10; cf.

v. 9). John's command to **repent** could therefore be rendered "be converted."

John's message of preparation for the coming of the King was repentance, conversion, the demand for a completely different life. That must have been startling news for Jews who thought that, as God's chosen people—the children of Abraham, the people of the covenant—they deserved and were unconditionally assured of the promised King. Knowing what they must have been thinking, John later told his listeners, "Do not suppose that you can say to yourselves, 'We have Abraham for our father'; for I say to you, that God is able from these stones to raise up children to Abraham" (3:9). God was not interested in His people's human heritage but in their spiritual life. "What the King wants from you," John was saying, "is that you make a complete turnaround from the way you are, that you be totally converted, totally changed." God calls for radical change and transformation that affects the mind, the will, and the emotions—the whole person. John's point was simple: "You are in the same condition as the Gentiles. You have no right to the kingdom unless you repent and are converted from sin to righteousness." He called for a true repentance that results in the fruit of a translated life (v. 8) and that includes baptism with water (v. 11a). Failure to repent would result in severe judgment, as Matthew 11:20-24 and 12:38-41 demonstrate.

Repentance was exactly the same message with which Jesus began His preaching and the apostles began theirs. "The time is fulfilled, and the kingdom of God is at hand," Jesus proclaimed; "repent and believe in the gospel" (Mark 1:15; cf. Matt. 3:2; 4:17; Luke 5:32). Mark 6:12 says of the twelve: "And they went out and preached that men should repent." In his Pentecost sermon, Peter's concluding words were, "Repent, and let each of you be baptized in the name of Jesus Christ for the forgiveness of your sins" (Acts 2:38; cf. Acts 3:19; 20:21; 26:18).

The close connection between repentance and conversion is also indicated in texts that do not specifically use the word repentance, yet convey the same idea (see Matt. 18:3; Luke 14:33). The best summary statement may be that of Paul in Acts 26:20, where he states that the objective of his ministry was that men "should repent and turn to God, performing deeds appropriate to repentance."

THE MOTIVE

The motive John gave for repentance was: **the kingdom of heaven is at hand** (3:2b). The people should repent and be converted because the King was coming, and He deserves and requires no less. The unrepentant and unconverted cannot give the heavenly King the glory He deserves, do not belong to the heavenly King, and are unfit for His heavenly kingdom.

After four hundred years, the people of Israel again heard God's prophetic word. Malachi's prophecy was followed by four centuries of silence, with no new or direct word from the Lord. Now, when His word came to Israel again, proclaiming the coming of the King, it was not the expected word of joy and comfort and celebration but a message of warning and rebuke. **The kingdom of heaven is at hand,** waiting to be ushered in, but Israel was not ready for it.

Despite many similar warnings by the prophets, many of the people and most of the leaders were not prepared for John's message. What he said was shocking; it was unexpected and unacceptable. It was inconceivable to them that, as God's people, they had anything to do to inherit God's kingdom but simply wait for and accept it. The Messiah was *their* Messiah, the King was *their* King, the Savior was *their* Savior, the promise was *their* promise. Every Jew was destined for the kingdom, and every Gentile was excluded, except for a token handful of proselytes. That was the common Jewish thinking of the day, which John totally shattered.

But John's message was God's message, and he would not compromise it or clutter it with the popular misconceptions and delusions of his own day and his own people. He had no word but God's word, and he proclaimed no kingdom but God's kingdom and no preparation but God's preparation. That preparation was repentance. God's standard would not change, even if every Jew were excluded and every Gentile saved. God knew that some Jews would be saved, but none apart from personal repentance and conversion.

Although the precise phrase is not found there, **the kingdom of heaven** is basically an Old Testament concept. David declares that "the Lord is King forever and ever" (Ps. 10:16; cf. 29:10), that His kingdom is everlasting, and that His dominion "endures throughout all generations" (Ps. 145:13). Daniel speaks of "the God of heaven [who] will set up a kingdom which will never be destroyed" (Dan. 2:44; cf. Ezek. 37:25), a "kingdom [that] is an everlasting kingdom" (Dan. 4:3). The God of heaven is the King of heaven, and the heavenly kingdom is God's kingdom.

Matthew uses the phrase **kingdom of heaven** thirty-two times, and is the only gospel writer who uses it at all. The other three use "the kingdom of God." It is probable that Matthew used **kingdom of heaven** because it was more understandable to his primarily Jewish readers. Jews would not speak God's name (Yahweh, or Jehovah), and would often substitute *heaven* when referring to Him—much as we do in such expressions as "heaven smiled on me today."

There is no significant difference between "the kingdom of God" and **the kingdom of heaven**. The one phrase emphasizes the sovereign Ruler of the kingdom and the other emphasizes the kingdom itself, but they are the same kingdom. Matthew 19:23-24 confirms the equality of the phrases by using them interchangeably.

The **kingdom** has two aspects, the outer and the inner, both of which are spoken of in the gospels. Those aspects are evident as one moves through Matthew. In the broadest sense, the kingdom includes everyone who professes to acknowledge God. Jesus' parable of the sower represents the kingdom as including both genuine and superficial believers (Matt. 13:3-23), and in His following parable (vv. 24-30) as including both wheat (true believers) and tares (false believers). That is the outer kingdom, the one we can see but cannot accurately evaluate ourselves, because we cannot know people's hearts.

The other kingdom is the inner, the kingdom that includes only true believers, only those who, as John the Baptist proclaimed, repent and are converted. God rules over both aspects of the kingdom, and He will one day finally separate the superficial from the real. Meanwhile He allows the pretenders to identify themselves outwardly with His kingdom.

God's kingly rule over the hearts of men and over the world may be thought of as having a number of phases. The first is the *prophesied* kingdom, such as that foretold by Daniel. The second phase is the *present* kingdom, the one that existed at the time of John the Baptist and that he mentions. It is the kingdom that both John and Jesus spoke of as being **at hand** (cf. 4:17). The third phase may be referred to as the *interim* kingdom, the kingdom that resulted because of Israel's rejection of her King. The King returned to heaven and His kingdom on earth now exists only in a mystery form. Christ is Lord of the earth in the sense of His being its Creator and its ultimate Ruler; but He does not presently exercise His full divine will over the earth. He is, so to speak, in a voluntary exile in heaven until it is time for Him to return again. He reigns only in the hearts of those who know Him as Savior and Lord. For those "the kingdom of God is . . . righteousness and peace and joy in the Holy Spirit" (Rom. 14:17).

The fourth phase can be described as the *manifest* kingdom, in which Christ will rule, physically, directly, and fully on earth for a thousand years, the Millennium. In that kingdom He will rule both externally and internally— externally over all mankind, and internally in the hearts of those who belong to Him by faith. The fifth, and final, phase is the "*eternal* kingdom of our Lord and Savior Jesus Christ," which "will be abundantly supplied" to all of His own (2 Pet. 1:11).

Had God's people Israel accepted their King when He first came to them, there would be no interim kingdom. The kingdom **at hand** would have become the kingdom of a thousand years, which, in turn, would have ushered in the eternal kingdom. But because they killed the forerunner of the King and then the King Himself, the millennial kingdom, and consequently the eternal kingdom, were sovereignly postponed.

The Mission

For this is the one referred to by Isaiah the prophet, saying, "The voice of one crying in the wilderness, 'Make ready the way of the Lord, make His paths straight!'" (3:3)

The mission of John the Baptist had long before been described by **Isaiah the prophet** (see Isa. 40:3-4). Here Matthew again emphasizes fulfilled prophecy in the coming of Jesus Christ as divine King (cf. 1:22; 2:5, 15, 17). But as herald of the great King, John did not clear the roads and highways of obstacles, but sought to clear men's hearts of the obstacles that kept them from the King. **The way of the Lord** is the way of repentance, of turning from sin to righteousness, of turning moral and spiritual **paths** that are crooked into ones that are **straight**, ones that are fit for the King. "Let every valley be lifted up, and every mountain and hill be made low," Isaiah continues, "and let the rough ground become a plain, and the rugged terrain a broad valley; then the glory of the Lord will be revealed, and all flesh will see it together" (Isa. 40:4-5). The call of John's **voice** that was **crying** [*bōntos*] **in the wilderness** of Judea was the shouting of urgency commanding people to repent, to confess sin and the need of a Savior. **His paths** (*tribous*) are well known, as the Greek term implies, because they are clearly revealed in Scripture.

THE MANNER

Now John himself had a garment of camel's hair, and a leather belt about his waist; and his food was locusts and wild honey. (3:4)

John must have been a startling figure to those who saw him. He claimed to be God's messenger, but he did not live, dress, or talk like other religious leaders. Those leaders were proper, well-dressed, well-fed, sophisticated, and worldly. John obviously cared for none of those things and even made a point of forsaking them. His **garment of camel's hair** and his **leather belt about his waist** were as plain and drab as the wilderness in which he lived and preached. His clothes were practical and long-wearing, but far from being comfortable or fashionable. He was much like the first Elijah in that regard (2 Kings 1:8). His diet of **locusts and wild honey** was as spartan as his clothing. It was nourishing but little else.

John's very dress, food, and life-style were in themselves a rebuke to the self-satisfied and self-indulgent religious leaders of Israel—the scribes, Pharisees, Sadducees, and priests. It was also a rebuke to most of the people, who, though they may not have been able to indulge in the privileges of their leaders, nonetheless admired and longed for the same advantages.

John's purpose was not to turn the people into hermits or ascetics. He called on no one, not even his disciples, to live and dress as he did. But his manner of living was a dramatic reminder of the many loves and pleasures that keep people from exchanging their own way for God's.

THE MINISTRY

Then Jerusalem was going out to him, and all Judea, and all the district around the Jordan; and they were being baptized by him in the Jordan River, as they confessed their sins. (3:5-6)

The immediate effect of John's preaching was dramatic. People were coming from the great city of **Jerusalem**, which was a considerable distance away. They came, in fact, from **all Judea, and all the district around the Jordan**. In other words they were coming from all over southern Palestine, including both sides of the **Jordan River**. As Matthew reports later in his gospel, the people recognized John as a prophet (21:26).

That those Jews submitted to **being baptized** was more than a little significant, because that was not a traditional Jewish ceremony. It was completely different from the Levitical washings, which consisted of washing the hands, feet, and head. The Essenes, a group of Jewish ascetics who lived on the northwest shore of the Dead Sea, practiced a type of ceremonial washing that more nearly resembled baptism. But both the Levitical and the Essene washings were repeated, those of the Essenes as much as several times a day or even hourly. They represented repeated purification for repeated sinning.

John's washing, however, was one-time. The only one-time washing the Jews performed was for Gentiles, signifying their coming as outsiders into the true faith of Judaism. A Jew who submitted to such a rite demonstrated, in effect, that he was an outsider who sought entrance into the people of God—an amazing admission for a Jew. Members of God's chosen race, descendants of Abraham, heirs of the covenant of Moses, came to John to be **baptized** like a Gentile!

That act symbolized before the world that they realized their national and racial descent, or even their calling as God's chosen and covenant people, could not save them. They had to repent, forsake sin, and trust in the Lord for salvation. It is that of which the baptism was a public witness, **as they confessed their sins.** They had to come into the kingdom just like the Gentiles, through repentance and faith—which included a public admission of sins (cf. the same Greek term [*exomologeō*] in Phil. 2:11, where it refers to a verbal confession).

We know from subsequent accounts in the gospels that many of those acts of repentance must have been superficial and hypocritical, because John soon lost much of his following, just as Jesus would eventually lose most of His popularity. But the impact of John's ministry on the Jewish people was profound and unforgettable. The way of the King had been announced to them, and they had no excuse for not being ready for His coming.

Six things demonstrate the true greatness of John. (1) He was filled with and controlled by the Spirit, even from "his mother's womb" (Luke 1:15*b*). (2) He was obedient to God's Word. From childhood he followed God's will, and from it he never wavered. (3) He was self-controlled, drinking neither "wine or liquor" (Luke 1:15*a*). In his food, dress, and life-style he was temperate and austere. (4) He was humble. His purpose was to announce the king, not to act kingly or take for himself any of the king's prerogatives. Speaking of Jesus, John said, "After me One is coming who is mightier than I, and I am not fit to stoop down and untie the thong of His sandals" (Mark 1:7), and on a later occasion, "He must increase, but I must decrease" (John 3:30). (5) He courageously and faithfully proclaimed God's Word, thundering it across the wilderness as long as he was free to preach, to whomever would listen. (6) Finally, he was faithful in winning people to Christ, in turning "back many of the sons of Israel to the Lord their God" (Luke 1:16). He stands as a pattern for all who seek genuine greatness.

The Fruits of
True Repentance (3:7-12)

But when he saw many of the Pharisees and Sadducees coming for baptism, he said to them, "You brood of vipers, who warned you to flee from the wrath to come? Therefore bring forth fruit in keeping with repentance; and do not suppose that you can say to yourselves, 'We have Abraham for our father'; for I say to you, that God is able from these stones to raise up children to Abraham. And the axe is already laid at the root of the trees; every tree therefore that does not bear good fruit is cut down and thrown into the fire. As for me, I baptize you with water for repentance, but He who is coming after me is mightier than I, and I am not fit to remove His sandals; He will baptize you with the Holy Spirit and fire. And His winnowing fork is in His hand, and He will thoroughly clear His threshing floor; and He will gather His wheat into the barn, but He will burn up the chaff with unquenchable fire." (3:7-12)

Matthew records but this one sample of the preaching of John the Baptist. The parallel account in Luke (3:1-18) gives more details, but the message is the same: a call to repentance and baptism, an inner change of mind and heart, along with an outward act that symbolized that change—and, even more importantly, a manner of living that *demonstrated* the change. The "many other exhortations" that

John preached (Luke 3:18) possibly consisted primarily of more examples of the fruit in keeping with repentance (v. 8) that he gave in addition to those mentioned in verses 11-14.

John's preaching was simple and his message was limited to that which was most essential, but he faithfully fulfilled his singular calling as the herald of God's coming great King. He performed his ministry with a boldness, courage, power, and single-minded devotion that caused that King to say of him, "Truly, I say to you, among those born of women there has not arisen anyone greater than John the Baptist" (Matt. 11:11).

In the narrative of 3:7-12 Matthew focuses on four elements: the congregation, the confrontation, the condemnation, and the consolation.

THE CONGREGATION

But when he saw many of the Pharisees and Sadducees coming for baptism, (3:7a)

Among the great number of people who came out to see John in the wilderness (v. 5) were **many of the Pharisees and Sadducees**, whom the Baptist singled out for special warning and rebuke.

By New Testament times three groups, or sects, had developed that were quite distinct from the rest of Judaism. Besides the two mentioned here (and frequently in the gospels and Acts), were the Essenes. Most of the Essenes were unmarried, but they often adopted children from other Jewish families. These secretive and ascetic Jews lived for the most part in isolated, exclusive, and austere communities such as the now-famous Qumran, on the northwest shore of the Dead Sea. They spent much of their time copying the Scriptures, and it is to them that we owe the valuable and helpful Dead Sea Scrolls—discovered by accident in 1947 by an Arab shepherd boy. But the Essenes had little contact with or influence on the society of their own day and are nowhere mentioned in the New Testament.

THE PHARISEES

The **Pharisees**, however, were a great contrast to the Essenes. They were equally, if not more, exclusive, but were found for the most part in the larger cities such as Jerusalem. They were an association very much in the mainstream of Jewish life and made a point of being noticed and admired. Jesus exposed them as doing "all their deeds to be noticed by men . . . and they love the place of honor at banquets, and the chief seats in the synagogues, and respectful greetings in the market places, and being called by men, Rabbi" (Matt. 23:5-7; cf. 6:2, 5).

We have no specific documentation as to exactly how or when the Pharisee sect began, but it is likely that it developed out of a former group called the Hasidim, whose name means "pious ones" or "saints." The Hasidim came into being in the second century B.C., during the intertestamental period. Palestine had been under the Hellenistic (Greek) rule of the Seleucid Syrian kings for many years. Jewish patriots, under the leadership of Judas Maccabaeus, revolted when Antiochus Epiphanes tried to force his pagan culture and religion on the Jews. That despicable tyrant even profaned the Temple by sacrificing a pig on the altar and forcing the sacrificed meat down the throats of the priests—a double abomination to Jews, because the law of Moses forbade them to eat pork (Lev. 11:4-8; Deut. 14:7-8). The Hasidim were among the strongest supporters of the revolt, until its leaders began to become worldly and politicized.

Many scholars believe that the **Pharisees**, and likely the Essenes also, descended from the Hasidim. The word *Pharisee* means "separated ones," and members of the sect diligently tried to live up to their name. Admission to the group was strictly controlled by periods of probation lasting up to one year, during which the applicant had to prove his ability to follow ritual law. They separated themselves not only from Gentiles but from tax collectors and any others whom they considered to be base "sinners" (Luke 7:39). They even looked with disdain on the common Jewish people, whom a group of Pharisees in Jerusalem once referred to as "accursed" (John 7:49). After leaving the marketplace or any public gathering, they would as soon as possible perform ceremonial washings to purify themselves of possible contamination from touching some unclean person.

The Pharisees formed a self-righteous, "holy" community within the community; they were legalistic isolationists who had no regard or respect for those outside their sect. They believed strongly in God's sovereignty and in divine destiny and that they alone were the true Israel. They considered themselves to be superspiritual, but their "spirituality" was entirely external, consisting of the pursuit of meticulous observance of a multitude of religious rituals and taboos, most of which they and various other religious leaders had devised over the previous several centuries as supplements to the law of Moses. These were known collectively as "the tradition of the elders," concerning which Jesus gave the Pharisees one of His strongest rebukes, charging them with "teaching as doctrines the precepts of men" (Matt. 15:2-9).

By the time of Christ, the **Pharisees** had lost most of whatever nationalism they may earlier have had. Another sect, the Zealots, had become the association for those whose primary concern was Jewish independence. The Pharisees' single loyalty was to themselves, to their traditions and to their own influence and prestige. By their strict adherence to those traditions they expected to reap great reward in heaven. But they were the epitome of religious emptiness and hypocrisy, as Jesus often pointed out (Matt. 15:7; 22:18; 23:13, 23, 25; etc.). The Pharisees "outwardly [appeared] righteous to men, but inwardly [were] full of hypocrisy and lawlessness" (Matt. 23:28).

THE SADDUCEES

The **Sadducees** were at the other end of the Jewish religious spectrum— the ultraliberals. The origin of their name is uncertain, but many modern scholars believe it is derived from Zadok (Sadok in the Septuagint, the Greek Old Testament), the name of a man who was priest under David (2 Sam. 8:17) and chief priest under Solomon (1 Kings 1:32). This sect also arose during the intertestamental period, but from among the priestly aristocracy. They were compromisers, both religiously and politically. They cared little for Greek culture, with its emphasis on philosophy and intellectualism, but were greatly attracted to the pragmatic, practical Romans.

The Sadducees claimed to accept the law of Moses as the supreme and only religious authority, and they scorned the legalistic traditions of their antagonists, the Pharisees. In New Testament times they were still closely associated with the priestly class (see Acts 5:17), to the extent that the terms *chief priest* and *Sadducee* were used almost synonymously (as were the terms *scribe* and *Pharisee*). But they cared little for religion, especially doctrine, and denied the existence of angels, the resurrection, and most things supernatural (Acts 23:6-8). Consequently they lived only for the present, getting everything they could from whomever they could— Gentiles and fellow Jews alike. They believed in extreme human autonomy and in the unlimited freedom of the will. They considered themselves masters of their own destinies.

The Sadducees were much fewer in number than the Pharisees and were extremely wealthy. Among other things, under the leadership of Annas they ran the Temple franchises—the money exchanging and the sale of sacrificial animals— and charged exorbitantly for those services. It was therefore the Sadducees' business that Jesus damaged when he drove the moneychangers and sacrifice sellers out of the Temple (Matt. 21:12-13).

Because of their great wealth, Temple racketeering, and affiliation with the Romans, the Sadducees were much less popular with their fellow Jews than were the Pharisees, who were strongly religious and had some measure of national loyalty.

Religiously, politically, and socially the **Pharisees and Sadducees** had almost nothing in common. The Pharisees were ritualistic; the Sadducees were rationalistic. The Pharisees were strict separatists; the Sadducees comprising collaborators. The Pharisees were commoners (most of them had a trade), while the Sadducees were aristocrats. Both groups had members among the scribes and were represented in the priesthood and in the Jewish high council, the Sanhedrin; yet they were in almost constant opposition to each other. During New Testament times about the only common ground they exhibited was opposition to Christ and His followers (Matt. 22:15-16, 23, 34-35; Acts 4:1; 23:6).

They had one other common religious and spiritual ground. The Pharisees expected their reward in heaven, while the Sadducees expected theirs in this life, but the trust of both groups was in personal works and self-effort. Both emphasized the superficial and nonessential, and had no concern for the genuine inner spiritual life or for the welfare of their fellow man. That was "the leaven of the Pharisees and Sadducees," the hypocritical, self-serving, dead externalism about which Jesus warned His disciples (Matt. 16:6).

Throughout most of its history the church has had its own brands of Pharisees and Sadducees, its ritualists and its rationalists. The one looks for salvation and blessing through prescribed ceremonies and legalistic practices; the other finds religious meaning and purpose in private, existential beliefs and standards. One is conservative and the other is liberal, but the hope and trust of both groups is in themselves, in what they can perform or accomplish by their own actions and wills.

It is probably because of that deeper spiritual commonness that Matthew speaks of them as one group, emphasized by the use of a single definite article (**the**) rather than two ("*the* Pharisees and *the* Sadducees"). It is clear from John's response to them that he considered their basic problem and need to be exactly the same.

This group was **coming for baptism**, the Greek preposition *epi* (**for**) being used in a construction that clearly indicates purpose. In light of John's unorthodox dress and style and his prophetic and authoritative exhortations, it is hard to imagine why the self-righteous and proud Pharisees and Sadducees would ask to be baptized by him. Some of them may simply have been curious. It seems more probable, however, that they suspected that John might indeed be a prophet, as many of the people believed (Matt. 14:5), and that they wanted to check him out as thoroughly as they could. If he were a genuine prophet perhaps they could gain his approval, parade the pretense of repentant spirituality, and capitalize on or even take over the movement—in the way religious opportunists still do today. Whatever their reasons were, they were wrong, wicked reasons. They were not seeking God's truth or God's working in their own lives. They were not repentant; they had not confessed their sins; they had not changed at all—as John well knew. They were not genuinely seeking the true righteousness that delivers from judgment. They were the same smug, self-righteous hypocrites they had been when they started out to find John.

THE CONFRONTATION

he said to them, "You brood of vipers, who warned you to flee from the wrath to come?" (3:7b)

John's awareness of the insincerity and lack of repentance of the Pharisees and Sadducees is evident in those strong words. They intended to carry their hypocrisy even to the extent of submitting to John's baptism, out of whatever corrupt motives they may have had. *Gennēma* (**brood**) may also be translated "offspring," signifying descendants or children. Jesus used the same epithet (**brood of vipers**) to describe the Pharisees on several occasions (Matt. 12:34; 23:33). **Vipers** (*echidna*) were small but very poisonous desert snakes, which would have been quite familiar to John the Baptist. They were made even more dangerous by the fact that, when still, they looked like a dead branch and were often picked up unintentionally. That is exactly what Paul did on the island of Malta when he went to gather wood for a fire after the shipwreck. As indicated by the response of the natives who were befriending Paul and the others, the bite of the **viper** was often fatal, though Paul miraculously "suffered no harm" (Acts 28:3-5).

Calling the Pharisees and Sadducees a **brood of vipers** pointed up the danger of their religious hypocrisy—as well as the fact that their wicked work had been passed on to them by the original serpent (Gen. 3:1-13) through their spiritual forefathers, of whom they were the **brood**, or offspring. Like the desert viper, they often appeared to be harmless, but their brand of godliness (cf. 2 Tim. 3:5) was venomous and deadly. In His series of woes against the scribes and Pharisees, Jesus said, "You shut off the kingdom of heaven from men; for you do not enter in yourselves, nor do you allow those who are entering to go in" (Matt. 23:13). They were responsible for keeping countless Jews out of the kingdom, and therefore from salvation and spiritual life.

In Matthew 23:33 Jesus calls the scribes and Pharisees "serpents" as well as a "brood of vipers," suggesting even more directly that their true spiritual father was Satan—as He specifically charges in John 8:44 (cf. Rev. 12:9; 20:2). These religious hypocrites were Satan's children doing Satan's deceitful work.

The question **Who warned you to flee** continues the viper figure. A brush fire or a farmer's burning the stalks in his field after the harvest would cause vipers and other creatures to **flee** before the flames in order to escape. It was a common sight in many of the Mediterranean and Arab regions, and one that John the Baptist doubtlessly had seen many times. The implication is that the Pharisees and Sadducees were expecting John's baptism to be a kind of spiritual fire insurance, giving protection from the flames of **the wrath to come**. True repentance and conversion *do* protect from God's **wrath** and judgment, but superficial and insincere professions or acts of faith tend only to harden a person against genuine belief, giving a false sense of security. John would not be party to such hypocrisy and sham. It was the deceitfulness of their true master, Satan, and not genuine fear of God's judgment, that led them out to hear John and to seek his baptism as a pretentious formality.

John's indictment must have deeply stung those false religious leaders, who considered themselves to be far above the common man in their relationship to God and His kingdom. John, and Jesus after him, characterized them as deceivers rather than leaders, perpetuators of spiritual darkness rather than spiritual light, children of the devil rather than sons of God.

The Condemnation

Therefore bring forth fruit in keeping with repentance; and do not suppose that you can say to yourselves, 'We have Abraham for our father'; for I say to you, that God is able from these stones to raise up children to Abraham. And the axe is already laid at the root of the trees; every tree therefore that does not bear good fruit is cut down and thrown into the fire. (3:8-10)

The marks of a truly repentant heart are **fruit in keeping with repentance**, or as Paul described them to King Agrippa, "deeds appropriate to repentance" (Acts 26:20). In his parallel account Luke mentions several examples of the kind of **fruit** John was talking about. To the general multitude he said, "Let the man who has two tunics share with him who has none; and let him who has food do likewise" (Luke 3:11). To the tax-gatherers he said, "Collect no more than what you have been ordered to" (v. 13), and to some soldiers he said, "Do not take money from anyone by force, or accuse anyone falsely, and be content with your wages" (v. 14).

As James points out, "Faith, if it has no works, is dead" (James 2:17). John says in his first epistle, "The one who practices righteousness is righteous, just as He is righteous" (1 John 3:7); and that "if someone says, 'I love God,' and hates his brother, he is a liar; for the one who does not love his brother whom he has seen, cannot love God whom he has not seen" (4:20). Our actions toward our fellow men are indicators of our true attitude toward God.

Axios (**in keeping with**) has the root idea of having equal weight or worth, and therefore of being appropriate. True **repentance** not only should but *will* have correspondingly genuine works, demonstrated in both attitudes and actions. Right relationship to God brings right relationship to our fellow human beings, at least as far as our part is concerned (cf. Rom. 12:18). Those who claim to know Christ, who claim to be born again, will demonstrate a new way of living that corresponds to the new birth.

The Pharisees and Sadducees knew a great deal about repentance. That God fully and freely remits the sins of a penitent is a basic doctrine of Judaism. The ancient rabbis said, "Great is repentance, for it brings healing upon the world. Great is repentance, for it reaches to the throne of God," and, "A man can shoot an arrow for a few furlongs, but repentance reaches to the throne of God." Some rabbis maintained that the law was created two thousand years before the world, but that repentance was created even before the law. The clear meaning of repentance in Judaism has always been a change in man's attitude toward God that results in a moral and religious reformation of the individual's conduct. The great medieval Jewish scholar Maimonides said of the traditional Jewish concept of repentance: "What is repentance? Repentance is that the sinner forsakes his sin, puts it out of his thoughts, and fully resolves in his mind that he will never do it again."

Such understanding of repentance is basically consistent with the teaching of the Old Testament. Repentance always involves a changed life, a renouncing of sin and doing righteousness. The Lord declared through Ezekiel, "When the righteous turns from his righteousness and commits iniquity, then he shall die in it. But when the wicked turns from his wickedness and practices justice and righteousness, he will live by them" (Ezek. 33:18-19). Hosea pleaded, "Return, O Israel, to the Lord your God, for you have stumbled because of your iniquity. Take words with you and return to the Lord. Say to Him, 'Take away all iniquity, and receive us graciously'" (Hos. 14:1-2). After Jonah's reluctant but powerful warning to Nineveh, "God saw their deeds, that they turned from their wicked way, [and] then God relented concerning the calamity which He had declared He would bring upon them. And He did not do it" (Jonah 3:10). Nineveh brought **forth fruit in keeping with repentance.**

The idea that repentance is evidenced by renunciation of sin and by righteous living did not originate with John the Baptist, but had long been an integral part of orthodox Judaism. Faithful rabbis had taught that one of the most important passages in Scripture was, "Wash yourselves, make yourselves clean; remove the evil of your deeds from My sight. Cease to do evil, learn to do good; seek justice, reprove the ruthless; defend the orphan, plead for the widow" (Isa. 1:16-17).

Theologian Erich Sauer, in *The Triumph of the Crucified* (Grand Rapids: Eerdmans, 1951, p. 67), speaks of repentance as "a threefold action. In the understanding it means knowledge of sin; in the feelings it means pain and grief; and in the will it means a change of mind." True repentance first of all involves understanding and insight, intellectual awareness of the need for moral and spiritual cleansing and change. Second, it involves our emotions. We come to *feel* the need that our mind knows. Third, it involves appropriate actions that result from what our mind knows and our heart feels.

Recognition of personal sin is the important first step. But by itself it is useless, even dangerous, because it tends to make a person think that mere recognition is all that is necessary. A hardened pharaoh admitted his sin (Ex. 9:27), a double-minded Balaam admitted his (Num. 23:34), a greedy Achan acknowledged his (Josh. 7:20), and an insincere Saul confessed his (1 Sam. 15:24). The rich young ruler who asked Jesus how to have eternal life went away sorrowful but not repentant (Luke 18:23). Even Judas, despairing over his betrayal of Jesus, said to the chief priests and elders, "I have sinned by betraying innocent blood" (Matt. 27:4). All of those men recognized their sin, yet none of them repented. They were experiencing what Paul called "the sorrow of the world" that "produces death" instead of the "godly sorrow" that "produces a repentance" (2 Cor. 7:10-11).

True repentance will include a deep *feeling* of wrongdoing and of sin against God. David begins his great penitential psalm by crying out, "Be gracious to me, O God, according to Thy lovingkindness; according to the greatness of Thy compassion blot out my transgressions" (Ps. 51:1). He not only clearly saw his sin but deeply felt his need to be rid of it. In another psalm he declared, "When I kept silent about my sin, my body wasted away through my groaning all day long" (Ps. 32:3).

The sorrow of true repentance is like David's; it is sorrow for offense against a holy God, not simply regret over the personal consequences of our sin. Sorrow over being found out or over suffering hardship or discipline because of our sin is not godly sorrow, and has nothing to do with repentance. That sort of sorrow is but selfish regret, concern for self rather than for God. It merely adds to the original sin.

Even acknowledgement of sin and feeling of offense against God do not complete repentance. If it is genuine, it will result in a changed life that bears **fruit**

in keeping with repentance. David, after confessing and expressing great remorse for his sin against God, determined that, with God's help, he would forsake his sin and turn to righteousness. "Create in me a clean heart, O God, and renew a steadfast spirit within me, . . . Then I will teach transgressors Thy ways, and sinners will be converted to Thee" (Ps. 51:10, 13). **Fruit** is always seen in Scripture as manifested behavior (cf. Matt. 7:20).

The great Puritan Thomas Goodwin called for repentance with these striking words:

> Fall down upon thy knees afore him, and with a heart broken to water, acknowledge, as Shimei, thy treason and rebellions against him who never did thee hurt; and acknowledge, with a rope ready fitted to thy neck by thy own hands, as they Benhadad's servants wore; that is, confessing that if he will hang thee up, he may. . . . Tell Him that He may shew his justice on thee, if he will; and present thy naked breast, thy hateful soul, as a butt and mark for him, if He please, to shoot his arrows into and sheathe his sword in. Only desire him to remember that he sheathed his sword first in the bowels of his Son, Zech. 13:7, when he made his soul an offering for sin. (*The Works of Thomas Goodwin* [Edinburgh: James Nichol, 1863], 7:231)

Another Puritan, William Perkins, wrote, "Godly sorrow causeth grief for sin, because it is sin. It makes any man in whom it is to be of this disposition and mind, that if there were no conscience to accuse, no devil to terrify, no Judge to arraign and condemn, no hell to torment, yet he would be humbled and brought on his knees for his sins, because he hath offended a loving, merciful, and long-suffering God."

Ultimately, of course, repentance like that is a gift of God. Speaking to the Sanhedrin, the supreme Jewish council, Peter and some of the other apostles said, "He [Jesus] is the one whom God exalted to His right hand as a Prince and a Savior, to grant repentance to Israel, and forgiveness of sins" (Acts 5:31). Some while later, after he himself had finally been persuaded by God that the Gentiles were eligible for the kingdom (10:1-35), Peter managed to convince skeptical Jewish Christians in Jerusalem, who then "glorified God, saying, 'Well then, God has granted to the Gentiles also the repentance that leads to life'" (11:18). Paul called Timothy to be a gentle bond-servant of the Lord in proclaiming the truth to the lost in the hope that "God may grant them repentance leading to the knowledge of the truth, and they may come to their senses and escape from the snare of the devil, having been held captive by him to do his will" (2 Tim. 2:25-26).

It was clearly not God-given repentance that the Pharisees and Sadducees professed before John. Of all people they should have known the meaning of true repentance, but they did not. They were hypocrites and phonies, as John well knew. He had seen absolutely no evidence of true repentance, and he demanded to see such evidence before he would baptize them. As in the case of all baptisms since John, they are to be outward signs of inward transformation.

John's words to those religious leaders was at once a rebuke and an invitation: **Therefore bring forth fruit in keeping with repentance.** "You have shown no evidence of it," he was saying, "but now you have opportunity to truly repent if you mean it. Show me that you have turned from your wicked hypocrisy to genuine godliness, and I will be glad to baptize you." The rabbis taught that the gates of repentance never close, that repentance is like the sea, because a person can bathe in it at any hour. Rabbi Eleezar said, "It is the way of the world, when a man has insulted his fellow in public, and after a time seeks to be reconciled to him, that the other says, 'You insult me publicly, and now you would be reconciled to me between us two alone! Go bring the men in whose presence you insulted me, and I will be reconciled to you.' But God is not so. A man may stand and rail and blaspheme in the market place and the Holy One says, 'Repent between us two alone, and I will receive you.'" (cited in William Barclay, *The Gospel of Matthew* [Philadelphia: Westminster, 1975], 1:56).

Some years ago a well-known man in public ministry openly and repeatedly ridiculed a fellow minister. After many months of criticism, the first man decided that he was wrong in what he had done and went to the other minister asking his forgiveness. It was reported that the one who had been criticized replied, "You attacked me publicly and you should apologize publicly. When you do I will forgive you."

There is no reason to believe that John the Baptist intended to humiliate the Pharisees and Sadducees or demand some sort of public demonstration of their sincerity. But he insisted on seeing valid evidence of true repentance and would not be party to their using him to promote their own selfish and ungodly purposes.

Knowing what they were probably thinking, John continued, **and do not suppose that you can say to yourselves, "We have Abraham for our father."** They believed that simply being Abraham's descendants, members of God's chosen race, made them spiritually secure. Not so, John said, **for I say to you, that God is able from these stones to raise up children to Abraham.** Descent from Abraham was not a passport to heaven. It was a great advantage in knowing and understanding God's will (Rom. 3:1-2; 9:4-5), but without faith in Him that advantage becomes a more severe condemnation. If Abraham himself was justified only by his personal faith (Gen. 15:6; Rom. 4:1-3), how could his descendants expect to be justified in any other way (Rom. 3:21-22)?

Many Jews of New Testament times believed, and many Orthodox Jews of our own day still believe, that simply their Jewishness assures them a place in God's kingdom. The rabbis taught that "all Israelites have a portion in the world to come." They spoke of the "delivering merits of the fathers," who passed on spiritual merit to their descendants. Some even taught that Abraham stood guard at the gates of Gehenna, or hell, turning back any Israelite who happened that way. They claimed that it was Abraham's merit that enabled Jewish ships to sail safely on the seas, that sent rain on their crops, that enabled Moses to receive the law and to enter heaven, and that caused David's prayers to be heard.

That was the sort of presumption John the Baptist rebuked. No descent from Abraham, no matter how genetically pure, could make a person right with God. Jesus contradicted the similar claims of another group of Pharisees, except in even stronger terms than John's. After they self-righteously asserted, "Abraham is our father," Jesus said, "If you are Abraham's children, do the deeds of Abraham. But as it is, you are seeking to kill Me, a man who has told you the truth, which I heard from God; this Abraham did not do" (John 8:39-40). Our Lord went on to say that their deeds proved their father was actually Satan. In Jesus' story of the rich man and Lazarus, it is overlooked that the rich man in hell addresses Abraham as "Father," and Abraham, speaking from heaven, calls the rich man his "Child." But the rich man was then told by Abraham, "Between us and you there is a great chasm fixed, in order that those who wish to come over from here to you may not be able, and that none may cross over from there to us" (Luke 16:25-26). A child of Abraham in hell was beyond their thinking.

The Jews generally considered Gentiles to be the occupants of hell, spiritually lifeless and hopeless, dead stones as far as a right relationship with God is concerned. It may be that John played on that figure in declaring that **God is able from these stones to raise up children to Abraham**, that is, true children of Abraham who come to the Lord as Abraham did, by faith. When the Roman centurion asked Jesus to heal his servant simply by saying the word, Jesus replied, "Truly I say to you, I have not found such great faith with anyone in Israel. And I say to you, that many shall come from east and west, and recline at the table with Abraham, and Isaac, and Jacob, in the kingdom of heaven; but the sons of the kingdom [i.e., Israelites] shall be cast out into the outer darkness; in that place there shall be weeping and gnashing of teeth" (Matt. 8:10-12).

In John's preaching, as in the Old Testament prophets, judgment was closely connected with salvation in the coming of the Messiah. Those men of God saw no gap between His coming to save and His coming to judge. Isaiah wrote of the "shoot" that would "spring from the stem of Jesse, and a branch from his roots" who would "decide with fairness for the afflicted of the earth; and He will strike the earth with the rod of His mouth, and with the breath of His lips He will slay the wicked" (Isa. 11:1, 4). Speaking again of the Messiah, Isaiah wrote, "The Spirit of the Lord God is upon me, because the Lord has anointed me to bring good news to the afflicted; . . . to proclaim the favorable year of the Lord, and the day of vengeance of our God" (Isa. 61:1-2; cf. Joel 3). In his blessing of the infant Jesus in the Temple, Simeon said of Him, "Behold, this Child is appointed for the fall and rise of many in Israel" (Luke 2:34).

Israel experienced a foretaste of God's judgment in the ravaging of Jerusalem and the destruction of the Temple in A.D. 70, only about forty years after John the Baptist preached. Every unbeliever likewise faces a certain judgment when he dies, and even before death people may suffer foretaste judgments from God because of sin and rebellion. As the book of Proverbs repeatedly reminds us (1:32-33; 2:3-22; 3:33-35; etc.), God makes certain that ultimately, and even to a great extent in this life, the good will reap goodness and the evil will reap evil (cf. Rom. 2:5-11).

John apparently believed that God's ultimate judgment was imminent. Because the Messiah had arrived, **the axe is already laid at the root of the trees; every tree therefore that does not bear good fruit is cut down and thrown into the fire.**

At the end of every harvest season the farmer would go through his vineyard or orchard looking for plants that had borne no good fruit. These would be cut down to make room for productive vines and trees and to keep them from taking nutrients from the soil that were needed by the good plants. A fruitless tree was a worthless and useless tree, fit only to be **cut down and thrown into the fire.** Jesus used a similar figure in describing false disciples. "If anyone does not abide in Me, he is thrown away as a branch, and dries up; and they gather them, and cast them into the fire, and they are burned" (John 15:6). Fruitless repentance is worthless and useless; it means absolutely nothing to God.

Fire is a frequent biblical symbol of the torment of divine punishment and judgment. Because of their exceptional wickedness, Sodom and Gomorrah were destroyed by "brimstone and fire from the Lord out of heaven" (Gen. 19:24). After Korah, his men, and their households were swallowed up by the earth and "went down alive to Sheol . . . fire also came forth from the Lord and consumed the two hundred and fifty men who were offering the incense" (Num. 16:32-33, 35). In His role as a righteous Judge, God is frequently called "a consuming fire" (Ex. 24:17; Deut. 4:24; 9:3; etc.). In the last chapter in the Old Testament, Malachi speaks of the coming day that will be "burning like a furnace; and all the arrogant and every evildoer will be chaff; and the day that is coming will set them ablaze" (Mal. 4:1). John's preaching picked up where Malachi left off, and Jesus Himself often spoke of the fires of hell (Matt. 5:22, 29; Mark 9:43, 47; Luke 3:17; etc.).

John was speaking specifically to the unrepentant Pharisees and Sadducees, but his message of judgment was to every person, **every tree . . . that does not bear good fruit,** who refuses to turn to God for forgiveness and salvation and therefore has no evidence, no **good fruit,** of genuine repentance. Salvation is not verified by a past act, but by present fruitfulness.

THE CONSOLATION

As for me, I baptize you with water for repentance, but He who is coming after me is mightier than I, and I am not fit to remove His sandals; He will baptize you with the Holy Spirit and fire. And His winnowing fork is in His hand, and He will thoroughly clear His threshing floor; and He will gather His wheat into the barn, but He will burn up the chaff with unquenchable fire. (3:11-12)

With the message of judgment John also gives a measure of hope and consolation. Here he speaks specifically of the Messiah, who had come in order that no one need face God's judgment.

First, John explains how his baptism differed from that of the Messiah: **I baptize you with water for repentance**. John's baptism reflected a ritual the Jews often used when a Gentile accepted the God of Israel. The ceremony was the mark of an outsider's becoming a part of the chosen people. In John's ministry it marked the outward profession of inward **repentance**, which prepared a person for the coming of the King. As the apostle Paul explained many years later, "John baptized with the baptism of repentance, telling the people to believe in Him who was coming after him, that is, in Jesus" (Acts 19:4).

The second baptism mentioned here is by the Messiah, a baptism by the One John says **is coming after me** and who **is mightier than I**, whose **sandals** John was **not fit to remove**. One of the lowliest tasks of a slave in that day was removing the sandals of his master and any guests and then washing their feet. It was the symbol Jesus Himself used in teaching His disciples to be servants (John 13:5-15). The humility of John, one mark of his spiritual stature, is evident in this description of the One he heralded and is consistent with his expression in John 3:30 that "He must increase, but I must decrease."

Among the ways in which the Messiah would be **mightier** than John would be in His baptism **with the Holy Spirit**. The Holy Spirit was promised by Jesus to His disciples as "another Helper, that He may be with you forever; that is the Spirit of truth, whom the world cannot receive, because it does not behold Him or know Him, but you know Him because He abides with you, and will be in you" (John 14:16-17). At Pentecost (Acts 2:1-4) and during the initial formation of the church (Acts 8:5-17; 10:44-48; 19:1-7), the promised Holy Spirit did come upon the disciples, baptizing them and establishing them in the body of Christ. Though without such dramatic attending signs, every believer since that time is baptized into the church by Christ with God's Spirit. "For by one Spirit we were all baptized into one body, whether Jews or Greeks, whether slaves or free" (1 Cor. 12:13).

John's word about the Holy Spirit must have been comforting and thrilling to the faithful Jews among his hearers, those who hoped for the day when God would "pour out [His] Spirit on all mankind" (Joel 2:28), when He would "sprinkle clean water on [them]," and "give [them] a new heart and put a new spirit within [them]" (Ezek. 36:25-26). In that day they would at last be baptized in the very power and person of God Himself.

The third baptism mentioned here is that of **fire**. Many interpreters take this to be a part of the Holy Spirit baptism, which began at Pentecost and which in that instance was accompanied by "tongues of fire" (Acts 2:3). But the Acts account says that those tongues "appeared to them" (that is, the waiting disciples) "*as of fire.*" They were not fire, but looked like licks of fire. In his last promise of the soon-coming baptism with the Holy Spirit, Jesus said nothing about actual fire being a part of the experience (Acts 1:5). And when, a short time later, Cornelius and his household were baptized with the Holy Spirit, no fire was present (Acts 10:44; 11:16; cf. 8:17; 19:6).

Other interpreters take the **fire** to represent a spiritual cleansing, as described in the quotation above from Ezekiel. But nothing in Ezekiel's text, in the context of John's message here, or in the Pentecost reference to the tongues "as of fire" relates to such cleansing.

Consequently, it seems best to consider **fire** as representing God's coming judgment, which, as we have seen, is so frequently in Scripture symbolized by fire. In both the preceding and following verses (10, 12) John clearly uses fire to represent judgment and punishment. It is impossible that the middle reference to fire would concern an entirely different subject. Both of the adjoining verses contrast the fates of believers and unbelievers, those who bear good fruit and those who do not (v. 10) and the valuable wheat and the worthless chaff (v. 12). It therefore seems logical and natural to take verse 11 also as a contrast between believers (those baptized **with the Holy Spirit**) and unbelievers (those baptized with the **fire** of God's judgment).

As in the preceding two verses, John again gives consolation to believers but warning to unbelievers: **And His winnowing fork is in His hand, and He will thoroughly clear His threshing floor; and He will gather His wheat into the barn, but He will burn up the chaff with unquenchable fire**. The figure is changed to that of a farmer who has just harvested his grain crop.

In Palestine, as in many other parts of the ancient world, farmers made a **threshing floor** by picking out a slight depression in the ground, or digging one if necessary, usually on a hill where breezes could be caught. The soil would then be wetted and packed down until it was very hard. Around the perimeter of the floor, which was perhaps thirty or forty feet in diameter, rocks would be stacked to keep the grain in place. After the stalks of grain were placed onto the floor, an ox, or a team of oxen, would drag heavy pieces of wood around over the grain, separating the **wheat** kernels from the **chaff**, or straw. Then the farmer would take a **winnowing fork** and throw a pile of grain into the air. The wind would blow the chaff away, while the kernels, being heavier, would fall back to the floor. Eventually, nothing would be left but the good and useful **wheat**.

In a similar way the Messiah will separate out everyone who belongs to Him and, like a farmer, **He will gather His wheat into the barn**, where it will be forever safe and protected. Also in a similar way to the farmer's, **He will burn up the chaff with unquenchable fire**. The long-awaited Messiah would Himself perform both functions, though not in the time and sequence that John and the prophets before him may have thought. The final separation and the ultimate judgment will be only at Christ's second coming, when the unsaved "will go away into eternal punishment, but the righteous into eternal life" (Matt. 25:46). That scene is dramatically presented by our Lord in the parable of the tares (Matt. 13:36-43) and the parable of the dragnet (Matt. 13:47-50).

John's introduction to the person and ministry of the Messiah prepared the people for the arrival of their King.

The Coronation of the King (3:13-17)

7

Then Jesus arrived from Galilee at the Jordan coming to John, to be baptized by him. But John tried to prevent Him, saying, "I have need to be baptized by You, and do You come to me?" But Jesus answering said to him, "Permit it at this time; for in this way it is fitting for us to fulfill all righteousness." Then he permitted Him. And after being baptized, Jesus went up immediately from the water; and behold, the heavens were opened, and he saw the Spirit of God descending as a dove, and coming upon Him, and behold, a voice out of the heavens, saying, "This is My beloved Son, in whom I am well-pleased." (3:13-17)

Though Matthew does not use the terms, we see in this passage what might be called the divine commissioning, or the coronation, of the King. The gospel writer has given us the King's ancestry (1:1-17), His arrival (1:18-25), His adoration (2:1-12), His attestation (2:13-23), and His announcement (3:1-12). Now we see His anointing, His coronation.

There is something strikingly majestic about this great event that brings all the preceding events into focus. Here, for the first time, the Lord Jesus Christ comes fully onto the stage of the gospel story. Here is where His ministry and work truly begin. Everything before this, even those events which directly involved the young

Jesus, were introductory and preparatory. Bethlehem, Egypt, and Nazareth are all behind. From this day on the Son of Man would call no place His earthly home (8:20), but was to move about fulfilling His mission.

After an eternity of glory in heaven and some thirty years of virtual obscurity on earth, the Messiah-King is manifested publicly for the world to see and know. As "the voice of one crying in the wilderness," John the Baptist had faithfully prepared the way for the King, even as Isaiah had prophesied (3:3; Isa. 40:3). The herald of the King had announced the coming of the King, and now the King Himself appears for His coronation.

One cannot fail to be aware that in these few verses Matthew reports the three central and absolutely critical aspects of Jesus' coronation as King of kings: the baptism of the Son, the anointing of the Spirit, and the confirmation of the Father. As clearly as in any passage in Scripture we see here the revelation and the working of the Trinity—the Son, the Spirit, and the Father. Because He is no earthly King and His is no earthly kingdom, no men crowned Him—only God, while men watched.

BAPTISM OF THE SON

Then Jesus arrived from Galilee at the Jordan coming to John, to be baptized by him. But John tried to prevent Him, saying, "I have need to be baptized by You, and do You come to me?" But Jesus answering said to him, "Permit it at this time; for in this way it is fitting for us to fulfill all righteousness." Then he permitted Him. (3:13-15)

We will first look at some of the details of the baptism and then at its significance.

We are not told the exact time to which the **then** refers, and Matthew no doubt uses the term simply to show the general sequence of events. We do not know the precise length of John's ministry, but according to Luke he began preaching "in the fifteenth year of the reign of Tiberius Caesar, when Pontius Pilate was governor of Judea, and Herod was tetrarch of Galilee . . . in the high priesthood of Annas and Caiaphas" (3:1-2). The best assumption is that it occurred in the year A.D. 29, quite a few months, perhaps nearly a year, before Jesus' baptism. John also continued to preach for a while afterward, causing his ministry to be ending as Jesus' ministry was beginning.

We know that John was about six months older than Jesus (Luke 1:26) and that Jesus began His ministry when He "was about thirty years of age" (Luke 3:23). If John began preaching at the same age, he would have been ministering for about six months when Jesus came to him for baptism. But we have no reason to believe that the two began ministering at the same age. And though we know how old Jesus was when He began, we are given no reason as to why He began at that age.

Some scholars suggest that the age of 30 was the generally accepted age for

Jewish religious leaders to begin their ministry. According to Numbers 4:30, priests entered the priesthood at that age. But that provision was temporary, because a short while later the age was lowered to 25 (Num. 8:24) and later to 20 (1 Chron. 23:24)—where it continued to be through the reign of Hezekiah (2 Chron. 31:17) and even through the Captivity (Ezra 3:8). We therefore lack clear insight, either biblical or traditional, as to why either John or Jesus began to minister when they did.

We know from the parallel passage in Luke that when **Jesus arrived from Galilee at the Jordan**, He did not come for a private ceremony. "Now it came about when all the people were baptized, that Jesus also was baptized" (Luke 3:21). Jesus was not to have a private, secret anointing as David first did (1 Sam. 16:13; cf. 2 Sam. 2:4).

Arrived is from *paraginomai*, which, as we saw in relation to the magi (2:1) and John the Baptist ("came," 3:1), was often used to indicate an official arrival or public appearance. We learn from Mark 1:9 that Jesus not only came from **Galilee**, but specifically from Nazareth, when He came to see **John**. It is clear from all the gospel accounts (cf. Mark 1:9; Luke 3:21; John 1:29) that Jesus came alone. No family members or friends accompanied Him, and He had as yet called no disciples.

We do not know exactly where on **the Jordan** River John was then baptizing, though it seems likely it was toward the southern end, and therefore near Jericho and the Dead Sea. John tells us that it was near "Bethany beyond the Jordan" (John 1:28), but the precise location of that town is uncertain.

We know from John's greeting to Jesus that he recognized Him immediately, but we have no idea how well they knew each other at this time. They were cousins, and before their births Mary stayed with Elizabeth for three months in the hill country of Judah, where the two women shared with each other their wonderful blessings (Luke 1:39-56). Elizabeth knew before Jesus' birth that Mary's child would be the Messiah, because she addressed Mary as "the mother of my Lord" (Luke 1:43). Surely Elizabeth would often have shared this wonderful news with her son John, the one whom the angel had told her husband would be "the forerunner before Him in the spirit and power of Elijah" (Luke 1:17; cf. v. 66). Both boys grew physically and spiritually (Luke 1:80; 2:40), but they did so separately— Jesus in Nazareth and John in the wilderness. It may be, therefore, that they had little, if any, ongoing firsthand acquaintance with one another.

Jesus came **to John** specifically **to be baptized by him**, as indicated by the aorist passive infinitive (*baptisthēnai*), which emphasizes purpose. But the idea of Jesus' being baptized by him was unthinkable to John. He not only knew Jesus' human identity but His divine identity. The apostle John tells us that John the Baptist "saw Jesus coming to him, and said, 'Behold, the Lamb *of God!*'" (John 1:29). John knew that this was God's own anointed Messiah, come to fulfill God's redemptive purpose. The Baptist's first reaction to Jesus' request for baptism was **I have need to be baptized by You.**

It is not difficult to understand John's concern. His baptism was for confession of sin and repentance (3:2, 6, 11), of which he himself had need; but

Jesus had no sins to confess or be forgiven of. John's baptism was for those who turned from their sin and thereby became fit for the arrival of the great King. Why, then, would the sinless King Himself want to be baptized?

An ancient apocryphal book called *The Gospel According to the Hebrews* suggests that Jesus asked for baptism because His mother and brothers wanted Him to: "Behold, the mother of the Lord and His brethren said to Him, 'John the Baptist baptizeth for the remission of sins, let us go and be baptized by him.' But He said to them, 'What sin have I committed that I should go and be baptized by him, except perchance this very thing that I have said in ignorance?'" The writer of that spurious gospel saw the problem, but his solution was purely speculative and is incongruous with the rest of the New Testament.

For others in the early centuries, Jesus' coming for baptism seemed to pose no problem at all. Those who were strongly influenced by Gnostic philosophy believed that until His baptism Jesus was just an ordinary man, sinful like every other man. At His baptism he was endowed with deity by the divine *logos* (Word), the "Christ Spirit." His baptism was therefore necessary to purify Him and make Him suitable to receive the divine endowment. Like the rest of the Gnostic views, that idea does not square with Scripture. Jesus was *born* the Son of God (Luke 1:32, 35) and was called "'Immanuel,' which translated means 'God with us,'" even before His birth (Matt. 1:23).

It was because John the Baptist was fully aware of Jesus' deity and sinlessness that he **tried to prevent Him**. The Greek verb is in the imperfect tense (*diekōluen*) and suggests a continued effort by John—"he kept trying to prevent Him." The verb is also a compound, whose prepositional prefix (*dia*) intensifies it. The pronouns in John's statement are all emphatic, giving evidence of his bewilderment. **I have need to be baptized by You, and do You come to me?** He did not directly contradict Jesus, as Peter would do (Matt. 16:22), but he thought that somehow he surely misunderstood what Jesus intended, that He could not possibly mean what He seemed to be saying.

John resisted baptizing Jesus for exactly the opposite reason that he resisted baptizing the Pharisees and Sadducees. They were in great need of repentance but were unwilling to ask for it and gave no evidence of having it. John therefore refused to baptize them, calling them a "brood of vipers" (3:7). Jesus, by contrast, came for baptism, though He alone of all mankind had no need of repentance. John refused to baptize the Pharisees and Sadducees because they were totally unworthy of it. Now he was almost equally reluctant to baptize Jesus, because He was too worthy for it.

John knew that his baptism for repentance from sin was totally inappropriate for Jesus. John acknowledged Jesus as the Christ, "the Lamb of God who takes away the sin of the world!" (John 1:29). Why should the One who takes away sin submit Himself to a ceremony that represents confession and repentance of sin?

John's attempt to **prevent** Jesus from being baptized is therefore a testimony to Jesus' sinlessness. This prophet, of whom the Lord Himself said there had "not arisen anyone greater" (Matt. 11:11), knew that he himself was not sinless. I

have need to be baptized by You, he told Jesus, **and do You come to me?** "I am only a prophet of God," John was saying, "and I am sinful like everyone whom I baptize. But You are the Son of God and sinless. You are not a sinner. Why, then, do you ask me to baptize You?" Among John's many God-given insights into who Jesus was, what He was like, and what He had come to do, was his knowledge that the One who now stood before Him was without sin. In a less direct but yet definite way, John declared with the writer of Hebrews that Jesus, though "tempted in all things as we are, [is] yet without sin" (Heb. 4:15). So even in his reluctance to baptize Christ, John was fulfilling the role of a herald and the office of a prophet by proclaiming the perfection of the Savior.

Why did Jesus, who was even more aware of His own sinlessness than John was, want to submit Himself to an act that testified to confession and repentance of sin? Some interpreters suggest that He intended His baptism to be a sort of initiatory rite for His high priesthood, reflecting the ceremony which prepared the Old Testament priests for their ministry. Others suggest that Jesus wanted to identify Himself with the Gentiles, who were initiated into Judaism as proselytes by the act of baptism. Still others take Jesus' baptism to be His recognition and endorsement of John's authority, His accrediting of John as a true prophet of God and the genuine forerunner of His own ministry. A fourth view is that the Lord intended to be baptized vicariously for the sins of mankind, making His baptism, along with His atoning death on the cross, a part of His sin-bearing, redemptive work.

But none of those views is supported by Scripture, and none fits the context of the present passage. Jesus Himself explains to John His reason for wanting to be baptized. In His first recorded words since the age of twelve, when He told His parents, "Did you not know that I had to be in My Father's house?" (Luke 2:49), Jesus said, **Permit it at this time; for in this way it is fitting for us to fulfill all righteousness.** These are words of royal dignity and humility.

Jesus did not deny that He was spiritually superior to John or that He was sinless. **Permit it at this time** was an idiom meaning that the act of His baptism, though not seemingly appropriate, was indeed appropriate for this special **time.** Jesus understood John's reluctance and knew that it came from deep spiritual commitment and sincerity. He gave permission for John to do what, without divine instruction, he would never have been willing to do. He assured the prophet that **in this way it is fitting,** and went on to explain to John that His baptism was important for both of their ministries, **for us to fulfill all righteousness.** For God's plan to be perfectly fulfilled, it was necessary for Jesus to be baptized and to be baptized specifically by John.

It seems that one reason Jesus submitted to baptism was to give an example of obedience to His followers. As the King of kings Jesus recognized that He had no ultimate obligation to pay taxes to a human government. When Peter on one occasion asked about the matter, Jesus replied, "'What do you think, Simon? From whom do the kings of the earth collect customs or poll-tax, from their sons or from strangers?' And upon his saying, 'From strangers,' Jesus said to him, 'Consequently the sons are exempt. But, lest we give them offense, . . . give it [a stater coin] to them for you and Me'" (Matt. 17:25-27). As Scripture makes clear in many places, it is proper and right for believers, even though they are sons of God, to honor and pay taxes to human governments (see Rom. 13:1-7; Titus 3:1; 1 Pet. 2:13-15). In every case, Jesus modeled obedience. In His baptism He acknowledged that John's standard of righteousness was valid and in action affirmed it as the will of God to which men are to be subject.

Jesus came into the world to identify with men; and to identify with men is to identify with sin. He could not purchase righteousness for mankind if He did not identify with mankind's sin. Hundreds of years before Christ's coming, Isaiah had declared that the Messiah "was numbered with the transgressors; yet He Himself bore the sin of many, and interceded for the transgressors" (Isa. 53:12). Jesus' baptism also represented the willing identification of the sinless Son of God with the sinful people He came to save.

That was the first act of His ministry, the first step in the redemptive plan that He came to fulfill. He who had no sin took His place among those who had no righteousness. He who was without sin submitted to a baptism for sinners. In this act the Savior of the world took His place among the sinners of the world. The sinless Friend of sinners was sent by the Father "in the likeness of sinful flesh and as an offering for sin, He condemned sin in the flesh" (Rom. 8:3); and He "made Him who knew no sin to be sin on our behalf, that we might become the righteousness of God in Him" (2 Cor. 5:21; cf. Isa. 53:11). There was no other way **to fulfill all righteousness.**

Jesus' baptism not only was a symbol of His identity with sinners but was also a symbol of His death and resurrection, and therefore a prefigurement of Christian baptism. Jesus made only two other references to personal baptism, and each related to His death. Not long before His final trip to Jerusalem He told His disciples, "I have a baptism to undergo, and how distressed I am until it is accomplished!" (Luke 12:50). On the other occasion He was responding to the request by James and John that they be given the top positions in His heavenly kingdom. "You do not know what you are asking for. Are you able to drink the cup that I drink, or to be baptized with the baptism with which I am baptized?" (Mark 10:38). Jesus' supreme identification with sinners was His taking their sin upon Himself, which He did at Calvary.

Though John, having been given such a brief explanation, could not possibly have comprehended the full meaning of Jesus' baptism, he accepted His Lord's word and obeyed. **Then he permitted Him.**

And after being baptized, Jesus went up immediately from the water; and behold, the heavens were opened, and he saw the Spirit of God descending as a dove, and coming upon Him, (3:16)

John's baptism, and that of Jesus' disciples during His earthly ministry (John 4:1-2), represented cleansing, or washing, from sin. Christian baptism represents the believer's identification with Christ's death and resurrection (Rom. 6:4; Col. 2:12). In both cases the significance of the act is lost if it does not involve immersion. Sprinkling or pouring does not fit either the symbolism of cleansing or of dying and being raised.

The Greek word itself (*baptizō*) means literally to dip an object into water or other liquid, not to have the liquid put on the object. If all the forms of this word in Scripture had been translated (as "immersed") instead of being simply transliterated (as "baptized")—first into Latin and then into modern languages— the confusion we now see regarding the mode of baptism would never have arisen. In relation to other things the same word *is* translated—as we see in Luke 16:24, where the rich man in Hades asks that Lazarus might "dip [from *baptizō*] the tip of his finger in water and cool off my tongue," and John 13:26, where Jesus "dipped [also from *baptizō*] the morsel." As can be determined from any Greek lexicon, the original word never had a meaning other than dipping or submerging, and no other term is used for baptizing.

The Christian church knew no form of baptism but immersion until the Middle Ages, when the practice of sprinkling or pouring was introduced by the Roman Catholic church—which itself had previously always baptized by immersion. The great Catholic theologian Thomas Aquinas (1225-1274) said, "In immersion the setting forth of the burial of Christ is more plainly expressed, in which this manner of baptizing is more commendable." The Catholic church did not recognize other modes until the Council of Ravenna, held in France in 1311. It was from the Catholic church that Lutheran and Reformed churches inherited the form of sprinkling or pouring. The Church of England did not begin the practice of sprinkling until 1645. The Eastern Orthodox church has never permitted any mode but immersion.

That Jesus **went up immediately from the water** indicates that He had been all the way into the water. John was baptizing *in* the Jordan (3:6), and his custom was to baptize where "there was much water" (John 3:23), which would have been pointless if only sprinkling were used (cf. Acts 8:38-39).

At the moment Jesus came out of the river, **behold, the heavens were opened**. When Ezekiel saw the heavens opened and had the vision of God, he saw such things as the four living creatures, the chariot, and the wheels (Ezek. 1:1-19). Just before he died, Stephen saw "the heavens opened up and the Son of Man standing at the right hand of God" (Acts 7:56), and John the apostle had several heavenly visions (Rev. 4:1; 11:19; 19:11). Paul's experience of being "caught up to the third heaven" was so wonderful and amazing as to be "inexpressible" (2 Cor. 12:2-4).

As one commentator suggests, "Just as the veil of the Temple was rent in twain to symbolize the perfect access of all men to God, so here the heavens are rent asunder to show how near God is to Jesus, and Jesus is to God."

When the heavens opened before John the Baptist, **he saw the Spirit of God descending as a dove, and coming upon Him**, just as the Lord had promised (John 1:33). The confirming sign was that of **a dove**, the only instance in which the Holy Spirit was ever so represented. To the Jewish mind of that day the dove was associated with sacrifice. Bullocks were sacrificed by the rich and lambs by the middle class, but most of the people were poor and could only afford a dove.

Why did the Holy Spirit come upon Jesus? When He became a man, Jesus did not lose His divinity. He was still fully God in every way. In His deity He needed nothing. But in His humanity He was here being anointed for service and granted strength for ministry. The Spirit anointed Him for His kingly service, as Isaiah had predicted: "The Spirit of .the Lord God is upon me, because the Lord has anointed me to bring good news to the afflicted; He has sent me to bind up the brokenhearted, to proclaim liberty to captives, and freedom to prisoners" (Isa. 61:1). Among other things, the Spirit of God came upon Jesus in His humanness in a special way (John 3:34) that empowered Him to cast out demons (Matt. 12:28), to do miraculous signs and wonders (Acts 2:22), and to preach (cf. Acts 10:38). Like every human being, Jesus became tired and hungry and sleepy. His humanness needed strengthening, and that needed strength was given by the Holy Spirit (cf. Matt. 4:1; Luke 4:14).

Jesus' anointing with the Holy Spirit was unique. It was given to empower Him in His humanness, but it was also given as a visible, confirming sign to John the Baptist and to everyone else watching. Jesus was indeed the Messiah, the great King whose coming the Lord had called John to announce and to prepare men for.

CONFIRMATION BY THE FATHER

and behold, a voice out of the heavens, saying, "This is My beloved Son, in whom I am well-pleased." (3:17)

All the Trinity participated in Jesus' baptism. The Son had confirmed His own kingship by saying, "It is fitting for us to fulfill all righteousness" (v. 15), and the Spirit had confirmed His right of messiahship by resting on Him (v. 16). The final aspect of Jesus' coronation, or commissioning, was the Father's confirming word. For a sacrifice to be acceptable to God it must be pure, spotless, without blemish (Ex. 12:5; Lev. 1:3; Deut. 17:1; etc.). Of this One who willingly identified Himself with sinners by His baptism and who was marked by the Holy Spirit as the dove of sacrifice, the Father now said, **This is My beloved Son, in whom I am well-pleased.**

No Old Testament sacrifice, no matter how carefully selected, had ever been truly pleasing to God. It was not possible to find an animal that did not have some blemish, some imperfection. Not only that, but the blood of those animals was at best only symbolic, "for it is impossible for the blood of bulls and goats to take away sins" (Heb. 10:4; cf. 9:12). But the sacrifice Jesus would make on the cross would be "with precious blood, as of a lamb unblemished and spotless, the blood of Christ" (1 Pet. 1:19). Thus God could say He was **well-pleased** with the perfection of Jesus Christ (cf. Matt. 17:5; John 12:28, where God repeats this superlative commendation).

Beloved (*agapētos*) connotes a deep, rich, and profound relationship. It is used here of the Father's great love for His **Son**, but it is also used elsewhere of His love for believers (Rom. 1:7) and for what believers' love toward each other should be (1 Cor. 4:14). Jesus is the Father's **beloved** above all those He loves, the beloved apart from whom no other could ever be beloved (cf. Eph. 1:6). Only in His **Son** could the Father ever be fully **well-pleased** (*eudokeō*). God had examined, as it were, His **beloved Son**, who would offer Himself as a sacrifice for the sins of those with whom He was willing to identify Himself. No imperfection could be found in Him, and God was delighted.

As believers, we too are a delight to the Father, because we are now in the Son. Because the Father finds no imperfection in His Son, He now by His grace finds no imperfection in those who trust in Him (cf. Rom. 3:26; 5:17, 21; Gal. 2:20; 3:27; Eph. 1:3-6; etc.).

The fact that Jesus Christ is the Son of God is central to the gospel. In no passage is that made more clear than in Hebrews 1:1-8:

> God, after He spoke long ago to the fathers in the prophets in many portions and in many ways, in these last days has spoken to us in His Son, whom He appointed heir of all things, through whom also He made the world. And He is the radiance of His glory and the exact representation of His nature, and upholds all things by the word of His power. When He had made purification of sins, He sat down at the right hand of the Majesty on high; having become as much better than the angels, as He has inherited a more excellent name than they. For to which of the angels did He ever say, "Thou art My Son, today I have begotten Thee"? And again, "I will be a Father to Him, and He shall be a Son to Me"? And when He again brings the first-born into the world, He says, "And let all the angels of God worship Him." And of the angels He says, "Who makes His angels winds, and His ministers a flame of fire." But of the Son He says, "Thy throne, O God, is forever and ever, and the righteous scepter is the scepter of His kingdom."

Jesus Christ is the fullest expression of God, superior to and exalted above everything and everyone else. He is the beginning of all things, Creator; the middle of all things, Sustainer and Purifier; and the end of all things, Heir (see also Rom. 11:36; Col. 1:16).

The Son is the manifestation of God, the radiance of God's personal glory, the image of God (2 Cor. 4:4). In Him all deity dwells (Col. 1:15-19; 2:9). Because of His deity, He is superior to the angels who worship Him. (For a fuller explanation of Jesus' sonship, see the author's *Hebrews* [Chicago: Moody Press, 1983], pp. 27-29.)

Even God's title as Father is a reference to His essential relationship to Jesus Christ. God is presented in the New Testament more as the Father of the Lord Jesus

Christ (Matt. 11:27; John 5:17-18; 10:29-33; 14:6-11; 17:1-5; Rom. 15:6; 2 Cor. 1:3; Eph. 1:3, 17; Phil. 2:9-11; 1 Pet. 1:3; 2 John 3) than as the Father of believers (Matt. 6:9).

When Jesus called God "Father," He was not emphasizing primarily submission or generation but sameness of essence—that is, deity. John 5:23 sums it up by demanding "that all may honor the Son, even as they honor the Father." No one can worship God unless he worships Him as the God who is one with King Jesus—"the God and Father of our Lord Jesus Christ."

The Crisis
of Temptation (4:1-11)

8

Then Jesus was led up by the Spirit into the wilderness to be tempted by the devil. And after He had fasted forty days and forty nights, He then became hungry. And the tempter came and said to Him, "If You are the Son of God, command that these stones become bread." But He answered and said, "It is written, 'Man shall not live on bread alone, but on every word that proceeds out of the mouth of God.'" Then the devil took Him into the holy city; and he had Him stand on the pinnacle of the temple, and said to Him, "If You are the Son of God throw Yourself down; for it is written, 'He will give His angels charge concerning You'; and 'On their hands they will bear You up, lest You strike Your foot against a stone.'" Jesus said to him, "On the other hand, it is written, 'You shall not put the Lord your God to the test.'" Again, the devil took Him to a very high mountain, and showed Him all the kingdoms of the world, and their glory; and he said to Him, "All these things will I give You, if You fall down and worship me." Then Jesus said to him, "Begone, Satan! For it is written, 'You shall worship the Lord your God, and serve Him only.'" Then the devil left Him; and behold, angels came and began to minister to Him. (4:1-11)

Since the Fall in the Garden of Eden, temptation has been a constant, unrelenting part of human life. Men have tried to avoid and resist it with self-inflicted pain to make themselves uncomfortable and presumably humble, or by isolating themselves from other people and from physical comforts. But no person has ever found a place or a circumstance that can make him safe from temptation.

Throughout the history of the church much has been written and spoken about overcoming temptation. A fifth-century Christian wrote,

> Fly from all occasions of temptation, and if still tempted, fly further still. If there is no escape possible, then have done with running away and show a bold face and take the two-edged sword of the Spirit. Some temptations must be taken by the throat as David killed the lion; others must be stifled as David hugged the bear to death. Some you had better keep to yourselves and not give air. Shut them up as a scorpion in a bottle. Scorpions in such confinement die soon, but if allowed out for a crawl and then put back into the bottle and corked down, they will live a long while and give you trouble. Keep the cork on your temptations, and they will die of themselves.

Benedict of Nursia (c. 480-543) sought an increase of grace and exemption from temptation by wearing a rough hair shirt and living for three years in a desolate cave, where his scant food was lowered to him on a cord. Once he threw himself into a clump of thorns and briars until his body was covered with bleeding wounds. But he found no escape from temptation. It followed him wherever he went and in whatever he did.

Others have tried to overcome temptation by, in effect, denying it. Jovinian, a heretical fifth-century monk, taught that after a person was baptized he was forever free of the devil's power and from temptation. Jerome, his most outstanding opponent, wisely commented that baptism does not drown the devil.

In Matthew 4:1-11 one of the most monumental and mysterious spiritual battles of all time is recounted—the personal confrontation between Jesus Christ and Satan. The devil's temptations directed at Jesus in the wilderness of Judea were observed by no other human being. He was entirely alone, and it is therefore obvious that we could know nothing of what transpired there unless Jesus Himself had told His disciples of it. Here He reveals the victory secret, as it were, of His momentous struggle with Satan.

The encounter occurred immediately after Jesus' baptism, which, in the terms of His kingship, represented His coronation, His commissioning. Now, after His proclamation as King comes the test of His kingliness. His baptism in the Jordan declared His royalty; His testing in the wilderness demonstrated it. Here Jesus proved He was worthy to receive and to reign over the kingdom His Father would give Him. The One of whom the Father had just said, "This is My beloved Son, in whom I am well-pleased" (3:17), here shows why He was well-pleasing to His Father. He shows that, even in the extreme of temptation, He consistently lived in perfect harmony with the divine plan. Here He first demonstrated His power over hell. His absolute sovereignty forbade Him to bow to the "god of this world," so He faced the full force of Satan's wicked deception, yet remained untouched and uncontaminated. Evil at its lowest was overcome by Him, and goodness at its highest commended Him. The combination of both accredited Him as King.

In this struggle of the Son of God with the son of perdition we are given clear and applicable insights into Satan's strategy against God and His people and also into Christ's way of victory over the tempter. Side by side we are shown the way of danger and the way of escape, the way that leads to defeat and death and the way that leads to victory and life—in short, the way of Satan and the way of God.

It seems that Matthew had two primary purposes in presenting Jesus' temptations in the wilderness. First, as mentioned above, Jesus' victory demonstrated His divine kingship, His royal power to resist the only other great ruler and dominion in the universe, Satan himself. Christ here won His first direct battle with His great enemy, and thereby gave evidence of His glorious right and power as the King of kings and Lord of lords, the supreme Ruler of all creation, the only God. By so doing, He sealed His final victory yet to come. Satan's purpose in the temptations was, of course, just the opposite: to conquer the newly commissioned King, to overthrow the Messiah, and to claim all His royal rights and prerogatives for himself.

Matthew's other purpose was to demonstrate the pattern found in Jesus' human victory over sin, a pattern that He longs to share with all who belong to Him. When we face testing and temptation in the same way our Lord did, we too can be victorious over the adversary's attempts to corrupt us and to usurp the Lord's rightful place in our lives.

The momentous encounter that Matthew here describes, and from which believers can gain such help and encouragement, may be divided into three parts for study: the preparation, the temptation, and the triumph.

THE PREPARATION

Then Jesus was led up by the Spirit into the wilderness to be tempted by the devil. And after He had fasted forty days and forty nights, He then became hungry. (4:1-2)

We learn from Mark that "immediately the Spirit impelled Him to go out into the wilderness" (Mark 1:12). The "immediately," of course, is sequential to the baptism. As soon as Jesus' baptism was completed, His forty-day wilderness experience began. Mark's use of *ekballō* ("impelled") indicates the necessity of Jesus' temptation. Although the temptations were given by Satan, they were a part of God's perfect plan for the redemptive work of His Son.

One of the great truths of life, from which even the Son of God was not exempt on earth, is that after every victory comes temptation. God's Word warns, "Let him who thinks he stands take heed lest he fall" (1 Cor. 10:12). When we have just succeeded in something important, we are invariably tempted to think that we made the accomplishment in our own power and that it is rightfully and permanently ours. When we are most exhilarated with success we are also most vulnerable to pride—and to failure.

In one of my high school football games we were ahead by some fifty points in the fourth quarter, and the coach was letting everyone play. We were on about the five-yard line, and a touchdown was certain. The coach decided to let a fourth-string runningback carry the ball, so that he could have at least one touchdown to his credit before he graduated the next spring. He easily ran through the hole the line opened up for him, and he scored. As the crowd cheered he turned to wave, but kept running. He hit the goal post and was knocked cold. He was so carried away with his triumph that he completely lost his perspective and his sense of reality. Consequently his victory was short-lived.

At other times success causes us to feel invincible and to let down our guard, and when testings come we are not prepared for them. In the contest between Elijah and the 450 prophets of Baal on Mt. Carmel, the Lord gave dramatic and miraculous evidence that He was the true God and that Elijah was His true prophet. First He sent fire from heaven to consume the sacrifices and wood that Elijah had soaked with water. Then, in answer to the prophet's prayer, He sent rain to drought-stricken Judah (1 Kings 18:16-46). But within less than a day Elijah was in despair and asked the Lord to take his life. After being courageous and immovable before the 450 false prophets, he shriveled before the threats of Jezebel (19:1-4). From the height of exhilarating victory he quickly fell into deep despair.

No sooner had Israel been delivered from Egypt than Pharaoh came pursuing her with his army. No sooner had Hezekiah left the solemn Passover than Sennacherib came against him. No sooner had Paul received an abundance of revelations than he was assaulted with vile temptations.

And no sooner had Jesus experienced the first great testimony to His ministry than He faced the first great test of His ministry. After being anointed by the Holy Spirit and attested by the Father, "Jesus, full of the Holy Spirit, returned from the Jordan and was led about by the Spirit in the wilderness" (Luke 4:1). Jesus now was in full consciousness of His divine mission, and His sacred humanity was filled through and through with the abiding presence and power of God. As never before, He was deeply satisfied as He contemplated the redemptive work He was sent to accomplish. After thirty years of waiting in obscurity He now was fully commissioned to begin His task. Then the devil tried to turn Him away.

One of Satan's most common scriptural names is **the devil**, from *diabolos,* which means accuser or slanderer. Among the many other names given him are: the ruler of this world (John 12:31; 14:30; 16:11), the prince of the power of the air (Eph. 2:2), the god of this world (2 Cor. 4:4), the serpent of old and the deceiver of the whole world (Rev. 12:9), Abaddon and Apollyon, both of which mean "destroyer" (Rev. 9:11), and the tempter, as seen in the next verse of our text (Matt. 4:3; cf. 1 Thess. 3:5).

Many people, including some professing Christians, do not believe in a personal devil. But Satan has never made himself more personally manifest than he did to Jesus in the wilderness. The Lord's own account shows unmistakably that the opponent He faced was personal in every sense. Satan was so real even to Martin Luther that it is reported that on one occasion Luther threw an inkwell at his adversary.

Having been cast out of heaven by the Lord, Satan's full fury has ever since been turned against God and His work. During Jesus' incarnation that wrath was specially focused in all its intensity against the Son and against His divine mission of salvation. The devil's single purpose is to frustrate the plan of God and to usurp the place of God. He therefore continually attacks Christ and all who belong to Him. He also pursues every effort to keep others from coming to Christ.

The wilderness of Judea is a hot, barren, and desolate area that extends west from the Dead Sea almost to Jerusalem, and is some thirty-five miles long and fifteen miles wide. George Adam Smith described it as an area of yellow sand and crumbling limestone. It is an area of contorted strata, where the ridges run in all directions as if they were warped and twisted. The hills are like dust heaps, the limestone is blistered and peeling, the rocks are bare and jagged, and often the ground sounds hollow (cited in William Barclay, *The Gospel of Matthew* [Philadelphia: Westminster, 1975], 1:63). Nowhere in Palestine could Jesus have been more isolated or in less comfort.

Satan met Adam in the paradise of Eden, where everything good was provided and nothing harmful existed. Adam lost his battle with Satan while in the perfect situation. The Second Adam met Satan in the desolate, forbidding **wilderness**, where "He was with the wild beasts" (Mark 1:13) and was without food for forty days (Luke 4:2). Yet what the first Adam lost in an ideal environment the Second Adam won back in a terribly imperfect environment. What better proof can there be that spiritual and moral failure are not caused by circumstances but by the character and response of the one who is tempted?

The temptations did not catch God by surprise. Jesus specifically went there **to be tempted by the devil.** The Greek *peirazō* is a morally neutral word that simply means "to test." Whether the testing is for a good or evil purpose depends on the intent of the one giving the test. When the scriptural context clearly indicates the testing is an enticement to evil, the word is most frequently translated by a form of the English *tempt,* which carries that negative connotation. The fact that **the devil** was here doing the testing clearly indicates that Jesus was being **tempted,** enticed to do evil.

Yet God often uses Satan's tempting to evil as His own means of testing for good. What Satan intended to lead the Son into sin and disobedience, the Father used to demonstrate the Son's holiness and worthiness. That is God's plan for all of His children. Christians cannot be tempted in a way that God cannot use for their good and His glory. James even tells us to "consider it all joy, my brethren, when you encounter various trials [*peirasmos*], knowing that the testing of your faith produces endurance. And let endurance have its perfect result, that you may be perfect and complete, lacking in nothing" (James 1:2-4). That is God's plan and purpose—to use Satan's temptations as a means of testing and strengthening our faith in Him and of our growing stronger in righteousness. God allows testings in our lives in order that our spiritual "muscles" may be exercised and strengthened. Whether the testing is by God's initiative or is sent by Satan, God will always use it to produce good in us when we meet the test in His power.

God never tests in the sense of enticing to evil. "Let no one say when he is tempted, 'I am being tempted by God'; for God cannot be tempted by evil, and He Himself does not tempt anyone. But each one is tempted when he is carried away and enticed by his own lust" (James 1:13). All five of the forms of "to tempt" in those verses are from *peirazō,* and all five indicate the negative side of testing, the inducement to evil. God never has a part in that sort of testing, but He can and will turn even the worst sort of testing into the right sort, when it is surrendered to His will and power. It is God's great desire to turn into victory what Satan intends for failure, to strengthen us at the very point where the adversary wants to find us weak.

Joseph's being sold into slavery by his brothers, along with the false accusations and imprisonment he endured as a slave in Egypt, could easily have driven him to despair and bitterness. Most people, faced with such mistreatment and misfortune, would ask, "Why me, Lord? What have I done to deserve this?" They would seethe over their circumstances and possibly dream of revenge. That, no doubt, was the devil's desire for Joseph, but it was not God's. As Joseph told his brothers many years later, "You meant evil against me, but God meant it for good in order to bring about this present result, to preserve many people alive" (Gen. 50:20). What Satan and the brothers had intended for evil, God, through Joseph's obedience, turned to good.

Before the three strong temptation efforts were directed to Jesus, **He had fasted forty days and forty nights.** We are not told what He did during that period, but He no doubt spent most of the time communing with His heavenly Father. Between His baptism and the temptations perhaps He needed the special preparation of being entirely alone and undisturbed with His Father. Even in His perfect humanity, Jesus needed time for thought and for prayer, as we all do. Moses spent forty years in Midian being prepared to lead Israel from Egypt to Canaan. Between his conversion and the beginning of his ministry, Paul spent three years of preparation in Nabataen Arabia (Gal. 1:17-18).

It seems a great understatement to say that, after Jesus' long period of fasting, **He became hungry.** Yet Matthew's simple and direct words give strong evidence that the story was not manufactured by the disciples or the early church. The writings of virtually every false religion and cult are characterized by exaggeration and overdramatization of events relating to the lives of its founders and key leaders. By contrast, even the most astounding events in Scripture are reported with restraint and simplicity.

Hunger not only makes us physically weak but also tends to weaken our moral and spiritual resistance as well. When we are tired, hungry, or sick we are usually less concerned about other needs and dangers and tend to be vulnerable to anything that might provide relief from our present distress. Satan therefore usually attacks most fiercely in such times of weakness and unpreparedness. Temptations that have been anticipated, guarded against, and prayed about have little power to harm us. Jesus tells us to "keep watching and praying, that you may not come into temptation" (Mark 14:38). Victory over temptation comes from being constantly prepared for it, which, in turn, comes from constantly relying on the Lord.

It is said that a person traveling in tiger country will not be attacked if he sees the tiger before the tiger sees him. Tigers attack from behind in order to surprise their victims, and therefore one of the best defenses against that vicious animal is to face it.

Jesus, though having fasted for over a month, was no less alert to spiritual danger. Because He had spent the time in communion with His Father, even in His weakest physical moments He did not allow Satan to gain any foothold. The accounts in Mark (1:13) and Luke (4:2) seem to indicate that Jesus was in some way tempted throughout His stay in the wilderness. Possibly it was the devil's strategy to gradually wear the Lord down little by little before confronting Him with the three great temptations that are specifically recorded. But Jesus would not yield to His adversary on even the slightest point.

THE TEMPTATION

And the tempter came and said to Him, "If You are the Son of God, command that these stones become bread." But He answered and said, "It is written, 'Man shall not live on bread alone, but on every word that proceeds out of the mouth of God.'" Then the devil took Him into the holy city; and he had Him stand on the pinnacle of the temple, and said to Him, "If You are the Son of God throw Yourself down; for it is written, 'He will give His angels charge concerning You'; and 'On their hands they will bear You up, lest You strike Your foot against a stone.'" Jesus said to him, "On the other hand, it is written, 'You shall not put the Lord your God to the test.'" Again, the devil took Him to a very high mountain, and showed Him all the kingdoms of the world, and their glory; and he said to Him, "All these things will I give You, if You fall down and worship me." Then Jesus said to him, "Begone, Satan! For it is written, 'You shall worship the Lord your God, and serve Him only.'" (4:3-10)

Satan is here spoken of as **the tempter,** one of his descriptive names and titles in Scripture. We are not told what form the devil may have taken on this occasion, but his confrontation with Jesus was direct and personal. They spoke to each other and even moved about together, first to the pinnacle of the Temple in Jerusalem and then to a high mountain.

Satan's first great frontal attack on Jesus Christ as He began His earthly ministry was in the form of three temptations, each designed to weaken and destroy the Messiah in an important area of His mission. The temptations became progressively worse. The first was for Jesus to distrust the providential care of His Father and to use His own divine powers to serve Himself. The second was to presume on the Father's care by putting Him to the test. The third was for Him to renounce the way of His Father and to substitute the way of Satan.

SERVING SELF

And the tempter came and said to Him, "If You are the Son of God, command that these stones become bread." But He answered and said, "It is written, 'Man shall not live on bread alone, but on every word that proceeds out of the mouth of God.'" (4:3-4)

The devil's first approach to Jesus had also been his first approach to Eve— to cast doubt on God's Word. He asked Eve, "Indeed, has God said, 'You shall not eat from any tree of the garden'?" (Gen. 3:1), causing her to question God's command. His first word to Jesus was, **If you are the Son of God**—the Greek conditional phrase assumes that Jesus is indeed the divine Son whom the Father had just proclaimed Him to be at His baptism (3:17). Before he gave the direct temptation, Satan gave this one simply to set up the rest. Satan was hoping to persuade Jesus to demonstrate His power to verify that it was real. That would mean violating God's plan that He set that power aside in humiliation and use it only when the Father willed. Satan wanted Jesus to disobey God. Affirming His deity and rights as the Son of God would have been to act independently of God.

The first direct temptation in the wilderness was for Jesus to act against God's plan and to **command that these stones become bread.** This temptation involved a great deal more than Jesus' satisfying His hunger. After forty days and nights of fasting, He certainly was hungry and thirsty, and He had the right to have something to eat and drink. The most obvious part of the temptation was for Jesus to fulfill His legitimate physical needs by miraculous means. But the deeper temptation was Satan's appeal to Jesus' supposed rights as the Son of God. "Why," Satan seemed to say, "should you starve in the wilderness if you are really God's Son? How could the Father allow His Son to go hungry, when He even provided manna for the rebellious children of Israel in the wilderness of Sinai? And had not Isaiah written of the righteous that 'His bread will be given him; his water will be sure'" (Isa. 33:16)? You are a man, and you need food to survive. If God had let His people die in the wilderness, how could His plan of redemption have been fulfilled? If He lets you die in this wilderness, how can you fulfill your divine mission on His behalf?

The purpose of the temptation was not simply for Jesus to satisfy His physical hunger, but to suggest that His being hungry was incompatible with His being the Son of God. He was being tempted to doubt the Father's Word, the Father's love, and the Father's provision. He had every right, Satan suggested, to use

His own divine powers to supply what the Father had not. The Son of God certainly was too important and dignified to have to endure such hardship and discomfort. He had been born in a stable, had to flee to Egypt for His life, spent thirty years in an obscure family in a obscure village in Galilee, and forty days and nights unattended, unrecognized, and unpitied in the wilderness. Surely that was more than enough ignominy to allow Him to identify with mankind. But now that the Father Himself had publicly declared Him to be His Son, it was time for Jesus to use some of His divine authority for His own personal benefit.

This first temptation in the wilderness implied essentially the same mocking taunt that the crowds made at the crucifixion: "If You are the Son of God, come down from the cross" (Matt. 27:40; cf. vv. 42-43). It also included the wicked attempt to cause the Second Adam to fail where the first Adam had failed—in relation to food. Satan wanted Christ to fail because of bread just as Adam had failed because of fruit. Above all, however, he wanted to solicit the Son's rebellion against the Father.

But Jesus had come in His incarnation to do the Father's will and only the Father's will; indeed His will and the Father's were exactly the same (John 5:30; cf. 10:30; Heb. 10:9). He testified, "My food is to do the will of Him who sent Me, and to accomplish His work" (John 4:34), and on another occasion, "For I have come down from heaven, not to do My own will, but the will of Him who sent Me" (John 6:38). In the Garden of Gethsemane, just before His betrayal and arrest, He said, "My Father, if it is possible, let this cup pass from Me; yet not as I will, but as Thou wilt," and a short while later, "My Father, if this cannot pass away unless I drink it, Thy will be done" (Matt. 26:39, 42).

It was that absolute trust and submission that Satan sought to shatter. To have succeeded would have put an irreparable rift in the Trinity. They would no longer have been Three in One, no longer have been of one mind and purpose. In his incalculable pride and wickedness, Satan tried to fracture the very nature of God Himself.

But Jesus, in His incalculable humility and righteousness, **answered and said, "It is written, 'Man shall not live on bread alone, but on every word that proceeds out of the mouth of God.'"** All three of Jesus' responses to the devil were begun with an appeal to God's Word: **It is written.** Even more than David, He could say, "Thy word I have treasured in my heart, that I may not sin against Thee" (Ps. 119:11). In quoting Deuteronomy 8:3 to Satan, Jesus declared that we are better off to obey and depend on God, waiting on His provision, than to grab satisfaction for ourselves when and as we think we need it. Moses had originally said those words to Israel as he recounted to her the great love and blessing God had bestowed on her during her own wilderness experience (Deut. 8:1-18).

God's people are never justified in complaining and worrying about their needs. If we live by faith in Him and in obedience to His Word, we will never lack anything we really need. "And my God shall supply all your needs," Paul assures us, "according to His riches in glory in Christ Jesus" (Phil. 4:19). Jesus tells us that God knows what we need even before we ask Him (Matt. 6:8). Later in the same discourse He says, "But seek first His kingdom and His righteousness; and all these things shall be added to you" (6:33). We are *always* better off to obey God and to trust in His gracious sustenance than to impatiently and selfishly provide for ourselves in ways that disobey, or in any way compromise, His Word. Underlying our readiness to justify much of what we do is the common but self-centered and carnal notion that, as God's children, we deserve the earthly best and that it is inappropriate and even unspiritual to be satisfied with anything less. Grabbing or demanding what we think we deserve may be an act of rebellion against sovereign God.

To try to circumvent or modify God's revealed will not only is unfaithful and fleshly but is based on the false assumption that our physical well-being is our most crucial need, without which we cannot exist. Jesus contradicts that assumption, which is so natural to fallen man. **Man shall not live on bread alone, but on every word that proceeds out of the mouth of God**. "It is not food," Jesus says, "that is the most necessary part of life. The creative, energizing, and sustaining power of God is the only real source of man's existence."

James reminds us that we do not know what we will be able to do in the future, or even if we will have a future in this life. Every person is "just a vapor that appears for a little while and then vanishes away," he says. When planning what we want to do, we "ought to say, 'If the Lord wills, we shall live and also do this or that'" (James 4:14-15). Like Jesus, the purposes and intentions of our lives should only be the purposes and intentions of our heavenly Father. The guiding principle of His life should be the guiding principle of ours. The central motive of our lives should be to please God and to trust Him to supply everything we need—to follow without reservation Jesus' command to "seek first His kingdom and His righteousness" and to believe without reservation that He will provide everything we need (Matt. 6:33). Before He gave that command, Jesus had asked, "Why are you anxious about clothing? Observe how the lilies of the field grow; they do not toil nor do they spin, yet I say to you that even Solomon in all his glory did not clothe himself like one of these. But if God so arrays the grass of the field, which is alive today and tomorrow is thrown into the furnace, will He not much more do so for you, O men of little faith?" (6:28-30).

We can never please God, or even serve our own best interests, by complaining about and demanding what we do not have, or by violating or ignoring His will in order to get something we want. If we persist in disobeying God He may severely discipline us, or even take us off the scene, as John warns in his first letter (1 John 5:16). Ananias and Sapphira lost their lives because they lied to the Holy Spirit by telling the apostles they had received less than they actually did from the sale of some property (Acts 5:1-11). Certain members of the Corinthian church became weak and sick, and several even died, because they profaned the Lord's Supper (1 Cor. 11:27-30).

Even when our disobedience does not reach such extremes, we always suffer when we willfully bypass God's Word. Following our Lord's example in the wilderness, no matter how urgent and important a need seems to be, we are to wait for our heavenly Father's provision, knowing that expedience and self-effort cannot bring good for ourselves, and certainly not glory to God.

TESTING GOD

Then the devil took Him into the holy city; and he had Him stand on the pinnacle of the temple, and said to Him, "If You are the Son of God throw Yourself down; for it is written, 'He will give His angels charge concerning You'; and 'On their hands they will bear You up, lest You strike Your foot against a stone.'" Jesus said to him, "On the other hand, it is written, 'You shall not put the Lord your God to the test.'" (4:5-7)

Having failed to induce Jesus to use His divine powers to serve His own self-interests and thereby rebel against the will of His Father, Satan proceeded to tempt the Son to put His heavenly Father's love and power to a test.

By some means **the devil took Him into the holy city; and he had Him stand on the pinnacle of the temple.** The location and form of the **pinnacle of the temple** in Jerusalem has not been identified with certainty. It must have been part of the reconstruction ordered by Herod the Great and most likely was on the eastern side of the Temple, overlooking the Kidron Valley. **The pinnacle** may have been the roof that extended out over Herod's portico. Josephus reports that the drop to the valley floor was some 450 feet. According to early tradition, James, the head of the Jerusalem church, was martyred by being thrown from that portico.

Still hoping to undermine Jesus' relation to God in His divine sonship, the devil again introduced his temptation with the words **if You are the Son of God.** "Prove to yourself and to the world that you are the Son of God," Satan taunted, and **throw Yourself down.**

In the first temptation a need (lack of food) already existed; in the second a need was to be created. To make the temptation more persuasive, the devil quoted Scripture, as Jesus had just done. Quoting Psalm 91:11-12, he said, **for it is written, "He will give His angels charge concerning You"; and "On their hands they will bear You up, lest You strike Your foot against a stone."**

With that subtle and clever twist, the tempter thought He had backed Jesus into a corner. If Jesus lived only by the Word of God, then He would be confronted by something from the Word of God. "You claim to be God's Son and You claim to trust His Word," Satan was saying. "If so, why don't you demonstrate your sonship and prove the truth of God's Word by putting Him to a test—a scriptural test? If you won't use your *own* divine power to help yourself, let your Father use *His* divine power to help you. If you won't act independently of the Father, let the Father act. Give your Father a chance to fulfill the Scripture I just quoted to you."

For Jesus to have followed Satan's suggestion would have been, in the eyes of many Jews, sure proof of His messiahship. According to William Barclay, that is exactly the sort of proof many purported messiahs of that day were trying to give. A man named Theudas led a group of people from the Temple to the Jordan River, promising to split the waters. After he failed, no one listened to him anymore. An Egyptian pretender claimed he would lay flat the walls of Jerusalem, which, of course, he was not able to do. Tradition holds that Simon the magician (see Acts 8:9) tried the very feat with which Satan tempted Jesus: jumping off the top of the Temple—for which he lost his life as well as his following (*The Gospel of Matthew* [Philadelphia: Westminster, 1975], 1:69).

Sensationalism has always appealed to the flesh, and many people are willing to believe almost anyone or anything as long as the claims are accompanied by fantastic happenings. Jesus warned that "false Christs and false prophets will arise and will show great signs and wonders, so as to mislead, if possible, even the elect" (Matt. 24:24). But such dramatic signs, even when they are from God, do not produce faith; they only strengthen the faith of those who already believe. The many miracles by which God provided for Israel in the wilderness drove many of the people to presumption and greater disbelief. Jesus' miracles only hardened the opposition of His enemies. He declared that "an evil and adulterous generation craves for a sign" (Matt. 12:39; cf. 16:4). When Jesus was dedicated in the Temple as an infant, Simeon "said to Mary His mother, 'Behold, this Child is appointed for the fall and rise of many in Israel, and for a sign to be opposed'" (Luke 2:34). Jesus Himself was the greatest sign ever given by God to mankind, yet, as Isaiah had predicted hundreds of years earlier, He "was despised and forsaken of men" (Isa. 53:3; Luke 18:31-33).

Those who acclaimed Jesus only because of His miracles and impressive words later turned against Him. When the crowd from Galilee, astounded by Jesus' multiplying the bread and fish, tried to make Him king, He would have nothing of it (John 6:14-15). Those who scattered their garments before Jesus and waved palm branches in His honor as He came into Jerusalem did so because He had raised Lazarus from the dead (John 12:13, 17-18). A short while later Jesus hid Himself from the Jerusalem crowd, about whom John says, "But though He had performed so many signs before them, yet they were not believing in Him" (John 12:37). Demanding sensational proof is not evidence of faith but of doubt. To long for the visible sign, the big miracle, the dramatic proof is nothing but masked unbelief. It is the farthest thing from faith.

Jesus would have no part of cheap, faithless sensationalism. He therefore replied to Satan, **It is written, "You shall not put the Lord your God to the test."** For those who believe in God, it is more than evident that He already has proved Himself. Jesus did not need to prove to Himself that His Father cared and protected, and He knew that the Father's care and protection could not be proved to others by any means but faith.

For at least two reasons Jesus refused to take part in a spectacle such as throwing Himself off the Temple roof. First, any sensationalism inevitably is frustrated by the law of diminishing returns. People are never satisfied. They always want one more sign, one more miracle, one more show. To have maintained His influence over the people by the use of miracles, Jesus would have had to produce greater and greater sensations. Because the natural, carnal heart can never be satisfied, this year's miracle would have become next year's bore. His followers would only have been lovers of sensation, not lovers of God.

Second, and more significant, no matter how noble and important we may think our reasons are, to test God is to doubt God. And to doubt God is not to trust Him, and not to trust Him is sin. That, of course, is what Satan wanted Jesus to do. To induce Jesus to sin, if that were possible, would shatter His perfect holiness, and therefore shatter His divinity and man's hope of salvation. Had Jesus put His Father to such a test, He would have separated Himself from His Father and perverted the divine plan of redemption—the very purpose for which He had come to earth.

Not only that, but to have tested the Father by putting Him under pressure to provide by extraordinary means, especially a means of Jesus' own choosing, would have been for the Son to put His judgment and will above the Father's— which He would never do (Matt. 26:39, 42; John 5:30; 6:30; etc.). It would also have questioned the Father's gracious providence and love. How much more should we, mere creatures who are so imperfect, never place our will or judgment above God's. To live recklessly and carelessly, and then expect God to bail us out when we get into trouble, is to presume upon his grace.

Those who willingly put themselves in the way of danger and temptation often end up blaming God when harm comes from their foolishness. When the Lord confronted Adam about his eating the forbidden fruit, Adam's response was to blame God even more than he blamed his wife. "The woman whom Thou gavest to be with me, she gave me from the tree, and I ate" (Gen. 3:12). It was true that Eve gave Adam the fruit, but because God gave Eve to Adam, the primary blame was God's—according to Adam's perverted logic. Our need is not to prove God's faithfulness but to demonstrate our own, by trusting Him both to determine and to supply our needs according to His own will.

God expects us to take risks, any risks necessary, in order to obey His will. When we risk our prestige, our money, our lives, our families, or anything else to fulfill the Lord's calling, we can rest confidently in His divine provision for all that we need—if we accept the truth that only He knows what our needs really are. But when we take risks simply to fulfill our own ambitions or to put God to the test, He gives no promise on which we can rest.

WORSHIPING SATAN

Again, the devil took Him to a very high mountain, and showed Him all the kingdoms of the world, and their glory; and he said to Him, "All these things will I give You, if You fall down and worship me." Then Jesus said to him, "Begone, Satan! For it is written, 'You shall worship the Lord your God, and serve Him only.'" (4:8-10)

Satan now drops his pretense and makes one final, desperate effort to corrupt Jesus. He finally reveals his supreme purpose: to induce Jesus Christ to worship him. He had first suggested what Jesus ought to do for Himself. Next he suggested what the Father ought to do for Jesus. Now he suggests what Satan could do for Jesus—in exchange for what Jesus could do for him.

We are not told what **very high mountain** it was to which **the devil took him.** The significance, however, lies in the fact that this location gave a vast view of the earth. But the view extended far beyond what physical vision could perceive from *any* vantage point, no matter how high. By some supernatural accommodation the devil showed Jesus the glories of Egypt—its pyramids, temples, libraries, and vast treasures. He showed the power and splendor of Rome, with its mighty empire spread over the known world. He showed great Athens, magnificent Corinth, and of course wondrous Jerusalem, the royal city of David, and more—**all the kingdoms of the world, and their glory.**

As God's own proclaimed King of kings, Jesus had a divine right to all kingdoms, and it was to that right that Satan appealed in this last temptation. "Why should you have to wait for what is already rightfully yours?" he suggested to Jesus. "You deserve to have it now. Why do you submit as a Servant when you could reign as a King? I am only offering you what the Father has already promised." Perhaps he reminded Jesus that God had said to the Son, "Ask of Me, and I will surely give the nations as Thine inheritance, and the very ends of the earth as Thy possession" (Ps. 2:8).

But Satan was offering the world to Jesus on his own corrupt terms, not God's. That which the Father promised to the Son because of His righteous obedience, Satan offered to the Son in exchange for His unrighteous disobedience. God's plan in testing the Son was to prove the Son's worthiness to inherit and rule the world. Satan's plan was to draw the Son away from that worthiness by enticing Him to grab the kingdom the Father promised to give Him. Instead of enduring the long, bitter, humiliating, and painful road to the cross—and the even longer wait in heaven for God's time to be completed—Jesus could rule the world now!

Satan always comes at us in that way. He suggests that the world of business, the world of politics, the world of fame, or the world of whatever our heart desires can be ours—if only . . . ! We can get what we want; we can fulfill our lusts and our fantasies; we can *be* somebody. All we must do to get those things of the world is to go after them in the way of the world—which is Satan's way.

That, in essence, is what the tempter always promises. He promised Eve that by eating the forbidden fruit she would not die as God had warned, but that, in fact, she would become a god herself. "For God knows that in the day you eat from it your eyes will be opened, and you will be like God" (Gen. 3:4-5). He tempts each of us in the same way. "Why set your standards so high? What's the use? You can get what you want by cutting a corner here and shading the truth there. Why wait for heavenly reward, when you can have what you want now?" When we set our hearts on money, prestige, popularity, power, or selfish happiness, we are doing exactly what Satan wanted Jesus to do—put self first and God last. Self-will is Satan's will and is therefore by definition the opposite of God's will, which is for us to "seek first His kingdom and His righteousness" (Matt. 6:33). Abraham sought what God promised in his own self-styled act with Hagar, and tragedy resulted. It always does.

Satan is a counterfeiter. He offers what seems to be the same as what God offers, and his price is much cheaper. "God wants you to prosper, doesn't He?" Satan asks. "Well, I'll give you prosperity a lot sooner and for a lot less. Just turn your head a little at questionable practices. Give in when it's advantageous; don't be a prude; follow the crowd. That's the way to success." The basic argument is always a form of the idea that the end justifies the means.

But Satan is also the father of lies. What he really demanded in the wilderness was Jesus' own soul: **All these things I will give You, if You fall down and worship me.** Satan had rebelled against God in the first place because he could not tolerate being second to the Trinity. Here, he thought, was his great opportunity: he would bribe the Son to worship at his feet. Satan's price is always immeasurably more than he leads us to believe.

And what he gives is always immeasurably less than he promises. For Jesus to have given in to this third temptation would have brought the same ultimate result as His having succumbed to either of the other two. He would have disqualified Himself not only as King but as Savior. The statement of those who mocked at the foot of the cross would have had to have been reversed: "He saved Himself; others He cannot save" (see Matt. 27:42). Instead of redeeming the world He would have joined the world. Instead of inheriting the world, He would have lost the world. The Christ would have played the antichrist, and the Lamb would have become the beast.

As before, Jesus' reply was from Scripture, and is again from Deuteronomy. **Then Jesus said to him, "Begone, Satan! For it is written, 'You shall worship the Lord your God, and serve Him only.'"** The tempter's last proposal was so preposterous that Jesus dismissed him with **Begone, Satan!** The devil had stepped beyond all bounds in proposing such unutterable wickedness. Because Satan's present power is only by God's permission, when the Son commanded him to leave, Satan had no choice but to obey. Therein Christ demonstrated the very sovereign power Satan wanted Him to misuse!

If the Son of God would not compromise even the least important truth in the universe, He would surely not compromise the greatest: that God, and God alone, is to be worshiped and served. Jesus had heard enough from the enemy. Though Satan would be back as soon as he had "an opportune time" (Luke 4:13), for now he was forced to leave.

Jesus will inherit the kingdom in God's time, and we will inherit the kingdom with Him (Matt. 5:5; 25:34; Rom. 8:17; James 2:5). In the eternal, heavenly state all the universe will be ours! Who would want to sacrifice that for the deceptive, disappointing, and short-lived imitations Satan offers?

There are many good things that God will give us even in this life. No one desires our happiness more than our heavenly Father. "If you then, being evil," Jesus says, "know how to give good gifts to your children, how much more shall your Father who is in heaven give what is good to those who ask Him!" (Matt. 7:11). We can have the happiness God gives; why should we settle for the cheap substitute

Satan proffers? We can have the success of living righteously and pleasing our heavenly Father; why should we settle for the brief and disappointing successes sin produces? By God's grace we can have the peace that passes understanding; why should we settle for the cheap satisfactions that everyone understands but that will soon pass?

THE TRIUMPH

Then the devil left Him; and behold, angels came and began to minister to Him. (4:11)

When Jesus said, "Begone," **the devil left Him,** because he had no choice. The Lord gives all of His children the power to resist Satan. "Resist the devil," James assures us, "and he will flee from you" (James 4:7). As he did with Jesus, Satan will not long stay away from us; but with *every* temptation God "will provide a way of escape" (1 Cor. 10:13). For every temptation Satan leads us into, a way out is provided by the Father.

Satan's temptations failed, but God's testings succeeded. Jesus' responses to the tempter were, in essence, "I will trust the Father; I will not presume on His Word; and I will not circumvent His will. I will take the Father's good gifts from the Father's own hand, in the Father's own way, and in the Father's own time." Thus the King was accredited by the severest test.

After Satan left, **angels came.** How much better is the ministry of angels than the deceptions of Satan. At Jesus' baptism the Father acknowledged Jesus' worthiness by proclaiming, "This is My beloved Son, in whom I am well-pleased." Now the Father acknowledges Jesus' worthiness by sending angels **to minister to Him.** At any time during His wilderness experience Jesus could have asked for and received the aid of "more than twelve legions of angels" (Matt. 26:53). But He waited for His Father to send them in His Father's time.

We are not told what the ministry of the angels included, but surely they brought Jesus food to satisfy His hunger. We know they could not have been in the presence of the Son of God without offering Him worship. And certainly they could not have come from heaven without bringing strengthening words of assurance and love from His Father.

Satan tempts us in the same basic ways he tempted Jesus in the wilderness. First, he will try to get us to distrust God's providential care and to try to solve our problems, win our struggles, and meet our needs by our own plans and in our own power. Second, he will try to get us to presume on God's care and forgiveness by willingly putting ourselves in the way of danger—whether physical, economic, moral, spiritual, or any other. Third, he will appeal to selfish ambitions and try to get us to use our own schemes to fulfill the promises God has made to us—which amounts to trying to fulfill God's plan in Satan's way.

Those three ways are reflected in 1 John 2:16—"For all that is in the world, the lust of the flesh and the lust of the eyes and the boastful pride of life, is not from the Father, but is from the world." The temptation for Jesus to turn stones into bread was to fulfill "the lust of the flesh" by using His divine powers for selfish means. The temptation to throw Himself off the pinnacle of the Temple was to fulfill "the lust of the eyes" by showing off to the world and seeking fame through sensationalism. The temptation to grab immediate control of the kingdoms of the world was to satisfy the "boastful pride of life" by yielding to Satan's power and will.

The story is told of a man who was trying to teach his dog obedience. He would take a large piece of meat and put it in the middle of the floor. Each time the dog attempted to take the meat the man would swat the dog and say, "No." Soon the dog began to associate the swatting with the word *no* and learned to stop simply when the word was said. When meat was placed on the floor the dog would not look at it but rather at his master, waiting for his word of approval or denial.

That is essentially the message God teaches in this passage: "When temptation comes, don't look at the temptation but at Jesus Christ. Keep your eyes on His example and do what he did. Look at the ways He was tempted and at the way He resisted, and learn from Him." The writer of Hebrews, perhaps with Jesus' wilderness temptations particularly in mind, tells us, "For we do not have a high priest who cannot sympathize with our weaknesses, but one who has been tempted in all things as we are, yet without sin" (Heb. 4:15). Even more encouraging is the earlier declaration: "For since He Himself was tempted in that which He has suffered, He is able to come to the aid of those who are tempted" (Heb. 2:18).

Jesus has been there before us; He has met the worst Satan can give and has been victorious. More than that, He is eager to share that victory with His own people when they are tempted. "No temptation has overtaken you but such as is common to man; and God is faithful, who will not allow you to be tempted beyond what you are able, but with the temptation will provide the way of escape also, that you may be able to endure it" (1 Cor. 10:13).

We can have victory over temptation only by resisting in the way that Jesus resisted—by holding with complete obedience to God and His Word. Jesus endured temptation to the very limit of Satan's power, and He resisted to that very limit. He did not in the least degree allow temptation to develop into desire, much less into sin (cf. James 1:13-15). He did not think the matter over or give it any consideration. He simply stood firmly in His Father's will and said no!

We find help against temptation, just as we find help for everything else in the Christian life, by "fixing our eyes on Jesus, the author and perfecter of faith" (Heb. 12:2). A hurdler soon learns that if he looks at the hurdles as he runs, he will trip and fall. From start to finish he looks only at the goal, and when he does that the hurdles are cleared in stride as each one is encountered. Keeping our eyes on our Lord Jesus Christ is our only hope of conquering temptation and faithfully running "with endurance the race that is set before us" (Heb. 12:1).

The Light Dawns (4:12-17)

9

Now when He heard that John had been taken into custody, He withdrew into Galilee; and leaving Nazareth, He came and settled in Capernaum, which is by the sea, in the region of Zebulun and Naphtali. This was to fulfill what was spoken through Isaiah the prophet, saying, "The Land of Zebulun and the land of Naphtali, by the way of the sea, beyond the Jordan, Galilee of the Gentiles—The people who were sitting in darkness saw a great light, and to those who were sitting in the land and shadow of death, upon them a light dawned."

From that time Jesus began to preach and say, "Repent, for the kingdom of heaven is at hand." (4:12-17)

One of the most beautiful metaphors used to describe Jesus' nature and character is that of light. It conveys the idea of the illuminating, truth-revealing, and sin-exposing ministry of the Son of God. After first presenting Jesus Christ as the creative Word of God, John tells us, "In Him was life, and the life was the light of men. And the light shines in the darkness, and the darkness did not comprehend it" (John 1:4-5). He then tells us that John the Baptist "came that he might bear witness of the light . . . the true light which, coming into the world, enlightens every man" (vv. 8-9). He continues to say that "this is the judgment, that the light is come into the world, and men loved the darkness rather than the light; for their deeds were evil. For everyone who does evil hates the light, and does not come to the light, lest his deeds should be exposed. But he who practices the truth comes to the light, that his deeds may be manifested as having been wrought in God" (John 3:19-21).

Speaking of Himself, Jesus said, "I am the light of the world; he who follows Me shall not walk in the darkness, but shall have the light of life" (John 8:12). Jesus spoke those words "in the treasury, as He taught in the temple" (v. 20). The Temple treasury was the outer court, the court of the women, and Jesus was there at the conclusion of the feast of Tabernacles. At that feast the Jews celebrated what they called the illumination of the Temple. A massive series of candelabra was placed in the middle of the court of the women, and for a week a great stream of light shinned out continuously—to commemorate the pillar of fire that led Israel during the wilderness wanderings under Moses. As Jesus entered the court of the women, the light had just been extinguished. The candelabra were still in place, but they now gave no light. Jesus' declaration that He Himself was the light of the world that would never go out must have struck His hearers with great force.

In the Old Testament, walking in the light was often used as a figure of righteousness and obedience to God, and walking in darkness as a figure of wickedness and disobedience (see Prov. 2:13; 4:18-19; etc.). Now Jesus presents Himself as the embodiment of righteousness and godliness, the very "light of the world." "While I am in the world," He said, "I am the light of the world" (John 9:5), and again, "For a little while longer the light is among you. Walk while you have the light, that darkness may not overtake you" (12:35; cf. v. 46). Paul proclaimed, "For God, who said, 'Light shall shine out of darkness,' is the One who has shone in our hearts to give the light of the knowledge of the glory of God in the face of Christ" (2 Cor. 4:6). Peter speaks of Christians as "a chosen race, a royal priesthood, a holy nation, a people for God's own possession, that you may proclaim the excellencies of Him who has called you out of darkness into His marvelous light" (1 Pet. 2:9).

After the Fall, mankind had two "candles," as it were, that continued to give light about God and His will—the candle of creation and the candle of conscience. But man paid little attention to either, preferring to walk in the darkness of his own corrupted will (see Rom. 1:18-21). In his sinfulness man continually extinguished the only two lights he had that revealed God's nature and His will for His creatures.

Modern research has shown that, contrary to what had always been assumed, leprosy, now often called Hansen's disease, does not itself cause the decay and deformity so often found in the extremities of its victims. The ulceration and decay are caused by abrasion, infection, external heat, and other secondary causes. The disease itself causes certain parts of the body to become insensitive to pain, and the person therefore has no warning of danger or harm. People with leprosy will therefore often reach into a fire to retrieve something, or will tear their feet to shreds walking on sharp stones they cannot feel.

The disease of sin has a similar effect. It desensitizes man's spiritual and moral nature, destroying even the limited natural protection he has against evil, snuffing out the residual light that remains after the Fall. And Satan endeavors to shut out the light of the saving good news (2 Cor. 4:3-4).

Jesus Christ came not only to make man sensitive again to sin, but to restore the life and health that sin has destroyed. He came not only to reveal the darkness that sin causes, but also to bring the light that overcomes the darkness. That is how Matthew introduces the active ministry of Jesus: He is Himself the great light that has dawned upon mankind. As the aged Simeon said of Jesus as He held the infant Lord in his arms in the Temple, "My eyes have seen Thy salvation, which Thou hast prepared in the presence of all peoples, a light of revelation to the Gentiles, and the glory of Thy people Israel" (Luke 2:30-32; cf. Isa. 42:6; 49:6; 52:10).

We learn from the apostle John (1:19—4:42) that about a year elapsed between Jesus' wilderness temptations and the events recorded in Matthew 4:12-17. Probably because it does not relate directly to Jesus' kingship, that period is not mentioned by Matthew.

What Jesus did during that time was nevertheless significant. For some three days Jesus had remained near the Jordan where John was baptizing. During that time John gave progressively greater testimony to Jesus' messiahship. The first day he spoke of Jesus as "He who comes after me, the thong of whose sandal I am not worthy to untie" (John 1:27). The second day he proclaimed, "Behold, the Lamb of God who takes away the sin of the world" (v. 29) and "This is the Son of God" (v. 34). The third day, when John again declared, "Behold, the Lamb of God," the two disciples of John who were with him left to follow Jesus (v. 35-37). In effect, John said, "The Messiah has come," then, "Behold, the Messiah," and finally, "Follow the Messiah." Those two disciples of John, one of whom was Andrew, now became the disciples of Jesus (vv. 37-40).

John was a bridge between the Old Testament and the New, and that bridge had now almost completed its service. He himself would soon say of Jesus, "He must increase, but I must decrease" (John 3:30). During that first year of Jesus' ministry, John continued to preach, and their two ministries overlapped. As John's work began to phase out, Jesus' work began to build.

Among the other highlights of that year were Jesus' first miracle at the wedding at Cana (John 2:1-11), His cleansing of the Temple (2:12-25), His testimony to Nicodemus (3:1-21), the final public testimony of John the Baptist (3:22-36), and Jesus' ministry in Samaria at Sychar (4:1-42).

In 4:12-17, Matthew picks up the story of that first year where the apostle John leaves off, giving three features of Jesus' early ministry that show God's perfect work through His Son. It was at the right time; it was in the right place; and it was the right proclamation.

THE RIGHT TIME

Now when He heard that John had been taken into custody, (4:12a)

In Matthew's presentation, Jesus' official ministry began when the herald of the King went to jail. The Son of God always worked on His Father's divine timetable. He had, as it were, a divine clock ticking in His mind and heart that regulated everything He said and did. Paul affirms that "when the fulness of the time came, God sent forth His Son" (Gal. 4:4). Jesus spoke of His hour as not having yet come (John 7:30; 8:20) and then of its having arrived (Matt. 26:45; John 12:23; 17:1).

Jesus chose not to use His supernatural powers to accomplish things that could be accomplished by ordinary human means. He submitted Himself to human limitations. Although He knew what was in every man's heart (John 2:24-25), He learned of John's imprisonment by common report, just as did everyone else. It was only **when He heard** of John's arrest that He went back to Galilee.

John had been taken into custody by Herod Antipas and thrown into the dungeon at the palace at Machaerus, on the eastern shore of the Dead Sea. John's reproof of Herod for his great wickedness, including the taking of his half-brother Philip's wife, Herodias, for himself (14:3-4; Luke 3:19-20), cost the prophet his freedom and eventually his life. This non-Jewish Idumean was tetrarch of Galilee and Perea and, like his father before him, held office by Rome's appointment. He was one of several sons (by several wives) of Herod the Great who were appointed over parts of the region ruled by their father before his death. Herodias was the woman—vile even by Roman standards—who would induce her daughter, Salome, to trick Herod into serving the head of John the Baptist on a platter before his guests at a royal dinner (14:6-11). The act was so unusually barbaric that even the hardened Herod himself "was distressed" (v. 9, NIV).

It is always dangerous to confront evil, and John's fearless condemnation of moral wickedness in high places led to his being beheaded. With similar bravery John Knox of Scotland stood ground against a corrupt monarchy. Standing before the repressive and corrupt Queen Mary, who had just rebuked him for resisting her authority, he said, "If princes exceed their bounds, madam, they may be resisted and even deposed."

John the Baptist's imprisonment and death, just as his heralding the King of kings, were in God's divine plan and timetable. The end of the herald's work signaled the beginning of the King's. Herod and Herodias believed they freely controlled their province, and certainly the destiny of the insignificant Jewish preacher who dared condemn them. It is amazing how the proud and arrogant think they act in perfect freedom to accomplish their selfish ends, when in truth their decisions and actions only trigger events that God scheduled before the foundation of the world.

THE RIGHT PLACE

He withdrew into Galilee; and leaving Nazareth, He came and settled in Capernaum, which is by the sea, in the region of Zebulun and Naphtali. This was to fulfill what was spoken through Isaiah the prophet, saying, "The Land of Zebulun and the land of Naphtali, by the way of the sea, beyond the Jordan,

Galilee of the Gentiles—The people who were sitting in darkness saw a great light, and to those who were sitting in the land and shadow of death, upon them a light dawned." (4:12b-16)

Nothing is accidental or circumstantial in the Lord's work. Jesus did not go from Judea, through Samaria, and into Galilee because He was forced to do so by Herod or by the Jewish leaders or because He had nowhere else to go. He left Judea because His work there was finished for that period of His ministry. He went through Samaria in order to bring light to the half-Jew, half-Gentile Samaritans. He then **withdrew** (*anachōreō,* used often to convey the thought of escaping danger) **into Galilee** because that was the next place where the divine plan scheduled Him to minister. By divine determination Jesus went to the right place at the right time.

When Jesus **withdrew into Galilee** after hearing of John's arrest, it was not out of fear of Herod. He feared no man, and was surely no less brave than John. Had He wanted to escape possible trouble from Herod, He would not have gone to **Galilee**, because that, too, was under Herod's control.

We again find additional information in John's gospel. "When therefore the Lord knew that the Pharisees had heard that Jesus was making and baptizing more disciples than John, . . . He left Judea, and departed again into Galilee" (John 4:1, 3). Jesus left the lower Jordan region for Galilee because of the Jewish leaders, particularly the Pharisees, and not because of Herod. Though Jesus had not yet begun preaching, His close association with John the Baptist made Him suspect to the Pharisees and Sadducees, whom John had so scathingly rebuked (Matt. 3:7). Those religious leaders had come to hate John, but did not dare take action against him because he was so highly regarded by most of the people. Even several years after John's death they would not speak ill of him for "fear [of] the multitude" (Matt. 21:26). They were therefore greatly pleased when Herod did to John what they themselves wanted, but were afraid, to do. When they learned that Jesus was gaining a larger following even than John, their hatred would soon turn against Him as well. Jesus had no fear of their hatred, but it was not yet time for that hatred to be unleashed against Him.

Jesus was no more afraid of the Pharisees than was John, but He wanted to avoid a premature confrontation. When the time came, Jesus faced the Jewish religious leaders without a wince, and His denunciations of them were longer-lasting and immeasurably harder than those of John the Baptist had been (see, e.g., Matt. 23:1-36). Jesus knew that He was eternally safe from any danger that men could devise. His life would be forfeited, but by His own divine will, not by the wills or power of His enemies (John 10:17-18). And He would live again!

The Roman region of **Galilee** was primarily to the west, but also extended north and south, of the Sea of Galilee—which was really a lake, sometimes called Tiberias (John 6:1) or Gennesaret (Luke 5:1). The region is some 60 miles long, north to south, and about 30 miles wide. The area around the lake was heavily populated (estimated by some to have had as many as two million people in Jesus' day) and had long been the breadbasket of central Palestine. The soil was extremely fertile, and the lake furnished great quantities of edible fish. The Jewish historian Josephus, who at one time was governor of Galilee, said of the area, "It is throughout rich in soil and pasture, producing every variety of tree, and inviting by its productivity even those who have the least inclination for agriculture. It is everywhere tilled and everywhere productive" (*The Wars of the Jews* 3. 3.2).

The Jews who lived in **Galilee** were less sophisticated and traditional than those in Judea, especially those in the great metropolis of Jerusalem. Josephus observed that Galileans "were fond of innovations and by nature disposed to change, and they delighted in seditions." They even had a distinct accent in their speech (Matt. 26:73). Perhaps Jesus chose His disciples from that area because they would be less bound to Jewish tradition and more open to the newness of the gospel.

It is evident from the text that Jesus was in **Nazareth** for a while. Luke explains that, after Jesus came from Judea through Samaria, He "returned to Galilee in the power of the Spirit, . . . and He came to Nazareth, where He had been brought up; and as was His custom, He entered the synagogue on the Sabbath, and stood up to read" (Luke 4:14, 16). At first "all were speaking well of Him, and wondering at the gracious words which were falling from His lips; and they were saying, 'Is this not Joseph's son?'" (v. 22). But after Jesus exposed their true spiritual condition, "all in the synagogue were filled with rage as they heard these things." They would have thrown Him over a cliff to His death had He not escaped (vv. 23-30).

After Jesus' hometown rejected Him, just as He had said they would (Luke 4:23-27), **He came and settled in Capernaum, which is by the sea, in the region of Zebulun and Naphtali.**

Capernaum means "village of Nahum" and was possibly named for the prophet Nahum. But Nahum means "compassion," and it may be that the town simply had been named for its compassionate people. By Jesus' day it was a flourishing, prosperous city. It was here that Matthew had his tax office (Matt. 9:9), and it was this place that Matthew refers to as "His city," that is, Jesus' own city (9:1). Yet a short while later Jesus would say of it, "And you, Capernaum, will not be exalted to heaven, will you? You shall descend to Hades; for if the miracles had occurred in Sodom which occurred in you, it would have remained to this day. Nevertheless I say to you that it shall be more tolerable for the land of Sodom in the day of judgment, than for you" (Matt. 11:23-24). Today **Capernaum**, though a popular attraction for Christian visitors, is virtually uninhabited.

As we learn from Matthew's quotation of Isaiah 9:1 in verse 15, **the land of Zebulun and Naphtali, by the way of the sea, beyond the Jordan,** had long been known as **Galilee of the Gentiles** (*ethnoi,* heathen, or nations). All of Galilee was cosmopolitan, with the Syrians to the north and east and the descendants of the ancient Phoenicians to the west. It was more of a crossroads than Jerusalem, which was isolated from much trade traffic. A famous trade route was actually known as **the way of the sea.** It went through **Galilee** on its way from Damascus to the Mediterranean coast and then down to Egypt. One ancient writer said that Judea was on the way to nowhere, whereas Galilee was on the way to everywhere. The Galilean Jews' constant association with Gentiles contributed greatly to their nontraditional character.

The region of Galilee originally had been given by the Lord to the tribes of Asher, **Zebulun and Naphtali** when Israel began to settle in Canaan (see Josh. 19:10-39). But, contrary to God's command, **Zebulun and Naphtali** failed to expel all of the Canaanites from their territories. From the beginning, therefore, these unfaithful Jews suffered the problem of mixed marriages and the inevitable pagan influence which that practice brought.

In the eighth century B.C. the Assyrians, under Tiglath-pileser, took away a large part of those tribes as captives (2 Kings 15:29) and replaced them with Assyrians and other non-Jews. Until it was temporarily liberated by Judas Maccabaeus in 164 B.C., the region of Galilee was largely under foreign control and was even largely populated by non-Jews. Another Jewish leader, Aristobulus, reconquered Galilee in 104 B.C. and tried unsuccessfully to establish an entirely Jewish nation by forcibly circumcizing all the male inhabitants. Through those disrupting centuries, the Jews that remained in Galilee had been greatly weakened in both biblical and traditional Judaism—giving even greater significance to the name **Galilee of the Gentiles.**

It is not strange, then, that the reaction of many Jews in Jerusalem was, "Surely the Christ is not going to come from Galilee, is He?" (John 7:41). The idea of a Galilean Messiah seemed ludicrous. When Nicodemus tried to convince the Pharisees that Jesus should be given a fair hearing, "They answered and said to him, 'You are not also from Galilee, are you? Search, and see that no prophet arises out of Galilee'" (vv. 51-52).

Yet, as Matthew here reminds his readers, Isaiah had long before prophesied that in **Galilee of the Gentiles—The people who were sitting in darkness saw a great light, and to those who were sitting in the land and shadow of death, upon them a light dawned** (cf. Isa. 9:1-2). The fact alone that Jesus so accurately and completely fulfilled Old Testament prophecy should be enough to convince an honest mind of the Bible's truthfulness and authority. Just as Isaiah had predicted eight centuries earlier, the despised, sin-darkened, and rebellious Galileans were the first to glimpse the Messiah, the first to see the dawning of God's New Covenant! Not mighty and beautiful Jerusalem, the queen city of the Jews, but **Galilee of the Gentiles** would first hear Messiah's message. Not the learned, proud, and pure Jews of Jerusalem, but the mongrel, downcast, nontraditional mixed multitude of Samaria and Galilee had that great honor. To those who were neediest, and who were most likely to recognize their need, Jesus went first.

The fact that Jesus began His ministry in Samaria and Galilee, rather than in Jerusalem and Judea, emphasizes the fact that His gospel of salvation was for the whole world. It was the fulfillment of Old Testament truth, which God had chosen to reveal through the Jews (cf. Rom. 3:1-2), but it was in no way an accommodation to the traditional, proud, and exclusive Judaism that had developed during the intertestamental period and that was so dominant in Jesus' day. The Son of God was sent to be "a light of revelation of the Gentiles, and the glory of Thy people Israel" (Luke 2:32; cf. Isa. 42:6; 49:6; 52:10). It was no coincidence of history that "the light of the world" (John 8:12) first proclaimed Himself in **Galilee of the Gentiles.**

It was in and around Galilee that Jesus had spent all but a small part of His childhood and early manhood, and it was there that His ministry first developed and began to spread. As the new day of the gospel dawned, the first rays of light shined in **Galilee.** Into this land of oppression, dispersion, and corrosive moral and spiritual influences—and impending death at the word of divine judgment—Jesus came with words and deeds of mercy, truth, love, and hope: **"To those who were sitting in the land and shadow of death, upon them a light dawned."**

THE RIGHT PROCLAMATION

From that time Jesus began to preach and say, "Repent, for the kingdom of heaven is at hand." (4:17)

Preaching was a central part of Jesus' ministry and remains a central part of the ministry of His church. **From that time,** when He went to Galilee, **Jesus began to preach.** *Kērussō* **(to preach)** means "to proclaim" or "to publish," that is, to publicly make a message known. R. C. H. Lenski comments, "The point to be noted is that to preach is not to argue, reason, dispute, or convince by intellectual proof, against all of which a keen intellect may bring counterargument. We simply state in public or testify to all men the truth which God bids us state. No argument can assail the truth presented in this announcement or testimony. Men either believe the truth, as all sane men should, or refuse to believe it, as only fools venture to do" (*The Interpretation of St. Matthew's Gospel* [Minneapolis: Augsburg, 1964], p. 168).

Jesus preached His message with certainty. He did not come to dispute or to argue, but to proclaim, **to preach.** Preaching is the proclamation of certainties, not the suggestion of possibilities. Jesus also preached "as one having authority, and not as their scribes" (Matt. 7:29). What He proclaimed not only was certain but was of the utmost authority. The scribes could not teach authoritatively because they had so mingled biblical truth with the interpretations and traditions of various rabbis that all certainty and authority had long vanished. They could no longer distinguish God's Word from men's words, and all that remained were opinions and speculations. For God's people once again to hear someone preach as the prophets had preached was astonishing (cf. Matt. 7:28-29).

Jesus not only preached with certainty and authority but preached only what He was commissioned by His Father to preach. John the Baptist said of Jesus, "For He whom God has sent speaks the words of God" (John 3:34). Jesus Himself said, "I speak the things which I have seen with My Father" (John 8:38). Later he gave the same testimony even more pointedly: "For I did not speak on My own initiative, but the Father Himself who sent Me has given Me commandment, what to say, and what to speak" (John 12:49).

In His high priestly prayer Jesus spoke to His Father of His disciples, saying, "Now they have come to know that everything Thou hast given Me is from Thee; for the words which Thou gavest Me I have given to them; and they received them" (John 17:7-8). And it is in His own authority that Jesus sends out His ministers to the world: "All authority has been given to Me in heaven and on earth. Go therefore and make disciples of all the nations" (Matt. 28:18-19). That is God's commission to everyone who preaches in His name. The faithful preacher and teacher will proclaim God's certain truth, with God's delegated authority, and under God's divine commission.

When the King's light dawned, the message that His light brought was clear. He began where His herald, John the Baptist, had begun: **Repent, for the kingdom of heaven is at hand** (cf. 3:2).

The darkness in which the people lived was the darkness of sin and evil. Jesus was saying, "The great darkness has been upon you because of the great darkness that is within you. You must be willing to turn from that darkness before the light can shine in you." To turn from sin is to **repent**, to change one's orientation, to turn around and seek a new way. *Metanoeō* literally means a change of perception, a change in the way we see something. To **repent**, therefore, is to change the way a person looks at sin and the way he looks at righteousness. It involves a change of opinion, of direction, of life itself. To repent is to have a radical change of heart and will—and, consequently, of behavior (cf. Matt. 3:8).

That was, and has always continued to be, the first demand of the gospel, the first requirement of salvation, and the first element of the saving work of the Spirit in the soul. The conclusion of Peter's Pentecost sermon was a call to repentance: "Repent, and let each of you be baptized in the name of Jesus Christ for the forgiveness of your sins" (Acts 2:38). Many years later Paul reminded Timothy that repentance leads "to the knowledge of the truth" (2 Tim. 2:25).

Israel would not be ready for or worthy of the King until she repented. Repentance, of course, had always been in order and had always been needed, but now that **the kingdom of heaven** [was] **at hand**, it was all the more imperative. The King had arrived, and the kingdom was near. Messiah's time had come—to usher in the age of righteousness and rest, to subdue Israel's enemies, to bring all of God's people back to their land, and to reign on the throne of David.

Tragically, because most of Israel did not repent and did not recognize and accept the King, the promised earthly kingdom had to be postponed. As Matthew later explains, the literal, physical kingdom was set aside for a period of time. The spiritual kingdom presently exists only in the hearts of those who have trusted in Jesus Christ, the King. He is not ruling the nation Israel and the world as He one day will, but He rules the lives of those who belong to Him by faith. The world does not have peace, but those do who know the Prince of Peace. The external kingdom has not yet come, yet the King Himself indwells those that are His. The Messiah, the Christ, now rules in those who have received Him who is "the light of men."

Fishing
for Men (4:18-22)

10

And walking by the Sea of Galilee, He saw two brothers, Simon who was called Peter, and Andrew his brother, casting a net into the sea; for they were fishermen. And He said to them, "Follow Me, and I will make you fishers of men." And they immediately left the nets, and followed Him. And going on from there He saw two other brothers, James the son of Zebedee, and John his brother, in the boat with Zebedee their father, mending their nets; and He called them. And they immediately left the boat and their father, and followed Him. (4:18-22)

The following widely told story is a sobering parable of what the church's concern for evangelism has often been like.

On a dangerous seacoast where shipwrecks were frequent, a crude little life-saving station was built. The building was just a hut, and there was only one boat, but the few devoted crewmen kept a constant watch over the sea. With no thought for themselves, they went out day or night, tirelessly searching for any who might need help. Many lives were saved by their devoted efforts. After a while the station became famous. Some of those who were saved, as well as others in the surrounding area, wanted to become a part of the work. They gave time and money for its support. New boats were bought, additional crews were trained, and the

111

station grew. Some of the members became unhappy that the building was so crude. They felt a larger, nicer place would be more appropriate as the first refuge of those saved from the sea. So they replaced the emergency cots with hospital beds and put better furniture in the enlarged building. Soon the station became a popular gathering place for its members to discuss the work and to visit with each other. They continued to remodel and decorate until the station more and more took on the look and character of a club. Fewer members were interested in going out on lifesaving missions, so they hired professional crews to do the work on their behalf. The lifesaving motif still prevailed on the club emblems and stationery, and there was a liturgical lifeboat in the room where the club held its initiations. One day a large ship was wrecked off the coast, and the hired crews brought in many boatloads of cold, wet, half-drowned people. They were dirty, bruised, and sick; and some had black or yellow skin. The beautiful new club was terribly messed up, and so the property committee immediately had a shower house built outside, where the shipwreck victims could be cleaned up before coming inside. At the next meeting there was a split in the club membership. Most of the members wanted to stop the club's lifesaving activities altogether, as being unpleasant and a hindrance to the normal social life of the club. Some members insisted on keeping lifesaving as their primary purpose and pointed out that, after all, they were still called a lifesaving station. But those members were voted down and told that if they wanted to save lives they could begin their own station down the coast somewhere. As the years went by, the new station gradually faced the same problems the other one had experienced. It, too, became a club, and its lifesaving work became less and less of a priority. The few members who remained dedicated to lifesaving began another station. History continued to repeat itself; and if you visit that coast today you will find a number of exclusive clubs along the shore. Shipwrecks are still frequent in those waters, but most of the people drown.

What a striking illustration of the history of the church. Yet the work of evangelism, of spiritual lifesaving, is nonetheless the purest, truest, noblest, and most essential work the church will ever do. The work of fishing men and women out of the sea of sin, the work of rescuing people from the breakers of hell, is the greatest work the church is called by God to do.

Rescuing men from sin is God's great concern. Evangelism has been called the sob of God. Concern for the lost caused Jesus to grieve over unbelieving Jerusalem: "O Jerusalem, Jerusalem, who kills the prophets and stones those who are sent to her! How often I wanted to gather your children together, the way a hen gathers her chicks under her wings, and you were unwilling" (Matt. 23:37).

God sent His Son to earth—to preach, die, and be raised—for the very purpose of saving men from sin. The Father "so loved the world, that He gave His only begotten Son, that whoever believes in Him should not perish, but have eternal life. For God did not send the Son into the world to judge the world, but that the world should be saved through Him" (John 3:16-17). The Son Himself came "to seek and to save that which was lost" (Luke 19:10). The Holy Spirit gives to those who believe "the washing of regeneration and renewing" (Titus 3:5). The whole

Trinity is at work in the ministry of saving mankind from sin. Evangelism is the great concern of the Father, of the Son, and of the Holy Spirit.

God's concern for redeeming mankind did not, of course, begin when He sent His Son to earth. In the Garden of Eden He promised that one day sin would be destroyed, that Satan's very head would be bruised (Gen. 3:15). In His covenant with Abraham He promised that in him "all the families of the earth shall be blessed" (Gen. 12:3). In the covenant at Sinai God called Israel to "be to Me a kingdom of priests and a holy nation" (Ex. 19:6), a kingdom of His witnesses to the world to draw all mankind to Himself.

God's people were to share His concern for the lost. Moses was so desperate for the salvation of his own rebellious people that he cried to God, "But now, if Thou wilt, forgive their sin—and if not, please blot me out from Thy book which Thou hast written!" (Ex. 32:32). The writer of Proverbs reminded Israel that "he who is wise wins souls" (Prov. 11:30). The Lord told Daniel, "Those who have insight will shine brightly like the brightness of the expanse of heaven, and those who lead the many to righteousness, like the stars forever and ever" (Dan. 12:3).

Evangelism was the great concern of the New Testament church. Immediately after Pentecost, the new believers were totally dedicated to God and to winning others to Him. As they studied at the apostles' feet, shared with each other, and praised God, they came to have "favor with all the people. And the Lord was adding to their number day by day those who were being saved" (Acts 2:42-47). When the first great persecution of the church in Jerusalem began under the direction of Saul, "those who had been scattered went about preaching the word" (Acts 8:1-4). They did not despair over their hardship but took it as an opportunity to expand the Lord's work.

After Saul himself was converted, his own great concern was evangelism— for building up the movement he had formerly tried to destroy. "I am under obligation both to Greeks and to barbarians, both to the wise and to the foolish," he would one day write. "Thus, for my part, I am eager to preach the gospel to you also who are in Rome. For I am not ashamed of the gospel, for it is the power of God for salvation to everyone who believes" (Rom. 1:14-16). Though he was called to be God's special apostle to the Gentiles (Acts 9:15; Eph. 3:8), Paul had such an overwhelming desire for the salvation of his fellow Jews that he said, "I could wish that I myself were accursed, separated from Christ for the sake of my brethren, my kinsmen according to the flesh" (Rom. 9:3). His "heart's desire and [his] prayer to God for them [was] for their salvation" (10:1). He wanted *everyone* to be saved, and was willing to "become all things to all men, that [he might] by all means save some" (1 Cor. 9:22).

Evangelism has been the heartthrob of faithful Christians throughout the history of the church. John Knox pleaded with God, "Give me Scotland or I die." John Wesley considered the whole world his parish.

Like the Christian life in general, soul-winning involves a paradox. Jesus said, "For whoever wishes to save his life shall lose it; but whoever loses his life for My sake shall find it" (Matt. 16:25). In other words, in saving others we lose ourselves; in losing ourselves in the task we will be used to win others. Jesus warned His disciples that the Jewish leaders would soon "make you outcasts from the synagogue, but an hour is coming for everyone who kills you to think that he is offering service to God" (John 16:2)—just as they hated Jesus Himself "without a cause" (15:25). Those who would reach the world must be willing to be rejected by the world, just as our Lord conquered death by yielding to death.

In a sense, the life of evangelism involves sacrificing the greater for the lesser, the worthy for the unworthy. It is the opposite of the loveless and brutal survival of the fittest—the way of the fallen, sinful world. God's way, the way of redemption, is that of the strong being willing to die that the weak might live. God's Word is clear that, if we are committed to the salvation of those without Jesus Christ, we will lose ourselves in order to reach them. Preaching the saving gospel is essential, and so is personal witnessing.

Forms of *evangelize* are used over fifty times in the New Testament. Evangelization is the primary thrust of the Great Commission: "Go therefore and make disciples of all the nations" (Matt. 28:19). To make disciples is to evangelize, to bring men and women under the Saviorhood and lordship of Jesus Christ. When Jesus called His disciples to Himself, He also called them to call others.

By comparing the gospel accounts we discover that there were at least five different phases of Jesus' calling of the twelve. Each gospel writer emphasized those phases which best suited his particular purpose. As would be expected, the first call was to salvation, to faith in the Messiah (see John 1:35-51; 2:11). The calling that Matthew mentions here was the second calling, the calling to witness. After neither the first nor the second call did the disciples permanently leave their occupations. At the time of the third call (Luke 5:1-11), Peter, James, and John were again back fishing. Jesus repeated the call to be fishers of men, and the disciples then realized the call was permanent and "they *left everything* and followed Him" (v. 11).

In Luke's account, Simon and the others are still fishermen, and the Lord is teaching the crowd on shore from Simon's boat (v. 3). After the teaching, He instructed the disciples to go out to the deep water and let down their nets for a catch. Simon protested that a full night of fishing had yielded nothing, but said that he would obey nonetheless. When the fish came into the net to the point of breaking it, and the catch filled both boats so that they almost sank with the weight of the fish, Simon knew who Jesus was—the presence of the holy God. His reaction, "Depart from me, for I am a sinful man, O Lord" (v. 8), reveals the same attitude Isaiah had when he saw God (Isa. 6:1-5)—an overwhelming sense of sinfulness. The sinner in the presence of God sees only his sin, and shrinks back in fear of judgment. But instead of consuming fire, Peter received a call to discipleship and evangelism. When the call came he responded with the other three men in total commitment to follow the Lord.

Mark tells us of the fourth level, or phase, of the call. "And He went up to the mountain and summoned those whom He Himself wanted, and they came to Him. And He appointed twelve, that they might be with Him, and that He might send them out to preach, and to have authority to cast out the demons" (Mark 3:13-15). The fifth phase, anticipated in the previous one, is recorded in Matthew 10:1—"And having summoned His twelve disciples, He gave them authority over unclean spirits, to cast them out, and to heal every kind of disease and every kind of sickness."

God calls all believers in a similar way. First He calls us to salvation, apart from which no other call could be effective. He then calls us progressively to more specific and ever-expanding service.

CALLING PETER AND ANDREW

And walking by the Sea of Galilee, He saw two brothers, Simon who was called Peter, and Andrew his brother, casting a net into the sea; for they were fishermen. And He said to them, "Follow Me, and I will make you fishers of men." And they immediately left the nets, and followed Him. (4:18-20)

The Sea of Galilee is an oval-shaped body of water about eight miles wide and thirteen miles long, and is nearly 700 feet below sea level. Luke, who was well traveled, always referred to it more properly as a lake. Yet Josephus reports that in the first century A.D. some 240 boats regularly fished the waters of that lake. Much additional fishing was done along the shore, as **Simon who was called Peter** [see Matt. 16:16-18], **and Andrew his brother** were doing on this occasion, **casting a net into the sea.**

In that day, three methods of fishing were used. One was by hook and line, the second was by a throw net cast from the shallow water along the shore, and the third was by a large dragnet strung between two or more boats in the deep water. **Peter and Andrew** were here obviously using the second method. That **net** was probably about nine feet in diameter, and the two brothers were skilled in its use, **for they were fishermen** by trade. The Greek term for that particular net was *amphiblēstron* (related to our *amphibious,* an adjective describing something related to both land and water)—so named because the person using the net would stand on or near shore and throw the net into the deeper water where the fish were.

When Jesus called those first disciples, He gathered together the first fish-catching crew of His church. They were the first of the original band of evangelists He called to fulfill the Great Commission. They were Jesus' first partners in ministry. He had the power and the right to accomplish the work of proclaiming the gospel by Himself. But that was not His plan. He could have done it alone, but He never intended to do it alone. From the beginning of His ministry, His plan was to use disciples to win disciples. He would command His disciples to do other things, but His first call to them was, **Follow Me, and I will make you fishers of men.**

We are given specific details of the callings of only seven of the original twelve. But Jesus individually selected those who would become part of the first marvelous ministry of winning people to Himself. "He called His disciples to Him; and chose twelve of them, whom He also named as apostles" (Luke 6:13). God always chooses His partners. He chose Noah and Abraham, Moses and David. He chose the prophets. He chose Israel herself to be a whole nation of partners, "a kingdom of priests and a holy nation" (Ex. 19:6). Jesus told His disciples, "You did not choose Me, but I chose you, and appointed you, that you should go and bear fruit" (John 15:16; cf. 6:70; 13:18). Paul called Epaenetus "the first convert [lit., "firstfruit," *aparchē*] to Christ from Asia" (Rom. 16:5).

That calling to bear fruit in evangelism is extended to everyone who belongs to Jesus Christ. The called ones are themselves to become callers. Speaking of all Christians, Peter wrote, "But you are a chosen race, a royal priesthood, a holy nation, a people for God's own possession, that you may proclaim the excellencies of Him who has called you out of darkness into His marvelous light" (1 Pet. 2:9). Christ mandates that all of His followers be **fishermen**. The command, **Follow Me** (in the Greek an adverb of place expressing a command), literally means "come here." The term *after* is used in the original to show the place they are to come: "Your place is following after Me!"

The disciples' obedience was instant: **And they immediately left the nets, and followed Him**. The sovereign authority of the Lord had spoken. **Followed** is from *akoloutheō*, which conveys the idea of following as a disciple who is committed to imitating the one he follows.

Many years ago an Italian recluse was found dead in his house. He had lived frugally all his life, but when friends were going through his house to sort out the few possessions he had accumulated they discovered 246 expensive violins crammed into his attic. Some even more valuable ones were in a bureau drawer in his bedroom. Virtually all of his money had been spent buying violins. Yet his misdirected devotion to the instruments had robbed the world of their beautiful sounds. Because he selfishly treasured those violins, the world never heard the music they were meant to play. It is even reported that the first violin the great Stradivarius ever made was not played until it was 147 years old!

Many Christians treat their faith like that man treated his violins. They hide their light; they squirrel away their great treasure. By not sharing their light and their treasure, many to whom they could have witnessed are left in spiritual darkness and poverty.

Some researchers estimate that as many as ninety-five percent of all Christians have never led another person to Jesus Christ. If that is true, ninety-five percent of the world's spiritual violins have never been played! True love of our riches in Christ leads us to shine and share, not to hide and hoard.

When D. L. Moody once visited an art gallery in Chicago he was especially impressed by a painting called "The Rock of Ages." The picture showed a person with both hands clinging to a cross firmly embedded in a rock. While the stormy sea smashed against the rock, he hung tightly to the cross. Years later Mr. Moody saw a similar picture. This one also showed a person in a storm holding to a cross, but with one hand he was reaching out to someone who was about to drown. The great evangelist commented that, though the first painting was beautiful, the second was even lovelier.

CALLING JAMES AND JOHN

And going on from there He saw two other brothers, James the son of Zebedee, and John his brother, in the boat with Zebedee their father, mending their nets; and He called them. And they immediately left the boat and their father, and followed Him. (4:21-22)

When Jesus called **James** and **John** they were tough, crusty outdoorsmen—uncut jewels. They were **in the boat with Zebedee their father, mending their nets,** a routine but important task in the fishing business. They had already been called to faith in the Savior (see John 1:35-51; 2:11); here **He called them** to the work of evangelism alongside Himself. And they **immediately left the boat and their father, and followed Him.**

These disciples had little education, little spiritual perception, and possibly little religious training of any sort. As their new Master began to teach them, even when He spoke in parables, they often lacked full comprehension of His meaning.

They were often self-centered and inhospitable. When the multitude who had walked a long way around the Sea of Galilee to be with Jesus became hungry, the disciples thought only of sending them away on their own to find food (Matt. 14:15). When some little children were brought to Jesus for blessing, the disciples rebuked those who brought them (19:13). Peter thought he would be extremely generous to forgive someone "up to seven times" (18:21). Even on the night of Jesus' betrayal, as their Lord agonized in the Garden of Gethsemane, Peter, James, and John could not stay awake with Him (26:40, 45). The disciples were selfish, proud, weak, and cowardly. They showed little potential even for dependability, much less for greatness. Yet Jesus chose them for disciples, even to be His inner circle of twelve. They were raw material that He would make into useful instruments.

All the disciples were probably not as rough and unpromising as the first and most dominant four Jesus called, but not one was chosen from among the Jewish religious leaders—the scribes, Pharisees, Sadducees, priests, or rabbis. It was no doubt partly that fact that caused those leaders to reject Jesus. They could not believe that anyone who Himself was not an official leader, and who chose no official leaders to be His personal students and co-workers, could possibly be the Messiah. It was beyond their comprehension that God's own Son would bypass the proper leaders of His chosen people when He came to establish His kingdom.

The only apostle who had been a Jewish religious leader was not among the original twelve, and he considered himself "one untimely born." He knew that his own calling was exceptional and reflected God's exceeding grace (1 Cor. 15:8-10). He reminded the Corinthian believers, "For consider your calling, brethren, that there were not many wise according to the flesh, not many mighty, not many noble; but God has chosen the foolish things of the world to shame the wise, and God has chosen the weak things of the world to shame the things which are strong, and the base things of the world and the despised, God has chosen, the things that are not, that He might nullify the things that are, that no man should boast before God" (1 Cor. 1:26-29).

Jesus did not simply command His disciples to become **fishers of men**, but promised that He would **make** them fishermen for men's souls. As He later would make clear on more than one occasion, that promise was also a caution. Not only was He willing to make them into disciplers, but they could never be effective disciplers—or effective disciples in any way—without His power. "I am the vine, you are the branches; he who abides in Me, and I in him, he bears much fruit; for apart from Me you can do nothing" (John 15:5).

A number of qualities that make a good fisherman can also help make a good evangelist. First, a fisherman needs to be patient, because he knows that it often takes time to find a school of fish. Fishermen learn to wait. Second, a fisherman must have perseverance. It is not simply a matter of waiting patiently in one place, hoping some fish will eventually show up. It is a matter of going from place to place, and sometimes back again, over and over—until the fish are found. Third, fishermen must have good instinct for going to the right place and dropping the net at the right moment. Poor timing has lost many a catch, both of fish and of men. A fourth quality is courage. Commercial fishermen, certainly ones such as those on the Sea of Galilee, frequently face considerable danger from storms and various mishaps.

A good fisherman also keeps himself out of sight as much as possible. It is very easy for ourselves to get in the way of our witnessing, causing people to turn away. A good soul-winner keeps himself out of the picture as much as possible.

When Jesus called the disciples to commit themselves to evangelism, He also committed Himself to train them and empower them. Following the Lord's example, the church not only must call its members to evangelize, but must continually train and encourage them in that calling. The Lord not only empowers his disciples to witness but empowers them to train others to witness. In other words, He empowers His disciples to disciple, just as He promised in the Great Commission. "All authority has been given to Me in heaven and on earth. Go therefore and make disciples of all the nations" (Matt. 28:18-19).

Jesus first sent the disciples out two-by-two on brief missions, instructing them about what they should and should not do and say (Mark 6:7-11). After three years of teaching and training in short-term assignments, He finally left them permanently on their own. Yet they were not on their own, because He would henceforth not only be with them but in them (Matt. 28:20; John 16:13-15).

Both in Jesus' teaching and in His example we can see principles that every soul-winner must emulate. First of all, Jesus was available. It seems incredible that the Son of God, who had so very little time to teach and train the slow-learning disciples, would be so open to those who came to Him for comfort or healing. He never turned down a request for help.

Second, Jesus showed no favoritism. The poor and outcast could approach Him as easily as the wealthy and powerful. The influential Jairus and the powerful Roman centurion had no advantage over the Samaritan woman of Sychar or the woman taken in adultery.

Third, Jesus was totally sensitive to the needs of those around Him. He always recognized an open heart, a repentant sinner. Even when the crowd pressed around Him, He noticed the woman who touched the hem of His garment. "Jesus turning and seeing her said, 'Daughter, take courage; your faith has made you well.' And at once the woman was made well" (Matt. 9:20-22). When we are sensitive to Christ's Spirit, He will make us sensitive to others, and will lead us to them or them to us.

Fourth, Jesus usually secured a public profession or testimony. Sometimes He gave specific instruction, as He did to the man He delivered from demons (Mark 5:19), whereas at other times the desire to witness was spontaneous, as with the woman of Sychar (John 4:28-29).

Fifth, Jesus showed love and tenderness to those He sought to win. Again His experience with the woman at Sychar gives a beautiful example. She not only was a religious outcast in the eyes of Jews but was an adulteress. She had had five husbands and was then living with a man to whom she was not married. Yet Jesus firmly but gently led her to the place of faith. Through her, many other Samaritans were led to salvation (John 4:7-42).

Finally, Jesus always took time. In contrast to many of His followers, Jesus always had time for others. Some Christian workers are so busy with "the Lord's work" that they have no time for others—though that was a primary characteristic of Jesus' own ministry. Even while on His way to heal Jairus' daughter, Jesus took time to heal the woman who had suffered from a hemorrhage for twelve years (Mark 5:21-34).

The response of Peter, Andrew, James, and John to Jesus' call was the same. **They immediately left** what they were doing **and followed Him**. Their obedience was instant and without hesitation. At this time they had little knowledge of Jesus' teaching or of what following Him would cost. But it was enough for them to know who He was and that His call to them was a divine call.

From many subsequent accounts in the gospels we know that none of the disciples at this time had a passion for souls, or a passion for any part of the Lord's work. In fact, their response to unbelief was to call for instant divine destruction (see Luke 9:51-56). Passion came only after understanding and obedience. They developed compassion, humility, understanding, patience, and love as they learned from and obeyed Jesus. Obedience is the spark that lights the fire of passion. The way to develop a love for souls is to obey Jesus' call to win souls. As we do that, God will kindle that spark of obedience into a great flame of passion. This is the time of gracious evangelism, not of consuming judgment, as our Lord made clear in the parable of the tares (Matt. 13:24-30, 36-43).

David Brainerd, the great missionary to the American Indians, who died while still in his twenties, said, "Oh, that I were a flame of fire in my Master's cause." His selfless obedience proved the sincerity of that desire, and God gave him a burning heart for lost souls that has few parallels in the history of the church. Henry Martyn, missionary to India and Persia, prayed that he might "burn out for God," and that is what God graciously allowed him to do.

Such burning desire comes only from the pilot light of obedience. Like David Brainerd, Robert Murray McCheyne died before he was thirty. Of him Courtland Myers wrote: "Everywhere he stepped Scotland shook. Whenever he opened his mouth a spiritual force swept in every direction. Thousands followed him to the feet of Christ." Visitors who came to see the church where McCheyne had preached were shown a table, chair, and open Bible. They were then told how that man of God spent hours with his head buried in the Bible, weeping for those to whom he would preach. Myers then comments, "With such a passion for souls, is it any wonder that the Holy Spirit gave McCheyne a magnetic personality which drew so many to the Savior?"

The hymn "Let the Lower Lights Be Burning" is based on a story told by D. L. Moody. A ship was coming into Cleveland harbor on Lake Erie on a stormy night. The harbor had two sets of lights to guide incoming vessels. One set was high on the bluff above the harbor and could be seen for many miles. The other set was down near the coastline and was used to guide the ships through the rocks as they came nearer to port. On that particular night the wind and rain had extinguished the lower lights, and the pilot suggested they stay out in the lake until daylight. The captain, however, was afraid of the ship's being destroyed by the storm and decided to risk making the harbor. But without the lower lights to guide it, the ship was wrecked on the rocks, and many of the men drowned. In applying that story to Christian witnessing, Moody said, "The upper lights in heaven are burning as brightly as ever they've burned. But what about the lower lights?"

The King's Divine Credentials (4:23-25)

11

And Jesus was going about in all Galilee, teaching in their synagogues, and proclaiming the gospel of the kingdom, and healing every kind of disease and every kind of sickness among the people. And the news about Him went out into all Syria; and they brought to Him all who were ill, taken with various diseases and pains, demoniacs, epileptics, paralytics; and He healed them. And great multitudes followed Him from Galilee and Decapolis and Jerusalem and Judea and from beyond the Jordan. (4:23-25)

One of the ways in which Jesus demonstrated His divine character and power was through miracles of healing, which served as messianic credentials. John was especially concerned with those credentials, and his gospel features them. He makes it clear that "many other signs therefore Jesus also performed in the presence of the disciples, which are not written in this book; but these have been written that you may believe that Jesus is the Christ, the Son of God; and that believing you may have life in His name" (John 20:30-31). Matthew also confirms that through His mighty works Jesus presented Himself as the Messiah, the great coming King.

The primary purpose of all four gospel writers was to present Jesus as being more than a man. He was the very Son of God. Apart from that central truth everything else about Him would be of little consequence. It would be of absolutely *no* consequence as far as salvation is concerned. But in light of that truth, *everything* about Him is of supreme significance. What He said was the Word of God, and what He did was the work of God.

> He who believes in Me does not believe in Me, but in Him who sent Me. And he who beholds Me beholds the One who sent Me. I have come as light into the world, that everyone who believes in Me may not remain in darkness. And if anyone hears My sayings, and does not keep them, I do not judge him; for I did not come to judge the world, but to save the world. He who rejects Me, and does not receive My sayings, has one who judges him; the word I spoke is what will judge him at the last day. For I did not speak on My own initiative, but the Father Himself who sent Me has given Me commandment, what to say, and what to speak. And I know that His commandment is eternal life; therefore the things I speak, I speak just as the Father has told Me. (John 12:44-50)

Jesus' claims were so astounding that His enemies desperately suggested that He must be demon-possessed or insane. But others were wiser, "saying, 'These are not the sayings of one demon-possessed. A demon cannot open the eyes of the blind, can he?'" (John 10:19-21). The man healed of blindness told the disbelieving Pharisees, "Well, here is an amazing thing, that you do not know where He is from, and yet He opened my eyes. We know that God does not hear sinners; but if anyone is God-fearing, and does His will, He hears him. Since the beginning of time it has never been heard that anyone opened the eyes of a person born blind. If this man were not from God, He could do nothing" (9:30-33). Jesus' amazing words were backed up by His amazing works.

On another occasion the officers of the chief priests and Pharisees reported, "Never did a man speak the way this man speaks" (John 7:46). At the end of the Sermon on the Mount, "the multitudes were amazed at His teaching; for He was teaching them as one having authority, and not as their scribes" (Matt. 7:28-29). The words Jesus said were also overpowering marks of His messiahship and His majesty.

Matthew focuses both on Jesus' words and His works as, in 4:23-25, he introduces His ministry of teaching, preaching, and healing. He has already demonstrated that Jesus came at the right time and place and with the right message (4:12-17), and that for His work He chose the right partners (vv. 18-22). Now he shows that He came with the right plan—to establish His deity by His words and His works.

TEACHING

And Jesus was going about in all Galilee, teaching in their synagogues (4:23a)

Was going about (from *periagō*) is in the imperfect tense, indicating repeated and continuous action. This verse summarizes Jesus' entire Galilean ministry. His going **about in all Galilee** is given in detail in chapters 5-9. His words are the subject of chapters 5-7 (the Sermon on the Mount), and His works are the focus of chapters 8-9.

Matthew does not imply that Jesus visited every village in **Galilee**, but emphasizes that He ministered throughout the region. Because the entire region was only some sixty by thirty miles, and Jesus moved about in it, anyone interested in seeing and hearing Him would not have had far to travel. In the time that He had, He ministered to as many people as He possibly could.

Though that vicinity had long been known as "Galilee of the Gentiles" (see 4:15; Isa. 9:1), Jesus' ministry there apparently concentrated in the Jewish **synagogues**. The synagogue is believed to have developed during the Babylonian exile, and its use was greatly expanded during the intertestamental period. By New Testament times it had become the most important institution in Jewish life. Although the Temple remained by far the holiest shrine of Judaism, many Jews lived thousand of miles from Jerusalem and could never expect to visit there. But synagogues could be established anywhere in Israel or beyond, and around them virtually all Jewish religious and social life centered.

The synagogue not only was the primary place of worship but also of study, community fellowship, and of legal activity. The greatest tragedy for most Jews was to be disfellowshiped from the synagogue, to be unsynagogued (*aposunagōgos,* John 12:43). That is what happened to Jews who became Christians. It was such a terrible prospect that, as we assume from the repeated warnings of the book of Hebrews (6:4-6; 10:35-39; etc.), many Jews who recognized the truth of the gospel refused to become Christians because of the certainty of being ostracized from the Jewish community.

Most synagogues were built on a hill, often on the highest point of a town. Many had a tall pole jutting into the sky, much like a church steeple, making them stand out and be easy to find. Frequently they were built on banks of rivers, sometimes—as the one whose ruins are a popular attraction in modern Capernaum—without a roof.

Worship was held every Sabbath, which began at sundown on Friday and ended at sundown on Saturday. The Jews had special services on the second and fifth days of every week and observed the festivals prescribed in the law as well as numerous others that had developed by tradition. During the Sabbath services, sections of the Torah (law) and the prophets were read. That was followed by various prayers, singing, and responses. Then a text of Scripture would be expounded, possibly following the pattern begun by Ezra after the return from Babylon (see Neh. 8:1-8). Often visiting dignitaries or rabbis would be given the honor of expounding the Scripture, a practice of which both Jesus and Paul took advantage on numerous occasions (see Luke 4:16-17; Acts 13:15-16).

The affairs of the average village synagogue were usually administered by ten elders of the congregation, of whom three were called rulers. The rulers decided whether or not to admit a proselyte into fellowship and settled disputes of all sorts.

A fourth ruler, called the angel, served as chairman of the synagogue. Some of the elders functioned as servers, carrying out the decisions of the four rulers. One elder interpreted the ancient Hebrew into the vernacular, one headed the theological school, which every synagogue had, and one served as a popular instructor, teaching on a level that the average member could understand.

During Roman rule the synagogue officials had the power to settle virtually every legal dispute within their congregations and even to inflict punishment, with the one exception of execution. That is why the Jewish leaders needed Pilate's permission to crucify Jesus. Even the Sanhedrin, the supreme council of Jerusalem, had no such right.

The synagogue served as public school for boys, where they studied the Talmud and learned to read, write, and do basic arithmetic. For men, the synagogue was a place of advanced theological study.

The **synagogues** of **Galilee** provided Jesus with His first platforms for **teaching**. In almost every community of any size He would have found a synagogue, and in the early part of His ministry He was welcomed in most of them. As a visiting rabbi He was often asked to read and expound Scripture, as He readily did (see Luke 4:16-21).

It was in the synagogues that believing, sincere Israelites would be found. Here, if anywhere, Jesus could expect to find those who would hear and accept His divine message. Here is where God's faithful remnant came to worship God and to be taught His Word.

Teaching is from *didaskō,* from which we get didactic and which refers to the passing on of information—often, but not necessarily, in a formal setting. It focused on content, with the purpose of discovering the truth—contrary to the forums so popular among Greeks, where discussion and the bantering about of various ideas and opinions was the primary concern (see Acts 17:21). Synagogue teaching, as illustrated by that of Jesus, was basically expository. Scripture was read and explained section by section, often verse by verse.

Preaching

and proclaiming the gospel of the kingdom (4:23b)

Proclaiming is from a term (*kērussō*) often translated "to preach." The root idea is to herald, or cry out. Whereas *didaskō* relates to explaining a message, *kērussō* relates simply to announcing it. While interpreting the Old Testament in His teaching He also was **proclaiming the gospel of the kingdom**, announcing the fact that God's long-promised Messiah and King had come to establish His **kingdom.** He continued and extended the heralding that John the Baptist had begun.

That which is proclaimed is the *kērugma* (Matt. 12:41; Rom. 16:25; Titus

1:3; etc.), and that which is taught is the *didachē* (Matt. 7:28; Rom. 16:17; etc.). The message proclaimed needs to be explained, and vice versa.

Gospel means "good news," and it was the good news that the **kingdom** was coming that Jesus preached throughout Galilee. That was the supreme truth, the great good news, around which all of His teaching centered. From His baptism to His ascension Jesus preached the kingdom. "Until the day when He was taken up," Luke tells us, Jesus was "speaking of the things concerning the kingdom of God" (Acts 1:2-3). He never allowed Himself to get sidetracked into economics, social issues, politics, or personal disputes. His teaching and preaching focused entirely on expounding God's Word and proclaiming God's kingdom—a sound pattern for every faithful messenger of the gospel.

John the Baptist heralded the kingdom, but not **the gospel of the kingdom.** Good news as such was not the primary feature in his preaching. His preaching called men to repent of their sins and to prepare themselves for the coming of the King (3:1-10). He focused on sin and judgment. His was the bad news that pointed up the graciousness of the good news about to come. When Jesus' ministry was more and more resisted by the Jewish leaders, His preaching became more and more stern, even sterner than that of John the Baptist. As hypocrisy became more evident and hostility became more vehement, Jesus' words became more harsh.

But the King's first proclamation was of good news, God's marvelous offer to deliver "us from the domain of darkness, and [to transfer] us to the kingdom of His beloved Son, in whom we have redemption, the forgiveness of sins" (Col. 1:13-14). The **gospel** is the good news of salvation through Jesus Christ, the good news that God's **kingdom** (the sphere of God's rule by the grace of salvation) is open to anyone who puts his trust in the King.

The Jews were then under the rule of Rome, and before that they had been under the Greeks, the Medes and Persians, and the Babylonians. Even when they had their own kingdom and their own kings, their condition was far from ideal. Because they were not satisfied to have the Lord as their King, they insisted on having human kings, like all the other nations (1 Sam. 12:12). But those kings brought little peace, prosperity, or happiness, and much sorrow, tragedy, and corruption.

When Jesus preached and taught, He was announcing that He was the King who had come to bring God's promised perfect kingdom. Had they accepted the One who now proclaimed the good news of the kingdom to them, the Jews could have had that kingdom established in their midst. Had they accepted Jesus as the Messiah, His kingdom then would have come on earth. But because they rejected the King and His **gospel,** they rejected the earthly, promised **kingdom.**

Jesus spoke powerful words, eternal words, words like no man before had ever spoken. Even the people in His hometown of Nazareth "were speaking well of Him, and wondering at the gracious words which were falling from His lips" (Luke 4:22). When He went down to Capernaum, "they were amazed at His teaching, for

His message was with authority" (v. 32). Jesus' cleverest enemies could never trap Him in His words, or confuse Him or confound Him or find any error in what He said. His teaching and His preaching about the kingdom were the divine credentials of His words.

HEALING

and healing every kind of disease and every kind of sickness among the people. And the news about Him went out into all Syria; and they brought to Him all who were ill, taken with various diseases and pains, demoniacs, epileptics, paralytics; and He healed them. And great multitudes followed Him from Galilee and Decapolis and Jerusalem and Judea and from beyond the Jordan. (4:23c-25)

Some people are sick and unhealthy because of their own foolish habits, whereas others suffer as a direct consequence of their sin. God sometimes uses physical affliction to discipline His people. Many of the Corinthian Christians were weak, sick, and had even died because they profaned the Lord's Supper (1 Cor. 11:30). Ananias and Sapphira lost their lives for lying to the Holy Spirit (Acts 5:1-10). Yet Scripture makes it equally clear that all suffering and disease are not caused by sin, ignorance, errors in judgment, or God's discipline. Job suffered greatly, though he was blameless, upright, feared God, and turned away from evil (Job 1:1). When Jesus' disciples assumed that the man who was born blind was being punished either for his own sin or that of his parents, Jesus corrected them. "It was neither that this man sinned, nor his parents; but it was in order that the works of God might be displayed in him" (John 9:1-3).

Jesus' **healing** was a divine verification. His words should have been sufficient evidence of His messiahship, as they were for those who truly believed. The disciples left everything to follow Jesus before He performed a miracle of any sort. Many heard Him and believed in Him who had no need of healing for themselves or for their family or friends. It is possible that many who heard and believed in Christ never saw Him perform a miracle—just as many believed John the Baptist's message, although "John performed no sign" (John 10:41).

Yet Jesus' healing ministry was a powerful addition to the evidence of His teaching and preaching. Alexander Maclaren said, "It may be doubted whether we have an adequate notion of the immense number of Christ's miracles. Those recorded are but a small portion of those done. Those early ones were illustrations of the nature of His kingdom; they were His first gifts to His kingdom subjects." The writer of Hebrews says of the gospel of the kingdom that "after it was at the first spoken through the Lord, it was confirmed to us by those who heard, God also bearing witness with them, both by signs and wonders and by various miracles and by gifts of the Holy Spirit according to His own will" (Heb. 2:3-4). Like Jesus' words, the miracles were a foretaste of His glorious, earthly kingdom. To get some idea of what the millennial kingdom will be like we need only multiply His words and His miracles ten-thousandfold.

Jesus healed **every kind of disease and every kind of sickness among the people.** This universal character of the healings is expanded and illustrated in the following verse: **And the news about Him went out into all Syria; and they brought to Him all who were ill, taken with various diseases and pains, demoniacs, epileptics, paralytics; and He healed them.**

In Jesus' day **Syria** was a Roman province that took in all of Palestine, including Galilee. In the context of this verse, however, it may refer only to the northern part, of which Damascus was the major city. In any case, the point is that Jesus' fame spread well beyond the area in which He was ministering. From a wide surrounding area the people **brought to Him all who were ill,** in hope that He would heal them.

Until modern times, with our great advances in sanitary and medical knowledge, disease was frequently rampant. Plagues stopped only when they had run their natural course, leaving behind countless dead and many others who were disfigured or crippled. Simple infections often became life-threatening. It is not strange, therefore, that news of a healer who could cure any affliction spread like wildfire.

As representative of the **various diseases and pains,** Matthew mentions three specific types that Jesus healed. **Diseases** signifies the many maladies, whereas **pains** refers to the many symptoms.

The first type of malady was that suffered by **demoniacs,** those whose afflictions were caused by demons. It is clear from Scripture, especially the New Testament, that many physical and mental afflictions are caused directly by Satan through the operation of his demons. Chapters 9, 12, and 17 of Matthew, and chapters 9 of Mark and 13 of Luke give abundant evidence of demon-related afflictions. The ability to cast out demons is often referred to as the gift of miracles (literally, "powers"; 1 Cor. 12:10, 28-29), the divine power given specifically to combat the demonic powers of darkness (see Luke 9:1; 10:17-19; Acts 8:6-7; cf. Eph. 6:12).

The second group that Jesus healed were **epileptics.** The King James renders the original (*selēniazō*) as "lunatic," which, like the Greek, literally means "moonstruck." In many cultures the mentally ill and those who have convulsions or seizures have been thought to be under the influence of the moon. From other biblical references, such as Matthew 17:15, as well as from descriptions of the affliction in other ancient literature, it is almost certain that the disease was epilepsy, which involves disorder of the central nervous system.

The third group were the **paralytics,** a general term representing a wide range of crippling handicaps. The three terms Matthew uses characterize the three broad areas of man's afflictions—the spiritual, the mental/nervous, and the physical. Jesus was able to overpower whatever evil afflicted those who came to Him. The earthly aspect of His kingdom will have no place for anything harmful, anything wicked, anything less than perfect wholeness and perfect goodness. "On that day the deaf shall hear, . . . the eyes of the blind shall see. The afflicted also shall increase their gladness in the Lord, and the needy of mankind shall rejoice in the Holy One of Israel" (Isa. 29:18-19; cf. 11:6-9). **They brought to Him all who were ill, . . . and He healed them.**

The great reformed theologian B. B. Warfield said, "When our Lord came down to earth He drew heaven with Him. The signs which accompanied His ministry were but the trailing clouds of glory which He brought from heaven, which is His home. The number of the miracles which He wrought may easily be underrated. It has been said that in effect He banished disease and death from Palestine for the three years of His ministry. One touch of the hem of His garment that He wore could heal whole countries of their pain. One touch of His hand could restore life."

Jesus' miracles accomplished four things above and beyond the immediate and obvious benefit to those who were healed. First, they proved that He was divine, because no mere human being could do such things. "Believe Me that I am in the Father, and the Father in Me," Jesus told Philip; "otherwise believe on account of the works themselves" (John 14:11).

Second, the wondrous healings showed that God is compassionate toward those who suffer.

Third, the miracles showed that Jesus was the prophesied Messiah, because the Old Testament predicted that the Messiah would perform miracles. When John the Baptist was imprisoned and began to have doubts about Jesus' messiahship, Jesus told John's disciples, "Go and report to John what you hear and see: the blind receive sight and the lame walk, the lepers are cleansed and the deaf hear, and the dead are raised up, and the poor have the gospel preached to them" (Matt. 11:4-5). That Jesus did these things predicted of the Messiah (see Isaiah 35:5-10; 61:1-3; etc.) proved His messiahship.

Fourth, the miracles proved that the coming kingdom was a reality, the wonders and signs being a foretaste of the marvelous realm God has in store for those who are His. "And Jesus was going about all the cities and the villages, teaching in their synagogues, and proclaiming the gospel of the kingdom, and healing every kind of sickness" (Matt. 9:35). A short while later Jesus committed the same message and accompanying powers to His disciples: "And as you go, preach, saying, 'The kingdom of heaven is at hand.' Heal the sick, raise the dead, cleanse the lepers, cast out demons; freely you received, freely give" (Matt. 10:7-8). A while after that, He pointedly told the disbelieving Pharisees, "If I cast out demons by the Spirit of God, then the kingdom of God has come upon you" (12:28).

I am convinced that the only time such miracles will again be performed is just before the millennial kingdom arrives, when the Lord regathers Israel and the tribulation begins. Then, just as at Christ's (Messiah's) first coming, "the eyes of the blind will be opened, and the ears of the deaf will be unstopped. Then the lame will leap like a deer, and the tongue of the dumb will shout for joy" (Isa. 35:5-6). When Israel rejected the King at His first coming she also rejected the kingdom. But when the King comes again, the coming of His kingdom will not depend on men's response. He *will* establish it then. It will be announced "among the nations, 'The Lord reigns; indeed, the world is firmly established, it will not be moved'" (Ps. 96:10).

To demonstrate the absoluteness of His power and authority, Jesus **healed** everyone who came to Him during His earthly ministry, without exception and without limit. He still has power to heal today, with the same absoluteness and completeness; and, as He sovereignly chooses, He does so. But He does not promise to heal everyone who now asks Him, not even those who belong to Him. The healing miracles He performed while on earth, like His other miracles and those of the apostles, were temporary authenticating signs to Israel that her Messiah had come. The Scripture now stands to attest to the promise of a coming earthly kingdom.

Six features of Jesus' healing have never been duplicated since New Testament times. First, Jesus healed directly, with a word or a touch, without prayer and sometimes even without being near the afflicted person. Second, Jesus healed instantaneously. There was no waiting for restoration to come in stages. Third, He healed completely, never partially. Fourth, He healed everyone who came to Him, everyone who was brought to Him, and everyone for whom healing was asked by another. He healed without discrimination as to person or affliction. Fifth, Jesus healed organic and congenital problems, no matter how severe or longstanding. Sixth, He brought people back to life. He healed even after disease had run its full course and taken the life of its victim.

Those six features also characterized the healing ministry of the apostles. At the beginning of the book of Acts we are told of many miracles and signs that the apostles performed. Yet before the end of the book the accounts of miracles cease. The same diminishing is seen in the epistles. In his early ministry Paul performed many miracles of healing, but years later he simply advised Timothy to take some wine for his stomach ailment (1 Tim. 5:23). At the end of his next letter to Timothy the apostle reports that "Trophimus I left sick at Miletus" (2 Tim. 4:20), apparently beyond the power of Paul to help. There is no scriptural evidence that, by the end of the apostolic age, miracles of any sort were still performed. Once Israel had turned her back on her Messiah, her divine King, the authenticating signs of the kingdom had no more purpose. They faded and then disappeared altogether.

The **great multitudes** who **followed Him** no doubt came for many reasons besides healing for themselves or others. Many came primarily to hear Him teach and preach, and many no doubt came out of mere curiosity. But they came in great numbers and from great distances. **Decapolis** was a region composed of ten major cities (hence the name, which literally means "ten cities") located east and south of **Galilee. Beyond the Jordan** probably referred to areas such as Perea, which was south of **Decapolis** and east of **Jerusalem and Judea.**

Many of that **great multitude** believed in Jesus and were saved, experiencing the kingdom inwardly, the rule of God through the grace of salvation. The vast majority, however, Jew and Gentile alike, did not believe in Him. They listened to what He said, watched what He did, and received temporary blessings. But they did not accept the One who spoke and who healed, whose words and works not only give blessing but eternal life.

The Great Sermon of the Great King (5:1-2)

12

And when He saw the multitudes, He went up on the mountain; and after He sat down, His disciples came to Him. And opening His mouth He began to teach them, saying, (5:1-2)

Until this point in Matthew, Jesus' words have been limited (4:17, 19) and reference to His teachings general (4:23). Now, in one powerfully comprehensive yet compact message, the Lord sets forth the foundational truths of the gospel of the kingdom He came to proclaim.

Here begins what has traditionally been called the Sermon on the Mount. Though Jesus repeated many of these truths on other occasions, chapters 5-7 record one continuous message of the Lord, delivered at one specific time. As we will see, these were revolutionary truths to the minds of those Jewish religionists who heard them, and have continued to explode with great impact on the minds of readers for nearly two thousand years.

Here is the manifesto of the new Monarch, who ushers in a new age with a new message.

THE CONTEXT

THE BIBLICAL CONTEXT

The King's new message was closely related to the message of the Old

Testament and was, in fact, a reaffirmation of it. Yet the emphasis of the gospel (which means "good news") was radically different from the current understanding of the Old Testament—an astounding clarification of what Moses, David, the prophets, and other inspired writers of God's Word had revealed. In addition to that, Christ's message struck violently against the Jewish tradition of His day.

The last message in the Old Testament is, "And he will restore the hearts of the fathers to their children, and the hearts of the children to their fathers, lest I come and smite the land with a curse" (Mal. 4:6). By contrast, this first great sermon of the New Testament begins with a series of blessings, which we call the Beatitudes (5:3-12). The Old Testament ends with the warning of a curse; the New Testament begins with the promise of blessing. The Old Testament was characterized by Mount Sinai, with its law, its thunder and lightning, and its warnings of judgment and cursing. The New Testament is characterized by Mount Zion, with its grace, its salvation and healing, and its promises of peace and blessing (cf. Heb. 12:18-24).

The Old Testament law demonstrates man's need of salvation, and the New Testament message offers the Savior, the Lord Jesus Christ. Our Lord had to begin with a proper presentation of the law, so the people would recognize their sin— then could come the offer of salvation. The Sermon on the Mount clarifies the reasons for the curse and shows that man has no righteousness that can survive the scrutiny of God. The new message offers blessing, and that is the Lord's opening offer.

As will be developed in the next chapter, however, the blessedness Christ offers is not dependent on self-effort or self-righteousness, but on the new nature God gives. In God's Son man comes to share God's very nature, which is characterized by true righteousness and its consequence—blessedness, or happiness. In Christ we partake of the very bliss of God Himself! That is the kind and the extent of the contentment God wants His children to have—His very own peace and happiness. So the Lord begins with the offer of blessedness and then proceeds to demonstrate that human righteousness, such as the Jews sought, cannot produce it. The good news is that of blessing. The bad news is that man cannot achieve it, no matter how self-righteous and religious he is.

The Old Testament is the book of Adam, whose story is tragic. Adam not only was the first man on earth but the first king. He was given dominion over all the earth, to subdue and rule it (Gen. 1:28). But that first monarch fell soon after he began to rule, and his fall brought a curse—the curse with which the Old Testament both begins and ends.

The New Testament begins with the presentation of the new sovereign Man, One who will not fall and One who brings blessing rather than cursing. The second Adam is also the last Adam, and after Him will come no other ruler, no other sovereign. The first king sinned and left a curse; the second King was sinless and leaves a blessing. As one writer has put it, the first Adam was tested in a beautiful garden and failed; the last Adam was tested in a threatening wilderness and succeeded. Because the first Adam was a thief, he was cast out of paradise; but the last Adam turned to a thief on a cross and said, "Today you shall be with Me in paradise" (Luke 23:43). The Old Testament, the book of the generations of Adam, ends with a curse; the New Testament, the book of the generations of Jesus Christ, ends with the promise, "There shall no longer be any curse" (Rev. 22:3). The Old Testament gave the law to show man in his misery, and the New Testament gives life to show man in his bliss.

In Jesus Christ a new reality dawned on history. A new Man and new King of the earth came to reverse the terrible curse of the first king. The Sermon on the Mount is the masterful revelation from the great King, offering blessing instead of cursing to those who come on His terms to true righteousness.

THE POLITICAL CONTEXT

Most Jews of Jesus' day expected the Messiah to be, first of all, a military and political leader who would deliver them from the yoke of Rome and establish a prosperous Jewish kingdom that would lead the world. He would be greater than any king, leader, or prophet in their history. After Jesus miraculously fed the multitude on the far side of the Sea of Galilee, the people tried "to come and take Him by force, to make Him king" (John 6:15). They saw Jesus as the anticipated leader of a great welfare state in which even their routine physical needs would be provided. But Jesus would not allow Himself to be mistaken for that sort of king, and He disappeared from the crowd. Later, when Pilate asked Jesus, "Are You the King of the Jews?" the Lord replied, "My kingdom is not of this world. If My kingdom were of this world, then My servants would be fighting, that I might not be delivered up to the Jews; but as it is, My kingdom is not of this realm" (John 18:36).

The thrust of the Sermon on the Mount is that the message and work of the King are first and most importantly internal and not external, and spiritual and moral rather than physical and political. Here we find no politics or social reform. His concern is for what men are, because what they are determines what they do.

The ideals and principles in the Sermon on the Mount are utterly contrary to those of human societies and governments. In Christ's kingdom the most exalted persons are those who are the lowliest in the world's estimation, and vice versa. Jesus declared that John the Baptist was the greatest man who had ever lived until that time. Yet John had no possessions and no home, lived in the wilderness, dressed in a hair garment, and ate locusts and wild honey. He was not a part of the religious system, and he had no financial, military, or political power. In addition to that, he preached a message that in the world's eyes was completely irrelevant and absurd. By worldly standards he was a misfit and a failure. Yet he received the Lord's highest praise.

In Jesus' kingdom the least are greater even than John the Baptist (Matt. 11:11). They are characterized in this sermon as being humble, compassionate, meek, yearning for righteousness, merciful, pure in heart, peacemakers—and persecuted for the sake of the very righteousness they practice. In the world's eyes those characteristics are the marks of losers. The world says, "Assert yourself, stand up for yourself, be proud of yourself, elevate yourself, defend yourself, avenge yourself, serve yourself." Those are the treasured traits of the world's people and the world's kingdoms.

THE RELIGIOUS CONTEXT

Jesus lived in a highly complex religious society, one that included many professional religionists. Those professionals were in four primary groups: the Pharisees, the Sadducees, the Essenes, and the Zealots. At this point, it is only necessary to introduce these groups briefly. Later chapters will unfold more of their distinctives.

The Pharisees believed that right religion consisted in divine laws and religious tradition. Their primary concern was for fastidious observance of the Mosaic law and of every minute detail of the traditions handed down by various rabbis over the centuries. They focused on adhering to the laws of the past.

The Sadducees focused on the present. They were the religious liberals who discounted most things supernatural and who modified both Scripture and tradition to fit their own religious philosophy.

The Essenes were ascetics who believed that right religion meant separation from the rest of society. They led austere lives in remote, barren areas such as Qumran, on the northwest edge of the Dead Sea.

The Zealots were fanatical nationalists who thought that right religion centered in radical political activism. These Jewish revolutionaries looked down on fellow Jews who would not take up arms against Rome.

In essence, the Pharisees said, "Go back"; the Sadducees said, "Go ahead"; the Essenes said, "Go away"; and the Zealots said, "Go against." The Pharisees were traditionalists; the Sadducees were modernists; the Essenes were separatists; and the Zealots were activists. They represented the same primary types of religious factions that are common today.

But Jesus' way was not any of those. To the Pharisees He said that true spirituality is internal, not external. To the Sadducees He said that it is God's way, not man's way. To the Essenes He said that it is a matter of the heart, not the body. To the Zealots He said that it is a matter of worship, not revolution. The central thrust of His message to every group and every person, of whatever persuasion or inclination, was that the way of His kingdom is first and above all a matter of the inside—the soul. That is the central focus of the Sermon on the Mount. True religion in God's kingdom is not a question of ritual, of philosophy, of location, or of military might—but of right attitude toward God and toward other people. The Lord summed it up in the words "I say to you, that unless your righteousness surpasses that of the scribes and Pharisees, you shall not enter the kingdom of heaven" (5:20).

The dominant message of the Sermon on the Mount is that one must not find comfort merely in right theology, much less in contemporary philosophy, geographical separation, or military and political activism. Right theology is essential; so are being contemporary in the right way, separating ourselves from worldliness, and taking stands on moral issues. But those external things must flow from right internal life and attitudes if they are to serve and please God. That has always been God's way. He told Samuel, "God sees not as man sees, for man looks at the outward appearance, but the Lord looks at the heart" (1 Sam. 16:7). In Proverbs, wisdom says, "Watch over your heart with all diligence, for from it flow the springs of life" (4:23).

When the Pharisees with whom Jesus was having lunch were bothered that He did not ceremonially wash His hands before eating, Jesus said, "Now you Pharisees have the habit of cleaning the outside of your cups and dishes, but inside you yourselves are full of greed and wickedness. You fools! Did not the One who made the outside make the inside too? But dedicate once for all your inner self, and at once you will have everything clean" (Luke 11:39-41, Williams). That was His message for every sect of Judaism.

THE IMPORTANCE

In light of the preceding truths we can see at least five reasons why the Sermon on the Mount is important. First, it shows the absolute necessity of the new birth. Its standards are much too high and demanding to be met by human power. Only those who partake of God's own nature through Jesus Christ can fulfill such demands. The standards of the Sermon on the Mount go far beyond those of Moses in the law, demanding not only righteous actions but righteous attitudes—not just that men *do* right but that they *be* right. No part of Scripture more clearly shows man's desperate situation without God.

Second, the sermon intends to drive the listener to Jesus Christ as man's only hope of meeting God's standards. If man cannot live up to the divine standard, he needs a supernatural power to enable him. The proper response to the sermon leads to Christ.

Third, the sermon gives God's pattern for happiness and for true success. It reveals the standards, the objectives, and the motivations that, with God's help, will fulfill what God has designed man to be. Here we find the way of joy, peace, and contentment.

Fourth, the sermon is perhaps the greatest scriptural resource for witnessing, for reaching others for Christ. A Christian who personifies these principles of Jesus will be a spiritual magnet, attracting others to the Lord who empowers him to live as he does. The life obedient to the principles of the Sermon on the Mount is the church's greatest tool for evangelism.

Fifth, the life obedient to the maxims of this proclamation is the only life that is pleasing to God. That is the believer's highest reason for following Jesus' teaching—it pleases God.

The Setting

And when He saw the multitudes, He went up on the mountain; and after He sat down, His disciples came to Him. (5:1)

Jesus was always concerned for **the multitudes,** for whom He had great compassion—whether they were "distressed and downcast" (Matt. 9:36), sick (14:14; cf. 4:23), hungry (15:32), or in any other need. Whether the people were physically ill or healthy, emotionally stable or demon-possessed, financially poor or rich, politically oppressed or powerful, religiously insignificant or influential, intellectually ignorant or educated, Jesus had compassion on them. Jesus attracted all strata of people because He loved them all.

Everything Jesus said on this occasion was spoken publicly, to **the multitudes** (cf. 7:28-29). His intention was to drive them to a recognition of their sin, and thus to the need of a Savior, which He had come to be. Until they believed in Him, the demands of the sermon could only show them how terribly far they were from meeting God's standards. This masterful evangelistic sermon is designed to confront men with their desperate condition of sinfulness.

THE PREACHER

It was Jesus who **saw the multitudes,** . . . **went up on the mountain; and** . . . **sat down.** God's own Son delivered the sermon. The greatest Preacher who ever lived preached the greatest sermon ever preached. When **He** concluded, "the multitudes were amazed at His teaching; for He was teaching them as one having authority, and not as their scribes" (7:28-29). He quoted no sources, no ancient rabbis, no revered tradition. What He spoke, He spoke on His own authority. That was unheard of among the Jews, who always derived their authority from recognized sources.

The Sermon on the Mount is the supreme model of good preaching, a homiletical masterpiece. It beautifully and powerfully flows from the introduction (5:3-12) to the first point (the citizens of the kingdom, 5:13-16), to the second point (the righteousness of the kingdom, 5:17—7:12), to the third point (the exhortation to enter the kingdom, 7:13-27), and to the conclusion (the effect of the sermon on its hearers, 7:28-29). The transitions from point to point are clear and unmistakable.

At the beginning of his ministry Ezekiel was told by the Lord, "I will make your tongue stick to the roof of your mouth so that you will be dumb, and cannot be a man who rebukes them, for they are a rebellious house" (Ezek. 3:26). Much later the same prophet testified, "Now the hand of the Lord had been upon me in the evening, before the refugees came. And He opened my mouth at the time they came to me in the morning; so my mouth was opened, and I was no longer speechless" (33:22). Like Ezekiel, Jesus did not display His truth, His wisdom, and His power until it was time in God's sovereign will for Him to do so.

THE LOCATION

The sanctuary for the greatest sermon ever preached was **the mountain**. As far as we know, this mountain—really a large hill—had no name until Jesus preached there. Until then it had been but one of many hills that slope up gently from the north shore of the Sea of Galilee. What had been simply *a* mountain among many other mountains now became **the mountain**, sanctified and set apart by the presence of the Lord. For many centuries the traditional site has been called the Mount of Beatitudes.

THE STYLE

A rabbi commonly **sat down** when he taught. If he spoke while standing or walking, what he said was considered to be informal and unofficial. But when he sat down, what he said was authoritative and official. Even today we speak of professors holding a "chair" in a university, signifying the honored position from which they teach. When the Roman Catholic pope gives an official pronouncement, he is said to speak ex cathedra, which literally means to speak from his chair. When Jesus **sat down** and delivered the Sermon on the Mount, He spoke from His divine chair with absolute authority as the sovereign King.

As mentioned above, the multitudes were an important audience for this evangelistic sermon. But the standards of spiritual life that Jesus gave here could not apply to them or be followed by them unless they belonged to Him.

That **His disciples came to Him** indicates they were also His audience. In fact, the twelve were the only ones at that time who, to any real extent, could know the blessedness of which the Lord spoke and follow the perfect way of righteousness which He set forth. They were the only ones who had partaken of the inner divine power and presence that are absolutely necessary for obeying God's perfect will. So the sermon not only showed the multitude the standard of God's righteousness that they could not keep, but it also showed the disciples the possible standard they could now keep because of His coming and their faith in Him.

An archbishop of the Church of England once remarked that it would be impossible to conduct the affairs of Britain on the basis of the Sermon on the Mount, because the nation was not loyal to the King. The sermon of the King can be understood and followed only by faithful subjects of the King.

The famous historian Will Durant said that in any given generation only a handful of people make an impression on the world that lasts more than a few years. The person who stands out above all others, he said, is Jesus Christ. Jesus undoubtedly has had the most powerful and permanent influence on the thought of mankind. But, the historian went on to say, His teachings have not had a corresponding effect on man's actions.

Trying to apply Jesus' teachings without receiving Him as Lord and Savior is futile. Those, for example, who promote the social gospel, endeavoring to institute Jesus' teachings apart from His saving and regenerating work, prove only that His principles cannot work for those who do not have a transformed nature and God's indwelling power. One cannot behave like Christ until one becomes like Christ. Those who do not love the King cannot live like the King.

THE CONTENT

And opening His mouth He began to teach them, saying, (5:2)

Matthew's speaking of Jesus' **opening His mouth** as **He began to teach them** was not a superfluous statement of the obvious, but was a common colloquialism used to introduce a message that was especially solemn and important. It was also used to indicate intimate, heartfelt testimony or sharing. Jesus' sermon was both authoritative and intimate; it was of the utmost importance and was delivered with the utmost concern.

In this sermon our Lord establishes a standard of living counter to everything the world practices and holds dear. To live by the standards He gives here is to live a life of blessed happiness. Here is an utterly new approach to living, one that results in joy instead of despair, in peace instead of conflict—a peace that the world does not understand and cannot have (John 14:27; Phil. 4:7). It is a blessedness not produced by the world or by circumstances, and it cannot be taken away by the world or by circumstances. It is not produced externally and cannot be destroyed externally.

Because of its seemingly impossible demands, many evangelicals maintain that the Sermon on the Mount pertains only to the kingdom age, the Millennium. Otherwise, they argue, how could Jesus command us to be perfect, just as our "heavenly Father is perfect" (Matt. 5:48)? For several reasons, however, that interpretation cannot be correct. First of all, the text does not indicate or imply that these teachings are for another age. Second, Jesus demanded them of people who were not living in the Millennium. Third, many of the teachings themselves become meaningless if they are applied to the Millennium. For example, there will be no persecution of believers (see 5:10-12, 44) during the kingdom age. Fourth, every principle taught in the Sermon on the Mount is also taught elsewhere in the New Testament in contexts that clearly apply to believers of our present age. Fifth, there are many New Testament passages that command equally impossible standards, which unglorified human strength cannot continually achieve (see Rom. 13:14; 2 Cor. 7:1; Phil. 1:9-10; Col. 3:1-2; Heb. 12:14; 1 Pet. 1:15-16).

The teachings of the Sermon on the Mount are for believers today, marking the distinctive life-style that should characterize the direction, if not the perfection, of the lives of Christians of every age. Unfortunately, those standards do not always characterize Christians. The world's standards and objectives too often have engulfed believers and conformed them to its own image, squeezed them into its own mold (see Rom. 12:2, Phillips).

Jesus' new way of living comes from a new way of thinking, and the new way of thinking comes from new life. Here are God's standards for those created in His own image and recreated into the image of His own dear Son (Rom. 8:29; 1 Cor. 15:49; 2 Cor. 3:18). Those who do not follow them as a general direction of life have an unacceptable righteousness (Matt. 5:20).

Who knows more about a product than the manufacturer? When you buy a new power tool or appliance the first sensible thing to do is read the owner's manual. The manufacturer prints those manuals to explain what the item is designed to do and not do, how it is to be cared for, what its limitations are, and so on. God has made every human being, yet few turn to their Maker to find meaning, purpose, and fulfillment in their lives, to learn how they are to live and how they are to take care of themselves—how they can function properly and happily as they were designed to do.

As the Sermon on the Mount itself makes clear, internal changes also bring external changes. When our attitudes and thinking are right, our actions will fall in line. If our inner life does not make our outer life better, our inner life is deficient or nonexistent. "Faith without works is useless," James says (James 2:20). Paul tells us that we are "created in Christ Jesus for good works, which God prepared beforehand, that we should walk in them" (Eph. 2:10).

But the true outside life can only be produced from a true inside life. David Martyn Lloyd-Jones compares the Christian life to playing music. A person may play Beethoven's *Moonlight Sonata* accurately and without a single mistake—yet not really play what the composer had in mind. Even though the notes are played correctly, they do not produce the sonata. The pianist may mechanically strike the right notes at the right time, yet miss the essence, the soul, of the composition. He may not at all express what Beethoven meant to be expressed. The true artist must play the right notes at the right time. He is not exempt from the rules and principles of music. But accurate playing is not what makes him a great musician. It is his expression of what lies behind the notes that enthralls his listeners. In the same way, faithful Christians are concerned about the letter of God's Word; but beyond that they are also concerned about the spirit, the deeper will and purpose that lie behind the letter. That concern reveals an obedient heart filled with the desire to glorify the Lord.

To claim to follow the spirit without obeying the letter is to be a liar. To follow the letter without following the spirit is to be a hypocrite. To follow the spirit in the right attitude and the letter in the right action is to be a faithful child of God and a loyal subject of the King.

Happy Are the Humble (5:3)

13

Blessed are the poor in spirit, for theirs is the kingdom of heaven. (5:3)

THE BEATITUDES

The series of conditional blessings promised in Matthew 5:3-12 have long been called the Beatitudes, a name derived from Latin and referring to a state of happiness or bliss. Jesus presents the possibility of people being genuinely happy, and that available happiness is the opening theme of the Sermon on the Mount. Many people, including some Christians, find that hard to believe. How could a message as demanding and impossible as the Sermon on the Mount be intended to make people happy? Yet the first and greatest sermon preached by Jesus Christ begins with the resounding and repeated theme of happiness, a fitting start for the New Testament's "good news."

Far from being the cosmic killjoy that many accuse Him of being, God desires to save men from their tragic lostness, to give them power to obey His will, and to make them happy. In this great sermon, His Son carefully and clearly sets forth the way of blessedness for those who come to Him.

Makarios (**blessed**) means happy, fortunate, blissful. Homer used the word to describe a wealthy man, and Plato used it of one who is successful in business. Both Homer and Hesiod spoke of the Greek gods as being happy (*makarios*) within themselves, because they were unaffected by the world of men—who were subject to poverty, disease, weakness, misfortune, and death. The fullest meaning of the term, therefore, had to do with an inward contentedness that is not affected by circumstances. That is the kind of happiness God desires for His children, a state of joy and well-being that does not depend on physical, temporary circumstances (cf. Phil. 4:11-13).

The word **blessed** is often used of God Himself, as when David ended one of his psalms with the declaration "Blessed be God!" (Ps. 68:35). His son Solomon sang, "Blessed be the Lord God, the God of Israel, who alone works wonders" (Ps. 72:18). Paul spoke of "the glorious gospel of the blessed God" (1 Tim. 1:11) and of Jesus Christ "who is the blessed and only Sovereign, the King of kings and Lord of lords" (6:15). Blessedness is a characteristic of God, and it can be a characteristic of men only as they share in the nature of God. There is no blessedness, no perfect contentedness and joy of the sort of which Jesus speaks here, except that which comes from a personal relationship to Him, through whose "magnificent promises" we "become partakers of the divine nature" (2 Pet. 1:4).

Because blessedness is fundamentally an element of the character of God, when men partake of His nature through Jesus Christ they partake of His blessedness. So it becomes clear at the very beginning of the Sermon on the Mount that Jesus is speaking of a reality that is only for believers. Others can see the kingdom standards and get a glimpse of kingdom blessings, but only those who belong to the kingdom have the promise of personally receiving and experiencing the blessings. To be **blessed** is not a superficial feeling of well-being based on circumstance, but a deep supernatural experience of contentedness based on the fact that one's life is right with God. Blessedness is based on objective reality, realized in the miracle of transformation to a new and divine nature.

The Beatitudes seem paradoxical. The conditions and their corresponding blessings do not seem to match. By normal human standards such things as humility, mourning, desire for righteousness, mercy, and persecution are not the stuff of which happiness is made. To the natural man, and to the immature or carnal Christian, such happiness sounds like misery with another name. As one commentator has observed, it is much as if Jesus went into the great display window of life and changed all the price tags.

In a way, happiness *is* misery with another name; Jesus *has* changed the price tags. He teaches that misery endured for the right purpose and in the right way *is* the key to happiness. That basic principle summarizes the Beatitudes. The world says, "Happy are the rich, the noble, the successful, the macho, the glamorous, the popular, the famous, the aggressive." But the message from the King does not fit the world's standards, because His kingdom is not of this world but of heaven. His way to happiness, which is the *only* way to true happiness, is by a much different route.

Seneca, the first-century Roman philosopher who tutored Nero, wisely wrote, "What is more shameful than to equate the rational soul's good with that which is irrational?" His point was that you cannot satisfy a rational, personal need with an irrational, impersonal object. External things cannot satisfy internal needs.

Yet that is exactly the philosophy of the world: things satisfy. Acquiring things brings happiness, achieving things brings meaning, doing things brings satisfaction.

Solomon, the wisest and most magnificent of ancient kings, tried the world's way to happiness for many years. He had the royal blood of his father, David, coursing through his veins. He had vast amounts of gold and jewels and "made silver as common as stones in Jerusalem" (1 Kings 10:27). He had fleets of ships and stables filled with thousands of the finest horses. He had hundreds of wives, gathered from the most beautiful women of many lands. He ate the most sumptuous of foods on the finest of tableware in the most elegant of palaces with the most distinguished people. He was acclaimed throughout the world for his wisdom, power, and wealth. Solomon should have been immeasurably happy. Yet that king, so great and blessed by earthly standards, concluded that his life was purposeless and empty. The theme of Ecclesiastes, Solomon's personal testimony on the human situation, is "Vanity of vanities! All is vanity. What advantage does man have in all his work which he does under the sun?" (1:2-3).

Jesus came to announce that the tree of happiness cannot grow in a cursed earth. Earthly things cannot bring even lasting earthly happiness, much less eternal happiness. "Beware, and be on your guard against every form of greed," Jesus warned; "for not even when one has an abundance does his life consist of his possessions" (Luke 12:15). Physical things simply cannot touch the soul, the inner person.

It should be pointed out that the opposite is also true: spiritual things cannot satisfy physical needs. When someone is hungry he needs food, not a lecture on grace. When he is hurt he needs medical attention, not moral advice. True spiritual concern for such people will express itself first of all in providing for their physical needs. "Whoever has the world's goods, and beholds his brother in need and closes his heart against him, how does the love of God abide in him?" (1 John 3:17).

But the more common danger is trying to meet almost *every* need with physical things. That philosophy is as futile as it is unscriptural. When King Saul was distressed, his jewels and his army could give him no help. When King Belshazzar was having a great feast with his nobles, wives, and concubines, he suddenly saw a hand writing on the wall, "MENE, MENE, TEKEL, UPHARSIN." He was so terrified that his "face grew pale, and his thoughts alarmed him; and his hip joints went slack, and his knees began knocking together." His military power, his influential allies, and his great possessions could give him no solace (Dan. 5:3-6, 25).

The great Puritan saint Thomas Watson wrote, "The things of the world will no more keep out trouble of spirit, than a paper sconce will keep out a bullet. . . . Worldly delights are winged. They may be compared to a flock of birds in the garden, that stay a little while, but when you come near to them they take their flight and are gone. So 'riches make themselves wings; they fly away as an eagle toward heaven'" (*The Beatitudes* [Edinburgh: Banner of Truth Trust, 1971], p. 27). The writer of Proverbs said, "Do not weary yourself to gain wealth, cease from your consideration of it. When you set your eyes on it, it is gone" (Prov. 23:4-5).

Tragically, many preachers, teachers, and writers today "who must be silenced" (Titus 1:11) are passing off worldly philosophy in the name of Christianity—claiming that faithfulness to Christ guarantees health, wealth, success, prestige, and prosperity. But Jesus taught no such thing. What He taught was nearer the opposite. He warned that physical, worldly advantages most often limit true happiness. The things of the world become fuel for pride, lust, and self-satisfaction—the enemies not only of righteousness but of happiness. "The worry of the world, and the deceitfulness of riches choke the word, and it becomes unfruitful," Jesus said (Matt. 13:22).

To expect happiness from the things of this world is like seeking the living among the dead, just as the women sought Christ at the garden tomb on that first Easter morning. The angels told the women, "He is not here, but He has risen" (Luke 24:6). Paul said, "If then you have been raised up with Christ, keep seeking the things above, where Christ is, seated at the right hand of God. Set your mind on the things above, not on the things that are on earth" (Col. 3:1-2). John said, "Do not love the world, nor the things in the world. . . . And the world is passing away, and also its lusts; but the one who does the will of God abides forever" (1 John 2:15, 17).

True blessedness is on a higher level than anything in the world, and it is to that level that the Sermon on the Mount takes us. Here is a completely new way of life, based on a completely new way of thinking. It is in fact based on a new way of being. The standard of righteousness, and therefore the standard of happiness, is the standard of selflessness—a standard that is completely opposite to man's fallen impulses and unregenerate nature.

It is impossible to follow Jesus' new way of living without having His new life within. As someone has suggested, one might as well try in our own day to fulfill Isaiah's prophecy that in the Millennium the wolf, lamb, leopard, kid, lion, and cow will live together peaceably (Isa. 11:6-7). If we were to go to a zoo and lecture a lion on the new peaceable way he was expected to live, and then placed a lamb in the cage with him, we know exactly what would happen as soon as the lion became hungry. The lion will not lie down peaceably with the lamb until the day when the lion's nature is changed.

It is important to remember that the Beatitudes are pronouncements, not probabilities. Jesus does not say that if men have the qualities of humility, meekness, and so on that they are more likely to be happy. Nor is happiness simply Jesus' wish for His disciples. The Beatitudes are divine judgmental pronouncements, just as surely as are the "woes" of chapter 23. *Makarios* is, in fact, the opposite of *ouai* (woe), an interjection that connotes pain or calamity. The opposite of the blessed life is the cursed life. The **blessed** life is represented by the true inner righteousness of those who are humble, **poor in spirit**, whereas the cursed life is represented by the outward, hypocritical self-righteousness of the proud religionists (5:20).

The Beatitudes are progressive. As will be seen as each one is discussed in detail, they are not in a random or haphazard order. Each leads to the other in logical succession. Being poor in spirit reflects the right attitude we should have to our sinful condition, which then should lead us to mourn, to be meek and gentle, to hunger and thirst for righteousness, to be merciful, pure in heart, and have a peacemaking spirit. A Christian who has all those qualities will be so far above the level of the world that his life will rebuke the world—which will bring persecution from the world (5:10-12) and light to the world (vv. 14-16).

THE POOR IN SPIRIT

Blessed are the poor in spirit, for theirs is the kingdom of heaven. (5:3)

Discussion of this first beatitude demands that it be looked at from five perspectives: the meaning of **poor in spirit**, the location of this virtue in the list, the way to achieve that attitude, how to know if we have that attitude, and the result promised for having it.

THE MEANING OF POOR IN SPIRIT

Ptōchos (**poor**) is from a verb meaning "to shrink, cower, or cringe," as beggars often did in that day. Classical Greek used the word to refer to a person reduced to total destitution, who crouched in a corner begging. As he held out one hand for alms he often hid his face with the other hand, because he was ashamed of being recognized. The term did not mean simply poor, but begging poor. It is used in Luke 16:20 to describe the beggar Lazarus.

The word commonly used for ordinary poverty was *penichros,* and is used of the widow Jesus saw giving an offering in the Temple. She had very little, but she did have "two small copper coins" (Luke 21:2). She was poor but not a beggar. One who is *penichros* poor has at least some meager resources. One who is *ptōchos* poor, however, is completely dependent on others for sustenance. He has absolutely no means of self-support.

Because of a similar statement in Luke 6:20—"Blessed are you who are poor, for yours is the kingdom of God"—some interpreters have maintained that the beatitude of Matthew 5:3 teaches material poverty. But sound hermeneutics (the interpretation of Scripture) requires that, when two or more passages are similar but not exactly alike, the clearer one explains the others, the more explicit clarifies the less explicit. By comparing Scripture with Scripture we see that the Matthew account is the more explicit. Jesus is speaking of a spiritual poverty that corresponds to the material poverty of one who is *ptōchos.*

If Jesus were here advocating material poverty He would have contradicted many other parts of His Word—including the Sermon on the Mount itself (5:42)—that teach us to give financial help to the poor. If Jesus was teaching the innate blessedness of material poverty, then the task of Christians would be to help make everyone, including themselves, penniless. Jesus did not teach that material poverty is the path to spiritual prosperity.

Those who are materially poor *do* have some advantages in spiritual matters by not having certain distractions and temptations; and the materially rich have some disadvantage by *having* certain distractions and temptations. But material possessions have no necessary relationship to spiritual blessings. Matthew makes clear that Jesus is here talking about the condition of the **spirit**, not of the wallet.

After He began His public ministry, Jesus often had "nowhere to lay His head" (Matt. 8:20), but He and His disciples were not destitute and never begged for bread. Paul was beaten, imprisoned, shipwrecked, stoned, and often economically hard pressed; but neither did he ever beg for bread. It was, in fact, a badge of honor for him that he worked in order to pay his own expenses in the ministry (Acts 20:34; 1 Cor. 9:6-18). The Lord and the apostles were accused of being ignorant, troublemakers, irreligious, and even mad; but they were never charged with being indigent or beggars.

On the other hand, no New Testament believer is condemned for being rich. Nicodemus, the Roman centurion of Luke 7, Joseph of Arimathea, and Philemon were all wealthy and faithful. That "not many mighty, not many noble" are called (1 Cor. 1:26) is not because they are rejected due to their positions or possessions but because so many of them trust only in those things (1 Tim. 6:6-17).

To be **poor is spirit** is to recognize one's spiritual poverty apart from God. It is to see oneself as one really is: lost, hopeless, helpless. Apart from Jesus Christ every person is spiritually destitute, no matter what his education, wealth, social status, accomplishments, or religious knowledge.

That is the point of the first beatitude. The **poor in spirit** are those who recognize their total spiritual destitution and their complete dependence on God. They perceive that there are no saving resources in themselves and that they can only beg for mercy and grace. They know they have no spiritual merit, and they know they can earn no spiritual reward. Their pride is gone, their self-assurance is gone, and they stand empty-handed before God.

In spirit also conveys the sense that the recognition of poverty is genuine, not an act. It does not refer to outwardly acting like a spiritual beggar, but to recognizing what one really is. It is true humility, not mock humility. It describes the person about whom the Lord speaks in Isaiah 66:2—"To this one I will look, to him who is humble and contrite of spirit, and who trembles at My word." It describes the person who is "brokenhearted" and "crushed in spirit" (Ps. 34:18), who has "a broken and a contrite heart" before the Lord (Ps. 51:17).

Jesus told the parable of the Pharisee and the tax-gatherer to "certain ones who trusted in themselves that they were righteous, and viewed others with contempt." As the Pharisee stood praying in the Temple, he proudly recited his virtues and gave thanks that he was not like those who are sinful, especially the tax-gatherer who was nearby. The tax-gatherer, however, "was even unwilling to lift up his eyes to heaven, but was beating his breast, saying, 'God be merciful to me, the sinner!'" The tax-gatherer, Jesus said, "went down to his house justified rather than the other; for everyone who exalts himself shall be humbled, but he who humbles himself shall be exalted" (Luke 18:9-14). The Pharisee was proud in spirit; the tax-gatherer was **poor in spirit**.

When God called Moses to lead Israel out of Egypt, Moses pleaded his unworthiness, and God was able to use him mightily. Peter was still aggressive, self-assertive, and proud, but when Jesus miraculously provided the great catch of fish, Peter was so overawed that he confessed, "Depart from me, for I am a sinful man, O Lord!" (Luke 5:8). Even after he became an apostle, Paul recognized that "nothing good dwells in me, that is, in my flesh" (Rom. 7:18), that he was the chief of sinners (1 Tim. 1:15), and that the best things he could do in himself were rubbish (Phil. 3:8).

In his *Confessions* Augustine makes clear that pride was his greatest barrier to receiving the gospel. He was proud of his intellect, his wealth, and his prestige. Until he recognized that those things were less than nothing, Christ could do nothing for him. Until Martin Luther realized that all his sacrifice, rituals, and self-abuse counted for nothing before God, he could find no way to come to God or to please Him.

Even at Sinai, when the law was given, it was evident that God's own chosen people could not fulfill its demands on their own. As Moses was receiving the law on the mountain, Aaron was leading the people in a pagan orgy in the valley below (Ex. 32:1-6).

Israelites who were spiritually sensitive knew they needed God's power to keep God's law. In humility they confessed their helplessness and pleaded for His mercy and strength. David began his great penitential psalm with the plea "Be gracious to me, O God, according to Thy lovingkindness; according to the greatness of Thy compassion blot out my transgressions. . . . For I know my transgressions, and my sin is ever before me" (Ps. 51:1, 3).

Other Israelites, however, took another approach to the law. Knowing they could not fulfill its demands, they simply brought the law down to a level that was more manageable and acceptable. They piled interpretation upon interpretation, creating man-made traditions that were possible to keep in the flesh. Those traditions came to be known as the Talmud, a commentary on the law that leading rabbis developed over many centuries and that eventually superseded the law in the minds of most Jews. They exchanged the Torah (God's revealed law) for the Talmud (man's modification of the law). In the name of interpreting and protecting the law they contradicted and weakened it. They brought God's standards down to men's standards—which they could keep without God's help. They then taught as doctrine those precepts of men (Matt. 15:9). They made the fatal error of thinking that God was less holy than He is and that they were more holy than they were. The result was the illusion that they were sufficiently righteous to please God.

Traditions have to do with what we can see and measure. They involve only the outer man, whereas God's law involved the whole man. The Ten Commandments cannot be fulfilled simply by doing or not doing outward acts. They not only forbid making idols but also require love of God (Ex. 20:4, 6). Honoring father and mother is first of all an attitude, a matter of the heart, as is covetousness (vv. 12, 17).

Every thoughtful Jew knew that God's law was far above his own human power to obey. The proud and self-satisfied responded by diluting the law. The humble and penitent responded by calling to God for help.

If God's Old Testament standards are impossible for man to meet by himself, how much less attainable by one's own power are the standards of the Sermon on the Mount. Jesus here teaches not only that people must love God but that they "are to be perfect, as [their] heavenly Father is perfect" (5:48), and that unless their righteousness exceeds the external, man-originated "righteousness . . . of the scribes and Pharisees, [they] shall not enter the kingdom of heaven" (5:20).

WHY HUMILITY IS FIRST

Jesus puts this beatitude first because humility is the foundation of all other graces, a basic element in becoming a Christian (Matt. 18:3-4). Pride has no part in Christ's kingdom, and until a person surrenders pride he cannot enter the kingdom. The door into His kingdom is low, and no one who stands tall will ever go through it. We cannot be filled until we are empty; we cannot be made worthy until we recognize our unworthiness; we cannot live until we admit we are dead. We might as well expect fruit to grow without a tree as to expect the other graces of the Christian life to grow without humility. We cannot begin the Christian life without humility, and we cannot live the Christian life with pride.

Yet in the church today there is little emphasis on humility, little mention of self-emptying. We see many Christian books on how to be happy, how to be successful, how to overcome problems, and on and on. But we see very few books on how to empty ourselves, how to deny ourselves, and how to take up our crosses and follow Jesus—in the way that He tells us to follow Him.

Until a soul is humbled, until the inner person is **poor in spirit**, Christ can never become dear, because He is obscured by self. Until one knows how helpless, worthless, and sinful he is in himself, he can never see how mighty, worthy, and glorious Christ is in Himself. Until one sees how doomed he is, he cannot see what a Redeemer the Lord is. Until one sees his own poverty he cannot see God's riches. Only when one admits to his own deadness can Christ give him His life. "Everyone who is proud in heart is an abomination to the Lord" (Prov. 16:5).

Being **poor in spirit** is the first beatitude because humility must precede everything else. No one can receive the kingdom until he recognizes that he is unworthy of the kingdom. The church in Laodicea said proudly, "I am rich, and have become wealthy, and have need of nothing," not knowing that she was instead "wretched and miserable and poor and blind and naked" (Rev. 3:17). Those who refuse to recognize that they are lost and helpless are like the blind Roman slave girl who insisted that she was not blind but that the world was permanently dark.

Where self is exalted, Christ cannot be. Where self is king, Christ cannot be. Until the proud in spirit become **poor in spirit**, they cannot receive the King or inherit His kingdom.

ACHIEVING HUMILITY

How, then, do we become **poor in spirit?** Almost by definition, it cannot start with us, with anything we can do or accomplish in our own power. Nor does it involve putting ourselves down. We are already down; humility simply recognizes the truth. And simply *being* hopeless, helpless, and in need obviously is no virtue. That is not God's will for anyone. His will is to get us out of that condition and into blessing. The fulfillment of that goal depends on His sovereign, gracious work of humbling.

Humility is not a necessary human work to make us worthy, but a necessary divine work to make us see that we *are* unworthy and cannot change our condition without God. That is why monasticism, asceticism, physical self-denial, mutilation, and other such self-efforts are so foolish and futile. They feed pride rather than subdue it, because they are works of the flesh. They give a person a reason to boast in what he has done or not done. Such self-imposed efforts are enemies of humility.

Yet even though genuine humility is produced by the Lord as an element of the work of salvation, it is also commanded of men. There are numerous divine commands to humble oneself (Matt. 18:4; 23:12; James 4:10; 1 Pet. 5:5), which the Lord perfectly harmonizes with His sovereign work of humbling. Sovereign saving work is never without personal cooperation. Because of that it is helpful to look at some of the steps from the human side of the divine paradox.

The first step in experiencing humility is to turn our eyes off ourselves and to look to God. When we study His Word, seek His face in prayer, and sincerely desire to be near Him and please Him, we move toward being **poor in spirit**. It is the vision of the infinitely Holy God in all His sinless purity and perfection that allows us to see ourselves as sinners by contrast. To seek humility, we do not look at ourselves to find the faults, but at God Almighty to behold His perfection.

Second, we must starve the flesh by removing the things on which it feeds. The essence of the fleshly nature is pride, and to starve the flesh is to remove and avoid those things that promote pride. Rather than looking for praise, compliments, and popularity, we should we be wary of them. Yet because our human sinfulness has a way of turning even the best intentions to its advantage, we need to be careful not to make an issue of avoiding praise and recognition. The evil is not in being given praise but in seeking it and glorying in it. When, without having sought it, we are praised or honored, to ungraciously reject the recognition may be an act of pride rather than of humility.

The third and balancing principle in coming to humility is asking God for it. With David we should pray, "Create in me a clean heart, O God, and renew a steadfast spirit within me" (Ps. 51:10). Humility, like every other good gift, comes only from God. Also as with every other good thing, He is more willing to give it than we are to ask for it, and He stands ready to give it long before we ask for it.

KNOWING WHEN WE ARE HUMBLE

How can we know if we are genuinely humble, if we are **poor in spirit?** There are at least seven principles we may apply in determining humility.

First, if we are humble we will be weaned from ourselves. We will be able to say with David, "My soul is like a weaned child within me" (Ps. 131:2). One who is poor in spirit loses his self-preoccupation. Self is nothing, and Christ is everything. Paul's humility is nowhere more beautifully expressed than in his saying, "I have been crucified with Christ; and it is no longer I who live, but Christ lives in me; and the life which I now live in the flesh I live by faith in the Son of God, who loved me, and delivered Himself up for me" (Gal. 2:20). To the Philippian believers he wrote, "For to me, to live is Christ, and to die is gain" (Phil. 1:21).

Second, humility will lead us to be lost in the wonder of Christ, "with unveiled face beholding as in a mirror the glory of the Lord, . . . being transformed into the same image from glory to glory" (2 Cor. 3:18). Our satisfaction will be in the prospect of one day being fully in the likeness of our Lord.

Third, we will not complain about our situation, no matter how bad it may become. Because we know we deserve worse than anything we can experience in this life, we will consider no circumstance to be unfair. When tragedy comes we will not say, "Why me, Lord?" When our suffering is for Christ's sake we not only will not complain or feel ashamed but will glorify God for it (1 Pet. 4:16), knowing that we will "also be glorified with Him" and realizing "that the sufferings of this present time are not worthy to be compared with the glory that is to be revealed to us" (Rom. 8:17-18).

Fourth, we will more clearly see the strengths and virtues of others as well as our own weaknesses and sins. With "humility of mind" we will "regard one another as more important than [ourselves]" (Phil. 2:3) and will "give preference to one another in honor" (Rom. 12:10).

Fifth, we will spend much time in prayer. Just as the physical beggar begs for physical sustenance, the spiritual beggar begs for spiritual. We will knock often at heaven's gate because we are always in need. Like Jacob wrestling with the angel, we will not let go until we are blessed.

Sixth, we will take Christ on His terms, not on ours or any other. We will not try to have Christ while keeping our pride, our pleasures, our covetousness, or our immorality. We will not modify His standards by ecclesiastical traditions or by our own inclinations or persuasions. His Word alone will be our standard.

Thomas Watson said, "A castle that has long been besieged and is ready to be taken will deliver up on any terms to save their lives. He whose heart has been a garrison for the devil, and has held out long in opposition against Christ, when once God has brought him to poverty of spirit and he sees himself damned without

Christ, let God propound what articles he will, he will readily subscribe to them. 'Lord, what wilt Thou have me to do?'" (*The Beatitudes* [Edinburgh: Banner of Truth Trust, 1971], p. 47).

Seventh, when we are poor in spirit we will praise and thank God for His grace. Nothing more characterizes the humble believer than abounding gratitude to his Lord and Savior. He knows that he has no blessing and no happiness but that which the Father gives in love and grace. He knows that God's grace is "more than abundant, with the faith and love which are found in Christ Jesus" (1 Tim. 1:14).

THE RESULT OF BEING POOR IN SPIRIT

Those who come to the King in this humility inherit His kingdom, **for theirs is the kingdom of heaven.** God has gladly chosen to give the kingdom to those who humbly come to Him and trust Him (Luke 12:32).

When the Lord called Gideon to deliver Israel from the Midianites, Gideon replied, "O Lord, how shall I deliver Israel? Behold, my family is the least in Manasseh, and I am the youngest in my father's house"—to which God answered, "Surely I will be with you, and you shall defeat Midian as one man" (Judg. 6:15-16). When Isaiah "saw the Lord sitting on a throne, lofty and exalted," he cried in despair, "Woe is me, for I am ruined! Because I am a man of unclean lips." Then an attending seraph touched the prophet's mouth with a burning coal and said, "Behold, this has touched your lips; and your iniquity is taken away, and your sin is forgiven" (Isa. 6:1, 5-7).

Those who come to the Lord with broken hearts do not leave with broken hearts. "For thus says the high and exalted One who lives forever, whose name is Holy, 'I dwell on a high and holy place, and also with the contrite and lowly of spirit in order to revive the spirit of the lowly and to revive the heart of the contrite'" (Isa. 57:15). God wants us to recognize our poverty so that He can make us rich. He wants us to recognize our lowliness so that He can raise us up. "Humble yourselves in the presence of the Lord," James says, "and He will exalt you" (James 4:10).

In giving up their own kingdom, the poor in spirit inherit God's.

Happy Are the Sad (5:4)

14

Blessed are those who mourn, for they shall be comforted. (5:4)

In Psalm 55 David cries out, "Oh, that I had wings like a dove! I would fly away and be at rest. Behold, I would wander far away, I would lodge in the wilderness. I would hasten to my place of refuge from the stormy wind and tempest" (vv. 6-8).

Such a cry comes from the lips of almost everyone at some time or another. David echoes the cry of humanity—a cry for release, a cry for freedom, a cry for escape from things that weigh heavy on us. When we face great sorrow, disappointment, tragedy, or failure, we wish that we could escape the trouble like we escape a thunderstorm by running inside. But comfort from the troubles of life is much harder to find than shelter from rain. The deeper the sorrow, the harder the pressure, the worse the despair, the more elusive comfort seems to be.

As pointed out in the previous chapter, all of the Beatitudes are paradoxical, because what they promise for what they demand seems incongruous and upside down in the eyes of the natural man. The paradox of the second beatitude is obvious. What could be more self-contradictory than the idea that the sad are happy, that the path to happiness is sadness, that the way to rejoicing is in mourning?

In the routine of ordinary, day-by-day living, the idea seems absurd. The whole structure of most human living—whether by the primitive or sophisticated, the wealthy or the poor, the educated or the uneducated—is based on the seemingly incontrovertible principle that the way to happiness is having things go your own way. Pleasure brings happiness, money brings happiness, entertainment brings happiness, fame and praise bring happiness, self-expression brings happiness. On the negative side, avoiding pain, trouble, disappointment, frustration, hardships, and other problems brings happiness. Sidestepping those things is necessary before the other things can bring full happiness. Throughout history a basic axiom of the world has been that favorable things bring happiness, whereas unfavorable things bring unhappiness. The principle seems so self-evident that most people would not bother to debate it.

But Jesus said, "Happy are the sad." He even went so far as to say, "Woe to you who laugh now, for you shall mourn and weep" (Luke 6:25)—the converse beatitude of Matthew 5:4. Jesus turned the world's principles exactly upside down. He reversed the path to happiness.

To discover what Jesus meant, and did not mean, in this beatitude we will look at the meaning of mourning as it is used here, the result of mourning, the way to mourn as Jesus teaches, and the way to know if we are truly mourning.

The Meaning of Mourning

Certain kinds of sorrow are common to all mankind, experienced by believer and unbeliever alike. Some of these sorrows are normal and legitimate, sorrows which concern the Lord and for which He knows our need. Others are abnormal and illegitimate, brought about solely because of sinful passions and objectives.

IMPROPER MOURNING

Improper mourning is the sorrow of those who are frustrated in fulfilling evil plans and lusts, or who have misguided loyalties and affection. To those who mourn in that way the Lord offers no help or solace.

David's son "Amnon was so frustrated because of his sister Tamar that he made himself ill, for she was a virgin, and it seemed hard to Amnon to do anything to her" (2 Sam. 13:2). Amnon's grief was caused by incestuous, unfulfilled lust.

Others carry legitimate sorrow to illegitimate extremes. When a person grieves so hard and so long over the loss of a loved one that he cannot function normally, his grief becomes sinful and destructive. Such depressing sorrow is usually related to guilt, essentially selfish, and, for a Christian, is a mark of unfaithfulness and lack of trust in God.

David grieved that way, in part to try to atone for his guilt. When the rebellious Absalom, another of David's sons, was killed, his father went into inconsolable mourning (2 Sam. 18:33—19:4). Joab finally rebuked the king, saying, "Today you have covered with shame the faces of all your servants, who today have saved your life and the lives of your sons and daughters, the lives of your wives, and the lives of your concubines, by loving those who hate you, and by hating those who love you. For you have shown today that princes and servants are nothing to you; for I know this day that if Absalom were alive and all of us were dead today, then you would be pleased" (19:5-6). The wickedly ambitious Absalom had raised a rebel army, driven the king—his own father—out of Jerusalem, and taken over the palace.

David's love for his son was understandable, but his judgment had been perverted. Probably because of his great feeling of guilt for having been such a poor father, and because he knew that Absalom's tragedy was part of the judgment God sent because of David's adulterous and murderous affair with Bathsheba, the king's mourning over Absalom was abnormal. The judgment that came on Absalom was entirely deserved.

PROPER MOURNING

There are also, of course, other kinds of sorrow, legitimate sorrows that are common to all mankind and for which reasonable mourning is appropriate. To express these sorrows and to cry over them opens an escape valve that keeps our feelings from festering and poisoning our emotions and our whole life. It provides the way for healing, just as washing out a wound helps prevent infection.

An Arab proverb says, "All sunshine makes a desert." The trouble-free life is likely to be a shallow life. We often learn more and mature more from times of sorrow than from times when everything is going well. A familiar poem by Robert Browning Hamilton expresses the truth:

> I walked a mile with Pleasure,
>   She chattered all the way,
> But left me none the wiser
>   For all she had to say.
> I walked a mile with Sorrow,
>   And ne'er a word said she,
> But, oh, the things I learned from her
>   When Sorrow walked with me.

> (Cited in William Barclay, *The Gospel of Matthew* [rev. ed.; Philadelphia: Westminster, 1975], 1:94)

Sarah's death caused Abraham to mourn (Gen. 23:2). But the "father of the faithful" did not weep from lack of faith but for the loss his beloved wife, which he had every right to do.

Loneliness for God, from whom he felt separated for a time, caused the psalmist to declare, "As the deer pants for the water brooks, so my soul pants for

Thee, O God. My soul thirsts for God, for the living God; when shall I come and appear before God? My tears have been my food day and night, while they say to me all day long, 'Where is your God?'" (Ps. 42:1-3).

Defeat and discouragement caused Timothy to mourn, leading Paul, his spiritual father, to write, "I thank God, whom I serve with a clear conscience the way my forefathers did, as I constantly remember you in my prayers night and day, longing to see you, even as I recall your tears, so that I may be filled with joy" (2 Tim. 1:3-4).

Anguished concern about the sins of Israel and God's coming judgment on His people caused Jeremiah to mourn. "Oh, that my head were waters, and my eyes a fountain of tears," he cried, "that I might weep day and night for the slain of the daughter of my people!" (Jer. 9:1).

Concern for the spiritual welfare of the Ephesian believers had caused Paul to mourn. "Night and day for a period of three years I did not cease to admonish each one with tears," he said (Acts 20:31). Because of their great love for him the elders from the Ephesus church later mourned for Paul as he prayed with them on the beach near Miletus, "grieving especially over the word which he had spoken, that they should see his face no more" (v. 38).

The earnest love of a father caused him to be grief-stricken over his demon-possessed son, even as he brought him to Jesus for healing. No doubt tears ran down the man's face as He implored Jesus to help, confessing "I do believe; help my unbelief" (Mark 9:24).

Repentant, worshipful devotion caused a woman to mourn over her sins as she went into the Pharisee's house and washed Jesus' feet with her tears and wiped them with her hair. To the proud host who resented her contaminating his house and interrupting his dinner party, Jesus said, "I say to you, her sins, which are many, have been forgiven, for she loved much; but he who is forgiven little, loves little" (Luke 7:47).

Immeasurable divine love caused our Lord to weep at the death of Lazarus (John 11:35) and over the sinning people of Jerusalem, whom He wanted to gather into His care as a mother hen gathers her chicks (Matt. 23:37).

GODLY MOURNING

The mourning about which Jesus is talking in the second beatitude, however, has nothing to do with the types just discussed, proper or improper. The Lord is concerned about all of the legitimate sorrows of His children, and He promises to console, comfort, and strengthen us when we turn to Him for help. But those are not the kind of sorrow at issue here. Jesus is speaking of godly sorrow, godly mourning, mourning that only those who sincerely desire to belong to Him or who already belong to Him can experience.

Paul speaks of this sorrow in his second letter to Corinth. "For the sorrow that is according to the will of God produces a repentance without regret, leading to salvation; but the sorrow of the world produces death. For behold what earnestness this very thing, this godly sorrow, has produced in you" (2 Cor. 7:10-11). The only sorrow that brings spiritual life and growth is godly sorrow, sorrow over sin that leads to repentance. Godly sorrow is linked to repentance, and repentance is linked to sin.

As the first beatitude makes clear, entrance into the kingdom of heaven begins with being "poor in spirit," with recognition of total spiritual bankruptcy. The only way any person can come to Jesus Christ is empty-handed, totally destitute and pleading for God's mercy and grace. Without a sense of spiritual poverty no one can enter the kingdom. And when we enter the kingdom we should never lose that sense, knowing "that nothing good dwells in [us], that is, in [our] flesh" (Rom. 7:18).

Spiritual poverty leads to godly sorrow; the poor in spirit become **those who mourn.** After his great sin involving Bathsheba and Uriah, David repented and expressed his godly sorrow in Psalm 51: "For I know my transgressions, and my sin is ever before me. Against Thee, Thee only, I have sinned, and done what is evil in Thy sight" (vv. 3-4). Job was a model believer, "blameless, upright, fearing God, and turning away from evil" (Job. 1:1). Yet he still had something to learn about God's greatness and his own unworthiness, about God's infinite wisdom and his own very imperfect understanding. Only after God allowed everything dear to Job to be taken away and then lectured His servant on His sovereignty and His majesty, did Job finally come to the place of godly sorrow, of repenting of and mourning over his sin. He confessed, "I have heard of Thee by the hearing of the ear; but now my eye sees Thee; therefore I retract, and I repent in dust and ashes" (42:5-6). God loves and honors a morally righteous life, but it is no substitute for a humble and contrite heart, which God loves and honors even more (Isa. 66:2).

As seen in the discussion of the first beatitude, makarios (**blessed**) means to be happy, blissful. That happiness is a divine pronouncement, the assured benefit of those who meet the conditions God requires.

The condition of the second beatitude is mourning: **blessed are those who mourn.** Nine different Greek words are used in the New Testament to speak of sorrow, reflecting its commonness in man's life. It is woven into the cloth of the human situation. The story of history is the story of tears. And before the earth's situation gets better it will get worse. Jesus tells us that before He comes again, "nation will rise against nation, and kingdom against kingdom, and in various places there will be famines and earthquakes. But all these things are merely the beginning of birth pangs" (Matt. 24:7-8). Until the Lord returns, history is destined to go from tragedy to greater tragedy, from sorrow to still greater sorrow.

Of the nine terms used for sorrow, the one used here (pentheō, **mourn**) is the strongest, the most severe. It represents the deepest, most heart-felt grief, and was generally reserved for grieving over the death of a loved one. It is used in the Septuagint (Greek Old Testament) for Jacob's grief when he thought his son Joseph was killed by a wild animal (Gen. 37:34). It is used of the disciples' mourning for Jesus before they knew He was raised from the dead (Mark 16:10). It is used of the mourning of world business leaders over the death of its commerce because of the destruction of the world system during the Tribulation (Rev. 18:11, 15).

The word carries the idea of deep inner agony, which may or may not be expressed by outward weeping, wailing, or lament. When David stopped hiding his sin and began mourning over it and confessing it (Ps. 32:3-5), he could declare, "How blessed is he whose transgression is forgiven, whose sin is covered! How blessed is the man to whom the Lord does not impute iniquity, and in whose spirit there is no deceit!" (vv. 1-2).

Happiness, or blessedness, does not come in the mourning itself. Happiness comes with what God does in response to it, with the forgiveness that such mourning brings. Godly mourning brings God's forgiveness, which brings God's happiness. Mourning is not merely a psychological or emotional experience that makes people feel better. It is a communion with the living, loving God who responds to the mourner with an objective reality—the reality of divine forgiveness!

David experienced and expressed many kinds of common human sorrow, both proper and improper. He mourned over being lonely, over being rejected, over being discouraged and disappointed, and over losing an infant child. He also mourned inordinately over the death of Absalom, whom God had removed to protect Israel and the messianic throne of David. But nothing broke the heart of David like his own sin. No anguish was as deep as the anguish he felt when he finally saw the awfulness of his offenses against the Lord. That is when David became happy, when he became truly sad over his transgressions.

The world says, "Pack up your troubles in your old kit bag, and smile, smile, smile." Hide your problems and pretend to be happy. The same philosophy is applied to sin. But Jesus says, "Confess your sins, and mourn, mourn, mourn." When we do that, our smiles can be genuine, because our happiness will be genuine. Godly mourning brings godly happiness, which no amount of human effort or optimistic pretense, no amount of positive thinking or possibility thinking, can produce.

Only mourners over sin are happy because only mourners over sin have their sins forgiven. Sin and happiness are totally incompatible. Where one exists, the other cannot. Until sin is forgiven and removed, happiness is locked out. Mourning over sin brings forgiveness of sin, and forgiveness of sin brings a freedom and a joy that cannot be experienced in any other way.

"Draw near to God and He will draw near to you," James tells us. "Cleanse your hands, you sinners; and purify your hearts, you double-minded. Be miserable and mourn and weep; let your laughter be turned into mourning, and your joy to gloom. Humble yourselves in the presence of the Lord, and He will exalt you" (James 4:8-10).

There is great need in the church today to cry instead of laugh. The frivolity, silliness, and foolishness that go on in the name of Christianity should themselves make us mourn. God's counsel to the frivolous happy, the self-satisfied happy, the indulgent happy is: "Be miserable and mourn and weep; let your laughter be turned into mourning, and your joy into gloom."

The faithful child of God is constantly broken over his sinfulness, and the longer he lives and the more mature he becomes in the Lord, the harder it is for him to be frivolous. He sees more of God's love and mercy, but he also sees more of his own and the world's sinfulness. To grow in grace is also to grow in awareness of sin. Speaking to Israel, the prophet Isaiah said, "In that day the Lord God of hosts called you to weeping, to wailing, to shaving the head, and to wearing sackcloth. Instead, there is gaiety and gladness, killing of cattle and slaughtering of sheep, eating of meat and drinking of wine." Following the world's philosophy, which still prevails today, God's ancient people said, "Let us eat and drink, for tomorrow we may die" (Isa. 22:12-13).

We follow that philosophy vicariously, if not actually, when we laugh at the world's crude and immoral jokes even though we do not retell them, when we are entertained by a sin even though we do not indulge in it, when we smile at ungodly talk even though we do not repeat the words. To joke about divorce, to make light of brutality, to be intrigued by sexual immorality is to rejoice when we should be mourning, to be laughing when we should be crying. To "rejoice in the perversity of evil" is placed alongside "delight in doing evil" (Prov. 2:14). To take "pleasure in wickedness" (2 Thess. 2:12) is to be a part of the wickedness, whether or not we commit the specific sin.

Much of the church today has a defective sense of sin, which is reflected in this defective sense of humor. When even its own members make the church the butt of jokes, make light of its beliefs and ordinances, caricature its leaders as inept and clownish, and make its high standards of purity and righteousness the subject of humorous commentary, the church has great need to turn its laughter into mourning.

The Bible recognizes a proper sense of humor, humor that is not at the expense of God's name, God's Word, God's church, or any person, except perhaps ourselves. God knows that "a joyful heart is good medicine" (Prov. 17:22), but a heart that rejoices in sin is taking poison, not medicine. The way to happiness is not in ignoring sin, much less in making light of it, but rather in sorrow over it that cries to God.

We can react to our spiritual bankruptcy in one of several ways. Like the Pharisees we can deny our spiritual destitution and pretend we are spiritually rich. Or, like monastics and advocates of moral rearmament, we can admit our condition and try to change it in our own power and by our own efforts. Or we can admit our condition and then despair over it to such a degree that we try to drown it in drink, escape it by drugs or by activity, or give up completely and commit suicide, as Judas did. Because they can find no answer in themselves or in the world, these people conclude that there is no answer. Or, like the prodigal son, we can admit our condition, mourn over it, and turn to the heavenly Father to remedy our poverty (see Luke 15:11-32).

Mourning over sin is not being engulfed in despair. Even the person who has been severely disciplined by the church should be forgiven, comforted, and loved, "lest somehow such a one be overwhelmed by excessive sorrow" (2 Cor.

2:7-8). Nor is godly mourning wallowing in self-pity and false humility, which are really badges of pride.

True mourning over sin does not focus on ourselves, not even on our sin. It focuses on God, who alone can forgive and remove our sin. It is an attitude that begins when we enter the kingdom and lasts as long as we are on earth. It is the attitude of Romans 7. Contrary to some popular interpretation, Paul is not here speaking simply about his former condition. The problems of chapter 7 were not one-time experiences that were completely replaced by the victories of chapter 8. The apostle clearly says, "For that which I am doing I do not understand; for I am not practicing what I would like to do, but I am doing the very thing I hate" (7:15). Here he uses the present tense, as he does throughout the rest of the chapter: "For I know that nothing good dwells in me, that is, in my flesh; . . . for the good that I wish, I do not do; but I practice the very evil that I do not wish" (vv. 18-19); "I find then the principle that evil is present in me" (v. 21); "Wretched man that I am! . . . So then, on the one hand I myself with my mind am serving the law of God, but on the other, with my flesh the law of sin" (vv. 24-25).

Paul wrote those words at the height of his ministry. Yet righteousness and sin were still fighting a battle in his life. As he acknowledges in verse 25, the way of victory is "through Jesus Christ our Lord," but the rest of the verse makes clear that, at that time, the victory was not yet complete. He knew where the victory was, and he had tasted the victory many times. But he knew that, in this life, it is never a permanent victory. The presence of the flesh sees to that. Permanent victory is assured to us now, but it is not given to us now.

Paul not only spoke of the creation anxiously longing for restoration, but of his own longing for complete restoration. "And not only this, but also we ourselves, having the first fruits of the Spirit, even we ourselves groan within ourselves, waiting eagerly for our adoption as sons, the redemption of our body" (Rom. 8:19, 22-23). Paul was tired of sin, tired of fighting it in himself, as well as in the church and in the world. He longed for relief. "For indeed in this house we groan," he said, "longing to be clothed with our dwelling from heaven." He greatly preferred "rather to be absent from the body and to be at home with the Lord" (2 Cor. 5:2, 8).

The mark of the mature life is not sinlessness, which is reserved for heaven, but growing awareness of sinfulness. "If we say that we have no sin," John warns, "we are deceiving ourselves, and the truth is not in us. If we confess our sins, He is faithful and righteous to forgive us our sins and to cleanse us from all unrighteousness" (1 John 1:8-9). The subjects of God's kingdom—the forgiven ones, the children of God and joint heirs with the Son—are characterized by continual confession of sin.

Several years ago a college student said to me, "I've been liberated. Someone explained to me the true meaning of 1 John 1:9, and now I realize that I no longer have to confess my sins." I asked him, "Well, do you still confess your sins?" "I just told you that I don't have to anymore," he replied. "I know you did," I said, "but do you still confess your sins?" When he replied, "Yes, that's what bothers me," I stopped being bothered. I said, "I'm very glad to hear that," and then told him that I knew that, despite the false teaching to which he had been exposed, he was a genuine Christian. His redeemed nature refused to go along with the false teaching his mind had temporarily accepted.

Penthountes (**mourn**) is a present participle, indicating continuous action. In other words, those who are continually mourning are those who will be continually comforted. In his ninety-five theses Martin Luther said that the Christian's entire life is a continuous act of repentance and contrition. In his psalms David cried out, "For my iniquities are gone over my head; as a heavy burden they weigh too much for me" (38:4) and, "I know my transgressions, and my sin is ever before me" (51:3).

There is no record in the New Testament of Jesus laughing. We are told of His weeping, His anger, His hunger and thirst, and many other human emotions and characteristics. But if He laughed, we do not know of it. We do know that, as Isaiah predicted, He was "a man of sorrows, and acquainted with grief" (Isa. 53:3). Yet today we often hear of another Jesus, who laughs and cajoles and draws people into the kingdom by His nonjudgmental spirit and His winsome way. The fun-loving, escapist world of comedians is found plying its trade even in the church—and finding ready acceptance.

THE RESULT OF MOURNING

The result of godly mourning is comfort: **they shall be comforted.** That is why they are **blessed.** It is not the mourning that blesses, but the comfort God gives to those who mourn in a godly way.

The emphatic pronoun *autos* (**they**) indicates that *only* those who mourn over sin will be comforted. The blessing of God's comfort is reserved exclusively for the contrite of heart. It is only those who mourn for sin who will have their tears wiped away by the loving hand of Jesus Christ.

Comforted is from *parakaleō*, the same word that, as a noun, is rendered Comforter, or Helper, in John 14:16, where we are told that Jesus was the first Helper, and the Holy Spirit is "another Helper."

The Old Testament also speaks of God comforting those who mourn. Isaiah tells of the Messiah's coming, among other things, "to comfort all who mourn, to grant those who mourn in Zion, giving them a garland instead of ashes, the oil of gladness instead of mourning" (Isa. 61:2-3). David was comforted by the rod and staff of his divine Shepherd (Ps. 23:4).

As our mourning rises to the throne of God, His unsurpassed and matchless comfort descends from Him by Christ to us. Ours is the "God of all comfort" (2 Cor. 1:3), who is always ready to meet our need, admonishing, sympathizing, encouraging, and strengthening. God is a God of comfort, Christ is a Christ of comfort, and the Holy Spirit is a Spirit of comfort. As believers we have the comfort of the entire Trinity!

Shall be does not refer to the end of our lives or the end of the age. Like all other blessings of God, it will be completed only when we see our Lord face-to-face.

In the eternal heavenly state God "shall wipe away every tear from their eyes; and there shall no longer be any death; there shall no longer be any mourning, or crying, or pain" (Rev. 21:4).

But the comfort of Matthew 5:4 is future only in the sense that the blessing comes after the obedience; the comfort comes after the mourning. As we continually mourn over our sin, we **shall be** continually comforted—now, in this present life. God is not only the God of future comfort but of present comfort. "God our Father" already has "given us eternal comfort and good hope by grace" (2 Thess. 2:16).

Even God's written Word is a present comforter, given for our encouragement and hope (Rom. 15:4). And as God Himself gives us comfort and His Word gives us comfort, we are called to comfort each other with the promises of His Word (1 Thess. 4:18; cf. 2 Cor. 1:6; 7:13; 13:11; etc.).

Happiness comes to sad people because their godly sadness leads to God's comfort. "Come to Me, all who are weary and heavy-laden," Jesus says, "and I will give you rest" (Matt. 11:28). He will lift the burden from those who mourn over sin, and He will give rest to those who are weary of sin. As often as we confess our sin, He is faithful to forgive, and for as long as we mourn over sin He is faithful to comfort.

How to Mourn

What does true mourning over sin involve? How can we become godly mourners?

ELIMINATE HINDRANCES

The first step requires removing the hindrances that keep us from mourning, the things that make us content with ourselves, that make us resist God's Spirit and question His Word, and that harden our hearts. A stony heart does not mourn. It is insensitive to God, and His plow of grace cannot break it up. It only stores up wrath till the day of wrath.

Love of sin is the primary hindrance to mourning. Holding on to sin will freeze and petrify a heart. *Despair* hinders mourning because despair is giving up on God, refusing to believe that He can save and help. Despair is putting ourselves outside God's grace. Of such people Jeremiah writes, "They will say, 'It's hopeless! For we are going to follow our own plans, and each of us will act according to the stubbornness of his evil heart'" (Jer. 18:12). The one who despairs believes he is destined to sin. Because he believes God has given up on him, he gives up on God. Despair excuses sin by choosing to believe that there is no choice. Despair hides God's mercy behind a self-made cloud of doubt.

Another hindrance is *conceit,* which tries to hide the sin itself, choosing to believe that there is nothing over which to mourn. It is the spiritual counterpart of a doctor treating a cancer as if it were a cold. If it was necessary for Jesus Christ to shed His blood on the cross to save us from our sin, our sin must be great indeed!

Presumption hinders mourning because it is really a form of pride. It recognizes the need for grace, but not much grace. It is satisfied with cheap grace, expecting God to forgive little because it sees little to be forgiven. Sins are bad, but not bad enough to be confessed, repented of, and forsaken. Yet the Lord declared through Isaiah, "Let the wicked forsake his way, and the unrighteous man his thoughts; and let him return to the Lord, and He will have compassion on him; and to our God, for He will abundantly pardon" (Isa. 55:7). No pardon is offered to the unrepentant, presumptuous person who refuses to forsake his sin. The gospel that teaches otherwise has always been popular, as it clearly is in our own day; but it is a false gospel, "a different gospel" (Gal. 1:6), a distortion and contradiction of the gospel of Scripture.

Procrastination hinders godly mourning simply by putting it off. It says, "One of these days, when things are just right, I'll take a hard look at my sins, confess them, and ask God's forgiveness and cleansing." But procrastination is foolish and dangerous, because we "do not know what [our] life will be like tomorrow. [We] are just a vapor that appears for a little while and then vanishes away" (James 4:14). The sooner the disease of sin is dealt with the sooner comfort will come. If it is not dealt with, we have no assurance that comfort will ever come, because we have no assurance we will have time to confess it later.

The most important step we can take in getting rid of hindrances to mourning, whatever they are, is to look at the holiness of God and the great sacrifice of sin-bearing at the cross. If seeing Christ die for our sins does not thaw a cold heart or break up a hardened heart, it is beyond melting or breaking. In her poem "Good Friday," Christina Rossetti gives these moving lines:

> Am I a stone and not a sheep,
>   That I can stand, O Christ, beneath Thy cross,
>   To number drop by drop Thy Blood's slow loss
> And yet not weep?
>
> Not so those women loved
>   Who with exceeding grief lamented Thee;
>   Not so fallen Peter weeping bitterly;
> Not so the thief was moved;
>
> Not so the Sun and Moon
>   Which hid their faces in a starless sky.
>   A horror of great darkness at broad noon—
> I, only I.
>
> Yet give not oe'r
>   But seek Thy sheep, true Shepherd of the flock;
>   Greater than Moses, turn and look once more
> And smite a rock.

STUDY GOD'S WORD

The second step toward godly mourning is to study sin in Scripture, to learn what an evil and repulsive thing it is to God and what a destructive and damning thing it is to us. We should learn from David to keep our sin ever before us (Ps. 51:3) and from Isaiah to say, "Woe is me, for I am ruined! Because I am a man of unclean lips" (Isa. 6:5). We should learn from Peter to say, "I am a sinful man" (Luke 5:8) and from Paul to confess that we are the chief of sinners (1 Tim. 1:15). As we hear those great men of God talking about their sin, we are forced to face the reality and the depth of our own.

Sin tramples on God's laws, makes light of His love, grieves His Spirit, spurns His forgiveness and blessing, and in every way resists His grace. Sin makes us weak and makes us impure. It robs us of comfort and, much more importantly, robs God of glory.

PRAY

The third step toward godly mourning is to pray for contriteness of heart, which only God can give and which He never refuses to give those who ask. It must always be recognized that humility depends on the working of the Lord. The way to godly mourning lies not in pre-salvation human works, but in God's saving grace.

How to Know if We Are Mourning as Christ Commands

Knowing whether or not we have godly mourning is not difficult. First, we need to ask ourselves if we are sensitive to sin. If we laugh at it, take it lightly, or enjoy it, we can be sure we are not mourning over it and are outside the sphere of God's blessing.

The mock righteousness of hypocrites who make every effort to appear holy on the outside (see Matt. 6:1-18) has no sensitivity to sin, only sensitivity to personal prestige and reputation. Nor does the mock gratitude of those who thank God they are better than other people (Luke 18:11). Saul regretted that he had disobeyed God by not slaying King Agag and by sparing the best of the Amalekite animals. But he was not repentant; he did not mourn over his sin. He instead tried to excuse his actions by claiming that the animals were spared so that they could be sacrificed to God and that the people made him do what he did. He twice admitted that he had sinned, and even asked Samuel for pardon. But his real concern was not for the Lord's honor but for his own. "I have sinned; but please honor me now before the elders of my people and before Israel" (1 Sam. 15:30). Saul had ungodly regret, not godly mourning.

The godly mourner will have true sorrow for his sins. His first concern is for the harm his sin does to God's glory, not the harm its exposure might bring to his own reputation or welfare.

If our mourning is godly we will grieve for the sins of fellow believers and for the sins of the world. We will cry with the psalmist, "My eyes shed streams of water, because they do not keep Thy law" (Ps. 119:136). We will wish with Jeremiah that our heads were fountains of water that we could have enough tears for weeping (Jer. 9:1; cf. Lam. 1:16). With Ezekiel we will search out faithful believers "who sigh and groan over all the abominations which are being committed" around us (Ezek. 9:4; cf. Ps. 69:9). We will look out over the community where we live and weep, as Jesus looked out over Jerusalem and wept (Luke 19:41).

The second way to determine if we have genuine mourning over sin is to check our sense of God's forgiveness. Have we experienced the release and freedom of knowing our sins are forgiven? Do we have His peace and joy in our life? Can we point to true happiness He has given in response to our mourning? Do we have the divine comfort He promises to those who have forgiven, cleansed, and purified lives?

The godly mourners "who sow in tears shall reap with joyful shouting. He who goes to and fro weeping, carrying his bag of seed, shall indeed come again with a shout of joy, bringing his sheaves with him" (Ps. 126:5-6).

Happy Are the Meek (5:5)

15

Blessed are the gentle, for they shall inherit the earth. (5:5)

Like the first two beatitudes, this one must have been shocking and perplexing to Jesus' hearers. He taught principles that were totally foreign to their thinking.

Jesus' audience knew how to act spiritually proud and spiritually self-sufficient. They were proficient in erecting a pious facade. They actually believed that the Messiah was coming soon and would commend them for their goodness. He would, at last, give the Jewish people their rightful place in the world—a position above all other people, because they were the chosen of God.

They eagerly anticipated that the Messiah would deal gently with them and harshly with their oppressors, who for nearly a hundred years had been the Romans. After the Maccabean revolution that freed them from Greece, the Jews had a brief time of independence. But Rome's rule, though not as cruel and destructive, was much more powerful than that of Greece. Since 63 B.C., when Pompey annexed Palestine to Rome, the region had been ruled primarily by puppet kings of the Herodian family and by Roman governors, or procurators, the best known of which to us was Pilate.

The Jews so despised Roman oppression that sometimes they even refused to admit it existed. One day as He taught on the Mount of Olives, Jesus had one of His strongest exchanges with the Pharisees. When He said "to those Jews who had believed Him, 'If you abide in My word, then you are truly disciples of Mine; and you shall know the truth, and the truth shall make you free,'" the Pharisees' response was strange. "We are Abraham's offspring," they said, "and have never yet been enslaved to anyone; how is it that You say, 'You shall become free?'" (John 8:31-33). The fact was, of course, that Israel's history was one of repeated conquest and oppression—by Egypt, Assyria, the Medes and Persians, the Greeks, and, at that very time, Rome. Apparently pride would not allow those Pharisees to acknowledge one of the most obvious facts of their nation's history and of their present situation.

All Jews hoped for deliverance of some sort, by some means. Many were expecting deliverance to come through the Messiah. God had directly promised the godly Simeon "that he would not see death before he had seen the Lord's Christ," that is, the Messiah (Luke 2:26). Simeon's expectation was fulfilled when he was given the privilege of seeing the true Messiah as an infant. Others, however, such as the Pharisees, expected the Messiah to come with great fanfare and a mighty show of supernatural power. They assumed He would miraculously throw off the yoke of Rome and establish a Jewish state, a revived theocracy and holy commonwealth that would rule the world. Others, such as the materialistic Sadducees, hoped for change through political compromise, for which they were despised by many fellow Jews. The monastic Essenes, isolated both physically and philosophically from the rest of Judaism, lived largely as if Rome and the rest of the world did not exist.

The Zealots, as their name implies, were the most vocal and active proponents of deliverance. Many of them expected the Messiah to come as a powerful, irresistible military leader who would conquer Rome in the same way that Rome had conquered them. They were not, however, waiting passively for their Deliverer, but were determined that, whenever and however He might come, they would do their part to make His job easier. Their numbers, influence, and power continued to grow until Rome brutally attempted to crush Jewish resistance. In A.D. 70 Titus totally destroyed Jerusalem and massacred over a million Jews. Three years later Flavius Silva finally succeeded in his long siege against the stronghold at Masada. When Jewish rebelliousness continued to frustrate Rome, Hadrian swept through Palestine during the years 132-35 and systematically destroyed most of the cities and slaughtered the Jews living there.

In Jesus' day the aggressive, rebellious Zealots were not many in number, but they had the sympathy and moral support of many of the people, who wanted Rome to be overthrown, however it was done.

Consequently, in whatever way various groups of people expected the Messiah to come, they did not anticipate His coming humbly and meekly. Yet those were the very attitudes that Jesus, the one whom John the Baptist had announced as the Messiah, was both teaching and practicing. The idea of a meek Messiah leading meek people was far from any of their concepts of the messianic kingdom. The Jews understood military power and miracle power. They even understood the power of compromise, unpopular as it was. But they did not understand the power of meekness.

The people as a whole eventually rejected Jesus because He did not fulfill their messianic expectations. He even preached *against* the means in which they had put their hope. They first rejected, then hated, and finally killed Him because, instead of approving their religion He condemned it, and instead of leading them to independence from Rome He disdained revolutionary acts and offered a way of even greater subservience.

In their minds Jesus could not possibly be the Messiah, and the final evidence was His crucifixion. The Old Testament taught that anyone hanged on a tree was "accursed of God" (Deut. 21:23), yet that is exactly where Jesus' life ended—ignominiously on a cross, and a Roman cross at that. As He hung dying, some of the Jewish leaders could not resist a last taunt against His claim to be Savior and Messiah: "He saved others; He cannot save Himself. He is the King of Israel; let Him now come down from the cross, and we shall believe in Him. He trusts in God; let Him deliver Him now, if He takes pleasure in Him; for He said, 'I am the Son of God'" (Matt. 27:42-43).

In the early days of apostolic preaching, the death and resurrection of Christ were the greatest hindrances to belief in the gospel. The ideas were foolishness to Gentiles and a stumbling block to Jews (1 Cor. 1:23). The gospel was foolishness to those Gentiles who considered the body to be inherently evil and thought it absurd that the Savior of the world not only would allow Himself to be killed but would come back from the dead in bodily form. To the Jews the gospel was a stumbling block because the idea of the Messiah dying at all, much less on a cross, was unthinkable. How could a Messiah who taught for a few years, accomplished absolutely nothing as far as anyone could see, and then was rejected by the religious teachers and put to death be worth believing in? (cf. Acts 3:17-18).

But rejection of Jesus started long before His crucifixion. When He began the Sermon on the Mount by teaching humility, mourning, and meekness, the people sensed something was wrong. This strange preacher could hardly be the deliverer they were looking for. Great causes are fought by the proud, not the humble. You cannot win victories while mourning, and you certainly could never conquer Rome with meekness. In spite of all the miracles of His ministry, the people never really believed in Him as the Messiah, because He failed to act in military or miracle power against Rome.

The Jews were not looking for the Messiah that God had told them was coming. They disregarded such parts of His Word as Isaiah 40-60, which so clearly and vividly portrays the Messiah as the Suffering Servant as well as the conquering Lord. They could not accept the idea that such descriptions as, "He has no stately form or majesty . . . He was despised and forsaken of men . . . He was oppressed and He was afflicted . . . like a lamb that is led to slaughter . . . that He was cut off out of the land of the living," and "His grave was assigned with wicked men" (Isa. 53:2-3, 7-9) could apply to the Messiah, to the coming great deliverer of the Jews.

Jesus' teaching seemed new and unacceptable to most of His hearers simply because the Old Testament was so greatly neglected and misinterpreted. They did not recognize the humble and self-denying Jesus as the Messiah because they did not recognize God's predicted Suffering Servant as the Messiah. That was not the kind of Messiah they wanted.

THE MEANING OF MEEKNESS

Gentle is from *praos,* which basically means mild or soft. The term sometimes was used to describe a soothing medicine or a soft breeze. It was used of colts and other animals whose naturally wild spirits were broken by a trainer so that they could do useful work. As a human attitude it meant being gentle of spirit, meek, submissive, quiet, tenderhearted. During His triumphal entry into Jerusalem, Jesus was hailed as the coming King, though He was "gentle, and mounted on a donkey" (Matt. 21:5). Paul lovingly referred to the "meekness and gentleness of Christ" (2 Cor. 10:1) as the pattern for his own attitude.

The essential difference between being poor in spirit and being meek, or **gentle**, may be that poverty in spirit focuses on our sinfulness, whereas meekness focuses on God's holiness. The basic attitude of humility underlies both virtues. When we look honestly at ourselves, we are made humble by seeing how sinful and unworthy we are; when we look at God, we are made humble by seeing how righteous and worthy He is.

We again can see logical sequence and progression in the Beatitudes. Poverty of spirit (the first) is negative, and results in mourning (the second). Meekness (the third) is positive, and results in seeking righteousness (the fourth). Being poor in spirit causes us to turn away from ourselves in mourning, and meekness causes us to turn toward God in seeking His righteousness.

The blessings of the Beatitudes are for those who are realistic about their sinfulness, who are repentant of their sins, and who are responsive to God in His righteousness. Those who are unblessed, unhappy, and shut out of the kingdom are the proud, the arrogant, the unrepentant—the self-sufficient and self-righteous who see in themselves no unworthiness and feel no need for God's help and God's righteousness.

Most of Jesus' hearers, like fallen men throughout history, were concerned about justifying their own ways, defending their own rights, and serving their own ends. The way of meekness was not their way, and therefore the true kingdom was not their kingdom. The proud Pharisees wanted a miraculous kingdom, the proud Sadducees wanted a materialistic kingdom, the proud Essenes wanted a monastic kingdom, and the proud Zealots wanted a military kingdom. The humble Jesus offered a meek kingdom.

Meekness has always been God's way for man. It is the way of the Old Testament. In the book of Job we are told that God "sets on high those who are lowly, and those who mourn are lifted to safety" (5:11). Moses, the Jews' great deliverer and law-giver, "was very humble, more than any man who was on the face of the earth" (Num. 12:3). The Jews' great King David, their supreme military hero, wrote, "He [the Lord] leads the humble in justice, and He teaches the humble His way" (Ps. 25:9).

Meekness is the way of the New Testament. It is taught by Jesus in the Beatitudes as well as elsewhere and is continued to be taught by the apostles. Paul entreated the Ephesians to "walk in a manner worthy of the calling with which you have been called, with all humility and gentleness, with patience, showing forbearance to one another in love" (Eph. 4:1-2). He told the Colossians to "put on a heart of compassion, kindness, humility, gentleness and patience" (Col. 3:12). He told Titus to remind those under his leadership "to be subject to rulers, to authorities, to be obedient, to be ready for every good deed, to malign no one, to be uncontentious, gentle, showing every consideration for all men" (Titus 3:1-2).

Meekness does not connote weakness. The word was used in much extrabiblical literature to refer to the breaking of an animal. Meekness means power put under control. A person without meekness is "like a city that is broken into and without walls" (Prov. 25:28). "He who is slow to anger is better than the mighty, and he who rules his spirit, than he who captures a city" (Prov. 16:32). An unbroken colt is useless; medicine that is too strong will harm rather than cure; a wind out of control destroys. Emotion out of control also destroys, and has no place in God's kingdom. Meekness uses its resources appropriately.

Meekness is the opposite of violence and vengeance. The meek person, for example, accepts joyfully the seizing of his property, knowing that he has infinitely better and more permanent possessions awaiting him in heaven (Heb. 10:34). The meek person has died to self, and he therefore does not worry about injury to himself, or about loss, insult, or abuse. The meek person does not defend himself, first of all because that is His Lord's command and example, and second because he knows that he does not deserve defending. Being poor in spirit and having mourned over his great sinfulness, the **gentle** person stands humbly before God, knowing he has nothing to commend himself.

Meekness is not cowardice or emotional flabbiness. It is not lack of conviction nor mere human niceness. But its courage, its strength, its conviction, and its pleasantness come from God, not from self. The spirit of meekness is the spirit of Christ, who defended the glory of His Father, but gave Himself in sacrifice for others. Leaving an example for us to follow, He "committed no sin, nor was any deceit found in His mouth; and while being reviled, He did not revile in return; while suffering, He uttered no threats, but kept entrusting Himself to Him who judges righteously" (1 Pet. 2:21-23).

Though He was sinless, and therefore never deserved criticism or abuse, Jesus did not resist slander or repay injustice or threaten His tormentors. The only human being who did no wrong, the One who always had a perfect defense, never defended Himself.

When His Father's house was profaned by moneychangers and sacrifice sellers, "He made a scourge of cords, and drove them all out of the temple, with the sheep and the oxen; and He poured out the coins of the moneychangers, and overturned their tables" (John 2:14-15). Jesus scathingly and repeatedly denounced the hypocritical and wicked religious leaders; He twice cleansed the Temple by force; and He fearlessly uttered divine judgment on those who forsook and corrupted God's Word.

But Jesus did not once raise a finger or give a single retort in His own defense. Though at any time He could have called legions of angels to His side (Matt. 26:53), He refused to use either natural or supernatural power for His own welfare. Meekness is not weakness, but meekness does not use its power for its own defense or selfish purposes. Meekness is power completely surrendered to God's control.

THE MANIFESTATION OF MEEKNESS

The best way to describe meekness is to illustrate it, to see it in action. Scripture abounds with instructive accounts of meekness.

After God had called Abraham from Ur of the Chaldeans to the Promised Land and had made the marvelous unconditional covenant with him, a dispute about grazing lands arose between the servants of Abraham and those of his nephew Lot. All the land of Canaan had been promised to Abraham. He was God's chosen man and the Father of God's chosen people. Lot, on the other hand, was essentially a hanger-on, an in-law who was largely dependent on Abraham for his welfare and safety. Besides that, Abraham was Lot's uncle and his elder. Yet Abraham willingly let Lot take whatever land he wanted, thus giving up his rights and prerogatives for the sake of his nephew, for the sake of harmony between their households, and for the sake of their testimony before "the Canaanite and the Perizzite [who] were dwelling then in the land" (Gen. 13:5-9). Those things were much more important to Abraham than standing up for his own rights. He had both the right and the power to do as he pleased in the matter, but in meekness he gladly waived his rights and laid aside his power.

Joseph was abused by his jealous brothers and eventually sold into slavery. When, by God's gracious plan, he came to be second only to Pharaoh in Egypt, he was in a position to take severe vengeance on his brothers. When they came to Egypt asking for grain for their starving families, Joseph could easily have refused and, in fact, could have put his brothers into more severe slavery than that into which they had sold him. Yet he had only forgiveness and love for them. When he finally revealed to them who he was, "he wept so loudly that the Egyptians heard it, and the household of Pharaoh heard of it" (Gen. 45:2). Then he said to them, "Do not be grieved or angry with yourselves, because you sold me here; for God sent me before you to preserve life. . . . Now, therefore, it was not you who sent me here, but God" (vv. 5, 8). Later he told them, "Do not be afraid, for am I in God's place? And as for you, you meant evil against me, but God meant it for good in order to bring about this present result, to preserve many people alive" (50:19-20). In meekness Joseph understood that it was God's place to judge and his to forgive and help.

Moses killed an Egyptian who was beating some Hebrew slaves; faced up to

Pharaoh to demand the release of his people; and was so angry at the orgy that Aaron and the people were having around the golden calf that he smashed the first set of tablets of the Ten Commandments. Yet he was called "very humble, more than any man who was on the face of the earth" (Num. 12:3). Moses vented his anger against those who harmed and enslaved his people and who rebelled against God, but he did not vent his anger against those who abused him or demand personal rights and privileges.

When God called him to lead Israel out of Egypt, Moses felt completely inadequate, and pleaded, "Who am I, that I should go to Pharaoh, and that I should bring the sons of Israel out of Egypt?" (Ex. 3:11). After God explained His plan for Moses to confront Pharaoh, Moses again pleaded, "Please, Lord, I have never been eloquent, neither recently nor in time past, nor since Thou hast spoken to Thy servant; for I am slow of speech and slow of tongue" (4:10). Moses would defend God before anyone, but he did not defend himself before God.

David was chosen by God and anointed by Samuel to replace Saul as Israel's king. But when, in the cave of Engedi, he had the opportunity to take Saul's life, as Saul often had tried to take his, David refused to do so. He had such great respect for the king's office, despite that particular king's wickedness and abuse of him, that "David's conscience bothered him because he had cut off the edge of Saul's robe. So he said to his men, 'Far be it from me because of the Lord that I should do this thing to my lord, the Lord's anointed, to stretch out my hand against him, since he is the Lord's anointed'" (1 Sam. 24:5-6).

Many years later, after David's rebellious son Absalom had routed his father from Jerusalem, a member of Saul's family named Shimei cursed David and threw stones at him. When one of David's soldiers wanted to cut off Shimei's head, David prevented him, saying, "Behold, my son who came out from me seeks my life; how much more now this Benjamite? Let him alone and let him curse, for the Lord has told him. Perhaps the Lord will look on my affliction and return good to me instead of his cursing this day" (2 Sam. 16:5-12).

By contrast, King Uzziah, who began to reign at the age of sixteen and who "did right in the sight of the Lord," and "continued to seek God" (2 Chron. 26:4-5), became self-confident after the Lord gave him great victories over the Philistines, Ammonites, and other enemies. "When he became strong, his heart was so proud that he acted corruptly, and he was unfaithful to the Lord his God, for he entered the temple of the Lord to burn incense on the altar of incense" (v. 16). Uzziah thought he could do no wrong, and arrogantly performed a rite that he knew was restricted to the priests. He was so concerned with exalting himself and glorying in his greatness, that he disobeyed the God who had made him great and even profaned His Temple. As a consequence "King Uzziah was a leper to the day of his death; and he lived in a separate house, being a leper, for he was cut off from the house of the Lord" (v. 21).

Of the many examples of meekness in the New Testament, the greatest other than Jesus Himself was Paul. He was by far the most educated of the apostles and the one, as far as we can tell, that God used most widely and effectively. Yet he refused to put any confidence in himself, "in the flesh" (Phil. 3:3). He knew that he could do all things, but only "through Him who strengthens me" (4:13).

THE RESULT OF MEEKNESS

As with the other beatitudes, the general result of meekness is being **blessed**, being made divinely happy. God gives the meek His own joy and gladness.

More specifically, however, the **gentle . . . shall inherit the earth.** After creating man in His own image, God gave man dominion over the whole earth (Gen. 1:28). The subjects of His kingdom are going to come someday into that promised inheritance, largely lost and perverted after the Fall. Theirs will be paradise regained.

One day God will completely reclaim His earthly domain, and those who have become His children through faith in His Son will rule that domain with Him. And the only ones who become His children and the subjects of His divine kingdom are those who are **gentle**, those who are meek, because they understand their unworthiness and sinfulness and cast themselves on the mercy of God. The emphatic pronoun *autos* (**they**) is again used (see vv. 3, 4), indicating that *only* those who are meek **shall inherit the earth.**

Most Jews thought that the coming great kingdom of the Messiah would belong to the strong, of whom the Jews would be the strongest. But the Messiah Himself said that it would belong to the meek, and to Jew and Gentile alike.

Klēronomeō (to **inherit**) refers to the receiving of one's allotted portion, one's rightful inheritance. This beatitude is almost a direct quotation of Psalm 37:11—"But the humble will inherit the land." For many generations faithful Jews had wondered, as God's people today sometimes wonder, why the wicked and godless seem to prosper and the righteous and godly seem to suffer. Through David, God assured His people, "Yet a little while and the wicked man will be no more; and you will look carefully for his place, and he will not be there" (v. 10). The wicked person's time of judgment was coming, as was the righteous person's time of blessing.

Our responsibility is to trust the Lord and obey His will. The settling of accounts, whether in judgment or blessing, is in His hands and will be accomplished exactly in the right time and in the right way. In the meanwhile, God's children live in faith and hope based on the certain promise, the divine pronouncement, that **they shall inherit the earth.**

Paul both warns and assures the Corinthians, saying, "So then let no one boast in men. For all things belong to you, whether Paul or Apollos or Cephas or the world or life or death or things present or things to come; all things belong to you, and you belong to Christ; and Christ belongs to God" (1 Cor. 3:21-23). Because we belong to Christ, our place in the kingdom is as secure as His.

It is also certain "that the unrighteous shall not inherit the kingdom of God" (1 Cor. 6:9). One day the Lord will take the earth from the hands of the wicked and give it to His righteous people, whom He will use "to execute vengeance on the nations, and punishment on the peoples; to bind their kings with chains, and their nobles with fetters of iron; to execute on them the judgment written" (Ps. 149:7-9).

Our inheritance of the earth is not entirely future, however. The promise of the future inheritance itself gives us hope and happiness now. And we are able to appreciate many things, even earthly things, in ways that only those who know and love the Creator can experience.

In the beautiful words of Wade Robinson,

> Heav'n above is softer blue,
>   Earth around is sweeter green;
> Something lives in ev'ry hue
>   Christless eyes have never seen!
> Birds with gladder songs o'erflow,
>   Flow'rs with deeper beauties shine,
> Since I know, as now I know,
>   I am His and He is mine.

Nearly a century ago George MacDonald wrote, "We cannot see the world as God means it in the future, save as our souls are characterized by meekness. In meekness we are its only inheritors. Meekness alone makes the spiritual retina pure to receive God's things as they are, mingling with them neither imperfection nor impurity."

THE NECESSITY FOR MEEKNESS

Meekness is necessary first of all because it is required for salvation. Only the meek will inherit the earth, because only the meek belong to the King who will rule the future kingdom of the earth. "For the Lord takes delight in His people," says the psalmist; "he crowns the humble with salvation" (Ps. 149:4, NIV). When the disciples asked Jesus who was the greatest in the kingdom, "He called a child to Himself and set him before them, and said, 'Truly I say to you, unless you are converted and become like children, you shall not enter the kingdom of heaven. Whoever then humbles himself as this child, he is the greatest in the kingdom of heaven'" (Matt. 18:2-4).

Meekness is also necessary because it is commanded. "Seek the Lord, all you humble of the earth who have carried out His ordinances; seek righteousness, seek humility" (Zeph. 2:3). James commands believers, "Therefore putting aside all filthiness and all that remains of wickedness, in humility receive the word implanted, which is able to save your souls" (James 1:21). Those who do not have a humble spirit are not able even to listen rightly to God's Word, much less understand and receive it.

Meekness is necessary because we cannot witness effectively without it. Peter says, "Sanctify Christ as Lord in your hearts, always being ready to make a defense to everyone who asks you to give an account for the hope that is in you, yet with gentleness and reverence" (1 Pet. 3:15). Pride will always stand between our testimony and those to whom we testify. They will see us instead of the Lord, no matter how orthodox our theology or how refined our technique.

Meekness is necessary because only meekness gives glory to God. Pride seeks its own glory, but meekness seeks God's. Meekness is reflected in our attitude toward other children of God. Humility in relation to fellow Christians gives God glory. "Now may the God who gives perseverance and encouragement grant you to be of the same mind with one another according to Christ Jesus; that with one accord you may with one voice glorify the God and Father of our Lord Jesus Christ. Wherefore, accept one another, just as Christ also accepted us to the glory of God" (Rom. 15:5-7).

Happy Are the Hungry (5:6)

16

Blessed are those who hunger and thirst for righteousness, for they shall be satisfied. (5:6)

This beatitude speaks of strong desire, of driving pursuit, of a passionate force inside the soul. It has to do with ambition—ambition of the right sort—whose object is to honor, obey, and glorify God by partaking of His righteousness. This holy ambition is in great contrast to the common ambitions of men to gratify their own lusts, accomplish their own goals, and satisfy their own egos.

As no other creature, Lucifer basked in the splendor and radiance of God's glory. The name Lucifer means "star of the morning" or, more literally, "the bright one." But he was not satisfied with living in God's glory, and he said in his heart, "I will ascend to heaven; I will raise my throne above the stars of God, and I will sit on the mount of assembly in the recesses of the north. I will ascend above the heights of the clouds; I will make myself like the Most High" (Isa. 14:13-14). His ambition was not to reflect God's glory but to usurp God's sovereign power—while forsaking righteousness. Therefore when Satan declared his intention to make himself like the Most High, the Most High responded by declaring to His adversary, "You will be thrust down to Sheol, to the recesses of the pit" (v. 15).

As king of Babylon, Nebuchadnezzar ruled over the greatest of all world empires. One day as he walked on the roof of the royal palace of Babylon, "the king reflected and said, 'Is this not Babylon the great, which I myself have built as a royal residence by the might of my power and for the glory of my majesty?'" (Dan. 4:29-30). Nebuchadnezzar lusted after praise just as Lucifer lusted after power. God's reaction was immediate: "While the word was in the king's mouth, a voice came from heaven, saying, 'King Nebuchadnezzar, to you it is declared: sovereignty has been removed from you, and you will be driven away from mankind, and your dwelling place will be with the beasts of the field. You will be given grass to eat like cattle, and seven periods of time will pass over you, until you recognize that the Most High is ruler over the realm of mankind, and bestows it on whomever He wishes'" (vv. 31-32).

Jesus told a parable about a rich farmer whose crops were so abundant that he did not have enough space to store them. After planning to tear down his old barns and build bigger ones, he said, "'I will say to my soul, "Soul, you have many goods laid up for many years to come; take your ease, eat, drink and be merry."' But God said to him, 'You fool! This very night your soul is required of you; and now who will own what you have prepared?' So is the man who lays up treasure for himself, and is not rich toward God" (Luke 12:16-21).

Lucifer hungered for power; Nebuchadnezzar hungered for praise; and the rich fool hungered for pleasure. Because they hungered for wrong things and rejected God's good things, they forfeited both.

Jesus declares that the deepest desire of every person ought to be to **hunger and thirst for righteousness**. That is the Spirit-prompted desire that will lead a person to salvation and keep him strong and faithful once he is in the kingdom. It is also the only ambition that, when fulfilled, brings enduring happiness.

The American Declaration of Independence asserts that citizens have the right to the pursuit of happiness. The founding fathers did not presume to guarantee that all who pursue it would find it, because that is beyond the power of any government to provide. Each person is free to seek whatever kind of happiness he wants in the way he wants within the law. Sadly, most US citizens, like most people throughout all of history, have chosen to pursue the wrong kind of happiness in ways that provide *no* kind of happiness.

Jesus says that the way to happiness, the way to being truly **blessed**, is the way of spiritual hunger and thirst.

THE NECESSITY FOR SPIRITUAL HUNGER

Hunger and thirst represent the necessities of physical life. Jesus' analogy demonstrates that **righteousness** is required for spiritual life just as food and water are required for physical life. **Righteousness** is not an optional spiritual supplement but a spiritual necessity. We can no more live spiritually without righteousness than we can live physically without food and water.

Since the great famine in Egypt during the time of Joseph, and probably long before then, the world has been periodically plagued by famines. Rome experienced a famine in 436 B.C., which was so severe that thousands of people threw themselves into the Tiber River to drown rather than starve to death. Famine struck England in A.D. 1005, and all of Europe suffered great famines in 879, 1016, and 1162. In our own century, despite the advances in agriculture, many parts of the world still experience periodic famines. In recent years Africa has seen some of the most devastating famines in the world's history. In the last 100 years tens of millions throughout the world have died from starvation or from the many diseases that accompany severe malnutrition.

A starving person has a single, all-consuming passion for food and water. Nothing else has the slightest attraction or appeal; nothing else can even get his attention.

Those who are without God's righteousness are starved for spiritual life. But tragically they do not have the natural desire for spiritual life that they do for physical. The tendency of fallen mankind is to turn to itself and to the world for meaning and life, just as "'a dog returns to its own vomit,' and 'a sow, after washing, returns to wallowing in the mire'" (2 Pet. 2:22; cf. Prov. 26:11).

The heart of every person in the world was created with a sense of inner emptiness and need. Yet apart from God's revelation men do not recognize what the need is or know what will satisfy it. Like the prodigal son, they will eat pigs' food, because they have nothing else. "Why," God asks, "do you spend money for what is not bread, and your wages for what does not satisfy?" (Isa. 55:2). The reason is that men have forsaken God, "the fountain of living waters, to hew for themselves cisterns, broken cisterns, that can hold no water" (Jer. 2:13). Though God has created men with a need for Himself, they try to satisfy that need through lifeless gods of their own making.

Again like the prodigal son, men are prone to take good things God has given—such as possessions, health, freedom, opportunities, and knowledge—and spend them on pleasure, power, popularity, fame, and every other form of self-satisfaction. But unlike the prodigal, they are often content to stay in the far country, away from God and away from His blessings.

People are warned not to "love the world, nor the things in the world. If anyone loves the world, the love of the Father is not in him. For all that is in the world, the lust of the flesh and the lust of the eyes and the boastful pride of life, is not from the Father, but is from the world. And the world is passing away, and also its lusts; but the one who does the will of God abides forever" (1 John 2:15-17).

Seeking satisfaction only in God and in His provision is a mark of those who come into His kingdom. Those who belong to the King **hunger and thirst for the King's righteousness.** They desire sin to be replaced with virtue and disobedience to be replaced by obedience. They are eager to serve the Word and will of God.

Jesus' call to spiritual hunger and thirst also follows logically in the progression of the Beatitudes. The first three are essentially negative, commands to forsake evil things that are barriers to the kingdom. In poverty of spirit we turn away from self-seeking; in mourning we turn away from self-satisfaction; and in meekness we turn away from self-serving.

The first three beatitudes are also costly and painful. Becoming poor in spirit involves death to self. Mourning over sin involves facing up to our sinfulness. Becoming meek involves surrendering our power to God's control.

The fourth beatitude is more positive and is a consequence of the other three. When we put aside self, sins, and power and turn to the Lord, we are given a great desire for righteousness. The more we put aside what we have, the more we long for what God has.

Martyn Lloyd-Jones says, "This Beatitude again follows logically from the previous ones; it is a statement to which all the others lead. It is the logical conclusion to which they come, and it is something for which we should all be profoundly thankful and grateful to God. I do not know of a better test that anyone can apply to himself or herself in this whole matter of the Christian profession than a verse like this. If this verse is to you one of the most blessed statements of the whole of Scripture, you can be quite certain you are a Christian. If it is not, then you had better examine the foundations again" (*Studies in the Sermon on the Mount* [Grand Rapids: Eerdmans, 1971], 1:73-74).

The person who has no hunger and thirst for righteousness has no part in God's kingdom. To *have* God's life within us through the new birth in Jesus Christ is to *desire* more of His likeness within us by growing in righteousness. This is readily clear from David's confession in Psalm 119:97, "O how I love Thy law." Paul echoes David's passion for righteousness in Romans 7:22, where he testifies, "I joyfully concur with the law of God in the inner man." The true believer desires to obey, even though he struggles with unredeemed flesh (cf. Rom. 8:23).

The Meaning of Spiritual Hunger

Most of us have never faced life-threatening hunger and thirst. We think of hunger as missing a meal or two in a row, and of thirst as having to wait an hour on a hot day to get a cold drink. But the **hunger and thirst** of which Jesus speaks here is of a much more intense sort.

During the liberation of Palestine in World War I, a combined force of British, Australian, and New Zealand soldiers was closely pursuing the Turks as they retreated from the desert. As the allied troops moved northward past Beersheba they began to outdistance their water-carrying camel train. When the water ran out, their mouths got dry, their heads ached, and they became dizzy and faint. Eyes became bloodshot, lips swelled and turned purple, and mirages became common. They knew that if they did not make the wells of Sheriah by nightfall, thousands of them would die—as hundreds already had done. Literally fighting for their lives, they managed to drive the Turks from Sheriah.

As water was distributed from the great stone cisterns, the more able-bodied were required to stand at attention and wait for the wounded and those who would take guard duty to drink first. It was four hours before the last man had his drink. During that time the men stood no more than twenty feet from thousands of gallons of water, to drink of which had been their consuming passion for many agonizing days. It is said that one of the officers who was present reported, "I believe that we all learned our first real Bible lesson on the march from Beersheba to Sheriah Wells. If such were our thirst for God, for righteousness and for His will in our lives, a consuming, all-embracing, preoccupying desire, how rich in the fruit of the Spirit would we be?" (E. M. Blaylock, "Water," *Eternity* (August 1966), p. 27)

That is the kind of hunger and thirst of which Jesus speaks in this beatitude. The strongest and deepest impulses in the natural realm are used to represent the depth of desire the called of God and redeemed have for righteousness. The present participle is used in each case and signifies continuous longing, continuous seeking. Those who truly come to Jesus Christ come hungering and thirsting for righteousness, and those who are in Him continue to know that deep longing for holiness.

The parallel passage in Luke says, "Blessed are you who hunger now" (6:21). Desire for righteousness is to characterize our life *now* and in the rest of our earthly existence.

When Moses was in the wilderness, God appeared to him in a burning bush. When he went back to Egypt to deliver his people, he saw God's might and power in the miracles and the ten plagues. He saw God part the Dead Sea and swallow up their Egyptian pursuers. He saw God's glory in the pillar of cloud and the pillar of fire which led Israel in the wilderness. He built a Tabernacle for God and saw the Lord's glory shining over the Holy of Holies. Over and over Moses had sought and had seen God's glory. "Thus the Lord used to speak to Moses face to face, just as a man speaks to his friend" (Ex. 33:11). But Moses was never satisfied and always wanted to see more. He continued to plead, "I pray Thee, show Thy glory" (v. 18).

Moses never had enough of the Lord. Yet from that dissatisfaction came satisfaction. Because of his continual longing for God, Moses found favor in His sight (v. 17), and God promised him, "I Myself will make all My goodness pass before you, and will proclaim the name of the Lord before you" (v. 19).

David declared, "O God, Thou art my God," but continued, "I shall seek Thee earnestly; my soul thirsts for Thee, my flesh yearns for Thee, in a dry and weary land where there is no water" (Ps. 63:1).

Paul had great visions of God and great revelations from God, yet he was not satisfied. He had given up his own righteousness "derived from the law" and was growing in "the righteousness which comes from God on the basis of faith." But still he longed to "know Him, and the power of His resurrection and the fellowship of His sufferings, being conformed to His death" (Phil. 3:9-10). Peter expressed his own great desire and hunger when he counseled those to whom he wrote to "grow in the grace and knowledge of our Lord and Savior Jesus Christ" (2 Pet. 3:18).

John Darby wrote, "To be hungry is not enough; I must be really starving to know what is in God's heart toward me. When the prodigal son was hungry, he went to feed on the husks, but when he was starving, he turned to his father." That is the hunger of which the fourth beatitude speaks, the hunger for righteousness that only the Father can satisfy.

Several years ago someone told me of a friend who had begun coming to a Bible study but soon gave it up, explaining that she wanted to be religious but did not want to make the commitment that Scripture demands. She had little hunger for the things of God. She wanted to pick and choose, to nibble at whatever suited her fancy—because basically she was satisfied with the way she was. In her own eyes she had enough, and thereby became one of the self-adjudged rich whom the Lord sends away empty-handed. It is only the hungry that He fills with good things (Luke 1:53).

The Object of Spiritual Hunger

As with the other beatitudes, the goal of hungering and thirsting for righteousness is twofold. For the unbeliever the goal is salvation; for the believer it is sanctification.

FOR SALVATION

When a person initially hungers and thirsts for righteousness he seeks salvation, the righteousness that comes when one turns from sin to submit to the lordship of Jesus Christ. In poverty of spirit he sees his sin; in mourning he laments and turns from his sin; in meekness he submits his own sinful way and power to God; and in hunger and thirst he seeks God's righteousness in Christ to replace his sin.

In many Old Testament passages righteousness is used as a synonym for salvation. "My righteousness is near, My salvation has gone forth," the Lord said through Isaiah (51:5). Daniel wrote of the time when "those who have insight will shine brightly like the brightness of the expanse of heaven, and those who lead the many to righteousness, like the stars forever and ever" (Dan. 12:3).

When a person abandons all hope of saving himself, all confidence in self-righteousness, and begins to hunger for the salvation that brings God's righteousness and the obedience that God requires, he will be **blessed**, be made divinely happy.

The Jews' greatest obstacle to receiving the gospel was their self-righteousness, their confidence in their own purity and holiness, which they imagined was created by good works. Because they were God's chosen race, and as keepers of the law—or, more often, keepers of men's interpretations of the law—they felt heaven was assured.

The Messiah told them, however, that the only way to salvation was by hungering and thirsting for God's righteousness to replace their own self-righteousness, which was really unrighteousness.

FOR SANCTIFICATION

For believers, the object of hungering and thirsting is to grow in the righteousness received from trusting in Christ. That growth is sanctification, which more than anything else is the mark of a Christian.

No believer "arrives" in his spiritual life until he reaches heaven, and to claim perfection of any sort before then is the ultimate presumption. Children of the kingdom never stop needing or hungering for more of God's righteousness and holiness to be manifest in them through their obedience. Paul prayed for believers in Philippi that their love might "abound still more and more in real knowledge and all discernment, so that you may approve the things that are excellent, in order to be sincere and blameless until the day of Christ" (Phil. 1:9-10).

In the Greek language, verbs such as hunger and thirst normally have objects that are in the partitive genitive, a case that indicates incompleteness, or partialness. A literal English rendering would be: "I hunger for of food" or "I thirst for of water." The idea is that a person only hungers for *some* food and *some* water, not for all the food and water in the world.

But Jesus does not here use the partitive genitive but the accusative, and **righteousness** is therefore the unqualified and unlimited object of **hunger and thirst**. The Lord identifies those who desire all the righteousness there is (cf. Matt. 5:48; 1 Pet. 1:15-16).

Jesus also uses the definite article (*tēn*), indicating that He is not speaking of just any righteousness, but *the* righteousness, the only true righteousness—that which comes from God and, in fact, is God's very own righteousness which He has in Himself.

It becomes obvious, then, that we cannot possibly have our longing for godliness satisfied in this life, so we are left to continually hunger and thirst until the day we are clothed entirely in Christ's righteousness.

THE RESULT OF SPIRITUAL HUNGER

The result of hungering and thirsting for righteousness is being **satisfied**. *Chortazō* was frequently used of the feeding of animals until they wanted nothing more. They were allowed to eat until they were completely satisfied.

Jesus' divine pronouncement is that those who hunger and thirst for righteousness will be given total satisfaction. The giving of satisfaction is God's work, as the future passive tense indicates: **they shall be satisfied**. Our part is to seek; His part is to satisfy.

Again there is a marvelous paradox, because though saints continually seek God's righteousness, always wanting more and never getting all, they nevertheless will be satisfied. We may eat steak or our favorite pie until we can eat no more, yet our taste for those things continues and even increases. It is the very satisfaction that makes us want more. We want to eat more of those things because they are so satisfying. The person who genuinely hungers and thirsts for God's righteousness finds it so satisfying that he wants more and more.

God's satisfying those who seek and love Him is a repeated theme in the Psalms. "For He has satisfied the thirsty soul, and the hungry soul He has filled with what is good" (Ps. 107:9). "The young lions do lack and suffer hunger; but they who seek the Lord shall not be in want of any good thing" (34:10). The best-loved of all psalms begins, "The Lord is my shepherd, I shall not want," and later declares, "Thou dost prepare a table before me . . . my cup overflows" (23:1, 5).

Predicting the great blessings of Christ's millennial kingdom, Jeremiah assured Israel that in that day, "'My people shall be satisfied with My goodness,' declares the Lord" (Jer. 31:14). Jesus told the Samaritan woman at the well in Sychar that "whoever drinks of the water that I shall give him shall never thirst; but the water that I shall give him shall become in him a well of water springing up to eternal life" (John 4:14). To the crowds near Capernaum, many of whom had been among the five thousand He fed with the five barley loaves and the two fish, Jesus said, "I am the bread of life; he who comes to Me shall not hunger, and he who believes in Me shall never thirst" (John 6:35).

THE TESTING OF SPIRITUAL HUNGER

There are several marks of genuine hunger and thirst for God's righteousness. First is dissatisfaction with self. The person who is pleased with his own righteousness will see no need for God's. The great Puritan Thomas Watson wrote, "He has most need of righteousness that least wants it." No matter how rich his spiritual experience or how advanced his spiritual maturity, the hungering Christian will always say, "Wretched man that I am! Who will set me free from the body of this death?" (Rom. 7:24).

Second is freedom from dependence on external things for satisfaction. A hungry man cannot be satisfied by an arrangement of lovely flowers, or beautiful music, or pleasant conversation. All of those things are good, but they have no ability to satisfy hunger. Neither can anything but God's own righteousness satisfy the person who has true spiritual hunger and thirst.

Third is craving for the Word of God, the basic spiritual food He provides His children. A hungry man does not have to be begged to eat. Jeremiah rejoiced, "Thy words were found and I ate them, and Thy words became for me a joy and the delight of my heart" (Jer. 15:16). The more we seek God's righteousness, the more we will want to devour Scripture. Feeding on God's Word increases our appetite for it.

Fourth is the pleasantness of the things of God. "To a famished man any bitter thing is sweet" (Prov. 27:7). The believer who seeks God's righteousness above all other things will find fulfillment and satisfaction even in those things that humanly are disastrous. Thomas Watson comments that "the one who hungers and thirsts after righteousness can feed on the myrrh of the gospel as well as the honey." Even the Lord's reproofs and discipline bring satisfaction, because they are signs of our Father's love. "For those whom the Lord loves He disciplines, and He scourges every son whom He receives" (Heb. 12:6).

A final mark of true spiritual hunger is unconditionality. When our spiritual hunger and thirst are genuine they will make no conditions; they will seek and accept God's righteousness in whatever way He chooses to provide it and will obey His commands no matter how demanding they may be. The least of God's righteousness is more valuable than the greatest of anything we possess in ourselves or that the world can offer. The rich young ruler wanted only the part of God's kingdom that fit his own plans and desires, and he was therefore unfit for the kingdom. He thirsted more for other things than for the things of God. His conditions for God's blessings barred him from them.

The spiritually hungry do not ask for Christ and economic success, Christ and personal satisfaction, Christ and popularity, or Christ and anything else. They want *only* Christ and what God in His wisdom and love sovereignly provides through Christ—whatever that may or may not be.

The spiritually hungry cry, "My soul is crushed with longing after Thine ordinances at all times" (Ps. 119:20), and they confess, "At night my soul longs for Thee, indeed, my spirit within me seeks Thee diligently" (Isa. 26:9).

Happy Are the Merciful (5:7)

17

Blessed are the merciful, for they shall receive mercy. (5:7)

The first four beatitudes deal entirely with inner principles, principles of the heart and mind. They are concerned with the way we see ourselves before God. The last four are outward manifestations of those attitudes. Those who in poverty of spirit recognize their need of mercy are led to show mercy to others (v. 7). Those who mourn over their sin are led to purity of heart (v. 8). Those who are meek always seek to make peace (v. 9). And those who hunger and thirst for righteousness are never unwilling to pay the price of being persecuted for righteousness' sake (v. 10).

The concept of mercy is seen throughout Scripture, from the Fall to the consummation of history at the return of Christ. Mercy is a desperately needed gift of God's providential and redemptive work on behalf of sinners—and the Lord requires His people to follow His example by extending mercy to others.

To discover its essence we will look at three basic aspects of mercy: its meaning, its source, and its practice.

THE MEANING OF MERCY

For the most part, the days in which Jesus lived and taught were not characterized by mercy. The Jewish religionists themselves were not inclined to show mercy, because mercy is not characteristic of those who are proud, self-righteous, and judgmental. To many—perhaps most—of Jesus' hearers, showing mercy was considered one of the least of virtues, if it was thought to be a virtue at all. It was in the same category as love—reserved for those who had shown the virtue to you. You loved those who loved you, and you showed mercy to those who showed mercy to you. That attitude was condemned by Jesus later in the Sermon on the Mount. "You have heard that it was said, 'You shall love your neighbor, and hate your enemy'" (Matt. 5:43). But such a shallow, selfish kind of love that even the outcast tax-gatherers practiced (v. 46) was not acceptable to the Savior. He said, "Love your enemies, and pray for those who persecute you in order that you may be sons of your Father who is in heaven. . . . For if you love those who love you, what reward have you? . . . And if you greet your brothers only, what do you do more than others? Do not even the Gentiles do the same?" (vv. 44-47).

Yet many people have interpreted this beatitude in another way that is just as selfish and humanistic: they maintain that our being merciful causes those around us, especially those to whom we show mercy, to be merciful to us. Mercy given will mean mercy received. For such people, mercy is shown to others purely in an effort toward self-seeking.

The ancient rabbi Gamaliel is quoted in the Talmud as saying, "Whenever thou hast mercy, God will have mercy upon thee, and if thou hast not mercy, neither will God have mercy on thee." Gamaliel's idea is right. When God is involved there will be mercy for mercy. "If you forgive men for their transgressions," Jesus said, "your heavenly Father will also forgive you. But if you do not forgive men, then your Father will not forgive your transgressions" (Matt. 6:14-15).

But as a platitude applied among men, the principle does not work. One writer sentimentally says, "This is the great truth of life: if people see us care, they will care." Yet neither Scripture nor experience bears out that idea. God works that way, but the world does not. With God there is always proper reciprocation, and with interest. If we honor God, He will honor us; if we show mercy to others, especially to His children, He will show even more abundant mercy to us. But that is not the world's way.

A popular Roman philosopher called mercy "the disease of the soul." It was the supreme sign of weakness. Mercy was a sign that you did not have what it takes to be a real man and especially a real Roman. The Romans glorified manly courage, strict justice, firm discipline, and, above all, absolute power. They looked down on mercy, because mercy to them was weakness, and weakness was despised above all other human limitations.

During much of Roman history, a father had the right of *patria opitestas,* of deciding whether or not his newborn child would live or die. As the infant was held up for him to see, the father would turn his thumb up if he wanted the child to live, down if he wanted it to die. If his thumb turned down the child was immediately drowned. Citizens had the same life-or-death power over slaves. At any time and for any reason they could kill and bury a slave, with no fear of arrest or reprisal.

Husbands could even have their wives put to death on the least provocation. Today abortion reflects the same merciless attitude. A society that despises mercy is a society that glorifies brutality.

The underlying motive of self-concern has characterized men in general and societies in general since the Fall. We see it expressed today in such sayings as, "If you don't look out for yourself, no one else will." Such popular proverbs are generally true, because they reflect the basic selfish nature of fallen man. Men are not naturally inclined to repay mercy for mercy.

The best illustration of that fact is the Lord Himself. Jesus Christ was the most merciful human being who ever lived. He reached out to heal the sick, restore the crippled, give sight to the blind, hearing to the deaf, and even life to the dead. He found prostitutes, tax collectors, the debauched and the drunken, and drew them into His circle of love and forgiveness. When the scribes and Pharisees brought the adulteress to Him to see if He would agree to her stoning, He confronted them with their merciless hypocrisy: "He who is without sin among you, let him be the first to throw a stone at her." When no one stepped forward to condemn her, Jesus said to her, "Neither do I condemn you; go your way. From now on sin no more" (John 8:7-11). Jesus wept with the sorrowing and gave companionship to the lonely. He took little children into His arms and blessed them. He was merciful to everyone. He was mercy incarnate, just as He was love incarnate.

Yet what was the response to Jesus' mercy? He shamed the woman's accusers into inaction, but they did not become merciful. By the time the accounts of John 8 ended, Jesus' opponents "picked up stones to throw at Him" (v. 59). When the scribes and Pharisees saw Jesus "eating with the sinners and tax-gatherers," they asked His disciples why their Master associated with such unworthy people (Mark 2:16).

The more Jesus showed mercy, the more He showed up the unmercifulness of the Jewish religious leaders. The more He showed mercy, the more they were determined to put Him out of the way. The ultimate outcome of His mercy was the cross. In Jesus' crucifixion, two merciless systems—merciless government and merciless religion—united to kill Him. Totalitarian Rome joined intolerant Judaism to destroy the Prince of mercy.

The fifth beatitude does not teach that mercy to men brings mercy from men, but that mercy to men brings mercy from God. If we are merciful to others, God will be merciful to us, whether men are or not. God is the subject of the second clause, just as in the other beatitudes. It is God who gives the kingdom of heaven to the poor in spirit, comfort to those who mourn, the earth to the meek, and satisfaction to those who hunger and thirst for righteousness. Those who are **merciful . . . shall receive mercy** from God. God gives the divine blessings to those who obey His divine standards.

Merciful is from *eleēmōn*, from which we also get eleemosynary, meaning beneficial or charitable. Hebrews 2:17 speaks of Jesus as our "merciful and faithful high priest." Christ is the supreme example of mercy and the supreme dispenser of mercy. It is from Jesus Christ that both redeeming and sustaining mercy come.

In the Septuagint (the Greek Old Testament) the same term is used to translate the Hebrew *ḥesed,* one of the most commonly used words to describe God's character. It is usually translated as mercy, love, lovingkindness, or steadfast love (Ps. 17:7; 51:1; Isa. 63:7; Jer. 9:24; etc.). The basic meaning is to give help to the afflicted and to rescue the helpless. It is compassion in action.

Jesus is not speaking of detached or powerless sentiment that is unwilling or unable to help those for whom there is sympathy. Nor is He speaking of the false mercy, the feigned pity, that gives help only to salve a guilty conscience or to impress others with its appearance of virtue. And it is not passive, silent concern which, though genuine, is unable to give tangible help. It is genuine compassion expressed in genuine help, selfless concern expressed in selfless deeds.

Jesus says in effect, "The people in My kingdom are not takers but givers, not pretending helpers but practical helpers. They are not condemners but mercy givers." The selfish, self-satisfied, and self-righteous do not bother to help anyone—unless they think something is in it for them. Sometimes they even justify their lack of love and mercy under the guise of religious duty. Once when the Pharisees and scribes questioned why His disciples did not observe the traditions of the elders, Jesus replied, "Moses said, 'Honor your father and your mother'; and 'He who speaks evil of father or mother, let him be put to death'; but you say, 'If a man says to his father or his mother, anything of mine you might have been helped by is Corban (that is to say, given to God),' you no longer permit him to do anything for his father or his mother; thus invalidating the word of God by your tradition which you have handed down" (Mark 7:10-13). In the name of hypocritical religious tradition, compassion toward parents in such a case was actually forbidden.

Mercy is meeting people's needs. It is not simply feeling compassion but showing compassion, not only sympathizing but giving a helping hand. Mercy is giving food to the hungry, comfort to the bereaved, love to the rejected, forgiveness to the offender, companionship to the lonely. It is therefore one of the loveliest and noblest of all virtues.

In Shakespeare's *The Merchant of Venice* (4.1.180-85) Portia says,

> The quality of mercy is not strain'd;
> It droppeth, as the gentle rain from heaven,
> Upon the place beneath: it is twice bless'd.
> It blesseth him that gives, and him that takes:
> 'Tis mightiest in the mightiest; it becomes
> The throned monarch better than his crown:

MERCY AND FORGIVENESS

A clearer understanding of mercy can be gained by working through some comparisons. Mercy has much in common with forgiveness but is distinct from it.

Paul tells us that Jesus "saved us, not on the basis of deeds which we have done in righteousness, but according to His mercy, by the washing of regeneration and renewing by the Holy Spirit" (Titus 3:5). God's forgiveness of our sins flows from His mercy. But mercy is bigger than forgiveness, because God is merciful to us even when we do not sin, just as we can be merciful to those who have never done anything against us. God's mercy does not just forgive our transgressions, but reaches to all our weakness and need.

"The Lord's lovingkindnesses [mercies, KJV] indeed never cease, for His compassions never fail. They are new every morning; great is Thy faithfulness" (Lam. 3:22). God's mercy to His children never ceases.

MERCY AND LOVE

Forgiveness flows out of mercy, and mercy flows out of love. "But God, being rich in mercy, because of His great love with which He loved us, even when we were dead in our transgressions, made us alive together with Christ" (Eph. 2:4-5). Just as mercy is more than forgiveness, love is more than mercy. Love manifests itself in many ways that do not involve either forgiveness or mercy. Love loves even when there is no wrong to forgive or need to meet. The Father loves the Son and the Son loves the Father, although they both are without sin and without need. They both love the holy angels, although the angels are without sin and need. When we enter heaven we, too, will be without sin or need, yet God's love for us will, in comparison to eternity, only be just beginning.

Mercy is the physician; love is the friend. Mercy acts because of need; love acts because of affection, whether there is need or not. Mercy is reserved for times of trouble; love is constant. There can be no true mercy apart from love, but there can be true love apart from mercy.

MERCY AND GRACE

Mercy is also related to grace, which flows out of love just as forgiveness flows out of mercy. In each of his three pastoral epistles Paul includes the words "grace, mercy and peace" in his salutations (1 Tim. 1:2; 2 Tim. 1:2; Titus 1:4, KJV). Grace and mercy have the closest possible relationship; yet they are different. Mercy and its related terms all have to do with pain, misery, and distress—with the consequences of sin. Whether because of our individual sins or because of the sinful world in which we live, all of our problems, in the last analysis, are sin problems. It is with those problems that mercy gives help. Grace, on the other hand, deals with sin itself. Mercy deals with the symptoms, grace with the cause. Mercy offers relief from punishment; grace offers pardon for the crime. Mercy eliminates the pain; grace cures the disease.

When the good Samaritan bound up the wounds of the man who had been beaten and robbed, he showed mercy. When he took him to the nearest inn and paid for his lodging until he was well, he showed grace. His mercy relieved the pain; his grace provided for healing.

Mercy relates to the negative; grace relates to the positive. In relation to salvation, mercy says, "No hell," whereas grace says, "Heaven." Mercy says, "I pity you"; grace says, "I pardon you."

MERCY AND JUSTICE

Mercy is also related to justice, although, on the surface, they seem to be incompatible. Justice gives exactly what is deserved; whereas mercy gives less punishment and more help than is deserved. It is difficult, therefore, for some people to understand how God can be both just and merciful at the same time to the same person. If God is completely just, how could He ever not punish sin totally? For Him to be merciful would seem to negate His justice. The truth is that God does *not* show mercy without punishing sin; and for Him to offer mercy without punishment *would* negate His justice.

Mercy that ignores sin is false mercy and is no more merciful than it is just. It is that sort of false mercy that Saul showed to King Agag after God had clearly instructed Saul to kill every Amalekite (1 Sam. 15:3, 9). It is that sort of false mercy that David showed to his rebellious and wicked son Absalom when he was young. Because David did not deal with Absalom's sin, his attitude toward his son was unrighteous sentimentality, neither justice nor mercy—and it served to confirm Absalom in his wickedness.

That sort of false mercy is common in our day. It is thought to be unloving and unkind to hold people responsible for their sins. But that is a cheap grace that is not just and is not merciful, that offers neither punishment nor pardon for sin. And because it merely overlooks sin, it leaves sin; and the one who relies on that sort of mercy is left in his sin. To cancel justice is to cancel mercy. To ignore sin is to deny the truth; and mercy and truth are inseparable, they "are met together" (Ps. 85:10, KJV). In every true act of mercy, someone pays the price. God did, the Good Samaritan did, and so do we. To be merciful is to bear the load for someone else.

To expect to enter the sphere of God's mercy without repenting from our sin is but wishful thinking. And for the church to offer hope of God's mercy apart from repentance from sin is to offer false hope through a false gospel. God offers nothing but merciless judgment to those who will not turn from their sin to the Savior. Neither relying on good works nor relying on God's overlooking sin will bring salvation. Neither trusting in personal goodness nor presuming on God's goodness will bring entrance into the kingdom. Those who do not come to God on His terms have no claim on His mercy.

God's mercy is grounded not only in His love but in His justice. It is not grounded in sentiment but in Christ's atoning blood, which paid the penalty for and cleanses from sin those who believe in Him. Without being punished and removed, even the least of our sin would eternally separate us from God.

The good news of the gospel is that Christ paid the penalty for all sins in order that God might be merciful to all sinners. On the cross Jesus satisfied God's justice, and when a person trusts in that satisfying sacrifice God opens the floodgates of His mercy. The good news of the gospel is not that God winked at justice, glossed over sin, and compromised righteousness. The good news is that in the shedding of Christ's blood justice was satisfied, sin was forgiven, righteousness was fulfilled, and mercy was made available. There is never an excuse for sin, but always a remedy.

Mercy, therefore, is more than forgiveness and less than love. It is different from grace and is one with justice. And what is true of God's mercy should be true of ours.

Mercy led Abraham to rescue his selfish nephew Lot from Chedorlaomer and his allies. Mercy led Joseph to forgive his brothers and to provide them food for their families. Mercy led Moses to plead with the Lord to remove the leprosy with which his sister Miriam had been punished. Mercy led David to spare the life of Saul.

Those who are unmerciful will not receive mercy from God. In one of his imprecatory psalms David says of an unnamed wicked man, "Let the iniquity of his fathers be remembered before the Lord, and do not let the sin of his mother be blotted out. Let them be before the Lord continually, that He may cut off their memory from the earth." David's anger was not vengeful or retaliatory. That man and his family did not deserve mercy because they were not themselves merciful. "He did not remember to show lovingkindness, but persecuted the afflicted and needy man, and the despondent in heart, to put them to death" (Ps. 109:14-16).

Paul characterizes godless men as unrighteous, wicked, greedy, evil, envious, murderous, deceitful, malicious, gossiping, slanderous, haters of God, insolent, arrogant, boastful, disobedient to parents, without understanding, untrustworthy, and unloving. The climaxing evil of that long list, however, is being unmerciful (Rom. 1:29-31). Mercilessness is the capstone marking those who reject God's mercy.

"The merciful man does himself good, but the cruel man does himself harm" (Prov. 11:17). The way to happiness is through mercy; the way to misery is through cruelty. The truly merciful person is even kind to animals, whereas the merciless person is cruel to everything. "A righteous man has regard for the life of his beast, but the compassion of the wicked is cruel" (Prov. 12:10).

In His Olivet discourse Jesus warned that those who claim to belong to Him but who have not served and shown compassion on the hungry, the thirsty, the stranger, the naked, the sick, and the imprisoned will not be allowed to enter His kingdom. He will say to them, "Depart from Me, accursed ones, into the eternal fire which has been prepared for the devil and his angels; for I was hungry, and you gave Me nothing to eat; I was thirsty, and you gave Me nothing to drink; I was a stranger, and you did not invite Me in; naked, and you did not clothe Me; sick, and in prison, and you did not visit Me." When they say, " 'Lord, when did we see You hungry,' . . . He will answer them, saying, 'Truly I say to you, to the extent that you did not do it to one of the least of these, you did not do it to Me' " (Matt. 25:41-45).

James writes, "Whoever keeps the whole law and yet stumbles in one point, he has become guilty of all. For He who said, 'Do not commit adultery,' also said, 'Do not commit murder.' Now if you do not commit adultery, but do commit murder, you have become a transgressor of the law. So speak and so act, as those who are to be judged by the law of liberty. For judgment will be merciless to one who has shown no mercy" (James 2:10-13a).

In the midst of our corrupt, ego-centered, and selfish society that tells us to grab everything we can get, the voice of God tells us to give everything we can give. The true character of mercy is in giving—giving compassion, giving help, giving time, giving forgiveness, giving money, giving ourselves. The children of the King are merciful. Those who are merciless face judgment; but "mercy triumphs over judgment" (James 2:13b).

The Source of Mercy

Pure mercy is a gift of God. It is not a natural attribute of man but is a gift that comes with the new birth. We can be merciful in its full sense and with a righteous motive only when we have experienced God's mercy. Mercy is only for those who through grace and divine power have met the requirements of the first four beatitudes. It is only for those who by the work of the Holy Spirit bow humbly before God in poverty of spirit, who mourn over and turn from their sin, who are meek and submissive to His control, and who hunger and thirst above all else for His righteousness. The way of mercy is the way of humility, repentance, surrender, and holiness.

Balaam continually prostituted his ministry, trying to keep within the letter of God's will while conspiring with a pagan king against God's people. He presumptuously prayed, "Let me die the death of the upright, and let my end be like his!" (Num. 23:10). As one Puritan commentator observed, Balaam wanted to die like the righteous, but he did not want to live like the righteous. Many people want God's mercy but not on God's terms.

God has both absolute and relative attributes. His absolute attributes— such as love, truth, and holiness—have characterized Him from all eternity. They were characteristic of Him before He created angels, or the world, or man. But His relative attributes—such as mercy, justice, and grace—were not expressed until His creatures came into being. In fact they were not manifest until man, the creature made in His own image, sinned and became separated from his Creator. Apart from sin and evil, mercy, justice, and grace have no meaning.

When man fell, God's love was extended to His fallen creatures in mercy. And only when they receive His mercy can they reflect His mercy. God is the source of mercy. "For as high as the heavens are above the earth, so great is His lovingkindness [mercy] toward those who fear Him" (Ps. 103:11). It is because we have the resource of God's mercy that Jesus commanded, "Be merciful, just as your Father is merciful" (Luke 6:36).

Donald Barnhouse writes,

> When Jesus Christ died on the cross, all the work of God for man's salvation passed out of the realm of prophecy and became historical fact. God has now had mercy upon us. For anyone to pray, "God have mercy on me" is the equivalent of asking Him to repeat the sacrifice of Christ. All the mercy that God ever will have on man He has already had, when Christ died. That is the totality of mercy. There could not be any more. . . . The fountain is now opened, and it is flowing, and it continues to flow freely. (*Romans* [Grand Rapids: Eerdmans, 1983], 4:4)

We cannot have the blessing apart from the Blesser. We cannot even meet the condition apart from the One who has set the condition. We are **blessed** by God when we are **merciful** to others, and we are able to be merciful to others because we have already received salvation's mercy. And when we share the mercy received, we **shall receive mercy** even beyond what we already have.

We never sing more truthfully than when we sing, "Mercy there was great and grace was free; pardon there was multiplied to me; there my burdened soul found liberty, at Calvary."

THE PRACTICE OF MERCY

The most obvious way we can show mercy is through physical acts, as did the good Samaritan. As Jesus specifically commands, we are to feed the hungry, clothe the naked, visit the sick and imprisoned, and give any other practical help that is needed. In serving others in need, we demonstrate a heart of mercy.

It is helpful to note that the way of mercy did not begin with the New Testament. God has always intended for mercy to characterize His people. The Old Testament law taught, "You shall not harden your heart, nor close your hand from your poor brother; but you shall freely open your hand to him, and shall generously lend him sufficient for his need in whatever he lacks" (Deut. 15:7-8). Even in the year of release, when all debts were canceled, Israelites were to give their poor countrymen whatever they needed. They were warned, "Beware, lest there is a base thought in your heart, saying 'The seventh year, the year of remission, is near,' and your eye is hostile toward your poor brother, and you give him nothing" (v. 9).

Mercy is also to be shown in our attitudes. Mercy does not hold a grudge, harbor resentment, capitalize on another's failure or weakness, or publicize another's sin. On a great table at which he fed countless hundreds of people, Augustine inscribed,

> Whoever thinks that he is able,
> To nibble at the life of absent friends,
> Must know that he's unworthy of this table.

The vindictive, heartless, indifferent are not subjects of Christ's kingdom. When they pass need by on the other side, as the priest and the Levite did in the story of the good Samaritan, they show they have passed Christ by.

Mercy is also to be shown spiritually. First, it is shown through pity. Augustine said, "If I weep for the body from which the soul is departed, should I not weep for the soul from which God is departed?" The sensitive Christian will grieve more for lost souls than for lost bodies. Because we have experienced God's mercy, we are to have great concern for those who have not.

Jesus' last words from the cross were words of mercy. For His executioners He prayed, "Father, forgive them; for they do not know what they are doing" (Luke 23:34). To the penitent thief hanging beside Him He said, "Truly I say to you, today you shall be with Me in Paradise" (v. 43). To His mother He said, "'Woman, behold your son!' Then He said to the disciple [John], 'Behold, your mother!' And from that hour the disciple took her into his own household" (John 19:26-27). Like his Master, Stephen prayed for those who were taking his life, "Lord, do not hold this sin against them!" (Acts 7:60).

Second, we are to show spiritual mercy by confrontation. Paul says that, as Christ's servants, we should gently correct "those who are in opposition, if perhaps God may grant them repentance leading to the knowledge of the truth" (2 Tim. 2:25). We are to be willing to confront others about their sin in order that they might come to God for salvation. When certain teachers were "upsetting whole families, teaching things they should not teach, for the sake of sordid gain," Paul told Titus to "reprove them severely that they may be sound in the faith" (Titus 1:11, 13). Love and mercy will be severe when that is necessary for the sake of an erring brother and for the sake of Christ's church. In such cases it is cruel to say nothing and let the harm continue.

As Jude closed his letter with the encouragement to "keep yourselves in the love of God, waiting anxiously for the mercy of our Lord Jesus Christ to eternal life," he also admonished, "And have mercy on some, who are doubting; save others, snatching them out of the fire; and on some have mercy with fear, hating even the garment polluted by the flesh" (Jude 21-23). Extreme situations require extreme care, but we are to show mercy even to those trapped in the worst systems of apostasy.

Third, we are to show spiritual mercy by praying. The sacrifice of prayer for those without God is an act of mercy. Our mercy can be measured by our prayer for the unsaved and for Christians who are walking in disobedience.

Fourth, we are to show spiritual mercy by proclaiming the saving gospel of Jesus Christ—the most merciful thing we can do.

THE RESULT OF MERCY

Reflecting on the fact that when we are **merciful** we **receive mercy**, we see God's cycle of mercy. God is merciful to us by saving us through Christ; in obedience we are merciful to others; and God in faithfulness gives us even more mercy, pouring out blessing for our needs and withholding severe chastening for our sin.

As in the other beatitudes, the emphatic pronoun *autos* (**they**) indicates that *only* those who are merciful qualify to **receive mercy**. David sang of the Lord, "With the kind Thou dost show Thyself kind" (2 Sam. 22:26). Speaking of the opposite side of the same truth, James says, "For judgment will be merciless to one who has shown no mercy" (James 2:13). At the end of the disciples' prayer Jesus explained, "For if you forgive men for their transgressions, your heavenly Father will also forgive you. But if you do not forgive men, then your Father will not forgive your transgressions" (Matt. 6:14-15). Again the emphatic truth is that God will respond with chastening for an unforgiving disciple.

Neither in that passage nor in this beatitude is Jesus speaking of our mercy gaining us salvation. We do not earn salvation by being merciful. We must be saved by God's mercy before we can truly *be* merciful. We cannot work our way into heaven even by a lifetime of merciful deeds, any more than by good works of any sort. God does not give mercy for merit; He gives mercy in grace, because it is needed, not because it is earned.

To illustrate the working of God's mercy Jesus told the parable of a slave who had been graciously forgiven a great debt by the king. The man then went to a fellow slave who owed him a pittance by comparison and demanded that every cent be repaid and had him thrown into prison. When the king heard of the incident, he called the first man to him and said, "'You wicked slave, I forgave you all that debt because you entreated me. Should you not also have had mercy on your fellow slave, even as I had mercy on you?' And his lord, moved with anger, handed him over to the torturers until he should repay all that was owed him. So shall My heavenly Father also do to you, if each of you does not forgive his brother from your heart" (Matt. 18:23-35).

In that parable Jesus gives a picture of God's saving mercy in relation to forgiving others (vv. 21-22). The first man pleaded with God for mercy and received it. The fact that he, in turn, was unmerciful was so inconsistent with his own salvation that he was chastened until he repented. The Lord will chasten, if need be, to produce repentance in a stubborn child. Mercy to others is a mark of salvation. When we do not show it, we may be disciplined until we do. When we hold back mercy, God restricts His flow of mercy to us, and we forfeit blessing. The presence of chastening and the absence of blessing attend an unmerciful believer.

If we have received from a holy God unlimited mercy that cancels our unpayable debt of sin—we who had no righteousness but were poor in spirit, mourning over our load of sin in beggarly, helpless condition, wretched and doomed, meek before almighty God, hungry and thirsty for a righteousness we did not have and could not attain—it surely follows that we should be merciful to others.

Happy Are the Holy (5:8)

18

Blessed are the pure in heart, for they shall see God. (5:8)

Here is one of those passages of Scripture whose depths are immeasurable and whose breadth is impossible to encompass. This incredible statement of Jesus is among the greatest utterances in all of the Bible.

The subject of holiness, of purity of heart, can be traced from Genesis to Revelation. The theme is infinitely vast and touches on virtually every other biblical truth. It is impossible to exhaust its meaning or significance, and the discussion in this chapter is nothing more than introductory.

THE CONTEXT

THE HISTORICAL CONTEXT

As discussed in some detail in earlier chapters, when Jesus began His earthly ministry, Israel was in desperate condition—politically, economically, and spiritually. For hundreds of years, with only brief respites, she had been under the oppression of foreign conquerors. The country had limited freedom to develop its economy, and a large part of income and profit was paid to Rome in taxes. Those were problems that every person saw and felt.

The less obvious problem, however, was by far the worst. For longer than she had suffered political and economic oppression, Israel had suffered spiritual weakness and faithlessness. Yet that problem was not recognized by many Jews. Jewish leaders thought their religion was in fine shape, and believed the Messiah would soon solve the political and economic problems. But when He came, His only concern was for the spiritual problem, the problem of their hearts.

At the time of Christ the most influential religious force in Judaism was the Pharisees. They were the chief managers and promoters of the pervasive legalistic and ritualistic system that dominated Jewish society. Over the centuries various rabbis had interpreted and reinterpreted the Jewish Scriptures, especially the law, until those interpretations—known as the traditions of the elders—became more authoritative than Scripture itself. The essence of the traditions was a system of dos and don'ts that gradually expanded to cover almost every aspect of Jewish life.

To conscientious and honest Jews it had become obvious that total observance of all the religious requirements was impossible. Because they could not keep all of the law, they doubtlessly developed terrible feelings of guilt, frustration, and anxiety. Their religion was their life, but they could not fulfill everything their religion demanded. Consequently, some of the religious leaders devised the idea that, if a person could perfectly keep just a few of the laws, God would understand. When even that proved impossible, some narrowed the requirement to one law perfectly kept.

That idea may have been in the mind of the lawyer who tested Jesus with the question, "Teacher, which is the great commandment in the Law?" (Matt. 22:36). Perhaps he wanted to see which of the many hundreds of laws Jesus believed was the single most important one to keep—the one that would satisfy God even if a person failed to keep the others.

This oppressive and confusing religious system probably contributed to the initial popularity of John the Baptist. He was radically different from the scribes, Pharisees, Sadducees, and priests, and it was obvious that he did not bother to observe most of the religious traditions. He was a breath of fresh air in a stifling, never-ending system of demands and prohibitions. Perhaps in this prophet's teaching they would find some relief. They did not want another rabbi with another law, but someone who could show them how to be forgiven for those laws they had already broken. They wanted to know the real way of salvation, the real way to please God, the true way of peace and relief from sin. They knew that the Scriptures taught of One who would come not simply to demand but to redeem, not to add to their burdens but to help carry them, not to increase their guilt but to remove it. No doubt it was such expectations as those that caused many people to think John the Baptist might be the Messiah.

The people knew from Ezekiel that someday God was going to come and sprinkle their souls with water, cleanse them from their sin, and replace their hearts of stone with hearts of flesh (Ezek. 36:25-26). They knew the testimony of David, who cried out, "How blessed is he whose transgression is forgiven, whose sin is covered! How blessed is the man to whom the Lord does not impute iniquity, and in whose spirit there is no deceit!" (Ps. 32:1-2). They knew of those truths, and they longed to experience the reality of them.

Nicodemus was one such person. He was a Pharisee and "a ruler of the Jews," that is, a member of the Sanhedrin, the Jewish high court. We are not told specifically what his intentions were in coming to Jesus, because his first words were not a question but a testimony. The fact that he came at night suggests he was ashamed of being seen with Jesus. But there is no reason to doubt the sincerity of his words, which showed unusual spiritual insight: "Rabbi, we know that You have come from God as a teacher; for no one can do these signs that You do unless God is with him" (John 3:2). Nicodemus knew that, whatever else Jesus might be, He was a teacher truly sent from God.

Though he does not state it, the question that was on his mind is implied both from his testimony and from Jesus' reply. The Lord knew Nicodemus's mind, and He said to him, "Truly, truly, I say to you, unless one is born again, he cannot see the kingdom of God" (v. 3). Nicodemus wanted to know how to please God, to be forgiven. "How can I be made righteous?" he wondered. "How can I be redeemed and become a child of God? How can I become part of God's kingdom?" Had he not had a deep, compelling desire to know God's will, he would not have risked coming to Jesus even at night. Nicodemus was honest enough to admit his sinfulness. He was a Pharisee, a teacher of the law, and a ruler in the Sanhedrin; but he knew in his heart that all of that did not make him right with God.

After Jesus had fed the great multitude near the Sea of Galilee, some of the people who had seen the miracle asked Jesus, "What shall we do, that we may work the works of God?" (John 6:28). The same question troubled them that had troubled Nicodemus: "How can a person get right with God? What must we do to truly please Him?" Like Nicodemus, they had been through all the ceremonies and rituals. They had attended the feasts and offered the required sacrifices. They had tried to keep the law and the traditions. But they knew that something was missing—something crucial that they did not know of, much less had experienced.

Luke tells of another lawyer who asked Jesus, "Teacher, what shall I do to inherit eternal life?" (Luke 10:25). He asked the question to test Jesus (v. 25*a*), and after Jesus gave an answer the man tried "to justify himself" (v. 29). But despite his insincerity, he had asked the right question, the question that was on the minds of many Jews who *were* sincere.

A rich ruler asked Jesus the same question: "Good Teacher, what shall I do to inherit eternal life?" (Luke 18:18). This man apparently asked sincerely, but he was unwilling to pay the cost. He wanted to keep the wealth of this life more than he wanted to gain the wealth of eternal life, and he went away "very sad" (v. 23). He knew he needed something more than outward obedience to the law, at which he had been diligent since childhood (v. 21). He knew that, with all his devotion and effort to please God, he had no assurance of possessing eternal life. He was seeking the kingdom, but he was not seeking it first (Matt. 6:33).

Others were asking, "What must I be to belong to the kingdom of God? What is the standard for eternal life?" All of those people, at various levels of understanding and sincerity, knew that they had not found what they sought. Many knew that they had not kept even a single law perfectly. If honest, they became more and more convinced that they *could* not keep even a single law perfectly, and that they were powerless to please God.

It was to answer that need that Jesus came to earth. It was to answer that need that He gave the Beatitudes. He shows simply and directly how sinful man can be made right with holy God.

THE LITERARY CONTEXT

At first glance this beatitude seems out of place, inserted indiscriminately into an otherwise orderly development of truths. Because of its supreme importance, a more strategic place—either at the beginning as the foundation, or at the end as the culmination—might seem more appropriate.

But the sixth beatitude, like every part of God's Word, is in the right place. It is part of the beautiful and marvelous sequence of truths that are here laid out according to the mind of God. It is the climax of the Beatitudes, the central truth to which the previous five lead and from which the following two flow.

THE MEANING

Blessed are the pure in heart, for they shall see God. (5:8)

The word **blessed** implies the condition of well-being that results from salvation, the status of one who has a right relation to God. Being accepted by Him is a matter of internal transformation.

Heart translates *kardia,* from which we get cardiac and similar terms. Throughout Scripture, as well as in many languages and cultures throughout the world, the heart is used metaphorically to represent the inner person, the seat of motives and attitudes, the center of personality. But in Scripture it represents much more than emotion, feelings. It also includes the thinking process and particularly the will. In Proverbs we are told, "As [a man] thinketh in his heart, so is he" (Prov. 23:7, KJV). Jesus asked a group of scribes, "Why are you thinking evil in your hearts?" (Matt. 9:4; cf. Mark 2:8; 7:21). The heart is the control center of mind and will as well as emotion.

In total contrast to the outward, superficial, and hypocritical religion of the scribes and Pharisees, Jesus said that it is in the inner man, in the core of his very being, that God requires purity. That was not a new truth, but an old one long forgotten amidst ceremony and tradition. "Watch over your heart with all diligence, for from it flow the springs of life," the writer of Proverbs had counseled (Prov. 4:23). The problem that caused God to destroy the earth in the Flood was a heart problem. "Then the Lord saw that the wickedness of man was great on the earth, and that every intent of the thoughts of his heart was only evil continually" (Gen. 6:5).

David acknowledged before the Lord, "Behold, Thou dost desire truth in the innermost being, and in the hidden part Thou wilt make me know wisdom"; and then he prayed "Create in me a clean heart, O God, and renew a steadfast spirit within me" (Ps. 51:6, 10). Asaph wrote, "Surely God is good to Israel, to those who are pure in heart!" (Ps. 73:1). Jeremiah declared, "The heart is more deceitful than all else and is desperately sick; who can understand it? I, the Lord, search the heart, I test the mind, even to give to each man according to his ways, according to the results of his deeds" (Jer. 17:9-10). Evil ways and deeds begin in the heart and mind, which are here used synonymously. Jesus said, "For out of the heart come evil thoughts, murders, adulteries, fornications, thefts, false witness, slanders. These are the things which defile the man" (Matt. 15:19).

God has always been concerned above all else with the inside of man, with the condition of his heart. When the Lord called Saul to be Israel's first king, "God changed his heart" (1 Sam. 10:9). Until then Saul had been handsome, athletic, and not much more. But the new king soon began to revert to his old heart patterns. He chose to disobey God and to trust in himself. Among other things, he presumed to take for himself the priestly role of offering sacrifice (13:9) and refused to destroy all of the Amalekites and their possessions as God had commanded (15:3-19). Consequently, the Lord took the kingdom from Saul and gave it to David (15:23, 28). Saul's actions were wrong because his heart rebelled, and it is by our hearts that the Lord judges us (16:7). It was said of David's leadership over Israel, "He shepherded them according to the integrity of his heart, and guided them with his skillful hands" (Ps. 78:72).

God took the kingdom from Saul because he refused to live by the new heart God had given him. He gave the kingdom to David because David was "a man after [God's] own heart" (1 Sam. 13:14). David pleased God's heart because God pleased David's heart. "I will give thanks to the Lord with all my heart," he sang (Ps. 9:1). His deepest desire was, "Let the words of my mouth and the meditation of my heart be acceptable in Thy sight, O Lord, my rock and my Redeemer" (Ps. 19:14). He prayed, "Examine me, O Lord, and try me; test my mind and my heart" (Ps. 26:2). When God told David, "Seek My face," David's heart replied, "Thy face, O Lord, I shall seek" (Ps. 27:8).

Once when David was fleeing from Saul he went to Gath, a Philistine city, for help. When he realized that his life was also in danger there, he "acted insanely in their hands, and scribbled on the doors of the gate, and let his saliva run down into his beard" (1 Sam. 21:13). Thinking him to be mad, the Philistines let him go, and he went to hide in the cave of Adullum. He came to his senses and realized how foolish and unfaithful he had been to trust the Philistines for help instead of the Lord. It was there that he wrote Psalm 57, in which he declared, "My heart is steadfast, O God, my heart is steadfast" (v. 7). He rededicated his heart, his innermost being, single-mindedly to God. David often failed, but his heart was fixed on God. The evidence of his true-hearted commitment to God is found in all the first 175 verses of Psalm 119. The fact that his flesh sometimes overruled his heart is the final admission of verse 176: "I have gone astray like a lost sheep; seek Thy servant."

Pure translates *katharos,* a form of the word from which we get catharsis. The basic meaning is to make pure by cleansing from dirt, filth, and contamination. Catharsis is a term used in psychology and counseling for a cleansing of the mind or emotions. The Greek word is related to the Latin *castus,* from which we get chaste. The related word chasten refers to discipline given in order to cleanse from wrong behavior.

The Greek term was often used of metals that had been refined until all impurities were removed, leaving only the pure metal. In that sense, purity means unmixed, unalloyed, unadulterated. Applied to the heart, the idea is that of pure motive—of single-mindedness, undivided devotion, spiritual integrity, and true righteousness.

Double-mindedness has always been one of the great plagues of the church. We want to serve the Lord and follow the world at the same time. But that, says Jesus, is impossible. "No one can serve two masters; for either he will hate the one and love the other, or he will hold to one and despise the other" (Matt. 6:24). James puts the same truth in another way: "Do you not know that friendship with the world is hostility toward God? Therefore whoever wishes to be a friend of the world makes himself an enemy of God" (James 4:4). He then gives the solution to the problem: "Cleanse your hands, you sinners; and purify your hearts, you double-minded" (v. 8).

Christians have the right heart motive concerning God. Even though we often fail to be single-minded, it is our deep desire to be so. We confess with Paul, "For that which I am doing, I do not understand; for I am not practicing what I would like to do, but I am doing the very thing I hate. . . . I find then the principle that evil is present in me, the one who wishes to do good. . . . So then, on the one hand I myself with my mind am serving the law of God, but on the other, with my flesh the law of sin" (Rom. 7:15, 21, 25). Paul's deepest spiritual desires were pure, although the sin dwelling in his flesh sometimes overrode those desires.

Those who truly belong to God will be motivated to purity. Psalm 119 is the classic illustration of that longing, and Romans 7:15-25 is the Pauline counterpart. The deepest desire of the redeemed is for holiness, even when sin halts the fulfillment of that desire.

Purity of heart is more than sincerity. A motive can be sincere, yet lead to worthless and sinful things. The pagan priests who opposed Elijah demonstrated great sincerity when they lacerated their bodies in order to induce Baal to send fire down to consume their sacrifices (1 Kings 18:28). But their sincerity did not produce the desired results, and it did not enable them to see the wrongness of their paganism—because their sincere trust was in that very paganism. Sincere devotees walk on nails to prove their spiritual power. Others crawl on their knees for hundreds of yards, bleeding and grimacing in pain, to show their devotion to a saint or a shrine. Yet their sincere devotion is sincerely wrong and is completely worthless before God.

The scribes and Pharisees believed they could please God by such superficial practices as tithing "mint and dill and cummin"; but they "neglected the weightier provisions of the law: justice and mercy and faithfulness" (Matt. 23:23). They were meticulously careful about what they did outwardly but paid no attention to what they were inwardly. "Woe to you, scribes and Pharisees, hypocrites!" Jesus told them, "For you clean the outside of the cup and of the dish, but inside they are full of robbery and self-indulgence. You blind Pharisee, first clean the inside of the cup and of the dish, so that the outside of it may become clean also" (vv. 25-26).

Even genuinely good deeds that do not come from a genuinely good heart are of no spiritual value. Thomas Watson said, "Morality can drown a man as fast as vice," and, "A vessel may sink with gold or with dung." Though we may be extremely religious and constantly engaged in doing good things, we cannot please God unless our hearts are right with Him.

The ultimate standard for purity of heart is perfection of heart. In the same sermon in which He gave the Beatitudes Jesus said, "Therefore you are to be perfect, as your heavenly Father is perfect" (Matt. 5:48). One hundred percent purity is God's standard for the heart.

Man's tendency is to set the opposite standard. We are inclined to judge ourselves by the worst instead of the best. The Pharisee who prayed in the Temple, thanking God that he was not like other men, considered himself to be righteous simply because he was not a swindler, an adulterer, or a tax-gatherer (Luke 18:11). We are all tempted to feel better about ourselves when we see someone doing a terrible thing that we have never done. The "good" person looks down on the one who seems to be less good than himself, and that person looks down on those worse than he is. Carried to its extreme, that spiral of judgment would go down and down until it reached the most rotten person on earth—and that last person, the worst on earth, would be the standard by which the rest of the world judged itself!

God's standard for men, however, is Himself. They cannot be fully pleasing to God until they are pure as He is pure, until they are holy as He is holy and perfect as He is perfect. Only those who are pure in heart may enter the kingdom. "Who may ascend into the hill of the Lord?" David asks, "and who may stand in His holy place? He who has clean hands and a pure heart" (Ps. 24:3-4).

It is impurity of heart that separates man from God. "Behold, the Lord's hand is not so short that it cannot save; neither is His ear so dull that it cannot hear. But your iniquities have made a separation between you and your God, and your sins have hidden His face from you, so that He does not hear" (Isa. 59:1-2). And just as impurity of heart separates men from God, only purity of heart through Jesus Christ will reconcile men to God.

Basically there are but two kinds of religion—the religion of human achievement and the religion of divine accomplishment. There are many variations of the first kind, which includes every religion but biblical Christianity. Within the religions of human accomplishment are two basic approaches: head religion, which trusts in creeds and religious knowledge, and hand religion, which trusts in good deeds.

The only true religion, however, is heart religion, which is based on God's implanted purity. By faith in what God has done through His Son, Jesus Christ, "we have redemption through His blood, the forgiveness of our trespasses, according to the riches of His grace" (Eph. 1:7). When God imputes His righteousness to us He imputes His purity to us.

As we look at Scripture we discover six kinds of purity. One may be called *primal purity,* the kind that exists only in God. That purity is as essential to God as light is to the sun or wetness is to water.

Another form of purity is *created purity,* the purity that existed in God's creation before it was corrupted by the Fall. God created the angels in purity and He created man in purity. Tragically, some of the angels and all of mankind fell from that purity.

A third kind of purity is *positional purity,* the purity we are given the moment we trust in Jesus Christ as Savior. When we trust in Him, God imputes to us Christ's own purity, Christ's own righteousness. "To the one who does not work, but believes in Him who justifies the ungodly, his faith is reckoned as righteousness" (Rom. 4:5; cf. Gal. 2:16). From that day the Father sees us just as He sees the Son, perfectly righteous and without blemish (2 Cor. 5:21; Heb. 9:14).

Fourth, imputed purity is not just a statement without substance; with imputed purity God grants *actual purity* in the new nature of the believer (Rom. 6:4-5; 8:5-11; Col. 3:9-10; 2 Pet. 1:3). In other words, there is no justification without sanctification. Every believer is a new creation (2 Cor. 5:17). Paul affirms that when a believer sins, it is not caused by the pure new self, but by sin in the flesh (Rom. 7:17, 19-22, 25).

Fifth, there is *practical purity.* This, of course, is the hard part, the part that *does* require our supreme effort. Only God possesses or can possess primal purity. Only God can bestow created purity, ultimate purity, positional purity, and actual purity. But practical purity, though it too comes from God, demands our participation in a way that the other kinds of purity do not. That is why Paul implores, "Therefore, having these promises, beloved, let us cleanse ourselves from all defilement of flesh and spirit, perfecting holiness in the fear of God" (2 Cor. 7:1). It is why Peter pleads, "As obedient children, do not be conformed to the former lusts which were yours in your ignorance, but like the Holy One who called you, be holy yourselves also in all your behavior; because it is written, 'You shall be holy, for I am holy'" (1 Pet. 1:14-16).

We are not saved just for future heavenly purity but also for present earthly purity. At best it will be gold mixed with iron and clay, a white garment with some black threads. But God wants us now to be as pure as we can be. If purity does not characterize our living, we either do not belong to Christ, or we are disobedient to Him. We will have temptations, but God will always provide a way of escape (1 Cor. 10:13). We will fall into sin, but "if we confess our sins, He is faithful and righteous to forgive us our sins and to cleanse us from all unrighteousness" (1 John 1:9).

Finally, for believers there will also one day be *ultimate purity,* the perfected purity that God's redeemed people will experience when they are glorified in His presence. All sins will be totally and permanently washed away, and "we shall be like Him, because we shall see Him just as He is" (1 John 3:2).

THE WAY TO HOLINESS

Throughout the history of the church people have suggested various ways to achieve spiritual purity and holiness. Some have suggested monasticism, getting away from the normal cares and distractions of the world and devoting oneself entirely to meditation and prayer. Others claim that holiness is a second work of grace, by which God miraculously eradicates not only sins but the sin nature, allowing a sinless earthly life from that point onward. But neither Scripture nor experience supports either of those views. The problem of sin is not primarily the world around us but the worldliness within us, which we cannot escape by living in isolation from other people.

But God always provides for what He demands, and He has provided ways for us to live purely. First, we must realize that we are unable to live a single holy moment without the Lord's guidance and power. "Who can say, 'I have cleansed my heart, I am pure from my sin'?" (Prov. 20:9), the obvious answer to which is "No one." The Ethiopian cannot change his skin or the leopard its spots (Jer. 13:23). Cleansing begins with a recognition of weakness. Weakness then reaches out for the strength of God.

Second, we must stay in God's Word. It is impossible to stay in God's will apart from His Word. Jesus said, "You are already clean because of the word which I have spoken to you" (John 15:3).

Third, it is essential to be controlled by and walking in the will and way of the Holy Spirit. Galatians 5:16 says it clearly: "Walk by the Spirit, and you will not carry out the desire of the flesh."

Fourth, we must pray. We cannot stay in God's will or understand and obey His Word unless we stay near Him. "With all prayer and petition" we are to "pray at all times in the Spirit" (Eph. 6:18; cf. Luke 18:1; 1 Thess. 5:17). With David we cry, "Create in me a clean heart, O God" (Ps. 51:10).

THE RESULT OF HOLINESS

The great blessing of those who are pure in heart is that **they shall see God.** The Greek is in the future indicative tense and the middle voice, and a more literal translation is, "They shall be continuously seeing God for themselves." It is *only* **they** (the emphatic *autos*), the pure in heart, who **shall see God.** Intimate knowledge of and fellowship with God is reserved for the pure.

When our hearts are purified at salvation we begin to live in the presence of God. We begin to see and to comprehend Him with our new spiritual eyes. Like

Moses, who saw God's glory and asked to see more (Ex. 33:18), the one who is purified by Jesus Christ sees again and again the glory of God.

To see God was the greatest hope of Old Testament saints. Like Moses, David wanted to see more of God. "As the deer pants for the water brooks," he said, "so my soul pants for Thee, O God. My soul thirsts for God, for the living God; when shall I come and appear before God?" (Ps. 42:1). Job rejoiced when he was able to say, "I have heard of Thee by the hearing of the ear; but now my eye sees Thee" (Job 42:5).

Purity of heart cleanses the eyes of the soul so that God becomes visible. One sign of an impure heart is ignorance, because sin obscures the truth (John 3:19-20). Evil and ignorance come in a package. Other signs of an impure heart are self-centeredness (Rev. 3:17), pleasure in sin (2 Tim. 3:4), unbelief (Heb. 3:12), and hatred of purity (Mic. 3:2). Those who belong to God exchange all of those things for integrity and purity.

F. F. Bullard wrote,

> When I in righteousness at last
>   Thy glorious face shall see;
> When all the weary night has passed,
>   And I awake with Thee,
> To view the glories that abide,
>   Then and only then will I be satisfied.

> (Cited in William Hendriksen, *The Gospel of Matthew* [Grand Rapids: Baker, 1973], p. 278)

Happy Are the Peacemakers (5:9)

19

Blessed are the peacemakers, for they shall be called sons of God. (5:9)

The God of peace (Rom. 15:33; 2 Cor. 13:11; Phil. 4:9) has emphasized that cherished but elusive reality by making peace one of the dominant ideas of His Word. Scripture contains four hundred direct references to peace, and many more indirect ones. The Bible opens with peace in the Garden of Eden and closes with peace in eternity. The spiritual history of mankind can be charted based on the theme of peace. Although the peace on earth in the garden was interrupted when man sinned, at the cross Jesus Christ made peace a reality again, and He becomes the peace of all who place their faith in Him. Peace can now reign in the hearts of those who are His. Someday He will come as Prince of Peace and establish a worldwide kingdom of peace, which will eventuate in ultimate peace, the eternal age of peace.

But one of the most obvious facts of history and of human experience is that peace does not characterize man's earthly existence. There is no peace now for two reasons: the opposition of Satan and the disobedience of man. The fall of the angels and the fall of man established a world without peace. Satan and man are engaged with the God of peace in a battle for sovereignty.

The scarcity of peace has prompted someone to suggest that "peace is that glorious moment in history when everyone stops to reload." In 1968 a major newspaper reported that there had been to that date 14,553 known wars since thirty-six years before Christ. Since 1945 there have been some seventy or so wars and nearly two hundred internationally significant outbreaks of violence. Since 1958 nearly one hundred nations have been involved in some form of armed conflict.

Some historians have claimed that the United States has had two generations of peace—one from 1815 to 1846 and the other from 1865 to 1898. But that claim can only be made if you exclude the Indian wars, during which our land was bathed in Indian blood.

With all the avowed and well-intentioned efforts for peace in modern times, few people would claim that the world or any significant part of it is more peaceful now than a hundred years ago. We do not have economic peace, religious peace, racial peace, social peace, family peace, or personal peace. There seems to be no end of marches, sit-ins, rallies, protests, demonstrations, riots, and wars. Disagreement and conflict are the order of the day. No day has had more need of peace than our own.

Nor does the world honor peace as much by its standards and actions as it does by its words. In almost every age of history the greatest heroes have been the greatest warriors. The world lauds the powerful and often exalts the destructive. The model man is not meek but macho. The model hero is not self-giving but self-seeking, not generous but selfish, not gentle but cruel, not submissive but aggressive, not meek but proud.

The popular philosophy of the world, bolstered by the teaching of many psychologists and counselors, is to put self first. But when self is first, peace is last. Self precipitates strife, division, hatred, resentment, and war. It is the great ally of sin and the great enemy of righteousness and, consequently, of peace.

The seventh beatitude calls God's people to be peacemakers. He has called us to a special mission to help restore the peace lost at the Fall.

The peace of which Christ speaks in this beatitude, and about which the rest of Scripture speaks, is unlike that which the world knows and strives for. God's peace has nothing to do with politics, armies and navies, forums of nations, or even councils of churches. It has nothing to do with statesmanship, no matter how great, or with arbitration, compromise, negotiated truces, or treaties. God's peace, the peace of which the Bible speaks, never evades issues; it knows nothing of peace at any price. It does not gloss or hide, rationalize or excuse. It confronts problems and seeks to solve them, and after the problems are solved it builds a bridge between those who were separated by the problems. It often brings its own struggle, pain, hardship, and anguish, because such are often the price of healing. It is not a peace that will be brought by kings, presidents, prime ministers, diplomats, or international humanitarians. It is the inner personal peace that only He can give to the soul of man and that only His children can exemplify.

Four important realities about God's peace are revealed: its meaning, its Maker, its messengers, and its merit.

THE MEANING OF PEACE: RIGHTEOUSNESS AND TRUTH

The essential fact to comprehend is that the peace about which Jesus speaks is more than the absence of conflict and strife; it is the presence of righteousness. Only righteousness can produce the relationship that brings two parties together. Men can stop fighting without righteousness, but they cannot live peaceably without righteousness. Righteousness not only puts an end to harm, but it administers the healing of love.

God's peace not only stops war but replaces it with the righteousness that brings harmony and true well-being. Peace is a creative, aggressive force for goodness. The Jewish greeting *shalom* wishes "peace" and expresses the desire that the one who is greeted will have all the righteousness and goodness God can give. The deepest meaning of the term is "God's highest good to you."

The most that man's peace can offer is a truce, the temporary cessation of hostilities. But whether on an international scale or an individual scale, a truce is seldom more than a cold war. Until disagreements and hatreds are resolved, the conflicts merely go underground—where they tend to fester, grow, and break out again. God's peace, however, not only stops the hostilities but settles the issues and brings the parties together in mutual love and harmony.

James confirms the nature of God's peace when he writes, "But the wisdom from above is first pure, then peaceable" (James 3:17). God's way to peace is through purity. Peace cannot be attained at the expense of righteousness. Two people cannot be at peace until they recognize and resolve the wrong attitudes and actions that caused the conflict between them, and then bring themselves to God for cleansing. Peace that ignores the cleansing that brings purity is not God's peace.

The writer of Hebrews links peace with purity when he instructs believers to "pursue peace with all men, and the sanctification without which no one will see the Lord" (Heb. 12:14). Peace cannot be divorced from holiness. "Righteousness and peace have kissed each other" is the beautiful expression of the psalmist (Ps. 85:10). Biblically speaking, then, where there is true peace there is righteousness, holiness, and purity. Trying to bring harmony by compromising righteousness forfeits both.

Jesus' saying "Do not think that I came to bring peace on the earth; I did not come to bring peace, but a sword" (Matt. 10:34) seems to be the antithesis of the seventh beatitude. His meaning, however, was that the peace He came to bring is not peace at any price. There will be opposition before there is harmony; there will be strife before there is peace. To be peacemakers on God's terms requires being peacemakers on the terms of truth and righteousness—to which the world is in fierce opposition. When believers bring truth to bear on a world that loves falsehood, there will be strife. When believers set God's standards of righteousness before a world that loves wickedness, there is an inevitable potential for conflict. Yet that is the only way.

Until unrighteousness is changed to righteousness there cannot be godly peace. And the process of resolution is difficult and costly. Truth will produce anger before it produces happiness; righteousness will produce antagonism before it produces harmony. The gospel brings bad feelings before it can bring good feelings. A person who does not first mourn over his own sin will never be satisfied with God's righteousness. The sword that Christ brings is the sword of His Word, which is the sword of truth and righteousness. Like the surgeon's scalpel, it must cut before it heals, because peace cannot come where sin remains.

The great enemy of peace is sin. Sin separates men from God and causes disharmony and enmity with Him. And men's lack of harmony with God causes their lack of harmony with each other. The world is filled with strife and war because it is filled with sin. Peace does not rule the world because the enemy of peace rules the world. Jeremiah tells us that "the heart is more deceitful than all else and is desperately sick [or wicked]" (Jer. 17:9). Peace cannot reign where wickedness reigns. Wicked hearts cannot produce a peaceful society. "'There is no peace for the wicked,' says the Lord" (Isa. 48:22).

To talk of peace without talking of repentance of sin is to talk foolishly and vainly. The corrupt religious leaders of ancient Israel proclaimed, "Peace, peace," but there was no peace, because they and the rest of the people were not "ashamed of the abominations they had done" (Jer. 8:11-12).

"From within, out of the heart of men, proceed the evil thoughts, fornications, thefts, murders, adulteries, deeds of coveting and wickedness, as well as deceit, sensuality, envy, slander, pride and foolishness. All these evil things proceed from within and defile the man" (Mark 7:21-23). Sinful men cannot create peace, either within themselves or among themselves. Sin can produce nothing but strife and conflict. "For where jealousy and selfish ambition exist, there is disorder and every evil thing," James says. "But the wisdom from above is first pure, then peaceable, gentle, reasonable, full of mercy and good fruits, unwavering, without hypocrisy. And the seed whose fruit is righteousness is sown in peace by those who make peace" (James 3:16-18).

Regardless of what the circumstances might be, where there is conflict it is because of sin. If you separate the conflicting parties from each other but do not separate them from sin, at best you will succeed only in making a truce. Peacemaking cannot come by circumventing sin, because sin is the source of every conflict.

The bad news of the gospel comes before the good news. Until a person confronts his sin, it makes no sense to offer him a Savior. Until a person faces his false notions, it makes no sense to offer him the truth. Until a person acknowledges his enmity with God, it makes no sense to offer him peace with God.

Believers cannot avoid facing truth, or avoid facing others with the truth, for the sake of harmony. If someone is in serious error about a part of God's truth, he cannot have a right, peaceful relationship with others until the error is confronted and corrected. Jesus never evaded the issue of wrong doctrine or behavior. He treated the Samaritan woman from Sychar with great love and compassion, but He did not hesitate to confront her godless life. First He confronted her with her immoral living: "You have had five husbands, and the one whom you now have is not your husband" (John 4:18). Then He corrected her false ideas about worship: "Woman, believe Me, an hour is coming when neither in this mountain, nor in Jerusalem, shall you worship the Father. You worship that which you do not know; we worship that which we know, for salvation is from the Jews" (John 4:21-22).

The person who is not willing to disrupt and disturb in God's name cannot be a peacemaker. To come to terms on anything less than God's truth and righteousness is to settle for a truce—which confirms sinners in their sin and may leave them even further from the kingdom. Those who in the name of love or kindness or compassion try to witness by appeasement and compromise of God's Word will find that their witness leads away from Him, not to Him. God's peacemakers will not let a sleeping dog lie if it is opposed to God's truth; they will not protect the status quo if it is ungodly and unrighteous. They are not willing to make peace at any price. God's peace comes only in God's way. Being a peacemaker is essentially the result of a holy life and the call to others to embrace the gospel of holiness.

THE MAKER OF PEACE: GOD

Men are without peace because they are without God, the source of peace. Both the Old and New Testaments are replete with statements of God's being the God of peace (Lev. 26:6; 1 Kings 2:33; Ps. 29:11; Isa. 9:6; Ezek. 34:25; Rom. 15:33; 1 Cor. 14:33; 2 Thess. 3:16). Since the Fall, the only peace that men have known is the peace they have received as the gift of God. Christ's coming to earth was the peace of God coming to earth, because only Jesus Christ could remove sin, the great barrier to peace. "But now in Christ Jesus you who formerly were far off have been brought near by the blood of Christ. For He Himself is our peace" (Eph. 2:13-14).

I once read the story of a couple at a divorce hearing who were arguing back and forth before the judge, accusing each other and refusing to take any blame themselves. Their little four-year-old boy was terribly distressed and confused. Not knowing what else to do, he took his father's hand and his mother's hand and kept tugging until he finally pulled the hands of his parents together.

In an infinitely greater way, Christ brings back together God and man, reconciling and bringing peace. "For it was the Father's good pleasure for all the fulness to dwell in Him, and through Him to reconcile all things to Himself, having made peace through the blood of His cross" (Col. 1:19-20).

How could the cross bring peace? At the cross all of man's hatred and anger was vented against God. On the cross the Son of God was mocked, cursed, spit upon, pierced, reviled, and killed. Jesus' disciples fled in fear, the sky flashed lightning, the earth shook violently, and the veil of the Temple was torn in two. Yet through that violence God brought peace. God's greatest righteousness confronted man's greatest wickedness, and righteousness won. And because righteousness won, peace was won.

In his book *Peace Child* (Glendale, Calif.: Regal, 1979), Don Richardson tells of his long struggle to bring the gospel to the cannibalistic, headhunting Sawi tribe of Irian Jaya, Indonesia. Try as he would, he could not find a way to make the people understand the gospel message, especially the significance of Christ's atoning death on the cross.

Sawi villages were constantly fighting among themselves, and because treachery, revenge, and murder were highly honored there seemed no hope of peace. The tribe, however, had a legendary custom that if one village gave a baby boy to another village, peace would prevail between the two villages as long as the child lived. The baby was called a "peace child."

The missionary seized on that story as an analogy of the reconciling work of Christ. Christ, he said, is God's divine Peace Child that He has offered to man, and because Christ lives eternally His peace will never end. That analogy was the key that unlocked the gospel for the Sawis. In a miraculous working of the Holy Spirit many of them believed in Christ, and a strong, evangelistic church soon developed—and peace came to the Sawis.

If the Father is the source of peace, and the Son is the manifestation of that peace, then the Holy Spirit is the agent of that peace. One of the most beautiful fruits the Holy Spirit gives to those in whom He resides is the fruit of peace (Gal. 5:22). The God of peace sent the Prince of Peace who sends the Spirit of peace to give the fruit of peace. No wonder the Trinity is called Yahweh Shalom, "The Lord is Peace" (Judg. 6:24).

The God of peace intends peace for His world, and the world that He created in peace He will one day restore to peace. The Prince of Peace will establish His kingdom of peace, for a thousand years on earth and for all eternity in heaven. "'For I know the plans that I have for you,' declares the Lord, 'plans for welfare and not for calamity to give you a future and a hope'" (Jer. 29:11). Jesus said, "These things I have spoken to you, that in Me you may have peace. In the world you have tribulation, but take courage; I have overcome the world" (John 16:33). The one who does not belong to God through Jesus Christ can neither have peace nor be a peacemaker. God can work peace through us only if He has worked peace in us.

Some of the earth's most violent weather occurs on the seas. But the deeper one goes the more serene and tranquil the water becomes. Oceanographers report that the deepest parts of the sea are absolutely still. When those areas are dredged they produce remnants of plant and animal life that have remained undisturbed for thousands of years.

That is a picture of the Christian's peace. The world around him, including his own circumstances, may be in great turmoil and strife, but in his deepest being he has peace that passes understanding. Those who are in the best of circumstances but without God can never find peace, but those in the worst of circumstances but with God need never lack peace.

THE MESSENGERS OF PEACE: BELIEVERS

The messengers of peace are believers in Jesus Christ. Only they can be

peacemakers. Only those who belong to the Maker of peace can be messengers of peace. Paul tells us that "God has called us to peace" (1 Cor. 7:15) and that "now all these things are from God, who reconciled us to Himself through Christ, and gave us the ministry of reconciliation" (2 Cor. 5:18). The ministry of reconciliation is the ministry of peacemaking. Those whom God has called to peace He also calls to make peace. "God was in Christ reconciling the world to Himself, not counting their trespasses against them, and He has committed to us the word of reconciliation. Therefore, we are ambassadors for Christ, as though God were entreating through us" (2 Cor. 5:19-20).

At least four things characterize a peacemaker. First, he is one who himself has made peace with God. The gospel is all about peace. Before we came to Christ we were at war with God. No matter what we may consciously have thought about God, our hearts were against Him. It was "while we were enemies" of God that "we were reconciled to God through the death of His Son" (Rom. 5:10). When we received Christ as Savior and He imputed His righteousness to us, our battle with God ended, and our peace with God began. Because he has made peace with God he can enjoy the peace of God (Phil. 4:7; Col. 3:15). And because he has been given God's peace he is called to share God's peace. He is to have his very feet shod with "the gospel of peace" (Eph. 6:15).

Because peace is always corrupted by sin, the peacemaking believer must be a holy believer, a believer whose life is continually cleansed by the Holy Spirit. Sin breaks our fellowship with God, and when fellowship with Him is broken, peace is broken. The disobedient, self-indulgent Christian is not suited to be an ambassador of peace.

Second, a peacemaker leads others to make peace with God. Christians are not an elite corps of those who have spiritually arrived and who look down on the rest of the world. They are a body of sinners cleansed by Jesus Christ and commissioned to carry His gospel of cleansing to the rest of the world.

The Pharisees were the embodiment of what peacemakers are not. They were smug, proud, complacent, and determined to have their own ways and defend their own rights. They had scant interest in making peace with Rome, with the Samaritans, or even with fellow Jews who did not follow their own party line. Consequently they created strife wherever they went. They cooperated with others only when it was to their own advantage, as they did with the Sadducees in opposing Jesus.

The peacemaking spirit is the opposite of that. It is built on humility, sorrow over its own sin, gentleness, hunger for righteousness, mercy, and purity of heart. G. Campbell Morgan commented that peacemaking is the propagated character of the man who, exemplifying all the rest of the beatitudes, thereby brings peace wherever he comes.

The peacemaker is a beggar who has been fed and who is called to help feed others. Having been brought to God, he is to bring others to God. The purpose of the church is to preach "peace through Jesus Christ" (Acts 10:36). To preach Christ is to promote peace. To bring a person to saving knowledge of Jesus Christ is the most peacemaking act a human being can perform. It is beyond what any diplomat or statesman can accomplish.

Third, a peacemaker helps others make peace with others. The moment a person comes to Christ he becomes at peace with God and with the church and becomes himself a peacemaker in the world. A peacemaker builds bridges between men and God and also between men and other men. The second kind of bridge building must begin, of course, between ourselves and others. Jesus said that if we are bringing a gift to God and a brother has something against us, we are to leave our gift at the altar and be reconciled to that brother before we offer the gift to God (Matt. 5:23-24). As far as it is possible, Paul says, "so far as it depends on [us]," we are to "be at peace with all men" (Rom. 12:18). We are even to love our enemies and pray for those who persecute us, "in order that [we] may be sons of [our] Father who is in heaven" (Matt. 5:44-45).

By definition a bridge cannot be one-sided. It must extend between two sides or it can never function. Once built, it continues to need support on both sides or it will collapse. So in any relationship our first responsibility is to see that our own side has a solid base. But we also have a responsibility to help the one on the other side build his base well. Both sides must be built on righteousness and truth or the bridge will not stand. God's peacemakers must first be righteous themselves, and then must be active in helping others become righteous.

The first step in that bridge-building process is often to rebuke others about their sin, which is the supreme barrier to peace. "If your brother sins," Jesus says, "go and reprove him in private; if he listens to you, you have won your brother. But if he does not listen to you, take one or two more with you, so that by the mouth of two or three witnesses every fact may be confirmed. And if he refuses to listen to them, tell it to the church" (Matt. 18:15-17). That is a difficult thing to do, but obeying that command is no more optional than obeying any of the Lord's other commands. The fact that taking such action often stirs up controversy and resentment is no excuse for not doing it. If we do so in the way and in the spirit the Lord teaches, the consequences are His responsibility. Not to do so does not preserve peace but through disobedience establishes a truce with sin.

Obviously there is the possibility·of a price to pay, but any sacrifice is small in order to obey God. Often confrontation will bring more turmoil instead of less— misunderstanding, hurt feelings, and resentment. But the only way to peace is the way of righteousness. Sin that is not dealt with is sin that will disrupt and destroy peace. Just as any price is worth paying to obey God, any price is worth paying to be rid of sin. "If your right eye makes you stumble," Jesus said, "tear it out, and throw it from you; . . . And if your right hand makes you stumble, cut it off, and throw it from you; for it is better for you that one of the parts of your body perish, than for your whole body to go into hell" (Matt. 5:29-30). If we are unwilling to help others confront their sin, we will be unable to help them find peace.

Fourth, a peacemaker endeavors to find a point of agreement. God's truth and righteousness must never be compromised or weakened, but there is hardly a person so ungodly, immoral, rebellious, pagan, or indifferent that we have absolutely no point of agreement with him. Wrong theology, wrong standards, wrong beliefs, and wrong attitudes must be faced and dealt with, but they are not usually the best places to start the process of witnessing or peacemaking.

God's people are to contend without being contentious, to disagree without being disagreeable, and to confront without being abusive. The peacemaker speaks the truth in love (Eph. 4:15). To start with love is to start toward peace. We begin peacemaking by starting with whatever peaceful point of agreement we can find. Peace helps beget peace. The peacemaker always gives others the benefit of the doubt. He never assumes they will resist the gospel or reject his testimony. When he does meet opposition, he tries to be patient with other people's blindness and stubbornness just as he knows the Lord was, and continues to be, patient with his own blindness and stubbornness.

God's most effective peacemakers are often the simplest and least noticed people. They do not try to attract attention to themselves. They seldom win headlines or prizes for their peacemaking, because, by its very nature, true peacemaking is unobtrusive and prefers to go unnoticed. Because they bring righteousness and truth wherever they go, peacemakers are frequently accused of being troublemakers and disturbers of the peace—as Ahab accused Elijah of being (1 Kings 18:17) and the Jewish leaders accused Jesus of being (Luke 23:2, 5). But God knows their hearts, and He honors their work because they are working for His peace in His power. God's peacemakers are never unfruitful or unrewarded. This is a mark of a true kingdom citizen: he not only hungers for righteousness and holiness in his own life but has a passionate desire to see those virtues in the lives of others.

THE MERIT OF PEACE: ETERNAL SONSHIP IN THE KINGDOM

The merit, or result, of peacemaking is eternal blessing as God's children in God's kingdom. Peacemakers **shall be called sons of God.**

Most of us are thankful for our heritage, our ancestors, our parents, and our family name. It is especially gratifying to have been influenced by godly grandparents and to have been raised by godly parents. But the greatest human heritage cannot match the believer's heritage in Jesus Christ, because we are "heirs of God and fellow heirs with Christ" (Rom. 8:17). Nothing compares to being a child of God.

Both *huios* and *teknon* are used in the New Testament to speak of believers' relationship to God. *Teknon* (child) is a term of tender affection and endearment as well as of relationship (see John 1:12; Eph. 5:8; 1 Pet. 1:14; etc.). **Sons,** however, is from *huios,* which expresses the dignity and honor of the relationship of a child to his parents. As God's peacemakers we are promised the glorious blessing of eternal sonship in His eternal kingdom.

Peacemaking is a hallmark of God's children. A person who is not a peacemaker either is not a Christian or is a disobedient Christian. The person who is continually disruptive, divisive, and quarrelsome has good reason to doubt his relationship to God altogether. God's **sons**—that is, all of His children, both male and female—are peacemakers. Only God determines who His children are, and He has determined that they are the humble, the penitent over sin, the gentle, the seekers of righteousness, the merciful, the pure in heart, and the peacemakers.

Shall be called is in a continuous future passive tense. Throughout eternity peacemakers will go by the name "children of God." The passive form indicates that all heaven will call peacemakers **sons of God**, because God Himself has declared them to be His children.

Jacob loved Benjamin so much that his whole life came to be bound up in the life of that son (Gen. 44:30). Any parent worthy of the name loves his children more than his own life, and immeasurably more than all of his possessions together. God loves His children today as He loved Israel of old, as "the apple of His eye" (Zech. 2:8; cf. Ps. 17:8). The Hebrew expression "apple of the eye" referred to the cornea, the most exposed and sensitive part of the eye, the part we are the most careful to protect. That is what God's children are to Him: those whom He is most sensitive about and most desires to protect. To attack God's children is to poke a finger in God's eye. Offense against Christians is offense against God, because they are His very own children.

God puts the tears of His children in a bottle (Ps. 56:8), a figure reflecting the Hebrew custom of placing into a bottle the tears shed over a loved one. God cares for us so much that He stores up His remembrances of our sorrows and afflictions. God's children matter greatly to Him, and it is no little thing that we can call Him Father.

God's peacemakers will not always have peace in the world. As Jesus makes clear by the last beatitude, persecution follows peacemaking. In Christ we have forsaken the false peace *of* the world, and consequently we often will not have peace *with* the world. But as God's children we may always have peace even while we are *in* the world—the peace of God, which the world cannot give and the world cannot take away.

Happy Are the Harassed (5:10-12)

Blessed are those who have been persecuted for the sake of righteousness, for theirs is the kingdom of heaven. Blessed are you when men cast insults at you, and persecute you, and say all kinds of evil against you falsely, on account of Me. Rejoice, and be glad, for your reward in heaven is great, for so they persecuted the prophets who were before you." (5:10-12)

Of all the beatitudes, this last one seems the most contrary to human thinking and experience. The world does not associate happiness with humility, mourning over sin, gentleness, righteousness, mercy, purity of heart, or peacemaking holiness. Even less does it associate happiness with persecution.

Some years ago a popular national magazine took a survey to determine the things that make people happy. According to the responses they received, happy people enjoy other people but are not self-sacrificing; they refuse to participate in any negative feelings or emotions; and they have a sense of accomplishment based on their own self-sufficiency.

The person described by those principles is completely contrary to the kind of person the Lord says will be authentically happy. Jesus says a **blessed** person is not one who is self-sufficient but one who recognizes his own emptiness and need, who comes to God as a beggar, knowing he has no resources in himself.

He is not confident in his own ability but is very much aware of his own inability. Such a person, Jesus says, is not at all positive about himself but mourns over his own sinfulness and isolation from a holy God. To be genuinely content, a person must not be self-serving but self-sacrificing. He must be gentle, merciful, pure in heart, yearn for righteousness, and seek to make peace on God's terms—even if those attitudes cause him to suffer.

The Lord's opening thrust in the Sermon on the Mount climaxes with this great and sobering truth: those who faithfully live according to the first seven beatitudes are guaranteed at some point to experience the eighth. Those who live righteously will inevitably be persecuted for it. Godliness generates hostility and antagonism from the world. The crowning feature of the happy person is persecution! Kingdom people are rejected people. Holy people are singularly **blessed**, but they pay a price for it.

The last beatitude is really two in one, a single beatitude repeated and expanded. **Blessed** is mentioned twice (vv. 10, 11), but only one characteristic (**persecuted**) is given, although it is mentioned three times, and only one result (**for theirs is the kingdom of heaven**) is promised. **Blessed** apparently is repeated to emphasize the generous blessing given by God to those who are persecuted. "Double-blessed are those who are persecuted," Jesus seems to be saying.

Three distinct aspects of kingdom faithfulness are spoken of in this beatitude: the persecution, the promise, and the posture.

THE PERSECUTION

Those who have been persecuted are the citizens of the kingdom, those who live out the previous seven beatitudes. To the degree that they fulfill the first seven they may experience the eighth.

"All who desire to live godly in Christ Jesus will be persecuted" (2 Tim. 3:12). Before writing those words Paul had just mentioned some of his own "persecutions, and suffering, such as happened to me at Antioch, at Iconium and at Lystra" (v. 11). As one who lived the kingdom life he had been persecuted, and all others who live the kingdom life can expect similar treatment. What was true in ancient Israel is true today and will remain true until the Lord returns. "As at that time he who was born according to the flesh persecuted him who was born according to the Spirit, so it is now also" (Gal. 4:29).

Imagine a man who accepted a new job in which he had to work with especially profane people. When at the end of the first day his wife asked him how he had managed, he said, "Terrific! They never guessed I was a Christian." As long as people have no reason to believe that we are Christians, at least obedient and righteous Christians, we need not worry about persecution. But as we manifest the standards of Christ we will share the reproach of Christ. Those born only of the flesh will persecute those born of the Spirit.

To live for Christ is to live in opposition to Satan in his world and in his system. Christlikeness in us will produce the same results as Christlikeness did in the apostles, in the rest of the early church, and in believers throughout history. Christ living in His people today produces the same reaction from the world that Christ Himself produced when He lived on earth as a man.

Righteousness is confrontational, and even when it is not preached in so many words, it confronts wickedness by its very contrast. Abel did not preach to Cain, but Abel's righteous life, typified by his proper sacrifice to the Lord, was a constant rebuke to his wicked brother—who in a rage finally slew him. When Moses chose to identify with his own despised Hebrew people rather than compromise himself in the pleasures of pagan Egyptian society, he paid a great price. But he considered "the reproach of Christ greater riches than the treasures of Egypt" (Heb. 11:26).

The Puritan writer Thomas Watson said of Christians: "Though they be never so meek, merciful, pure in heart, their piety will not shield them from sufferings. They must hang their harp on the willows and take the cross. The way to heaven is by way of thorns and blood. . . . Set it down as a maxim, if you will follow Christ you must see the swords and staves" (*The Beatitudes* [Edinburgh: Banner of Truth Trust, 1971], pp. 259-60).

Savonarola was one of the greatest reformers in the history of the church. In his powerful condemnation of personal sin and ecclesiastical corruption, that Italian preacher paved the way for the Protestant Reformation, which began a few years after his death. "His preaching was a voice of thunder," writes one biographer, "and his denunciation of sin was so terrible that the people who listened to him went about the streets half-dazed, bewildered and speechless. His congregations were so often in tears that the whole building resounded with their sobs and their weeping." But the people and the church could not long abide such a witness, and for preaching uncompromised righteousness Savonarola was convicted of "heresy," he was hanged, and his body was burned.

Persecution is one of the surest and most tangible evidences of salvation. Persecution is not incidental to faithful Christian living but is certain evidence of it. Paul encouraged the Thessalonians by sending them Timothy, "so that no man may be disturbed by these afflictions; for you yourselves know that we have been destined for this. For indeed when we were with you, we kept telling you in advance that we were going to suffer affliction; and so it came to pass, as you know" (1 Thess. 3:3-4). Suffering persecution is part of the normal Christian life (cf. Rom. 8:16-17). And if we never experience ridicule, criticism, or rejection because of our faith, we have reason to examine the genuineness of it. "For to you it has been granted for Christ's sake," Paul says, "not only to believe in Him, but also to suffer for His sake, experiencing the same conflict which you saw in me, and now hear to be in me" (Phil. 1:29-30). Persecution for Christ's sake is a sign of our own salvation just as it is a sign of damnation for those who do the persecuting (v. 28).

Whether Christians live in a relatively protected and tolerant society or whether they live under a godless, totalitarian regime, the world will find ways to persecute Christ's church. To live a redeemed life to its fullest is to invite and to expect resentment and reaction from the world.

The fact that many professed believers are popular and praised by the world does not indicate that the world has raised its standards but that many who call themselves by Christ's name have lowered theirs. As the time for Christ's appearing grows closer we can expect opposition from the world to increase, not decrease. When Christians are not persecuted in some way by society it means that they are reflecting rather than confronting that society. And when we please the world we can be sure that we grieve the Lord (cf. James 4:4; 1 John 2:15-17).

When (*hotan*) can also mean whenever. The idea conveyed in the term is not that believers will be in a constant state of opposition, ridicule, or persecution, but that, whenever those things come to us because of our faith, we should not be surprised or resentful. Jesus was not *constantly* opposed and ridiculed, nor were the apostles. There were times of peace and even popularity. But every faithful believer will at times have *some* resistance and ridicule from the world, while others, for God's own purposes, will endure more extreme suffering. But whenever and however affliction comes to the child of God, his heavenly Father will be there with him to encourage and to bless. Our responsibility is not to seek out persecution, but to be willing to endure whatever trouble our faithfulness to Jesus Christ may bring, and to see it as a confirmation of true salvation.

The way to avoid persecution is obvious and easy. To live like the world, or at least to "live and let live," will cost us nothing. To mimic the world's standards, or never to criticize them, will cost us nothing. To keep quiet about the gospel, especially the truth that apart from its saving power men remain in their sins and are destined for hell, will cost us nothing. To go along with the world, to laugh at its jokes, to enjoy its entertainment, to smile when it mocks God and takes His name in vain, and to be ashamed to take a stand for Christ will not bring persecution. Those are the habits of sham Christians.

Jesus does not take faithlessness lightly. "For whoever is ashamed of Me and My words, of him will the Son of Man be ashamed when He comes in His glory, and the glory of the Father and of the holy angels" (Luke 9:26). If we are ashamed of Christ, He will be ashamed of us. Christ also warned, "Woe to you when all men speak well of you, for in the same way their fathers used to treat the false prophets" (Luke 6:26). To be popular with everyone is either to have compromised the faith or not to have true faith at all.

Though it was early in His ministry, by the time Jesus preached the Sermon on the Mount He had already faced opposition. After He healed the man on the Sabbath, "the Pharisees went out and immediately began taking counsel with the Herodians against Him, as to how they might destroy Him" (Mark 3:6). We learn from Luke that they were actually hoping Jesus would heal on the Sabbath "in order that they might find reason to accuse Him" (Luke 6:7). They already hated His teaching and wanted Him to commit an act serious enough to warrant His arrest.

Our Lord made it clear from His earliest teaching, and His opponents made it clear from their earliest reactions, that following Him was costly. Those who entered His kingdom would suffer for Him before they would reign with Him. That is the hard honesty that every preacher, evangelist, and witness of Christ should exemplify. We do the Lord no honor and those to whom we witness no benefit by hiding or minimizing the cost of following Him.

The cost of discipleship is billed to believers in many different ways. A Christian stonemason in Ephesus in Paul's day might have been asked to help build a pagan temple or shrine. Because he could not do that in good conscience, his faith would cost him the work and possibly his job and career. A believer today might be expected to hedge on the quality of his work in order to increase company profits. To follow His conscience in obedience to the Lord could also cost his job or at least a promotion. A Christian housewife who refuses to listen to gossip or to laugh at the crude jokes of her neighbors may find herself ostracized. Some costs will be known in advance and some will surprise us. Some costs will be great and some will be slight. But by the Lord's and the apostles' repeated promises, faithfulness always has a cost, which true Christians are willing to pay (contrast Matt. 13:20-21).

The second-century Christian leader Tertullian was once approached by a man who said, "I have come to Christ, but I don't know what to do. I have a job that I don't think is consistent with what Scripture teaches. What can I do? I must live." To that Tertullian replied, "Must you?" Loyalty to Christ is the Christian's only true choice. To be prepared for kingdom life is to be prepared for loneliness, misunderstanding, ridicule, rejection, and unfair treatment of every sort.

In the early days of the church the price paid was often the ultimate. To choose Christ might mean choosing death by stoning, by being covered with pitch and used as a human torch for Nero, or by being wrapped in animal skins and thrown to vicious hunting dogs. To choose Christ could mean torture by any number of excessively cruel and painful ways. That was the very thing Christ had in mind when He identified His followers as those willing to bear their crosses. That has no reference to mystical devotion, but is a call to be ready to die, if need be, for the cause of the Lord (see Matt. 10:35-39; 16:24-25).

In resentment against the gospel the Romans invented charges against Christians, such as accusing them of being cannibals because in the Lord's Supper they spoke of eating Jesus' body and drinking His blood. They accused them of having sexual orgies at their love feasts and even of setting fire to Rome. They branded believers as revolutionaries because they called Jesus Lord and King and spoke of God's destroying the earth by fire.

By the end of the first century, Rome had expanded almost to the outer limits of the known world, and unity became more and more of a problem. Because only the emperor personified the entire empire, the caesars came to be deified, and their worship was demanded as a unifying and cohesive influence. It became compulsory to give a verbal oath of allegiance to caesar once a year, for which a person would be given a verifying certificate, called a libellus. After publicly proclaiming, "Caesar is Lord," the person was free to worship any other gods he chose. Because faithful Christians refused to declare such an allegiance to anyone but Christ, they were considered traitors—for which they suffered confiscation of property, loss of work, imprisonment, and often death. One Roman poet spoke of them as "the panting, huddling flock whose only crime was Christ."

In the last beatitude Jesus speaks of three specific types of affliction endured for Christ's sake: physical persecution, verbal insult, and false accusation.

PHYSICAL PERSECUTION

First, Jesus says, we can expect physical persecution. **Have been persecuted** (v. 10), **persecute** (v. 11), and **persecuted** (v. 12) are from *diōkō*, which has the basic meaning of chasing, driving away, or pursuing. From that meaning developed the connotations of physical persecution, harassment, abuse, and other unjust treatment.

All of the other beatitudes have to do with inner qualities, attitudes, and spiritual character. The eighth beatitude speaks of external things that happen to believers, but the teaching behind these results also has to do with attitude. The believer who has the qualities required in the previous beatitudes will also have the quality of willingness to face persecution **for the sake of righteousness**. He will have the attitude of self-sacrifice for the sake of Christ. It is the lack of fear and shame and the presence of courage and boldness that says, "I will be in this world what Christ would have me be. I will say in this world what Christ will have me say. Whatever it costs, I will be and say those things."

The Greek verb is a passive perfect participle, and could be translated "allow themselves to be persecuted." The perfect form indicates continuousness, in this case a continuous willingness to endure persecution if it is the price of godly living. This beatitude speaks of a constant attitude of accepting whatever faithfulness to Christ may bring.

It is in the demands of this beatitude that many Christians break down in their obedience to the Lord, because here is where the genuineness of their response to the other beatitudes is most strongly tested. It is here where we are most tempted to compromise the righteousness we have hungered and thirsted for. It is here where we find it convenient to lower God's standards to accommodate the world and thereby avoid conflicts and problems that we know obedience will bring.

But God does not want His gospel altered under pretense of its being less demanding, less righteous, or less truthful than it is. He does not want witnesses who lead the unsaved into thinking that the Christ life costs nothing. A synthetic gospel, a man-made seed, produces no real fruit.

VERBAL INSULTS

Second, Jesus promises that kingdom citizens are **blessed . . . when men cast insults** at them. *Oneidizō* carries the idea of reviling, upbraiding, or seriously insulting, and literally means to cast in one's teeth. To **cast insults** is to throw abusive words in the face of an opponent, to mock viciously.

To be an obedient citizen of the kingdom is to court verbal abuse and reviling. As He stood before the Sanhedrin after His arrest in the Garden of Gethsemane, Jesus was spat upon, beaten, and taunted with the words "Prophesy to us, You Christ; who is the one who hit You?" (Matt. 26:67-68). As He was being sentenced to crucifixion by Pilate, Jesus was again beaten, spit upon, and mocked, this time by the Roman soldiers (Mark 15:19-20).

Faithfulness to Christ may even cause friends and loved ones to say things that cut and hurt deeply. Several years ago I received a letter from a woman who told of a friend who had decided to divorce her husband for no just cause. The friend was a professed Christian, but when she was confronted with the truth that what she was doing was scripturally wrong, she became defensive and hostile. She was reminded of God's love and grace, of His power to mend whatever problems she and her husband were having, and of the Bible's standards for marriage and divorce. But she replied that she did not believe the Bible was really God's Word but was simply a collection of men's ideas about God that each person had to accept, reject, or interpret for himself. When her friend wanted to read some specific Bible passages to her, she refused to listen. She had made up her mind and would not give heed to Scripture or to reason. With hate in her eyes she accused the other woman of luring her into her house in order to ridicule and embarrass her, saying she could not possibly love her by questioning her right to get a divorce. As she left, she slammed the door behind her.

The woman who wrote the letter concluded by saying, "I love her, and it is with a heavy heart that I realize the extent of her rejection of Christ. Painful as this has been, I thank God. For the first time in my life I know what it is to be separate from the world."

Paul told the Corinthian church, whose members had such a difficult time separating themselves from the world, "For, I think, God has exhibited us apostles last of all, as men condemned to death; because we have become a spectacle to the world, both to angels and to men" (1 Cor. 4:9). Paul drew the expression "become a spectacle" from the practice of Roman generals to parade their captives through the street of the city, making a spectacle of them as trophies of war who were doomed to die once the general had used them to serve his proud and arrogant purposes. That is the way the world is inclined to treat those who are faithful to Christ.

In a note of strong sarcasm to enforce his point, Paul continues, "We are fools for Christ's sake, but you are prudent in Christ; we are weak, but you are strong; you are distinguished, but we are without honor" (v. 10). Many in the Corinthian church suffered none of the ridicule and conflict the apostle suffered because they prized their standing before the world more than their standing before the Lord. In the world's eyes they were prudent, strong, and distinguished— because they were still so much like the world.

God does not call His people to be sanctified celebrities, using their worldly reputations in a self-styled effort to bring Him glory, using their power to supplement His power and their wisdom to enhance His gospel. We can mark it down as a cardinal principle that to the extent the world embraces a Christian cause or person—or that a Christian cause or person embraces the world—to that extent that cause or person has compromised the gospel and scriptural standards.

If Paul had capitalized on his human credentials he could have drawn greater crowds and certainly have received greater welcome wherever he went. His credentials were impressive. "If anyone else has a mind to put confidence in the flesh, I far more," he says. He was "circumcised the eighth day, of the nation of Israel, of the tribe of Benjamin, a Hebrew of Hebrews; as to the Law, a Pharisee" (Phil. 3:4-5). He had been "caught up to the third heaven, . . . into Paradise" (2 Cor. 12:2, 4) and had spoken in tongues more than anyone else (1 Cor. 14:18). He had studied under the famous rabbi Gamaliel and was even a free-born Roman citizen (Acts 22:3, 29). But all those things the apostle "counted as loss for the sake of Christ, . . . but rubbish in order that I may gain Christ" (Phil. 3:7-8). He refused to use worldly means to try to achieve spiritual purposes, because he knew they would fail.

The marks of authenticity Paul carried as an apostle and minister of Jesus Christ were his credentials as a servant and a sufferer, "in far more labors, in far more imprisonments, beaten times without number, often in danger of death. Five times I received from the Jews thirty-nine lashes. Three times I was beaten with rods, once I was stoned, three times I was shipwrecked, a night and a day I have spent in the deep. I have been on frequent journeys, in dangers from rivers, dangers from robbers, dangers from my countrymen, dangers from the Gentiles, dangers in the city, dangers in the wilderness, dangers on the sea, dangers among false brethren; I have been in labor and hardship, through many sleepless nights, in hunger and thirst, often without food, in cold and exposure" (2 Cor. 11:23-27).

The only thing of which he would boast was his weakness (12:5), and when he preached he was careful not to rely on "superiority of speech or of wisdom" (1 Cor. 2:1), which he could easily have done. "For I determined to know nothing among you except Jesus Christ, and Him crucified," he told the Corinthians. "And I was with you in weakness and in fear and in much trembling. And my message and my preaching were not in persuasive words of wisdom, but in demonstration of the Spirit and of power, that your faith should not rest on the wisdom of men, but on the power of God" (vv. 2-5).

We live in a day when the church, more than ever before, is engaged in self-glorification and an attempt to gain worldly recognition that must be repulsive to God. When the church tries to use the things of the world to do the work of heaven, it only succeeds in hiding heaven from the world. And when the world is pleased with the church, we can be sure that God is not. We can be equally sure that when we are pleasing to God, we will not be pleasing to the system of Satan.

FALSE ACCUSATION

Third, faithfulness to Christ will bring enemies of the gospel to **say all kinds of evil against** [us] **falsely.** Whereas **insults** are abusive words said to our faces, these **evil** things are primarily abusive words said behind our backs.

Jesus' critics said of Him, "Behold, a gluttonous man and a drunkard, a friend of tax-gatherers and sinners" (Matt. 11:19). If the world said that of the sinless Christ, what things can His followers expect to be called and accused of?

Slander behind our backs is harder to take partly because it is harder to defend against than direct accusation. It has opportunity to spread and be believed before we have a chance to correct it. Much harm to our reputations can be done even before we are aware someone has slandered us.

We cannot help regretting slander, but we should not grieve about it. We should count ourselves **blessed**, as our Lord assures us we shall be when the slander is **on account of Me**.

Arthur Pink comments that "it is a strong proof of human depravity that men's curses and Christ's blessings should meet on the same persons" (*An Exposition of the Sermon on the Mount* [Grand Rapids: Baker, 1950], p. 39). We have no surer evidence of the Lord's blessing than to be cursed for His sake. It should not seriously bother us when men's curses fall on the head that Christ has eternally blessed.

The central theme of the Beatitudes is righteousness. The first two have to do with recognizing our own unrighteousness, and the next five have to do with our seeking and reflecting righteousness. The last beatitude has to do with our suffering **for the sake of righteousness**. The same truth is expressed in the second part of the beatitude as **on account of Me**. Jesus is not speaking of every hardship, problem, or conflict believers may face, but those that the world brings on us *because of* our faithfulness to the Lord.

It is clear again that the hallmark of the **blessed** person is **righteousness**. Holy living is what provokes persecution of God's people. Such persecution because of a righteous life is joyous. Peter identifies such experience as a happy honor.

> And who is there to harm you if you prove zealous for what is good? But even if you should suffer for the sake of righteousness, you are blessed. And do not fear their intimidation, and do not be troubled, but sanctify Christ as Lord in your hearts, always being ready to make a defense to everyone who asks you to give an account for the hope that is in you, yet with gentleness and reverence; and keep a good conscience so that in the thing in which you are slandered, those who revile your good behavior in Christ may be put to shame. For it is better, if God should will it so, that you suffer for doing what is right rather than for doing what is wrong. For Christ also died for sins once for all, the just for the unjust, in order that He might bring us to God, having been put to death in the flesh, but made alive in the spirit." (1 Pet. 3:13-18)

With those words, the apostle extols the privilege of suffering for holiness, and thus of sharing in a small way in the same type of suffering Christ endured. In the next chapter, Peter emphasizes the same thing.

> Beloved, do not be surprised at the fiery ordeal among you, which comes upon you for your testing, as though some strange thing were happening to you; but to the degree that you share the sufferings of Christ, keep on rejoicing; so that also at the revelation of His glory, you may rejoice with exultation. If you are reviled for the name of Christ, you are blessed, because the Spirit of glory and of God rests upon you. . . . If anyone suffers as a Christian, let him not feel ashamed, but in that name let him glorify God. . . . Therefore, let those also who suffer according to the will of God entrust their souls to a faithful Creator in doing what is right." (4:12-14, 16, 19)

When we are hated, maligned, or afflicted as Christians, the real animosity is not against us but against Christ. Satan's great enemy is Christ, and he opposes us because we belong to Jesus Christ, because He is in us. When we are despised and attacked by the world, the real target is the righteousness for which we stand and which we exemplify. That is why it is easy to escape persecution. Whether under pagan Rome, atheistic Communism, or simply a worldly boss, it is usually easy to be accepted if we will denounce or compromise our beliefs and standards. The world will accept us if we are willing to put some distance between ourselves and the Lord's righteousness.

In the closing days of His ministry Jesus repeatedly and plainly warned His disciples of that truth. "If the world hates you," He said, "you know that it has hated Me before it hated you. If you were of the world, the world would love its own; but because you are not of the world, but I chose you out of the world, therefore the world hates you. Remember the word that I said to you, 'A slave is not greater than his master.' If they persecuted Me, they will also persecute you; if they kept My word, they will keep yours also. But all these things they will do to you for My name's sake, because they do not know the One who sent Me" (John 15:18-21).

The world went along for thousands of years before it ever saw a perfect man. Until Christ came, every person, even God's best, were sinful and flawed. All had feet of clay. To see God's people fail and sin is often taken as an encouragement by the wicked. They point a finger and say, "He claims to be righteous and good, but look at what he did." It is easy to feel smug and secure in one's sinfulness when everyone else is also sinful and imperfect. But when Christ came, the world finally saw the perfect Man, and all excuse for smugness and self-confidence vanished. And instead of rejoicing in the sinless Man, sinful men resented the rebuke that His teaching and His life brought against them. They crucified Him for His very perfection, for His very righteousness.

Aristides the Just was banished from ancient Athens. When a stranger asked an Athenian why Aristides was voted out of citizenship he replied, "Because we became tired of his always being just." A people who prided themselves in civility and justice chafed when something or someone was *too* just.

Because they refused to compromise the gospel either in their teaching or in their lives, most of the apostles suffered a martyr's death. According to tradition, Andrew was fastened by cords to a cross in order to prolong and intensify his agony. We are told that Peter, by his own request, was crucified head down, because he felt unworthy to die in the same manner as Jesus. Paul presumably was beheaded by Nero. Though John escaped a violent death, he died in exile on Patmos.

THE PROMISE

But compared to what is gained, even a martyr's price is small. Each beatitude begins with **blessed** and, as already suggested, Jesus pronounces a double blessing on those who are persecuted for the sake of righteousness, which is for His own sake. The specific blessing promised to those who are so persecuted is that **theirs is the kingdom of heaven**. The citizens of the kingdom are going to inherit the kingdom. Paul expresses a similar thought in 2 Thessalonians 1:5-7— "This a plain indication of God's righteous judgment so that you may be considered worthy of the kingdom of God, for which indeed you are suffering. For after all it is only just for God to repay with affliction those who afflict you, and to give relief to you who are afflicted and to us as well when the Lord Jesus shall be revealed from heaven with His mighty angels in flaming fire."

I believe that the blessings of the **kingdom** are threefold: present, millennial, and eternal. Jesus said, "Truly I say to you, there is no one who has left house or brothers or sisters or mother or father or children or farms, for My sake and for the gospel's sake, but that he shall receive a hundred times as much now in the present age, houses and brothers and sisters and mothers and children and farms, along with persecutions; and in the age to come, eternal life" (Mark 10:29-30).

First, we are promised blessings here and now. Joseph was sold into slavery by his brothers, was falsely accused by Potiphar's wife, and was imprisoned. But the Lord raised him to be the prime minister of Egypt and used him to save His chosen people from starvation and extinction. Daniel was thrown into a den of lions because of his refusal to stop worshiping the Lord. Not only was his life spared, but he was restored to his high position as the most valued commissioner of King Darius, and the king made a declaration that "in all the dominion of my kingdom men are to fear and tremble before the God of Daniel; for He is the living God and enduring forever" (Dan. 6:26).

Not every believer is rewarded in this life with the things of this life. But every believer is rewarded in this life with the comfort, strength, and joy of His indwelling Lord. He is also blessed with the assurance that no service or sacrifice for the Lord will be in vain.

As a sequel to his book *Peace Child,* Don Richardson has written *Lords of the Earth* (Glendale, Calif.: Regal, 1977). He tells the story of Stan Dale, another missionary to Irian Jaya, Indonesia, who ministered to the Yali tribe in the Snow Mountains. The Yali had one of the strictest known religions in the world. For a tribe member even to question, much less disobey, one of its tenets brought instant death. There could never be any change or modification. The Yali had many sacred spots scattered throughout their territory. If even a small child were to crawl onto one of those sacred pieces of ground, he was considered defiled and cursed. To keep the whole village from being involved in that curse, the child would be thrown into the rushing Heluk River to drown and be washed downstream.

When Stan Dale came with his wife and four children to that cannibalistic people he was not long tolerated. He was attacked one night and miraculously survived being shot with five arrows. After treatment in a hospital he immediately returned to the Yali. He worked unsuccessfully for several years, and the resentment and hatred of the tribal priests increased. One day as he, another missionary named Phil Masters, and a Dani tribesman named Yemu were facing what they knew was an imminent attack, the Yali suddenly came upon them. As the others ran for safety, Stan and Yemu remained back, hoping somehow to dissuade the Yali from their murderous plans. As Stan confronted his attackers, they shot him with dozens of arrows. As the arrows entered his flesh he would pull them out and break them in two. Eventually he no longer had the strength to pull the arrows out, but he remained standing.

Yemu ran back to where Phil was standing, and Phil persuaded him to keep running. With his eyes fixed on Stan, who was still standing with some fifty arrows in his body, Phil remained where he was and was himself soon surrounded by warriors. The attack had begun with hilarity, but it turned to fear and desperation when they saw that Stan did not fall. Their fear increased when it took nearly as many arrows to down Phil as it had Stan. They dismembered the bodies and scattered them about the forest in an attempt to prevent the resurrection of which they had heard the missionaries speak. But the back of their "unbreakable" pagan system was broken, and through the witness of the two men who were not afraid to die in order to bring the gospel to this lost and violent people, the Yali tribe and many others in the surrounding territory came to Jesus Christ. Even Stan's fifth child, a baby at the time of this incident, was saved reading the book about his father.

Stan and Phil were not rewarded in this life with the things of this life. But they seem to have been double-blessed with the comfort, strength, and joy of their indwelling Lord—and the absolute confidence that their sacrifice for Him would not be in vain.

There is also a millennial aspect to the kingdom blessing. When Christ establishes His thousand-year reign on earth, we will be co-regents with Him over that wonderful, renewed earth (Rev. 20:4).

Finally, there is the reward of the eternal kingdom, the blessing of all blessings of living forever in our Lord's kingdom enjoying His very presence. The ultimate fruit of kingdom life is eternal life. Even if the world takes from us every possession, every freedom, every comfort, every satisfaction of physical life, it can take nothing from our spiritual life, either now or throughout eternity.

The Beatitudes begin and end with the promise of **the kingdom of heaven** (cf. v. 3). The major promise of the Beatitudes is that in Christ we become kingdom citizens now and forever. No matter what the world does to us, it cannot affect our possession of Christ's kingdom.

THE POSTURE

Rejoice, and be glad, for your reward in heaven is great, for so they persecuted the prophets who were before you. (5:12)

The believer's response to persecution and affliction should not be to retreat and hide. To escape from the world is to escape responsibility. Because we belong to Christ, we are no longer *of* this world, but He has sent us *into* this world to serve just as He Himself came into this world to serve (John 17:14-18).

His followers are "the salt of the earth" and the "light of the world" (Matt. 5:13-14). For our salt to flavor the earth and our light to lighten the world we must be active in the world. The gospel is not given to be hidden but to enlighten. "Let your light shine before men in such a way that they may see your good works, and glorify your Father who is in heaven" (vv. 15-16).

When we become Christ's salt and Christ's light, our salt will sting the world's open wounds of sin and our light will irritate its eyes that are used to darkness. But even when our salt and light are resented, rejected, and thrown back in our face, we should **rejoice, and be glad.**

Be glad is from *agalliaō,* which means to exult, to rejoice greatly, to be overjoyed, as is clear in the King James Version, "be exceeding glad." The literal meaning is to skip and jump with happy excitement. Jesus uses the imperative mood, which makes His words more than a suggestion. We are *commanded* to **be glad.** Not to be glad when we suffer for Christ's sake is to be untrusting and disobedient.

The world can take away a great deal from God's people, but it cannot take away their joy and their happiness. We know that nothing the world can do to us is permanent. When people attack us for Christ's sake, they are really attacking Him (cf. Gal. 6:17; Col. 1:24). And their attacks can do us no more permanent damage than they can do Him.

Jesus gives two reasons for our rejoicing and being glad when we are persecuted for His sake. First, He says, **your reward in heaven is great.** Our present life is no more than "a vapor that appears for a little while and then vanishes away" (James 4:14); but **heaven** is forever. Small wonder that Jesus tells us not to lay up treasures for ourselves here on earth, "where moth and rust destroy, and where thieves break in and steal. But lay up for yourselves treasures in heaven, where neither moth nor rust destroys, and where thieves do not break in or steal" (Matt. 6:19-20). Whatever we do for the Lord now, including suffering for Him—in fact, especially suffering for Him—reaps eternal dividends.

God's dividends are not ordinary dividends. They are not only eternal but are also **great.** If God "is able to do exceedingly abundantly beyond all that *we* ask or think" (Eph. 3:20), how much more abundantly is He able to grant what He Himself promises to us?

We often hear, and perhaps are tempted to think, that it is unspiritual and crass to serve God for the sake of rewards. But that is one of the motives that God Himself gives for serving Him. We first of all serve and obey Christ because we love Him, just as on earth He loved and obeyed the Father because He loved Him. But it was also because of "the joy set before Him" that Christ Himself "endured the cross, despising the shame" (Heb. 12:2). It is neither selfish nor unspiritual to do the Lord's work for a motive that He Himself gives and has followed.

Second, we are to **rejoice** because the world **persecuted the prophets who were before** us in the same way that it persecutes us. When we suffer for Christ's sake, we are in the best possible company. To be afflicted for righteousness's sake is to stand in the ranks of the prophets. Persecution is a mark of our faithfulness just as it was a mark of the prophets' faithfulness. When we suffer for Christ's sake we know beyond a doubt that we belong to God, because we are experiencing the same reaction from the world that the prophets experienced.

When we suffer for our Lord we join with the prophets and the other saints of old who "experienced mockings and scourgings, yes, also chains and imprisonment. They were stoned, they were sawn in two, they were tempted, they were put to death with the sword; they went about in sheepskins, in goatskins, being destitute, afflicted, ill-treated (men of whom the world was not worthy), wandering in deserts and mountains and caves and holes in the ground" (Heb. 11:36-38). Though the world is not worthy of their company, every persecuted believer is. To be persecuted verifies that we belong to the line of the righteous.

Our assurance of salvation does not come from knowing we made a decision somewhere in the past. Rather, our assurance that the decision was a true decision for Jesus Christ is found in the life of righteousness that results in suffering for the sake of Christ. Many will claim to have preached Christ, cast out demons, and done mighty works for His sake, but will be refused heaven (Matt. 7:21-23). But none who have suffered righteously for Him will be left out.

The world cannot handle the righteous life that characterizes kingdom living. It is not understandable and acceptable to them, and they cannot stomach it even in others. Poverty of spirit runs counter to the pride of the unbelieving heart. The repentant, contrite disposition that mourns over sin is never appreciated by the callous, indifferent, unsympathetic world. The meek and quiet spirit that takes wrong and does not strike back is regarded as pusillanimous, and it rasps against the militant, vengeful spirit characteristic of the world. To long after righteousness is repugnant to those whose fleshly cravings are rebuked by it, as is a merciful spirit to those whose hearts are hard and cruel. Purity of heart is a painful light that exposes hypocrisy and corruption, and peacemaking is a virtue praised by the contentious, self-seeking world in words but not in heart.

John Chrysostom, a godly leader in the fourth-century church preached so strongly against sin that he offended the unscrupulous Empress Eudoxia as well as many church officials. When summoned before Emperor Arcadius, Chrysostom was threatened with banishment if he did not cease his uncompromising preaching. His response was, "Sire, you cannot banish me, for the world is my Father's house." "Then I will slay you," Arcadius said. "Nay, but you cannot, for my life is hid with Christ in God," came the answer. "Your treasures will be confiscated" was the next threat, to which John replied, "Sire, that cannot be, either. My treasures are in heaven, where none can break through and steal." "Then I will drive you from man, and you will have no friends left!" was the final, desperate warning. "That you cannot do, either," answered John, "for I have a Friend in heaven who has said, 'I will never leave you or forsake you.'" Chrysostom was indeed banished, first to Armenia and then farther away to Pityus on the Back Sea, to which he never arrived because he died on the way. But neither his banishment nor his death disproved or diminished his claims. The things that he valued most highly not even an emperor could take from him.

Salt of the Earth and Light of the World
(5:13-16)

21

You are the salt of the earth; but if the salt has become tasteless, how will it be made salty again? It is good for nothing anymore, except to be thrown out and trampled under foot by men. You are the light of the world. A city set on a hill cannot be hidden. Nor do men light a lamp, and put it under the peck-measure, but on the lampstand; and it gives light to all who are in the house. Let your light shine before men in such a way that they may see your good works, and glorify your Father who is in heaven. (5:13-16)

In these four verses the Lord summarizes the function of believers in the world. Reduced to one word, that function is *influence*. Whoever lives according to the Beatitudes is going to function in the world as salt and light. Christian character consciously or unconsciously affects other people for better or for worse. As John Donne reminds us, "No man is an island."

An ancient Greek myth tells of a goddess who came to earth unseen but whose presence was always known by the blessings she left behind in her pathway. Trees burned by forest fires sprouted new leaves, and violets sprang up in her footprints. As she passed a stagnant pool its water became fresh, and parched fields turned green as she walked through them. Hills and valleys blossomed with new life and beauty wherever she went. Another Greek story tells of a princess sent as a present to a king. She was as beautiful as Aphrodite and her breath was as sweet as perfume. But she carried with her the contagion of death and decay. From infancy she had fed on nothing but poison and became so permeated with it that she poisoned the very atmosphere around her. Her breath would kill a swarm of insects; she would pick a flower and it would wither. A bird flying too close would fall dead at her feet.

Andrew Murray lived an exceptionally holy life. Among those on whom his influence was the greatest were his children and grandchildren. Five of his six sons became ministers of the gospel and four of his daughters became minister's wives. Ten grandsons became ministers and thirteen grandchildren became missionaries.

Woodrow Wilson told the story of being in a barbershop one time. "I was sitting in a barber chair when I became aware that a powerful personality had entered the room. A man had come quietly in upon the same errand as myself to have his hair cut and sat in the chair next to me. Every word the man uttered, though it was not in the least didactic, showed a personal interest in the man who was serving him. And before I got through with what was being done to me I was aware I had attended an evangelistic service, because Mr. D. L. Moody was in that chair. I purposely lingered in the room after he had left and noted the singular affect that his visit had brought upon the barber shop. They talked in undertones. They did not know his name, but they knew something had elevated their thoughts, and I felt that I left that place as I should have left a place of worship."

Many years ago Elihu Burrit wrote, "No human being can come into this world without increasing or diminishing the sum total of human happiness, not only of the present but of every subsequent age of humanity. No one can detach himself from this connection. There in no sequestered spot in the universe, no dark niche along the disc of nonexistence to which he can retreat from his relations with others, where he can withdraw the influence of his existence upon the moral destiny of the world. Everywhere his presence or absence will be felt. Everywhere he will have companions who will be better or worse because of him. It is an old saying, and one of the fearful and fathomless statements of import, that we are forming characters for eternity. Forming characters? Whose? Our own or others? Both. And in that momentous fact lies the peril and responsibility of our existence. Who is sufficient for the thought? Thousands of my fellow beings will yearly enter eternity with characters differing from those they would have carried thither had I never lived. The sunlight of that world will reveal my finger marks in their primary formations and in their successive strata of thought and life."

In Matthew 5:13-16 Jesus talks about the influence of His people on the world for God and for good. In His high priestly prayer Jesus said to His Father, "I do not ask Thee to take them out of the world, but to keep them from the evil one. They are not of the world, even as I am not of the world. . . . As Thou didst send Me into the world, I also have sent them into the world" (John 17:15-16, 18). John wrote, "Do not love the world, nor the things in the world" (1 John 2:15). Christ's kingdom people are not to reflect the world but they are to influence the world; they are to be in it but not of it.

When we live the life of the Beatitudes some people will respond favorably and be saved, whereas others will ridicule and persecute us. In the words of Paul, we will manifest "the sweet aroma of the knowledge of [Christ] in every place. For we are a fragrance of Christ to God among those who are being saved and among those who are perishing; to the one an aroma from death to death, to the other an aroma from life to life" (2 Cor. 2:14-16). In either case our lives have profound effects, and even persecution is not to alter our function in the world. We "are a chosen race, a royal priesthood, a holy nation, a people for God's own possession, that [we] may proclaim the excellencies of Him who has called [us] out of darkness into His marvelous light" (1 Pet. 2:9).

Though Jesus was speaking before a great multitude of people on the hillside, His teaching about kingdom life was primarily for His disciples, for those who believed in Him. His concern was for the all of the multitude, and in hearing His teaching on godly living many of them may have been drawn to faith. But the principles He teaches here are appropriate only for believers, for they are impossible to follow apart from the power of God's own Spirit.

Here is a mandate for Christians to influence the world. The Beatitudes are not to be lived in isolation or only among fellow believers, but everywhere we go. God's only witnesses are His children, and the world has no other way of knowing of Him except through the testimony of what we are.

The figures of salt and light emphasize different characteristics of influence, but their basic purpose is the same. They will both be studied from the aspects of the presupposition of the world's corruption and darkness, the plan for believers' godly dominion in the world, the problem of the danger of failure, and the purpose of glorifying God.

THE PRESUPPOSITION: CORRUPTION AND DARKNESS

The world needs salt because it is corrupt and it needs light because it is dark. G. Campbell Morgan said, "Jesus, looking out over the multitudes of His day, saw the corruption, the disintegration of life at every point, its breakup, its spoilation; and, because of His love of the multitudes, He knew the thing that they needed most was salt in order that the corruption should be arrested. He saw them also wrapped in gloom, sitting in darkness, groping amid mists and fogs. He knew that they needed, above everything else, . . . light" (*The Gospel According to Matthew* [New York: Revell, 1929], p. 46).

The biblical world view is that the world is corrupted and decayed, that it is dark and darkening. "Evil men and impostors will proceed from bad to worse, deceiving and being deceived," Paul warns (2 Tim. 3:13). The world cannot do anything but get worse, because it has no inherent goodness to build on, no inherent spiritual and moral life in which it can grow. Year after year the system of evil accumulates a deeper darkness.

A college student told me his professor had recently told the class that marriage was on the decline because man was evolving to a higher level. Marriage was something that man needed only at the lower stages of his evolutionary development. Now that man had ascended farther up the evolutionary scale, marriage was falling off just as his prehensile tail had done millions of years ago.

Any person who knows the history of mankind, even the history of the past hundred years, and thinks that man is evolving upward is "deceiving and being deceived," just as Paul said. Man has increased in scientific, medical, historical, educational, psychological, and technological knowledge to an astounding degree. But he has not changed his own basic nature and he has not improved society. Man's knowledge has greatly improved, but his morals have progressively degenerated. His confidence has increased, but his peace of mind has diminished. His accomplishments have increased, but his sense of purpose and meaning have all but disappeared. Instead of improving the moral and spiritual quality of his life, man's discoveries and accomplishments have simply provided ways for him to express and promote his depravity faster and more destructively. Modern man has simply invented more ways to corrupt and destroy himself.

Many philosophers, poets, and religious leaders at the end of the last century had great optimism about man's having come of age, about his inevitable moral and social improvement. They believed that Utopia was around the corner and that man was getting better and better in every way. The golden age of mankind was near. Wars would be a bad memory, crime and violence would disappear, ignorance would be gone, and disease would be eradicated. Peace and brotherhood would reign completely and universally. Few people today hold to such blind, unrealistic ideas.

It was not many generations after the Fall that "the Lord saw that the wickedness of man was great on the earth, and that every intent of the thoughts of his heart was only evil continually" (Gen. 6:5). Because wickedness was so great, God destroyed every person but eight—and they were far from perfect. A few generations after that, the cities of Sodom and Gomorrah became so rotten from the offspring of those eight that God destroyed them with fire and brimstone. Another day of judgment is coming when God will again rain fire on earth, but that destruction will be a holocaust such as men have never dreamed of. "The present heavens and earth by His word are being reserved for fire, kept for the day of judgment and destruction of ungodly men. . . . the heavens will pass away with a roar and the elements will be destroyed with intense heat, and the earth and its works will be burned up" (2 Pet. 3:7, 10).

Man is infected with the deadly virus of sin, which has no cure apart from God. Yet unlike their attitude toward physical diseases, most men do not want their sin cured. They love their decadence and they hate God's righteousness (cf. John 3:19-21). They love their own way and they hate God's.

Man's knowledge is increasing by quantum leaps, but his increased knowledge is mechanical knowledge, inanimate knowledge, lifeless knowledge, knowledge that has no bearing on the inner man (cf. 2 Tim. 3:7). His knowledge does not retard his corruption but rather is used to intensify and defend it.

Bertrand Russell devoted most of his 96 years to the study of philosophy.

Yet at the end of his life he acknowledged that philosophy proved to be a washout, and had taken him nowhere. Nothing he had thought or had heard that other philosophers had thought had changed the world for the better. He felt that the basic causes of man's problems, not to mention the solutions, had evaded the best minds of every age including his own.

Some scientists have proposed that by surgery or careful electronic stimulation of the brain, a person's bad impulses can be eradicated, leaving only the better part of his nature. Others propose that the ideal, crime-free, problem-free person will be developed by genetic engineering. But every part of every man is corrupt. He has no inherent, naturally good traits that can be isolated from the bad. His total nature is depraved. David knew that he was sinful from the moment of his conception. "Behold, I was brought forth in iniquity, and in sin my mother conceived me" (Ps. 51:5). There is no good part in man from which a better can be constructed or from which his corrupt part can be isolated. Isaiah said, "The whole head is sick, and the whole heart is faint" (Isa. 1:5), and Jeremiah labeled the heart as "more deceitful than all else" and as "desperately sick" (Jer. 17:9).

We go on from war to greater war, from crime to greater crime, from immorality to greater immorality, from perversion to greater perversion. The spiral is downward, not upward (see Rom. 1:18-32). Despair and pessimism reign in our day, because the honest person knows that man has not been able to retard his descent. He hopes that he can just live out his own life before someone pushes the button that blows mankind into oblivion.

A leading news magazine reported a few years ago that Americans tend to see themselves as potential saints rather than real-life sinners. Another leading magazine reported, "Today's young radicals in particular are almost painfully sensitive to . . . wrongs of their society, and they denounce them violently. But at the same time they are typically American in that they fail to place evil in its historic and human perspective. To them evil is not an irreducible component of man; it is not an inescapable fact of life, but something committed by the older generation, attributable to a particular class or the establishment and eradicable through love or revolution" (*Time,* 5 December 1969).

Just as every person is affected by the sin problem, every person also contributes to the sin problem.

THE PLAN: THE DOMINION OF HIS DISCIPLES

The church cannot accept the world's self-centeredness, easy solutions, immorality, amorality, and materialism. We are called to minister to the world while being separated from its standards and ways. Sadly, however, the church today is more influenced by the world than the world is influenced by the church.

In both verse 13 and verse 14 the pronoun **you** is emphatic. The idea is, "You are the only salt of the earth" and "You are the only light of the world." The world's corruption will not be retarded and its darkness will not be illumined unless God's people are its salt and light. The very ones who are despised by the world and persecuted by the world are the world's only hope.

The **you** in both verses is also plural. It is His whole body, the church, that is called to be the world's salt and light. Each grain of salt has its limited influence, but it is only as the church collectively is scattered in the world that change will come. One ray of light will accomplish little, but when joined with other rays a great light is created.

Some years ago a magazine carried a series of pictures that graphically depicted a tragic story. The first picture was of a vast wheat field in western Kansas. The second showed a distressed mother sitting in a farmhouse in the center of the field of wheat. The accompanying story explained that her four-year-old son had wandered away from the house and into the field when she was not looking. The mother and father looked and looked all day but the little fellow was too short to see or be seen over the wheat. The third picture showed dozens of friends and neighbors who had heard of the boy's plight and who had joined hands the next morning to make a long human chain as they walked through the field searching. The final picture was of the heartbroken father holding his lifeless son who had been found too late and had died of exposure. The caption underneath read, "O God, if only we had joined hands sooner."

The world is full of lost souls who cannot see their way above the distractions and barriers of the world and cannot find their way to the Father's house until Christians join together as salt and light and sweep through the world in search of them. Our work is not simply as individual grains of salt or as individual rays of light but as the whole church of Jesus Christ.

Are stresses being rather than doing. Jesus is stating a fact, not giving a command or request. Salt and light represent what Christians *are*. The only question, as Jesus goes on to say, is whether or not we are tasteful salt and effective light. The very fact that we belong to Jesus Christ makes us His salt and light in the world.

Christ is the source of our savor and of our light. He is "the true light which, coming into the world, enlightens every man" (John 1:9). "While I am in the world, I am the light of the world," He said (John 9:5). But now that He has left the world His light comes to the world through those whom He has enlightened. We shine forth the reflected light of Christ. "You were formerly darkness, but now you are light in the Lord," Paul tells us; "walk as children of light" (Eph. 5:8). "For He delivered us from the domain of darkness, and transferred us to the kingdom of His beloved Son" (Col. 1:13).

We are God's salt to retard corruption and His light to reveal truth. One function is negative, the other positive. One is silent, the other is verbal. By the indirect influence of the way we live we retard corruption, and by the direct influence of what we say we manifest light.

Both salt and light are unlike that which they are to influence. God has changed us from being part of the corrupted and corrupting world to being salt that can help preserve it. He has changed us from our own darkness to be His agents of giving light to others. By definition, an influence must be different from that which it influences, and Christians therefore must be different from the world they are called to influence. We cannot influence the world for God when we are worldly ourselves. We cannot give light to the world if we revert to places and ways of darkness ourselves.

The great blessings emphasized in verses 3-12 lead to the great responsibilities of verses 13-16. The blessings of heaven, comfort, inheriting the earth, being filled with righteousness, being given mercy, being called God's children, and being given heavenly reward bring the responsibility of being His salt and light in the world.

BEING SALT

Salt has always been valuable in human society, often much more so than it is today. During a period of ancient Greek history it was called *theon,* which means divine. The Romans held that, except for the sun, nothing was more valuable than salt. Often Roman soldiers were paid in salt, and it was from that practice that the expression "not worth his salt" originated.

In many ancient societies salt was used as a mark of friendship. For two persons to share salt indicated a mutual responsibility to look after one another's welfare. Even if a worst enemy ate salt with you, you were obliged to treat him as a friend.

Salt was frequently used in the ancient Near East to bind a covenant, somewhat in the way an agreement or contract is notarized in our day. When the parties to a covenant ate salt together before witnesses, the covenant was given special authentication. Though no particulars are given in the account, we learn from 2 Chronicles 13:5 that God made a covenant of salt with David. God prescribed that all sacrificial offerings in Israel were to be offered with salt "so that the salt of the covenant of your God shall not be lacking" (Lev. 2:13).

In numerous ways Jesus' hearers—whether Greek, Roman, or Jewish—would have understood **salt of the earth** to represent a valuable commodity. Though most could not have understood His full meaning, they knew He was saying that His followers were to have an extremely important function in the world. Whatever else it may have represented, salt always stood for that which was of high value and importance.

Many suggestions have been made as to the particular characteristics of salt that Jesus intended to associate with this figure. Some interpreters point out that salt is white and therefore represents purity. As the "pure in heart" (v. 8), Jesus' disciples are to be pure before the world and are to be God's means of helping purify the rest of the world. Their glistening white moral and spiritual purity is to contrast with the moral discolor of the world. Christians are to exemplify the divine standards of righteousness in thought, speech, and actions, remaining "unstained by the world" (James 1:27). All that is certainly true; but it does not seem to the point, because saltiness, not the color of salt, is the issue.

Others emphasize the characteristic of flavor. That is, Christians are to add divine flavor to the world. Just as many foods are tasteless without salt, the world is drab and tasteless without the presence of Christians. Someone has even said, "We Christians have no business being boring. Our function is to add flavor and excitement to the world." Christians are a means of God's blessing mankind, including unbelievers, just as He sends His sun and rain on the righteous and unrighteous alike.

There are certain senses in which that principle is true. An unbelieving marriage partner is sanctified by a believing spouse (1 Cor. 7:14), and God offered to spare Sodom for the sake of only ten righteous people, if that many could be found within it (Gen. 18:32).

The problem with that view, however, is that, from the earliest days of the church, the world has considered Christianity to be anything but attractive and "flavorful." It has, in fact, often found the most spiritual Christians to be the most unpalatable. In the world's eyes, Christians, almost above all others, take the flavor *out* of life. Christianity is stifling, restrictive, and a rain on the world's parade.

After Christianity became a recognized religion of the Roman Empire, the emperor Julian lamented, "Have you looked at these Christians closely? Hollow-eyed, pale-cheeked, flat-breasted, they brood their lives away unspurred by ambition. The sun shines for them, but they don't see it. The earth offers them its fullness, but they desire it not. All their desire is to renounce and suffer that they may come to die."

Oliver Wendell Holmes reportedly once said that he might have entered the ministry if certain clergymen he knew had not looked and acted so much like undertakers. Sometimes the world is turned away from the church because Christians are hypocritical, self-righteous, judgmental, and truly boring by any standard. But even when the church is faithful—indeed, especially when it is faithful—the world does not value whatever taste or aroma it sees in Christianity. Paul reminds us that Christians are an "aroma from life to life" and "a fragrance of Christ to God among those who are being saved," but are an "aroma of death to death" among "those who are perishing" (2 Cor. 2:15-16).

Because salt stings when placed in a wound, some interpreters believe that Jesus meant to illustrate just the opposite characteristic to that of flavor. Christians are to sting the world, prick its conscience, make it uncomfortable in the presence of God's holy gospel.

That analogy also has merit. The church frequently is so concerned with trying to please, attract, and excuse that its witness against sin is obscured and all but lost. We may be so concerned with not offending others that we fail to confront them with their lostness and their desperate need to be saved from their sin. A gospel that does not confront sin is not the gospel of Jesus Christ.

Some years ago a young couple who came to me to be married said they knew the Lord had brought them together and given them to each other. The woman claimed to have been a Christian all her life, but her concept of salvation was that of trying to please God by doing the best she could. She admitted that, although she had filed for divorce because her husband had been unfaithful, she was still married to him. On further questioning, she admitted that she had been committing fornication with the young man she now wanted to marry. The young man claimed to be born again, but he saw no great wrong in their relationship and no reason why they should not be married in a Christian service. I told them that God could not possibly have brought them together because they were living contrary to His revealed will—and worse, trying to justify it. At that point they both got up and angrily stormed out of the office.

The church cannot stand for the Lord if it does not stand for His Word, and when it stands for His Word its witness will often sting.

Salt also creates thirst. Partly because it increases the body's craving for water, salt tablets often are given to those who do hard work in excessive heat. Without proper intake of fluids, dehydration and even death may result. God intends for His people so to live and testify before the world that others will be made more aware of their spiritual dehydration and danger. A person may see our peace in a trying circumstance, or our confidence in what we believe, and thereby be persuaded to try our faith.

I believe that all of the foregoing analogies have some validity. Christians are to be pure; they should add a certain attractiveness to the gospel; they should be true to God's Word even when it stings; and their living should create a thirst for God in those who do not know Him.

But I believe the primary characteristic Jesus emphasizes is that of preservation. Christians are a preserving influence in the world; they retard moral and spiritual spoilage. When the church is taken out of the world at the rapture, Satan's perverse and wicked power will be unleashed in an unprecedented way (see 2 Thess. 2:7-12). Evil will go wild and demons will be almost unbridled. Once God's people are removed it will take only seven years for the world to descend to the very pits of hellishness (see Dan. 9:27; Rev. 6-19).

Until that day Christians can have a powerful influence on the welfare of the world. Martyn Lloyd-Jones writes, "Most competent historians are agreed in saying that what undoubtedly saved [England] from a revolution such as that experienced in France at the end of the eighteenth century was nothing but the Evangelical Revival. This was not because anything was done directly, but because masses of individuals had become Christians and were living this better life and had this higher outlook. The whole political situation was affected, and the great Acts of Parliament which were passed in the last century were mostly due to the fact that there were such large numbers of individual Christians found in the land" (*Studies in the Sermon on the Mount* [Grand Rapids: Eerdmans, 1971], 1:157).

As God's children and as the temples of His Holy Spirit, Christians represent God's presence in **the earth**. We are the salt that prevents the entire earth from degenerating even faster than it is.

Helen Ewing was saved as a young girl in Scotland and gave her life completely to the lordship of Christ. When she died at the age of 22 it is said that all Scotland wept. She had expected to serve God as a missionary in Europe and had become fluent in the Russian language. But she was not able to fulfill that dream.

She had no obvious gifts such as speaking or writing, and she had never traveled far from home. Yet by the time she died she had won hundreds of people to Jesus Christ. Countless missionaries mourned her death because they knew that a great channel of their spiritual strength was gone. She had risen every morning at five in order to study God's Word and to pray. Her diary revealed that she regularly prayed for over three hundred missionaries by name. Everywhere she went the atmosphere was changed. If someone was telling a dirty story, he would stop if he saw her coming. If people were complaining, they would become ashamed of it in her presence. An acquaintance reported that while she was at Glasgow University she left the fragrance of Christ wherever she went. In everything she said and did she was God's salt.

BEING LIGHT

Jesus also calls us to be light. **You are the light of the world**. Whereas salt is hidden, light is obvious. Salt works secretly, while light works openly. Salt works from within, light from without. Salt is more the indirect influence of the gospel, while light is more its direct communication. Salt works primarily through our living, while light works primarily through what we teach and preach. Salt is largely negative. It can retard corruption, but it cannot change corruption into incorruption. Light is more positive. It not only reveals what is wrong and false but helps produce what is righteous and true.

In his introduction to the book of Acts, Luke refers to his gospel as "the first account I composed, Theophilus, about all that Jesus began to do and teach" (1:1). Christ's work always has to do with both doing and speaking, with living and teaching.

David wrote, "For with Thee is the fountain of life; in Thy light we see light" (Ps. 36:9). "God is light," John reminds us, "and in Him there is no darkness at all. If we say that we have fellowship with Him and yet walk in the darkness, we lie and do not practice the truth; but if we walk in the light as He Himself is in the light, we have fellowship with one another, and the blood of Jesus His Son cleanses us from all sin" (1 John 1:5-7). Light is not given simply to have but to live by. "Thy word is a lamp to my feet, and a light to my path," the psalmist tells us (Ps. 119:105). God's light is to walk by and to live by. In its fullest sense, God's light is the full revelation of His Word—the written Word of Scripture and the living Word of Jesus Christ.

God's people are to proclaim God's light in a world engulfed in darkness, just as their Lord came "to shine upon those who sit in darkness and the shadow of death" (Luke 1:79). Christ is the true light, and we are His reflections. He is the Sun, and we are His moons. A free rendering of 2 Corinthians 4:6 could be, "God, who first ordered the light to shine in the darkness has flooded our hearts with His light. We now can enlighten men only because we can give them knowledge of the glory of God as we have seen it in the face of Jesus Christ." God sheds His light on the world through those who have received His light through Jesus Christ.

The Jews had long claimed to have God's light, and He had long called them to be His light. But because they had ignored and rejected His light, they could not be His light. They were confident that they were guides "to the blind, a light to those who are in darkness," but Paul told them they were blind guides and lamps without light. "You, therefore, who teach another, do you not teach yourself?" he asks (Rom. 2:19-21). They had the light, but they were not living by it. "You who preach that one should not steal, do you steal?" Paul continues by way of illustration. "You who say that one should not commit adultery, do you commit adultery?" (vv. 21-22). We are to prove ourselves "to be blameless and innocent, children of God above reproach in the midst of a crooked and perverse generation, among whom [we are to] appear as lights in the world" (Phil. 2:15).

By its nature and by definition light must be visible in order to illuminate. Christians must be more than the largely indirect influence of salt; they must also be the direct and noticeable instruments of light.

Both in the daytime and at night, **a city set on a hill cannot be hidden.** It is exposed for all to see. By day its houses and buildings stand out on the landscape, and at night the many lights shining out of its windows make it impossible to miss. A secret Christian is as incongruous as a hidden light. Lights are to illuminate, not to be hidden; to be displayed, not to be covered. Christians are to be both subtle salt and conspicuous light.

God did not give the gospel of His Son to be the secret, hidden treasure of a few but to enlighten every person (John 1:9). Many reject the light and reject those who bring it, but just as God offers His light to the whole world, so must His church. It is not our gospel but God's, and He gives it to us not only for our own sakes but the entire world's. True believers *are* salt and light, and must fulfill that identity.

THE PROBLEM: DANGER OF FAILURE

but if the salt has become tasteless, how will it be made salty again? It is good for nothing anymore, except to be thrown out and trampled under foot by men. (5:13*b*)

Much salt in Palestine, such as that found on the shores of the Dead Sea, is contaminated with gypsum and other minerals that make it taste flat and even repulsive. When a batch of such contaminated salt would find its way into a household and be discovered, it was thrown out. People would be careful not to throw it on a garden or field, because it would kill whatever was planted. Instead it would be thrown onto a path or road, where it would gradually be ground into the dirt and disappear.

There is a sense in which salt cannot really become unsalty. But contamination can cause it to lose its value as salt. Its saltiness can no longer function.

Jesus is not speaking of losing salvation. God does not allow any of His own to be taken from Him. "My sheep hear My voice, and I know them, and they follow Me; and I give eternal life to them, and they shall never perish; and no one shall snatch them out of My hand," Jesus assures us (John 10:27). Christians cannot lose their salvation, just as salt cannot lose its inherent saltiness. But Christians can lose their value and effectiveness in the kingdom when sin and worldliness contaminate their lives, just as salt can become **tasteless** when contaminated by other minerals. It is a common New Testament truth that although true believers are identified as righteous, godly, and salty, there are times when they fail to be what they are (cf. Rom. 7:15-25), which Peter says leads to loss of assurance (2 Pet. 1:9-10), not loss of salvation.

With great responsibility there is often great danger. We cannot be an influence for purity in the world if we have compromised our own purity. We cannot sting the world's conscience if we continually go against our own. We cannot stimulate thirst for righteousness if we have lost our own. We cannot be used of God to retard the corruption of sin in the world if our own lives become corrupted by sin. To lose our saltiness is not to lose our salvation, but it is to lose our effectiveness and to become disqualified for service (see 1 Cor. 9:27).

Pure salt does not lose its saltiness, that which makes it valuable and effective. Christians who are pure in heart do not become **tasteless**, ineffective, and useless in the kingdom of God.

Light, too, is in danger of becoming useless. Like salt, it cannot lose its essential nature. A hidden light is still light, but it is useless light. That is why people do not **light a lamp, and put it under the peck-measure, but on a lampstand; and it gives light to all who are in the house.** The exemplary woman praised in Proverbs 31 does not let her lamp go out at night (v. 18). There was always illumination for anyone in the household who had to get up or find his way home during the night. A light that is hidden under a **peck**-sized basket cannot even be used to read by; it helps neither the person who hides it nor anyone else.

Whether we hide our light because of fear of offending others, because of indifference and lovelessness, or because of anything else, we demonstrate unfaithfulness to the Lord.

THE PURPOSE: TO GLORIFY GOD

Let your light shine before men in such a way that they may see your good works, and glorify your Father who is in heaven. (5:16)

The word (*kalos*) for **good** that Jesus uses here does not so much emphasize quality—though that obviously is important—as it does attractiveness, beautiful appearance. Letting our **light shine before men** allows them to see our **good works,** the beauty the Lord has worked in us. To see good works by us is to see Christ in us. That is why Jesus says, **let your light shine.** It is not something we create or make up, but something we allow the Lord to do through us. It is God's light; our choice is whether to hide it or let it shine.

The purpose of letting our light shine and reveal our good works is not to bring attention or praise to ourselves but to God. Our intent should be that, in what we are and in what we do, others may see God in order that they may **glorify** [our] **Father who is in heaven**. Jesus' speaking of the **Father** emphasizes God's tenderness and intimacy, and speaking of His being **in heaven** emphasizes His majesty and holiness, as He is pictured dwelling in the splendor of His eternal holy home. Our good works are to magnify God's grace and power. This is the supreme calling of life: glorifying God. Everything we do is to cause others to give praise to the God who is the source of all that is good. The way we live should lead those around us to **glorify** (*doxazō,* from which we get *doxology*) the heavenly **Father**.

When what we do causes people to be attracted to us rather than to God, to see our human character rather than His divine character, we can be sure that what they see is not His light.

It is said of Robert Murray McCheyne, a godly Scottish minister of the last century, that his face carried such a hallowed expression that people were known to fall on their knees and accept Jesus Christ as Savior when they looked at him. Others were so attracted by the self-giving beauty and holiness of his life that they found his Master irresistible.

It was also said of the French pietist Francois Fenelon that his communion with God was such that his face shined with divine radiance. A religious skeptic who was compelled to spend the night in an inn with Fenelon, hurried away the next morning, saying, "If I spend another night with that man I'll be a Christian in spite of myself."

That is the kind of salt and light God wants His kingdom people to be.

Christ and the Law —part 1 The Preeminence of Scripture (5:17)

22

Do not think that I came to abolish the Law or the Prophets; I did not come to abolish, but to fulfill. (5:17)

In a recent book titled *The Interaction of Law and Religion* (Nashville: Abingdon, 1974), Harold J. Berman, professor of law at Harvard University, has developed a significant thesis. He notes that Western culture has had a massive loss of confidence in law and in religion. One of the most important causes of this double loss of confidence is the radical separation that has been made between the two. Berman concludes that you cannot have workable rules for behavior without religion, because only religion provides an absolute base on which morality and law can be based. The author fears that western society is doomed to relativism in law because of the loss of an absolute. When men break away from the idea of an authoritative religion, and even from the concept of God, they break away from the possibility of absolute truth. Their only remaining resource is existential relativism, a slippery, unstable, and ever-changing base on which no authoritative system of law or morals can be built. Religionless law can never command authority.

In that book Professor Berman notes that "Thomas Franck of New York University [has observed that law] in contrast to religion 'has become undisguisedly a pragmatic human process. It is made by men and it lays no claim to divine origin or eternal validity.'" (p. 27). Berman says that this observation

> leads Professor Franck to the view that a judge, in reaching a decision, is not propounding a truth but is rather experimenting in the solution of a problem, and if his decision is reversed by a higher court or if it is subsequently overruled, that does not mean it was wrong but only that it was, or became in the course of time, unsatisfactory. Having broken away from religion, Franck states, law is now characterized by "existential relativism." Indeed, it is now generally recognized "that no judicial decision is ever 'final,' that the law both follows the event (is not eternal or certain) and is made by man (is not divine or True)." (pp. 27-28)

Professor Berman goes on to ask, "If law is merely an experiment, and if judicial decisions are only hunches, why should individuals or groups of people observe those legal rules or commands that do not conform to their own interests?" (p. 28)

He is right. Rules without absolutes are rules without authority, except the authority of force and coercion. When God is abandoned, truth is abandoned; and when truth is abandoned, the basis for morals and law is abandoned. A consistent, coherent legal system cannot be built on philosophical humanism, on the principle that right and wrong fluctuate according to man's ideas and feelings.

In an article in *Esquire* magazine titled "The Reasonable Right," Peter Steinfels asks, "How can moral principles be grounded and social institutions ultimately legitimized in the absence of a religiously based culture?" (13 February 1979). The obvious answer is that they cannot be.

If there is no religious absolute there can be no basis for real law. People will not respect or long obey laws that are only judicial guesses. An evil, godless society, floating about on a sea of relativism, realizes that it has no foundation, no anchor, no unmoving point of reference. Law becomes a matter of preference and order a matter of power. A democracy where power is ultimately vested in the people is particularly vulnerable to chaos.

Is there an absolute basis for truth, for law, for morals, for real right and wrong; and if so, what is it? Those questions are the essence of what Jesus teaches in Matthew 5:17-20. The absolute, He says, is the law of the eternally sovereign God. God has laid down His absolute, eternal, abiding law and made it known to men. And as God's own Son, Jesus declared unequivocally that He did not come to teach or practice anything contrary to that law in even the slightest way, but to uphold it entirely.

We continually hear the idea that because times have changed the Bible does not fit our day. The truth, of course, is the opposite. The Bible always fits, because the Bible is God's perfect, eternal, and infallible Word. It is the standard by which true "fit" is measured. It is the world that does not fit the Bible, and not because the world has changed but because the Bible has *not* changed. Outwardly the world has changed a great deal since biblical days, but in its basic nature and orientation it has always been opposed to God and has never conformed to His Word. The world has never fit Scripture.

The argument is also proposed that Scripture is but a collection of various men's ideas about God and about right and wrong. One person's interpretation of the Bible is therefore just as good as another's, and there is no place for dogmatism. Men have been left free to believe or not believe, to follow or not follow, any or all of Scripture as it suits them. Each person becomes his own judge over Scripture, and the end result for most is to disregard it altogether.

It is impossible, however, to take Jesus seriously and not take Scripture seriously. It is impossible to believe Jesus spoke absolute truth and not to consider Scripture to be that absolute truth, because that is precisely what Jesus taught it to be. If Jesus was mistaken or deluded on this point, there would be no reason to accept anything else that He said. At the outset of His ministry He makes clear that His authority and Scripture's authority are the same; His truth and Scripture's truth are identical and inseparable.

God's revealed Word, Jesus says, not only is truth, but is truth conveyed with absolute, inviolable authority. It is in that authority that He came to teach and to minister, and it is to that authority that He commands His kingdom citizens to bow and obey. "Let it speak," He says. "Let it rebuke, correct, shatter, overturn all your evil ways and let it show the absolute, inerrant, and perfect will of God—and the way to eternal life."

For thirty years Jesus lived in privacy and obscurity. Only Mary and intimates to the family would have remembered the miraculous events that surrounded His birth and early years. As far as His friends and neighbors were concerned, He was but a unique Jewish carpenter. It was when He began His ministry, when He was immersed in the Jordan by John the Baptist and started to preach, that all eyes suddenly turned on Him. At that point, even the leaders of Israel could not ignore Him.

Jesus' meekness, humility, gentleness, and love marked Him out in great contrast to the proud, selfish, and arrogant scribes, Pharisees, Sadducees, and priests. His call to repentance and His proclamation of the gospel of the kingdom made people listen, even if they did not understand or agree. They wondered if He was just another prophet, a special prophet, or a false prophet. They wondered if He was a political or military revolutionary who might be the Messiah they anxiously awaited, who would break the yoke of Rome. He did not talk or act like anyone else they had ever heard or seen. He did not identify Himself with any of the scribal schools, or with any of the sects or movements of the time. Nor did He identify Himself with Herod or with Rome. Instead, Jesus openly and lovingly identified Himself with the outcast, the sick, the sinful, and the needy of every sort. He proclaimed grace and dispensed mercy. Whereas all the other rabbis and religious leaders talked only about the religious externals, He taught about the heart. They focused on ceremonies, rituals, and outward acts of every kind, whereas He focused on the heart. They set themselves above other men and demanded their service, while He set Himself below other men and became their Servant.

Of primary concern to every faithful Jew seeking to evaluate Jesus was, "What does He think of the law; what does He think of Moses and the prophets?" The leaders often confronted Jesus on matters of the law. Many Jews believed that the Messiah would radically revise or completely overturn the Mosaic law and establish His own new standards. They interpreted Jeremiah 31:31 as teaching that God's new promised covenant would annul the old covenant and start over on a completely new moral basis. Sickened of the demanding, hypocritical legalism of the Pharisees, many people hoped the Messiah would bring in a new day of freedom from the burdensome, mechanical, and meaningless demands of the traditional system.

Even the scribes and Pharisees realized God's revealed standards of righteousness were impossible to keep—which is one reason they invented traditions that were easier to keep than the law. The traditions were more involved, complicated, and detailed than God's law, but for the most part, they stayed within the bounds of human accomplishment, within what man could do in his own power and resources. Because of that, the traditions invariably and inevitably lowered the standards of God's scriptural teaching. The whole system of self-righteousness is built on reducing God's standards and elevating one's own imagined goodness.

It soon became obvious that Jesus fit none of the common molds of the religious leaders. He obviously had a high regard for the law, but at the same time He taught things completely contrary to the traditions. His teachings did not lower scriptural standards but upheld them in every way. He not only put God's standard at the height where it belonged but lived at that humanly impossible level.

The Law and **the Prophets** represent what we now call the Old Testament, the only written Scripture at the time Jesus preached (see Matt. 7:12; 11:13; 22:40; Luke 16:16; John 1:45; Acts 13:15; 28:23). It is therefore about the Old Testament that Jesus speaks in Matthew 5:17-20. Everything He taught directly in His own ministry, as well as everything He taught through the apostles, is based on the Old Testament. It is therefore impossible to understand or accept the New Testament apart from the Old.

As has been pointed out several times, each teaching in the Sermon on the Mount flows out of the teachings that have preceded it. Each beatitude logically follows the ones before it, and every subsequent teaching is related to previous teachings. What Jesus teaches in 5:17-20 also follows directly from what He has just said. Verses 3-12 depict the character of believers, who are kingdom citizens and children of God. Verses 13-16 teach the function of believers as God's spiritual salt and light in the corrupt and darkened world. Verses 17-20 teach the foundation for the inner qualities of the Beatitudes and for functioning as God's salt and light. That foundation is God's Word, the only standard of righteousness and of truth.

We cannot live the righteous life or be God's faithful witnesses by lowering His standards and claiming to follow a higher law of love and permissiveness. Whatever is contrary to God's law is beneath His law, not above it. No matter what the motive behind them, standards that are unbiblically permissive have no part either in God's love or His law, because His love and His law are inseparable. The key, and the only key, to a righteous life is keeping the Word of the living God.

Jesus' warning, **do not think**, indicates that most, if not all, of His hearers had a wrong conception about His teaching. Most traditionalistic Jews considered the rabbinic instructions to be the proper interpretations of the law of Moses, and they concluded that, because Jesus did not scrupulously follow those traditions, He obviously was doing away with the law or relegating it to minor importance. Because Jesus swept away the traditions of washings, special tithes, extreme Sabbath observance, and such things, the people thought He was thereby overthrowing God's law. From the outset, therefore, Jesus wanted to disabuse His hearers of any misconceptions about His view of Scripture.

Throughout the gospel of Matthew, more than in the other gospels, Jesus repeatedly uses Scripture to contradict and indict the superficial and hypocritical scribes and Pharisees. Though not always specifically identified as such, it is primarily their beliefs and practices that Jesus exposes in Matthew 5:21—6:18.

Kataluō (**abolish**) means to utterly overthrow or destroy, and is the same word used of the destruction of the Temple (Matt. 24:2; 26:61; etc.) and of the death of the physical body (2 Cor. 5:1). The basic idea is to tear down and smash to the ground, to obliterate completely. In several places, as here, the word is used figuratively to indicate bringing to naught, rendering useless, or nullifying (see Acts 5:38-39; Rom. 14:20). Doing that to God's law is the antithesis of the work and teaching of Jesus.

In the remainder of verse 17 Jesus focuses on the preeminence of Scripture as God's perfect, eternal, and wholly authoritative Word. By implication He suggests three reasons for that preeminence: it is authored by God, it is affirmed by the prophets, and it is accomplished by Christ.

AUTHORED BY GOD

By including the definite article (**the**) Jesus made clear to His Jewish audience what **Law** He was talking about—*the* Law of God. The giving of the Ten Commandments to Moses on Mt. Sinai was prefaced by the statement: "Then God spoke all these words, saying . . ." (Ex. 20:1). That God gave the law personally and directly is emphasized repeatedly in verses 2-6 by the use of the first person pronouns I and Me. The law given there is the only law because the Lord is the only God. The Lord does not change (Mal. 3:6), and His law does not change. It does not change to meet the whims of society or even of theologians. It was not given to be adapted and modified but to be obeyed. It was not given to suit man's will but to reveal God's.

Jews of that day referred to the law in four different ways. In its most limited sense it was used of the Ten Commandments. In a broader sense it was used of the Pentateuch, the five books written by Moses. In a still broader sense it was used to speak of the entire Scriptures, what we now call the Old Testament.

The fourth and most common use of the term law, however, was in reference to the rabbinical, scribal traditions—the thousands of detailed and external requirements that obscured the revealed Word of God the traditions were supposed to interpret. Jesus sternly told the scribes and Pharisees that they "invalidated the word of God for the sake of [their] tradition" (Matt. 15:6). On the surface it seemed that the traditions made the law harder, but in reality they made it much easier, because observance was entirely external. Keeping the traditions demanded a great deal of effort, but it demanded no heart obedience and no faith in God.

God's law had always required inward as well as outward obedience. "This people draw near with their words and honor Me with their lip service, but they remove their hearts far from Me, and their reverence for Me consists of tradition learned by rote" (Isa. 29:13). During the Exile and especially during the intertestamental period, the traditions were greatly multiplied and covered almost every conceivable activity a person could be involved in.

The rabbis looked through Scripture to find various commands and regulations, and to those they would add supplemental requirements. To the command not to work on the Sabbath they added the idea that carrying a burden was a form of work. They then faced the question of determining exactly what constituted a burden. They decided that a burden is food equal to the weight of a fig, enough wine for mixing in a goblet, milk enough for one swallow, honey enough to put on a wound, oil enough to anoint a small member of the body, water enough to moisten eyesalve, paper enough to write a customs house notice, ink enough to write two letters of the alphabet, reed enough to make a pen, and so on and on. To carry anything more than those prescribed amounts on the Sabbath was to break the law.

Since it was not possible to anticipate or provide for every contingency, much time was spent arguing about such things as whether a tailor committed a sin if he went out on the Sabbath with a needle stuck in his robe, or whether moving a lamp from one place in a room to another was permissible. Some strict interpreters believed that even wearing an artificial leg or using a crutch on the Sabbath constituted work and argued about whether or not a parent could lift a child on the Sabbath. They decided that to heal was work, but made exceptions for grave situations. But only enough treatment to keep the patient from getting worse was allowed; he could not be fully treated until after the Sabbath.

It was the keeping of such external minutia that had become the essence of religion for the scribes and Pharisees and for many other Jews as well. To the strict orthodox Jew of Jesus' day the law was a plethora of extra-Scriptural rules and regulations.

The phrase *the Law and the Prophets,* however, was always understood to refer to the Jewish Scriptures themselves, not the rabbinical interpretations. The phrase is used in that sense some fifteen times in the New Testament (see Matt. 11:13; Luke 16:16; cf. 24:27, 44; etc.), reflecting the common Jewish understanding. Therefore when Jesus said, **Do not think that I came to abolish the Law or the**

Prophets, His Jewish hearers knew He was speaking of the Old Testament Scripture.

The foundation of the Old Testament is the law given in the Pentateuch, which the prophets, psalmists, and other inspired writers preached, expounded, and applied. That law of God was composed of three parts: the moral, the judicial, and the ceremonial. The moral law was to regulate behavior for all men; the judicial law was for Israel's operation as a unique nation; and the ceremonial law was prescribed to structure Israel's worship of God. The moral law was based on the Ten Commandments, and the judicial and ceremonial laws were the subsequent legislation given to Moses. On the plains of Moab Moses reminded Israel that "He declared to you His covenant which He commanded you to perform, that is, the ten commandments; and He wrote them on two tablets of stone. And the Lord commanded me at that time to teach you statutes and judgments, that you might perform them in the land where you are going over to possess it" (Deut. 4:13-14).

Because Matthew does not qualify his use of **Law,** we are safe to say that it was God's whole law—the commandments, statutes, and judgments; the moral, judicial, and ceremonial—that Jesus came not to abolish but to fulfill. It was also the other Old Testament teachings based on the law, and all their types, patterns, symbols, and pictures that He came to fulfill. Jesus Christ came to accomplish every aspect and every dimension of the divinely authored Word (cf. Luke 24:44).

AFFIRMED BY THE PROPHETS

The law is also preeminent because it is affirmed by **the Prophets.** The prophets reiterated and reinforced the law. All of their warnings, admonitions, and predictions were directly or indirectly based on the Mosaic law. God's revelation to the prophets was an extension of His law. The prophets expounded the moral, the judicial, and the ceremonial law. They spoke on idolatry, adultery, lying, stealing, and all the other Ten Commandments. They warned the kings, the nobles, and the people in general about keeping the laws God had given for their government, their life-style, and their worship.

Though all the prophets did not have their mouths touched by God's own hand as did Jeremiah, they could all claim with him that the Lord had put His very words in their mouths (Jer. 1:9; Heb. 1:1). Clearly, the work of the prophet was to preach the law of God. Exodus 4:16 gives an excellent definition of a prophet when it records the word of the Lord to Moses regarding the service of Aaron: "He shall be as a mouth for you, and you shall be as God to him."

ACCOMPLISHED BY CHRIST

The culminating reason, however, for the law's preeminence was its fulfillment by Jesus Christ, God's own Son. **I did not come to abolish but to fulfill.** In His incarnation, in the work of His Holy Spirit through the church, and in His coming again Jesus would fulfill all of the law—moral, judicial, and ceremonial.

The Old Testament is complete; it is all God intended it to be. It is a wondrous, perfect, and complete picture of the coming King and His kingdom, and Jesus the King came to fulfill it in every detail. Five times in the New Testament we are told of Jesus' claiming to be the theme of the Old Testament: here, in Luke 24:27, 44; John 5:39; and in Hebrews 10:7.

Bible students have suggested a number of ways in which Jesus fulfilled the law. Some say He fulfilled it by His teaching. The law was the divine sketch or outline which He filled in with detail and color. In this view Jesus completed what was incomplete by giving it full dimension and meaning. There is a sense in which Jesus did that. Through His direct teaching in the gospels and through the apostles in the rest of the New Testament, Jesus elucidated more of the law of God than anyone ever had.

But that cannot be the primary meaning of **fulfill**, because that is not what the word means. It does not mean fill out but fill up. It does not mean to add to but to complete what is already present. Jesus did not add any basic new teaching but rather clarified God's original meaning.

Other commentators say that Jesus fulfilled the law by fully meeting its demands. In His life He perfectly kept every part of the law. He was perfectly righteous and did not violate the smallest part of God's law. Jesus, of course, did that. He was utterly flawless in His obedience, and He provided the perfect model of absolute righteousness.

But most importantly, as the Spirit surely intends to emphasize here, Jesus fulfilled the Old Testament by *being* its fulfillment. He did not simply teach it fully and exemplify it fully—He *was* it fully. He did not come simply to teach righteousness and to model righteousness; He came *as* divine righteousness. What He said and what He did reflected who He *is*.

JESUS FULFILLED THE MORAL LAW

The moral law was God's foundational code. As already mentioned, Jesus fulfilled that law by His perfect righteousness. Every commandment He obeyed, every requirement He met, every standard He lived up to.

Because keeping the Sabbath is one of the Ten Commandments, it may be helpful to comment on that part of the moral law. The essence of Sabbath observance was holiness, not resting or refraining from work. It was a provision meant to remove the heart from earthly endeavors and to turn it toward God. Because Christ fulfilled all righteousness and has become our righteousness, the purpose of Sabbath observance ended at the cross. Christians possess the reality, and so no longer need the symbol. All believers have entered into permanent salvation rest, as the writer of Hebrews carefully points out (4:1-11). Every day has become holy to the Lord.

In demonstration of that fact the early church met together every day for worship (Acts 2:46). But before long their primary worship meetings were held on the first day of the week (see 1 Cor. 16:2), which came to be called the Lord's Day (Rev. 1:10) because of its association with Jesus' resurrection. That day was to stimulate them to holiness every other day as well (Heb. 10:24-25). As Paul made clear, however, there is no longer any special day of worship (Rom. 14:5-6; Col. 2:16-17). Worship on Tuesday, Thursday, or any other day of the week is no less biblical or spiritual than worship on the Lord's Day. Sunday is not the "Christian Sabbath," as some claim, but is simply the day of worship most Christians have observed since New Testament times, a special time set aside for spiritual exercises. The moral aspect inherent in the Sabbath law is the heart of true worship.

JESUS FULFILLED THE JUDICIAL LAW

God's judicial law was given to provide unique identity for Israel as a nation that belonged to Jehovah. The laws relating to agriculture, settlement of disputes, diet, cleanliness, dress, and such things were special standards by which His chosen people were to live before the Lord and apart from the world. That judicial law Jesus fulfilled on the cross. His crucifixion marked Israel's ultimate apostasy in the final rejection of her Messiah (see Matt. 27:25; John 19:15) and the interruption of God's dealing with that people as a nation. With that the judicial law passed away, because Israel no longer served as His chosen nation. Before His crucifixion Jesus warned the Jews, "I say to you, the kingdom of God will be taken away from you" (Matt. 21:43). Praise God, He will someday redeem and restore Israel (Rom. 9-11), but in the meanwhile the church is His chosen body of people on earth (1 Pet. 2:9-10). All the redeemed—those who receive the work of His cross—are His chosen ones.

JESUS FULFILLED THE CEREMONIAL LAW

The ceremonial law governed the form of Israel's worship. When Jesus died on the cross He fulfilled that law as well as the judicial. Sacrifice was the heart of all Old Testament worship, and as the perfect Sacrifice, Jesus brought all the other sacrifices to an end. While He was on the cross "the veil of the temple was torn in two from top to bottom" (Matt. 27:51). Christ Himself was the new and perfect way into the Holy of Holies, into which any man could come by faith. "Since therefore, brethren, we have confidence to enter the holy place by the blood of Jesus, by a new and living way which He inaugurated for us through the veil, that is, His flesh, and since we have a great priest over the house of God, let us draw near with a sincere heart in full assurance of faith" (Heb. 10:19-22). The Levitical, priestly, sacrificial system ended. Though the Temple was not destroyed until A.D. 70, every offering made there after Jesus died was needless.

Symbolically they had no more significance. The Tabernacle and Temple sacrifices even before Christ's death *never* had power to cleanse from sin. They were only pictures of the Messiah-Savior's work of cleansing, pictures that pointed to that supreme manifestation of God's mercy and grace. "When Christ appeared as a high priest of the good things to come, He entered through the greater and more perfect tabernacle, not made with hands, that is to say, not of this creation; and not through the blood of goats and calves, but through His own blood, He entered the holy place once for all, having obtained eternal redemption" (Heb. 9:11-12).

The ceremonial law ended because it was fulfilled. Because the reality had come, the pictures and symbols had no more place or purpose. On the final Passover night of our Lord's life, He instituted new symbols to commemorate His death. (The Prophet Ezekiel points to a future time in the kingdom when Old Testament symbols will be a renewed part of worship by the redeemed; see Ezek. 40-48.)

Aaron was the first and foremost high priest of the Old Covenant, but he could not compare with the great High Priest of the New Covenant. Aaron entered the earthly tabernacle, but Christ entered the heavenly. Aaron entered once a year, Christ once for all time. Aaron entered beyond the veil, Christ tore the veil in two. Aaron offered many sacrifices, Christ only one. Aaron sacrificed for his own sin, Christ only for the sins of others. Aaron offered the blood of bulls, Christ His own blood. Aaron was a temporary priest, Christ is an eternal one. Aaron was fallible, Christ infallible. Aaron was changeable, Christ unchangeable. Aaron was continual, Christ is final. Aaron's sacrifice was imperfect, Christ's was perfect. Aaron's priesthood was insufficient, Christ's is all-sufficient.

Nor could the Tabernacle and Temple compare with Christ. They each had a door, whereas Christ is the door. They had a brazen altar, but He is the altar. They had a laver, but He Himself cleanses from sin. They had many lamps that continually needed filling; He is the light of the world that shines eternally. They had bread that had to be replenished, but Christ is the eternal bread of life. They had incense, but Christ's own prayers ascend for His saints. They had a veil, but His veil was His own body. They had a mercy seat, but He is now the mercy seat.

Nor could the offerings compare with Christ. The burnt offering spoke of perfection, but Christ was perfection incarnate. The meal offering spoke of dedication, but Jesus was Himself wholly dedicated to the Father. The peace offering spoke of peace, but Jesus is Himself our peace. The sin and trespass offerings spoke of substitution, but He is our Substitute.

Nor could the feasts compare to Christ. The Passover spoke of deliverance from physical death, whereas Christ is our Passover who delivers from spiritual death. The unleavened bread spoke of holiness, but Christ fulfilled all holiness. The first fruits spoke of harvest, but Jesus rose from the dead and became "the first fruits of those who are asleep" (1 Cor. 15:20). The feast of Tabernacles spoke of reunion, but only Christ is able one day to gather all of His people together in His heavenly house forever.

From Genesis 1:1 through Malachi 4:6, the Old Testament is Jesus Christ. It was inspired by Christ, it points to Christ, and it is fulfilled by Christ.

Over and over the New Testament tells us that the law could not make anyone righteous. Jesus had to do what the law could not. "Therefore the Law has become our tutor to lead us to Christ, that we may be justified by faith" (Gal. 3:24). The law only pointed to righteousness, but Christ gives us righteousness, His own righteousness.

The judicial law and the ceremonial law were fulfilled and set aside. They ended at the cross. But the moral law fulfilled by Christ is still being fulfilled through His disciples. Because Christ fulfilled the law, so can those who belong to Him. God sent "His own Son in the likeness of sinful flesh and as an offering for sin, He condemned sin in the flesh, in order that the requirement of the Law might be fulfilled in us, who do not walk according to the flesh, but according to the Spirit" (Rom. 8:3-4). When we walk in the Spirit we fulfill the righteousness of the law, because Christ in us fulfills it with His own righteousness which He has given to us.

Christle and the Law —part 2 The Permanence of Scripture (5:18)

23

For truly I say to you, until heaven and earth pass away, not the smallest letter or stroke shall pass away from the Law, until all is accomplished. (5:18)

The honest Jew of Jesus' day knew he could not fulfill all the requirements of the Mosaic law, and that he could not even keep all the traditions developed over the years by the rabbis and scribes. Many hoped the Messiah would bring God's standards down to a level they could manage.

But as indicated in previous chapters, Jesus made it clear in His first major sermon that God's true standard was even higher than the traditions, and that, as the Messiah, He had not come to diminish the law in the least bit, but to uphold and fulfill it in every detail.

By introducing His statement with **truly I say to you**, Jesus confirmed the special importance of what He was about to say. *Amēn* (**truly**) was a term of strong, intense affirmation. Jesus was saying, "I say this to you absolutely, without qualification and with the fullest authority."

His teaching not only was absolute but was permanent. **Until heaven and earth pass away** represents the end of time as we know it, the end of earthly history. As God's Word, the law would outlast the universe, which someday will cease to exist. "The present heavens and earth by His word are being reserved for fire, kept for the day of judgment and destruction of ungodly men" (2 Pet. 3:7; cf. v. 10). Even the psalmist knew that "Of old Thou didst found the earth; and the heavens are the work of Thy hands. Even they will perish, but Thou dost endure; and all of them will wear out like a garment; like clothing Thou wilt change them, and they will be changed. But Thou art the same, and Thy years will not come to an end" (Ps. 102:25-26). Isaiah said, "Lift up your eyes to the sky, then look to the earth beneath; for the sky will vanish like smoke, and the earth will wear out like a garment, and its inhabitants will die in like manner, but My righteousness shall not wane" (Isa. 51:6; cf. 34:4; Rev. 6:13-14).

Jesus equated His own words with the Word of God: "Heaven and earth will pass away, but My words shall not pass away" (Matt. 24:35). What was true of the law, in its fullest meaning as the Old Testament, was also true of Jesus' teaching. It is timeless.

It is incredibly foolish to ask, "What does the Bible, a two-thousand-year-old book, have to say to us today?" The Bible is the eternal Word of the eternal God. It "is living and active and sharper than any two-edged sword" (Heb. 4:12). It has long preceded and will long outlast every person who questions its validity and relevancy.

Not the smallest letter or stroke shall pass away from the Law, Jesus continued. **The smallest letter** translates the word iōta, the smallest letter of the Greek alphabet. To Jesus' Jewish hearers it would have represented the yodh, the smallest letter of the Hebrew alphabet, which looks something like an apostrophe. A **stroke** (keraia) literally means "little horn" and refers to the small marks that help distinguish one Hebrew letter from another. It was a small extension of a letter similar to a serif in modern typefaces.

In other words, not only will the smallest letter not be erased, but even the smallest part of a letter will not be erased **from the Law.** Not even the tiniest, seemingly most insignificant, part of God's Word will be removed or modified **until all is accomplished.**

As discussed in the last chapter, Jesus brought to completion all the judicial and ceremonial law and certain parts of the moral law, such as Sabbath observance. But God's basic moral law, centered in the Ten Commandments, is still every bit as valid today as when God gave it to Moses at Sinai. During His earthly ministry, death, resurrection, and ascension, Jesus fulfilled many of the prophecies of the Old Testament. Others, such as the coming of the Holy Spirit at Pentecost, would be fulfilled in later New Testament times. Still other prophecies, both of the Old and New Testaments, are yet to be fulfilled. But without the smallest exception, every commandment, every prophecy, every figure and symbol and type would be **accomplished.**

No other statement made by our Lord more clearly states His absolute contention that Scripture is verbally inerrant, totally without error in the original form in which God gave it. That is, Scripture is God's own Word not only down to every single written word, but down to every letter and the smallest part of every letter.

"Fulfill" in verse 17 has the idea of completion, of filling up. **Accomplished** (from *ginomai*) has the similar meaning of becoming or taking place. Arthur Pink comments, "Everything in the Law must be fulfilled [or accomplished]: not only its prefigurations and prophecies, but its precepts and penalty: fulfilled, first, personally and vicariously, by and upon the Surety; fulfilled, second and evangelically, in and by His people; and fulfilled, third, in the doom of the wicked, who shall experience its awful curse forever and ever. Instead of Christ's being opposed to the law of God, He came here to magnify it and render it honourable.... And rather than His teachings being subversive thereof, they confirmed and enforced it" (*An Exposition of the Sermon on the Mount* [Grand Rapids: Baker, 1950], p. 57).

Jesus referred to the Old Testament at least sixty-four times, and always as authoritative truth. In the course of defending His messiahship and divinity before the unbelieving Jewish leaders in the Temple, He said, "The Scripture cannot be broken" (John 10:35).

When the Sadducees tried to trip Him up by asking which of seven successive husbands would be a woman's husband in the resurrection, that is in heaven, He replied, "You are mistaken, not understanding the Scriptures, or the power of God" (Matt. 22:29). The question itself was foolish, He said, because its very premise was wrong, "For in the resurrection they neither marry, nor are given in marriage, but are like angels in heaven" (v. 30). He then went on to correct the Sadducees' view of resurrection, in which they did not believe. "But regarding the resurrection of the dead, have you not read that which was spoken to you by God, saying, 'I am the God of Abraham, and the God of Isaac, and the God of Jacob'? He is not the God of the dead but of the living" (vv. 31-32).

In that confrontation with the Sadducees, Jesus' whole argument is based on a single verb tense. In the book of Exodus, which He was here quoting, God told Moses that He *is,* not *was,* "the God of Abraham, the God of Isaac, and the God of Jacob" (3:6). Hundreds of years after those patriarchs had died, the Lord was still their God. Obviously those men were still alive. God's Word is therefore authoritative not only down to the smallest part of every letter, but also to the grammatical forms of every word. Because Scripture itself is without error, when it is believed and obeyed it will save us from error.

Over and over again, Jesus confirmed the accuracy and the authenticity of the Old Testament. He confirmed the standard of marriage that God established in the Garden of Eden (Matt. 19:4), the murder of Abel (Luke 11:51), Noah and the flood (Matt. 24:38-39), Abraham and his faith (John 8:56), Sodom, Lot, and Lot's wife (Luke 17:29), the call of Moses (Mark 12:26), the manna from heaven (John 6:31, 58), and the bronze serpent (John 3:14).

Jesus also made clear that Scripture was given to lead men to salvation. In Jesus' parable of the rich man and Lazarus, Abraham told the rich man that if his brothers, whom he hoped to save from hell, "do not listen to Moses and the Prophets, neither will they be persuaded if someone rises from the dead" (Luke 16:31). In other words, they had God's Word, which was sufficient to bring them to

God and to salvation—if they would believe it.

Jesus also used Scripture in His own defense. When He was tempted by Satan in the wilderness at the outset of His ministry, Jesus countered each temptation with quotations from Deuteronomy (Matt. 4:4, 7, 10; cf. Deut. 8:3; 6:16, 13). He could have challenged the devil in the power and authority of new words spoken simply for that occasion. But in quoting the Scriptures, He testified to their divine origin and authority.

I heard a preacher once say, "The one thing I've learned is that when you get into the pulpit you've got to somehow communicate without using the Bible, because the Bible turns people off. I've spent a long time developing the ability to communicate to people without ever using the Bible. I started out in my ministry saying this verse says this and this verse says that, and I finally realized that wouldn't get me anywhere. Now I say it in my own way and people will accept it."

What that preacher said is true. Many people today are very much turned off by the Bible. But men's being turned off by God's Word is hardly a new phenomenon. It has been turning off unbelievers for thousands of years. Many people today, just as in Jesus' day—and in the days of Moses and of the prophets— would much rather hear the opinions of men than the Word of God. But those opinions cannot lead them to the truth or to salvation. Opinions that do not square with Scripture will often leave men superficially contented and satisfied, but they will also leave them in darkness and sin.

Shortly after His temptation, Jesus went into the synagogue at Nazareth "on the Sabbath, and stood up to read. And the book of the prophet Isaiah was handed to Him. And He opened the book, and found the place where it was written, 'The Spirit of the Lord is upon Me, because He anointed Me to preach the gospel to the poor. He has sent Me to proclaim release to the captives, and recovery of sight to the blind, to set free those who are downtrodden, to proclaim the favorable year of the Lord.' And He closed the book, and gave it back to the attendant, and sat down; and the eyes of all in the synagogue were fixed upon Him. And He began to say to them, 'Today this Scripture has been fulfilled in your hearing'" (Luke 4:16-21; cf. Isa. 61:1).

The Lord used Scripture's authority to establish His own. When John the Baptist sent some of his disciples to ask Jesus, "Are You the Expected One, or shall we look for someone else? . . . Jesus answered and said to them, 'Go and report to John what you hear and see: the blind receive sight and the lame walk, the lepers are cleansed and the deaf hear, and the dead are raised up, and the poor have the gospel preached to them" (Matt. 11:3-5). In that reply Jesus again referred to the same passage from Isaiah which predicted the Messiah and His work.

When He cleansed the Temple on returning to Jerusalem for the last time, Jesus defended His action on the basis of Scripture. "Is it not written, 'My house shall be called a house of prayer for all the nations'? But you have made it a robbers' den" (Mark 11:17).

It is impossible to accept Christ's authority without accepting Scripture's authority, and vice versa. They stand together. To accept Jesus Christ as Savior and

Lord is to accept what He taught about Scripture as binding. To be a kingdom citizen is to accept what the King says about God's Word. To have a kingdom character and a kingdom testimony is to obey the King's manifesto, the Scriptures. Scripture's authority is Christ's authority, and to obey the Lord is to obey His Word. "He who is of God hears the words of God; for this reason you do not hear them, because you are not of God" (John 8:47). To trust in Christ is to say of Him as Peter did, "You have words of eternal life" (John 6:68).

If the Old Testament contains any errors we must conclude one of two things about Jesus Christ. One possibility is that He was ignorant of those errors, in which case He was not omniscient and was therefore not God. The other possibility is that He knew of the errors but denied them, in which case He would have been a liar and a hypocrite, and therefore not holy God.

If not a single letter or stroke or tense of God's Word is going to pass away, we first should receive it for what it is, "the word implanted, which is able to save [our] souls" (James 1:21). We should receive it because of the infinite majesty of the Author and His authoritative statements about it. We should receive it because of the price that God paid to get it to us, and because it is the standard of truth, joy, blessing, and salvation. And we should receive it because not to receive it brings judgment.

Second, we are called to honor God's Word. "How sweet are Thy words to my taste!" said the psalmist, "Yes, sweeter than honey to my mouth!" (Ps. 119:103). Charles Spurgeon said, "They called George Fox a Quaker. Why? Because when he spoke he would quake exceedingly through the force of the truth he so thoroughly apprehended." He went on to say, "It were better to break stones on a road than to be a preacher, unless God had given the Holy Spirit to sustain him. The heart and soul of a man who speaks for God will know no ease, for he hears in his ears that warning admonition, 'If the watchman warned them not, they perished, but their blood will I require at the watchman's hands.' Is the infallible revelation of the infallible Jehovah to be moderated, to be shaped, to be toned down to the fancies and fashions of the hour? God forbid us if we ever alter His Word."

Martin Luther never feared men, but when he stood up to preach he often felt his knees knock together under a sense of great responsibility to be true to the Word of God.

Third, we should obey God's Word. We should be diligent to present ourselves approved to God as workmen who do "not need to be ashamed, handling accurately the word of truth" (2 Tim. 2:15). Like Jeremiah, we should find God's words and eat them (Jer. 15:16), and "let the word of Christ richly dwell within" us (Col. 3:16).

Fourth, we must defend God's Word. We are to "contend earnestly for the faith which was once for all delivered to the saints" (Jude 3). Like Jude, we should fight for the integrity, purity, and authority of Scripture. Spurgeon said, "The everlasting gospel is worth preaching even if one stood on a burning fagot and addressed the crowds from a pulpit of flames. The truths revealed in Scripture are worth living for and they are worth dying for. I count myself thrice happy, to bear reproach for the sake of the faith. It is an honor of which I feel myself to be unworthy, and yet most truly I can say the words of our hymn, 'Shall I to soothe the unholy throng, soften Thy truths and smooth my tongue to gain earth's gilded toys, or flee the cross endured my God by Thee?'"

Finally, we live to proclaim God's Word. Says Spurgeon again, "I cannot speak out my whole heart on this theme which is so dear to me, but I would stir you all up to be instant in season and out of season in telling out the gospel message, especially to repeat such a word as this: 'God so loved the world that He gave His only begotten Son, that whosoever believeth in Him shall not perish but have everlasting life.' Whisper it in the ear of the sick, shout it in the corner of the streets, write it on your tablet, send it forth from the press, but everywhere let this be your great motive and warrant. You preach the gospel because the mouth of the Lord hath spoken it."

Christic and the Law —part 3 The Pertinence of Scripture (5:19)

Whoever then annuls one of the least of these commandments, and so teaches others, shall be called least in the kingdom of heaven; but whoever keeps and teaches them, he shall be called great in the kingdom of heaven. (5:19)

In the last several decades the expression "do your own thing" has described a popular approach to behavior. Freedom has been equated with doing what you want. The philosophical corollary of that attitude is antinomianism, the rejection of law, regulations, and rules of every sort. Such was the attitude in ancient Israel during the time of the judges, when "everyone did what was right in his own eyes" (Judg. 21:25).

Antinomianism is reflected in our own day in personal existentialism, the concept that teaches the fulfillment only of the present moment, regardless of standards or codes or consequences. Rejection of authority follows logically from personal existentialism: we want no one else making rules for us or holding us accountable for what we say or do. The inevitable consequence of that philosophy is breakdown of the home, of school, of church, of government, and of society in general. When no one wants to be accountable to anyone else, the only thing to survive is anarchy.

Even the church has not escaped such attitudes. Many congregations hesitate or even refuse to discipline members who are flagrantly immoral, dishonest, or heretical. For fear of offending, of losing financial support, of being thought old-fashioned or legalistic, or even for fear of stepping on someone else's presumed rights, there is widespread failure to maintain God's clear standards of righteousness in His own church. In the name of grace, love, forgiveness, and other "positive" biblical teachings and standards, sin is dismissed or excused.

Some Christians claim that, because God's grace covers every offense a believer can ever commit, there is no need to bother about holy living. Some even argue that, because the sinful flesh is presently unredeemed in its corruption and is going to be done away with at glorification, it does not make any difference what that part of us does now. Our new divine, incorruptible nature is good and eternal, and that is all that counts. That idea is simply a rebirth of the Greek dualism that wreaked so much havoc in the early church, and that Paul dealt with in the Corinthian letters.

But even the sincere Christian cannot help wondering about the relation between law and grace. The New Testament plainly teaches that in some very important ways believers are freed from the law. But what, exactly, is our freedom in Christ? In Matthew 5:19 the Lord confronts that question and reaffirms what that freedom cannot mean.

In Matthew 5:17 Jesus had pointed out the law's preeminence, because it was authored by God, affirmed by the prophets, and accomplished by the Messiah, the Christ. In verse 18 He showed its permanence, its lasting without the smallest change or reduction "until heaven and earth pass away." Now in verse 19 He shows its pertinence. The Jews were still under the full requirements of the Old Testament law.

In verses 17 and 18 Jesus declared that He came to fulfill and not diminish or disobey the law, and in verse 19 He declares that citizens of His kingdom are also not to diminish or disobey it. In light of His own attitude about and response to the law, Jesus now teaches what the attitude and response of His followers should be.

The law is pertinent for those who believe in Christ because of its own character, because of the consequences of obeying or disobeying, and because its demands are clarified and enforced throughout the rest of the New Testament.

THE CHARACTER OF THE LAW

The **then**, or therefore, refers to what Jesus has just said about the law. The law is utterly pertinent to those who trust in God, because it is His Word and is exalted by the prophets and accomplished by the Messiah Himself. Because the Bible is not a collection of men's religious ideas but God's revelation of divine truth, its teachings are not speculations to be judged but truths to be believed; its commands are not suggestions to be considered but requirements to be followed.

Because Scripture is given by God for man, nothing could be more relevant to man than this revelation. Scripture is the standard of relevance by which all other relevance is measured.

THE CONSEQUENCES OF MEN'S RESPONSES TO THE LAW

The consequences of the law depend on a person's response to it. Whoever responds to it positively will receive a positive result, but whoever responds to it negatively will receive a negative result.

THE NEGATIVE CONSEQUENCE

Jesus mentions the negative result first: **Whoever then annuls one of the least of these commandments, and so teaches others, shall be called least in the kingdom of heaven.**

Luō (**annuls**) is a common word in the New Testament and can mean to break, set loose, release, dissolve, or even to melt. The idea here is that of annulling God's law, or making it void, by loosing ourselves from its requirements and standards. Jesus used a compounded and stronger form of that term (*kataluō*) in verse 17 in asserting that He had not come "to abolish the Law or the Prophets."

Fallen human nature resents prohibitions and demands. Even Christians are tempted to modify and weaken God's standards. Because of ignorance, misunderstanding, or outright disregard, believers find reasons to make God's commands less demanding than they are. But when a Christian ceases to revere and obey God's Word in even the slightest degree, to that degree He is being un-Christlike, because that is something Christ refused to do.

The Jews of Jesus' day had divided the Old Testament laws into two categories. Two hundred forty-eight were positive commands, and three hundred sixty-five—one for each day of the year—were negative. The scribes and Pharisees would have long, heated debates about which laws in each category were the most important and which were the least.

Scripture itself makes clear that all of God's commands are not of equal importance. When a lawyer among the Pharisees asked which commandment was the greatest, Jesus replied without hesitation: "You shall love the Lord your God with all your heart, and with all your soul, and with all your mind. This is the great and foremost commandment." He then went on to say, "The second is like it, 'You shall love your neighbor as yourself'" (Matt. 22:37-39). Jesus acknowledged that one commandment is supreme above all others and that another is second in importance. It follows that all the other commandments fall somewhere below those two and that, like them, they vary in importance.

In His series of woes Jesus gives another indication of the relative importance of God's commands. "Woe to you, scribes and Pharisees, hypocrites! For you tithe mint and dill and cummin, and have neglected the weightier provisions of the law: justice and mercy and faithfulness; but these are the things you should have done without neglecting the others" (Matt. 23:23). The tithing of herbs was required; but being just, merciful, and faithful are much more spiritually important.

Jesus' point here, however, is that it is not permissible to **annul**—by ignoring, modifying, or disobeying—even **one of the least of these command-ments.** Some commands are greater than others, but none are to be disregarded.

Paul reminded the Ephesian elders that while he had ministered among them, he "did not shrink from declaring to [them] the whole purpose of God" (Acts 20:27). The apostle did not pick and choose what he would teach and exhort. He stressed some things more than others, but he left nothing out.

The person who **teaches others** to disregard or disobey any part of God's word is an even worse offender. He not only annuls the law himself but causes others to annul it. Besides that, his disobedience obviously is intentional. It is possible to break God's commands by being ignorant of them or forgetting them. But to teach others to break them has to be conscious and intentional.

James cautions, "Let not many of you become teachers, my brethren, knowing that as such we shall incur a stricter judgment" (James 3:1). Every believer is accountable for himself, but those who teach are also accountable for those whom they teach. "The head is the elder and honorable man," writes Isaiah, "and the prophet who teaches falsehood is the tail. For those who guide this people are leading them astray; and those who are guided by them are brought to confusion" (Isa. 9:15-16).

Jesus' warning does not simply apply to official or formal teachers. Every person teaches. By our example we continually help those around us either to be more obedient or more disobedient. We also teach by what we say. When we speak lovingly and respectfully of God's Word, we teach love and respect for it. When we speak disparagingly or slightingly of God's Word, we teach disregard and disrespect for it. When we ignore its demands, we give loud testimony to its unimportance to us.

Just after Paul reminded the elders from Ephesus that he had been faithful in teaching them God's full Word, he warned them, "Be on guard for yourselves and for all the flock. . . . I know that after my departure savage wolves will come in among you, not sparing the flock; and from among your own selves men will arise, speaking perverse things, to draw away the disciples after them" (Acts 20:28-30).

The consequence of practicing or teaching disobedience of any of God's Word is to **be called least in the kingdom of heaven.** I do not believe, as some commentators suggest, that **called** refers to what men say about us, but to what God says about us. Our reputation among other people, including other Christians, may or may not be adversely affected. Often other people do not know about our disobedience, and often when they know they do not care. But God always knows, and He always cares. It is only what we are **called** by God that is of any ultimate importance. It should be the concern of every believer who loves his Lord that He never have cause to call him **the least.**

Determining rank in **the kingdom of heaven** is entirely God's prerogative (cf. Matt. 20:23), and Jesus declares that He will hold those in lowest esteem who hold His Word in lowest esteem. There is no impunity for those who disobey, discredit, or belittle God's law.

That Jesus does not refer to loss of salvation is clear from the fact that, though offenders will **be called least**, they will still be **in the kingdom of heaven**. But blessing, reward, fruitfulness, joy, and usefulness will all be sacrificed to the extent that we are disobedient. "Watch yourselves," John warns, "that you might not lose what we have accomplished, but that you may receive a full reward" (2 John 8). It is possible to lose in the second phase of our Christian lives what we built up in the first.

To disdain even the smallest part of God's Word is to demonstrate disdain for all of it, because its parts are inseparable. James teaches that "whoever keeps the whole law and yet stumbles in one point, he has become guilty of all" (James 2:10). To ignore or reject the least of God's law is therefore to cheapen all of it and to become **the least** in His kingdom. Such Christians receive their rank because of their ill treatment of Scripture, not, as some imagine, because they may have lesser gifts.

THE POSITIVE CONSEQUENCE

The positive result is that **whoever keeps and teaches them, he shall be called great in the kingdom of heaven**. Here again Jesus mentions the two aspects of doing and teaching. Kingdom citizens are to uphold every part of God's law, both in their living and in their teaching.

Paul could tell the Thessalonians, "You are witnesses, and so is God, how devoutly and uprightly and blamelessly we behaved toward you believers; just as you know how we were exhorting and encouraging and imploring each one of you as a father would his own children, so that you may walk in a manner worthy of the God who calls you into His own kingdom and glory" (1 Thess. 2:10-12). Paul had been faithful to live and teach among them all of God's Word, just as he had done at Ephesus and everywhere else he ministered.

God's moral law is a reflection of God's very character and is therefore changeless and eternal. The things it requires will not have to be commanded in heaven, but they will be manifested in heaven because they manifest God. While God's people are still on earth, however, they do not naturally reflect the character of their heavenly Father, and His moral standards continue to be commanded and supernaturally produced (cf. Rom. 8:2-4).

"Prescribe and teach these things," Paul tells Timothy, "[and] in speech, conduct, love, faith and purity, show yourself an example of those who believe" (1 Tim. 4:11-12). Near the end of the same letter Paul tells Timothy to flee from all evil things and, as a man of God, to "pursue righteousness, godliness, faith, love, perseverance and gentleness. Fight the good fight of faith; take hold of the eternal life to which you were called" (6:11-12).

Paul both kept and taught the full Word of God, and he is therefore among those who will **be called great in the kingdom of heaven**. No one who does not do the same will be in the ranks of God's great saints.

Greatness is not determined by gifts, success, popularity, reputation, or size of ministry—but by a believer's view of Scripture as revealed in his life and teaching.

Jesus' promise is not simply to great teachers such as Paul—or Augustine, Calvin, Luther, Wesley, or Spurgeon. His promise applies to every believer who teaches others to obey God's Word by faithfully, carefully, and lovingly living by and speaking of that Word. Every believer does not have the gift of teaching the deep doctrines of Scripture, but every believer is called and is able to teach the right attitude toward it.

THE CLARIFICATION OF THE LAW

We know from the thrust of the New Testament epistles that Jesus is speaking here of God's permanent moral law. The Sermon on the Mount is just as valid for believers today as it was for those to whom Jesus preached it directly, because every principle and standard taught here is also taught in the epistles. The other writers make absolutely clear that believers' obligation to obey God's moral law not only did not cease at Christ's coming but was reaffirmed by Christ and remains energized by the Holy Spirit for the entire church age.

There is indeed a paradox in regard to the law, and it is especially evident in Paul's letters. On the one hand we are told of the law's being fulfilled and done away with, and on the other that we are still obliged to obey it. Speaking of the Jews and Gentiles, Paul says that Christ "is our peace, who made both groups into one, and broke down the barrier of the dividing wall, by abolishing in His flesh the enmity, which is the Law of commandments contained in ordinances, that in Himself He might make the two into one new man, thus establishing peace" (Eph. 2:14-15). When the church came into existence the "dividing wall" of civil, judicial law crumbled and disappeared.

In God's eyes Israel was temporarily set aside as a nation at the cross, when she crucified her King and rejected His kingdom. In the world's eyes Israel ceased to exist as a nation in A.D. 70, when all of Jerusalem, including the Temple, was razed to the ground by the Romans under Titus. (Her restoration nationally is but a preparation for her restoration spiritually, as Romans 9-11 teaches.)

The ceremonial law also came to an end. While Jesus was still hanging on the cross, "the veil of the temple was torn in two from top to bottom" (Mark 15:38). The Temple worship and the sacrifices were no longer valid, even symbolically. That part of the law was finished, accomplished, and done away with by Christ.

There is even a sense in which God's moral law is no longer binding on believers. Paul speaks of our not being under law but under grace (Rom. 6:14). But just before that he had said, "do not let sin reign in your mortal body that you should obey its lusts" (v. 12), and immediately after verse 14 he says, "What then? Shall we sin because we are not under law but under grace? May it never be!" (v. 15). Those in Christ are no longer under the ultimate penalty of the law, but are far from free of its requirement of righteousness.

To the Romans Paul said, "For Christ is the end of the law for righteousness to everyone who believes" (Rom. 10:4), and to the Galatians he wrote, "But if you are led by the Spirit, you are not under the Law" (Gal. 5:18). But he had just made it clear that Christians are not in the least free from God's moral standards. "For the flesh sets its desire against the Spirit, and the Spirit against the flesh; for these are in opposition to one another, so that you may not do the things that you please" (v. 17). The law that was once "our tutor to lead us to Christ" (Gal. 3:24) now leads us as "sons of God through Christ Jesus" to be clothed with Christ (vv. 26-27), and His clothing is the clothing of practical righteousness. If Christ's own righteousness never diminished or disobeyed God's moral law, how can His disciples be free to do so?

Paul harmonized the idea when he spoke of himself as being "without the law of God but under the law of Christ" (1 Cor. 9:21). In Christ we are anything but lawless. Christ's law is totally different from the Jewish judicial and ceremonial law and different from the Old Testament moral law, with its penalties and curses for disobedience. But it is not different in the slightest from the holy, righteous standards that the Old Testament law taught.

The Old Testament law is still a moral guide, as in revealing sin (Rom. 7:7). Even when it provokes sin (v. 8), it helps us see the wickedness of our own flesh and our helplessness apart from Christ. And even when we see the condemnation of the law (vv. 9-11), it should remind us that our Savior took that condemnation upon Himself on the cross (5:18; 8:1; 1 Pet. 2:24; etc.). Whenever a Christian looks at God's moral law with humility, meekness, and a sincere desire for righteousness, the law will invariably point him to Christ—as it was always intended to do. And for believers to live by it is for them to become like Christ. It could not possibly be otherwise, because it is *God's* law, and it reflects God's character. "So then," Paul is careful to remind us, "the Law is holy, and the commandment is holy and righteous and good" (v. 12).

Paul concludes Romans 7 by thanking "God through Jesus Christ our Lord" that even though his flesh served "the law of sin," his mind served "the law of God" (7:25). The penalty of the law has been paid for us by Jesus Christ, but also in Him the righteousness of the law is "fulfilled in us, who do not walk according to the flesh, but according the Spirit" (Rom. 8:4; cf. Gal. 5:13-24).

Christic and the Law
—part 4
The Purpose
of Scripture (5:20)

For I say to you, that unless your righteousness surpasses that of the scribes and Pharisees, you shall not enter the kingdom of heaven. (5:20)

It is the false teaching of salvation by self-effort that Jesus confronts head-on in this verse and which all of Scripture, from beginning to end, contradicts. As Paul makes clear in the Book of Romans, even Abraham, the father of the Jewish people, was saved by his faith, not by his works (Rom. 4:3; cf. Gen. 15:6). In Galatians the apostle explains that "the Scripture has shut up all men under sin, that the promise by faith in Jesus Christ might be given to those who believe" (Gal. 3:22). Outside of sin itself, the Bible opposes nothing more vehemently than the religion of human achievement.

Jesus told a "parable to certain ones who trusted in themselves that they were righteous and viewed others with contempt" (Luke 18:9). In that well-known story a Pharisee and a tax-gatherer went to the Temple to pray. The Pharisee prayed self-righteously, "'God, I thank Thee that I am not like other people: swindlers, unjust, adulterers, or even like this tax-gatherer. I fast twice a week; I pay tithes of all that I get.' But the tax-gatherer, standing some distance away, was even unwilling to lift up his eyes to heaven, but was beating his breast, saying 'God, be merciful to me, the sinner!' I tell you, this man went down to his house justified rather than the other," Jesus said, "for everyone who exalts himself shall be humbled, but he who humbles himself shall be exalted" (vv. 10-14).

The least-esteemed and most-hated man in Jewish society was the tax-gatherer, a fellow Jew who had sold out to Rome for the purpose of collecting taxes from his brethren. He extorted all he could get from the people, keeping for himself everything he purloined above what Rome required. He had forsaken both national, social, family, and religious loyalty for the sake of money. The Pharisee, on the other hand, was the model Jew, highly religious, moral, and respectable. Yet Jesus said that, despite the tax-gatherer's treachery and sin, he would be justified by God because of his penitent faith, whereas the Pharisee, despite his high morals and religiousness, would be condemned, because he trusted in his own righteousness and good works.

In the present passage Jesus teaches that the sort of righteousness exemplified by the Pharisees was not sufficient to gain entrance into His kingdom. To Jesus' legalistic, works-oriented hearers, this was doubtlessly the most radical thing He had yet taught. If the meticulously religious and moral Pharisees could not get into heaven, who could?

After showing the preeminence (v. 17), permanence (v. 18), and pertinence (v. 19) of Scripture, Jesus now shows its purpose. From the context of those preceding three verses it is clear that He is still speaking of "the Law and the Prophets," the Old Testament Scriptures. In saying that true righteousness exceeds the kind displayed by the scribes and Pharisees, Jesus said that, whatever they did with man-made tradition, they did not live up to the standards of Scripture.

The implied truth of Matthew 5:20 is this: The purpose of God's law was to show that, to please God and to be worthy of citizenship in His kingdom, more righteousness is required than anyone can possibly have or accomplish in himself. The purpose of the law was not to show what to do in order to make oneself acceptable, much less to show how good one already is, but to show how utterly sinful and helpless all men are in themselves. (That is one of Paul's themes in Romans and Galatians.) As the Lord pointed out to the Jews in the first beatitude, the initial step toward kingdom citizenship is poverty of spirit, recognizing one's total wretchedness and inadequacy before God.

THE IDENTITY OF THE SCRIBES AND PHARISEES

Like Ezra (Ezra 7:12), the earliest *grammateōn* (**scribes**) were found only among the priests and Levites. They recorded, studied, interpreted, and often taught Jewish law. Although there were scribes among the Sadducees, most were associated with the Pharisees.

Israel had two kinds of scribes, civil and ecclesiastical. The civil scribes functioned somewhat like notaries, and were involved in various governmental duties. Shimshai (Ezra 4:8) was such a scribe. The ecclesiastical scribes devoted their time to study of the Scriptures, and came to be its primary interpreters and articulators.

Yet, as Jesus repeatedly made plain, they failed to understand what they studied and taught. With all their exposure to God's Word, being superficially immersed in it continually, they missed its profound spiritual intent.

The influential, rigid **Pharisees** were particularly confident in their system of righteousness. The Jews had a saying, "If only two people go to heaven, one will be a scribe and the other a Pharisee." Those men were completely convinced that God was obligated to honor their devoted and demanding works. In comparing themselves with the standards they had established—and especially in comparing themselves with the average Jew, not to mention Gentile—they could not imagine God was not favorably impressed with their goodness.

Yet, like many serious and capable scholars throughout the history of the church, the Pharisees of Judaism were also blind to the meaning of the words they diligently studied and discussed.

THE RIGHTEOUSNESS OF THE SCRIBES AND PHARISEES

The standard of **righteousness** that **the scribes and Pharisees** taught and practiced differed from God's righteousness in several important ways. It was external, partial, redefined, and self-centered.

EXTERNAL

First of all the scribes and Pharisees concerned themselves entirely with external observance of the law and tradition. They took little consideration of motives or attitudes. No matter how much they may have hated a person, if they did not kill him they were not guilty of breaking the commandment. No matter how much they may have lusted, they did not consider themselves guilty of adultery or fornication as long as they did not commit the physical act.

In Matthew 23 our Lord gives a graphic picture of the external character of that religion. "You clean the outside of the cup and of the dish, but inside they are full of robbery and self-indulgence" (v. 25). The Lord prefaced those words with, "Woe to you, . . . hypocrites," labeling those leaders with their sin. They saw nothing wrong with having evil thoughts as long as they did not carry out those thoughts externally. They did not think God would judge them for what they thought but only for what they did.

Yet that is precisely the sort of righteousness Jesus declared to be the worst sort. He condemned such externalism because those who practiced it were really thieves, self-indulgent, unclean, lawless, murderous, and enemies of God's true spokesmen (Matt. 23:25-31). Jesus' next teachings in the Sermon on the Mount show that God's first concern is with the heart—with such things as anger, hatred, and lust—not just with their outward manifestations in murder or adultery (Matt. 5:22, 27-28). Hypocrisy cannot substitute for holiness.

God's concern about religious ceremony is the same. Jesus is soon to teach that if, for example, our giving, our prayer, and our fasting are not done out of a humble, loving spirit, they count for nothing with Him (6:5-18). Ritual cannot substitute for righteousness.

The scribes and Pharisees were proud that they had "seated themselves in the chair of Moses" (Matt. 23:2), that is, that they were the custodians and teachers of the law God gave to Moses. "All that they tell you, do and observe, but do not do according to their deeds; for they say things, and do not do them" (v. 3). By their ungodly system of works righteousness, Jesus told them, "You shut off the kingdom of heaven from men; for you do not enter in yourselves, nor do you allow those who are entering to go in" (v. 13). On another occasion He told the Pharisees, "You are those who justify yourselves in the sight of men, but God knows your hearts; for that which is highly esteemed among men is detestable in the sight of God" (Luke 16:15).

PARTIAL

The righteousness practiced by the scribes and Pharisees also fell short of God's righteousness because it was partial, woefully incomplete. Again Matthew 23 gives an example: "Woe to you, scribes and Pharisees, hypocrites! For you tithe mint and dill and cummin, and have neglected the weightier provisions of the law: justice and mercy and faithfulness" (v. 23). Those religious leaders were meticulous in tithing the smallest plants and seeds from their gardens, though that was not specifically commanded in the law. Yet they had total disregard for showing justice and mercy to other people and for being faithful in their hearts to God. They were much concerned about making long, pretentious prayers in public, but had no compunction about taking a widow's house away from her (v. 14).

To some extent this second evil was caused by the first. They disregarded such things as justice, mercy, and faithfulness because those things are essentially the reflections of a transformed heart. It is impossible to be merciful, just, and faithful without a divinely wrought change. No external formality can produce that.

Quoting God's scathing words to their forefathers, Jesus told them, "In vain do they worship Me, teaching as doctrines the precepts of men. Neglecting the commandment of God, you hold to the tradition of men" (Mark 7:7-8). Yet they considered themselves to be Israel's religious elite and the objects of God's special affection.

REDEFINED

In many ways the scribes and Pharisees were like neoorthodox and liberal theologians of our own day. They took biblical terms and redefined them to suit their own human perspectives and philosophy. They reworked biblical teachings, commands, and standards to produce variations in keeping with their own desires and capabilities.

Even such commands as "Consecrate yourselves therefore, and be holy; for

I am holy" (Lev. 11:44) they interpreted not as a call to pure attitude of heart but as a requirement to perform certain rituals. They knew they could not be holy in the same way God is holy—and had no desire to be—so they simply changed the meaning of holiness.

SELF-CENTERED

Not only was the righteousness of the scribes and Pharisees external, partial, and redefined, but it was also completely self-centered. It was produced by self for the purposes of self-glory. Above all else, those leaders sought to be self-satisfied, and their system of religion was designed to enhance that self-satisfaction by providing ways to accomplish external, showy things about which they could boast and be proud. Their satisfaction came when they received approval and commendation from men.

In stark contrast, the godly person is broken about his sin and mourns over the wicked condition of his inner life, the unrighteousness he sees in his heart and mind. He has absolutely no confidence in what he is or in what he can do, but longs for the righteousness only God can give out of His mercy and grace.

But the person who is righteous in his own eyes sees no need for any other righteousness, no need for salvation, mercy, forgiveness, or grace. Just as their self-righteous forefathers had not wanted the grace God offered in the Old Testament, the scribes and Pharisees of Jesus' day did not want the grace the Messiah now offered. They wanted to rule their own lives and determine their own destinies and were not ready to submit to a King who wanted to rule their inner as well as their outward lives. "Not knowing about God's righteousness, and seeking to establish their own, they did not subject themselves to the righteousness of God" (Rom. 10:3).

THE RIGHTEOUSNESS GOD REQUIRES

The **righteousness** God requires of His kingdom citizens far **surpasses that of the scribes and Pharisees.** The term **surpasses** is used of a river overflowing its banks, emphasizing that which is far in excess of the normal. The Lord requires genuine righteousness, real holiness that far exceeds anything human and that exists only in the redeemed heart. The psalmist wrote, "The King's daughter is all glorious within; her clothing is interwoven with gold" (Ps. 45:13). When the inside is beautiful, outward beauty is appropriate; but without inner beauty, outward adornment is pretense and sham.

God has always been concerned first of all with inner righteousness. When Samuel was ready to anoint Jesse's oldest son, Eliab, to be Saul's successor, the Lord said, "Do not look at his appearance or at the height of his stature, because I have rejected him; for God sees not as man sees, for man looks at the outward appearance, but the Lord looks at the heart" (1 Sam. 16:7).

God not only requires inner righteousness but perfect righteousness.

"Therefore you are to be perfect, as your heavenly Father is perfect" (Matt. 5:48). To be qualified for God's kingdom we must be as holy as the King Himself. That standard is so infinitely high that even the most self-righteous person would not dare claim to possess it or be able to attain it.

THE RIGHTEOUSNESS GOD GIVES

That impossibility leads the sincere person to wonder how such a holy heart is obtained, to ask the question Jesus' disciples one day asked Him, "Then who can be saved?" (Matt. 19:25). And the only answer is the one Jesus gave on that occasion: "With men this is impossible, but with God all things are possible" (v. 26).

The One who demands perfect righteousness gives perfect righteousness. The One who tells us of the way into the kingdom is Himself that way. "I am the way, and the truth, and the life; no one comes to the Father, but through Me" (John 14:6), Jesus said. The King not only sets the standard of perfect righteousness, but will Himself bring anyone up to that standard who is willing to enter the kingdom on the King's terms.

"A man is not justified by the works of the Law but through faith in Christ Jesus, . . . since by the works of the Law shall no flesh be justified" (Gal. 2:16). To be justified is to be made righteous, and to be made righteous by Christ is the only way to become righteous.

"But now apart from the Law the righteousness of God has been manifested, being witnessed by the Law and Prophets, even the righteousness of God through faith in Jesus Christ for all those who believe" (Rom. 3:21-22). Faith had always been God's way to righteousness, a truth that the scribes and Pharisees, the experts on the Old Testament, should have known above all other people. As Paul reminded his Jewish readers in Rome, "For what does the Scripture say? 'And Abraham believed God, and it was reckoned to him as righteousness'" (Rom. 4:3). He quoted from the Book of Genesis (15:6), the earliest book of the Old Testament. The first patriarch, the first Jew, was saved by faith, not by works (Rom. 4:2) or the act of circumcision (v. 10). Abraham "received the sign of circumcision, a seal of the righteousness of the faith which he had while uncircumcised, that he might be the father of all who believe without being circumcised, that righteousness might be reckoned to them" (v. 11).

The uncircumcised includes those before as well as after Abraham. He was the father of the faithful, but he was not the first of the faithful. "By faith Abel offered to God a better sacrifice than Cain, through which he obtained the testimony that he was righteous" and "by faith Enoch was taken up so that he should not see death; and he was not found because God took him up; for he obtained the witness that before his being taken up he was pleasing to God" (Heb. 11:4-5). It was also only by faith that Noah found salvation (v. 7).

"For if by the transgression of the one [that is, Adam], death reigned through the one, much more those who receive the abundance of grace and of the gift of righteousness will reign in life through the One, Jesus Christ" (Rom. 5:17).

"As sin reigned in death, even so grace might reign through righteousness to eternal life through Jesus Christ our Lord" (v. 21).

The righteousness God requires, God also gives. It cannot be deserved, earned, or accomplished, but only accepted. By offering Himself for sin, Christ "condemned sin in the flesh, in order that the requirement of the Law might be fulfilled in us" (Rom. 8:4-5). God gave the impossible standard and then Himself provided its fulfillment.

The writer of Romans had considerably more claim to man-made righteousness than most of the scribes and Pharisees to whom Jesus spoke. "If anyone else has a mind to put confidence in the flesh, I far more," wrote Paul; "circumcised the eighth day, of the nation of Israel, of the tribe of Benjamin, a Hebrew of Hebrews; as to the Law, a Pharisee; as to zeal, a persecutor of the church; as to the righteousness which is in the Law, found blameless" (Phil. 3:4-6).

But when the apostle was confronted by Christ's righteousness, he was also confronted by his own sinfulness. When he saw what God had done for him, he saw that what he had done for God was worthless. "Whatever things were gain to me, those things I have counted as loss for the sake of Christ. More than that, I count all things to be loss in view of the surpassing value of knowing Christ Jesus my Lord, for whom I have suffered the loss of all things, and count them but rubbish in order that I may gain Christ, and may be found in Him, not having a righteousness of my own derived from the Law, but that which is through faith in Christ, the righteousness which comes from God on the basis of faith" (vv. 7-9).

For those who trust in Him, Christ has become "to us wisdom from God, and righteousness and sanctification, and redemption" (1 Cor. 1:30). When God looks at imperfect, sinful believers, He sees His perfect, sinless Son. We have become "partakers of the divine nature" (2 Pet. 1:4) and possess in ourselves the very righteous life of the holy, eternal God. Admittedly, until our flesh is also redeemed (Rom. 8:23) that new righteous self is in a battle with sin. Even so, we are righteous in our standing before God in Christ, and have the new capacity to act righteously.

If even God's own law alone cannot make a person righteous, how much less can man-made traditions do so? Those who insist on coming to God in their own way and in their own power will never reach Him; they **shall not enter the kingdom of heaven**. No church, no ritual, no works, no philosophy, no system can bring a person to God. Those who, through a church, through a cult, or simply through their own personal standards, try to work their way into God's grace know nothing of what His grace is about.

It is tragic that many people today, like the scribes and Pharisees, will try any way to God but His way. They will pay any price, but will not accept the price He paid. They will do any work for Him, but they will not accept the finished work of His Son for them. They will accept any gift from God except the gift of His free salvation. Such people are religious but not regenerated, and they **shall not enter the kingdom of heaven**.

"I am not setting God's law aside," Jesus said. "I will uphold God's law, and I will strip it of all the barnacles of man-made tradition with which it has been encrusted. I will reestablish its preeminence, its permanence, and its pertinence. I will reaffirm the purpose God had for it from the beginning: to show that every person is a sinner and is incapable of fulfilling the law. The one who lowers the standards to a level he *can* fulfill will be judged by God's law and excluded from God's grace."

The Attitude Behind the Act (an Overview of 5:21-48)

From the beginning of the Sermon on the Mount Jesus focuses on the internal, on what men are like in their minds and hearts. That is the primary thrust of Matthew 5:21-48, as the Lord reemphasizes the divine standards for living in His kingdom, the divine standards already given in the law of the Old Testament, in contrast to Jewish tradition.

Contrary to the external, superficial, and hypocritical righteousness that typified the scribes and Pharisees, the righteousness God requires is first of all internal. If it does not exist in the heart, it does not exist at all. Though it had been long forgotten or neglected by most Jews of Jesus' day, that truth was presented to them throughout the Old Testament.

Solomon prayed, "Hear Thou in heaven Thy dwelling place, and forgive and act and render to each according to all his ways, whose heart Thou knowest, for Thou alone dost know the hearts of all the sons of men" (1 Kings 8:39). In David's last words to Solomon he said, "As for you, my son Solomon, know the God of your father, and serve Him with a whole heart and a willing mind; for the Lord searches all hearts, and understands every intent of the thoughts" (1 Chron. 28:9). Hanani the seer reminded King Asa, "For the eyes of the Lord move to and fro throughout the earth that He may strongly support those whose heart is completely His" (2 Chron. 16:9). "All the ways of a man are clean in his own sight," we are told in Proverbs, "but the Lord weighs the motives" (Prov. 16:2).

That God is first of all concerned about what men are like on the inside is a central truth of both testaments. A good outward act is validated before God only when it honestly represents what is on the inside. "I, the Lord, search the heart, I test the mind, even to give to each man according to his ways, according to the results of his deeds" (Jer. 17:10). In the last book of the Bible the Lord warns the church at Thyatira, "I am He who searches the minds and hearts; and I will give to each one of you according to your deeds" (Rev. 2:23). Right external behavior only pleases Him when it corresponds to right internal attitudes and motives. "I am conscious of nothing against myself," Paul said, "yet I am not by this acquitted; but the one who examines me is the Lord. Therefore do not go on passing judgment before the time, but wait until the Lord comes who will both bring to light the things hidden in the darkness and disclose the motives of men's hearts; and then each man's praise will come to him from God" (1 Cor. 4:4-5).

The presumed good deeds of the proud scribes and self-glorying Pharisees did not come from the heart attitudes Jesus says are characteristic of kingdom citizens: poverty of spirit, mourning over sin, gentleness, hunger and thirst for righteousness, and so on (vv. 3-12).

Because Jesus knew that His hearers, especially the self-righteous and self-satisfied religious leaders, could not possibly understand what He was saying, He devoted much of this sermon to exposing the faulty principles and motivations of the legalistic system that had replaced God's own revealed Word.

Jesus used the phrase "You have heard that the ancients were told," or a similar one, to introduce each of the six corrective illustrations He gives in this part of His sermon (see vv. 21, 27, 31, 33, 38, 43). The phrase has reference to rabbinical, traditional teaching, and in each illustration Jesus contrasts that human teaching with the divine Word of God. The examples show ways in which God's righteousness surpasses that of the scribes and Pharisees (see v. 20). They deal with the specific subjects of murder, sexual sin, divorce, speaking the truth, retaliation, and loving others. Yet they all illustrate the same basic principle, the principle Jesus says must be applied to every area of life: righteousness is a matter of the heart.

Jesus is not modifying the law of Moses, the teaching of the Psalms, the standards of the prophets, or any other part of Scripture. The essence of what He has just said in verses 17-20 is (1) that His teaching stands firmly in agreement with every truth, even every word, of the Old Testament, and (2) that the Jewish religious traditions *did not.*

In the six illustrations found in verses 21-48, Jesus first refers to two of the Ten Commandments, then to two more general principles in the law of Moses, and finally to the two broad principles of mercy and love. Murder and adultery deal with the foundational issues of individual and social preservation. Protection of life is the foundation of individual welfare, and protection of marriage is the foundation of social welfare. Divorce and truth-telling involve a wider area of social relationships, and mercy and love a wider area still. The illustrations progress from the protection of each human life to the love of all human life, including enemies.

Together, those illustrations affirm that every area of our lives should be characterized and measured by God's perfect standard of inner righteousness.

Patrick Fairbairn wrote,

> In the revelation of law there was a substratum of grace recognized in the words that prefaced the ten commandments, and promises of grace and blessing also intermingled with the stern prohibitions and injunctions of which they consist. And so, inversely, in the Sermon on the Mount, while it gives grace the priority and the prominence, [such as in the Beatitudes], it is far from excluding the severer aspect of God's character and government. No sooner, indeed, had grace poured itself forth in a succession of beatitudes, than there appear the stern demands of righteousness and law. (Cited in Arthur Pink, *An Exposition of the Sermon on the Mount* [Grand Rapids: Baker, 1950], p. 67)

The phrase "The ancients were told" could also be rendered "the ancients told, or said." In the first instance the implication would be that the ancients were told by God, in which case Jesus would be referring to God's revealed Word. That cannot be, because He contrasts His teaching, the teaching of God, with that of the ancients. For Him to contradict God's Word in any way would be totally out of the question in view of verses 17-19. In the second rendering the implication is that the ideas the ancients taught were primarily of their own devising. That must be the correct approach.

Jesus customarily referred to the Scriptures by such phrases as "Moses commanded," "the prophet Isaiah said," "it is written," and such. Here His words are much more general and therefore cannot refer directly to the Old Testament. He shows that, even in regard to the specific biblical commands against murder and adultery, their tradition was at variance with the holy Scripture, which reveals that God's primary concern has always been for inner purity, not simply outward compliance.

Fairbairn again observes, "The scribes and Pharisees of that age had completely inverted the order of things. Their carnality and self-righteousness had led them to exalt the precepts respecting ceremonial observances to the highest place and to throw the duties inculcated in the ten commandments comparatively into the background" (cited in Pink, *An Exposition on the Sermon on the Mount,* p. 69).

The rabbis of past generations were often called the "fathers of antiquity," or "the men of long ago," and it is to them that "the ancients" (vv. 21, 33) refers. Jesus was contrasting His teaching—and the true teaching of the Old Testament Scriptures themselves—with the Jewish written and oral traditions that had accumulated over the previous several hundred years and that had so terribly perverted God's revelation.

As Martyn Lloyd-Jones has pointed out, the condition of Judaism at the time of Christ was remarkably like that of the church in the early sixteenth century.

The Scriptures were not translated into the languages of the people. The liturgy, the prayers, the Scripture reading, and even most of the hymns and anthems were in Latin, which none of the common people knew or understood. When a priest gave a sermon or homily, the people had nothing by which to judge what he said. They had no idea as to whether or not his message was scriptural, or even whether or not being scriptural was important. The Bible taught what the church said it taught. The church, therefore, placed its own authority over that of Scripture (see *Studies in the Sermon on the Mount* [Grand Rapids: Eerdmans, 1971], 1:212).

Over the centuries the Roman Catholic church had developed a system of religion that departed further and further from Scripture. It was a system that the common man had no way of investigating or verifying. The greatest contribution of the Protestant Reformation was to give the Bible to the people in their own language. It put God's Word into the hands of God's people. It was the truth of Scripture that brought light to the Middle Ages and consequently an end to the Dark Ages.

In a less extreme way the Jews of Jesus' day had been separated from their Scriptures. During and after the Exile most Jews lost their use of the Hebrew language and had come to speak Aramaic, a Semitic language related to Hebrew. Parts of Ezra, Jeremiah, and Daniel were originally written in Aramaic, but the rest of the Old Testament was in Hebrew. The Septuagint, a Greek edition of the Old Testament, had been translated some two hundred fifty years earlier. But though it was widely used by Jews throughout the Roman Empire, the Septuagint was not used or understood by most Jews in Palestine. In addition to that, copies of the Scriptures were bulky, expensive, and far out of the financial reach of the average person. Therefore, when the Hebrew text was read and expounded in the synagogue services, most of the worshipers understood little of the text and consequently had no basis for judging the exposition. Their respect for the rabbis also led them to accept whatever those leaders said.

After the return from exile in Babylon, when Ezra and others read publicly from the law of Moses, they had to translate "to give the sense so that they [the people] understood the reading" (Neh. 8:8). Most later scribes and rabbis, however, did not attempt to translate or expound the scriptural text itself but rather taught from the Talmud, an exhaustive codification of the rabbinic traditions.

Therefore both the Jewish leaders and the rank and file of the people were amazed at Jesus' radical departure—in both content and delivery—from the type of teaching they were used to. Whether He was right or wrong, it was obvious to them that "He was teaching them as one having authority, and not as the scribes" (Mark 1:22).

Among Jesus' most amazing departures from traditional teaching were His insistence that tradition and Scripture were in conflict and that inner righteousness, not outward form, is the central and necessary characteristic of a right relationship to God.

In his *Institutes* (*Library of Christian Classics*, vol. 1, p. 372), John Calvin wrote,

Let us agree that through the law man's life is molded not only to outward honesty but to inward and spiritual righteousness. Although no one can deny this, very few duly note it. This happens because they do not look to the Lawgiver by whose character the nature of the law is to be appraised. If some king by edict forbids fornication, murder or theft, I admit that a man who does not commit such acts will not be bound by the penalty. That is because the mortal lawgiver's jurisdiction extends only to the outward political order. But God, whose eye nothing escapes and who is concerned not so much with outward appearance as with purity of heart, forbids not only fornication, murder and theft but lust, anger, hatred, coveting and deceit. For since He is a spiritual Lawgiver, He speaks not less to the soul than He does to the body.

Five basic principles summarize the central thrust of 5:21-48. The first principle is that the spirit of the law is more important than the letter. The law was not given as a mechanical set of rules by which men in their own power could govern their outward living. It was given as a guide to the type of character God requires.

The second principle is that the law is positive as well as negative. Its purpose not only is to prevent both inner and outward sin but to promote both inner and outward righteousness.

The third principle is that the law is not an end in itself. Its deeper purpose goes beyond purifying the lives of God's people. Its supreme purpose is to glorify God Himself.

The fourth principle is that God alone is qualified to judge men, because He alone can judge men's hearts. Only the Creator has the right and the ability to judge the deepest inner workings of His creatures.

The fifth principle is that every human being is commanded to live up to the perfect divine standard to which the law points. Because that command is impossible for man to fulfill, God Himself has provided fulfillment through His Son, Jesus Christ. The Demander of righteousness is also the Giver of righteousness; the Lawgiver is also the Redeemer.

Who Is a Murderer? (5:21-26)

You have heard that the ancients were told, "You shall not commit murder" and "Whoever commits murder shall be liable to the court." But I say to you that everyone who is angry with his brother shall be guilty before the court; and whoever shall say to his brother, "Raca," shall be guilty before the supreme court; and whoever shall say, "You fool," shall be guilty enough to go into the fiery hell. If therefore you are presenting your offering at the altar, and there remember that your brother has something against you, leave your offering there before the altar, and go your way; first be reconciled to your brother, and then come and present your offering. Make friends quickly with your opponent at law while you are with him on the way, in order that your opponent may not deliver you to the judge, and the judge to the officer, and you be thrown into prison. Truly I say to you, you shall not come out of there, until you have paid up the last cent. (5:21-26)

Man's first crime was homicide. "It came about when they were in the field, that Cain rose up against Abel his brother and killed him" (Gen. 4:8). Since that day murder has been a constant part of human society.

Recent years have seen the arrests and convictions of a number of mass murderers, whose names became household words. Over twenty-five thousand known murders are committed in the United States every year—averaging nearly seventy a day. The unknown murders no doubt would increase those figures considerably. Murders have become so commonplace that, unless they are bizarre or multiple or involve a famous person, they make no more than local news. If we were to add suicides (self-murder) and abortions (prebirth murder) the numbers would be staggering.

The first of six illustrations of heart-righteousness that Jesus gives in 5:21-48 deals with the sin of murder: **You have heard that the ancients were told, "You shall not commit murder."** As discussed in the previous chapter, **the ancients** refers to the rabbis and scribes of old who had devised the many traditions with which Judaism had become encumbered and which had virtually replaced the authority of the Scriptures. In the first two illustrations the ancient teachings to which Jesus refers are traditional interpretations of scriptural commands.

The murder of Abel was a terrible act, which Cain knew violated divine law (Gen. 4:9, 13). But the first specific prohibition of murder is found later in Genesis: "Whoever sheds man's blood, by man his blood shall be shed, for in the image of God He made man" (9:6). Here the penalty for murder and the reason for its seriousness are given. The penalty was death for the killer, and the reason for such severe punishment was that man is made in God's image. To take the life of a fellow human being is to assault the sacredness of the image of God.

The specific commandment to which Jesus here refers is from the Decalogue, which every Jew knew. The command "You shall not murder" (Ex. 20:13) does not prohibit every form of killing a human being. The term used has to do with criminal killing, and from many accounts and teachings in Scripture it is clear that capital punishment, just warfare, accidental homicide, and self-defense are excluded. The commandment is against the intentional killing of another human being for purely personal reasons, whatever those reasons might be.

Just as Satan is the father of lies and of those who reject and rebel against God, he is also the original murderer (John 8:44). Men are themselves accountable for murders they commit, just as they are accountable for every other sin; but every sin, including every murder, is inspired by the would-be murderer of God.

Even so, we cannot blame Satan for our sins, because fallen human nature shares the presence of evil that Satan personifies. Jesus said it is out of a person's own heart that "come evil thoughts, murders, adulteries, fornications, thefts, false witness, slanders" (Matt. 15:19). We do not sin simply because of Satan or because of social deprivation, stressful situations, bad influences, or any other external cause. Those things may tempt us to sin and make sinning easier, but when we commit sin—or even intend to commit sin—it is because we decide to sin. Sin is an act of the will. When in their rejection of God men "did not see fit to acknowledge God any longer, God gave them over to a depraved mind, to do those things which are not proper, being filled with all unrighteousness, wickedness, greed, evil; full of envy, murder, strife, deceit, malice; they are gossips, slanderers, haters of God, insolent, arrogant, boastful, inventors of evil, disobedient to parents, without understanding, untrustworthy, unloving, unmerciful" (Rom. 1:28-31).

"There are six things which the Lord hates, yes, seven which are an abomination to Him: haughty eyes, a lying tongue, and hands that shed innocent blood, a heart that devises wicked plans, feet that run rapidly to evil, a false witness who utters lies, and one who spreads strife among brothers" (Prov. 6:16-19). Murder is a despicable manifestation of a fleshly heart. The seriousness of the offense is seen in one of the last declarations in God's Word: "Outside [of heaven] are the dogs and the sorcerers and the immoral persons and the murderers and the idolaters, and everyone who loves and practices lying" (Rev. 22:15).

The Old and New Testaments are filled with the names of murderers. In the Old are Cain, Lamech, Pharaoh, Abimelech, Joab, the Amalekites, David, Absalom, Zimri, Jezebel, Haziel, Jehu, Athaliah, Joash, Manasseh, and many others. The New Testament list includes Herod, Judas, the high priests, Barabbas, Herodias and her daughter, and others. Biblical history, like human history in general, is filled with murderers.

Jesus' hearers were aware of the prevalence and seriousness of this sin. No doubt most of them were in full agreement with capital punishment for the crime and were convinced that they were innocent of that particular evil.

But now Jesus attacks such self-confidence by charging that no one is truly innocent of murder, because the first step in murder is anger. The anger that lies behind murder—anger which many people think is not really a sin—is one of the worst of sins. To one degree or another, it makes all men would-be murderers.

The Lord's teaching about murder, whether the act is committed outwardly or not, affects our view of ourselves, our worship of God, and our relation to others.

THE EFFECT ON OUR VIEW OF OURSELVES

You have heard that the ancients were told, "You shall not commit murder" and "Whoever commits murder shall be liable to the court." But I say to you that everyone who is angry with his brother shall be guilty before the court; and whoever shall say to his brother, "Raca," shall be guilty before the supreme court; and whoever shall say, "You fool," shall be guilty enough to go into the fiery hell. (5:21-22)

The first effect of Jesus' words is to shatter the illusion of self-righteousness. Like most people throughout history, the scribes and Pharisees thought that if there was any sin of which they were clearly not guilty it was murder. Whatever else they may have done, at least they had never committed murder.

According to rabbinic tradition, and to the beliefs of most cultures and religions, murder is strictly limited to the act of physically taking another person's life. Jesus had already warned that God's righteousness surpasses that of the scribes and Pharisees (v. 20). As the chosen custodians of God's Word (Rom. 3:2) the Jews, above all people, should have known that God commands heart-righteousness, not just external, legalistic behavior. But because most of them had come to converse in Aramaic rather than Hebrew, the language of the Old Testament, and because the rabbis had created a vast collection of traditions, which they taught in place of the Scripture itself, the Jews of Jesus' day were ignorant of much of the great revelation God had given them. Rabbinic interpretation of Scripture also obscured the divinely intended meaning.

As already pointed out, the traditional command **you shall not commit murder** was scriptural, being a rendering of Exodus 20:13. But the traditional Jewish penalty, **whoever commits murder shall be liable to the court,** fell short of the biblical standard in several ways. In the first place it fell short because it did not prescribe the scriptural penalty of death (Gen. 9:6; Num. 35:30-31; etc.). The traditional penalty for murder was liability before a civil court, which apparently used its own judgment as to punishment. In the second place, and more importantly, God's holy character was not even taken into consideration. Nothing was said of disobedience to His law, of desecrating His image in which man is made, or of His role in determining and dispensing judgment. In the third place nothing was said about the inner attitude, the heart offense of the murderer.

The rabbis, scribes, and Pharisees had confined murder to being merely a civil issue and had confined its prosecution to a human court. They had also confined its evil to the physical act. In doing so, they flagrantly disregarded what their own Scriptures taught. Long before the time of Christ, David had acknowledged, "Behold, Thou dost desire truth in the innermost being, and in the hidden part Thou wilt make me know wisdom" (Ps. 51:6; cf. 15:2). The Lord said to Samuel, "Man looks at the outward appearance, but the Lord looks at the heart" (1 Sam. 16:7).

In saying, **But I say to you,** Jesus was not contrasting His teaching with that of the Old Testament (cf. Matt. 5:17-19) but with that of rabbinic tradition. He was saying, in effect, "Let me tell what the Scriptures themselves say, what God's truth is on the matter. You cannot justify yourselves because you have not committed the physical act of murder. Murder goes much deeper than that. It originates in the heart, not in the hands. It starts with evil thoughts, regardless of whether or not those thoughts are brought to consummation in action."

Here Jesus begins to specifically point up the inadequacy of the righteousness in which the scribes, Pharisees, and many others trusted. Because their view of righteousness was external, their view of themselves was complimentary. But Jesus shatters that complacent self-righteousness by beginning with the accusation that a person is guilty of murder even if he is angry with, hates, curses, or maligns another person. In a statement that may have shocked His hearers more than anything He had yet said, Jesus declares that a person guilty of anger is guilty of murder and deserves a murderer's punishment.

It is possible for a model, law-abiding citizen to be as guilty of murder as anyone on death row. It is possible for a person who has never been involved in so much as a fist fight to have more of a murderous spirit than a multiple killer. Many people, in the deepest feelings of their hearts, have anger and hatred to such a degree that their true desire is for the hated person to be dead. The fact that fear, cowardice, or lack of opportunity does not permit them to take that person's life does not diminish their guilt before God. In fact, as the Lord makes plain in the following three illustrations of heart-murder, those who consciously desire the death of another person are not free from guilt.

All anger is incipient murder. "Everyone who hates his brother is a murderer" (1 John 3:15)—making all of us guilty, because who has never hated another person? In light of the context John used the term *brother* in the sense of a fellow believer. But Jesus' emphasis was wider than that. Most of those who heard the Sermon on the Mount made no pretense of belief in Christ, and He used **brother** in the broad ethnic sense of meaning any other Jewish person in that culture.

Jesus strips away every vestige of self-righteousness. Not only did He sweep aside all the rabbinical rubbish of tradition, but He also swept aside the self-justification that is common to all of us. His indictment is total.

In the spring of 1931 one of the most notorious criminals of that day was captured. Known as Two-gun Crowley, he had brutally murdered a great many people, including at least one policeman. It is said that when he finally was captured in his girl friend's apartment after a gun battle, the police found a blood-spattered note on him that read, "Under my coat is a weary heart, but a kind one, one that would do nobody any harm." Even the worst of men try to exonerate themselves. Such obvious self-deceit as that of Crowley's seems absurd, yet that is exactly the attitude the natural man has of himself. "I may have done some bad things," he thinks, "but down deep I'm not really bad."

In essence, that was the self-righteous attitude of the scribes and Pharisees, as it is of many people today. Comparing ourselves to a bloodthirsty criminal makes us seem very good in our own minds. Like the Pharisee in the Temple, we feel proud that we are "not like other people: swindlers, unjust, adulterers" (Luke 18:11). What Jesus says in the present passage is that we *are* just like those other people. Even if we do not take someone else's life, even if we never physically assault another person, we are guilty of murder.

Sociologists and psychologists report that hatred brings a person closer to murder than does any other emotion. And hatred is but an extension of anger. Anger leads to hatred, which leads to murder—in the heart if not in the act. Anger and hatred are so deadly that they can even turn to destroy the person who harbors them.

Jesus' main point here, and through verse 48, is that even the best of people, in their hearts, are sinful and so are in the same boat with the worst of people. Not to consider the state of our heart is not to consider that which the Lord holds to be the all-important measure of true guilt.

In verse 22 Jesus gives three examples that show the divine definition of murder: being **angry** with another person, saying **Raca** to him, and calling him a **fool**.

THE EVIL AND DANGER OF ANGER

everyone who is angry with his brother shall be guilty before the court. (5:22a)

We know from other Scripture, and from Jesus' own life, that He does not prohibit every form of anger. It was in righteous anger that He cleansed the Temple of those who defiled it (John 2:14-17; Matt. 21:12-13). Paul tells us to "be angry, and yet do not sin" (Eph. 4:26). Although the principle is often abused and misapplied, it is possible to have righteous anger. Faithfulness to Christ will sometimes demand it.

In our day of peace and harmony at any cost, of positive thinking, and of confusing godly love with human sentimentality, we often need to show more anger against certain things. There are things in our country, our communities, our schools, and even in our churches about which we have no excuse for *not* being angry, vocally angry. Many of the trends in our society, many of the philosophies and standards to which our children are exposed, and some of the unbiblical philosophies and standards within evangelicalism need to be challenged with righteous indignation, because they attack the kingdom and glory of God. God Himself is "angry with the wicked every day" (Ps. 7:11, KJV).

But Jesus is not talking about anger over God's being dishonored, but rather selfish anger, anger against a **brother**, whoever that might be, because he has done something against us, or simply irritates and displeases us. *Orgizō* (to be **angry**) has to do with brooding, simmering anger that is nurtured and not allowed to die. It is seen in the holding of a grudge, in the smoldering bitterness that refuses to forgive. It is the anger that cherishes resentment and does not want reconciliation. The writer of Hebrews identifies its depth and intensity as a "root of bitterness" (Heb. 12:15).

Such anger, Jesus says, is a form of murder. The person who harbors anger **shall be guilty before the court**. To be guilty before the civil court should have been to be guilty of murder and deserving of the death penalty. Anger merits execution, because the fruit of anger is murder.

THE EVIL AND DANGER OF SLANDER

and whoever shall say to his brother, "Raca," shall be guilty before the supreme court. (5:22b)

Raca was an epithet commonly used in Jesus' day that has no exact modern equivalent. Therefore in most Bible versions, as here, it is simply transliterated. A term of malicious abuse, derision, and slander, it has been variously rendered as brainless idiot, worthless fellow, silly fool, empty head, blockhead, and the like. It was a word of arrogant contempt. David spoke of persons who use such slander as those who "sharpen their tongues as a serpent; poison of a viper is under their lips" (Ps. 140:3). It was the type of word that would have been used by the soldiers who mocked Jesus as they placed the crown of thorns on His head and led Him out to be crucified (Matt. 27:29-31).

A Jewish legend tells of a young rabbi named Simon Ben Eleazar who had just come from a session with his famous teacher. The young man felt especially proud about how he handled himself before the teacher. As he basked in his feelings of erudition, wisdom, and holiness, he passed a man who was especially unattractive. When the man greeted Simon, the rabbi responded, "You Raca! How ugly you are. Are all men of your town as ugly as you?" "That I do not know," the man answered, "but go and tell the Maker who created me how ugly is the creature He has made."

To slander a creature made in God's image is to slander God Himself and is equivalent to murdering that person. Contempt, says Jesus, is murder of the heart. The contemptuous person **shall be guilty before the supreme court**, the Sanhedrin, the council of the seventy who tried the most serious offenses and pronounced the severest penalties, including death by stoning (see Acts 6:12— 7:60).

THE EVIL AND DANGER OF CONDEMNING CHARACTER

and whoever shall say, "You fool," shall be guilty enough to go into the fiery hell. (5:22c)

Mōros (**fool**) means "stupid" or "dull" and is the term from which we get moron. It was sometimes used in secular Greek literature of an obstinate, godless person. It was also possibly related to the Hebrew *mārâ,* which means "to rebel against." To call someone **You fool** was to accuse them of being both stupid and godless.

The three illustrations in this verse show increasing degrees of seriousness. To be angry is the basic evil behind murder; to slander a person with a term such as *Raca* is even more serious, because it gives expression to that anger; and to condemn a person's character by calling him a **fool** is more slanderous still.

The Psalms twice tell us that "the fool has said in his heart, 'There is no God'" (Ps. 14:1; 53:1; cf. 10:4). The book of Proverbs is filled with references and warnings to fools. On the road to Emmaus Jesus used a similar, but less severe, term when He called the two disciples "foolish men and slow of heart to believe in all that the prophets have spoken!" (Luke 24:25).

Because of the testimony of God's Word, we know that fools of the worst sort do exist. And it is our obligation to warn those who are clearly in opposition to God's will that they are living foolishly. We certainly are not wrong to show someone what Scripture says about a person who rejects God. Jesus' prohibition is against slanderously calling a person a **fool** out of anger and hatred. Such an expression of malicious animosity is tantamount to murder and makes us **guilty enough to go into the fiery hell.**

Geenna (**hell**) is derived from Hinnom, the name of a valley just southwest of Jerusalem used as the city dump. It was a forbidding place where trash was continually burned and where the fire, smoke, and stench never ceased. The location was originally desecrated by King Ahaz when "he burned incense in the valley of Ben-hinnom, and burned his sons in fire, according to the abominations of the nations whom the Lord had driven out before the sons of Israel" (2 Chron. 28:3). That wicked king had used the valley to erect an altar to the pagan god Molech, an altar on which one's own children sometimes were offered by being burned alive. It would later be called "the valley of Slaughter" (Jer. 19:6). As part of his godly reforms, King Josiah tore down all the altars there and turned the valley into the garbage incinerator it continued to be until New Testament times. The name of the valley therefore came to be a metonym for the place of eternal torment, and was so used by Jesus eleven times.

To call a person a fool is the same as cursing him and murdering him, and to be guilty of that sin is to be worthy of the eternal punishment of **fiery hell.**

THE EFFECT ON OUR WORSHIP OF GOD

If therefore you are presenting your offering at the altar, and there remember that your brother has something against you, leave your offering there before the altar, and go your way; first be reconciled to your brother, and then come and present your offering. (5:23-24)

Jesus' teaching not only affects our view of ourselves by shattering all self-righteousness and showing that we are guilty and worthy of hell, but it also shows how the sins of anger and hatred affect our relationship to God.

Worship was a major concern of the scribes and Pharisees, directly or indirectly the focus of almost everything they did. They spent much time in the synagogues and in the Temple. They made sacrifices, offered prayers, gave tithes, and carried on religious activities of every sort. But it was all heartless external ceremony.

Therefore refers back to Jesus' point that sin, just as righteousness, is first of all internal. As long as there is internal sin, outward acts of worship are not acceptable to God. Jesus continues to focus on the particular sin of hatred against someone else, a **brother** in the broadest sense. Reconciliation must precede worship.

Every Jew realized that sin caused a breach in one's relationship with God, and that the sacrifices and offerings were intended to restore a right relationship with Him. In their reliance on rabbinical tradition and its misinterpretation of the Old Testament, however, they no longer gave much consideration to sins that could not be seen. Although they would not have called such things as hatred and lust good, they nevertheless did not think of them as true sins. But now Jesus said that anger and hatred are every bit as sinful as murder and adultery.

The scene of **presenting your offering at the altar** was a familiar one to Jews. The Lord may have had in mind here the sacrifice made on the Day of Atonement, when the worshiper brought an animal sacrifice for his sins. When he came to the court of the priests he would stop, because only priests were allowed to enter the altar area. He would then lay his hands on the animal to identify with it and present it to the priest to offer on his behalf. "But do not hand the sacrifice to the priest," Jesus said, "if you **remember that your brother has something against you**." Unresolved conflict has priority and must be settled. **Leave your offering there before the altar, and go your way; first be reconciled to your brother, and then come and present your offering.** Settle the breach between you and your brother before you try to settle the breach between you and God. Not to do that is to be a hypocrite by asking for forgiveness without repenting.

That has always been God's requirement. He had told Israel, "'What are your multiplied sacrifices to Me?' says the Lord. 'I have had enough of burnt offerings of rams, and the fat of cattle. And I take no pleasure in the blood of bulls, lambs, or goats. . . . Wash yourselves, make yourselves clean; remove the evil of your deeds from My sight. Cease to do evil, learn to do good; seek justice, reprove the ruthless; defend the orphan, plead for the widow'" (Isa. 1:11, 16-17; cf. 58:5-7). "Will you steal, murder, and commit adultery, and swear falsely, and offer sacrifices to Baal, and walk after other gods that you have not known, then come and stand before Me in this house, which is called by My name, and say, 'We are delivered'?" (Jer. 7:9-10). The Jews knew, or should have known, that God demanded they be willing to forsake hatred and be made right with each other before they could be right with Him.

The phrase **your brother has something against you** could also refer to anger or hatred on the brother's part. That is, even if we hold nothing against him, if he is angry with or hates us, we should do everything in our power to be reconciled to him. Obviously we cannot change another person's heart or attitude, but our desire and effort should be to close the breach as much as is possible from our side and to hold no anger ourselves even if the other person does.

Regardless of who is responsible for the break in relationship—and often there is guilt on both sides—we should determine to make a reconciliation before we come before God to worship. True worship is not enhanced by better music, better prayers, better architecture, or even better preaching. True worship is enhanced by better relationships between those who come to worship. Worship may be improved by our staying away from church until we have made things right with those with whom we know our relationship is strained or broken.

When there is animosity or sin of any sort in our heart there cannot be integrity in our worship. Nearly a thousand years before Christ preached the

Sermon on the Mount the psalmist had declared, "If I regard wickedness in my heart, the Lord will not hear" (Ps. 66:18). Even before that Samuel said, "Has the Lord as much delight in burnt offerings and sacrifices as in obeying the voice of the Lord? Behold, to obey is better than sacrifice, and to heed than the fat of rams" (1 Sam. 15:22).

The Effect on Our Relations with Others

Make friends quickly with your opponent at law while you are with him on the way, in order that your opponent may not deliver you to the judge, and the judge to the officer, and you be thrown into prison. Truly I say to you, you shall not come out of there, until you have paid up the last cent. (5:25-26)

These verses are essentially a commentary on the previous two. Using an illustration from the common practice of imprisoning a person for an unpaid debt, Jesus teaches that if someone holds a debt of any sort against us, he is to make it good as soon as possible and before it is too late and he is imprisoned.

The time for reconciliation, just as the time for salvation, is always now. Tomorrow is often too late. We are not to allow bitterness, anger, hatred, or any other sin to keep us separated from other people, whoever they are.

Whereas in verses 23-24 the command for reconciliation is given to the innocent as well as the guilty party, here the focus is strictly on the one who is guilty. Roman law provided that a plaintiff could bring the accused with him to face the judge. The two themselves could settle the matter **on the way**, but not after the court became involved. If a man had wronged an **opponent at law** (indicating that the issue was headed for court) he should **make friends quickly**, that is, settle the account with his **opponent** before he had to face judgment. The sequence of going from the **judge** to the **officer** to **prison** shows the typical procedure in dealing with a guilty person. To avoid judgment and prison he had to pay **the last cent** (a small Roman coin) owed.

This illustration is a picture of sin against another person. Such sin must be resolved to avoid having to face a sentence from the divine Judge.

The precise penalty to which Jesus alludes is not made clear. Being **thrown into prison** and not being able to get **out of there until** the debt is paid is an analogy of God's punishment. The basic teaching is plain and unmistakable: we are to make every effort, with no delay, to make our relationship right with our brother before our relationship can be right with God and we can avoid chastening.

In the fullest sense, of course, because no one ever fully has right attitudes toward others, no worship is acceptable. Thus everything Jesus teaches in this passage, as in the rest of the Sermon on the Mount, is to show the absolutely perfect standard of God's righteousness and the absolutely impossible task of our meeting that standard in our own power. He shatters self-righteousness in order to drive us to His righteousness, which alone is acceptable to God.

Who Is an Adulterer?
(5:27-30)

28

You have heard that it was said, "You shall not commit adultery"; but I say to you, that everyone who looks on a woman to lust for her has committed adultery with her already in his heart. And if your right eye makes you stumble, tear it out, and throw it from you; for it is better for you that one of the parts of your body perish, than for your whole body to be thrown into hell. And if your right hand makes you stumble, cut it off, and throw it from you; for it is better for you that one of the parts of your body perish, than for your whole body to go into hell. (5:27-30)

Jesus continues to unmask the self-righteous externalism typified by the scribes and Pharisees by showing that the only righteousness acceptable to God is purity of heart. Without that purity, the outward life makes no difference. God's divine evaluation takes place in the heart. He judges the source and origin of sin, not its manifestation or lack of manifestation. "As [a person] thinks within himself, so he is" (Prov. 23:7), and so he is judged by God (1 Sam. 16:7).

Jesus' second illustration of heart righteousness has to do with adultery and sexual sin in general. In verses 27-30 He focuses on the deed of adultery, the desire behind it, and the deliverance from it.

The Deed

You have heard that it was said, "You shall not commit adultery." (5:27)

As with the one relating to the sin of murder (vv. 21-26), this illustration begins with a quotation of one of the Ten Commandments (Ex. 20:14). In both of those cases, Jewish tradition was based on the law of Moses, at least superficially.

The sixth commandment protects the sanctity of life and the seventh the sanctity of marriage. Those who rely on external righteousness break both of those commandments, because in their hearts they attack the sanctity of life and the sanctity of marriage, whether they do so outwardly or not. When they are angry or hate, they commit murder. When they lust sexually, they commit adultery. And when they do either of those things, they choose to despise God's law and God's name (see Ex. 20:14; Lev. 20:10; Deut. 5:18).

Anger and sexual lust are two of the most powerful influences on mankind. The person who gives them reign will soon find that he is more controlled than in control. Every person has experienced temptation to anger and to sexual sin, and every person has at some time and to some degree given in to those temptations. Because of that fact, every person is guilty before God of murder and of adultery.

Although sexual temptations have been strong since man's fall, our day of permissiveness and perversion has brought an increase in those destructive influences that no society in history has had before (see 2 Tim. 3:13). Ours is a day of unbridled indulgence in sexual passion. People propagate, promote, and exploit it through the most powerful and pervasive media ever known to man. It seems to be the almost uninterrupted theme of our society's entertainment. Even in academic and religious circles we see seminars, books, tapes, and programs of all sorts that promise to improve sexual knowledge, experience, freedom, and enjoyment.

Mass media uses sex to sell its products and to glamorize its programs. Sex crimes are at all-time highs, while infidelity, divorce, and perversion are justified. Marriage, sexual fidelity, and moral purity are scorned, ridiculed, and laughed at. We are preoccupied with sex to a degree perhaps never before seen in a civilized culture.

But the philosophy of sexual hedonism is not new to our day. It was common in New Testament times, and Paul faced it full force in Corinth. His comment "Food is for the stomach, and the stomach is for food" (1 Cor. 6:13a) expressed the common Greek notion that biological functions are just biological functions and have no moral significance. It was a belief many of the Corinthian believers had reverted to, or had never given up, in order to justify their sexual misconduct. Apparently they were arguing, as do many hedonists today, that sex is simply a biological act, no different morally from eating, drinking, or sleeping. But Paul strongly refutes that idea by going on to say, "God will do away with both of them [that is, food and the stomach]. Yet the body is not for immorality, but for the Lord; and the Lord is for the body" (v. 13b). The body is more than biological, as divine judgment will reveal. For Christians it is a member of Christ, a temple of the Holy Spirit, and belongs to the Lord rather than to us (vv. 15, 19). It is therefore never to be used for any purpose that dishonors the God who made and indwells it. Christians should have but one response to sexual temptation—running away from it (v. 18).

The same philosophy that corrupted Corinth is today engulfing most of western society in a sea of sexual excess and perversion. In its many forms, sexual license is destroying lives physically, morally, mentally, and spiritually. It is destroying marriages, families, and even whole communities.

Throughout history some Christians have reacted to sexual temptations and sins in ways that are unbiblical. Seeing the great power of the sex drive and the great damage its unbridled expression can cause, they have sometimes concluded that sex itself is evil and should be completely condemned and avoided. Commonly referred to today as the Victorian view, that philosophy was prevalent long before the age of Queen Victoria.

Origen (A.D. 185-254), one of the outstanding early church Fathers, was so convicted of his own sinfulness by reading Matthew 5:27-30 that he had himself castrated (*The New International Dictionary of the Christian Church,* ed. James D. Douglas [new edition; Grand Rapids, 1974, 1978], p. 733. Peter Abelard, a twelfth-century French theologian, had lived a godly life for many years. He fell in love with a young woman (Heloise) and caused her to become pregnant. To protect her and to try to rectify the wrong, he married her. Damaging rumors had begun to circulate, however, and, rather than harm Abelard's career still further, Heloise entered a convent. Her uncle, angry at all that had happened, hired men to break into Abelard's quarters and castrate him; Abelard then joined the monastery of St.-Denis (*New International Dictionary of the Christian Church,* p. 3).

But geographical escapism, physical mutilation, or any form of forced celibacy violate God's purpose (see Heb. 13:4) and are just as unscriptural as sexual immorality. The Lord wants His people to be in the world but not of it (John 17:15-18). And because our bodies belong to Christ and are temples of the Holy Spirit, they are not to be abused in *any* way. God created sex and gives it as a blessing to those who enjoy it within the bounds of marriage. Anyone who promotes abstinence from marriage on the basis that all sexual expression is evil is "paying attention to deceitful spirits and doctrines of demons" (see 1 Tim. 4:1-3). Speaking of the marriage relationship, Paul commands, "Let the husband fulfill his duty to his wife, and likewise also the wife to her husband. . . . Stop depriving one another, except by agreement for a time that you may devote yourselves to prayer, and come together again lest Satan tempt you because of your lack of self-control" (1 Cor. 7:3, 5). Sexual expression not only is a thrilling privilege but an obligation of marriage.

In the middle of a biblical warning against adultery, husbands are instructed, "Let your fountain be blessed, and rejoice in the wife of your youth. As a loving hind and a graceful doe, let her breasts satisfy you at all times; be exhilarated always with her love" (Prov. 5:18-19). The Song of Solomon is devoted to the beauty and wonder of marital love. God has designed and blessed sexual expression within marriage, and to malign or denigrate that proper expression by such practices as castration or forced celibacy is as much of a perversion as fornication, adultery, or homosexuality.

The solution to sexual impurity cannot be external because the cause is not external. Job proclaimed, "If my heart has been enticed by a woman, or I have lurked at my neighbor's doorway, may my wife grind for another, and let others kneel down over her. For that would be a lustful crime; moreover, it would be an iniquity punishable by judges" (Job 31:9-11). That ancient saint knew that physical infidelity is first of all a matter of the heart, and that lusting is just as sinful in God's eyes as the act of adultery.

The Mosaic law portrays adultery as one of the most despicable and heinous of sins, punishable by death (Lev. 20:10; Deut. 22:22). In strongly opposing adultery, Jewish tradition appeared to be entirely scriptural. When the scribes and Pharisees told Jesus that Moses commanded them to stone the woman caught in the act of adultery, they were correct (John 8:4-5). Had not Jesus forgiven her of her sin she would have deserved stoning.

Throughout the New Testament, prohibitions against sexual immorality are every bit as clear as those of the Old. "Neither fornicators, nor idolaters, nor adulterers, nor effeminate, nor homosexuals" will inherit the Kingdom of God (1 Cor. 6:9; cf. Gal. 5:19-21; Rev. 2:22). "Fornicators and adulterers God will judge" (Heb. 13:4). Regardless of how much a couple may care for each other and be deeply in love, sexual relations outside of marriage are forbidden. In every case, without exception, it is a heinous sin against God.

In its most technical sense, committing **adultery** (from *moichaō*) refers to sexual intercourse between a man and woman when one or both of them is married. In both the Old and New Testaments the word relates to sexual intercourse with anyone other than one's marriage partner. That Jesus here implies that the principle of sexual purity can be seen in a wider sense than adultery (though adultery is His point here) seems clear from the fact that both **everyone** and **a woman** are comprehensive terms that could also apply to the unmarried.

THE DESIRE

but I say to you, that everyone who looks on a woman to lust for her has committed adultery with her already in his heart. (5:28)

The pronoun **I** (*egō*) is emphatic, indicating that Jesus puts His own word above the authority of revered rabbinic tradition. **Looks** (from *blepō*) is a present participle and refers to the continuous process of looking. In this usage, the idea is not that of an incidental or involuntary glance but of intentional and repeated gazing. *Pros to* (**to**) used with the infinitive (*epithumēsai*, **lust for**) indicates a goal or an action that follows in time the action of the looking. Jesus is therefore speaking of intentional looking with the purpose of lusting. He is speaking of the man who looks so that he may satisfy his evil desire. He is speaking of the man who goes to an X-rated movie, who selects a television program known for its sexual orientation, who goes to a beach known for its scanty swimsuits, or who does any such thing with the expectation and desire of being sexually and sinfully titillated.

Looking at a woman lustfully does not cause a man to commit adultery in his thoughts. He already **has committed adultery in his heart.** It is not lustful looking that causes the sin in the heart, but the sin in the heart that causes lustful looking. The lustful looking is but the expression of a heart that is already immoral and adulterous. The heart is the soil where the seeds of sin are imbedded and begin to grow.

Jesus is not speaking of unexpected and unavoidable exposure to sexual temptation. When a man happens to see a woman provocatively dressed, Satan will surely try to tempt that man with lustful thoughts. But there is no sin if the temptation is resisted and the gaze is turned elsewhere. It is continuing to look in order to satisfy lustful desires that Jesus condemns, because it evidences a vile, immoral heart.

David was not at fault for seeing Bathsheba bathing. He could not have helped noticing her, because she was in plain view as he walked on the palace roof. His sin was in dwelling on the sight and in willingly succumbing to the temptation. He could have looked away and put the experience out of his mind. The fact that he had her brought to his chambers and committed adultery with her expressed the immoral desire that already existed in his heart (see 2 Sam. 11:1-4).

A popular proverb goes, "Sow a thought and reap an act. Sow an act and reap a habit. Sow a habit and reap a character. Sow a character and reap a destiny." That process perfectly illustrates Jesus' main thrust in this passage: No matter where it ends, sin always begins when an evil thought is sown in the mind and heart.

Although Jesus here uses a man as the example, His condemnation of lustful thoughts as well as actions applies equally to women. Women are equally susceptible to lustful looking, and even to inciting men to lust. As Arthur Pink observes,

> If lustful looking is so grievous a sin, then those who dress and expose themselves with the desire to be looked at and lusted after . . . are not less but perhaps more guilty. In this matter it is not only too often the case that men sin but women tempt them to do so. How great then must be the guilt of the great majority of modern misses who deliberately seek to arouse the sexual passions of young men. And how much greater still is the guilt of most of their mothers for allowing them to become lascivious temptresses. (*An Exposition of the Sermon on the Mount* [Grand Rapids: Baker, 1974], p. 83)

Job said, "I have made a covenant with my eyes; how then could I gaze at a virgin. . . . If my step has turned from the way, or my heart followed my eyes, or if any spot has stuck to my hands, let me sow and another eat, and let my crops be uprooted" (Job 31:1, 7-8). Job knew that sin begins in the heart and that he was just as deserving of God's punishment for looking at a woman lustfully as for committing adultery with her. He therefore determined in advance to guard himself by making a pact with his eyes not to gaze at a woman who might tempt him.

Just as the adulterous heart plans to expose itself to lust-satisfying situations, the godly heart plans to avoid them whenever possible and to flee from them when unavoidable. Just as the adulterous heart panders to itself in advance, so the godly heart protects itself in advance, praying with the psalmist, "Turn away my eyes from looking at vanity, and revive me in Thy ways. Establish Thy word to Thy servant, as that which produces reverence for Thee" (Ps. 119:37-38). Paul exhorted Timothy to "flee from youthful lusts" and to cultivate a "pure heart" (2 Tim. 2:22).

Like Job, therefore, we must make a covenant with our eyes—and with every other part of our bodies, minds, and spirits—to shun lust and pursue purity.

THE DELIVERANCE

And if your right eye makes you stumble, tear it out, and throw it from you; for it is better for you that one of the parts of your body perish, than for your whole body to be thrown into hell. And if your right hand makes you stumble, cut it off, and throw it from you; for it is better for you that one of the parts of your body perish, than for your whole body to go into hell. (5:29-30)

Here Jesus points the way to deliverance from heart sin. At first His advice seems incongruous with what He has just been saying. If the problem is in the heart, what good is plucking out an eye or cutting off a hand? If the right eye were lost, the left would continue to look lustfully, and if the right hand were cut off, the left would still remain to carry on sinful acts.

Obviously Jesus is speaking figuratively of those things, physical or otherwise, that cause us to be tempted or make us more susceptible to temptation. In Jewish culture, the right eye and right hand represented a person's best and most precious faculties. The right eye represented one's best vision, and the right hand one's best skills. Jesus' point is that we should be willing to give up whatever is necessary, even the most cherished things we possess, if doing that will help protect us from evil. Nothing is so valuable as to be worth preserving at the expense of righteousness. This strong message is obviously not to be interpreted in a wooden, literal way so that the Lord appears to be advocating mutilation. Mutilation will not cleanse the heart. The intent of these words is simply to call for dramatic severing of the sinful impulses in us which push us to evil action (cf. Matt. 18:8-9).

Skandalizō basically means to cause to fall, but in its substantive form, as here (**makes . . . stumble**), it was often used of the bait stick that springs the trap when an animal touches it. Anything that morally or spiritually traps us, that causes us to fall into sin or to stay in sin, should be eliminated quickly and totally. For example, a married person's falling in love with someone besides his or her spouse is wrong. The relationship may be mutually enjoyable and considered to be rewarding, fulfilling, and beautiful. But it is totally sinful and should be immediately severed. What is a pure and truly beautiful relationship between marriage partners is morally ugly and repulsive to God when it is shared between a man and woman if either or both are married to someone else.

The message of this hyperbolic statement of our Lord is clearly that sin must be dealt with radically. Paul said, "I buffet my body and make it my slave, lest possibly, after I have preached to others, I myself should be disqualified" (1 Cor. 9:27). If we do not consciously and purposefully control what is around us, where we go, what we do, what we watch and read, the company we keep, and the conversations we have, then those things will control us. And what we cannot control we should discard without hesitation.

Obviously getting rid of harmful influences will not change a corrupt heart into a pure heart. Outward acts cannot produce inner benefits. But just as the outward act of adultery reflects a heart that is already adulterous, the outward act of forsaking whatever is harmful reflects a heart that hungers and thirsts for righteousness. That outward act is effective protection, because it comes from a heart that seeks to do God's will instead of its own.

Like Origen, Saint Anthony sought to escape immorality and lust by separating himself from the rest of society. He became a hermit in the Egyptian desert, where he lived in poverty and deprivation for thirty-five years. Yet by his own testimony he was never freed in all that time from the cares and temptations he sought to escape. Because his heart was still in the world he could not escape the world, and he quickly discovered that Satan, the god of this world, had no difficulty finding him in the desert (William Barclay, *The Gospel of Matthew,* 2 vols. [Philadelphia: Westminster, 1956], 1:146-47).

Jesus again sets forth the impossible standards of His kingdom righteousness. All people are murderers and adulterers. Many do not realize that they are because of the subtlety of sin and its blinding effect on the mind. Jesus does not suggest that the scribes and Pharisees, or anyone else, could deliver themselves from the propensity to sin. As always, the impossibility that He sets forth has a twofold purpose: to make men and women despair of their own righteousness and to seek His. The Lord's remedy for a wicked heart is a new heart, and His answer for our helplessness is His sufficiency.

The story is told that during the Civil War a beautiful, highly educated, and popular young woman fell into prostitution. By the time she was twenty-two years old, she was friendless, broken, and lay dying in a hospital in Cincinnati. Just before she died on a cold winter day she wrote a poem lamenting her life. The poem was published in a newspaper the next day and soon drew the sympathetic attention of thousands across the country. The poem ended with the lines:

Fainting, freezing, dying alone,
    too wicked for prayer,
Too weak for a moan to be heard
    in the streets of the crazy town
Gone mad in the joy
    of the snow coming down.
To lie, and to die,
    in my terrible woe,
With a bed and a shroud
    of the beautiful snow.

Sometime later a verse was added by another pen.

Helpless and frail as the trampled snow,
    Sinner despair not, Christ stoopeth low
To rescue the soul that is lost in its sin,
    And raise it to life and enjoyment again.
Groaning, bleeding, dying for thee,
    The Crucified hung, made a curse on the tree.
His accents of mercy fall soft on thine ear.
    Is there mercy for me? Will He heed my prayer?
O God! in the stream that for sinners doth flow,
    Wash me and I shall be whiter than snow.
(A. Nainsmith, *1200 Notes, Quotes, and Anecdotes* [Chicago: Moody,
                                                            1962], p. 184)

Many men and women go to hell forever because of the deception of self-righteous religion. The illusion that sin is only an external issue is damning.

Divorce and Remarriage (5:31-32)

29

And it was said, "Whoever divorces his wife, let him give her a certificate of dismissal"; but I say to you that everyone who divorces his wife, except for the cause of unchastity, makes her commit adultery; and whoever marries a divorced woman commits adultery. (5:31-32)

The many confused and conflicting ideas in our day about the biblical teaching on divorce are not caused by any deficiency in God's revelation but by the fact that sin has clouded men's minds to the straightfoward simplicity of what God has said. When people read God's Word through the lenses of their own preconceptions or carnal dispositions, a confused and perplexing picture is the only possible outcome. The confusion is not with God but with man.

In a recent book, *The Death of the Family,* a British physician suggests the best thing human society could do would be to abolish the family altogether. He claims that it is the primary conditioning device for a Western imperialistic world view. A well-known advocate of women's liberation, Kate Millett, maintains in her book *Sexual Politics* (New York: Doubleday, 1970; Ballantine, 1978) that "the family unit must go, because it is the family that has oppressed and enslaved women." City after city, and even some states, are passing legislation that grants increasing rights to homosexuals. From every side the family is being directly attacked or indirectly undermined.

Yet the famous Harvard Medical School psychiatrist Armand Nicoli says that

> certain trends prevalent today will incapacitate the family, destroy its integrity, and cause its members to suffer such crippling emotional conflicts that they will become an intolerable burden to society. If any one factor influences the character development and emotional stability of an individual, it is the quality of the relationship he or she experiences as a child with *both* parents. Conversely, if people suffering from severe nonorganic emotional illness have one experience in common, it is the absence of a parent through death, divorce, or some other cause. A parent's inaccessibility, either physically, emotionally, or both, can profoundly influence a child's emotional health. ("The Fractured Family: Following It into the Future," *Christianity Today,* 25 May 1979)

Dr. Nicoli identifies six trends or situations that are the most destructive of the family. They include mothers of young children working outside the home, frequent family moves, the invasion of television, lack of moral control in society, and lack of communication in the home. But he says that by far the major cause of emotional problems and the major detriment to the family is divorce. "The trend toward quick and easy divorce, and the ever-increasing divorce rate, subject more and more children to physically and emotionally absent parents." If the trend is not reversed, he says, "the quality of family life will continue to deteriorate, producing a society with a higher incidence of mental illness than ever before."

The harmful effects of divorce on children, parents, and on the family and society as a whole would be more than enough reason to be concerned about the problem. But the supreme tragedy of divorce is that it violates God's Word.

In many churches the problems of divorce and remarriage are minimized or ignored. Church standards and policies either do not exist or they are accommodated to the whims of the congregation. Often when those problems *are* faced, they are not dealt with on a firm scriptural basis. Many church leaders admit having no clear understanding of what the Bible precisely teaches about the rightness and wrongness of divorce.

Only four basic interpretations of the biblical data on divorce and remarriage are possible, and all four are found to be held in various Christian circles. The strictest view is that divorce is not permissible under any circumstance or for any reason. The opposite position contends that both divorce and remarriage are permissible for any reason or none. The other two views lie between those extremes. One is that divorce is permitted under certain circumstances but remarriage is never permitted. The other is that both divorce and remarriage are permitted under certain circumstances.

The Bible, of course, actually teaches only one of those four possibilities, and that view is taught by Jesus here in Matthew 5:31-32. Like many people today, the Jews of Jesus' day, typified by the scribes and Pharisees, had developed their own standards for divorce and remarriage—which they taught as God's standards. In this passage Jesus continues to correct the erroneous doctrines and practices of the rabbinic traditions and to replace them with the truth.

THE TEACHING OF THE SCRIBES AND PHARISEES

And it was said, "Whoever divorces his wife, let him give her a certificate of dismissal." (5:31)

It was said continues to refer to "the ancients" mentioned in verse 21, the rabbis and scribes who had developed the commonly accepted Jewish traditions over the previous centuries—primarily during and after the Babylonian Exile. This is our Lord's way of setting in place what is antithetical to the teaching of God.

In Jesus' day the dominant rabbinic position on divorce, and by extension on remarriage, was the most liberal of the four views mentioned above: permissibility on any grounds. The only requirement was the giving of **a certificate of dismissal.**

By that period of Jewish history divorce had become so easy and casual that a man could dismiss his wife for such trivial things as burning his meal or embarrassing him in front of his friends. Often the husband did not bother to give a reason, since none was required.

The rabbinic justification for such easy divorce was based on an erroneous interpretation of Deuteronomy 24:1-4, the Bible's first mention of **a certificate of dismissal.**

> When a man takes a wife and marries her, and it happens that she finds no favor in his eyes because he has found some indecency in her, and he writes her a certificate of divorce and puts it in her hand and sends her out from his house, and she leaves his house and goes and becomes another man's wife, and if the latter husband turns against her and writes her a certificate of divorce and puts it in her hand and sends her out of his house, or if the latter husband dies who took her to be his wife, then her former husband who sent her away is not allowed to take her again to be his wife, since she has been defiled; for that is an abomination before the Lord, and you shall not bring sin on the land which the Lord your God gives you as an inheritance.

The focus of that passage is not the question of whether or not divorce is permitted. It does not provide for divorce, much less command it. It is rather the statement of a very narrow, specific law that was given to deal with the matter of adultery. It shows how improper divorce leads to adultery, which results in defilement. Through Moses, God recognized and permitted divorce under certain circumstances when it was accompanied by a certificate, but He did not thereby condone or command divorce. God's permission for divorce was but another accommodation of His grace to human sin (see Matt. 19:18). "Because of your hardness of heart," Jesus explained to the Pharisees on another occasion, "Moses permitted you to divorce your wives; but from the beginning it has not been this way" (Matt. 19:8).

The certificate did not make the divorce right, but only gave the woman some protection. It protected her reputation from slander and provided proof of her legal freedom from her former husband and her consequent right to remarry.

A literal rendering of the Hebrew word translated "indecency" in Deuteronomy 24:1 is "the nakedness of a thing." Some interpreters say it refers to repeated indecent exposure, but Alfred Edersheim (*Sketches of Jewish Social Life* [(Grand Rapids: Eerdmans, 1976], pp. 157-58) says that the word includes every kind of impropriety and describes a generally poor reputation.

The only other place in the entire Bible where that Hebrew term is used is in the previous chapter of Deuteronomy: "And you shall have a spade among your tools, and it shall be when you sit down outside, you shall dig with it and shall turn to cover up your excrement. Since the Lord your God walks in the midst of your camp to deliver you and to defeat your enemies before you, therefore your camp must be holy; and He must not see anything indecent among you lest He turn away from you" (23:13-14). "Anything indecent" comes from the same Hebrew word as "indecency" in 24:1.

The meaning of the word in Deuteronomy 24 includes every kind of improper, shameful, or indecent behavior unbecoming to a woman and embarrassing to her husband. It cannot refer to adultery, because death was the penalty for that, even if it occurred during the engagement period (Lev. 20:10; Deut. 22:22-24).

What kind of indecency, then, would lead to the **certificate of dismissal?** It must have been sins of unfaithfulness and promiscuity that stopped just short of actual adultery. At any rate, Deuteronomy 24 is clear that if the woman remarried and was divorced again, or even if her second husband died, she could not be remarried to her first husband, because she had been "defiled."

The Lord's primary purpose in Deuteronomy 24:1-4 was not to give an excuse for divorce but to show the potential evil of it. His intention was not to provide for it but to prevent it. Verses 1-3 are a series of conditional clauses that culminate in the prohibition of a man ever remarrying a woman he has divorced if she marries someone else and is separated from that second husband either by another divorce or by death. Because her first divorce had no sufficient grounds, her second marriage would be adulterous. Even if her second husband died, she could not go back to her first, "since she [had] been defiled" (v. 4). She was defiled (more literally, "disqualified") because of the adultery brought about by her second marriage—which is the primary point of the passage. Moses is saying, then, that the divorce for indecency or promiscuity creates an adulterous situation.

In God's eyes, therefore, the granting of a certificate did not in itself make a divorce legitimate. Far from approving divorce, Deuteronomy 24:1-4 is a strong warning about it. The passage suggests, or perhaps assumes, that a divorce on proper grounds, accompanied by a certificate, was permitted. It does not offer a divine provision for divorce, but rather shows that divorce often leads to adultery. Even on the grounds of adultery, divorce was tolerated in the law of Moses only as a gracious alternative to the capital punishment that adultery justly deserved (Lev. 20:10-14).

The most popular school of rabbinic tradition in Jesus' day, as reflected in the Targum of Palestine (written in the first century A.D.), interpreted Moses' words in Deuteronomy 24:1 as a command. What God had provided as reluctant permission had been turned into a legal right.

THE TEACHING OF THE OLD TESTAMENT

The Bible's teaching on divorce cannot be understood apart from its teaching on marriage. Immediately after woman was created, God declared, "For this cause a man shall leave his father and his mother, and shall cleave to his wife; and they shall become one flesh" (Gen. 2:24). Marriage was God's plan, not man's, and in the deepest sense every couple that has ever been married, whether believers or not, participates in a union established by the Creator Himself. Marriage is God's institution.

From the beginning, God intended monogamous, life-long marriage to be the only pattern of union between men and women. "Cleave to" carries the idea of firm, permanent attachment, as in gluing. In marriage a man and woman are so closely joined that they become "one flesh," which involves spiritual as well as physical oneness. In marriage God brings a husband and wife together in a unique physical and spiritual bond that reaches to the very depths of their souls. As God designed it, marriage is to be the welding of two people together into one unit, the blending of two minds, two wills, two sets of emotions, two spirits. It is a bond the Lord intends to be indissoluble as long as both partners are alive. The Lord created sex and procreation to be the fullest expression of that oneness, and the intimacies of marriage are not to be shared with any other human being.

One of the most immediate and damaging consequences of the Fall was the destruction of the blissful, loving, and caring relationship between husband and wife. In the garden, Adam and Eve had ruled together, with him as the head and her as his helper. Adam's headship was a loving, caring, understanding provision of leadership. Eve's role was that of loving, willing submission and support. Both were totally devoted to the Lord and to each other.

But problems in marriage, like problems in every other area of earthly existence, began with the Fall. Man's first sin brought a separation from God, a separation of man and nature, and a separation of husband and wife. God's curse on Eve and all women after her was, "I will greatly multiply your pain in childbirth, in pain you shall bring forth children; yet your desire shall be for your husband, and he shall rule over you" (Gen. 3:16). The curse on Adam and every man after him was, "Cursed is the ground because of you; in toil you shall eat of it all the days of your life. Both thorns and thistles it shall grow for you" (v. 17).

The Fall distorted and perverted the marriage relationship. Henceforth the wife's "desire" for her husband would no longer be the desire to help but the desire to control—the same desire that sin had for Cain (see Gen. 4:7, where the identical Hebrew construction is used). For the man's part, his "rule" over his wife henceforth would be one of stern control, in opposition to her desire to control him. At the Fall the battle of the sexes began, and women's liberation and male chauvinism have ever since been clouding and corrupting the divine plan for marriage.

One of the most tragic consequences of that battle is the propensity to divorce. But in light of God's perfect plan for marriage—the plan followed but for a brief while in the Garden of Eden—it is clear that divorce is like a person cutting off an arm or leg because he has a splinter in it. Instead of dealing with whatever trouble arises between husband and wife, divorce tries to solve the problem by destroying the union.

On an even deeper level, divorce destroys a union that God Himself has made. That is why Jesus said unequivocally, "What therefore God has joined together, let no man separate" (Matt. 19:6). The union of marriage is one which God, as its Creator, *never* desires to be broken. Divorce is a denial of His will and a destruction of His work.

The seriousness with which God takes marriage is seen in the penalty for adultery. All sexual intercourse outside of marriage is sinful and defiling, but any illicit sexual activity that involved married persons was punishable by death (Lev. 20:10-14). Two of the Ten Commandments relate to the sanctity of marriage. Not only is the act of adultery forbidden but even the intent of it in coveting another man's wife (Ex. 20:14, 17).

In fact, nowhere is God's high view of the sanctity of marriage more clearly emphasized than in the last of the Ten Commandments: "You shall not covet your neighbor's wife" (Ex. 20:17). For a married person even to desire another partner was a grievous sin. As Jesus affirms in Matthew 5:28, adultery is forbidden to both the body and the mind. In Leviticus 18:18 God went a step further and forbade polygamy. Every violation of lifelong, faithful, monogamous marriage was forbidden by the divine law.

God established marriage as the physical, spiritual, and social union of one man with one woman, a life-long, indivisible union that is never to be violated and never to be broken. He confirms His absolute hatred of divorce in Malachi 2:13-16.

And this is another thing you do: you cover the altar of the Lord with tears, with weeping and with groaning, because He no longer regards the offering or accepts it with favor from your hand. Yet you say, "For what reason?" Because the Lord has been a witness between you and the wife of your youth, against whom you have dealt treacherously, though she is your companion and your wife by covenant. But not one has done so who has a remnant of the Spirit. And what did that one do while he was seeking a godly offspring? Take heed then, to your spirit, and let no one deal treacherously against the wife of your youth. "For I hate divorce," says the Lord, the God of Israel, "and him who covers his garment with wrong," says the Lord of hosts. "So take heed to your spirit, that you do not deal treacherously."

The man who puts away his wife does what God hates. He "covers his garment with wrong," a literal rendering of which would be, "he covers his garment with violence." It brings to mind the picture of a man who murders someone and is caught with the blood of his victim spattered on his clothes. "Not one has done so [divorced] who has a remnant of the Spirit," Malachi tells us. That sentence represents a Hebrew phrase that is difficult to translate, but I believe that rendering gives the right sense of it. God's Holy Spirit is never a party to divorce.

Many people today claim to be led of the Lord to get a divorce and to have His peace after they leave their spouses. But, "I hate divorce," God continues to declare through Malachi, "so take heed to your spirit, that you do not deal treacherously" (v. 16). Without exception, divorce is a product of sin, and God hates it. He never commands it, endorses it, or blesses it.

The Pharisees used an erroneous interpretation of Deuteronomy 24:1-4 to defend their idea of divorce, conveniently interpreting that passage as a command for divorce (Matt. 19:7). In fact, the passage neither commands nor condones divorce. It simply recognizes it as a reality, as do other Old Testament passages. In Isaiah 50:1, for example, God challenges the nation of Israel for their spiritual fornication: "Thus says the Lord, 'Where is the certificate of divorce, by which I have sent your mother away? Or to whom of My creditors did I sell you? Behold, you were sold for your iniquities, and for your transgressions your mother was sent away.'"

Jeremiah 3:1 contains a similar reference: "God says, 'If a husband divorces his wife, and she goes from him, and belongs to another man, will he still return to her? Will not that land be completely polluted? But you are a harlot with many lovers; yet you turn to Me,' declares the Lord."

Far from encouraging divorce, most references to divorce in the Old Testament put restrictions on it. For example, Deuteronomy says about a husband who falsely accuses his bride of "shameful deeds" that "they shall fine him a hundred shekels of silver and give it to the girl's father, because he publicly defamed a virgin of Israel. And she shall remain his wife; he cannot divorce her all his days" (22:14, 19). In the same chapter we read: "If a man finds a girl who is a virgin, who is not engaged, and seizes her and lies with her and they are discovered, then the man who lay with her shall give to the girl's father fifty shekels of silver, and she shall become his wife because he has violated her; he cannot divorce her all his days" (vv. 28-29).

Divorce was clearly taught to be a defilement for a priest. "They [priests] shall not take a woman who is profaned by harlotry, nor shall they take a woman divorced from her husband; for he is holy to his God. . . . A widow, or a divorced woman, or one who is profaned by harlotry, these he may not take; but rather he is to marry a virgin of his own people" (Lev. 21:7, 14).

In the Old Testament God does not condone or bless divorce. In one unique case (Ezra 10:3-5) God actually commanded divorce through His priest, Ezra, because the existence of His covenant people was threatened (cf. Deut. 7:1-5); but that single exception did not negate His hatred of divorce. Ezra's call for divorce is an extreme historical example of following the lesser of two evils, and it applied only to the covenant nation of Israel in that one situation.

The entire book of Hosea is a picture of God's forgiving and patient love for Israel, dramatized by Hosea's forgiving and patient love for his wife, Gomer. Gomer prostituted herself, forsook Hosea, and was unfaithful to him in every possible way. But the heart of the story is that Hosea was faithful and forgiving no matter what she did, just as God is faithful and forgiving no matter what His people do. God looks on the union of husband and wife in the same way He looks on the union of Himself with believers. And the way of God should be the way of His people—to love, forgive, draw back, and seek to restore the partner who is willing to be restored.

Although Hosea's and Gomer's marriage is primarily a symbol of God's relationship to His people Israel, it is also an apt illustration of how to deal with a wayward marriage partner. God's forgiving love seeks to hold the union together. That is certainly Christ's attitude in His relationship to the church, as He repeatedly forgives His bride and never casts her away (Eph. 5:22-23).

There must be forgiving love and restoring grace in a marriage. That alone makes marriage a proper symbol of God's forgiving love and restoring grace. That is the magnificence of marriage. To pursue divorce is to miss the whole point of God's dramatization in the story of Hosea and Gomer, the whole point of our Lord's love for His church, and thus the whole point of marriage. God hates divorce.

THE TEACHING OF JESUS

but I say to you that everyone who divorces his wife, except for the cause of unchastity, makes her commit adultery; and whoever marries a divorced woman commits adultery. (5:31-32)

Jesus affirms exactly what Moses taught in Deuteronomy 24:1-4—that unjustified divorce inevitably leads to adultery. To the legalistic, self-righteous scribes and Pharisees Jesus was saying, "You consider yourselves to be great teachers and keepers of the law, but by allowing no-fault divorce you have caused a great blight of adultery to contaminate God's people. By lowering God's standards to meet your own, you have led many people into sin and judgment."

The Pharisees interpreted Moses' instructions to mean, "If you find something distasteful about your wife, divorce her." They saw the paperwork as the only issue. Jesus knew their warped interpretation and thus confronted them.

The error in their thinking is highlighted in 5:27-30. They prided themselves on the fact that they did not commit adultery. But Jesus said, "I say to you, that everyone who looks on a woman to lust for her has committed adultery with her already in his heart" (v. 28). In verses 29-30 He showed them that no sacrifice is too great to maintain moral purity. Then in these present verses (31-32), He again indicts them for adultery because they were committing it by putting away their wives. The ease of divorce made it possible to avoid open adultery. Only a little paperwork was required to legalize their lust.

But Jesus confronted them with a proper interpretation of God's law. He said that every time a man without proper cause turned his wife loose to remarry, he forced her into adultery, which made him guilty also. In addition, the man who married the former wife and the woman who married the former husband were likewise guilty of adultery. The result was multiplied adultery! Jesus' whole point is that divorce leads to adultery.

Some interpreters maintain that *apoluō* (**divorces**), which has the basic meaning of let loose, or let go free, refers only to separation, broken engagement, or desertion. A common view of this passage is that Jesus is referring only to divorce during the betrothal period, such as that mentioned in Matthew 1:18-19. But when used in the context of a man and wife, the common meaning of *apoluō* was always divorce—not merely separation or the breaking of an engagement (cf. Matt. 19:3, 7-9; Mark 10:2, 4, 11-12; Luke 16:18).

The term cannot refer only to a broken betrothal for several reasons. First, the background of the passage is Deuteronomy 24, which does not deal with broken betrothal but with broken marriage. To take the betrothal period as a limiting factor in a passage that deals strictly with marriage and divorce (based on its Old Testament roots) gives an illegitimate and nonhistorical restriction. If Christ has in mind the betrothal period He would then be adding something to the Old Testament standard, rather than commenting on and affirming it—which would have been out of step with His stated purpose for this section of the Sermon on the Mount (see 5:17-18).

Second, the indissoluble union in a Hebrew marriage began at betrothal, not consummation, as illustrated by Joseph and Mary. He was her "husband" during the betrothal period. The Old Testament punishment of death for adultery was the same for both participants, and it applied whether the adultery was committed during betrothal or after consummation of the marriage. Prior to betrothal, a man and woman who committed fornication were only required to marry each other (Deut. 22:28-29). In that cultural context betrothal was clearly an element of marriage.

Third, it is clear that the Jews who heard Jesus use the term understood Him to mean divorce, because there was never any need to clarify what was meant. Deuteronomy 24:1-4, to which Jesus refers in Matthew 5:31, had to do strictly with marriage and divorce, not betrothal, mere separation, or desertion. Jesus was not adding to or modifying what Moses had said, but simply clarifying it.

By divorcing his wife on grounds other than adultery, a husband **makes** his innocent former wife **commit adultery** if she remarries—as it is assumed she would. Further, as Jesus makes explicit in Mark 10:11-12, "Whoever divorces his wife and marries another woman commits adultery against her; and if she herself divorces her husband and marries another man, she is committing adultery." Jesus' statement that **whoever marries a divorced woman commits adultery** (cf. Luke 16:18) completes the picture. A man or woman who has no right to divorce has no right to remarry. To do so initiates a whole chain of adultery, because remarriage after illegitimate divorce results in illegitimate and adulterous relationships for all parties involved.

When the detrimental effects on children, other relatives, and society in general are added, we see that few practices match divorce for destructiveness. It not only causes further sin but also confusion, resentment, hatred, bitterness, despair, conflict, and hardships of every sort.

In Matthew 19 Jesus quotes God's declaration in Genesis 2:24 that "For this cause a man shall leave his father and mother, and shall cleave to his wife; and the two shall become one flesh" (Matt. 19:5). "Consequently," He goes on to say, "they are no longer two, but one flesh. What therefore God has joined together, let no man separate" (v. 6). The Pharisees' response, "Why then did Moses command to give her a certificate and divorce her?" (v. 7) again betrayed their misinterpretation of Deuteronomy 24:1-4. Jesus had to explain, "Because of your hardness of heart, Moses permitted you to divorce your wives; but from the beginning it has not been this way" (v. 8). God never "commanded" divorce but only "permitted" it as a concession to sinful, self-willed mankind. It is true that in Mark 10:5 Jesus speaks of Deuteronomy 24:1-4 as a commandment. But the teaching there is not a command to divorce but a command not to remarry the defiled person who has been divorced.

The condition **except for unchastity** is not a way out that God provides, but is the only grounds for divorce that He will recognize. Some say that this "exception clause" allows divorce for Jews only, and only in the case of the sin of consanguinity (marrying a near relative, a practice forbidden in Lev. 18). This view is propounded by those who wish to believe that there are no biblical grounds at all for divorce by Christians. They point out that the exception clause appears only in Matthew and maintain that to interpret it otherwise would be to contradict or add to the law governing the sin of adultery.

Of course, God has only to say a thing once for it to be true, so the fact that the exception clause appears only in Matthew has no bearing on proper interpretation. In fact, the exception clause would have been inappropriate in the contexts of Mark 10 and Luke 16. In Matthew 5 and 19 the clause is included to correct the Pharisees' misrepresentation of God's law regarding adultery. The exception clause in those passages amplifies Jesus' teaching on divorce in Mark 10 and Luke 16—it does not contradict it.

Jesus gives no more approval for divorce than did Moses. The Old Testament ideal has not been changed. The permissions for divorce in the Old Testament economy were designed to meet the unique, practical problems of an imperfect, sinful people. God never condoned divorce, because what He joins together is not to be separated by man (Matt. 19:6). Adultery, another reality that

God never intended, is the only thing that can break the bond of marriage. In fact, under the Old Testament law, adultery would necessarily dissolve a marriage, because the guilty party was put to death (Lev. 20:10).

Because Jesus specifically mentions divorce being permissible on the ground of adultery (Matt. 5:32; 19:9), and because He also specifically says that He did not come to contradict or annul the least part of the law (5:18-19), it seems evident that sometime during Israel's history divorce was allowed to take the place of execution as legitimate penalty for adultery. No Old Testament passage specifically authorizes divorce, but that does not mean God did not give specific revelation about it. Based on His own recognition and regulation of divorce, and His divorce of Israel and Judah (Jer. 3:8), we can assume that divine instructions for divorce had been given orally or by written revelation not preserved in Scripture. God divorced Israel and Judah for spiritual adultery rather than put them to death. Also Joseph, a righteous man, was prepared to divorce Mary rather than stone her for her presumed adultery (Matt. 1:19).

Why did God allow divorce to replace the death penalty? The answer may be that Israel had so completely immersed herself in immorality that there was not sufficient desire for righteousness left in the people to carry out executions for that offense. Ultimately, God in His mercy chose Himself not to enforce the death penalty. That is consistent with the divine nature revealed in Jesus, who challenged the Pharisees who were about to stone a woman for adultery and then forgave her Himself (John 8:7). Apart from the death penalty, divorce became the divine alternative, tolerated only because of the hardness of the human heart, as Jesus states in Matthew 19:8.

Divorce was never *commanded,* even for adultery. Otherwise God would have given His notice of divorce to Israel and Judah long before He did. A legitimate bill of divorce was allowable for adultery, but it was never commanded or required. It was a last resort—to be used only when unrepentant immorality had exhausted the patience of the innocent spouse, and the guilty one would not be restored.

If God permitted divorce rather than death as a merciful concession to man's sinfulness, why would He not also permit remarriage, since remarriage would be perfectly allowable under the original law of death for the adulterer? After all, the purpose of divorce was to show mercy to the guilty party, not to sentence the innocent party to a life of loneliness and misery.

Unchastity (*porneia*) refers to any illicit sexual intercourse, whether or not either of the parties is married. It was a broad term that included adultery, as other texts using a form of *porneia* indicate ("immorally," 1 Cor. 10:8; "immorality," Rev. 2:14; cf. 1 Cor. 5:1). Because Matthew 5:31-32 focuses on marriage and divorce, the primary **unchastity** involved here would be adultery. But *porneia* also included incest, prostitution, homosexuality, and bestiality—all of the sexual acts for which the Old Testament demanded the death penalty (Lev. 20:10-14). In other words, any of those corrupt and perverted sexual activities was a permissible ground for divorce.

Jesus does not advocate divorce in such cases, much less demand it. He simply says that divorce and remarriage on any other grounds always leads to adultery. As God, Jesus hates divorce (Mal. 2:16), but by implication He acknowledges that there are times when it does not result in adultery. The innocent party who has made every effort to maintain the marriage is free to remarry if his or her spouse insists on continued adultery or divorce.

Jesus sets the record straight that God still hates divorce and that His ideal is still monogamous, life-long marriage. But as a concession to sin and as a gracious provision for those who are innocent of defiling the marriage, He allows divorce on the single ground of **unchastity**.

In 1 Corinthians, Paul adds one more legitimate ground for divorce and subsequent remarriage. "But to the rest I say, not the Lord, that if any brother has a wife who is an unbeliever, and she consents to live with him, let him not send her away. And a woman who has an unbelieving husband, and he consents to live with her, let her not send her husband away" (7:12-13). After giving the reason for that instruction, he adds, "Yet if the unbelieving one leaves, let him leave; the brother or the sister is not under bondage in such cases, but God has called us to peace" (v. 15). The Greek word translated "leave" (*chōrizō*) was often used for divorce. Thus if an unbelieving spouse deserts or divorces a believer, the believer is no longer bound and is free to remarry. (For further study on this passage, see the author's commentary *First Corinthians* [Chicago: Moody, 1984], pp. 164-68.)

The Spiritual Credibility Gap
(5:33-37)

Again, you have heard that the ancients were told, "You shall not make false vows, but shall fulfill your vows to the Lord." But I say to you, make no oath at all, either by heaven, for it is the throne of God, or by the earth, for it is the footstool of His feet, or by Jerusalem, for it is the city of the great King. Nor shall you make an oath by your head, for you cannot make one hair white or black. But let your statement be, "Yes, yes" or "No, no"; and anything beyond these is of evil. (5:33-37)

Credibility gaps are not a creation of modern times. They have existed since the Fall and have continually been one of the major marks of the world system. Satan is the prince of this world, and since he not only is a liar himself but also "the father of lies" (John 8:44), it should not be surprising that the system he heads is characterized by lying. Because all men are born in sin, all men are born liars (see Ps. 58:3; 62:4; Jer. 9:3-5).

The natural credibility gap is widened even further by popular novels, movies, television, music, and advertising—in which truth, fantasy, and outright falsehood are blended into mixtures impossible to unscramble. Truth is so scarce that nearly everyone is suspect. Business people, advertisers, commentators, clerks, salesmen, lawyers, doctors, tradesmen, teachers, writers, politicians, and even many, if not most, preachers are suspect. Our whole society is largely built on a network of fabrication, of manufactured "truth." We shade the truth, we cheat, we exaggerate, we misrepresent income tax deductions, we make promises we have no intention of keeping, we make up excuses, and betray confidences—all as a matter of normal, everyday living.

So much of business, politics, government, the educational system, science, religion, and even family life is built on falsehoods and half-truths that a sudden revelation of the whole truth would cause society as we know it to disintegrate. It would be too devastating to handle.

Yet even the most corrupt and deceptive societies have always realized that, in certain areas at least, the "real truth" is necessary. Courts of law require witnesses to tell the truth, the whole truth, and nothing but the truth. Without truth, even a semblance of justice would be impossible. Because of the extreme importance of truthful testimony to justice, perjury itself is a crime that can bring severe penalties. Even gangs of criminals and conspirators, who use lying and cheating as their stock-in-trade, demand the truth among themselves, because it is necessary to their own survival.

Individually men are inclined to the truth only when it benefits them, yet collectively they have always known something of its importance and rightfulness—even outside courts of law. The great Roman orator Cicero said, "Truth is the highest thing a man may experience." Sadly, with most people it is an infrequent experience. Daniel Webster wrote, "There is nothing as powerful as truth and often nothing as strange."

Even the ancient Jewish rabbis, whose unbiblical traditions and flippancy with the truth Jesus challenges in the Sermon on the Mount, moralistically considered lying—along with scoffing, hypocrisy, and slander—to be one of the four great sins that would shut a person out of God's presence. In their consciences men know that truth is right and essential. That is one reason they go to such lengths to make what they say *appear* to be truthful. Our problem is in *being* truthful.

The Jews of Jesus' day revered the idea of truth in principle, but in practice it was buried under their system of tradition, which over the centuries had continually cut God's law down to fit their own sinful perspectives and purposes. In Matthew 5:33-37 the Lord proceeds to expose their convenient distortion and contradiction of the divine revelation they claimed to love and teach. In these five verses Jesus sets forth the original Mosaic teaching, the traditional perversion of that teaching, and His own reemphasis of what God's standard for truth has always been.

The Principle of Mosaic Law

Again, you have heard that the ancients were told, "You shall not make false vows, but shall fulfill your vows to the Lord." (5:33)

The traditional teaching that Jesus quotes here was a composite of ideas based on Leviticus 19:12, Numbers 30:2, and Deuteronomy 23:21. The two **vows** mentioned here are from two different, but related, Greek terms. The first is from the verb *epiorkeō*, which means to perjure oneself, to swear falsely, to **make false vows.** The second is from the noun *horkos*, which literally means to enclose, as with a fence, or to bind together. The truth of an oath or vow is enclosed, bound, and therefore strengthened by that which is invoked on its behalf.

A clear description of an oath is given in the book of Hebrews: "For men swear by one greater than themselves, and with them an oath given as confirmation is an end of every dispute" (6:16). The name of something or someone greater than the person making the oath is invoked to give greater credibility to what is said. Any oath calling on God invites Him to witness the truthfulness of what is said or to avenge if it is a lie. An oath was therefore generally taken to be the absolute truth, which made "an end of every dispute," because it invited judgment on the one who violated his word. The Jews who returned from the Babylonian Exile to Israel took "on themselves a curse and an oath to walk in God's laws" (Neh. 10:29).

God provided for making oaths by His name (Lev. 19:12) and many Old Testament saints, both before and after the giving of the law, followed the practice. Abraham confirmed his promises to the king of Sodom (Gen. 14:22-24) and to Abimelech (21:23-24) with oaths in the name of God. He also made his servant Eliezer "swear by the Lord, the God of heaven and the God of earth" that he would not take a wife for Isaac from among the pagan Canaanites around them but from among relatives in Abraham's homeland of Mesopotamia (24:1-4, 10). A similar oath is related involving Isaac (26:31). Jacob and Laban, his father-in-law, called on God as their witness when they made a covenant with each other at Mizpah (31:44-53). David and Jonathan did likewise when they covenanted together (1 Sam. 20:16). David himself "swore to the Lord, and vowed to the Mighty One of Jacob" (Ps. 132:2). All those great men of God, and many others, made oaths and covenants calling on God as witness to their truthfulness and sincerity (see Gen. 47:31; 50:25; Josh. 9:15; Judg. 21:5; Ruth 1:16-18; 2 Sam. 15:21; 2 Chron. 15:14-15).

Even God Himself made oaths on certain occasions. To Abraham He said, "By Myself I have sworn, declares the Lord, because you have done this thing, and have not withheld your son, your only son, indeed I will greatly bless you, and I will greatly multiply your seed as the stars of the heavens, and as the sand which is on the seashore; and your seed shall possess the gate of their enemies" (Gen. 22:16-17). As the writer of Hebrews explains, since God "could swear by no one greater, He swore by Himself" (Heb. 6:13-14, cf. v. 17). Obviously the Lord's promises made with an oath were no more truthful or binding than anything else He promised. It is not that God makes an oath because His word would otherwise be questionable or unreliable, but because He wishes to impress upon men a special importance or urgency related to the promise. (More references to divine oaths are mentioned in Ps. 89:3, 49; 110:4; Jer. 11:5; and Luke 1:73.)

Jesus many times used the phrase "Truly I say to you" (Matt. 5:18, 26; 6:2,

5, 16; etc.), and the even more emphatic "Truly, truly, I say to you" (John 1:51; 3:3, 5; 5:19, 24; etc.), to call attention to a teaching of special importance. As with God's oaths, the words Jesus introduces with "truly" are no more truthful than anything else He said, but emphasize the unique importance of certain of His teachings. It is important to note that Jesus Himself swore an oath before Caiaphas that He was the Christ, the Son of God (Matt. 26:63-64).

God provided for proper oath-giving in His name as an accommodation to sinful human nature, which is so prone to deceit and lying. Without any prohibition, Hebrews 6:16 affirms the place of proper oaths. He knows that men's inclination to lie causes them to distrust each other, and in serious situations an oath is permissible to give greater motivation to tell the truth or to keep a pledge. To make the wedding vow, with God as a witness, to love and cherish our mates for as long as we both live is to recognize and make a firm commitment to honor the special sanctity that God places on marriage. The psalmist, in describing the kind of person who may enter God's holy presence, makes clear that one mandatory requirement is that such a person be one who "swears to his own hurt, and does not change" (Ps. 15:1, 4). His word is more important than his welfare. Keeping oaths made to God is the mark of a true worshiper. To put it another way, true sons of the kingdom hate lies (Ps. 119:29, 163; 120:2).

Obviously an oath, no matter how strong the words used, is only as reliable as the one who makes it. As Peter sat in the courtyard outside the Sanhedrin while Jesus was being tried, a servant-girl said, "You too were with Jesus the Galilean"— to which Peter replied, "I do not know what you are talking about." When another servant-girl made a similar statement a short while later, Peter "denied it with an oath." Still later, when other bystanders made the same assertion, Peter "began to curse and swear, 'I do not know the man!'" (Matt. 26:69-74). That swearing was not profanity, but an oath given with special vehemence. Peter increased the strength of his oath, but that did not increase the truth of what he said. It was bad enough to have lied; it was even worse to call God as a witness to the lie. In addition to denying His Lord, Peter used God's name in vain. It is small wonder that he "went out and wept bitterly" (v. 75).

Sometimes oaths are made sincerely but foolishly, without considering their seriousness and possible consequences. Such rash oaths were made by Joshua (Josh. 9:15), Jephthah (Judg. 11:30-31), Saul (1 Sam. 14:24), and Herod (Matt. 14:7).

By Old Testament law, oaths were to be made only in God's name. "You shall fear only the Lord your God; and you shall worship Him, and swear by His name" (Deut. 6:13; cf. 10:20). "He who is blessed in the earth shall be blessed by the God of truth; and he who swears in the earth shall swear by the God of truth" (Isa. 65:16). Even Gentiles were to swear only by God's name. Of Israel's wicked neighbors, the Lord said, "Then it will come about that if they will really learn the ways of My people, to swear by My name, 'As the Lord lives,' . . . then they will be built up in the midst of My people" (Jer. 12:16).

God established the seriousness of keeping an oath. Even "if a person swears thoughtlessly with his lips to do evil or to do good, in whatever matter a man may speak thoughtlessly with an oath, and it is hidden from him, and then he comes to know it, . . . he shall confess that in which he has sinned. He shall also bring his guilt offering to the Lord for his sin which he has committed" (Lev. 5:4-6). Joshua 9:20 punctuates how essential keeping an oath is: ". . . lest wrath be upon us for the oath which we swore."

THE PERVERSION OF RABBINIC TRADITION

The tradition Jesus mentions in verse 33 seemed to be biblical, but it had several flaws that made it fall short of what the Old Testament actually taught. First, it had a missing ingredient, and second, it had a misplaced emphasis.

The missing ingredient was a proper circumstance for making an oath. Virtually any kind of oath, used for almost any kind of purpose, was acceptable— just as long as it was not **false** and the person would **fulfill** it. The missing ingredient of a serious circumstance led to frivolous, meaningless oath-making that completely vitiated the legitimate purpose of oaths. People would declare anything and promise anything with an oath, while having no qualms about providing means by which lying or breaking their word could still be done. Indiscriminate and insincere vows became so commonplace that no one took them seriously. Instead of being a mark of integrity they became a mark of deceit. Instead of prompting confidence they prompted skepticism.

The misplaced emphasis was in limiting the honest oaths to **vows to the Lord**, to oaths made directly to Him or in His name. The keeping of those oaths was mandatory, whereas the keeping of others they made optional.

The system of oaths between one person and another was like a giant game of King's X. People would swear by heaven, by the earth, by the Temple, by the hairs on their heads, and by any other thing they thought would impress those they wanted to take advantage of. That kind of routine oath-making was usually lie-making; and it was considered by those who practiced it to be perfectly acceptable as long as it was not in the name of the Lord.

The command "You shall not swear falsely by My name" (Lev. 19:12) was conveniently interpreted to mean that swearing falsely by any other name was allowed. The command "If a man makes a vow to the Lord, or takes an oath to bind himself with a binding obligation, he shall not violate his word; he shall do according to all that proceeds out of his mouth" (Num. 30:2) was interpreted as permitting the reneging on oaths made to anyone but God.

Thus, through rabbinic tradition, God's standard of absolute truthfulness was contradicted and lowered to a level that accommodated the sinful, selfish capacities and purposes of the people. They wanted to lie, and they did not want to be hampered by God's absolute standard of truth. Instead of calling on the Lord to help them live up to the divine standard, they reduced that standard to suit their own carnal abilities and interests.

THE PERSPECTIVE OF DIVINE TRUTH

But I say to you, make no oath at all, either by heaven, for it is the throne of God, or by the earth, for it is the footstool of His feet, or by Jerusalem, for it is the city of the great King. Nor shall you make an oath by your head, for you cannot make one hair white or black. But let your statement be, "Yes, yes" or "No, no"; and anything beyond these is of evil. (5:34-37)

In contrast to those alterations of the divine will, Jesus simply reasserts the Old Testament standard that had been misconstrued and perverted by tradition: **make no oath at all.** Oaths are to be used only on important occasions and are to be given only in the name of the Lord. Though the Greek construction here is an unconditional negative (*mē . . . holōs*), that does not preclude all oaths. Commentator William Hendriksen's explanation is helpful: "What we have here in Matthew 5:33-37 (cf. James 5:12) is the condemnation of the flippant, profane, uncalled for, and often hypocritical oath, used in order to make an impression or to spice daily conversation. Over against that evil Jesus commends simple truthfulness in thought, word and deed" (*Exposition of the Gospel According to Matthew* [Grand Rapids: Baker, 1973], p. 309).

In light of specific Old Testament teaching approving oaths, in light of Jesus' use of such phrases as "truly, truly," and in light of God Himself's making oaths that correspond to men's (Heb. 6:13-17; cf. Luke 1:73; Acts 2:30; etc.), it can hardly be correct, as many interpret this passage, that Jesus here forbids the making of any oath under any circumstance. (See Meredith G. Kline, *The Treaty of the Great King* [Grand Rapids: Eerdmans, 1963]; and *Zondervan Pictorial Encyclopedia of the Bible* [Grand Rapids: Zondervan, n.d.], p. 478, for a discussion of oaths.) He had just said that He did not come to destroy the smallest part of the law (Matt. 5:17-18), a law that taught proper oath-making by both precept and example. Additionally, in the early days of the church, even the apostle Paul gave a type of oath in saying to the Romans, "I am telling the truth in Christ, I am not lying, my conscience bearing me witness in the Holy Spirit" (Rom. 9:1). He called on Christ and the Holy Spirit as witnesses with his own conscience to the truthfulness of what he was about to say. That is swearing by God.

So, in accordance with the Old Testament standard, we are to swear by no other name but God's—not **by heaven, for it is the throne of God, or by earth, for it is the footstool of His feet, or by Jerusalem, for it is the city of the great King.** Appealing to **heaven, earth, Jerusalem,** and other such things was considered by most Jews to make their oaths less binding. Those were grand and great things, things that gave an aura of power, importance, and veracity to what was said or promised in their name. But because those things were far less than God, they made oaths given in their names far less binding than an oath made in His name. Still less binding would be an oath made merely **by your head.**

The common attitude toward oaths is also seen in Jesus' great series of woes in Matthew 23 against the hypocritical Jewish leaders. "Woe to you, blind guides, who say, 'Whoever swears by the temple, that is nothing; but whoever swears by the gold of the temple, he is obligated.' . . . And, 'Whoever swears by the altar, that is nothing, but whoever swears by the offering upon it, he is obligated'" (vv. 16, 18). First, Jesus exposed the utter illogic of their practice. "You fools and blind men; which is more important, the gold, or the temple that sanctified the gold? . . . You blind men, which is more important, the offering or the altar that sanctifies the offering? Therefore he who swears, swears both by the altar and by everything on it" (vv. 17, 19-20). By what twisted logic, He asks, should that which is *less* valuable make an oath *more* binding?

But the greatest error in the system was not in its illogic but in its basic deceptiveness and dishonesty. As a matter of accepted policy, some oaths were used to undermine the very purpose they purportedly were meant to serve: the truth. In spite of the fact that an oath is given to reinforce and emphasize the truthfulness of a statement or the reliability of a promise, over the years an intricate system of duplicity had been devised that virtually promoted the use of oaths for deception.

Jesus therefore went on to condemn the system still further: "He who swears by the temple, swears both by the temple and by Him who dwells within it. And he who swears by heaven, swears both by the throne of God and by Him who sits upon it" (vv. 21-22). However and whenever the truth is profaned, God's name is profaned.

Jesus' point was that God is the Creator and Lord of everything and is the God of truth in everything. To carelessly and dishonestly call any part of His creation as witness to a false oath was to dishonor God Himself, whether or not His name was invoked. To dishonor and compromise any truth is to dishonor and compromise His truth. **Heaven** is God's, the **earth** is God's, **Jerusalem** is God's, and every person's **head** is God's. It is therefore wicked and sinful to use anything of God's, whether His name or a part of His creation, as witness to anything that is dishonest, deceitful, insincere, or in the least way knowingly false. God has no separate categories of sacred and secular. Everything that pertains to Him is sacred, and all truth is His truth, just as all creation is His creation. Every lie is against God, and therefore *every* false oath dishonors His name.

Comments William Barclay, "Here is a great eternal truth. Life cannot be divided into compartments in some of which God is involved and in others of which he is not involved; there cannot be one kind of language in the Church and another kind of language in the shipyard or the factory or the office; there cannot be one kind of conduct in the Church and another kind of conduct in the business world. The fact is that God does not need to be invited into certain departments of life, and kept out of others. He is everywhere, all through life and in every activity of life. He hears not only the words which are spoken in his name; he hears all words; and there cannot be any such thing as a form of words which evades bringing God into any transaction. We will regard all promises as sacred if we remember that all promises are made in the presence of God" (*The Gospel of Matthew*, 2 vols. [rev. ed.; Philadelphia: Westminster, 1975], 1:160).

Truth has no degrees or shades. A half truth is a whole lie, and a white lie is really black. God has never had any standard lower than absolute truthfulness. Of every person He desires "truth in the innermost being" (Ps. 51:6). Among the things He especially hates is "a lying tongue" (Prov. 6:16-17), and "Lying lips are an abomination to the Lord" (12:22). And just as God hates lying, so do those who are faithful to Him (Ps. 119:163). Those "who speak lies go astray from birth. They have venom like the venom of a serpent" (Ps. 58:3-4). Jeremiah wept over Israel because "lies and not truth prevail in the land" (Jer. 9:3). The destiny of liars is the lake of fire (Rev. 21:8).

God's absolute, unchanging standard is truth and sincerity in *everything*. Not only should oaths be totally truthful and dependable, but even the most routine conversations should be truthful in every detail. **Let your statement be, "Yes, yes" or "No, no"; anything beyond these is of evil. Statement** is from *logos,* the basic meaning of which is simply "word." Every normal word in the course of daily speech should be a truthful word, unadorned and unqualified in regard to its truthfulness. A person's words, message, or speech (as *logos* is used in Acts 20:7; 1 Cor. 2:1; 4:19; and Titus 2:8) should be as good as his bond and as good as his oath or vow. "But above all, my brethren," James counsels, "do not swear, either by heaven or by earth or with any other oath; but let your yes be yes, and your no, no; so that you may not fall under judgment" (James 5:12).

God is a holy God, His kingdom is a holy kingdom, and the people of His kingdom are to be a holy people. His righteousness is to be their righteousness, and anything less than His righteousness, including anything less than absolute truth, is unacceptable to Him, because it **is of evil.** So our Lord shatters the fragile glass of their hypocritical oaths, which they used to cover lies.

An Eye for an Eye
(5:38-42)

31

You have heard that it was said, "An eye for an eye, and a tooth for a tooth." But I say to you, do not resist him who is evil; but whoever slaps you on your right cheek, turn to him the other also. And if anyone wants to sue you, and take your shirt, let him have your coat also. And whoever shall force you to go one mile, go with him two. Give to him who asks of you, and do not turn away from him who wants to borrow from you. (5:38-42)

One element of the great American philosophy of life is that we all have certain inalienable rights. Among the most important privileges that our Declaration of Independence espouses are life, liberty, and the pursuit of happiness. In our day the number of rights claimed has greatly expanded. Movements have developed for civil rights, women's rights, children's rights, workers' rights, prisoners' rights, and so on. Never has a society been more concerned about rights.

We idolize the hero who stands up for what is his no matter who it may offend. That self-interested, self-protecting spirit characterizes fallen human nature. Above all else, sinful man wants what he thinks is his own. And in the process of protecting what is his own, he is also inclined to wreak considerable trouble on anyone who takes what is his. Retaliation, usually with interest, is a natural extension of selfishness.

Inordinate concern for one's own rights comes from inordinate selfishness and leads to inordinate lawlessness. When our supreme concern is getting and keeping what we think is rightfully ours, then whoever or whatever gets in our way—including the law—becomes expendable. Since it is not possible for everyone to have everything he wants, to insist on our own way invariably tramples on the rights and welfare of others. Respect for law and for the welfare of others is always among the first and major casualties of self-assertion. When self is in the foreground, everything else and everyone else is pushed to the background.

When self-interest dominates, justice is replaced by vengeance. Impartial concern for justice becomes partial concern for personal revenge. Concern for protecting society becomes concern for protecting self-interest. As James points out, that perversion is the source of wars and every other human conflict. "What is the source of quarrels and conflicts among you? Is not the source your pleasures that wage war in your members? You lust and do not have; so you commit murder. And you are envious and cannot obtain; so you fight and quarrel" (James 4:1-2). When rights are first, righteousness suffers.

Few people have had their legitimate rights trampled on more than Paul. Yet to the selfish, indulgent Corinthians he wrote,

> Am I not free? Am I not an apostle? Have I not seen Jesus our Lord? Are you not my work in the Lord? . . . Do we not have a right to eat and drink? Do we not have a right to take along a believing wife, even as the rest of the apostles, and the brothers of the Lord, and Cephas? Or do only Barnabas and I not have a right to refrain from working? . . . If others share the right over you, do we not more? Nevertheless, we did not use this right, but we endure all things, that we may cause no hindrance to the gospel of Christ (1 Cor. 9:1, 4-6, 12)

Paul willingly set aside his rights for the sake of the gospel and the welfare of others.

But Paul did not always win the fight against his innate fallenness. When he was brought before the Sanhedrin during his last imprisonment in Jerusalem, he began his testimony by saying, "Brethren, I have lived my life with a perfectly good conscience before God up to this day." At that, "the high priest Ananias commanded those standing beside him to strike him on the mouth. Then Paul said to him, 'God is going to strike you, you whitewashed wall! And do you sit to try me according to the Law, and in violation of the Law order me to be struck?'" When Paul was informed that he was speaking to the high priest, he apologized and said, "I was not aware, brethren, that he was high priest; for it is written, 'You shall not speak evil of a ruler of your people'" (Acts 23:1-5). Because Paul's anger momentarily got the best of him, he retaliated with harsh words.

Ananias perhaps was not dressed in the customary high priestly garments, and therefore Paul failed to recognize him. But had he known he was speaking to Ananias, Paul would have had all the more justification, from a human standpoint, to righteously deride the one who ordered him struck. Ananias was an unusually vile, arrogant, and immoral man who continually profaned his high office. And, as Paul reminded him, to order a prisoner struck before he was convicted was against the very Jewish law Ananias was sworn to administer. Yet Paul acknowledged that his angry retort was wrong. In God's eyes he had no right to speak disparagingly of any ruler, and he condemned his own actions by Scripture.

Probably no part of the Sermon on the Mount has been so misinterpreted and misapplied as 5:38-42. It has been interpreted to mean that Christians are to be sanctimonious doormats. It has been used to promote pacifism, conscientious objection to military service, lawlessness, anarchy, and a host of other positions that it does not support. The Russian writer Tolstoy based one of his best-known novels on this passage. The thesis of *War and Peace* is that the elimination of police, the military, and other forms of authority would bring a utopian society.

But Jesus already had made plain that He did not come to eliminate even the smallest part of God's law (5:17-19), which includes respect for and obedience to human law and authority.

Among the many unrighteous things that the religion of the scribes and Pharisees (see Matt. 5:20) included was their insistence on personal rights and vengeance. In His fifth illustration contrasting their righteousness with God's, Jesus again shows how rabbinic tradition had twisted God's holy law to serve the selfish purposes of unholy men.

THE PRINCIPLE OF MOSAIC LAW

You have heard that it was said, "An eye for an eye, and a tooth for a tooth." (5:38)

This quotation is taken directly from the Old Testament (Ex. 21:24; Lev. 24:20; Deut. 19:21) and reflects the principle of *lex talionis,* one of the most ancient law codes. Simply put, it required that punishment exactly match the crime. The same idea is carried in the expressions *tit for tat* and *quid pro quo.* The earliest record of *lex talionis* is in the Code of Hammurabi, the great Babylonian king who lived a hundred or so years before Moses. It is likely, however, that the principle was in wide use long before that time.

In the Pentateuch **an eye for an eye, and a tooth for a tooth** are part of longer lists that include "hand for hand, foot for foot, burn for burn, wound for wound, bruise for bruise" (see Ex. 21:24-25) and "fracture for fracture" (Lev. 24:20). In both the law of Moses and the Code of Hammurabi the principle of punishment to match the crime had two basic purposes. The first was to curtail further crime. When a person is punished for his wrongdoing, "the rest will hear and be afraid, and will never again do such an evil thing among you" (Deut. 19:20). The second purpose was to prevent excessive punishment based on personal vengeance and angry retaliation of the type of which Lamech boasted: "For I have killed a man for wounding me; and a boy for striking me; if Cain is avenged sevenfold, then Lamech seventy-sevenfold" (Gen. 4:23-24). Punishment was to match, but not exceed, the harm done by the offense itself.

It is of the utmost significance that each of the three Pentateuch accounts that prescribe the **eye for an eye** principle has to do with the civil justice system. Exodus 21-23 deals entirely with God's provision for Israel's civil law, as do the similar teachings in Leviticus 24 and Deuteronomy 19. Punishment was sometimes carried out by the victim, but the trial and sentencing were always the responsibility of duly appointed judges or of a large, representative body of citizens (see Ex. 21:22; Deut. 19:18; Lev. 24:14-16).

The law of **an eye for an eye** was a just law, because it matched punishment to offense. It was a merciful law, because it limited the innate propensity of the human heart to seek retribution beyond what an offense deserved. It was also a beneficent law, because it protected society by restraining wrongdoing.

Selfish overreaction is the natural response of sinful human nature. We are tempted to get more than just even. Anger and resentment demand the sort of retaliation Lamech glorified. Human vengeance is never satisfied with justice; it wants a pound of flesh for an ounce of offense. That is one reason why God restricts vengeance to Himself. "Vengeance is Mine, and retribution" (Deut. 32:35; cf. Rom. 12:19; Heb. 10:30).

God's command for the individual has always been, "If your enemy is hungry, give him food to eat; and if he is thirsty, give him water to drink" (Prov. 25:21; cf. Matt. 5:44; Rom. 12:20). No individual has the right to say, "Thus I shall do to him as he has done to me; I will render to the man according to his work" (Prov. 24:29). In no instance did the Old Testament allow an individual to take the law into his own hands and apply it personally.

THE PERVERSION OF RABBINIC TRADITION

Yet that is exactly what rabbinic tradition had done. Each man was permitted, in effect, to become his own judge, jury, and executioner. God's law was turned to individual license, and civil justice was perverted to personal vengeance. Instead of properly acknowedging the law of **an eye for an eye, and a tooth for a tooth** as a limit on punishment, they conveniently used it as a mandate for vengeance—as it has often been wrongly viewed throughout history.

What God gave as a restriction on civil courts, Jewish tradition had turned into personal license for revenge. In still another way, the self-centered and self-asserted "righteousness" of the scribes and Pharisees had made a shambles of God's holy law.

THE PERSPECTIVE OF DIVINE TRUTH

But I say to you, do not resist him who is evil; but whoever slaps you on your right cheek, turn to him the other also. And if anyone wants to sue you, and

take your shirt, let him have your coat also. And whoever shall force you to go one mile, go with him two. Give to him who asks of you, and do not turn away from him who wants to borrow from you. (5:39-42)

In the command **do not resist him who is evil** Jesus rebuts the Pharisees' misinterpretation and forbids retaliation in personal relationships. He does not teach, as many have claimed, that no stand is to be taken against evil and that it should simply be allowed to take its course. Jesus and the apostles continually opposed evil with every means and resource. Jesus resisted the profaning of God's Temple by making a scourge of cords and physically driving out the sacrifice sellers and moneychangers (Matt. 21:12; John 2:15). We are to "resist the devil" (James 4:7; 1 Pet. 5:9) and all the evil that he stands for and inspires (Matt. 6:13; Rom. 12:9; 1 Thess. 5:22; 2 Tim. 4:18).

A proper resisting of evil includes resisting it in the church. When Peter compromised with the Judaizers, Paul "opposed him to his face, because he stood condemned" (Gal. 2:11). When there is immorality in the congregation, God says, "Remove the wicked man from among yourselves" (1 Cor. 5:13; cf. Deut. 13:5). Jesus said that a believer who sins should first be reproved in private, and then before two or three other church members if he does not repent. "And if he refuses to listen to them, tell it to the church; and if he refuses to listen even to the church, let him be to you as a Gentile and a tax-gatherer" (Matt. 18:15-17). Paul echoes Jesus' teaching when he says that those in the church who continue in sin should be rebuked "in the presence of all, so that the rest also may be fearful of sinning" (1 Tim. 5:20).

That the principle of nonresistance does not apply to governmental authorities is clear from many passages in the New Testament. Civil government "is a minister of God to you for good," Paul says. "But if you do what is evil, be afraid; for it does not bear the sword for nothing; for it is a minister of God, an avenger who brings wrath upon the one who practices evil" (Rom. 13:4). Peter commands, "Submit yourselves for the Lord's sake to every human institution, whether to a king as the one in authority, or to governors as sent by him for the punishment of evildoers and the praise of those who do right" (1 Pet. 2:13-14).

For the sake of God's righteousness, as well as for the sake of human justice, believers are obligated not only to uphold the law themselves but to insist that others do so as well. To report crime is an act of compassion, righteousness, and godly obedience as well as an act of civil responsibility. To belittle, excuse, or hide the wrongdoing of others is not an act of love but an act of wickedness, because it undermines civil justice and divine righteousness.

As long as the natural human heart exists, evil will have to be restrained by law. Our crime-wrecked society would do well to reexamine—and reapply—biblical law. When God is forsaken, His righteous standards are forsaken, and His law is forsaken. Antinomianism, the doing away with law, is as much an enemy of the gospel as legalism and works righteousness. The Old and New Testaments are never at odds in regard to law and grace, justice and mercy. The Old Testament teaches nothing of a righteous and just God apart from a merciful and loving God, and the New Testament teaches nothing of a merciful and loving God apart from a righteous and just God. The revelation of God is unchanging in regard to moral law.

When the church stopped preaching God's righteousness, justice, and eternal punishment of the lost, it stopped preaching the fullness of the gospel, and both society and the church have suffered greatly for it. And when the church stopped holding its own members accountable to God's standards and stopped disciplining its own ranks, a great deal of its moral influence on society was sacrificed. One of the legacies of theological liberalism is civil as well as religious lawlessness.

Not to restrain evil is neither just nor kind. It fails to protect the innocent and has the effect of encouraging the wicked in their evil. Proper restraint of evil, however, not only is just but is beneficent as well.

Arthur Pink says,

> Magistrates and judges were never ordained by God for the purpose of reforming reprobates or pampering degenerates, but to be His instruments for preserving law and order by being a terror to evil. As Romans chapter 13 says, they are to be "a revenger to execute wrath on him that doeth evil." . . . Conscience has become comatose. The requirements of justice are stifled; maudlin concepts now prevail. As eternal punishment was repudiated—either tacitly or in many cases openly— ecclesiastical punishments are shelved. Churches refuse to enforce sanctions and wink at flagrant offenses. The inevitable outcome has been the breakdown of discipline in the home and the creation of 'public opinion,' which is mawkish and spineless. School teachers are intimidated by foolish parents and children so that the rising generation are more and more allowed to have their own way without fear of consequences. And if some judge has the courage of his convictions, and sentences a brute for maiming an old woman, there is an outcry against the judge. (*An Exposition of the Sermon on the Mount* [Grand Rapids: Baker, 1974], p. 112-13)

To lower God's standard of justice is to lower God's standard of righteousness—which Jesus came to fulfill and clarify, not to obviate or diminish.

Anthistēmi (**resist**) means to set against or oppose, and in this context obviously refers to harm done to us personally by someone **who is evil**. Jesus is speaking of personal resentment, spite, and vengeance. It is the same truth taught by Paul when he said, "Never pay back evil for evil to anyone. . . . Never take your own revenge, beloved, but leave room for the wrath of God, for it is written, 'Vengeance is Mine, I will repay,' says the Lord" (Rom. 12:17, 19). Vengeful retaliation has no place in society at large, and even less place among those who belong to Christ. We are called to overcome someone's evil toward us by doing good to them (Rom. 12:21).

After establishing the basic principle in Matthew 5:39*a*, in verses 39*b*-42 Jesus picks out four basic human rights that He uses to illustrate the principle of nonretaliation: dignity, security, liberty, and property.

DIGNITY

but whoever slaps you on your right cheek, turn to him the other also. (5:39*b*)

As human beings we have the right to be treated with basic dignity, respect, and consideration. Because every person is created in His image, God demands that we treat one another with respect. But he knows that we will not always be so treated. Often for the very reason that we belong to God and go by the name of His Son, we will be mistreated, ridiculed, and held in contempt (see Matt. 10:16-23; John 15:18—16:3; 1 Pet. 2:20-21; 3:13-17; 4:12-19; cf. 2 Tim. 3:12). It is the way we react to mistreatment and insult that Jesus is talking about here.

Among Jews, a slap or other striking in the face was among the most demeaning and contemptuous of acts (cf. Matt. 26:67-68; Mark 14:65; John 18:22). To strike someone elsewhere on the body might cause more physical harm, but a slap in the face was an attack on one's honor and was considered to be a terrible indignity. It was to be treated with disdain, as being less than a human. Even a slave would rather have been stuck across the back with a whip than be slapped in the face by his master's hand.

To strike someone on the **right cheek** would then be a vicious angry reaction, indicating an act of insult. Yet when we are insulted, maligned, and treated with contempt—literally or figuratively struck on the cheek by someone— we are to **turn to him the other also**. But Jesus' point pertains more to what we are not to do than what we are to do. Turning the other cheek symbolizes the nonavenging, nonretaliatory, humble, and gentle spirit that is to characterize kingdom citizens (cf. vv. 3, 5).

Jesus strongly resisted evil that was directed against others, especially His Father—as when He cleansed the Temple of those who defiled His Father's house. But He did not resist by personal vengeance any evil directed at Himself. When the leaders of the Sanhedrin, and later the soldiers, physically abused Him and mocked Him, He did not retaliate either in words or in actions (Matt. 26:67-68). As Isaiah had predicted of Him, Christ gave His back to those who struck Him and His cheeks to those who plucked out His beard (Isa. 50:6). As Jesus hung from the cross, He prayed, "Father, forgive them; for they do not know what they are doing" (Luke 23:34). Peter sums up our Lord's example: "But if when you do what is right and suffer for it you patiently endure it, this finds favor with God. For you have been called for this purpose, since Christ also suffered for you, leaving you an example for you to follow in His steps, who committed no sin, nor was any deceit found in His mouth; and while being reviled, He did not revile in return; while suffering, He uttered no threats, but kept entrusting Himself to Him who judges righteously" (1 Pet. 2:20-23).

When someone attacks our right to dignity, we too are not to defend that right by retaliation. We are to leave the protection and defense of our dignity in God's hands, knowing that one day we will live and reign with him in His kingdom in great glory.

SECURITY

And if anyone wants to sue you, and take your shirt, let him have your coat also. (5:40)

The **shirt** mentioned here was a type of tunic worn as an undergarment, and the **coat** was an outer garment that also served as a blanket at night. Most people of that day owned only one coat and probably only one or two shirts. It was the outer garment, the **coat**, that Mosaic law required be returned to its owner "before the sun sets, for that is his only covering; it is his cloak for his body" (Ex. 22:26-27).

Jesus is not speaking of a robbery, in which a person tries to steal your clothes, but of the legitimate claim of **anyone who wants to sue you.** When a person had no money or other possessions, the court often would require the fine or judgment be paid by clothing. The attitude of a kingdom citizen, one who is truly righteous, should be willingness to surrender even one's **coat**, his extremely valuable outer garment, rather than cause offense or hard feelings with an adversary. The court could not demand the **coat**, but it could be voluntarily given to meet the requred debt. And that is precisely what Jesus says we should be willing to do.

If a legal judgment is fairly made against us for a certain amount, we should be willing to offer even more in order to show our regret for any wrong we did and to show that we are not bitter or resentful against the one who has sued us. In so doing we will show the love of Christ and that we are "sons of [our] Father who is in heaven" (v. 45). It is better even to be defrauded than to be resentful and spiteful. (Paul later instructs Christians regarding lawsuits in 1 Cor. 6:1-8, emphasizing a similar principle of willingness to forfeit one's due rather than be vengeful.)

LIBERTY

And whoever shall force you to go one mile, go with him two. (5:41)

The third right the Lord indicates kingdom citizens are to be willing to sacrifice is that of liberty. God's original intention was for everyone made in His image to live in freedom. Human bondage and slavery are consequences of the Fall and have no part in God's original plan for His creation. The best of human governments have always tried to protect the freedom of their citizens, and sometimes even of foreigners. In light of God's will and proper human justice, men have the right to certain freedoms. But like all other rights, freedom is not to be cherished and protected at the expense of righteousness or even of faithful witness.

Roman law gave a soldier the right to **force** a civilian to carry his pack for a *milion,* a Roman **mile,** which was slightly shorter than our modern mile. The law, designed to relieve the soldier, not only caused great inconvenience to civilians but was made even more despicable by the fact that the oppressed were made to carry the equipment and weapons of their oppressors. Outside of combat the Roman soldier was probably never more hated than when he forced someone to carry his pack.

Yet even so despised a burden should be carried willingly, Jesus says—not only willingly but with magnanimity. When we are forced to go **one mile**, we should willingly go **two**. When we are robbed of some of our cherished liberty, we should surrender even more of it rather than retaliate. In so doing we are obedient to our Lord and testify to His righteousness, knowing that in Him we have a dearer freedom that the world cannot take from us.

PROPERTY

Give to him who asks of you, and do not turn away from him who wants to borrow from you. (5:42)

The fourth right we are to surrender is that of property. Possessiveness is another characteristic of fallen human nature. We dislike giving up, even temporarily, that which belongs to us. Even as Christians, we often forget that nothing truly belongs to us and that we are only stewards of what belongs to God. But as far as other people are concerned, we *do* have a right to keep that which we possess. By right it is ours to use or dispose of as we see fit.

But that right, too, should be placed on the altar of obedience to Christ if required. When someone asks to **borrow** something from us, we should **not turn away from him**. In other words, we should give him what he wants. The implication is that the person who asks has a genuine need. We are not required to respond to every foolish, selfish request made of us. Sometimes to give a person what he wants but does not need is a disservice, doing him more harm than good.

Also implied is the principle that we should offer to give what is needed as soon as we know of the need, whether or not we are asked for help. Jesus is not speaking of begrudging acquiescence to a plea for help, but willing, generous, and loving desire to help others. He is speaking of generosity that genuinely wants to meet the other person's need, not tokenism that does a good deed to buy off one's own conscience.

Jesus does not undercut civil justice, which belongs in the courtroom. He undercuts personal selfishness (characteristic of the false religionists listening to Him on the mountain), which belongs nowhere and especially not in the hearts of His kingdom people.

A biographer of William Gladstone, the great British prime minister, wrote of him, "Of how few who have lived for more than sixty years in the full light of their countrymen and have, as party leaders, been exposed to angry and sometimes spiteful criticism, can it be said that there stands against them no malignant word and no vindictive act. This was due not perhaps entirely to Gladstone's natural sweetness of disposition but rather to self-control and a certain largeness of soul which would not condescend to anything mean or petty."

The only person who is nondefensive, nonvengeful, never bears a grudge, and has no spite in his heart is the person who has died to self. To fight for one's rights is to prove that self is still on the throne of the heart. The believer who is faithful to Christ lives for Him and, if necessary, dies for Him (Rom. 14:8). It is impossible to live for self and for Christ at the same time.

George Mueller wrote, "There was a day when I died, utterly died to George Mueller and his opinions, his preferences, and his tastes and his will. I died to the world, to its approval and its censure. I died to the approval or the blame of even my brethren and friends. And since then I have studied only to show myself approved unto God."

That is the spirit Jesus teaches in this passage, a spirit all men fail to possess apart from saving grace. It is the spirit Abraham manifested when he gave the best land to his nephew Lot. It is the spirit of Joseph when he embraced and kissed the brothers who had so terribly wronged him. Is the spirit that would not let David take advantage of the opportunity to take the life of Saul, who was then seeking to take David's life. It is the spirit that led Elisha to feed the enemy Assyrian army. It is the spirit that led Stephen to pray for those who were stoning him to death. It is the spirit of every believer who, by the Holy Spirit's power, seeks to be perfect even as our heavenly Father is perfect (v. 48).

Love Your Enemies
(5:43-48)

32

You have heard that it was said, "You shall love your neighbor, and hate your enemy." But I say to you, love your enemies, and pray for those who persecute you in order that you may be sons of your Father who is in heaven; for He causes His sun to rise on the evil and the good, and sends rain on the righteous and the unrighteous. For if you love those who love you, what reward have you? Do not even the tax-gatherers do the same? And if you greet your brothers only, what do you do more than others? Do not even the Gentiles do the same? Therefore you are to be perfect, as your heavenly Father is perfect. (5:43-48)

In His sixth, and last, illustration contrasting the false righteousness of the scribes and Pharisees with the true righteousness of God, Jesus contrasts their kind of love with God's. Nowhere did their humanistic, self-centered system of religion differ more from God's divine standards than in the matter of love. Nowhere had God's standard been so corrupted as in the way the self-righteous scribes and Pharisees viewed themselves in relation to others. Nowhere was it more evident that they lacked the humility, mourning over their own sin, meekness, yearning for true righteousness, mercy, purity of heart, and peacemaking spirit that are to belong to God's kingdom citizens.

As with the previous illustrations, we will look at the teaching of the Old Testament, the perversion of rabbinic tradition, and the perspective of Jesus Christ.

TEACHING OF THE OLD TESTAMENT

You shall love your neighbor. (5:43b)

That phrase is the only part of the tradition that was adapted from the Old Testament. Leviticus 19:18 requires that "you shall love your neighbor as yourself," a command often repeated in the New Testament (Matt. 19:19; 22:39; Mark 12:31; Luke 10:27; Rom. 13:9; Gal. 5:14; James 2:8). Love for others, shown in sympathetic concern and actual care for them, had always been God's standard for human relations.

In Deuteronomy the Israelites were commanded to help their fellow countrymen by returning a lost ox, sheep, donkey, or other such animal to its owner. If the owner was not known, the animal was to be kept and cared for until the owner was discovered. Likewise, a countryman was to be helped when his animal fell down or was injured (Deut. 22:1-4). But God's people were also commanded to do the same favors for an enemy. "If you meet your enemy's ox or his donkey wandering away, you shall surely return it to him. If you see the donkey of one who hates you lying helpless under its load, you shall refrain from leaving it to him, you shall surely release it with him" (Ex. 23:4-5).

As in all the teachings of the Sermon on the Mount, Jesus is speaking here about personal standards of righteousness, not civil law. The "enemy" spoken of in Exodus 23 is not the enemy soldier met on the battlefield, but an individual—whether fellow countryman or foreigner—who in some way or another is antagonistic. God has never had a double standard of righteousness. His "commandment is exceedingly broad" (Ps. 119:96), and in the fullest sense an Israelite's **neighbor** was anyone in need whom he might come across in his daily living. (See our Lord's answer to the question, "Who is my neighbor?" in Luke 10:30-37.)

Job testified, "Have I rejoiced at the extinction of my enemy, or exulted when evil befell him? No, I have not allowed my mouth to sin by asking for his life in a curse" (Job 31:29-30). He did nothing himself to harm his enemies and he did not rejoice when harm came to them from any other source. In other words, he did nothing, said nothing, and thought nothing against his enemies. Job did more than simply refrain from doing others harm; he gave them help. "Have the men of my tent not said, 'Who can find one who has not been satisfied with his meat'? The alien has not lodged outside, for I have opened my doors to the traveler" (vv. 31-32).

Job lived in the patriarchal period, perhaps during the time of Abraham and certainly hundreds of years before God gave his written law to Moses. Yet at that time God's standard of righteousness included merciful, kind, and loving care for others, a trait that characterized Job, who "was blameless, upright, fearing God, and turning away from evil" (Job. 1:1).

David prayed, "If I have rewarded evil to my friend, or have plundered him who without cause was my adversary, let the enemy pursue my soul and overtake it; and let him trample my life down to the ground, and lay my glory in the dust" (Ps. 7:4-5). David knew it was wrong to do evil against someone who had wronged him, just as it was wrong to do evil against a friend. In another psalm he said, "They repay me evil for good, to the bereavement of my soul. But as for me, when they were sick, my clothing was sackcloth; I humbled my soul with fasting; and my prayer kept returning to my bosom. I went about as though it were my friend or brother; I bowed down mourning, as one who sorrows for a mother. But at my stumbling they rejoiced" (Ps. 35:12-15). David grieved over and prayed for his enemies when they were sick and in need, despite the fact that they repaid him "evil for good" and rejoiced when he himself was in trouble.

Those were not mere words for David, because we know he lived out that spirit of love. When Saul was seeking to kill him, David had an easy opportunity to take Saul's life. To relieve himself, Saul went into a cave near Engedi where David and his men were hiding and became unknowingly at David's mercy. David stealthily cut off a piece of Saul's robe, but he was so sensitive about doing Saul any harm that "it came about afterward that David's conscience bothered him because he had cut off the edge of Saul's robe." His men interpreted the situation as a fulfillment of God's prophecy to give David's enemies into his hands; but David knew better. "So he said to his men, 'Far be it from me because of the Lord that I should do this thing to my lord, the Lord's anointed, to stretch out my hand against him, since he is the Lord's anointed.' And David persuaded his men with these words and did not allow them to rise up against Saul" (1 Sam. 24:3-7). David would not harm Saul directly, and he would not let anyone else do so in his behalf. David's conviction was deep and sincere. Though he had every human reason to hate Saul, David refused to return evil for evil. He would not hate his enemy.

On another occasion, after David had become king, a relative of Saul named Shimei threw rocks at David and cursed him. Again David would not retaliate or allow his men to do so on his behalf. Shimei was not God's anointed, and yet David refused to harm him or even give an angry retort. As king he had the legal right to kill Shimei on the spot, but his devotion to a higher law prevented him. In amazing humility he said instead, "If he curses, and if the Lord has told him, 'Curse David,' then who shall say, 'Why have you done so?'" (2 Sam. 16:5-10). David gave Shimei the benefit of any doubt, suggesting that Shimei may even have been acting on the Lord's behalf.

In Proverbs we read, "He who rejoices at calamity will not go unpunished" (Prov. 17:5). "Do not say, 'Thus I shall do to him as he has done to me'" (24:29); but, "If your enemy is hungry, give him food to eat; and if he is thirsty, give him water to drink" (25:21). Throughout the Old Testament, God's standard for His people was to treat even their enemies like their friends and families.

THE PERVERSION OF RABBINIC TRADITION

You have heard that it was said, "You shall love your neighbor, and hate your enemy." (5:43)

As in each of the five preceding illustrations, Jesus repeats the essence of the contemporary traditional teaching, in this case the teaching about love. Love, said the ancients, was to be reserved for those you get along with. Enemies were to be hated.

Satan's perversions of God's revelation almost always touch on the truth at some point. A little truth makes deception more believable and acceptable. The rabbis and scribes had kept a part of God's truth about love. As already indicated, **You shall love your neighbor** is a clear teaching of the Old Testament. "You shall not take vengeance, nor bear any grudge against the sons of your people, but you shall love your neighbor as yourself; I am the Lord" (Lev. 19:18).

In spite of such clear revelation, rabbinic tradition had perverted Old Testament teaching both by what was omitted and by what was added.

PERVERSION BY OMISSION

Omitted in the tradition was the phrase "as yourself," which was a key part of the Leviticus text but could not possibly fit into their scheme of proud self-righteousness. It simply was inconceivable that they should care for any other person as much as they cared for themselves.

The complete text of Leviticus 19:18 obviously was well known to the scribes and Pharisees. They were the supreme students, preservers, and interpreters of the law; and when copying or reading directly from Scripture they were meticulously accurate. The scribe who asked Jesus which was the greatest commandment confirmed Jesus' answer. "Right, Teacher," he said, "You have truly stated that . . . to love one's neighbor as himself is much more than all burnt offerings and sacrifices" (Mark 12:32-33). On another occasion, when Jesus asked a certain lawyer, "What is written in the Law? How does it read to you?" the lawyer accurately quoted Deuteronomy 6:5 and the end of Leviticus 19:18, including "and your neighbor as yourself" (Luke 10:26-27).

The words of Scripture were fully known but only partially taught and practiced; frequently they were even contradicted by rabbinic tradition. As with other scriptural standards that seemed too demanding, the one concerning love of neighbor was reduced to a humanly acceptable level.

The scribes and Pharisees knew how well they loved themselves. They loved to be honored, praised, and respected (Matt. 6:2, 5, 16; etc.), and believed they deserved it. The Pharisee who thanked God that he was "not like other people" (Luke 18:11) was typical of most Pharisees.

He was also typical of most people throughout history. For the natural man, and unfortunately for some Christians, self-love is real, active, and quite noticeable. Most people spend their lives doing and seeking things that are primarily in their own interest—their safety, comfort, income, pleasure, health, personal interests, and so on.

But the standard God had given the Jews was supernatural rather than natural, and they must have chafed under it, because they knew they could not live up to it in their own power. Besides that, they did not *want* to live up to it, and therefore simply excised "as yourself" from God's standard of love.

Along with that significant omission, tradition had narrowed the meaning of **neighbor** to include only those people they preferred and approved of—which amounted basically to their own kind. Such obviously profane people as tax-gatherers and ordinary sinners were despised as outcasts and as not being worthy even to be considered Jews.

Tax-gatherers were renegade Jews who had sold out to the Roman oppressors and made lucrative livings by extorting excessive taxes from their fellow citizens. "Sinners" were those such as criminals and prostitutes who were publicly known for their immorality. They were the "swindlers, unjust, adulterers," and such that the Pharisee thanked God for not being like (Luke 18:11). One of the things about Jesus that disgusted Jewish leaders the most was His open willingness to associate with, eat with, and even forgive such obviously unrighteous people (Matt. 9:11).

But even that restriction of **neighbor** was not narrow enough. The scribes and Pharisees also despised and looked down on the common people. They dismissed those who believed in Jesus by saying, "No one of the rulers or Pharisees has believed in Him, has he? But this multitude which does not know the Law is accursed" (John 7:48-49). Ironically, the proud and arrogant religious leaders who knew, but perverted, the law disdained as "accursed" the common people who they felt did not know it.

PERVERSION BY ADDITION

Rabbinic tradition also perverted the Old Testament teaching about love by adding something to it: **hate your enemy**. Their addition was even more perverse than their omission, but it was the logical extension of their all-consuming self-interest.

It goes without saying that Gentiles were not considered neighbors. A saying of the Pharisees has been discovered that reads, "If a Jew sees a Gentile fallen into the sea, let him by no means lift him out, for it is written, 'Thou shalt not rise up against the blood of thy neighbor,' but this man is not thy neighbor." It is little wonder that the Romans charged Jews with hatred of the human race.

One excuse the Jews may often have made to justify hatred of Gentiles was based on God's command for their forefathers to drive out the Canaanites, Midianites, Moabites, Ammonites, and other pagan peoples as they conquered and possessed the Promised Land under Joshua (Josh. 3:10; cf. Ex. 33:2; Deut. 7:1; etc.). But those ancient inhabitants of Palestine were among the most vile, corrupt, and depraved known to history. They were unbelievably immoral, cruel, and idolatrous. Human sacrifice was common among them, and even one's own children were sometimes burned alive as an offering to their pagan deities. They were a cancer that had to be cut out in order to save God's people from utter moral and spiritual corruption.

"The wars of Israel," writes Dietrich Bonhoeffer, "were the only 'holy wars' in history, for they were the wars of God against the world of idols. It is not this enmity which Jesus condemns, for then He would have condemned the whole history of God's dealing with His people. On the contrary, He affirms the Old Covenant" (*The Cost of Discipleship,* trans. R. H. Fuller [2d rev. ed.; Philadelphia: Westminster, 1960], p. 163).

Israel's harsh dealing with those people was entirely as the instrument of God's judgment. God's people were never to return evil for evil, cruelty for cruelty, hatred for hatred. The idea that Gentiles, even wicked ones, were to be personally despised and hated originated from the heretical Jews' own pride and self-righteousness, not from God's Word.

Rabbinic tradition no doubt also tried to justify hatred of enemies on the basis of the imprecatory psalms. David wrote, "May their table before them become a snare; and when they are in peace, may it become a trap. May their eyes grow dim so that they cannot see, and make their loins shake continually. Pour out Thine indignation on them, and may Thy burning anger overtake them" (Ps. 69:22-24).

Such words did not represent David's personal vendetta but his concern for God's holiness and justice to be executed on those who despised the Lord's glorious name and persecuted the Lord's people. The basis for David's imprecations is found in verse 9 of that same psalm: "For zeal for Thy house has consumed me, and the reproaches of those who reproach Thee have fallen on me." David was angered because of what was done against God. When Jesus cleansed the Temple in Jerusalem, "His disciples remembered" David's words, "that it was written, 'Zeal for Thy house will consume me'" (John 2:17). David and Jesus shared the same righteous indignation.

When David's own son Absalom raised an army and rebelled against his father, David prayed, "Arise, O Lord; save me, O my God! For Thou hast smitten all my enemies on the cheek; Thou hast shattered the teeth of the wicked" (Ps. 3:7; see also the superscription at the beginning of the psalm). David loved his son dearly and wept bitterly when he learned of his death (2 Sam. 18:33), but he knew Absalom was ungodly and the enemy of God's people and of His anointed king. As such, Absalom deserved defeat—and to that end his father David prayed.

The apostle John experienced similar tension of feelings when he "took the little book out of the angel's hand and ate it." "It was in my mouth sweet as honey," he said, "and when I had eaten it, my stomach was made bitter" (Rev. 10:10). He was glad because he knew the Lord would be absolutely victorious over His enemies;

but he was sad because of the millions who would be destroyed because they would not turn to God.

It is one thing to defend the honor and glory of God by seeking the defeat of His detracting enemies, but quite another to hate people personally as our own enemies. Our attitude toward even the worst pagans or heretics is to love them and pray that they will turn to God and be saved. But we also pray that, if they do not turn to Him, God will judge them and remove them in order to prepare the way for His Son Jesus Christ as the rightful ruler of this world.

We are to share God's own balance of love and justice. God loved Adam, but He cursed him. God loved Cain, but He punished him. God loved Sodom and Gomorrah, but He destroyed them. God loved Israel, but He allowed her to be conquered and exiled, and He set her aside for a while.

The scribes and Pharisees had no such balance. They had no love for justice, but only for vengeance. And they had no love for their enemies, but only for themselves. After David declared of God's enemies, "I hate them with the utmost hatred; they have become my enemies," he also prayed, "Search me, O God, and know my heart; try me and know my anxious thoughts; and see if there be any hurtful way in me, and lead me in the everlasting way" (Ps. 139:22-24).

The scribes and Pharisees, by contrast, knew nothing either of righteous indignation or righteous love. Their only indignation was that of personal hatred, and their only love was that of self-esteem.

THE PERSPECTIVE OF JESUS CHRIST

But I say to you, love your enemies, and pray for those who persecute you in order that you may be sons of your Father who is in heaven; for He causes His sun to rise on the evil and the good, and sends rain on the righteous and the unrighteous. For if you love those who love you, what reward have you? Do not even the tax-gatherers do the same? And if you greet your brothers only, what do you do more than others? Do not even the Gentiles do the same? Therefore you are to be perfect, as your heavenly Father is perfect. (5:44-48)

In five ascending statements Jesus proclaims the kind of love that God has always required of His people and that must characterize everyone who goes by the name of the Lord.

LOVE YOUR ENEMIES

But I say to you, love your enemies. (5:44a)

Here is the most powerful teaching in Scripture about the meaning of love.

The love that God commands of His people is **love** so great that it even embraces **enemies**.

William Hendriksen comments,

> All around him were those walls and fences. He came for the very purpose of bursting those barriers, so that love—pure, warm, divine, infinite—would be able to flow straight down from the heart of God, hence from his own marvelous heart, into the hearts of men. His love overleaped all the boundaries of race, nationality, party, age, sex. . . .
>
> When he said, "I tell you, love your enemies," he must have startled his audience, for he was saying something that probably never before had been said so succinctly, positively, and forcefully. (*The Gospel of Matthew* [Grand Rapids: Baker, 1973], p. 313)

The scribes and Pharisees were proud, prejudiced, judgmental, spiteful, hateful, vengeful men who masqueraded as the custodians of God's law and the spiritual leaders of Israel. To them, Jesus' command to **love your enemies** must have seemed naive and foolish in the extreme. They not only felt they had the right but the duty to hate their enemies. Not to hate those who obviously deserve to be hated would be a breach of righteousness.

Jesus again sets His divine standard against the perverted human standards of that heretical Jewish tradition and reinforces it with the emphatic **I**. In Greek verbs a pronominal suffix indicates the subject, as here with *lēgo* (I **say**), and the separate pronoun I would not have been necessary had Jesus intended simply to give information.

But here, as in each preceding instance in the sermon (vv. 22, 28, 32, 34, 39), the emphatic form (*egō . . . legō*) gives not only grammatical but theological emphasis. In placing what He said above what tradition said, He placed His word on a par with Scripture—as His hearers well understood. Jesus not only placed emphasis on what was said but on who said it. It was not just that His teaching was the standard of truth, but that He Himself was the standard of truth. "Your great rabbis, scribes, and scholars have taught you to love only those of your own preference and to hate your enemies," Jesus was saying. "But by My own authority, I declare that they are false teachers and have perverted God's revealed truth. The divine truth is My truth, which is that **you shall love your enemies.**"

As we have noted, the Old Testament concept of neighbor included even personal enemies. That is the truth Jesus expands in the parable of the Good Samaritan. The point of the parable is not primarily to answer the lawyer's question, "And who is my neighbor?" though it does that, but to show that God's requirement is for us to *be* neighbors to anyone who needs our help (Luke 10:29, 36-37).

The human tendency is to base love on the desirability of the object of our love. We love people who are attractive, hobbies that are enjoyable, a house or a car because it looks nice and pleases us, and so on. But true love is need-oriented. The Good Samaritan demonstrated great love because he sacrificed his own convenience, safety, and resources to meet another's desperate need.

The Greek language has four different terms that are usually translated "love." *Philia* is brotherly love and the love of friendship; *storgē* is the love of family; and *erōs* is desiring, romantic, sexual love. But the **love** of which Jesus speaks here, and which is most spoken of in the New Testament, is *agapē,* the love that seeks and works to meet another's highest welfare.

Agapē love *may* involve emotion but it *must* involve action. In Paul's beautiful and powerful treatise on love in 1 Corinthians 13, all fifteen of the characteristics of love are given in verb form. Obviously love must involve attitude, because, like every form of righteousness, it begins in the heart. But it is best described and best testified by what it does.

Above all, *agapē* love is the love that God is, that God demonstrates, and that God gives (1 John 4:7-10). "The love of God has been poured out within our hearts through the Holy Spirit who was given to us. . . . [and] God demonstrates His own love toward us, in that while we were yet sinners, Christ died for us" (Rom. 5:5, 8). Because of His love, we can love, and "if we love one another, God abides in us, and His love is perfected in us" (1 John 4:11-12).

When Jesus told the disciples, "A new commandment I give to you, that you love one another, even as I have loved you" (John 13:34), He had just finished washing their feet as an example of humble, self-giving love. The disciples had done nothing to inspire Jesus' love. They were self-centered, quarrelsome, jealous of each other, and sometimes even argued with and contradicted the One whom they confessed to be their God, Savior, and Lord. Yet everything that Jesus said to them and did for them was completely and without exception for their good. That was the kind of love He commanded them to have for Him and for each other. And that is the kind of love He commands all of His followers to have even for their enemies.

The commentator R. C. H. Lenski writes,

> [Love] indeed, sees all the hatefulness and the wickedness of the enemy, feels his stabs and his blows, may even have something to do toward warding them off; but all this simply fills the loving heart with the one desire and aim, to free its enemy from his hate, to rescue him from his sin, and thus to save his soul. Mere affection is often blind, but even then it thinks that it sees something attractive in the one toward whom it goes out; the higher love may see nothing attractive in the one so loved, . . . its inner motive is simply to bestow true blessing on the one loved, to do him the highest good. . . . I cannot like a low, mean criminal who may have robbed me and threatened my life; I cannot like a false, lying, slanderous fellow who, perhaps, has vilified me again and again; but I can by the grace of Jesus Christ love them all, see what is wrong with them, desire and work to do them only good, most of all to free them from their vicious ways. (*The Interpretation of St. Matthew's Gospel* [Minneapolis: Augsburg, 1964], p. 247)

Love's question is never who to love—because we are to love everyone—but only how to love most helpfully. We are not to love merely in terms of feeling but in terms of service. God's love embraces the entire world (John 3:16), and He loved each of us even while we were still sinners and His enemies (Rom. 5:8-10). Those who refuse to trust in God are His enemies; but He is not theirs. In the same way, we are not to be enemies of those who may be enemies to us. From their perspective, we are their enemies; but from our perspective, they should be our neighbors.

In 1567 King Philip II of Spain appointed the Duke of Alba as governor of the lower part of the nation. The Duke was a bitter enemy of the newly-emerging Protestant Reformation. His rule was called the reign of terror, and his council was called the Bloody Council, because it had ordered the slaughter of so many Protestants. It is reported that one man who was sentenced to die for his biblical faith managed to escape during the dead of winter. As he was being pursued by a lone soldier, the man came to a lake whose ice was thin and cracking. Somehow he managed to get safely across the ice, but as soon as he reached the other side he heard his pursuer screaming. The soldier had fallen through the ice and was about to drown. At the risk of being captured, tortured, and eventually killed—or of being drowned himself—the man went back across the lake and rescued his enemy, because the love of Christ constrained him to do it. He knew he had no other choice if he was to be faithful to His Lord (Elon Foster, *New Cyclopedia of Prose Illustrations: Second Series* [New York: T. Y. Crowell, 1877], p. 296).

The Scottish Reformer George Wishart, a contemporary and friend of John Knox, was sentenced to die as a heretic. Because the executioner knew of Wishart's selfless ministering to hundreds of people who were dying of the plague, he hesitated carrying out the sentence. When Wishart saw the expression of remorse on the executioner's face, he went over and kissed him on the cheek, saying, "Sir, may that be a token that I forgive you" (John Foxe, *Foxe's Book of Martyrs,* ed. W. Grinton Berry [Grand Rapids: Baker, 1978], p. 252).

Our "enemies," of course, do not always come in such life-threatening forms. Often they are ordinary people who are mean, impatient, judgmental, self-righteous, and spiteful—or just happen to disagree with us. In whatever personal relationships we have, God wants us to love. Whether a conflict is with our marriage partner, our children or parents, our friends and fellow church members, a devious business opponent, spiteful neighbor, political foe, or social antagonist, our attitude toward them should be one of prayerful love.

PRAY FOR YOUR PERSECUTORS

and pray for those who persecute you. (5:44b)

All men live with some sense of sin and guilt. And guilt produces fear, which in its ultimate form is fear of death and of what is beyond death. In various ways, therefore, most people have devised religious beliefs, rituals, and practices they are convinced will offer them some relief from guilt and judgment. Some people try to get rid of guilt simply by denying it or by denying the existence of a God who holds men accountable for sin.

Throughout history the worst persecutions have been religious. They have been the strongest against God's people, because the divine standards He has given to them and which are seen in them are a judgment on the wickedness and corruption of false religion. God's Word unmasks people at their most sensitive and vulnerable point, the point of their self-justification—whether that justification is religious, philosophical, or even atheistic.

Because persecution is so often the world's response to God's truth, the Lord assures us that, just as He was persecuted, so will we be (John 15:20). Therefore His command for us to pray for our persecutors is a command that every faithful believer may in some way have opportunity to obey. It is not reserved for believers who happen to live in pagan or atheistic lands where Christianity is forbidden or severely restricted.

Jesus taught that every disciple who makes his faith known is going to pay some price for it, and that we are to pray for those who exact that price from us. Spurgeon said, "Prayer is the forerunner of mercy," and that is perhaps the reason why Jesus mentions prayer here. Loving enemies is not natural to men and is sometimes difficult even for those who belong to God and have His love within them. The best way to have the right attitude, the *agapē* love attitude, toward those who **persecute** us is to bring them before the Lord in prayer. We may sense their wickedness, their unfairness, their ungodliness, and their hatred for us, and in light of those things we could not possibly love them for *what* they are. We must love them because of *who* they are—sinners fallen from the image of God and in need of God's forgiveness and grace, just as we were sinners in need of His forgiveness and grace before He saved us. We are to **pray** for them that they will, as we have done, seek His forgiveness and grace.

Our persecutors may not always be unbelievers. Christians can cause other Christians great trouble, and the first step toward healing those broken relationships is also prayer. Whoever persecutes us, in whatever way and in whatever degree, should be on our prayer list. Talking to God about others can begin to knit the petitioner's heart with the heart of God.

Chrysostom said that prayer is the very highest summit of self-control and that we have most brought our lives into conformity to God's standards when we can pray for our persecutors. Dietrich Bonhoeffer, the pastor who suffered and eventually was killed in Nazi Germany, wrote of Jesus' teaching in Matthew 5:44, "This is the supreme demand. Through the medium of prayer we go to our enemy, stand by his side, and plead for him to God" (*The Cost of Discipleship*, trans. R. H. Fuller [2d rev. ed.; New York: Macmillan, 1960], p. 166).

MANIFEST YOUR SONSHIP

in order that you may be sons of your Father who is in heaven; for He causes

His sun to rise on the evil and the good, and sends rain on the righteous and the unrighteous. (5:45)

To love our enemies and to pray for our persecutors shows that we are **sons of** [our] **Father who is in heaven.** The aorist tense of *genēsthe* (**may be**) indicates a once and for all established fact. God Himself is love, and the greatest evidence of our divine sonship through Jesus Christ is our love. "By this all men will know that you are My disciples, if you have love for one another" (John 13:35). "God is love, and the one who abides in love abides in God, and God abides in him" (1 John 4:16). In fact, "If someone says, 'I love God,' and hates his brother, he is a liar; for the one who does not love his brother whom he has seen, cannot love God whom he has not seen" (v. 20).

Loving as God loves does not *make* us **sons of** the **Father,** but gives evidence that we already are His children. When a life reflects God's nature it proves that life now *possesses* His nature by the new birth.

One of the commonest and most damaging criticisms of Christianity is the charge that Christians do not live up to their faith. Even though the world has a limited and often distorted idea of what the gospel is, they know enough about the teachings of Christ and the life of Christ to realize that most people who go by His name do not do all that He commanded and do not live as He lived.

But even a person who has never heard of Christ or the teachings of the New Testament would suspect there is divine power behind a life that loves and cares even to the point of loving enemies—simply because such a life is so utterly uncharacteristic of human nature. A life of self-giving love gives evidence of sonship of the **Father who is in heaven.** That phrase emphasizes the heavenly realm in which the Lord dwells, the realm that is the source of this kind of love.

Those who are God's children should show impartial love and care similar to what God shows. **He causes His sun to rise on the evil and the good, and sends rain on the righteous and the unrighteous.** Those blessings are given without respect to merit or deserving. If they were, no one would receive them. In what theologians traditionally have called common grace, God is indiscriminate in His benevolence. His divine love and providence in some forms benefit everyone, even those who rebel against Him or deny His existence.

An old rabbinic saying tells of the drowning of the Egyptians in the Red Sea. As the story goes, when the Egyptians were destroyed the angels began to rejoice; but God lifted up His hand and said, "The work of My hands are sunk in the sea and you would sing?" (William Barclay, *The Gospel of Matthew,* 2 vols. [rev. ed.; Philadelphia: Westminster, 1975], 1:176).

"The eyes of all look to Thee, and Thou dost give them their food in due time," the psalmist testifies. "Thou dost open Thy hand, and dost satisfy the desire of every living thing" (Ps. 145:15-16). There is no good thing—physical, intellectual, emotional, moral, spiritual, or of any other sort—that *anyone* possesses or experiences that does not come from the hand of God. If God does that for everyone, His children should reflect that same generosity.

EXCEED YOUR FELLOW MEN

For if you love those who love you, what reward have you? Do not even the tax-gatherers do the same? And if you greet your brothers only, what do you do more than others? Do not even the Gentiles do the same? (5:46-47)

If the scribes and Pharisees were certain of any one thing it was that they were far better than everyone else. But Jesus again cuts through their blind hypocrisy and shows that their type of love is nothing more than the ordinary self-centered love that was common even to **tax-gatherers** and **Gentiles**—to whom the scribes and Pharisees thought they were most undeniably superior.

Those were probably the most devastating and insulting words these religious leaders had ever heard, and they must have been enraged. **Tax-gatherers** were traitorous extortioners, and almost by definition were dishonest, heartless, and irreligious. In the eyes of most Jews, **Gentiles** were outside the pale of God's concern and mercy, fit only for destruction as His enemies and the enemies of those who thought they were His people.

But the love of the scribes and Pharisees, Jesus said, was no better than the love of those whom they despised above all other people. **You love those who love you,** and that is **the same** type of love that **even the tax-gatherers** and **the Gentiles** exhibit. "Your righteousness," He charged, "is therefore no better than theirs."

The citizens of God's kingdom are to have a much higher standard of love, and of every other aspect of righteousness, than does the rest of the world. Christians should be noticed on the job because they are more honest and more considerate. Christians should be noticed in their communities because they are more helpful and caring. Christians should be noticed anywhere in society they happen to be because the love they exhibit is a divine love. "Let your light shine before men," Jesus had already said, "in such a way that they may see your good works, and glorify your Father who is in heaven" (Matt. 5:16). As J. Oswald Sanders comments, "The Master expects from His disciples such conduct as can be explained only in terms of the supernatural."

BE LIKE YOUR HEAVENLY FATHER

Therefore you are to be perfect, as your heavenly Father is perfect. (5:48)

The sum of all that Jesus teaches in the Sermon on the Mount—in fact, the sum of all He teaches in Scripture—is in those words. The great purpose of salvation, the goal of the gospel, and the great yearning of the heart of God is for all men to become like Him.

Teleios (**perfect**) basically means to reach an intended end or a completion and is often translated "mature" (1 Cor. 2:6; 14:20; Eph. 4:13; etc.). But the meaning here is obviously that of perfection, because the **heavenly Father** is the standard. The "sons of [the] Father" (v. 45) are to be **perfect, as** [their] **heavenly Father is perfect**. That perfection is absolute perfection.

That perfection is also utterly impossible in man's own power. To those who wonder how Jesus can demand the impossible, He later says, "With men this is impossible, but with God all things are possible" (Matt. 19:26). That which God demands, He provides the power to accomplish. Man's own righteousness is possible, but is so imperfect that it is worthless; God's righteousness is impossible for the very reason that it is perfect. But the impossible righteousness becomes possible for those who trust in Jesus Christ, because He gives them His righteousness.

That is precisely our Lord's point in all these illustrations and in the whole sermon—to lead His audience to an overpowering sense of spiritual bankruptcy, to a "beatitude attitude" that shows them their need of a Savior, an enabler who alone can empower them to meet God's standard of perfection.

Giving Without Hypocrisy (6:1-4)

33

Beware of practicing your righteousness before men to be noticed by them; otherwise you have no reward with your Father who is in heaven.

When therefore you give alms, do not sound a trumpet before you, as the hypocrites do in the synagogues and in the streets, that they may be honored by men. Truly I say to you, they have their reward in full. But when you give alms, do not let your left hand know what your right hand is doing that your alms may be in secret; and your Father who sees in secret will repay you. (6:1-4)

Matthew 5:21-48 focuses on the teaching of the law, on what men believe, and 6:1-18 focuses on the practice of the law, what men do. The first section emphasizes inner moral righteousness—giving six representative illustrations regarding murder, adultery, divorce, oaths, revenge, and love. This second section emphasizes outward formal righteousness—giving three representative illustrations of religious activity. The first has to do with giving, our religion as it acts toward others (vv. 2-4); the second with praying, our religion as it acts toward God (vv. 5-15); and the third with fasting, our religion as it acts in relation to ourselves (vv. 16-18).

THE DANGER OF FALSE RIGHTEOUSNESS

Beware of practicing your righteousness before men to be noticed by them; otherwise you have no reward with your Father who is in heaven. (6:1)

This verse introduces the section on the forms of religious righteousness and applies to each of the three illustrations in 6:2-18.

The story is told of an eastern ascetic holy man who covered himself with ashes as a sign of humility and regularly sat on a prominent street corner of his city. When tourists asked permission to take his picture, the mystic would rearrange his ashes to give the best image of destitution and humility.

A great deal of religion amounts to nothing more than rearranging religious "ashes" to impress the world with one's supposed humility and devotion. The problem, of course, is that the humility is a sham, and the devotion is to self, not to God. Such religion is nothing more than a game of pretense, a game at which the scribes and Pharisees of Jesus' day were masters. Because their religion was mostly an act, and a mockery of God's true revealed way for His people, Jesus' most blistering denunciations were reserved for them.

But they were not the original or the last hypocrites. Since the fall of man there have been hypocrites. Hypocrites are mentioned in Scripture from Genesis through Revelation. Cain was the first hypocrite, feigning worship by offering a kind of sacrifice that God did not want. When his hypocrisy was unmasked, he killed his brother Abel out of resentment (Gen. 4:5-8). Absalom hypocritically vowed allegiance to his father, King David, while plotting the overthrow of his regime (2 Sam. 15:7-10).

The supreme hypocrite was Judas Iscariot, who betrayed the Lord with a kiss. Ananias and Sapphira hypocritically claimed to have given the church all the proceeds from the sale of some property, and lost their lives for lying to the Holy Spirit (Acts 5:1-10).

Hypocrites are found in paganism, in Judaism, and in Christianity. There were hypocrites in the early church, the medieval church, and the Reformation church. There are still hypocrites in the church today, and Paul assures us there will be hypocrites at the end of the age. "But the Spirit explicitly says that in later times some will fall away from the faith, paying attention to deceitful spirits and doctrines of demons, by means of the hypocrisy of liars seared in their own conscience as with a branding iron" (1 Tim. 4:1-2). Hypocrisy is endemic to fallen man, an integral part of his fleshly nature. Persecution of the church helps to diminish the number of hypocrites, but even that cannot completely eliminate them.

Hypocrisy is never treated lightly in Scripture. Through Amos, God said, "I hate, I reject your festivals, nor do I delight in your solemn assemblies. Even though you offer up to Me burnt offerings and your grain offerings, I will not accept them; and I will not even look at the peace offerings of your fatlings. Take away from Me the noise of your songs; I will not even listen to the sound of your harps. But let justice roll down like waters and righteousness like an ever-flowing stream" (Amos

(5:21-24) All of those religious acts had been prescribed by God; but because they were performed insincerely and were not accompanied by righteous living they were not acceptable to God. The sacrifices, offerings, and songs were not given to God's glory but to the people's own glory and self-satisfaction.

Outside of idolatry, the greatest sin both in Judah and Israel was hypocritical religion. The Jews were conquered and taken into captivity in large measure because they turned true worship of God into phoney mockery. In regard to that truth Isaiah says, "'What are your multiplied sacrifices to Me?' says the Lord. 'I have had enough of burnt offerings of rams, and the fat of fed cattle. And I take no pleasure in the blood of bulls, lambs, or goats'" (Isa. 1:11) The Lord continued by declaring His displeasure also with worthless offerings, incense, new moon and sabbath festivals, and hypocritical prayers (vv. 13-15). God wanted purity and righteousness, not perfunctory rituals. "Wash yourselves, make yourselves clean," He said; "remove the evil of your deeds from My sight. Cease to do evil, learn to do good; seek justice, reprove the ruthless; defend the orphan, plead for the widow. Come now, and let us reason together. . . . Though your sins are as scarlet, they will be as white as snow; though they are red like crimson, they will be like wool" (vv. 16-18).

Similar calls to replace superficial ceremony with genuine righteousness are found in the other literary prophets (Jer. 11:19-20; Amos 4:4-5; Mic. 6:6-8; etc.), as well as in the book of Job (8:13; 15:34; 36:13).

An Aesop's fable tells of a wolf who wanted to have a sheep for his dinner and decided to disguise himself as a sheep and follow the flock into the fold. While the wolf waited until the sheep went to sleep, the shepherd decided he would have mutton for his own meal. In the dark he picked out what he thought was the largest, fattest sheep; but after he had killed the animal he discovered it was a wolf. What that shepherd did inadvertently to a wolf in sheep's clothing, God does intentionally. The Lord judges hypocrisy.

Speaking to the scribes and Pharisees on one occasion, Jesus said, "Rightly did Isaiah prophesy of you hypocrites, as it is written, 'This people honors Me with their lips, but their heart is far away from Me. But in vain do they worship Me, teaching as doctrines the precepts of men'" (Mark 7:6-7).

Jesus used many figures to describe hypocrisy. He compared it to leaven (Luke 12:1), to whitewashed tombs (Matt. 23:27), concealed tombs (Luke 11:44), tares amidst the wheat (Matt. 13:25), and to wolves in sheep's clothing (Matt. 7:15).

In New Testament times some people made their living as professional mourners who were paid to weep, wail, and tear their garments at funerals and on other occasions of sadness (cf. Matt. 9:23). It is said that some mourners were careful to tear their clothing at a seam, so that the material could easily be sown back together for the next mourning. Both the professional mourners and those who hired them were hypocrites, hiring and being hired to put on a display of mourning that was entirely pretense.

Prosechō (**beware**) means to hold, or take hold of, something and pay attention to it, especially in the sense of being on guard. The scribes, Pharisees, and other hypocrites are warned by Jesus to **beware** of the religious activities in which they had such pride and confidence. He was about to show them again how worthless, meaningless, and unacceptable to God those activities were.

Theaomai (**to be noticed**) is related to the term from which we get theater. It has in mind a spectacle to be gazed at. In other words, Jesus is warning about **practicing** a form of **righteousness** (*dikaiosunē,* acts of religious devotion in general) whose purpose is to show off **before men**. Such religion is like a play; it is not real life but acting. It does not demonstrate what is in the minds and hearts of the actors, but is simply a performance designed to make a certain impression on those who are watching.

Such practices amount to theatrical **righteousness,** performed to impress rather than serve and to magnify the actors rather than God. The purpose is to please **men,** not God, and the activities are not real life but an exhibition. Such false righteousness, Jesus assures us, will never qualify a person for God's kingdom (Matt. 5:20).

False righteousness such as that does have a reward—the recognition and applause of other hypocrites and of ignorant people. That, however, is the limit of the honor, because Jesus tells those who practice such hypocritical righteousness, **you have no reward with your Father who is in heaven.** God does not reward men-pleasers (cf. Matt. 5:16), because they rob Him of glory. It should be noted that **your Father** is used in the same sense as in 5:16, as a reference to the Old Testament sense in which God was Israel's Father (Isa. 63:16), not in the New Testament sense of personal relationship by salvation (see Matt. 6:9).

The reference to God's dwelling **in heaven** distinguishes the eternal character of divine reward from the transient, shallow praise that hypocrites receive from other men.

THE PRACTICE AND REWARD OF FALSE GIVING

When therefore you give alms, do not sound a trumpet before you, as the hypocrites do in the synagogues and in the streets, that they may be honored by men. Truly I say to you, they have their reward in full. (6:2)

A *hupokritēs* (**hypocrite**) originally was a Greek actor who wore a mask that portrayed in an exaggerated way the role that was being dramatized. For obvious reasons the term came to be used of anyone who pretended to be what he was not.

John Calvin believed that in all virtues the entrance of [hypocrisy] was to be avoided, there being no work so praiseworthy as not to be in many instances corrupted and polluted by it (*A Harmony of the Evangelists Matthew, Mark, and Luke,* vol. 1 [Grand Rapids: Baker, 1979], pp. 308-9).

One of Satan's most common and effective ways of undermining the power of the church is through hypocrisy. Hypocrisy, therefore, is a great peril to the

church, and it comes in two forr
Christians. The second is that
spiritual. The warning Jesus g

Augustine said, "The ?
vices bring forth evil works
Hypocrisy is so dangerous be
good for purposes that are ?
homage that vice pays to vi

Eleēmosunē (**alms**) ?
used primarily of giving m
which we get the English ?

Jesus does not int
something He expects us
intentions or warm feelin
in the right spirit it not ?

6:3-4

was used by Jesus to describe the ?
that many wealthy **hypocrites**, ?
to themselves when they pre?
The reward they w?
men, and that became th?
a technical expressio?
carried the idea of ?
was owed or wou?
with their gene?
God. The L?
will be th?
their
do

God has always delighted in acts of ?
countryman of yours becomes poor and his means with regar?
you are to sustain him, like a stranger or a sojourner, that he may live with you?
(Lev. 25:35). When Israelites freed a slave they were told, "You shall not send him away empty-handed. You shall furnish him liberally from your flock and from your threshing floor and from your wine vat; you shall give to him as the Lord your God has blessed you" (Deut. 15:13-14). God's people were continually reminded in the Psalms, Proverbs, and prophetic writings to be considerate of and generous to the poor, whether fellow Israelites or Gentile strangers.

Jesus and the disciples had their own money bag from which they gave offerings to the poor (John 13:29). It is obvious, therefore, that it is only giving **alms** in the wrong spirit that is evil. The scribes and Pharisees gave them primarily to bring honor to themselves, not to serve others or to honor God.

The giving of alms had been carried to absurd extremes by rabbinic tradition. In the Jewish apocryphal books we read such things as, "It is better to give to charity than to lay up gold. For charity will save a man from death; it will expiate any sin" (Tobit 12:8) and, "As water will quench a flaming fire, so charity will atone for sin" (The Wisdom of Sirach 3:30). Consequently, many Jews believed that salvation was much easier for the rich, because they could buy their way into heaven by giving to the poor. The same mechanistic and unbiblical principle is seen in traditional Roman Catholic dogma. Pope Leo the Great declared, "By prayer we seek to appease God, by fasting we extinguish the lust of the flesh, and by alms we redeem our sins."

But just as a sympathetic feeling for someone in need does not help them unless something is given to meet their need, giving them money provides no spiritual benefit or blessing unless it is given from the heart. In any case, no act of charity or any other good work can atone for sin.

There seems to be no evidence from history or archaeology that a literal **trumpet** or other instrument was used by Jews to announce their giving. The figure

ttention **in the synagogues and in the streets**
ot just scribes and Pharisees, purposely attracted
ented their gifts.

anted was recognition and praise, to **be honored by**
eir **reward in full. They have their reward** was a form of
used at the completion of a commercial transaction, and
omething being paid for in full and receipted. Nothing more
ld be paid. Those who give for the purpose of impressing others
rosity and spirituality will receive no other reward, especially from
rd owes them nothing. When we give to please men, our only **reward**
at which men can give. Seeking men's blessings forfeits God's.

There are many more subtle trumpets people can use to call attention to
good works. When they make a point of doing publicly what they could easily
privately, they behave like the **hypocrites**, not like God's children.

A man came into my office one Sunday and told me it was his first time to
worship with us and that he intended to make our church his church home. He
then handed me a generous check, with the promise that I would receive one just
like it every week. I told him I did not want to receive his checks personally and
suggested that he should give anonymously as the rest of the church family did. If
he had continued to give a large amount every Sunday, there was no good reason for
him to have announced his generosity to me or to anyone else. How much better
for him simply to have put the check in the offering during a service.

Sometimes, of course, the pretense does not show. Knowing that it is wrong
to give ostentatiously and that fellow Christians are likely to resent it, we
sometimes try to make our good works "accidentally" noticed. But even if we only
want people to notice, and do nothing to attract their attention, our heart motive is
to **be honored by men.** The real trumpet blowing, the basic hypocrisy, is always on
the inside, and that is where God judges. Hypocritical righteousness, just as true
righteousness, begins in the heart.

Unfortunately, many Christian organizations use un-Christian methods to
motivate support of their ministries. When framed certificates, published names of
generous supporters, and other such recognitions are offered to stimulate giving,
hypocrisy is promoted in the name of Christ. It is just as wrong to appeal to wrong
motives as to have wrong motives. "It is inevitable that stumbling blocks come,"
Jesus said; "but woe to that man through whom the stumbling block comes!" (Matt.
18:7).

The Practice and Reward of True Giving

**But when you give alms, do not let your left hand know what your right hand
is doing that your alms may be in secret; and your Father who sees in secret
will repay you.** (6:3-4)

To **not let your left hand know what your right hand is doing** was possibly a proverbial expression that simply referred to doing something spontaneously, with no special effort or show. The right hand was considered the primary hand of action, and in a normal day's work the right hand would do many things as a matter of course that would not involve the left hand. Giving to help those in need should be a normal activity of the Christian, and he should do it as simply, directly, and discreetly as possible.

The most satisfying giving, and the giving that God blesses, is that which is done and forgotten. It is done in love out of response to a need, and when the need is met the giver goes on about his business, not waiting for or wanting recognition. What has been done should even be a **secret** to our **left hand**, not to mention to other people. Whether the person we help is grateful or ungrateful should not matter as far as our own purpose is concerned. If he is ungrateful, we are sorry for his sake, not our own.

It is said that there was a special, out-of-the-way place in the Temple where shy, humble Jews could leave their gifts without being noticed. Another place nearby was provided for the shy poor, who did not want to be seen asking for help. Here they would come and take what they needed. The name of the place was the Chamber of the Silent. People gave and people were helped, but no one knew the identities of either group. (Cf. Edersheim, *The Life and Times of Jesus the Messiah,* vol. 2 [Grand Rapids: Eerdmans, 1972], p. 387; Joachim Jeremias, *Jerusalem in the Time of Jesus* [Philadelphia: Fortress, 1969], p. 133; and William Barclay, *The Gospel of Matthew,* 2 vols. [rev. ed.; Philadelphia: Westminster, 1975], 1:171, 188.)

Matthew 6:3 has often been interpreted to mean that all good works are to be done in absolute secrecy. But true righteousness cannot be kept entirely secret, and should not be. "How blessed are those who keep justice, who practice righteousness at all times!" (Ps. 106:3). Isaiah says, "Yet they seek Me day by day, and delight to know My ways, as a nation that has done righteousness, and has not forsaken the ordinance of their God" (Isa. 58:2). John tells us, "If you know that He is righteous, you know that everyone also who practices righteousness is born of Him" (1 John 2:29).

Earlier in the Sermon on the Mount Jesus had specifically commanded, "Let your light shine before men in such a way that they may see your good works, and glorify your Father who is in heaven" (Matt. 5:16). The question is not whether or not our good works should be seen by others, but whether they are done for that end. When they are done "in such a way" that attention and glory are focused on our "Father who is in heaven" rather than on ourselves, God is pleased. But if they are done to be noticed by men (6:1), they are done self-righteously and hypocritically and are rejected by God. The difference is in purpose and motivation. When what we do is done in the right spirit and for the right purpose, it will almost inevitably be done in the right way.

The teachings of Matthew 5:16 and 6:1 are often thought to conflict with each other because it is not recognized that they relate to different sins. The discrepancy is only imaginary. In the first passage Jesus is dealing with cowardice, whereas in the second He is dealing with hypocrisy. A. B. Bruce gives the helpful explanation, "We are to show when tempted to hide and hide when tempted to show."

Never in the history of the church have Christians been so bombarded with appeals to give money, many of them to legitimate and worthwhile causes. Knowing how and where to give is sometimes extremely difficult. Christians are to give regularly and systematically to the work of their local church. "On the first day of every week let each one of you put aside and save, as he may prosper" (1 Cor. 16:2). But we are also called to give directly to those in need when we have opportunity and ability. Both the Old and New Testaments make it clear that willing, generous giving has always characterized the faithful people of God.

God does not need our gifts, because He is entirely sufficient in Himself. The need is on our part and on the part of those we serve in His name. Paul told the Philippian church, "Not that I seek the gift itself, but I seek for the profit which increases to your account" (Phil. 4:17).

Giving is described in the Old Testament as a part of God's cycle of blessing. "The generous man will be prosperous, and he who waters will himself be watered" (Prov. 11:25). As we give, God blesses, and when God blesses us we give again out of what He has given. "You shall celebrate the Feast of Weeks to the Lord your God with a tribute of a freewill offering of your hand, which you shall give just as the Lord your God blesses you" (Deut. 16:10). We are to give freely out of what God has given freely.

The cycle applies not only to material giving but to every form of giving that is done sincerely to honor God and to meet need. The way of God's people has always been the way of giving.

From Scripture we learn of at least seven principles to guide us in nonhypocritical giving. First, giving from the heart is investing with God. "Give, and it will be given to you; good measure, pressed down, shaken together, running over, they will pour into your lap. For by your standard of measure it will be measured to you in return" (Luke 6:38). Paul echoes Jesus' words: "Now this I say, he who sows sparingly shall also reap sparingly; and he who sows bountifully shall also reap bountifully" (2 Cor. 9:6).

Second, genuine giving is to be sacrificial. David refused to give to the Lord that which cost him nothing (2 Sam. 24:24). Generosity is not measured by the size of the gift itself, but by its size in comparison to what is possessed. The widow who gave "two small copper coins" to the Temple treasury gave more than all the "many rich people [who] were putting in large sums" because "they all put in out of their surplus, but she, out of her poverty, put in all she owned, all she had to live on" (Mark 12:41-44).

Third, responsibility for giving has no relationship to how much a person has. A person who is not generous when he is poor will not be generous if he becomes rich. He might then give a larger amount, but he will not give a larger proportion. "He who is faithful in a very little thing is faithful also in much; and he who is unrighteous in a very little thing is unrighteous also in much" (Luke 16:10). It is extremely important to teach children to give generously to the Lord with whatever small amounts of money they get, because the attitudes and patterns they develop as children are likely to be the ones they follow when they are grown. Giving is not a matter of how much money one has but of how much love and care is in the heart.

Fourth, material giving correlates to spiritual blessings. To those who are not faithful with mundane things such as money and other possessions, the Lord will not entrust things that are of far greater value. "If therefore you have not been faithful in the use of unrighteous mammon, who will entrust the true riches to you? And if you have not been faithful in the use of that which is another's, who will give you that which is your own?" (Luke 16:11-12).

Many young men have dropped out of seminary because they could not handle money, and the Lord did not want them in His ministry. Others have begun in the ministry but later dropped out for the same reason. Still others remain in the ministry but produce little fruit because God will not commit the care of eternal souls to them when they cannot even manage their own finances. Spiritual influences and effectiveness have a lot to do with how well finances are handled.

Fifth, giving is to be personally determined. "Let each one do just as he has purposed in his heart; not grudgingly or under compulsion; for God loves a cheerful giver" (2 Cor. 9:7). Righteous giving is done from a righteous and generous heart, not from legalistic percentages or quotas. The Macedonian Christians gave abundantly out of their deep financial poverty because spiritually they were rich in love (2 Cor. 8:1-2). The Philippian believers gave out of the spontaneous generosity of their hearts, not because they felt compelled (Phil. 4:15-18).

Sixth, we are to give in response to need. The early Christians in Jerusalem shared their resources without reservation. Many of their fellow believers had become destitute when they trusted in Christ and were ostracized from their families and lost employment because of their faith. Years later Paul collected money from the Galatian churches to help meet the great needs that continued to exist among the saints in Jerusalem and that had been intensified by famine.

There have always been charlatans who manufacture needs and play on the sympathy of others. And there have always been professional beggars, who are able to work but would rather not. A Christian has no responsibility to support such people and should take reasonable care to determine if and when real need exists before giving his money. "If anyone will not work," Paul says, "neither let him eat" (2 Thess. 3:10). Encouraging indolence weakens the character of the one who is indolent and also wastes the Lord's money. But where real need does exist, our obligation to help meet it also exists.

Seventh, giving demonstrates love, not law. The New Testament contains no commands for specified amounts or percentages of giving. The percentage we give will be determined by the love of our own hearts and the needs of others.

All of the previous principles point to the obligation to give generously because we are investing in God's work, because we are willing to sacrifice for Him who sacrificed Himself for us, because it has no bearing on how much we have, because we want spiritual riches more than financial riches, because we have personally determined to give, because we want to meet as much need as we can, and because our love compels us to give.

As in every area of righteousness, the key is the heart, the inner attitude that motivates what we say and do. Public righteousness is not to be rejected, but it is to be done in the spirit of humility, love, and sincerity. "For we are [God's] workmanship," Paul reminds us, "created in Christ Jesus for good works, which God prepared beforehand, that we should walk in them" (Eph. 2:10).

Also as in every area of righteousness, Jesus Himself is our supreme and perfect example. He preached His messages in public, He performed His miracles of healing, compassion, and power over nature in public. Yet He continually focused attention on His heavenly Father, whose will alone He came to do (John 5:30; cf. 4:34; 6:38). Even though He was one with the Father, while He lived on earth as a man Jesus did not seek His own glory but that of His Father (John 8:49-50).

When we give our **alms . . . in secret**, lovingly, unpretentiously, and with no thought for recognition or appreciation, our **Father who sees in secret will repay** us. The principle is this: if we remember, God will forget; but if we forget, God will remember. Our purpose should be to meet every need we are able to meet and leave the bookkeeping to God, realizing that "we have done only that which we ought to have done" (Luke 17:10).

God will not miss giving a single reward. "There is no creature hidden from His sight, but all things are open and laid bare to the eyes of Him with whom we have to do" (Heb. 4:13). The Lord knows our hearts, our attitudes, and our motives, and every reward that is due us will be given.

It is God's perfect plan and will to give rewards to those who faithfully trust and obey Him. And it is not unspiritual to expect and anticipate those rewards, if we do so in a spirit of humility and gratitude—knowing that God's rewards manifest His grace to the undeserving. We can meet His merciful requirements for rewards, but we can never truly earn them.

The greatest reward a believer can have is the knowledge that he has pleased his Lord. Our motive for looking forward to His rewards should be the anticipation of casting them as an offering at His feet, even as the twenty-four elders one day "will cast their crowns before the throne, saying, 'Worthy art Thou, our Lord and our God, to receive glory and honor and power'" (Rev. 4:10-11).

Praying Without Hypocrisy (6:5-8)

34

And when you pray, you are not to be as the hypocrites; for they love to stand and pray in the synagogues and on the street corners, in order to be seen by men. Truly I say to you, they have their reward in full. But you, when you pray, go into your inner room, and when you have shut your door, pray to your Father who is in secret, and your Father who sees in secret will repay you. And when you are praying, do not use meaningless repetition, as the Gentiles do, for they suppose that they will be heard for their many words. Therefore do not be like them; for your Father knows what you need, before you ask Him. (6:5-8)

None of us can comprehend exactly how prayer functions within the infinite mind and plan of God. The Calvinistic view emphasizes God's sovereignty, and in its extreme application holds that God will work according to His perfect will regardless of the way men pray or even whether they pray or not. Prayer is nothing more than tuning in to God's will. At the opposite extreme, the Arminian view holds that God's actions pertaining to us are determined largely on the basis of our prayers. On the one hand, prayer is seen simply as a way of lining up with God regarding what He has already determined to do, and on the other it is beseeching God to do what He otherwise would not do.

Scripture supports both of those views and holds them, as it were, in tension. The Bible is unequivocal about God's absolute sovereignty. But it is equally unequivocal in declaring that within His sovereignty God calls on His people to beseech Him in prayer—to implore His help in guidance, provision, protection, mercy, forgiveness, and countless other needs.

It is neither required nor possible to fathom the divine working that makes prayer effective. God simply commands us to obey the principles of prayer that His Word gives. Our Lord's teaching in the present passage contains some of those principles.

Jesus continues His contrast of true and false righteousness, in particular the false righteousness typified by the scribes and Pharisees. As 6:2-4 exposes their hypocritical giving and verses 16-18 their hypocritical fasting, verses 5-8 expose their equally hypocritical praying. The prayers were defective in their intended audience and in their content.

THE AUDIENCE OF PRAYER

THE FALSE AUDIENCE: OTHER MEN

And when you pray, you are not to be as the hypocrites; for they love to stand and pray in the synagogues and on the street corners, in order to be seen by men. Truly I say to you, they have their reward in full. (6:5)

No religion has ever had a higher standard and priority for prayer than Judaism. As God's chosen people the Jews were the recipients of His written Word, "entrusted with the oracles of God" (Rom. 3:2). God spoke directly to Abraham and to many of his descendants, and they had spoken directly to Him. No other people, as a race or as a nation, has ever been so favored by God or had such direct communication with Him. Of all people, they should have known how to pray. But they did not. Like every other aspect of their religious life, their praying had been corrupted and perverted by rabbinic tradition. Most Jews were completely confused about how to pray as God wanted.

William Barclay, in a most helpful discussion of this passage in *The Gospel of Matthew* ([Philadelphia: Westminster, 1958], 1:191-98), points out that over the years a number of faults had crept into Jewish prayer life. For one thing, prayer had become ritualized. The wording and forms of prayers were set, and were then simply read or repeated from memory. Such prayers could be given with almost no attention being paid to what was said. They were a routine, semiconscious religious exercise.

A faithful Jew would repeat the Shema early in the morning and again at night. That prayer, which began, "Hear, O Israel, the Lord our God is one Lord," was a composite of selected phrases from Deuteronomy 6:4-9, 11:13-21 and Numbers 15:37-41. Often an abbreviated version (Deut. 6:4 only) was used.

Another formalized prayer Barclay refers to was the Shemonēh 'esray, ("The Eighteen"), which embodied eighteen prayers for various occasions. Faithful Jews prayed all eighteen each morning, afternoon, and evening. It, too, had an abbreviated version.

Both the Shema and the Shemonēh 'esray were to be said every day, regardless of where one might be or what one was doing. Wherever one was— whether at home, in the field, at work, on a journey, in the synagogue, or visiting friends—at the appointed time the devout Jew stopped what he was doing and offered the appropriate prayer. The most common times were at the third, sixth, and ninth hours (9:00 A.M., 12:00 noon, and 3:00 P.M., according to the Palestinian mode of time).

The ritual prayers could be given with three basic attitudes: sincerity, indifference, or pride. Those Jews whose hearts were right used the times of prayer to worship and glorify God. They thought about the words and sincerely believed what they prayed. Others went through the words perfunctorily, mumbling the syllables as fast as possible in order to finish. Others, such as the scribes and Pharisees, recited the prayers meticulously, making sure to enunciate every word and syllable properly. Three times a day they had a ready-made opportunity to parade their piosity.

A second fault that had crept into Jewish prayer life was the development of prescribed prayers for every object and every occasion. There were prayers for light, darkness, fire, rain, the new moon, traveling, good news, bad news, and so on. No doubt the original intent was to bring every aspect of life into the presence of God; but by making the prayers prescribed and formalized that purpose was undermined.

A third fault, already mentioned, was the practice of limiting prayer to specific times and occasions. Prayer was offered when the given time came or situation arose, with no relation to genuine desire or need. As with prescribed wording, prescribed times did not prevent true prayer from being offered. Many faithful Jews like Daniel (Dan. 6:10) used those times as reminders to open their hearts to the Lord. Even in the early church, because most Christians were Jews and still worshiped at the Temple and in the synagogues, the traditional hours of prayer were often observed (see Acts 3:1; cf. 10:3, 30).

A fourth fault was in esteeming long prayers, believing that a prayer's sanctity and effectiveness were in direct proportion to its length. Jesus warned of the scribes who, "for appearance's sake offer long prayers" (Mark 12:40). A long prayer, of course, is not necessarily an insincere prayer. But a long public prayer lends itself to pretense, repetition, rote, and many other such dangers. The fault is in praying "for appearance's sake," to impress others with our religiosity.

Ancient rabbis maintained that the longer the prayer, the more likely it would be heard and heeded by God. Verbosity was confused with meaning, and length was confused with sincerity.

A fifth fault, singled out by Jesus in Matthew 6:7, was that of meaningless repetitions, patterned after those of pagan religions. In their contest with Elijah on

Mt. Carmel, the pagan prophets "called on the name of Baal from morning until noon saying, 'O Baal, answer us,'" and they "raved until the time of the offering of the evening sacrifice" (1 Kings 18:26, 29). Hour after hour they repeated the same phrase, trying by the very quantity of their words to make their god hear and respond.

Through the centuries the Jews had been influenced by such pagan practices. They often added adjective after adjective before God's name in their prayers, apparently trying to outdo one another in mentioning His divine attributes.

By far the worst fault, however, was that of wanting to be seen and heard by other people, especially their fellow Jews. Most of the other faults were not necessarily wrong in themselves, but were carried to extremes and used in meaningless ways. But this fault was intrinsically evil, because it both came from and was intended to satisfy pride. Whatever form the prayer may have taken, the motive was sinful self-glory, the ultimate perversion of this sacred means of glorifying God (John 14:13).

It is that despicable fault that Jesus zeroes in on. **And when you pray, you are not to be as the hypocrites.** Prayer that focuses on self is always hypocritical, because, by definition, the focus of every prayer should be on God. As mentioned in the last chapter, the term *hypocrite* originally referred to actors who used large masks to portray the roles they were playing. **Hypocrites** are actors, pretenders, persons who play a role. What they say and do does not represent what they themselves feel or believe but only the image they hope to create.

The hypocritical scribes and Pharisees prayed for the same purpose they did everything else—to attract attention and bring honor to themselves. That was the essence of their "righteousness," which Jesus said had no part in His kingdom (5:20).

An old commentator observed that the greatest danger to religion is that the old self simply becomes religious. The **hypocrites** of whom Jesus speaks had convinced themselves that by performing certain religious acts, including various types of prayer, they became acceptable to God. People today still deceive themselves into thinking they are Christians, when all they have done is dress their old nature in religious trappings.

Nothing is so sacred that Satan will not invade it. In fact, the more sacred something is, the more he desires to profane it. Surely few things please him more than to come between believers and their Lord in the sacred intimacy of prayer. Sin will follow us into the very presence of God; and no sin is more powerful or destructive than pride. In those moments when we would come before the Lord in worship and purity of heart, we may be tempted to worship ourselves.

Martyn Lloyd-Jones writes,

> We tend to think of sin as we see it in rags and in the gutters of life. We look at a drunkard, poor fellow, and we say, there is sin. But that is not the essence of sin. To have a real picture and a true understanding of sin, you must look at some great

saint, some unusually devout and devoted man, look at him there on his knees in the very presence of God. Even there self is intruding itself, and the temptation is for him to think about himself, to think pleasantly and pleasurably about himself and to really be worshiping himself rather than God. That, not the other, is the true picture of sin. The other is sin, of course, but there you do not see it at its acme, you do not see it in its essence. Or to put it in another form, if you really want to understand something about the nature of Satan and his activities, the thing to do is not to go to the dregs or the gutters of life. If you really want to know something about Satan, go away to that wilderness where our Lord spent forty days and forty nights. That's the true picture of Satan, where you see him tempting the very Son of God. (*Studies in the Sermon on the Mount* [Grand Rapids: Eerdmans, 1977], 2:22-23)

From what we know in the scriptural record, Jesus' two most intense times of spiritual opposition were during His forty days of solitude in the wilderness and during His prayer in the Garden of Gethsemane on the night He was betrayed and arrested. On both occasions He was alone praying to His Father. It was in the most private and holy place of communion that Satan presented his strongest temptations before the Son of God.

The hypocrites loved **to stand and pray.** Standing was a normal position for prayer among the Jews. In the Old Testament we see God's faithful praying while kneeling, while lying prostrate, and while standing. In New Testament times standing was the most common position and did not necessarily indicate a desire to be noticed.

The synagogues were the most appropriate and likely places for public prayers to be offered. It was the place where Jews worshiped most often, especially those who lived great distances from the Temple. The synagogue was the local place of assembly, not only for worship but for various civic and social gatherings. If done sincerely, prayer at any of those functions was appropriate.

The street corners were also a normal place for prayer, because devout Jews would stop wherever they were at the appointed hour for prayer, even if they were walking down the street or visiting at the corner. But the word used here for **street** is not the same as that in verse 2, which refers to a narrow street (*rhumē*). The word used here (*plateia*) refers to a wide, major street, and therefore to a major street corner, where a crowd was most likely to be. The implied fault here is that the **hypocrites** loved to pray where they would have the largest audience. There was nothing wrong with praying at a major intersection if that was where you happened to be at the time for prayer. But something was very much wrong if you planned to be there at prayer time for the specific purpose of praying where the most people could see you.

The real evil of those hypocritical worshipers, whether in **the synagogues** or **on the street corners,** was the desire to display themselves **in order to be seen of men.** It was not wrong to pray in those places, but they happened to afford the largest audiences, and were therefore the places where the hypocrites preferred to pray.

As always, the sin began in the heart. It was pride, the desire to exalt themselves before their fellow Jews, that was the root of the sin. Like the Pharisee in Jesus' parable, those hypocrites ended up praying to themselves (see Luke 18:11) and before other people. God had no part.

Some overly reactionary believers have used these warnings of Jesus as a reason to renounce all public prayer. But the Lord taught no such thing. He Himself often prayed in the presence of His disciples (Luke 11:1) and in public, as when He blessed food before feeding the multitudes (Matt. 14:19). Scripture records many public prayers that were entirely appropriate and sincere. At the dedication of the Temple, Solomon prayed an extended, detailed prayer before all the priests, Levites, and leaders of Israel (2 Chron. 6:1-42; cf. 5:2-7). When, under Ezra's leadership, the covenant was renewed after the Exile, a group of eight Levites offered a heartfelt, moving prayer of repentance before all the people (Neh. 9:5-38). After Peter and John were arrested, questioned, and then released by the Sanhedrin shortly after Pentecost, the whole group of their companions rejoiced and "lifted their voices to God with one accord" (Acts 4:24).

But the public prayers of the typical scribe or Pharisee were ritualistic, mechanical, inordinately long, repetitious, and above all ostentatious. Like the hypocrites who gave for the sake of men's praise (Matt. 6:2), those who prayed for the sake of men's praise also had **their reward in full**. They were concerned only about the reward men could give, and that is all the reward they received.

THE TRUE AUDIENCE: GOD

But you, when you pray, go into your inner room, and when you have shut your door, pray to your Father who is in secret, and your Father who sees in secret will repay you. (6:6)

The basic definition of prayer is "communion with God," and if He is not involved there is only the pretense of prayer. Not only must He be involved, but centrally involved. Prayer is God's provision; it is God's idea, not man's. There could be no prayer if God did not condescend to speak with us, and we could not know how to pray had He not chosen to instruct us.

Jesus' teaching here is simple, in contrast to the complicated and difficult traditions. The phrase **when you pray** implies great latitude. No prescribed time or occasion is given by the Lord. The *tameion* (**inner room**) could be any sort of small room or chamber, even a storage closet. Such rooms were often secret and used to store valued possessions for protection. The idea is that of going to the most private place available.

As already mentioned, Jesus does not forbid or condemn public prayer as such (cf. 1 Tim. 2:1-4). His purpose here seems to have been to make as great a contrast as possible to the practices of the scribes, Pharisees, and other hypocritical religionists. The primary point Jesus makes does not have to do with location but with attitude. If necessary, Jesus says, go to the most secluded, private place you can find so you will not be tempted to show off. Go there and **shut the door**. Shut out everything else so that you can concentrate on God and **pray to your Father**. Do whatever you have to do to get your attention away from yourself and others and on Him and Him alone.

Much of our prayer life should be literally **in secret**. Jesus regularly went away from His disciples to pray entirely alone. Our family members or friends may know that we are praying, but what we say is not meant for them to hear. Chrysostom commented that in his day (the fourth century A.D.) many Christians prayed so loud in their rooms that everyone down the hall heard what they said. If people sometimes happen to overhear our private prayers, it should not be by our intention. (Cf. John A. Broadus, *Matthew* [Valley Forge, Pa.: Judson, 1886], p. 140.)

But the **Father** being **in secret** does not mean He is not present when we pray in public, or with our families or other small groups of believers. He is very much present whenever and wherever His children call on Him. Jesus' point has to do with the singleness of intention. True prayer is always intimate. Even prayer in public, if the heart is right and concentrated on God, will in a real and profound way shut one up alone in the presence of God.

In the pattern of prayer Jesus taught His disciples, He begins with "Our Father" (Matt. 6:9), indicating that other believers may be present and that the prayer is corporate. But even when prayer represents the feelings and needs of others who are present, the supreme attention is to be on God. In that sense, even the most public prayer is **in secret**. Even if the whole world hears what we say, there is an intimacy and focus on God in that communion that is unaffected.

God also **sees in secret** in the sense that He never betrays a confidence. Many things we share with God in our private prayers are for Him alone to know. Confidences we share even with our dearest loved ones or closest friends may sometimes be betrayed. But we can be sure our secrets with God will forever be just that, and that one believer praying **in secret** with a pure heart has the full attention of the **Father**.

Furthermore, when our prayer is as it should be, **our Father who sees in secret will repay** us. The most important **secret** He **sees** is not the words we say in the privacy of our room, but the thoughts we have in the privacy of our heart. Those are the secrets about which He is supremely concerned, and about which only He can know with certainty (cf. 1 Cor. 4:3-5). Those secrets sometimes are hidden even from ourselves, because it is so easy to be deceived about our own motives.

When God is genuinely the audience of our prayer, we will have the reward only He can give. Jesus gives no idea in this passage as to what God's reward, or repayment, will be. The important truth is that God will faithfully and unfailingly bless those who come to Him in sincerity. Without question, the Lord **will repay**. Those who pray insincerely and hypocritically will receive the world's reward, and those who pray sincerely and humbly will receive God's.

THE CONTENT OF PRAYER

A second area in which much prayer of Jesus' day fell short was that of content. The hypocritical prayers of the scribes and Pharisees not only were given in the wrong spirit but were given in meaningless words. They had no substance, no significant content. To be acceptable to God, Jesus declared, prayers must be genuine expressions of worship and of heartfelt requests and petitions.

FALSE CONTENT: MEANINGLESS REPETITION

And when you are praying, do not use meaningless repetition, as the Gentiles do, for they suppose that they will be heard for their many words. (6:7)

The particular fault Jesus singles out here is that of **meaningless repetition**, which has already been discussed. This practice was common in many pagan religions of that day, as it is in many religions today, including some branches of Christendom.

Use meaningless repetition is one word (from *battalogeō*) in the Greek and refers to idle, thoughtless chatter. It was probably onomatopoetic, mimicking the sounds of meaningless jabber.

Those who used repetitious prayers were not necessarily hypocrites, at least not of the ostentatious type. The scribes and Pharisees used a great deal of repetition in their public displays of piety; but many other Jews used it even in private prayers. Some may have used repetition because their leaders had taught them to use it. Others, however, resorted to repetition because it was easy and demanded little concentration. To such people, prayer was simply a matter of required religious ceremony, and they could be entirely indifferent to its content. As long as it was officially approved, one pattern was as good as another.

Although this problem did not always involve hypocrisy, it always involved a wrong attitude, a wrong heart. The proud hypocrites tried to use God to glorify themselves, whereas those who used **meaningless repetition** were simply indifferent to real communion with God.

The Jews had picked up the practice from **the Gentiles**, who believed that the value of prayer was largely a matter of quantity. The longer the better. **They suppose they will be heard for their many words,** Jesus explained. Those who prayed to pagan gods thought their deities first had to be aroused, then cajoled, intimidated, and badgered into listening and answering—just as the prophets of Baal did on Mt. Carmel (1 Kings 18:26-29). In the New Testament we see a similar practice. Aroused against Paul and his companions by Demetrius and other silversmiths of Ephesus, a great crowd began chanting, "Great is Artemis of the Ephesians!" and continued incessantly for two hours (Acts 19:24-34).

Many Buddhists spin wheels containing written prayers, believing that each turn of the wheel sends that prayer to their god. Roman Catholics light prayer candles in the belief that their requests will continue to ascend repetitiously to God as long as the candle is lit. Rosaries are used to count off repeated prayers of Hail Mary and Our Father, the rosary itself coming to Catholicism from Buddhism by way of the Spanish Muslims during the Middle Ages. Certain charismatic groups in our own day repeat the same words or phrases over and over until the speaking degenerates to unintelligible confusion (John A. Broadus, *Matthew* [Valley Forge, Pa.: Judson, 1886], p. 130).

All of us, of course, have been guilty of repeating the same prayers meal after meal and prayer meeting after prayer meeting—with little or no thought of what we are saying or of the One to whom we are supposedly speaking. Prayer that is thoughtless and indifferent is offensive to God, and should also be offensive to us.

Again we must not jump to wrong conclusions. Jesus did not forbid the repetition of genuine requests. In the parable about the midnight visit to his neighbor, the persistent man was praised by Jesus as a model of our persistence before God. In His parable of the importunate widow, Jesus praised her persistence before the ungodly judge, saying, "Now shall not God bring about justice for His elect, who cry to Him day and night, and will He delay long over them?" (Luke 18:2-7). Paul "entreated the Lord three times" that the thorn in his flesh might be removed (2 Cor. 12:7-8). In the Garden of Gethsemane, as He faced the agony of the cross, Jesus cried out, "My Father, if it is possible, let this cup pass from Me; yet not as I will, but as Thou wilt." After rebuking the disciples for their sleep, He prayed the prayer again, and then, after a short while, He "prayed a third time, saying the same thing once more" (Matt. 26:39-44).

It is not honest, properly motivated repetition of needs or praise before God that is wrong, but the mindless, indifferent recital of spiritual-sounding incantations or magical formulas over and over. Not only must our hearts be right before God will hear our prayer, but also our minds. Thoughtless prayer is almost as offensive to God as heartless prayer. In most instances they go together.

TRUE CONTENT: SINCERE REQUESTS

Therefore do not be like them; for your Father knows what you need, before you ask Him. (6:8)

God does not have to be badgered and cajoled. Our **Father knows what** [we] **need, before** [we] **ask Him**. Martin Luther said, "By our praying . . . we are instructing ourselves more than we are him." The purpose of prayer is not to inform or persuade God, but to come before Him sincerely, purposely, consciously, and devotedly (John Stott, *Christian Counter-Culture: The Message of the Sermon on the Mount* [Downers Grove, Ill.: InterVarsity, 1978], p. 145).

Prayer is sharing the needs, burdens, and hunger of our hearts before our heavenly **Father**, who already **knows what** [we] **need** but who wants us to ask Him. He wants to hear us, He wants to commune with us, more than we could ever want to commune with Him—because His love for us is so much greater than our love for Him. Prayer is our giving God the opportunity to manifest His power, majesty, love, and providence (cf. John 14:13).

To pray rightly is to pray with a devout heart and with pure motives. It is to pray with single attention to God rather than to other men. And it is to pray with sincere confidence that our heavenly Father both hears and answers every request made to Him in faith. He always repays our sincere devotion with gracious response. If our request is sincere but not according to His will, He will answer in a way better than we want or expect. But He will always answer.

It is reported that D. L. Moody once felt so surfeited with God's blessings that he prayed, "God, stop." That is what God will do with every faithful believer who comes to Him as an expectant child to his father—smother him in more blessings than can be counted or named.

The Disciples' Prayer
—part 1 (6:9-15)

35

Pray, then, in this way: "Our Father who art in heaven, hallowed be Thy name. Thy kingdom come. Thy will be done, on earth as it is in heaven. Give us this day our daily bread. And forgive us our debts, as we also have forgiven our debtors. And do not lead us into temptation, but deliver us from evil. [For Thine is the kingdom, and the power, and the glory, forever. Amen.]" For if you forgive men for their transgressions, your heavenly Father will also forgive you. But if you do not forgive men, then your Father will not forgive your transgressions. (6:9-15) (For a more detailed study of the Disciples' Prayer, see the author's book *Jesus' Pattern of Prayer* [Chicago: Moody Press, 1981].)

Jesus' earthly ministry was remarkably brief, barely three years long. Yet in those three years, as must have been true in His earlier life, a great amount of time was spent in prayer. The gospels report that Jesus habitually rose early in the morning, often before daybreak, to commune with His Father. In the evening He would frequently go to the Mount of Olives or some other quiet spot to pray, usually alone. Prayer was the spiritual air that Jesus breathed every moment of His life.

Someone has said that many Christians offer their prayers like sailors use their pumps—only when the ship leaks. But to be obedient disciples of Christ, to experience the fullness of communion with God, and to open the floodgates of heaven's blessings, believers must pray as Jesus prayed. In addition to that, we must know *how* to pray. If we do not know how to pray and what to pray for, it does little good to go through the motions. But if we know how to pray, and then pray that way, every other part of our lives will be strengthened and put in proper perspective. As Martyn Lloyd-Jones has beautifully expressed it *Studies in the Sermon on the Mount,* "Man is at his greatest and highest when upon his knees he comes face to face to God" (2 vols. [Grand Rapids: Eerdmans, 1977], 2:45).

The Bible teaches a great deal about the importance and power of prayer. Prayer is effective; it makes a difference. "The effective prayer of a righteous man," James says, "can accomplish much" (James 5:16). Abraham's servant prayed, and Rebekah appeared. Jacob wrestled and prayed, and Esau's mind was turned from twenty years of revenge. Moses prayed, and Amalek was struck. Hannah prayed, and Samuel was born. Isaiah and Hezekiah prayed, and in twelve hours one hundred eighty-five thousand Assyrians were slain. Elijah prayed, and there were three years of drought; he prayed again, and rain came. Those are but a small sampling of answered prayer just from the Old Testament. The Jews to whom Jesus preached should have had unlimited confidence in the power of prayer.

Prayer is vital to every other aspect of kingdom living. We cannot, for example, give (see Matt. 6:2-4) or fast (see 6:16-18) properly unless we are in constant communion with God. The only giving that God wants is that which is sincere, willing, and done to His glory—giving that comes from a life of personal communion with Him. Fasting is meaningless apart from prayer, because apart from prayer it is apart from God. It will be a meaningless religious ritual. The greatest emphasis in this passage (6:1-18), therefore, is given to prayer.

God's Purpose

God's supreme purpose for prayer, the purpose beyond all other purposes, is to glorify Himself. Although nothing benefits a believer more than prayer, the purpose in praying must first of all be for the sake of God, not self. Prayer is, above all, an opportunity for God to manifest His goodness and glory. An old saint said, "True prayer brings the mind to the immediate contemplation of God's character and holds it there until the believer's soul is properly impressed." Jesus affirmed the purpose of prayer when He said, "And whatever you ask in My name, that will I do, that the Father may be glorified" (John 14:13).

Contrary to much emphasis in the evangelical church today, true prayer, like true worship, centers on God's glory, not on man's needs. It is not simply to lay claim on God's promises, much less make demands of Him, but to acknowledge His sovereignty, to see the display of His glory, and to obey His will.

Because prayer is so absolutely important and because we often do not have the wisdom to pray as we ought or for what we ought, God has commissioned His own Holy Spirit to help us. "We do not know how to pray as we should, but the Spirit Himself intercedes for us with groanings too deep for words" (Rom. 8:26).

That is surely what Paul means when he urges believers to "pray at all times in the Spirit" (Eph. 6:18).

In the few words of Matthew 6:9-15 our Lord gives a succinct but marvelously comprehensive outline of what true prayer should be. As we will discuss later, the second part of verse 13, a doxology, was possibly not a part of the original text. The prayer proper has two sections; the first section deals with God's glory (vv. 9-10) and the second with man's need (vv. 11-13*a*). Each section is composed of three petitions. The first three are petitions in behalf of God's name, His kingdom, and His will. The second three are petitions for daily bread, forgiveness, and protection from temptation.

It is significant that Jesus makes no mention of where prayer should take place. As pointed out in the previous chapter, Jesus' instruction to "go into your inner room" (6:6) was to stress the single-mindedness of prayer, the need to block out every other concern but God. Jesus Himself had no inner room to call His own during His earthly ministry, and we see Him praying in many places and in many situations, both public and private. Paul's desire was for believers to pray "in every place" (1 Tim. 2:8).

Nor does Jesus specify a time to pray. Jesus, as well as saints of both the Old and New Testaments, prayed at every hour of the day and night. They can be seen praying at regular, habitual times, on special occasions, when in special danger, when specially blessed, before meals and after meals, when arriving at a destination and when leaving, and in every other conceivable circumstance and for every other conceivable good purpose.

Neither are attire or posture specified. As Jesus had already emphasized (6:5-8), it is the attitude and content of prayer that are of supreme importance, and those two things are central to the pattern He now prescribes.

In any posture, in any attire, at any time, in any place, and under any circumstance prayer is appropriate. Prayer is to be a total way of life, an open and constant communion with God (Eph. 6:18; 1 Thess. 5:17). Because it is to be a way of life, we need to understand how to pray; and that is precisely why Jesus gave His followers this model prayer.

As with all of the Sermon on the Mount, what Jesus says about prayer was not essentially new. The Old Testament, and even Jewish tradition, taught all of the basic principles that Jesus presents here. Many faults and perversions—such as praying to be seen of men and meaningless repetitions (6:5, 7)—had crept into Jewish prayer life. But rabbinic tradition was truer to Scripture in its teaching about prayer than perhaps about anything else. Both the Talmud and the Midrash contain many lofty and helpful teachings about prayer.

From their knowledge of Scripture, Jews rightly believed God wanted them to pray, that He heard and responded to their prayers, and that praying should be continual. From Scripture they also knew that prayer should incorporate certain elements—such as adoration, praise, thanksgiving, a sense of awe at God's holiness, the desire to obey His commands, confession of sin, concern for others, perseverance, and humility.

But something had gone wrong, and by Jesus' day most Jews had forgotten the teachings of Scripture and even the sound, biblical teachings of their tradition. Most prayer had become formalized, mechanical, rote, and hypocritical.

After warning against those perversions that had so corrupted Jewish prayer life, our Lord now gives a divine pattern by which kingdom citizens can pray in a way that is pleasing to God.

That the prayer Jesus is about to give was not meant to be repeated as a prayer itself is clear for several reasons. First, in the present passage it is introduced with the words, **Pray, then, in this way.** In the account in Luke the disciples did not ask Jesus to teach them a prayer but to teach them *how* to pray (Luke 11:1). *Houtōs oun* (**then, in this way**) means literally, "Thus therefore," and frequently carried the idea of "along these lines" or "in the following manner." Second, Jesus had just warned His followers *not* to pray with "meaningless repetition" (v. 7). To then give a prayer whose primary purpose was to be recited verbatim would have been an obvious contradiction of Himself. Third, nowhere in the New Testament— gospels, Acts, or epistles—do we find an instance of that or any other prayer being repeated by anyone or used in a repetitious, ritualistic manner by a group.

The Lord's Prayer, or more accurately, the Disciples' Prayer, is not a set group of words to repeat. It is fine to recite it, as we recite many parts of Scripture. It is certainly fine to memorize it and to rehearse it in our minds and meditate on it in our hearts. But it is not so much a prayer in itself as it is a skeleton which believers are to flesh out with their own words of praise, adoration, petitions, and so on. It is not a substitute for our own prayers but a guide for them.

In fewer than seventy words we find a masterpiece of the infinite mind of God, who alone could compress every conceivable element of true prayer into such a brief and simple form—a form that even a young child can understand but the most mature believer cannot fully comprehend.

Another indication of the prayer's divine comprehensiveness is seen in the seemingly endless schemes by which it can be outlined. When outlined from the perspective of our relationship to God, we see: **Our Father** showing the father/ child relationship; **hallowed be Thy name**, the deity/worshiper; **Thy kingdom come**, the sovereign/subject; **Thy will be done**, the master/servant; **give us this day our daily bread**, the benefactor/beneficiary; **forgive us our debts**, the Savior/ sinner; and **do not lead us into temptation**, the guide/pilgrim.

From the perspective of the attitude and spirit of prayer, **Our** reflects unselfishness; **Father** reflects family devotion; **hallowed be Thy name**, reverence; **Thy kingdom come**, loyalty; **Thy will be done**, submission; **give us this day our daily bread**, dependence; **forgive us our debts**, penitence; **do not lead us into temptation**, humility; **Thine is the kingdom**, triumph; **and the glory**, exultation; and **forever**, hope.

In similar ways the prayer can be outlined to show (1) the balance of God's glory and our need; (2) the threefold purpose of prayer: to hallow God's name, bring in His kingdom, and do His will; and (3) the approach of present (**give us** this day our daily bread), past (**forgive us our debts**), and future (**do not lead us into temptation**).

Those are but a brief sampling of the ways in which Jesus' magnificent diamond of prayer may be cut.

The purpose of prayer is seen more in the overall thrust of these five verses than in any particular word or phrase. From beginning to end the focus is on God, on His adoration, worthiness, and glory. Every aspect of true righteousness, the righteousness that characterizes God's kingdom citizens, focuses on Him. Prayer could hardly be an exception. Prayer is not trying to get God to agree with us or to provide for our selfish desires. Prayer is affirming God's sovereignty, righteousness, and majesty and seeking to conform our desires and our purposes to His will and glory.

Every facet of the Disciples' Prayer focuses on the Almighty. Here Jesus gives a comprehensive view of all the essential elements of righteous prayer, every one of which centers on God—acknowledging His paternity, priority, program, plan, provision, pardon, protection, and preeminence. Each element is overloaded with meaning, its truths being impossible to exhaust.

GOD'S PATERNITY

Our Father who art in heaven. (6:9*b*)

God is **Father** only of those who have come to His family through His Son, Jesus Christ. Malachi wrote, "Do we not all have one father? Has not one God created us?" (Mal. 2:10), and Paul said to the Greek philosophers on Mars Hill, "As even some of your own poets have said, 'For we also are His offspring'" (Acts 17:28). But Scripture makes it unmistakably clear that God's fatherhood of unbelievers is only in the sense of being their Creator. Spiritually, unbelievers have another father. In His severest condemnation of the Jewish leaders who opposed and rejected Him, Jesus said, "You are of your father the devil" (John 8:44). It is only to those who receive Him that Jesus gives "the right to become children of God, even to those who believe in His name" (John 1:12; cf. Rom. 8:14; Gal. 3:26; Heb. 2:11-14; 2 Pet. 1:4; etc.). Because believers belong to the Son, they can come to God as His beloved children.

Faithful Jews had known of God as their Father in several ways. They saw Him as Father of Israel, the nation He chose to be His special people. Isaiah declared, "For Thou art our Father, . . . Thou, O Lord, art our Father" (Isa. 63:16; cf. Ex. 4:22; Jer. 31:9). They also saw Him in an even more intimate and personal way as their spiritual Father and Savior (Ps. 89:26; 103:13).

But over the centuries, because of their disobedience to the Lord and their repeated flirting with the pagan gods of the peoples around them, most Jews had lost the sense of God's intimate fatherhood. They saw God as Father only in a remote, distant, faded figure who had once guided their ancestors.

Jesus reaffirmed to them what their Scripture taught and what faithful, godly Jews had always believed: God is the **Father** . . . **in heaven** of those who trust in Him. He used the title **Father** in all of His prayers except the one on the cross when He cried "My God, My God" (Matt. 27:46), emphasizing the separation He experienced in bearing mankind's sin. Though the text uses the Greek *Patēr,* it is likely that Jesus' used the Aramaic *Abba* when He gave this prayer. Not only was Aramaic the language in which He and most other Palestinian Jews commonly spoke, but *Abba* (equivalent to our "Daddy") carried a more intimate and personal connotation than *Patēr.* In a number of passages the term *Abba* is used even in the Greek text, and is usually simply transliterated in English versions (see Mark 14:36; Rom. 8:15; Gal. 4:6).

To be able to go to God as our heavenly **Father** first of all means the end of fear, the fear that pagans invariably had for their deities. Second, knowledge of God's fatherhood settles uncertainties and gives hope. If an earthly father will spare no effort to help and protect his children, how much more will the heavenly Father love, protect, and help His children (Matt. 7:11; John 10:29; 14:21)?

Third, knowing God as our Father settles the matter of loneliness. Even if we are rejected and forsaken by our family, friends, fellow believers, and the rest of the world, we know that our heavenly Father will never leave us or forsake us. "He who has My commandments and keeps them, he it is who loves Me; and he who loves Me shall be loved by My Father, and I will love him, and will disclose Myself to him" (John 14:21; cf. Ps. 68:5-6).

Fourth, knowing God's fatherhood should settle the matter of selfishness. Jesus taught us to pray, **Our Father**, using the plural pronoun because we are fellow children with all the rest of the household of God. There is no singular personal pronoun in the entire prayer. We pray holding up to God what is best for all, not just for one.

Fifth, knowing God as our Father settles the matter of resources. He is **our Father who** [is] **in heaven**. All the resources of heaven are available to us when we trust God as our heavenly Supplier. Our Father "has blessed us with every spiritual blessing in the heavenly places in Christ" (Eph. 1:3).

Sixth, God's fatherhood should settle the matter of obedience. If Jesus, as God's true Son, came down from heaven not to do His own will but His Father's (John 6:38), how much more are we, as adopted children, to do only His will. Obedience to God is one of the supreme marks of our relationship to Him as His children. "For whoever does the will of My Father who is in heaven, he is My brother and sister and mother" (Matt. 12:50).

Yet in His grace, God loves and cares even for His children who are disobedient. The story of Luke 15 should be called the parable of the loving father rather than the prodigal son. It is first of all a picture of our heavenly Father, who can forgive a self-righteous child who remains moral and upright and also forgive one who becomes dissolute, wanders away, and returns.

Our Father, then, indicates God's eagerness to lend His ear, His power, and

His eternal blessing to the petitions of His children if it serves them best and further reveals His purpose and glory.

GOD'S PRIORITY

hallowed be Thy name. (6:9c)

At the beginning Jesus gives a warning against self-seeking prayer. God is to have priority in every aspect of our lives, and certainly in our times of deepest communion with Him. Praying is not to be a casual routine that gives passing homage to God, but should open up great dimensions of reverence, awe, appreciation, honor, and adoration. This phrase introduces a protection against any sentimentalism or overuse and abuse of **Father**, which is prone to being sentimentalized.

God's **name** signifies infinitely more than His titles or appellations. It represents all that He is—His character, plan, and will. When Moses went up on Mount Sinai to receive the commandments for the second time, he "called upon the name of the Lord. Then the Lord passed by in front of him and proclaimed, 'The Lord, the Lord God, compassionate and gracious, slow to anger, and abounding in lovingkindness and truth; who keeps lovingkindness for thousands, who forgives iniquity, transgression and sin'" (Ex. 34:5-7). The characteristics of God given in verses 6-7 are the equivalent of "the name of the Lord" mentioned in verse 5.

It is not because we simply know God's titles that we love and trust Him, but because we know His character. "Those who know Thy name will put their trust in Thee," David said, "for Thou, O Lord, hast not forsaken those who seek Thee" (Ps. 9:10). God's name is seen in His faithfulness. In another psalm David declared, "I will give thanks to the Lord according to His righteousness, and will sing praise to the name of the Lord Most High" (Ps. 7:17; cf. 113:1-4). In the typical form of Hebrew poetry, God's righteousness and His name are paralleled, showing their equivalence. When the psalmist said, "Some boast in chariots, and some in horses; but we will boast in the name of the Lord, our God" (20:7), he had much more in mind than the title by which God is called. He spoke of the fullness of God's person.

Each of the many Old Testament names and titles of God shows a different facet of His character and will. He is called, for example, *Elohim,* the Creator God; *El Elyon,* "possessor of heaven and earth"; *Jehovah-Jireh,* "the Lord will provide"; *Jehovah-Shalom,* "the Lord our peace"; *Jehovah-Tsidkenu,* "the Lord our righteousness"; and many others. All of those names speak of God's attributes. His names not only tell who He is but what He is like.

But Jesus Himself gives the clearest teaching about what God's name means, because *Jesus Christ* is God's greatest name. "I manifested Thy name to the men whom Thou gavest Me out of the world" (John 17:6). Everything the Son of God did on earth manifested God's name. As the perfect manifestation of God's

377

nature and glory (John 1:14), Jesus was the perfect manifestation of God's name.

Hallowed is an archaic English word used to translate a form of *hagiazō*, which means to make holy. Words from the same root are translated "holy, saint, sanctify, sanctification," etc. God's people are commanded to *be* holy (1 Pet. 1:16), but God is acknowledged as *being* holy. That is the meaning of praying **hallowed be Thy name**: to attribute to God the holiness that already is, and always has been, supremely and uniquely His. To hallow God's name is to revere, honor, glorify, and obey Him as singularly perfect. As John Calvin observed, that God's name should be hallowed was nothing other than to say that God should have His own honor, of which He was so worthy, that men should never think or speak of Him without the greatest veneration (cited in *A Harmony of the Gospels Matthew, Mark, and Luke* [Grand Rapids: Baker, 1979], p. 318).

Hallowing God's name, like every other manifestation of righteousness, begins in the heart. "Sanctify Christ as Lord in your hearts," Peter tells us (1 Pet. 3:15), using a form of the word that **hallowed** translates.

When we sanctify Christ in our hearts we will also sanctify Him in our lives. We hallow His name when we acknowledge that He exists. "He who comes to God must believe that He is, and that He is a rewarder of those who seek Him" (Heb. 11:6). To the honest and open mind, God is self-evident. Immanuel Kant had many strange ideas about God, but he was absolutely right when he said, "The law within us and the starry heavens above us drive us to God." (See William Barclay, *The Gospel of Matthew*, 2 vols. [Philadelphia: Westminster, 1975], 1:208.)

We also hallow God's name by having true knowledge about Him. False ideas about the Sovereign One are irreverent. Origen said, "The man who brings into his concept of God ideas that have no place there takes the name of the Lord God in vain." Discovering and believing truth about God demonstrate reverence for Him; and willing ignorance or wrong doctrine demonstrate irreverence. We cannot revere a God whose character and will we do not know or care about. But acknowledging God's existence and having true knowledge about Him are not enough to hallow His name. We must have a constant awareness of His presence. Spasmodic thinking of God does not hallow His name. To truly hallow His name is to consciously draw Him into every daily thought, every daily word, and every daily action. David put the focus of his life where it should always be—"I have set the Lord continually before me" (Ps. 16:8).

The Father's **name** is most **hallowed** when we behave in conformity to His will. For Christians to live in disobedience to God is to take His name in vain, claiming as Lord someone whom we do not follow as Lord. "Not everyone who says to Me, 'Lord, Lord,'" Jesus warned, "will enter the kingdom of heaven; but he who does the will of My Father who is in heaven" (Matt. 7:21). When we eat, drink, and do everything else to the glory of God (1 Cor. 10:31), that is hallowing His name. Finally, to hallow God's name is to attract others to Him by our commitment, to "let [our] light shine before men in such a way that they may see [our] good works, and glorify [our] Father who is in heaven" (Matt. 5:16). Psalm 34:3 sums up the teaching in this phrase with a lovely exhortation: "O magnify the Lord with me, and let us exalt His name together."

GOD'S PROGRAM

Thy kingdom come. (6:10*a*)

Frances Havergal wrote these beautiful words of tribute to her Lord:

> Oh, the joy to see Thee reigning,
> Thee, my own beloved Lord.
> Every tongue Thy name confessing,
> Worship, honor, glory, blessing,
> Brought to Thee with one accord.
> Thee, my Master and my Friend,
> Vindicated and enthroned,
> Unto earth's remotest end,
> Glorified, adored, and owned.

Our greatest desire should be to see the Lord reigning as King in His **kingdom,** to have the honor and authority that have always been His but that He has not yet come to claim. The King is inseparable from His kingdom. To pray **Thy kingdom come** is to pray for the program of the eternal Deity to be fulfilled, for Christ to come and reign as King of kings and Lord of lords. His program and His plan should be the preoccupation of our lives and of our prayers.

But how self-centered our prayers usually are, focused on our needs, our plans, our aspirations, our understandings. We are often like tiny infants, who know no world but the world of their own feelings and wants. One of the greatest struggles of the Christian life is to fight the old sinful habits, with their constant and unrelenting focus on self.

Even problems and issues outside of ourselves can cloud our supreme concern for God's **kingdom.** It is our responsibility to pray for our families, pastors, missionaries, national and other leaders, and for many other people and things. But our prayers in every case should be that God's will be done in and through those people, that they would think, speak, and act in accordance with God's will. The best we can pray for any person or for any cause is that God's kingdom be advanced in that person or that cause.

The holy purpose of the divine Father is to exalt Christ in the consummation of history when the Son rules and reigns in His **kingdom.** The Jewish Talmud is right in saying, "That prayer in which the kingdom of God is not named, is no prayer" (in John Broadus, *Matthew* [Valley Forge: Judson, 1886], p. 132).

The greatest opposition to Christ's kingdom, and the greatest opposition to

Christian living, is the kingdom of this present world, which Satan rules. The essence of Satan's kingdom is opposition to God's kingdom and God's people.

Basíleia (**kingdom**) does not refer primarily to a geographical territory but to sovereignty and dominion. Therefore when we pray **Thy kingdom come**, we are praying for God's rule through Christ's enthronement to come, His glorious reign on earth to begin. **Come** translates the aorist active imperative of *erchomai*, indicating a sudden, instantaneous coming (cf. Matt. 24:27). It is the coming millennial kingdom (Rev. 20:4) of which the Lord is speaking, not an indirect effort to create a more godly society on earth through the progressive, human-oriented work of Christians.

To pray **Thy kingdom come** is to pray for *God's* kingdom, the kingdom over which He, and He alone, is Lord and King. It will be a kingdom on earth (v. 10*a*), but it will not be a kingdom of this world—that is, of this present world system. "My kingdom is not of this world," Jesus told Pilate (John 18:36). No human kingdom could dovetail with God's kingdom, even partially. Sinful man could not be a part of a divine reign. That is why we do not advance God's kingdom by trying to improve human society. Many good and worthy causes deserve the support of Christians, but in supporting those causes we neither build the earthly kingdom of Jesus Christ or bring it closer. Even the best of such things are but holding actions that help retard the corruption that will always and inevitably characterize human societies and human kingdoms—until the Lord returns to establish His own perfect **kingdom**.

The kingdom of God, or of heaven, was the heart of Jesus' message. He came to "preach the kingdom of God" (Luke 4:43). There is no other gospel but the good news of the kingdom of our Lord and of His Christ. Always and everywhere He went, Jesus preached the message of salvation as entrance to the kingdom. He even stated that He "must preach the kingdom . . . for I was sent for this purpose" (Luke 4:43). For the forty days that Jesus remained on earth between His resurrection and ascension He spoke to His disciples "of the things concerning the kingdom of God" (Acts 1:3).

God's kingdom is past, in the sense that it embodied Abraham, Isaac, and Jacob (Matt. 8:11). It was present in the time of Jesus' earthly ministry, in the sense that the true divine King was present "in the midst of you" (Luke 17:21, lit.). But the particular focus of our praying is to be on the **kingdom** that is yet to **come**.

God now and always has ruled the kingdom of the universe. He created it, and He controls it, orders it, and holds it together. As James Orr comments, "There is therefore recognized in Scripture . . . a natural and universal kingdom or dominion of God embracing all objects, persons, and events, all doings of individuals and nations, all operations and changes of nature and history, absolutely without exception." . . . (cited by Alva J. McClain, *The Greatness of the Kingdom* [Winona Lake, Ind.: BMH Books, 1980], p. 22). God's is an "everlasting kingdom" (Ps. 145:13), and even now "His sovereignty rules over all" (Ps. 103:19; cf. 29:10; 1 Chron. 29:11-12; etc.).

But the most obvious fact of life is that God is not now ruling on earth as He rules in heaven (Matt. 6:10c)—and it is the divine *earthly* kingdom we are to pray will **come**. Our praying should be for Christ to return and to establish His earthly kingdom, to put down sin and enforce obedience to God's will. The Lord will then "rule them with a rod of iron" (Rev. 2:27; cf. Isa. 30:14; Jer. 19:11). After a thousand years His earthly kingdom will blend into His eternal kingdom, and there will be no distinction between His rule on earth and His rule in heaven (see Rev. 20-21).

The Greek of this verse could be translated "Let **Thy kingdom come** now." There is therefore a sense in which we pray for God's kingdom to come presently. In a present and limited, but real and miraculous way, God's kingdom is coming to earth each time a new soul is brought into the kingdom.

First of all, the kingdom comes in this way by conversion (Matt. 18:1-4). So prayer should be evangelistic and missionary—for new converts, new children of God, new kingdom citizens. Conversion to the kingdom involves an invitation (Matt. 22:1-14), repentance (Mark 1:14-15), and a willing response (Mark 12:28-34; Luke 9:61-62). The present existence of the kingdom on earth is internal, in the hearts and minds of those who belong to Jesus Christ, the King. We should pray for their number to mightily increase. Praying for the kingdom to come, in this sense, is praying for the salvation of souls. Every believer should seek others who can sing, "King of my life, I crown Thee now, Thine shall the glory be" ("Lead Me to Calvary," by Jennie Evelyn Hussey).

The **kingdom** for which we are to pray, and of which we now have a taste, is of infinite value. "The kingdom of heaven is like a treasure hidden in the field" or a "pearl of great value" which a person sells all his possessions to buy (Matt. 13:44-46). Its value is so great that each of those parables emphasizes that the procurer sold all he had to purchase salvation (cf. Matt. 10:37).

Second, the kingdom comes now through commitment. The desire of those already converted should be to respond to the rule of the Lord in their lives now so that He rules in them as He rules in heaven. When we pray as Jesus teaches, we will continually pray that our lives will honor and glorify our Father in heaven.

The call for the kingdom to come is also related to the second coming of the Lord. John says in the last chapter of Revelation: "He who testifies to these things says, 'Yes I am coming quickly.' Amen. Come, Lord Jesus" (22:20).

In that day, our prayers will finally be answered. As the hymn by Isaac Watts begins, "Jesus shall reign where 'ere the sun does its successive journeys run. His kingdom spread from shore to shore, 'til moon shall wax and wane no more." Paul emphasizes that waiting for the kingdom to come in its final form is not so much looking for an event as for a person—the King Himself (1 Thess. 1:10).

GOD'S PLAN

Thy will be done, on earth as it is in heaven. (10:b)

Many people wonder how God's sovereignty can be related to praying for

His will to be done. If He is sovereign, is not His will inevitably done? Does our will override His will when we pray earnestly and sincerely? That is one of the great paradoxes of Scripture, a paradox about which Calvinists and Arminians have debated for centuries. It should be evident that this paradox, like those of God's being three in one and Jesus' being wholly God and wholly man, must be left to the infinite mind of God, because it is far beyond the finite human mind to comprehend. But what seems a hopeless contradiction to us is no dilemma to God. We hold both truths, seemingly paradoxical, in perfect tension with faith in the infinite mind of God, who resolves all things in perfect, noncontradictory truth (Deut. 29:29).

It is absolutely clear from Scripture that God is sovereign and yet not only allows but commands that man exercise his own volition in certain areas. If man were not able to make his own choices, God's commands would be futile and meaningless and His punishments cruel and unjust. If God did not act in response to prayer, Jesus' teaching about prayer would also be futile and meaningless. Our responsibility is not to solve the dilemma but to believe and act on God's truths, whether some of them seem to conflict or not. To compromise one of God's truths in an effort to defend another is the stuff of which heresy is made. We are to accept every part of every truth in God's Word, leaving the resolution of any seeming conflicts to Him. Attempting on a human level to resolve all apparent paradoxes in Scripture is an act of arrogance and an attack on the truth and intent of God's revelation.

When we pray **Thy will be done**, we are praying first of all that God's will become our own will. Second, we are praying that His will prevail all over the **earth as it** [does] **in heaven.**

WRONG UNDERSTANDING OF GOD'S WILL

Many people, including many believers, wrongly understand this part of the Disciples' Prayer. Seeing God's sovereignty simply as the absolute imposition of a dictator's will, some believers are resentful. When, or if, they pray for His will to be done, they pray out of a feeling of compulsion. God's will has to be done, and He is too strong to resist; so what would be the point of praying otherwise? The logical conclusion of most people who look at God in that way is that there is no point to prayer—certainly not to petitions. Why ask for the inevitable?

Other people are more charitable in their feelings about God. But because they, too, believe His will is inevitable, they pray out of passive resignation. They pray for God's will to be done simply because that is what the Lord tells them to do. They are resignedly obedient. They do not pray so much out of faith as out of capitulation. They do not try to put their wills into accord with the divine will, but rather shift their own wills into neutral, letting God's will run its course.

It is easy for Christians to fall into praying that way. Even in the very early days of the church, when faith generally was strong and vital, prayer could be passive and unexpectant. A group of concerned disciples was praying in the house of Mary, John Mark's mother, for the release of Peter from prison. While they were praying, Peter was freed by an angel and came to the house and knocked on the door. When a servant girl named Rhoda came to the door and recognized Peter's voice, she rushed back inside to tell the others, forgetting to let Peter in. But the praying group did not believe her, and thought she had heard an angel. When Peter was finally admitted, "they saw him and were amazed" (Acts 12:16). They apparently had been praying for what they did not really believe would happen.

Our own prayer lives often are weak because we do not pray in faith; we do not expect prayer to change anything. We pray out of a sense of duty and obligation, subconsciously thinking that God is going to do just as He wants to do anyway. Jesus gave the parable of the importunate widow—who refused to accept the status quo and persisted in begging, despite receiving no response—for the very purpose of protecting us against that sort of passive and unspiritual resignation. "Now He was telling them a parable to show that at all times they ought to pray and not to lose heart" (Luke 18:1).

The very fact that Jesus tells us to pray **Thy will be done on earth** indicates that God's will is *not* always done on earth. It is not inevitable. In fact, lack of faithful prayer inhibits His will being done. In God's wise and gracious plan, prayer is essential to the proper working of His divine will on earth.

God is sovereign, but He is not independently deterministic. Looking at God's sovereignty in a fatalistic way, thinking "What will be will be," absolutely destroys faithful prayer and faithful obedience of every sort. That is not a "high" view of God's sovereignty, but a destructive and unbiblical view of it. That is not the divine sovereignty the Bible teaches. It is not God's **will** that people die, or why would Christ have come to destroy death? It is not God's **will** that people go to hell, or why would His only Son have taken the penalty of sin upon Himself so that men might escape hell? "The Lord is not slow about His promise, as some count slowness, but is patient toward you, not wishing for any to perish but for all to come to repentance" (2 Pet. 3:9). That sin exists on earth and causes such horrible consequences is not evidence of God's will but of His patience in allowing more opportunity for men to turn to Him for salvation.

Other people, overemphasizing the importance of man's will, look at prayer as a means of bending God's will to their own. They think of God's providence as a sort of cosmic vending machine, which they can operate simply by inserting the required claim on one of His promises. As Elton Trueblood observes, "In some congregations the Gospel has been diminished to the mere art of self-fulfillment. Some current religious authors, far from emphasizing what it means to believe that God was in Christ reconciling the world unto Himself, write chiefly of themselves. Egocentricity is all that is left when the objective truth about the revelation of Christ is lost or even obscured."

But Jesus undercuts that notion throughout His model prayer. True prayer focuses on **Thy** name, **Thy** kingdom, **Thy** will. Amy Carmichael wrote, "And shall I pray to change Thy will, my Father, until it accord to mine? But no, Lord, no; that shall never be. Rather I pray Thee blend my human will with Thine."

There is a tension between God's sovereignty and man's will, between God's grace and man's faith, but we dare not try to resolve it by modifying God's truth about either His sovereignty or our will, His grace or our faith. God is sovereign, but He gives us choices. God is sovereign, but He tells us to pray **Thy will be done on earth as it is in heaven.** And James reminds us that "the effective prayer of a righteous man can accomplish much" (5:16).

RIGHT UNDERSTANDING OF GOD'S WILL

David sang of the angels who did God's will. "Bless the Lord, you His angels, mighty in strength, who perform His word, obeying the voice of His word!" (Ps. 103:20). That is the way God's **will** is done **in heaven,** and that is the way believers are to pray for God's **will** to **be done on earth**—unwaveringly, completely, sincerely, willingly, fervently, readily, swiftly, and constantly. Our prayer should be that every person and thing on earth be brought into conformity with God's perfect will.

A part of the right understanding of and attitude toward God's will is what might be called a sense of righteous rebellion. To be dedicated to God's will is, by definition, to be opposed to Satan's. To pray **Thy will be done, on earth as it is heaven** is to rebel against the worldly idea that sin is normal and inevitable and should therefore be acquiesced to or at least tolerated. It is to rebel against the world system of ungodliness, the dishonoring and rejecting of Christ, and also the disobedience of believers. Impotence in prayer leads us, however unwillingly, to strike a truce with wrong. To accept what is, is to abandon a Christian view of God and His plan for redemptive history.

Jesus knew the end from the beginning, but He did not accept the situation as inevitable or irresistible. He preached against sin and He acted against sin. When His Father's house was profaned, "He made a scourge of cords, and drove them all out of the temple, with the sheep and the oxen; and He poured out the coins of the moneychangers, and overturned their tables; and to those who were selling the doves He said, 'Take these things away; stop making My Father's house a house of merchandise'" (John 2:14-16; cf. Matt. 21:12-13).

To pray for God's will to be done on earth is to rebel against the idea, heard today even among evangelicals, that virtually every wicked, corrupt thing that we do or that is done to us is somehow God's holy will and should be accepted from His hand with thanksgiving. Nothing wicked or sinful comes from the hand of God, but only from the hand of Satan. To pray for righteousness is to pray against wickedness. To pray for God's will to be done is to pray for Satan's will to be undone.

To pray for God's will to be done is to cry with David, "Let God arise, let His enemies be scattered; and let those who hate Him flee before Him" (Ps. 68:1) and with the saints under God's altar, "How long, O Lord, holy and true, wilt Thou refrain from judging and avenging our blood on those who dwell on the earth?" (Rev. 6:10).

To pray rightly is to pray in faith, believing that God will hear and answer our prayers. I think the greatest hindrance to prayer is not lack of technique, lack of biblical knowledge, or even lack of enthusiasm for the Lord's work, but lack of faith. We simply do not pray with the expectation that our prayers will make a difference in our lives, in other people's lives, in the church, or in the world.

There are three distinct aspects of God's will as He reveals it to us in His Word. First, is what may be called His will of purpose—the vast, comprehensive, and tolerating will of God expressed in the unfolding of His sovereign plan that embodies all of the universe, including heaven, hell, and the earth. This is God's ultimate will, of which Isaiah wrote, "The Lord of hosts has sworn saying 'Surely, just as I have intended so it has happened, and just as I have planned so it will stand'" (Isa. 14:24; cf. Jer. 51:29; Rom. 8:28; Eph. 1:9-11; etc.). This is the will of God that allows sin to run its course and Satan to have his way for a season. But in God's appointed time sin's course and Satan's way will end exactly according to God's plan and foreknowledge.

Second, is what may be called God's will of desire. This is within His will of purpose and completely consistent with it. But it is more specific and focused. Unlike God's will of purpose, His will of desire is not always fulfilled; in fact, it is very unfulfilled in comparison to Satan's will in this present age.

Jesus greatly desired that Jerusalem be saved, and He prayed, preached, healed, and ministered among its people to that end. But few believed in Him; most rejected Him, and some even crucified Him. "O Jerusalem, Jerusalem," He prayed. "I wanted to gather your children together, just as a hen gathers her brood under her wings, and you would not have it!" (Luke 13:34). That was the repeated experience of God's Son, who came to earth that men might have life, and have it more abundantly. Like the unbelieving Jews in Jerusalem, most people were not willing to come to Jesus for that abundant life (John 5:40; cf. 1 Tim. 2:4; 2 Pet. 3:9).

Third, is what may be called God's will of command. This will is entirely for His children, because only they have the capacity to obey. The will of command is the ardent desire of the heart of God that we who are His children obey Him completely and immediately with a willing heart. "Do you not know," Paul says, "that when you present yourselves to someone as slaves for obedience, you are slaves of the one whom you obey, either of sin resulting in death, or of obedience resulting in righteousness? But thanks be to God that though you were slaves of sin, you became obedient from the heart to that form of teaching to which you were committed, and having been freed from sin, you became slaves of righteousness" (Rom. 6:16-18).

God's will of purpose embraces the ultimate end of this world, Christ's second coming and the setting up of His eternal kingdom. His will of desire embraces conversion; and His will of command embraces the commitment and obedience of His children.

The great enemy of God's will is pride. Pride caused Satan to rebel against God, and pride causes unbelievers to reject God and believers to disobey Him. For God's will to be accepted and to be prayed for in sincerity and with faith, self-will must be forsaken in the power of the Holy Spirit. "I urge you therefore, brethren, by the mercies of God, to present your bodies a living and holy sacrifice, acceptable to God, which is your spiritual service of worship. And do not be conformed to this world, but be transformed by the renewing of your mind, that you may prove what the will of God is, that which is good and acceptable and perfect" (Rom. 12:1-2).

When we pray in faith and in conformity to God's will, our prayer is a sanctifying grace that changes our lives dramatically. Prayer is a means of progressive sanctification. John Hannah said, "The end of prayer is not so much tangible answers as a deepening life of dependency. . . . The call to prayer is a call to love, submission, and obedience, . . . the avenue of sweet, intimate, and intense fellowship of the soul with the infinite Creator."

The believer's call is to bring heaven to earth by hallowing the Lord's name, letting His kingdom come, and seeking to do His will.

In verses 11-13a Jesus gives three petitions. The first relates to our physical life and the present (**daily bread**), the second to our mental and emotional life and the past (**debts**), and the third to our spiritual life and the future (**temptation** and **evil**).

The Disciples' Prayer —part 2 (6:9-15)

36

Pray, then, in this way: "Our Father who art in heaven, hallowed be Thy name. Thy kingdom come. Thy will be done, on earth as it is in heaven. Give us this day our daily bread. And forgive us our debts, as we also have forgiven our debtors. And do not lead us into temptation, but deliver us from evil. [For Thine is the kingdom, and the power, and the glory, forever. Amen.]" For if you forgive men for their transgressions, your heavenly Father will also forgive you. But if you do not forgive men, then your Father will not forgive your transgressions. (6:9-15)

God's Provision

Give us this day our daily bread. (6:11)

Although it may have been a genuine concern in New Testament times, to many Christians in the western world today, such a request may seem needless and inappropriate. Why should we ask God for what we already have in such abundance? Why, when many of us need to consume less food than we do, ask God to supply our **daily bread**? What would be a completely understandable request of a Christian in Ethiopia or Cambodia, seems irrelevant on the lips of a well-fed American.

But this part of the Disciples' Prayer, like every other part, extends beyond the first century to all believers, in every age and in every situation. In this pattern for prayer our Lord gives all the necessary ingredients for praying. We can see five key elements in this request for God's provision: the substance, the source, the supplication, the seekers, and the schedule.

THE SUBSTANCE

Bread not only represents food but is symbolic of all of our physical needs. John Stott has observed that to Martin Luther, "everything necessary for the preservation of this life is bread, including food, a healthy body, good weather, house, home, wife, children, good government, and peace" (*Christian Counter-Culture: The Message of the Sermon on the Mount* [Downers Grove, Ill.: InterVarsity, 1978], p. 149).

It is marvelous to understand that the God who created the entire universe, who is the God of all space and time and eternity, who is infinitely holy and completely self-sufficient, should care about supplying our physical needs—and should be concerned that we receive enough food to eat, clothes to wear, and a place to rest. God obligates Himself to supply our needs.

This part of the prayer is in the form of a petition, but it is also an affirmation—which is why it is as appropriate for those who are well-fed as for those who have little to eat. Above all it is an affirmation that every good thing we have comes from the gracious hand of God (James 1:17).

THE SOURCE

That leads us to the source, who is God. The **Father** is the one addressed throughout the prayer, the One who is praised and petitioned.

When all our needs are met and all is going well in our lives, we are inclined to think we are carrying our own load. We earn our own money, buy our own food and clothes, pay for our own houses. Yet even the hardest-working person owes all that he earns to God's provision (see Deut. 8:18). Our life, breath, health, possessions, talents, and opportunities all originate from resources that God has created and made available to man (see Acts 17:24-28). After scientists have made all their observations and calculations, there remains the unexplained element of the design, origin, and operation of the universe. It is unexplained, that is, apart from God, who holds it all together (Heb. 1:2-3).

God provided for man even before He created man. Man was God's final creation, and after He made and blessed Adam and Eve He said, "Behold, I have given you every plant yielding seed that is on the surface of all the earth, and every tree which has fruit yielding seed; it shall be food for you" (Gen. 1:29). Since that time God has continued to provide an abundance of food for mankind, in almost unlimited variety.

Yet Paul tells us that "the Spirit explicitly says that in later times some will fall away from the faith, . . . and advocate abstaining from foods, which God has created to be gratefully shared in by those who believe and know the truth. For everything created by God is good, and nothing is to be rejected, if it is received with gratitude; for it is sanctified by means of the word of God and prayer" (1 Tim. 4:1, 3-5). The Word of God sanctifies it by way of creation, and we sanctify it when we receive it with grateful prayer.

Every physical thing we have comes from God's provision through the earth. It is therefore the sin of indifference and ingratitude not to daily recognize His gifts in thankful prayer.

SUPPLICATION

Supplication is expressed in the word **give**. That is the heart of the petition, because it recognizes need. Even though God may already have provided it, we ask Him for it in recognition of His past and present provision as well as in trust for His future provision.

The only thing that could make Jesus' instruction and our petitions valid is the promise of God. We could not expect God to give what He has not promised. We can pray confidently because God has promised abundantly. "Trust in the Lord, and do good," David counsels us; "dwell in the land and cultivate faithfulness. Delight yourself in the Lord; and He will give you the desires of your heart. . . . Yet a little while and the wicked man will be no more; . . . But the humble will inherit the land, and will delight themselves in abundant prosperity" (Ps. 37:3-4, 10-11).

God does not bind Himself to meet the physical needs of everyone, but only of those who trust in Him. In Psalm 37 David is speaking to believers who "trust in the Lord" (v. 3), "delight . . . in the Lord" (v. 4), "commit [their] way to the Lord" (v. 5), "rest in the Lord and wait patiently for Him" (v. 7), "cease from anger," and "do not fret" (v. 8). He says, "I have been young, and now I am old; yet I have not seen the righteous forsaken, or his descendants begging bread" (v. 25).

THE SEEKERS

The **us** of Jesus' model prayer are those who belong to Him. Speaking to believers, Paul wrote, "Now He who supplies seed to the sower and bread for food, will supply and multiply your seed for sowing and increase the harvest of your righteousness; you will be enriched in everything for all liberality, which through us is producing thanksgiving to God" (2 Cor. 9:10-11).

Jesus said, "Truly I say to you, there is no one who has left house or wife or brothers or parents or children, for the sake of the kingdom of God, who shall not receive many times as much at this time and in the age to come, eternal life" (Luke

18:29-30). God irrevocably commits Himself to meet the essential needs of His own.

The greatest cause of famine and its attendant diseases in the world is not poor agricultural practices or poor economic and political policies. Nor is the root problem lack of scientific and technological resources or even overpopulation. Those problems only aggravate the basic problem, which is spiritual. Only some fifteen percent of the arable land in the world is used for agriculture, and that for only half of the year. There is no major area of the world that with proper technology is not capable of supporting its own population and more.

Those parts of the world that have no Christian roots or heritage invariably place a low value on human life. The great poverty and starvation in India, for example, may be laid at the feet of Hinduism, the pagan religion that spawned a host of other religions—Shintoism, Buddhism, Zoroastrianism, Confucianism, Taoism, and various subcults. Those religious systems spiritually enslave the eastern world—and are rapidly spreading their influence in the west.

To the Hindu, man is but the incarnation of a soul on its way to *moksha,* a kind of "final emancipation," during which trip he goes through countless, perhaps unending, cycles of reincarnation in both animal and human form. He works his way up to higher forms by good deeds and regresses to lower forms by sinning. Poverty, disease, and starvation are therefore seen as divine punishments for which the persons involved must do penance in order to be born into a higher form. To help a person in poverty or sickness is to interfere with his karma and therefore do him spiritual harm. (For a discussion of *moksha,* or *mokṣa,* see *Encyclopedia Britannica,* Micropaedia, VI, p. 972; for a more general discussion, see *Encyclopaedia Britannica,* Macropaedia, vol. 8, pp. 888-908. Consult, also, *Eerdman's Handbook to World Religions* [Grand Rapids: Eerdmans, 1982].)

All animals are considered to be incarnations either of men or deities. Cows are held to be especially sacred because they are incarnated deities—of which Hinduism has some 330 million. Cows not only are not to be eaten but add to the food problem by consuming 20 percent of India's total food supply. Even rats and mice, which eat 15 percent of the food supply, are not killed because they might be one's reincarnated relatives.

Just as paganism is the great plague of India, Africa, and many other parts of the world, Christianity has been the blessing of the West. Europe and the United States, though never fully Christian in any biblical sense, have been immeasurably blessed because of the Christian influence on political, social, and economic philosophy and policy. The great concerns for human rights, care for the poor, orphanages, hospitals, prison reform, racial and slave reform, and a host of other concerns did not come from paganism or humanism but from biblical Christianity. On the other hand, the current degraded view of human life reflected in the low view of the family and growing legal and social approval of abortion, infanticide, and euthanasia are the legacy of humanism and practical atheism.

Without a proper view of God there cannot be a proper view of man. Those who have a right view of God and also a right relationship to Him through Jesus

Christ are promised the provision of their heavenly Father. "For this reason," Jesus says, "I say to you, do not be anxious for your life, as to what you shall eat, or what you shall drink; nor for your body, as to what you shall put on. Is not life more than food, and the body than clothing? . . . For all these things the Gentiles eagerly seek; for your heavenly Father knows that you need all these things. But seek first His kingdom and His righteousness; and all these things shall be added to you" (Matt. 6:25, 32-33).

God has sometimes provided for His children through miraculous means, but His primary way of provision is through work, for which He has given life, energy, resources, and opportunity. His primary way to care for those who cannot work is through the generosity of those who are able to work. Whether he does so directly or indirectly, God is always the source of our physical well-being. He makes the earth to produce what we need, and He gives us the ability to procure it.

THE SCHEDULE

The schedule of God's provision for His children is **daily**. The meaning here is simply that of regular, day-by-day supply of our needs. We are to rely on the Lord one day at a time. He may give us vision for work He calls us to do in the future, but His provision for our needs is **daily**, not weekly, monthly, or yearly. To accept the Lord's provision for the present day, without concern for our needs or welfare tomorrow, is a testimony of our contentment in His goodness and faithfulness.

GOD'S PARDON

And forgive us our debts, as we also have forgiven our debtors. (6:12)

Opheilēma (**debts**) is one of five New Testament Greek terms for sin. *Hamartia* is the most common and carries the root idea of missing the mark. Sin misses the mark of God's standard of righteousness. *Paraptōma*, often rendered "trespass," is the sin of slipping or falling, and results more from carelessness than from intentional disobedience. *Parabasis* refers to stepping across the line, going beyond the limits prescribed by God, and is often translated "transgression." This sin is more conscious and intentional than *hamartia* and *paraptōma*. *Anomia* means lawlessness, and is a still more intentional and flagrant sin. It is direct and open rebellion against God and His ways.

The noun *opheilēma* is used only a few times in the New Testament, but its verb form is found often. Of the some thirty times it is used in its verb form, twenty-five times it refers to moral or spiritual debts. Sin is a moral and spiritual debt to God that must be paid. In his account of this prayer, Luke uses *hamartia* ("sins"; Luke 11:4), clearly indicating that the reference is to sin, not to a financial debt. Matthew probably used **debts** because it corresponded to the most common

Aramaic term (ḥôbāʾ) for sin used by Jews of that day, which also represented moral or spiritual debt to God.

THE PROBLEM

Sin is that which separates man from God, and is therefore man's greatest enemy and greatest problem. Sin dominates the mind and heart of man. It has contaminated every human being and is the degenerative power that makes man susceptible to disease, illness, and every conceivable form of evil and unhappiness, temporal and eternal. The ultimate effects of sin are death and damnation, and the present effects are misery, dissatisfaction, and guilt. Sin is the common denominator of every crime, every theft, lie, murder, immorality, sickness, pain, and sorrow of mankind. It is also the moral and spiritual disease for which man has no cure. "Can the Ethiopian change his skin or the leopard his spots? Then you also can do good who are accustomed to do evil" (Jer. 13:23). The natural man does not *want* his sin cured, because he loves darkness rather than light (John 3:19).

Those who trust in the Lord Jesus Christ have received God's pardon for sin and are saved from eternal hell. And since, as we have seen, this prayer is given to believers, the **debts** referred to here are those incurred by Christians when they sin. Immeasurably more important than our need for daily bread is our need for continual forgiveness of sin.

Arthur Pink writes in *An Exposition of the Sermon on the Mount* (Grand Rapids: Baker, 1974), pp. 163-64:

> As it is contrary to the holiness of God, sin is a defilement, a dishonor, and a reproach to us as it is a violation of His law. It is a crime, and as to the guilt which we contact thereby, it is a debt. As creatures we owe a debt of obedience unto our maker and governor, and through failure to render the same on account of our rank disobedience, we have incurred a debt of punishment; and it is for this that we implore a divine pardon.

THE PROVISION

Because man's greatest problem is sin, his greatest need is forgiveness— and that is what God provides. Though we have been forgiven the ultimate penalty of sin, as Christians we need God's constant forgiveness for the sins we continue to commit. We are to pray, therefore, **forgive us**. Forgiveness is the central theme of this entire passage (vv. 9-15), being mentioned six times in eight verses. Everything leads to or issues from forgiveness.

Believers have experienced once-for-all God's judicial forgiveness, which they received the moment Christ was trusted as Savior. We are no longer condemned, no longer under judgment, no longer destined for hell (Rom. 8:1). The eternal Judge has declared us pardoned, justified, righteous. No one, human or satanic, can condemn or bring any "charge against God's elect" (Rom. 8:33-34).

But because we still fall into sin, we frequently require God's gracious forgiveness, His forgiveness not now as Judge but as Father. "If we say that we have no sin, we are deceiving ourselves, and the truth is not in us," John warns believers. But, he goes on to assure us, "If we confess our sins, He is faithful and righteous to forgive us our sins and to cleanse us from all unrighteousness" (1 John 1:8-9).

During the Last Supper, Jesus began washing the disciples' feet as a demonstration of the humble, serving spirit they should have as His followers. At first Peter refused, but when Jesus said, "If I do not wash you, you have no part with Me," Peter went to the other extreme, wanting to be bathed all over. Jesus replied, "'He who has bathed needs only to wash his feet, but is completely clean; and you are clean, but not all of you.' For He knew the one who was betraying Him; for this reason He said, 'Not all of you are clean'" (John 13:5-11).

Jesus' act of footwashing was therefore more than an example of humility; it was also a picture of the forgiveness God gives in His repeated cleansing of those who are already saved. Dirt on the feet symbolizes the daily surface contamination from sin that we experience as we walk through life. It does not, and cannot, make us entirely dirty, because we have been permanently cleansed from that. The positional purging of salvation that occurs at regeneration needs no repetition, but the practical purging is needed every day, because every day we fall short of God's perfect holiness.

As Judge, God is eager to forgive sinners, and as Father He is even more eager to keep on forgiving His children. Hundreds of years before Christ, Nehemiah wrote, "Thou art a God of forgiveness, gracious and compassionate, slow to anger, and abounding in lovingkindness" (Neh. 9:17). As vast and pervasive as the sin of man is, God forgiveness is more vast and greater. Where sin abounds, God's grace abounds even more (Rom. 5:20).

THE PLEA

Asking forgiveness implies confession. Feet that are not presented to Christ cannot be washed by Him. Sin that is not confessed cannot be forgiven. That is the condition John makes plain in the text just quoted above: "If we confess our sins, He is faithful and righteous to forgive us our sins and to cleanse us from all unrighteousness" (1 John 1:9). To confess means basically to agree with, and when we confess our sins we agree with God about them that they are wicked, evil, defiling, and have no part in those who belong to Him.

It is difficult to confess sins, and both Satan and our prideful nature fight against it. But it is the only way to the free and joyful life. "He who conceals his transgressions will not prosper, but he who confesses and forsakes them will find compassion" (Prov. 28:13). John Stott says, "One of the surest antidotes to the process of moral hardening is the disciplined practice of uncovering our sins of thought and outlook as well as word and deed and the repentant forsaking of the same" (*Confess Your Sins* [Waco, Tex.: Word, 1974], p. 19).

The true Christian does not see God's promise of forgiveness as a license to sin, a way to abuse His love and presume on His grace. Rather he sees God's gracious forgiveness as the means of spiritual growth and sanctification, and continually gives thanks to God for His great love and willingness to forgive and forgive and forgive. It is also important to realize that confessing sin gives God the glory when He chastens the disobedient Christian, because it removes any complaint that God is unfair when He disciplines (this is illustrated in Josh. 7:19-26), by admitting that the sinner deserves what God gives.

A Puritan saint of many generations ago prayed, "Grant me never to lose sight of the exceeding sinfulness of sin, the exceeding righteousness of salvation, the exceeding glory of Christ, the exceeding beauty of holiness, and the exceeding wonder of grace. I am guilty but pardoned. I am lost but saved. I am wandering but found. I am sinning but cleansed. Give me perpetual broken-heartedness. Keep me always clinging to Thy cross" (Arthur Bennett, *The Valley of Vision*).

THE PREREQUISITE

Jesus gives the prerequisite for receiving forgiveness in the words, **as we also have forgiven our debtors.** The principle is simple but sobering: if we have forgiven, we will be forgiven; if we have not forgiven, we will not be forgiven.

We are to forgive because it is the character of righteousness, and therefore of the faithful Christian life, to forgive. Citizens of God's kingdom are blessed and receive mercy because they themselves are merciful (Matt. 5:7). They love even their enemies because they have the nature of the loving heavenly Father within them (5:44-45, 48). Forgiveness is the mark of a truly regenerate heart. Still we fail to be consistent with that mark and need constant exhortation because of the strength of sinful flesh (Rom. 7:14-25).

We are also to be motivated to forgive because of Christ's example. "Be kind to one another," Paul says, "tender-hearted, forgiving each other, just as God in Christ also has forgiven you" (Eph. 4:32). John tells us, "The one who says he abides in Him ought himself to walk in the same manner as He walked" (1 John 2:6).

Because it reflects God's own gracious forgiveness, the forgiving of another person's sin expresses the highest virtue of man. "A man's discretion makes him slow to anger, and it is his glory to overlook a transgression" (Prov. 19:11).

Forgiving others also frees the conscience of guilt. Unforgiveness not only stands as a barrier to God's forgiveness but also interferes with peace of mind, happiness, satisfaction, and even the proper functioning of the body.

Forgiving others is of great benefit to the whole congregation of believers. Probably few things have so short-circuited the power of the church as unresolved conflicts among its members. "If I regard wickedness in my heart," the psalmist warns himself and every believer, "the Lord will not hear" (Ps. 66:18). The Holy Spirit cannot work freely among those who carry grudges and harbor resentment (see Matt. 5:23-24; 1 Cor. 1:10-13; 3:1-9).

Forgiving others also delivers us from God's discipline. Where there is an unforgiving spirit, there is sin; and where there is sin, there will be chastening

(Heb. 12:5-13). Unrepented sins in the church at Corinth caused many believers to be weak, sick, and even to die (1 Cor. 11:30).

But the most important reason for being forgiving is that it brings God's forgiveness to the believer. That truth is so important that Jesus reinforces it after the close of the prayer (vv. 14-15). Nothing in the Christian life is more important than forgiveness—our forgiveness of others and God's forgiveness of us.

In the matter of forgiveness, God deals with us as we deal with others. We are to forgive others as freely and graciously as God forgives us. The Puritan writer Thomas Manton said, "There is none so tender to others as they which have received mercy themselves, for they know how gently God hath dealt with them."

GOD'S PROTECTION

And do not lead us into temptation, but deliver us from evil. (6:13*a*)

Peirasmos (**temptation**) is basically a neutral word in the Greek, having no necessary connotation either of good or evil, as does our English *temptation,* which refers to inducement to evil. The root meaning has to do with a testing or proving, and from that meaning are derived the related meanings of trial and temptation. Here it seems to parallel the term **evil**, indicating that it has in view enticement to sin.

God's holiness and goodness will not allow His leading anyone, certainly not one of His children, into a place or experience in which they would purposely be induced to commit sin. "Let no one say when he is tempted," says James, "'I am being tempted by God'; for God cannot be tempted by evil, and He Himself does not tempt anyone" (James 1:13).

Yet James had just said, "Consider it all joy, my brethren, when you encounter various trials (*peirasmos*), knowing that the testing of your faith produces endurance" (vv. 2-3). There is an interpretive problem, therefore, as to whether *peirasmos* in Matthew 6:13 is translated temptation or trial. As James tells us, God does not tempt. So why ask Him not to do what He would never do anyway? Yet James also tells us we should rejoice when trials come and not seek to avoid them. So why should we pray, **do not lead us into temptation**?

I affirm with Chrysostom, the early church Father, that the solution to this issue is that Jesus is here not speaking of logic or theology but of a heart desire and inclination that cause a believer to want to avoid the danger and trouble sin creates. It is the expression of the redeemed soul that so despises and fears sin that it wants to escape all prospects of falling into it, choosing to avoid rather than having to defeat temptation.

Here is another paradox of Scripture. We know that trials are a means for our growing spiritually, morally, and emotionally. Yet we have no desire to be in a place where even the possibility of sin is increased. Even Jesus, when He prayed in the Garden of Gethsemane, first asked, "My Father, if it is possible, let this cup pass from Me," before He said, "yet not as I will, but as Thou wilt" (Matt. 26:39). He was horrified at the prospect of taking sin upon Himself, yet He was willing to endure it in order to fulfill the will of His Father to make possible the redemption of man.

Our proper reaction to times of temptation is similar to Christ's, but for us it is primarily a matter of self-distrust. When we honestly look at the power of sin and at our own weakness and sinful propensities, we shudder at the danger of temptation or even trial. This petition is another plea for God to provide what we in ourselves do not have. It is an appeal to God to place a watch over our eyes, our ears, our mouth, our feet, and our hands—that in whatever we see, hear, or say, and in any place we go and in anything we do, He will protect us from sin.

Like Joseph we know that what men and Satan mean for evil God will turn to the good of His children (see Gen. 50:20); but we are not certain that, like Joseph, we will be completely submissive to and dependent on God in our trials. The implication of this part of the prayer seems to be: "Lord, don't ever lead us into a trial that will present such a temptation that we will not be able to resist it." It is laying claim to the promise that "God is faithful, who will not allow you to be tempted beyond what you are able, but with the temptation will provide the way of escape also, that you may be able to endure it" (1 Cor. 10:13).

This petition is a safeguard against presumption and a false sense of security and self-sufficiency. We know that we will never have arrived spiritually, and that we will never be free of the danger of sin, until we are with the Lord. With Martin Luther we say, "We cannot help being exposed to the assaults, but we pray that we may not fall and perish under them." As our dear Lord prayed for us in His great intercessory prayer, we want, at all costs, to be kept from the evil one (John 17:15).

When we sincerely pray, **do not lead us into temptation, but deliver us from evil,** we also declare that we submit to His Word, which is our protection from sin. "Submit therefore to God," James says. "Resist the devil and he will flee from you" (James 4:7). Submitting to God is submitting to His Word. "Thy word I have treasured in my heart, that I may not sin against Thee" (Ps. 119:11). So the believer prays to be kept from overwhelming solicitation to sin, and if he falls into it, to be rescued from it. **Deliver** is actually in the form of a command.

In a cursed world where we are battered by evil all around us, we confess our inadequacy to deal with evil. We confess the weakness of our flesh and the absolute impotency of human resources to combat sin and rescue us from its clutches. Above all we confess our need for the protection and deliverance of our loving heavenly Father.

GOD'S PREEMINENCE

[For Thine is the kingdom, and the power, and the glory, forever. Amen.] (6:13*b*)

Because they are not found in the most reliable manuscripts, it is likely that these words were not in the original text. In many modern translations they are therefore given in footnotes or, as here, placed in brackets.

Although they may not have been in the original account, the words are perfectly fitting in this passage, and express truths that are thoroughly scriptural. They form a beautiful doxology, declaring the preeminence of God as seen in the greatness of His eternal **kingdom, . . . power, and . . . glory.** They are an echo of 1 Chronicles 29:11 and, to the minds and hearts of Matthew's Jewish readers, would have been a moving and appropriate climax.

GOD'S POSTSCRIPT

For if you forgive men for their transgressions, your heavenly Father will also forgive you. But if you do not forgive men, then your Father will not forgive your transgressions. (6:14-15)

The prayer lesson concludes with a reminder that follows the teaching of forgiveness in verse 12. This is the Savior's own commentary on our petition to God for forgiveness, and the only one of the petitions to which He gives added insight. Thus its importance is amplified.

For if you forgive men for their transgressions puts the principle in a positive mode. Believers should forgive as those who have received judicial forgiveness (cf. Eph. 1:7; 1 John 2:1-2) from God. When the heart is filled with such a forgiving spirit, **your heavenly Father will also forgive you.** Believers cannot know the parental forgiveness, which keeps fellowship with the Lord rich and blessings from the Lord profuse, apart from forgiving others in heart and word. **Forgive** (*aphiēmi*) means literally "to hurl away."

Paul had this in mind when he wrote, "I found mercy, in order that in me as the foremost [of sinners], Jesus Christ might demonstrate His perfect patience" (1 Tim. 1:16; cf. Matt. 7:11). An unforgiving spirit not only is inconsistent for one who has been totally forgiven by God, but also brings the chastening of God rather than His mercy. Our Lord illustrates the unmerciful response in the parable of Matthew 18:21-35. There a man is forgiven the unpayable debt representing sin and is given the mercy of salvation. He then refuses to forgive another and is immediately and severely chastened by God.

But if you do not forgive men, then your Father will not forgive your transgressions. That states the truth of verse 14 in a negative way for emphasis. The sin of an unforgiving heart and a bitter spirit (Heb. 12:15) forfeits blessing and invites judgment. Even the Talmud taught that "he who is indulgent toward others' faults will be mercifully dealt with by the Supreme Judge."

Every believer must seek to manifest the forgiving spirit of Joseph (Gen. 50:19-21) and of Stephen (Acts 7:60) as often as needed (Luke 17:3-4). To receive pardon from the perfectly holy God and then to refuse to pardon others when we are sinful men is the epitome of abuse of mercy. And "judgment will be merciless to one who has shown no mercy; mercy triumphs over judgment" (James 2:13).

There are petitions for the believer to ask from God, but there are also conditions for the answers to be received. Even more, our prayers are to be primarily concerned with the exaltation of the name, kingdom, and will of the Lord Jesus Christ. Prayer is primarily worship which inspires thanks and personal purity.

Fasting Without Hypocrisy (6:16-18)

37

And whenever you fast, do not put on a gloomy face as the hypocrites do, for they neglect their appearance in order to be seen fasting by men. Truly I say to you, they have their reward in full. But you, when you fast, anoint your head, and wash your face so that you may not be seen fasting by men, but by your Father who is in secret; and your Father who sees in secret will repay you. (6:16-18)

Fasting is the third area—after those of giving (6:2-4) and praying (vv. 5-15)—for which Jesus gives a corrective to the hypocritical religious practices typified by the scribes and Pharisees. In each case the perversion of God's standard was caused by the overriding desire to be seen and praised by men (v. 1).

Fasting has been practiced for various reasons throughout history. Many ancient pagans believed that demons could enter the body through food. When they felt they were under demonic attack they would fast to prevent more evil spirits from gaining access to their bodies. The yogis of most eastern religions and cults have always been committed to fasting—often for long periods of time, in which mystical visions and insights are claimed to be received. In modern western society fasting has become popular for purely physical and cosmetic reasons, and is recommended in some diet programs.

The Bible records no teaching or practice of fasting for practical reasons. Legitimate fasting always had a spiritual purpose and is never presented as having *any* value in and of itself.

During Old Testament times many faithful believers fasted—Moses, Samson, Samuel, Hannah, David, Elijah, Ezra, Nehemiah, Esther, Daniel, and many others. And the New Testament tells us of the fasting of Anna, John the Baptist and his disciples, Jesus, Paul, and numerous others. We know that many of the early church Fathers fasted, and that Luther, Calvin, Wesley, Whitefield, and many other outstanding Christian leaders have fasted.

But the only fast commanded in Scripture is the one connected with the Day of Atonement. On that day all the people were to "humble [their] souls" (Lev. 16:29; cf. 23:27), a Hebrew expression that included forsaking food as an act of self-denial. That was a national fast, involving every man, woman, and child in Israel. But it occurred only one time a year, and then only as an integral part of the Day of Atonement.

Because it is not elsewhere commanded by God, fasting is unlike giving and praying, for which there are many commands in both testaments. Both the Old and New Testaments speak favorably of fasting and record many instances of fasting by believers. But except for the yearly fast just mentioned, it is nowhere required. Beyond that, fasting is shown to be an entirely noncompulsory, voluntary act, not a spiritual duty to be regularly observed.

PRETENTIOUS FASTING

And whenever you fast, do not put on a gloomy face as the hypocrites do, for they neglect their appearance in order to be seen fasting by men. Truly I say to you, they have their reward in full. (6:16)

The phrase **and whenever you fast** supports the understanding that fasting is not commanded. But when it is practiced it is to be regulated according to the principles Jesus gives here.

Nēsteia (**fast**) literally means not to eat, to abstain from food. Fasts were sometimes total and sometimes partial, and ordinarily only water was drunk.

Two extreme views of eating were held among the Jews of Jesus' day. Many, like the ones mentioned in this passage, made an obvious display of fasting. Others believed that, because food is a gift from God, each person would have to give an account to Him on the day of judgment for every good thing he had not eaten. The first group not only was more prevalent but was more self-righteous and proud. Their fasting was not a matter of spiritual conviction but a means of self-gratification.

By the time of Christ, fasting, like almost every other aspect of Jewish religious life, had been perverted and twisted beyond what was scriptural and sincere. Fasting had become a ritual to gain merit with God and attention before men. Like praying and almsgiving, it was largely a hypocritical religious show.

Many Pharisees fasted twice a week (Luke 18:12), usually on the second and fifth days of the week. They claimed those days were chosen because they were the days Moses made the two separate trips to receive the tablets of law from God on Mount Sinai. But those two days also happened to be the major Jewish market days, when cities and towns were crowded with farmers, merchants, and shoppers. They were, therefore, the two days where public fasting would have the largest audiences.

Those wanting to call attention to their fasting would **put on a gloomy face**, and **neglect their appearance in order to be seen fasting by men**. They would wear old clothes, sometimes purposely torn and soiled, dishevel their hair, cover themselves with dirt and ashes, and even use makeup in order to look pale and sickly. As we have seen in previous chapters, **hypocrites** comes from a Greek word for the mask used by actors to portray a certain character or mood. In regard to fasting, some Jewish **hypocrites** literally resorted to theatrics.

When the heart is not right, fasting is a sham and a mockery. Those whom Jesus condemned for fasting **in order to be seen by men** were pretentiously self-righteous. Everything they did centered around themselves. God had no place in their motives or their thinking, and He had no part in their reward. The reward they wanted was recognition by men, and that reward, and only that reward, they received **in full**.

Unfortunately, throughout the history of the church fasting has most often been viewed in the two extremes that were common in Judaism. John Calvin said, "Many for want of knowing its usefulness undervalue its necessity. And some reject it all together as superfluous, while on the other hand, where the proper use of fasting is not well understood, it easily degenerates into superstition."

PROPER FASTING

But you, when you fast, anoint your head, and wash your face so that you may not be seen fasting by men, but by your Father who is in secret; and your Father who sees in secret will repay you. (6:17-18)

Fasting is mentioned some thirty times in the New Testament, almost always favorably. It is possible that fasting was even overemphasized in some parts of the early church. At least four times a reference to fasting seems to have been inserted into the original text where it is not found in the earliest and best manuscripts (Matt. 17:21; Mark 9:29; Acts 10:30; 1 Cor. 7:5). The other favorable accounts, however, both in the gospels and in the epistles, show that proper fasting is a legitimate form of spiritual devotion.

Jesus' statement **when you fast** (cf. v. 16) indicates that fasting is normal and acceptable in the Christian life. He assumes His followers will fast on certain occasions, but He does not give a command or specify a particular time, place, or method. Because the validity of the Day of Atonement ceased when Jesus made the once-for-all sacrifice on the cross (Heb. 10:10), the single prescribed occasion for fasting has ceased to exist.

Jesus' disciples did not fast while He was with them because fasting is associated primarily with mourning or other times of consuming spiritual need or anxiety. When the disciples of John the Baptist asked Jesus why His disciples did not fast like they and the Pharisees did, He replied, "The attendants of the bridegroom cannot mourn as long as the bridegroom is with them, can they? But the days will come when the bridegroom is taken away from them, and then they will fast" (Matt. 9:14-15). Fasting is there associated with mourning.

Fasting is never shown in Scripture to be the means to heightened spiritual experience, visions, or special insight or awareness—as many mystics, including some Christian mystics, claim. Fasting is appropriate in this age, because Christ is physically absent from the earth. But it is appropriate only as a response to special times of testing, trial, or struggle.

Fasting is appropriate during times of sorrow. When God caused the first child born to Bathsheba by David to be taken ill, David fasted while he pleaded for the infant's life (2 Sam. 12:16). He also fasted when Abner died (2 Sam. 3:35). David even fasted on behalf of his enemies. "When they were sick, my clothing was sackcloth; I humbled my soul with fasting; and my prayer kept returning to my bosom" (Ps. 35:13).

On such occasions of deep grief, fasting is a natural human response. Most people do not then feel like eating. Their appetite is gone, and food is the last thing they are concerned about. Unless a person is getting seriously weak from hunger or has some specific medical reason for needing to eat, we do them no favor by insisting that they eat.

Overwhelming danger often prompted fasting. King Jehoshaphat proclaimed a national fast in Judah when they were threatened with attack from the Moabites and Ammonites (2 Chron. 20:3). From a human standpoint they could not possibly win, and they cried out to God for help, forsaking food as they did so. Queen Esther, her servants, and all the Jews in the capital city of Susa fasted for three full days before she went before the king to plead for the Jews to be spared from Haman's wicked scheme against her people (Esther 4:16).

As the exiles were about to leave Babylon for the adventurous return to Jerusalem, Ezra declared a fast, "that we might humble ourselves before our God to seek from Him a safe journey for us, our little ones, and all our possessions" (Ezra 8:21). Ezra continues, "For I was ashamed to request from the king troops and horsemen to protect us from the enemy on the way, because we had said to the king, 'The hand of our God is favorably disposed to all those who seek Him, but His power and His anger are against all those who forsake Him.' So we fasted and sought our God concerning this matter, and He listened to our entreaty" (vv. 22-23).

Penitence was often accompanied by fasting. David fasted after his double sin of committing adultery with Bathsheba and then having her husband Uriah sent to the front of the battle to be killed. Daniel fasted as he prayed for God to forgive the sins of his people. When Elijah confronted Ahab with God's judgment for his great wickedness, the king "tore his clothes and put on sackcloth and fasted, and he lay in sackcloth and went about despondently" (1 Kings 21:27). Because of Ahab's sincerity, the Lord postponed the judgment (v. 29). Centuries later, after the exiles had returned safely to Jerusalem, the Israelites were convicted of their intermarrying with unbelieving Gentiles. As Ezra confessed that sin in behalf of his people, "he did not eat bread, nor drink water, for he was mourning over the unfaithfulness of the exiles" (Ezra 10:6).

When the people of Nineveh heard Jonah's preaching they were so convicted that they believed in God and "called a great fast and put on sackcloth from the greatest to the least of them. . . . By the decree of the king" they would "not let man, beast, herd, or flock taste a thing" (Jonah 3:5, 7). Rather than resent the warning of judgment and damnation, they repentantly turned to God and sought His forgiveness and mercy.

Fasting was sometimes associated with the receiving or proclaiming of a special revelation from God. As Daniel contemplated Jeremiah's prediction of the seventy year's desolation of Jerusalem, he gave his "attention to the Lord God to seek Him by prayer and supplications, with fasting, sackcloth, and ashes" (Dan. 9:2-3). As he continued "speaking in prayer," he reports, "then the man Gabriel, whom I had seen in the vision previously, came to me in my extreme weariness about the time of the evening offering. And he gave me instruction and talked with me, and said, 'O Daniel, I have now come forth to give you insight with understanding'" (vv. 21-22). A short time later, just before receiving another vision, Daniel made a partial fast—by forsaking "any tasty food, . . . meat or wine"—for three weeks (10:3). It is important to note that, though fasting was related to the revelations, it was not a means of achieving them. Daniel's fasting was simply a natural accompaniment to his deep and desperate seeking of God's will.

We often fail to understand God's Word as fully as we ought simply because, unlike those great people of God, we do not seek to comprehend it with their degree of intensity and determination. Skipping a few meals might be the small price we willingly pay for staying in the Word until understanding comes.

Fasting often accompanied the beginning of an important task or ministry. Jesus fasted forty days and nights before He was tempted in the wilderness and then began His preaching ministry. Intensity and zeal over proclaiming God's Word can so consume the mind and heart that food has no appeal and no place. Though abstaining from food has absolutely no spiritual value in itself, when eating is an intrusion on that which is immeasurably more important, it will be willingly, gladly, and unobtrusively forsaken.

Both before and after the Holy Spirit directed the church at Antioch to set apart Barnabas and Saul for special ministry, the people were praying and fasting (Acts 13:2-3). As those two men of God ministered God's Word they prayed and fasted as they appointed elders in the churches they founded (14:23).

Only the Lord knows how much the leadership of the church today could be strengthened if congregations were that determined to find and follow the Lord's will. The early church did not choose or send out leaders carelessly or by popular vote. Above all they sought and followed God's will. Fasting has no more power to assure godly leadership than it has to assure forgiveness, protection, or any other good thing from God. But it is likely to be a part of sincere dedication that is determined to know the Lord's will and have His power before decisions are made, plans are laid, or actions are taken. People who are consumed with concern before God do not take a lunch break.

In every scriptural account genuine fasting is linked with prayer. You can pray without fasting, but you cannot fast biblically without praying. Fasting is an affirmation of intense prayer, a corollary of deep spiritual struggle before God. It is never an isolated act or a ceremony or ritual that has some inherent efficacy or merit. It has no value at all—in fact becomes a spiritual hindrance and a sin—when done for any reason apart from knowing and following the Lord's will.

Fasting is also always linked with a pure heart and must be associated with obedient, godly living. The Lord told Zechariah to declare to the people, "When you fasted and mourned in the fifth and seventh months these seventy years, was it actually for Me that you fasted? . . . Thus has the Lord of hosts said, 'Dispense true justice, and practice kindness and compassion each to his brother; and do not oppress the widow or the orphan, the stranger or the poor; and do not devise evil in your hearts against one another'" (Zech. 7:5, 9-10). Seventy years of fasting meant nothing to the Lord, because it was done insincerely. Like the hypocrites that Jesus would later condemn, those Israelites lived only for themselves (v. 6).

After chastising the people in a similar way for their pretentious and unrighteous fasting, the Lord declared through Isaiah,

> Is this not the fast which I chose, to loosen the bonds of wickedness, to undo the bands of the yoke, and to let the oppressed go free, and break every yoke? Is it not to divide your bread with the hungry, and bring the homeless poor into the house; when you see the naked, to cover him; and not to hide yourself from your own flesh? Then your light will break out like the dawn, and your recovery will speedily spring forth; and your righteousness will go before you; the glory of the Lord will be your rear guard. Then you will call, and the Lord will answer; you will cry, and He will say, "Here I am." (Isa. 58:5-9)

There can be no right fasting apart from a right heart, right living, and a right attitude.

But you, when you fast, Jesus tells those who belong to Him, **anoint your head, and wash your face so that you may not be seen fasting by men.** To **anoint** the **head** with oil was commonly done as a matter of good grooming. The oil was often scented and used partly as a perfume. Like washing the **face,** it was associated with day-to-day living, but especially with more formal or important occasions. Jesus' point was that a person who fasts should do everything to make himself look normal and do nothing to attract attention to his deprivation and spiritual struggle.

The one who sincerely wants to please God will studiously avoid trying to impress men. He will determine **not** [to] **be seen fasting by men, but by** God the **Father who is in secret.** Jesus does not say we should fast for the purpose of being seen even by God. Fasting is not to be a display for anyone, including God. Genuine fasting is simply a part of concentrated, intense prayer and concern for the Lord, His will, and His work. Jesus' point is that the **Father** never fails to notice fasting that is heart-felt and genuine, and that He never fails to reward it. **Your Father who sees in secret will repay you.**

Treasure in Heaven (6:19-24)

38

Do not lay up for yourselves treasures upon earth, where moth and rust destroy, and where thieves break in and steal. But lay up for yourselves treasures in heaven, where neither moth nor rust destroys, and where thieves do not break in or steal; for where your treasure is, there will your heart be also. The lamp of the body is the eye; if therefore your eye is clear, your whole body will be full of light. But if your eye is bad, your whole body will be full of darkness. If therefore the light that is in you is darkness, how great is the darkness! No one can serve two masters; for either he will hate the one and love the other, or he will hold to one and despise the other. You cannot serve God and mammon. (6:19-24)

Human beings are naturally thing-oriented. We are strongly inclined to be wrapped up in seeking, acquiring, enjoying, and protecting material possessions. In prosperous cultures such as those in which most Westerners live, the propensity to build our lives around things is especially great.

The leading religionists of Jesus' day were preoccupied with things. They were materialistic, greedy, avaricious, covetous, grasping, and manipulative. That "the Pharisees . . . were lovers of money" (Luke 16:14) was not incidental to the other sins for which Jesus rebuked them. Because they did not have a right view of themselves (see Matt. 5:3-12), of their relation to the world (5:13-16), of the Word of God (5:17-20), of morality (5:21-48), and of religious duties (6:1-18), it was inevitable they would not have a right view of material things.

Jesus first shows how their view of nonessential material things was perverted (vv. 4-24) and then how their view of essential material things was also perverted (vv. 25-34). Their views both of luxuries and necessities were warped.

False doctrine leads to false standards, false behavior, and false values, and hypocritical religion seems always to be accompanied by greed and immorality (cf. 2 Pet. 2:1-3, 14-15). Hophni and Phinehas, the two sons of Eli the high priest, had no regard for the things of God, but they eagerly took advantage of their father's exalted office as well as their own priestly positions. They "were worthless men; they did not know the Lord" (1 Sam. 2:12). They took more than their prescribed share of the sacrificial meat for themselves, and they committed adultery "with the women who served at the doorway of the tent of meeting" (vv. 13-17, 22).

Annas and Caiaphas, who were high priests during Jesus' ministry, became extremely wealthy from the many concessions they ran or licensed in the Temple. It was of those concessions that Jesus twice cleansed His Father's house (John 2:14-16; Matt. 21:12-13).

Throughout the history of the church to the present day, religious charlatans have used the ministry as a means to garner wealth and to provide opportunity to indulge their sexual lusts.

Often such people, like the scribes and Pharisees, have used their material prosperity as imagined evidence of their spirituality, proclaiming without shame that they are materially blessed because they are spiritually superior. They turn upside down teachings such as those in Deuteronomy 28: "Now it shall be, if you will diligently obey the Lord your God, being careful to do all His commandments which I command you today, the Lord your God will set you high above all the nations of the earth. And all these blessings shall come upon you and overtake you, if you will obey the Lord your God. Blessed shall you be in the city, and blessed shall you be in the country" (vv. 1-3). Those blessings are clearly and repeatedly contingent on obedience to the Lord. Material or other earthly benefits that are accumulated by greed, dishonesty, deceit, or in any other immoral way are not to be conceived of as blessings from the Lord. To claim God's approval simply on the basis of one's wealth, health, prestige, or any other such thing is to pervert His Word and use His name in vain.

The Old Testament gives many warnings against accumulating wealth for its own sake. "Do not weary yourself to gain wealth, cease from your consideration of it" (Prov. 23:4).

Economic problems such as inflation, recessions, and depressions involve many complex factors—monetary, political, military, social, climatic, and so on. But with the exception of the climatic, over which men have little control, the root cause behind most economic difficulty is greed. The problems are brought about in the first place because of greed, and they are often seemingly impossible to solve for the same reason. As John Stott observes, "Worldly ambition has a strong fascination for us. The spell of materialism is very hard to break" (*Christian Counter-Culture* [Downers Grove, Ill.: InterVarsity, 1978], p. 154). Paul established the proper attitude when he said that "godliness actually is a means of great gain, when accompanied by contentment. For we have brought nothing into the world, so we cannot take anything out of it either. And if we have food and covering, with these we shall be content" (1 Tim. 6:6-8).

In the present passage Jesus looks at materialism—particularly in regard to luxuries—from the three perspectives of treasure, vision, and master.

A SINGLE TREASURE

Do not lay up for yourselves treasures upon earth, where moth and rust destroy, and where thieves break in and steal. But lay up for yourselves treasures in heaven, where neither moth nor rust destroys, and where thieves do not break in or steal; for where your treasure is, there will your heart be also. (6:19-21)

Lay up (*thēsaurizō*) and **treasures** (*thēsauros*) come from the same basic Greek term, which is also the source of our English *thesaurus,* a treasury of words. A literal translation of this phrase would therefore be, "do not treasure up treasures for yourselves."

The Greek also carries the connotation of stacking or laying out horizontally, as one stacks coins. In the context of this passage the idea is that of stockpiling or hoarding, and therefore pictures wealth that is not being used. The money or other wealth is simply stored for safekeeping; it is kept for the keeping's sake to make a show of wealth or to create an environment of lazy overindulgence (cf. Luke 12:16-21).

It is clear from this passage, as well as from many others in Scripture, that Jesus is not advocating poverty as a means to spirituality. In all of His many different instructions, He only once told a person to "sell your possessions and give to the poor" (Matt. 19:21). In that particular case, the young man's wealth was his idol, and therefore a special barrier between him and the lordship of Jesus Christ. It provided an excellent opportunity to test whether or not that man was fully committed to turning over the control of his life to Christ. His response proved that he was not. The problem was not in the wealth itself, but the man's unwillingness to part with it. The Lord did not specifically require His disciples to give up all their money and other possessions to follow Him, although it may be that some of them voluntarily did so. He did require obedience to His commands no matter what that cost. The price was too high for the wealthy young ruler, to whom possessions were the first priority.

Both testaments recognize the right to material possessions, including money, land, animals, houses, clothing, and every other thing that is honestly acquired. God has made many promises of material blessing to those who belong to and are faithful to Him. The foundational truth that underlies the commandments not to steal or covet is the right of personal property. Stealing and coveting are wrong because what is stolen or coveted rightfully belongs to someone else. Ananias and Sapphira did not forfeit their lives because they kept back some of the proceeds from the sale of their property, but because they lied to the Holy Spirit (Acts 5:3). Holding back some of the money was selfish, especially if they had other assets on which to live, but they had a right to keep it, as Peter makes plain: "While it remained unsold, did it not remain your own? And after it was sold, was it not under your control?" (v. 4).

God expects, in fact commands, His people to be generous. But He also expects, and even commands, them not only to be thankful for but to *enjoy* the blessings He gives—including the material blessings. The Lord "richly supplies us with all things to enjoy" (1 Tim. 6:17). That verse is specifically directed to "those who are rich in this present world," and yet it does not command, or even suggest, that they divest themselves of their wealth, but rather warns them not to be conceited about it or to trust in it.

Abraham was extremely rich for his day, a person who vied in wealth, influence, and military power with many of the kings in Canaan. When we first meet Job he is vastly wealthy, and when we leave him—after the testing that cost him everything he possessed outside of his own life—God has made him wealthier still, in flocks and herds, in sons and daughters, and in a healthy long life. "And the Lord blessed the latter days of Job more than his beginning" (Job 42:12-17).

The Bible gives considerable counsel for working hard and following good business practices (cf. Matt. 25:27). The ant is shown as a model of the good worker, who "prepares her food in the summer, and gathers her provision in the harvest" (Prov. 6:6-8). We are told that "in all labor there is profit, but mere talk leads only to poverty" (14:23) and "by wisdom a house is built, and by understanding it is established; and by knowledge the rooms are filled with all precious and pleasant riches" (24:3-4). "He who tills his land will have plenty of food, but he who follows empty pursuits will have poverty in plenty" (28:19).

Paul tells us that parents are responsible for saving up for their children (2 Cor. 12:14), that "if anyone will not work, neither let him eat" (2 Thess. 3:10), and that "if anyone does not provide for his own, and especially for those of his household, he has denied the faith, and is worse than an unbeliever" (1 Tim. 5:8).

During his exceptionally long ministry, which spanned most of the eighteenth century, John Wesley earned a considerable amount of money from his published sermons and other works. Yet he left only 28 pounds when he died, because he continually gave what he earned to the Lord's work.

It is right to provide for our families, to make reasonable plans for the future, to make wise investments, and to have money to carry on a business, give to the poor, and support the Lord's work. It is being dishonest, greedy, covetous, stingy, and miserly about possessions that is wrong. To honestly earn, save, and give is wise and good; to hoard and spend only on ourselves not only is unwise but sinful.

Some years ago, I happened to have contact with two quite wealthy men during the same week. One was a former professor at a major university who, through a long series of good investments in real estate, had accumulated a fortune of possibly a hundred million dollars. But in the process he lost his family, his happiness, his peace of mind, and had aged far beyond his years. The other man, a pastor, also acquired his wealth through investments, but they were investments to which he paid little attention. Because of his financial independence, he gave to his church over the years considerably more than he was paid for being its pastor. He is one of the godliest, happiest, most fruitful, and contented persons I have ever met.

The key to Jesus' warning here is **yourselves**. When we accumulate possessions simply for our own sakes—whether to hoard or to spend selfishly and extravagantly—those possessions become idols.

It is possible that both our **treasures upon earth** and our **treasures in heaven** can involve money and other material things. Possessions that are wisely, lovingly, willingly, and generously used for kingdom purposes can be a means of accumulating heavenly possessions. When they are hoarded and stored, however, they not only become a spiritual hindrance but are subject to loss through **moth, rust, and thieves**.

In ancient times, wealth was frequently measured in part by clothing. Compared to our day of mass-produced clothes, garments represented a considerable investment. Rich people sometimes had golden threads woven into their clothing, both to display and to store their wealth. But the best clothes were made of wool, which the **moth** loves to eat; and even the richest persons had difficulty protecting their clothes from the insects.

Wealth was also often held in grain, as we see from the parable of the rich farmer who said, "I will tear down my barns and build larger ones, and there I will store all my grain and my goods" (Luke 12:18). *Brōsis* (**rust**) literally means "an eating," and is translated with that meaning everywhere in the New Testament but here (see Rom. 14:17; 1 Cor. 8:4, "eating"; 2 Cor. 9:10, "food"; and Heb. 12:16, "meal"). It seems best to take the same meaning here, in reference to grain that is eaten by rats, mice, worms, and insects.

Almost any kind of wealth, of course, is subject to **thieves**, which is why many people buried their nonperishable valuables in the ground away from the house, often in a field (see Matt. 13:44). **Break in** is literally "dig through," and could refer to digging through the mud walls of a house or digging up the dirt in a field.

Nothing we own is completely safe from destruction or theft. And even if we keep our possessions perfectly secure during our entire lives, we are certainly separated from them at death. Many millionaires will be heavenly paupers, and many paupers will be heavenly millionaires.

But when our time, energy, and possessions are used to serve others and to further the Lord's work, they build up heavenly resources that are completely free from destruction or theft. There **neither moth nor rust destroys, and . . . thieves do not break in or steal**. Heavenly security is the only absolute security.

Jesus goes on to point out that a person's most cherished possessions and his deepest motives and desires are inseparable, **for where your treasure is, there will your heart be also.** They will either both be earthly or both be heavenly. It is impossible to have one on earth and the other in heaven (cf. James 4:4).

As always, the heart must be right first. In fact, if the heart is right, everything else in life falls into its proper place. The person who is right with the Lord will be generous and happy in his giving to the Lord's work. By the same token, a person who is covetous, self-indulgent, and stingy has good reason to question his relationship with the Lord.

Jesus is not saying that if we put our **treasure** in the right place our **heart** will then be in the right place, but that the location of our **treasure** indicates where our **heart** already is. Spiritual problems are *always* heart problems. Sinful acts come from a sinful heart, just as righteous acts come from a righteous heart.

When the exiles who came back to Jerusalem from Babylon began turning to God's Word, a revival also began. "Ezra opened the book in the sight of all the people" and various leaders took turns reading "from the law of God" (Neh. 8:5-8). Through hearing God's Word the people became convicted of their sin, began to praise God, and determined to begin obeying Him and to faithfully support the work of the Temple (chaps. 9-10).

Revival that does not affect the use of money and possessions is a questionable revival. As the Tabernacle was being built, "everyone whose heart stirred him and everyone whose spirit moved him came and brought the Lord's contribution for the work of the tent of meeting and for all its service and for the holy garments" (Ex. 35:21). As plans were being made to build the Temple, David himself gave generously to the work, and "the rulers of the fathers' households, and the princes of the tribes of Israel, and the commanders of thousands and of hundreds, with the overseers over the king's work, offered willingly. . . . Then the people rejoiced because they had offered so willingly, for they made their offering to the Lord with a whole heart, and King David also rejoiced greatly" (1 Chron. 29:2-6, 9).

G. Campbell Morgan wrote:

> You are to remember with the passion burning within you that you are not the child of to-day. You are not of the earth, you are more than dust; you are the child of tomorrow, you are of the eternities, you are the offspring of Deity. The measurements of your lives cannot be circumscribed by the point where blue sky kisses green earth. All the fact of your life cannot be encompassed in the one small sphere upon which you live. You belong to the infinite. If you make your fortune on the earth—poor, sorry, silly soul—you have made a fortune, and stored it in a place where you cannot hold it. Make your fortune, but store it where it will greet you in the dawning of the new morning. (*The Gospel According to Matthew* [New York: Revell, 1929], pp. 64-65)

When thousands of people, mostly Jews, were won to Christ during and soon after Pentecost, the Jerusalem church was flooded with many converts who had come from distant lands and who decided to stay on in the city. Many of them no doubt were poor, and many others probably left most of their wealth and possessions in their homelands. To meet the great financial burden suddenly placed on the church, local believers "began selling their property and possessions, and were sharing them with all, as anyone might have need" (Acts 2:45).

Many years later, during one of the many Roman persecutions, soldiers broke into a certain church to confiscate its presumed treasures. An elder is said to have pointed to a group of widows and orphans who were being fed and said, "There are the treasures of the church."

God's principle for His people has always been, "Honor the Lord from your wealth, and from the first of all your produce; so your barns will be filled with plenty, and your vats will overflow with new wine" (Prov. 3:9-10). Jesus said, "Give, and it will be given to you; good measure, pressed down, shaken together, running over, they will pour into your lap. For by your standard of measure it will be measured to you in return" (Luke 6:38). Paul assures us that "he who sows sparingly shall also reap sparingly; and he who sows bountifully shall also reap bountifully" (2 Cor. 9:6). That is God's formula for earning dividends that are both guaranteed and permanent.

At the end of His parable about the dishonest but shrewd steward, Jesus said, "I say to you, make friends for yourselves by means of the mammon of unrighteousness; that when it fails, they may receive you into the eternal dwellings" (Luke 16:9). Our material possessions are "unrighteous" in the sense of not having any spiritual value in themselves. But if we invest them in the welfare of human souls, the people who are saved or otherwise blessed because of them will someday greet us in heaven with thanksgiving.

A SINGLE VISION

The lamp of the body is the eye; if therefore your eye is clear, your whole body will be full of light. But if your eye is bad, your whole body will be full of darkness. If therefore the light that is in you is darkness, how great is the darkness! (6:22-23)

These verses expand on the previous three, and the **eye** becomes an illustration of the heart. **The lamp,** or lens, **of the body is the eye,** through which all light comes to us. It is the only channel of light we possess, and therefore our only means of vision.

The heart is the eye of the soul, through which the illumination of every spiritual experience shines. It is through our hearts that God's truth, love, peace, and every other spiritual blessing comes to us. When our hearts, our spiritual **eyes,** are **clear,** then our **whole body will be full of light.**

Haplous (**clear**) can also mean single, as it is translated in the King James

413

Version. An **eye** that is **clear** represents a heart that has single-minded devotion. Bishop John Charles Ryle said, "Singleness of purpose is one great secret of spiritual prosperity" (*Expository Thoughts on the Gospels: St. Matthew* [London: James Clarke, 1965], p. 56).

Words that are closely related to *haplous* mean "liberality" (Rom. 12:8; 2 Cor. 9:11) and "generously" (James 1:5). The implication in the present verse is that if our heart, represented by the **eye**, is generous (**clear**), our whole spiritual life will be flooded with spiritual understanding, or **light**.

If our **eye is bad**, however, if it is diseased or damaged, no light can enter, and the **whole body will be full of darkness**. If our hearts are encumbered with material concerns they become "blind" and insensitive to spiritual concerns. The eye is like a window which, when **clear**, allows light to shine through, but, when dirty, or **bad**, prevents light from entering.

Ponēros (**bad**) usually means evil, as it is translated here in the King James Version. In the Septuagint (Greek Old Testament) it is often used in translating the Hebrew expression "evil eye," a Jewish colloquialism that means grudging, or stingy (see Deut. 15:9, "hostile"; Prov. 23:6, "selfish"). "A man with an evil eye," for example, is one who "hastens after wealth" (Prov. 28:22).

The **eye** that is **bad** is the heart that is selfishly indulgent. The person who is materialistic and greedy is spiritually blind. Because he has no way of recognizing true light, he thinks he has light when he does not. What is thought to be **light** is therefore really **darkness**, and because of the self-deception, **how great is the darkness!**

The principle is simple and sobering: the way we look at and use our money is a sure barometer of our spiritual condition.

A Single Master

No one can serve two masters; for either he will hate the one and love the other, or he will hold to one and despise the other. You cannot serve God and mammon. (6:24)

The third choice relates to allegiance, to **masters**. Just as we cannot have our treasures both in earth and in heaven or our bodies both in light and in darkness, we cannot **serve two masters**.

Kurios (**masters**) is often translated lord, and refers to a slave owner. The idea is not simply that of an employer, of which a person may have several at the same time and work for each of them satisfactorily. Many people today hold two or more jobs. If they work the number of hours they are supposed to and perform their work as expected, they have fulfilled their obligation to their employers, no matter how many they may have. The idea is of **masters** of slaves.

But by definition, a slave owner has total control of the slave. For a slave there is no such thing as partial or part-time obligation to his master. He owes full-time service to a full-time master. He is owned and totally controlled by and obligated to his master. He has nothing left for anyone else. To give anything to anyone else would make his master less than master. It is not simply difficult, but absolutely impossible, to **serve two masters** and fully or faithfully be the obedient slave of each.

Over and over the New Testament speaks of Christ as Lord and Master and of Christians as His bondslaves. Paul tells us that before we were saved we were enslaved to sin, which was our master. But when we trusted in Christ, we became slaves of God and of righteousness (Rom. 6:16-22).

We cannot claim Christ as Lord if our allegiance is to anything or anyone else, including ourselves. And when we know God's will but resist obeying it, we give evidence that our loyalty is other than to Him. We can no more **serve two masters** at the same time than we can walk in two directions at the same time. We will **either . . . hate the one and love the other, or . . . hold to one and despise the other.**

John Calvin said, "Where riches hold the dominion of the heart, God has lost His authority" (*A Harmony of the Evangelists Matthew, Mark, and Luke,* vol. 1 [Grand Rapids: Baker, 1979], p. 337). Our treasure is either on earth or in heaven, our spiritual life is either full of light or of darkness, and our master is either **God** or **mammon** (possessions, earthly goods).

The orders of those two **masters** are diametrically opposed and cannot coexist. The one commands us to walk by faith and the other demands we walk by sight. The one calls us to be humble and the other to be proud, the one to set our minds on things above and the other to set them on things below. One calls us to love light, the other to love darkness. The one tells us to look toward things unseen and eternal and the other to look at things seen and temporal.

The person whose **master** is Jesus Christ can say that, when he eats or drinks or does anything else, he does "all to the glory of God" (1 Cor. 10:31). He can say with David, "I have set the Lord continually before me" (Ps. 16:8), and with Caleb when he was eighty-five years old, "I followed the Lord my God fully" (Josh. 14:8).

Overcoming Worry (6:25-34)

39

For this reason I say to you, do not be anxious for your life, as to what you shall eat, or what you shall drink; nor for your body, as to what you shall put on. Is not life more than food, and the body than clothing? Look at the birds of the air, that they do not sow, neither do they reap, nor gather into barns, and yet your heavenly Father feeds them. Are you not worth much more than they? And which of you by being anxious can add a single cubit to his life's span? And why are you anxious about clothing? Observe how the lilies of the field grow; they do not toil nor do they spin, yet I say to you that even Solomon in all his glory did not clothe himself like one of these. But if God so arrays the grass of the field, which is alive today and tomorrow is thrown into the furnace, will He not much more do so for you, O men of little faith? Do not be anxious then, saying, "What shall we eat?" or "What shall we drink?" or "With what shall we clothe ourselves?" For all these things the Gentiles eagerly seek; for your heavenly Father knows that you need all these things. But seek first His kingdom and His righteousness; and all these things shall be added to you. Therefore do not be anxious for tomorrow; for tomorrow will care for itself. Each day has enough trouble of its own. (6:25-34)

In Matthew 6:19-24 Jesus focuses on the attitude toward luxury, the unnecessary physical possessions men store and stockpile for selfish reasons. In verses 25-34 He focuses on the attitude toward what men eat, drink, and wear, the necessities of life that they absolutely must have to exist. The first passage is directed particularly at the rich and the second particularly at the poor. Both being rich and being poor have their special spiritual problems. The rich are tempted to trust in their possessions, and the poor are tempted to doubt God's provision. The rich are tempted to become self-satisfied in the false security of their riches, and the poor are tempted to worry and fear in the false insecurity of their poverty.

Whether men are wealthy or poor—or somewhere in between—their attitude toward material possessions is one of the most reliable marks of their spiritual condition. Man as an earthly creature is naturally concerned about earthly things. In Christ we are recreated as heavenly beings and, as children of our heavenly Father, our concerns should now focus primarily on heavenly things— even while we still live on earth. Christ sends us into the world to do His work, just as the Father sent Him into the world to do the Father's work. But we are not to be "of the world" even as Jesus Himself, while on earth, was "not of the world" (John 17:15-18). One of the supreme tests of our spiritual lives, then, is how we now relate to those two worlds. Sixteen of the thirty-eight parables of Jesus deal with money. One out of ten verses in the New Testament deals with that subject. Scripture offers about five hundred verses on prayer, fewer than five hundred on faith, and over two thousand on money. The believer's attitude toward money and possessions is determinative.

Ours is an age of unabashed materialism, an age guided by greed, ambition, success, prestige, self-indulgence, and conspicuous consumption. In his book *The Emerging Order: God in the Age of Scarcity,* Jeremy Rifkin says, "Emphasis on continuous economic growth is a black hole that has already sucked up a majority of the world's critical, nonrenewable resources." The author, who is not a Christian, makes the closing observation that "the only solution to our approach to life is the reemergence of the evangelical Christian ethic, which is an ethic of unselfishness and low consumption." The single alternative, Rifkin says, is a constrictive, totalitarian dictatorship that will control our society and our personal lives for us.

Unfortunately, there is little evidence that even most modern evangelicals themselves are any longer committed to such an ethic. We give much more evidence of following the worldly trends of our day than of setting, confronting, or modifying them. In light of that fact, it is difficult for most of us to identify with Jesus' warning not to worry about basic necessities. We are well fed, well clothed, and well fixed in all other necessary things, and in many things that are totally unnecessary.

The heart of Jesus' message in our present passage is: Don't worry—not even about necessities. He gives the command, **Do not be anxious** three times (vv. 25, 31, 34) and gives four reasons why worry, being **anxious,** is wrong: it is unfaithful because of our Master; it is unnecessary because of our Father; it is unreasonable because of our faith; and it is unwise because of our future.

WORRY IS UNFAITHFUL BECAUSE OF OUR MASTER

For this reason I say to you, do not be anxious for your life, as to what you shall eat, or what you shall drink; nor for your body, as to what you shall put on. Is not life more than food, and the body than clothing? (6:25)

For this reason refers back to the previous verse, in which Jesus declares that a Christian's only Master is God. He is therefore saying, "Because God is your Master, **I say to you, do not be anxious.**" A bondslave's only responsibility is to his master, and for believers to worry is to be disobedient and unfaithful to their Master, who is God. For Christians, worry and anxiety are forbidden, foolish, and sinful.

In the Greek, the command **do not be anxious** includes the idea of stopping what is already being done. In other words, we are to stop worrying and never start it again. **For your life** makes the command all-inclusive. *Psuchē* (**life**) is a comprehensive term that encompasses all of a person's being—physical, mental, emotional, and spiritual. Jesus is referring to **life** in its fullest possible sense. Absolutely nothing in any aspect of our lives, internal or external, justifies our being **anxious** when we have the Master we do.

Worry is the sin of distrusting the promise and providence of God, and yet it is a sin that Christians commit perhaps more frequently than any other. The English term *worry* comes from an old German word meaning to strangle, or choke. That is exactly what worry does; it is a kind of mental and emotional strangulation, which probably causes more mental and physical afflictions than any other single cause.

It has been reported that a dense fog extensive enough to cover seven city blocks a hundred feet deep is composed of less than one glass of water—divided into sixty thousand million droplets. In the right form, a few gallons of water can cripple a large city.

In a similar way, the substance of worry is nearly always extremely small compared to the size it forms in our minds and the damage it does in our lives. Someone has said, "Worry is a thin stream of fear that trickles through the mind, which, if encouraged, will cut a channel so wide that all other thoughts will be drained out."

Worry is the opposite of contentment, which should be a believer's normal and consistent state of mind. Every believer should be able to say with Paul, "I have learned to be content in whatever circumstances I am. I know how to get along with humble means, and I also know how to live in prosperity; in any and every circumstance I have learned the secret of being filled and going hungry, both of having abundance and suffering need" (Phil. 4:11-12; cf. 1 Tim. 6:6-8).

A Christian's contentment is found in God, and only in God—in His ownership, control, and provision of everything we possess and will ever need. First, God *owns* everything, including the entire universe. David proclaimed, "The earth is the Lord's, and all it contains, the world, and those who dwell in it" (Ps. 24:1). He also said, "Thine, O Lord, is the greatness and the power and the glory and the victory and the majesty, indeed everything that is in the heavens and the earth" (1 Chron. 29:11).

Everything we now have belongs to the Lord, and everything we will ever have belongs to Him. Why, then, do we worry about His taking from us what really belongs to Him?

One day when he was away from home someone came running up to John Wesley saying, "Your house has burned down! Your house has burned down!" To which Wesley replied, "No it hasn't, because I don't own a house. The one I have been living in belongs to the Lord, and if it has burned down, that is one less responsibility for me to worry about."

Second, a Christian should be content because God *controls* everything. Again David gives us the right perspective: "Thou dost rule over all, and in Thy hand is power and might; and it lies in Thy hand to make great, and to strengthen everyone" (1 Chron. 29:12). Daniel declared, "Let the name of God be blessed forever and ever, for wisdom and power belong to Him. And it is He who changes the times and the epochs; He removes kings and establishes kings; He gives wisdom to wise men, and knowledge to men of understanding" (Dan. 2:20-21).

Those were not idle words for Daniel, as became clear soon after he spoke them. When the jealous commissioners and satraps tricked King Darius into ordering Daniel thrown into the den of lions, it was the king, not Daniel, who was worried. "Slept fled from" the king during the night, but Daniel apparently slept soundly next to the lions, whose mouths had been closed by an angel (6:18-23).

Third, believers are to be content because the Lord *provides* everything. The supreme owner and controller is also the supreme provider—as indicated in one of His ancient names, Jehovah-Jireh, which means "the Lord who provides." That is the name Abraham ascribed to God when He provided a lamb to be sacrificed in place of Isaac (Gen. 22:14). If Abraham, with his limited knowledge of God, could be so trusting and content, how much more should we who know Christ and who have His whole written Word? As the apostle assures us, "God shall supply all your needs according to His riches in glory in Christ Jesus" (Phil. 4:19).

The needs that Jesus mentions here are the most basic—what we **eat**, what we **drink**, and what we **put on**. Those are things that every person in every age has needed; but because most western Christians have them in such abundance, they are not often worried about.

Throughout Bible times, however, food and water could seldom be taken for granted. When there was little snow in the mountains there was little water in the rivers, and inadequate rainfall was frequent. Shortage of water naturally brought shortage of food, which seriously affected the whole economy and made clothes harder to buy. Yet Jesus said, **do not be anxious** for any of those things.

Those things are important, and the Lord knows and cares about our need of them, as Jesus goes on to explain. But, He asks rhetorically, **Is not life more than food, and the body than clothing?** All three of those necessities pertain to the body, and Jesus says that the fullness of **life** is more than merely taking care of the body.

Yet taking care of the body has always been a common obsession with men. Even when we are not starving or thirsty or naked, we still give an inordinate amount of attention to our bodies. We pamper the body, decorate it, exercise it, protect it from disease and pain, build it up, slender it down, drape it with jewelry, keep it warm or keep it cool, train it to work and to play, help it get to sleep, and a hundred other things to serve and satisfy our bodies.

Even as Christians we are sometimes caught up in the world's idea that we live because of our bodies. And since we think we live because of our bodies, we live *for* our bodies. We know better, of course, but that is the way we often act. Our bodies in themselves are not the source of anything. They do not give us life but are given life by God, who is the source of all life—spiritual, emotional, intellectual, and physical.

Therefore, whether the Lord gives us more or gives us less of *anything,* it all belongs to Him, as owner, controller, and provider. It is our responsibility to thank Him for what He gives and to use it wisely and unselfishly for as long as He entrusts us with it.

WORRY IS UNNECESSARY BECAUSE OF OUR FATHER

Look at the birds of the air, that they do not sow, neither do they reap, nor gather into barns, and yet your heavenly Father feeds them. Are you not worth much more than they? And which of you by being anxious can add a single cubit to his life's span? And why are you anxious about clothing? Observe how the lilies of the field grow; they do not toil nor do they spin, yet I say to you that even Solomon in all his glory did not clothe himself like one of these. But if God so arrays the grass of the field, which is alive today and tomorrow is thrown into the furnace, will He not much more do so for you, O men of little faith? (6:26-30)

The basic thrust of these verses is that a believer has absolutely no reason to worry, because God is his **heavenly Father.** "Have you forgotten who your Father is?" He asks. To illustrate His point Jesus shows how unnecessary and foolish it is to worry about food, about life expectancy, or about clothing.

WORRY ABOUT FOOD

Look at the birds of the air, that they do not sow, neither do they reap, nor gather into barns, and yet your heavenly Father feeds them. Are you not worth much more than they? (6:26)

There are many birds in northern Galilee, and it is likely that Jesus pointed to some passing birds as He said, **Look at the birds of the air.** As an object lesson, He called attention to the fact that birds do not have intricate and involved processes for acquiring food. **They do not sow, neither do they reap, nor gather into barns.**

Like every creature, **birds** have their life from God. But God does not say to them, in effect, "I've done My part; from now on you're on your own." The Lord has provided them with an abundance of food resources and the instinct to find those resources for themselves and their offspring. **Your heavenly Father feeds them.** He "prepares for the raven its nourishment, when its young cry out to God" (Job 38:41; cf. Ps. 147:9).

If God so carefully takes care of such relatively insignificant creatures as birds, how much more will He take of those who are created in His own image and who have become His children through faith? **Are you not worth much more than they?**

Arthur Pink comments, "Here we may see how the irrational creatures, made subject to vanity by the sin of man, come nearer to their first estate and better observe the order of nature in their creation than man does. For they seek only for that which God has provided for them, and when they receive it they are content. This solemnly demonstrates that man is more . . . vile and more base than even the brute beasts" (*An Exposition of the Sermon on the Mount* [Grand Rapids: Baker, 1974], p. 229).

Jesus does not suggest that birds do nothing to feed themselves. Anyone who has observed them even for a little while is impressed with their diligence and persistence in foraging for food. Many birds spend the greater part of their time and energy finding food for themselves, their mates, and their young. But they do not worry about where their next meal is going to come from. They gather food until they have enough, and then go about whatever other business they may have until time for the next meal. Birds only eat excessively when humans put them in cages. They never worry about or stockpile their food. Certain species store seeds or nuts for winter, but they do so out of instinctive sense, not out of fear or worry. Much less do they stockpile simply for the sake of gloating over their hoard. In their own limited way they illustrate what we should know: that the **heavenly Father feeds them.**

Yet no bird is created in the image of God or recreated in the image of Christ. No bird was ever promised heirship with Jesus Christ throughout all eternity. No bird has a place prepared for him in heaven. And if God gives and sustains life for birds, will He not take care of us who are His children and who *have* been given all those glorious promises?

The idea that the world's food supply is rapidly diminishing is untrue. A recent bulletin of the U. S. Department of Agriculture states, "The world has more than enough food to feed every man, woman, and child in it. If the world's food supply had been evenly divided and distributed among the world's population for the last eighteen years, each person would have received more than the minimum number of calories. From 1960 to the present world food grain production never dropped below a hundred and three percent of the minimum requirement, and averaged a hundred and eight percent."

Nor has the per capita amount of food been dropping. The same bulletin reports, "World per capita food production declined only twice in the last twenty-five years. In fact production of grain, the primary food for most of the world's people, rose from two hundred and ninety kilograms per person during the early fifties to three hundred and sixty kilograms per person during the last five years." It is also stated that only ten percent of the agricultural land in the world could produce enough food to feed every human being on our planet, even by the standard of U. S. consumption!

WORRY ABOUT LONGEVITY

And which of you by being anxious can add a single cubit to his life's span? (6:27)

The second illustration has to do with life expectancy. Our culture is obsessed with trying to lengthen life. We exercise, eat carefully, supplement our diets with vitamins and minerals, get regular physical checkups, and do countless other such things in the hope of adding a few years to our lives.

Yet God has bounded the life of every person. Exercise, good eating, and other common-sense practices are beneficial when done in a reasonable way and looked at in the right perspective. They no doubt can improve the quality and productivity of our lives, but they will not force God into extending our life's span.

You can worry yourself to death, but not to life. Dr. Charles Mayo, of the famous Mayo Clinic, wrote, "Worry affects the circulation, the heart, the glands and the whole nervous system. I have never met a man or known a man to die of overwork, but I have known a lot who died of worry."

The gift of life is a gift from God to be used for His purposes, for spiritual and heavenly reasons, not selfish and earthly ones. Our concern should be to obey, honor, please, and glorify Him, leaving everything else to His wisdom and care.

WORRY ABOUT CLOTHING

And why are you anxious about clothing? Observe how the lilies of the field grow; they do not toil nor do they spin, yet I say to you that even Solomon in all his glory did not clothe himself like one of these. But if God so arrays the grass of the field, which is alive today and tomorrow is thrown into the furnace, will He not much more do so for you, O men of little faith? (6:28-30)

The third illustration has to do with clothing, using flowers as a model. Some of the people to whom Jesus spoke perhaps had little clothing, no more than one set of coverings for their bodies. He pointed again to their surroundings, this time to the flowers, to assure them of God's concern and provision.

The lilies of the field may have been a general term used of the wild flowers that in great variety and beauty grace the fields and hillsides of Galilee.

Those beautiful decorations of nature make no effort to grow and had no part in designing or coloring themselves. **They do not toil nor do they spin,** Jesus said, stating the obvious; **yet I say to you even Solomon in all his glory did not clothe himself like one of these.**

Even the naked eye can see much of the amazing detail, shading, and coloring of a flower. Under a microscope it shows itself to be even more marvelous and intricate than ancients could ever have imagined. Yet even **Solomon,** one of the most resplendent kings the world has ever known, **in all his glory did not clothe himself like one of these** little flowers which anyone there that day could have picked by the dozen.

It is an indictment of our day that we spend so much time, money, and effort to dress ourselves. Lusting after costly, stylish clothes is sinful, because its only purpose is to feed pride. The number of clothing stores we have today, and the vast amounts of clothes we find in them, is staggering. Many people have made a god out of fashion, and shamelessly waste money on expensive clothes they will wear but a few times.

Our worries today are seldom for necessary clothing. If Jesus told those who had but one simple garment not to worry about their clothing, what would He say to us?

Despite their beauty, however, flowers do not last long. Along with **the grass of the field,** they are **alive today and tomorrow** [are] **thrown into the furnace.**

Klibanos (**furnace**) is better translated "oven." Such ovens were made of hardened clay and were used primarily for baking bread. When a woman wanted to hurry the baking process, she would build a fire inside the oven as well as under it. Fuel for the inside heating was usually composed of dried grass and flowers gathered from nearby fields. Once the flower's beauty was gone it had little use except to be burned up as fuel for baking. Then it was gone.

But if God bothers to array the grass of the field with beautiful but short-lived flowers, how **much more** is He concerned to clothe and care for His very own children who are destined for eternal life?

To be anxious even about things which we need to survive, Jesus says, is sinful and shows **little faith.** A person who worries about those things may have saving faith, but he does not have faith that relies on God to finish what He has begun. It is significant that each of the four other times Jesus used the phrase "O men [or "you"] of little faith," it was also in relation to worry about food, clothing, or life span (see Matt. 8:26; 14:31; 16:8; Luke 12:28). "You believe that God can redeem you, save you from sin, break the shackles of Satan, take you to heaven where He has prepared a place for you, and keep you for all eternity," Jesus is saying; "and yet you do not trust Him to supply your daily needs?" We freely put our eternal destiny in His hands, but at times refuse to believe He will provide what we need to eat, drink, and wear.

Worry is not a trivial sin, because it strikes a blow both at God's love and at God's integrity. Worry declares our heavenly Father to be untrustworthy in His Word and His promises. To avow belief in the inerrancy of Scripture and in the next moment to express worry is to speak out of both sides of our mouths. Worry shows that we are mastered by our circumstances and by our own finite perspectives and understanding rather than by God's Word. Worry is therefore not only debilitating and destructive but maligns and impugns God.

When a believer is not fresh in the Word every day, so that God is in His mind and heart, then Satan moves into the vacuum and plants worry. Worry then pushes the Lord even further from our minds.

Paul counsels us as he did the Ephesians: "I pray that the eyes of your heart may be enlightened, so that you may know what is the hope of His calling, what are the riches of the glory of His inheritance in the saints, and what is the surpassing greatness of His power toward us who believe. These are in accordance with the working of the strength of His might" (Eph. 1:18-19).

WORRY IS UNREASONABLE BECAUSE OF OUR FAITH

Do not be anxious then, saying, "What shall we eat?" or "What shall we drink?" or "With what shall we clothe ourselves?" For all these things the Gentiles eagerly seek; for your heavenly Father knows that you need all these things. But seek first His kingdom and His righteousness; and all these things shall be added to you. (6:31-33)

Worry is inconsistent with our faith in God and is therefore unreasonable as well as sinful. Worry is characteristic of unbelief. *Ethnoi* (**Gentiles**) literally means simply "peoples," or "a multitude." In the plural form, as here, it usually referred to non-Jews, that is, to **Gentiles** and, by extension, to unbelievers or pagans. Worrying about **what** to **eat, drink,** and **clothe** themselves with are **things the Gentiles eagerly seek.** Those who have no hope in God naturally put their hope and expectations in things they can enjoy now. They have nothing to live for but the present, and their materialism is perfectly consistent with their religion. They have no God to supply their physical or their spiritual needs, their present or their eternal needs, so anything they get they must get for themselves. They are ignorant of God's supply and have no claim on it. No heavenly Father cares for them, so there is reason to worry.

The gods of the **Gentiles** were man-made gods inspired by Satan. They were gods of fear, dread, and appeasement who demanded much, promised little, and provided nothing. It was natural that those who served such gods would **eagerly seek** whatever satisfactions and pleasures they could while they could. Their philosophy is still popular in our own day among those who are determined

425

to grab all the gusto they can get. "Let us eat and drink, for tomorrow we die" is an understandable outlook for those who have no hope in the resurrection (1 Cor. 15:32).

But that is a completely foolish and unreasonable philosophy for those who *do* have hope in the resurrection, for those whose **heavenly Father knows that** [they] **need all these things.** To worry about our physical welfare and our clothing is the mark of a worldly mind, whether Christian or not. When we think like the world and crave like the world, we will worry like the world, because a mind that is not centered on God is a mind that has cause to worry. The faithful, trusting, and reasonable Christian is "anxious for nothing, but in everything by prayer and supplication with thanksgiving [lets his] requests be made known to God" (Phil. 4:6). He refuses in any way to "be conformed to this world" (Rom. 12:2).

Within this series of rebukes Jesus gives a positive command coupled with a beautiful promise: **But seek first His kingdom and His righteousness; and all these things shall be added to you.** The cause of worry is seeking the things of this world, and the cause of contentment is seeking the things of God's **kingdom and His righteousness.**

De is primarily a conjunction of contrast, for which **but** is a good rendering. In the present context it carries the idea of "rather," or "instead of." "Rather than seeking and worrying about food, drink, and clothing like unbelievers do," Jesus says, "focus your attention and hopes on the things of the Lord and He will take care of all your needs."

Out of all the options that we have, out of all the things we can seek for and be occupied with, we are to **seek first** the things of the One to whom we belong. That is the Christian's priority of priorities, a divine priority composed of two parts: God's **kingdom** and God's **righteousness.**

As we have seen in the discussion of the Disciples' Prayer (6:10), *basileia* (**kingdom**) does not refer to a geographical territory but to a dominion or rule. God's kingdom is God's sovereign rule, and therefore to **seek first His kingdom** is to seek first His rule, His will and His authority.

Seeking God's **kingdom** is losing ourselves in obedience to the Lord to the extent that we can say with Paul, "I do not consider my life of any account as dear to myself, in order that I may finish my course, and the ministry which I received from the Lord Jesus, to testify solemnly of the gospel of the grace of God" (Acts 20:24). To seek first God's kingdom is to pour out our lives in the eternal work of our heavenly Father.

To seek God's kingdom is seek to win people into that kingdom, that they might be saved and God might be glorified. It is to have our heavenly Father's own truth, love, and righteousness manifest in our lives, and to have "peace and joy in the Holy Spirit" (Rom. 14:17). We also seek God's kingdom when we yearn for the return of the King in His millennial glory to establish His kingdom on earth and usher in His eternal kingdom.

We are also to **seek . . . His righteousness.** Instead of longing after the things of this world, we are to hunger and thirst for the things of the world to come, which are characterized above all else by God's perfect **righteousness** and holiness. It is more than longing for something ethereal and future; it is also longing for something present and practical. We not only are to have heavenly expectations but holy lives (see Col. 3:2-3). "Since all these things [the earth and its works, v. 10] are to be destroyed in this way," Peter says, "what sort of people ought you to be in holy conduct and godliness, looking for and hastening the coming of the day of God" (2 Pet. 3:11).

Worry Is Unwise Because of Our Future

Therefore do not be anxious for tomorrow; for tomorrow will care for itself. Each day has enough trouble of its own. (6:34)

Making reasonable provisions for tomorrow is sensible, but to **be anxious for tomorrow** is foolish and unfaithful. God is the God of tomorrow as well as the God of today and of eternity. "The Lord's lovingkindnesses indeed never cease, for His compassions never fail. They are new every morning; great is Thy faithfulness" (Lam. 3:22-23).

It seems some people are so committed to worrying that, if they cannot find anything in the present to worry about, they think about possible problems in the future. **Tomorrow will take care of itself,** Jesus assures us. That is not the careless philosophy of the hedonist who lives only for his present enjoyment. It is the conviction of the child of God who knows that **tomorrow will take care of itself** because it is in his heavenly Father's hands.

That **each day has enough trouble of its own** is not a call to worry about that trouble, but to concentrate on meeting the temptations, trials, opportunities, and struggles we have today, relying on our Father to protect and provide as we have need. There is enough trouble in each day without adding the distress of worry to it.

God promises His grace for tomorrow and for every day thereafter and through eternity. But He does not *give* us grace for tomorrow now. He only gives His grace a day at a time as it is needed, not as it may be anticipated.

"The steadfast of mind Thou wilt keep in perfect peace," Isaiah says, "because he trusts in Thee. Trust in the Lord forever, for in God the Lord, we have an everlasting Rock" (Isa. 26:3-4).

Stop Criticizing (7:1-6)

40

Do not judge lest you be judged. For in the way you judge, you will be judged; and by your standard of measure, it will be measured to you. And why do you look at the speck that is in your brother's eye, but do not notice the log that is in your own eye? Or how can you say to your brother, "Let me take the speck out of your eye," and behold, the log is in your own eye? You hypocrite, first take the log out of your own eye, and then you will see clearly to take the speck out of your brother's eye.

Do not give what is holy to dogs, and do not throw your pearls before swine, lest they trample them under their feet, and turn and tear you to pieces. (7:1-6)

As with all the other elements of the Sermon on the Mount, the perspective of this passage is given in contrast to that of the scribes and Pharisees, whose hypocritical self-righteousness was in direct opposition to the true righteousness of God (see 5:20).

Here the comparison is in the area of human relations. Six verses (1-6) focus on the negative aspect of a self-righteous, judgmental spirit, and the following six verses (7-12) focus on the contrasting positive aspect of a spirit that is humble, trusting, and loving. These twelve verses form the divine summation of all the principles of right human relations.

When an individual or a group of people develop their own standards of religion and morality, they inevitably judge everyone by those self-made beliefs and standards. The scribes and Pharisees had done just that. Over the previous several centuries they had gradually modified God's revealed Word to suit their own thinking, inclinations, and abilities. By Jesus' time their tradition had taken such a hold on Judaism that it had actually replaced the authority of Scripture in the minds of many Jews (Matt. 15:6; cf. 15:2).

Along with the many other sins spawned by their self-righteousness, the scribes and Pharisees had become oppressively judgmental. They proudly looked down on everyone who was not a part of their elite system. They were unmerciful, unforgiving, unkind, censorious, and totally lacking in compassion and grace.

Their evaluation of others, like every other aspect of their hypocritical system, was based on appearances, on the external and superficial (John 7:24; 8:15). They lived to justify themselves in the eyes of other men; but Jesus told them that their judgment was utterly contrary to God's and was detestable in His sight (Luke 16:15).

The classic portrayal of self-righteous judgment is given in the parable of the Pharisee and the tax-gatherer who went to the Temple to pray. "The Pharisee stood and was praying thus to himself, 'God, I thank Thee that I am not like other people; swindlers, unjust, adulterers, or even like this tax-gatherer. I fast twice a week; I pay tithes of all that I get.' But the tax-gatherer, standing some distance away, was even unwilling to lift up his eyes to heaven, but was beating his breast, saying, 'God, be merciful to me, the sinner!'" Jesus' assessment of the two prayers is clear: "I tell you, this man went down to his house justified rather than the other; for everyone who exalts himself shall be humbled, but he who humbles himself shall be exalted" (Luke 18:11-14).

An inseparable corollary of justifying oneself is condemning others. When anyone elevates himself, everyone else is lowered accordingly. The Pharisees were doing all they could to lift themselves up in their own eyes, including acting as spiritual judges by condemning others.

It should be noted that this passage has erroneously been used to suggest that believers should never evaluate or criticize anyone for anything. Our day hates absolutes, especially theological and moral absolutes, and such simplistic interpretation provides a convenient escape from confrontation. Members of modern society, including many professing Christians, tend to resist dogmatism and strong convictions about right and wrong. Many people prefer to speak of all-inclusive love, compromise, ecumenism, and unity. To the modern religious person those are the only "doctrines" worth defending, and they are the doctrines to which every conflicting doctrine must be sacrificed.

Some years ago a church was looking for a pastor who would emphasize holiness rather than doctrine. I once received a manuscript to review whose primary thesis was that doctrine divides the church. Consequently, the author argued, all doctrine—at least all that might be disagreed with and therefore be divisive—should be eliminated for the sake of the higher goal of unity and fellowship. Right doctrine not only is compatible with true holiness, unity, and fellowship but is absolutely necessary for them to exist. Only right doctrine, biblical doctrine, can teach us what true holiness, unity, and fellowship are—and are not.

In many circles, including some evangelical circles, those who hold to strong convictions and who speak up and confront society and the church are branded as violators of this command not to judge, and are seen as troublemakers or, at best, as controversial. Yet at no time in the history of the church, or of ancient Israel, was spiritual and moral reformation achieved apart from confrontation and conflict. God's prophets have always been bold and controversial. And they have always been resisted, often by God's own people. The church reformers of the sixteenth century were men of strong doctrine, conviction, and principle—apart from which the Protestant Reformation would never have come about.

Reformation is needed when spiritual and moral life are low; and for the very reason they are low they will resist every effort to reform. The power of sin, whether in an unbeliever or believer, is opposed to righteousness and will always resist God's truth and God's standards. To the carnal person, absolute doctrine and high moral standards are inherently controversial.

Christ does not here or anywhere else forbid courts of law, as claimed by the Russian novelist Leo Tolstoy and others. Both the Old and New Testaments uphold not only the right but the divine necessity of human courts of law (e.g., Deut. 19:15-21; Rom. 13:1-7). Nor does this or any other part of Scripture teach that we are never to evaluate, criticize, or condemn the actions or teachings of another person.

The entire thrust of the Sermon on the Mount is to show the complete distinction between true religion and false religion, between spiritual truth and spiritual hypocrisy. Jesus places God's perfect and holy standards beside the unholy and self-righteous standards of the scribes and Pharisees and declares that those who follow those unholy and self-righteous standards have no part in God's kingdom (5:20). No more controversial or judgmental sermon has ever been preached.

If this greatest sermon by our Lord teaches anything, it teaches that His followers are to be discerning and perceptive in what they believe and in what they do, that they must make every effort to judge between truth and falsehood, between the internal and the external, between reality and sham, between true righteousness and false righteousness—in short, between God's way and all other ways.

A few verses later Jesus warns, "Beware of the false prophets" (Matt. 7:15). In other words, we are to judge who speaks for God and who does not. Jesus tells us to confront a sinning brother privately with his sin and, if he will not repent, to take one or two others with us to speak to him, and if that does not cause him to change, to bring him before the entire church. If he still does not repent, he is to be put out of the church and regarded "as a Gentile and a tax-gatherer" (Matt. 18:15-17).

Paul tells believers, "Now I urge you, brethren, keep your eye on those who cause dissensions and hindrances contrary to the teaching which you learned, and turn away from them. For such men are slaves, not of our Lord Christ but of their own appetites; and by their smooth and flattering speech they deceive the hearts of the unsuspecting" (Rom. 16:17-18). He also instructs saints not even "to associate with any so-called brother if he should be an immoral person, or covetous, or an idolater, or a reviler, or a drunkard, or a swindler—not even to eat with such a one" (1 Cor. 5:11). Obviously such commands demand that we employ a certain kind of judgment before we can obey.

Every message we hear is to be judged for the soundness of its doctrine. Paul told the Galatians, "But even though we, or an angel from heaven, should preach to you a gospel contrary to that which we have preached to you, let him be accursed" (Gal. 1:8). John says, "If anyone comes to you and does not bring this teaching, do not receive him into your house, and do not give him a greeting; for the one who gives him a greeting participates in his evil deeds" (2 John 10-11).

Not to rebuke sin is a form of hatred, not love. "You shall not hate your fellow countryman in your heart; you may surely reprove your neighbor" (Lev. 19:17). Refusing to warn a person about his sin is just as unloving as refusing to warn him about a serious disease he may have. A person who does not warn a friend about his sin cannot claim love as his motive (see Matt. 18:15). The author of Hebrews calls for a level of spiritual maturity wherein Christians "because of practice have their senses trained to discern good and evil" (5:14).

But Jesus is here talking about the self-righteous, egotistical judgment and unmerciful condemnation of others practiced by the scribes and Pharisees. Their primary concern was not to help others from sin to holiness, but to condemn them to eternal judgment because of actions and attitudes that did not square with their own worldly, self-made traditions.

Krinō (to **judge**) means basically to separate, choose, select, or determine, and has a dozen or more shades of meaning that must be decided from the context. In our present passage Jesus is referring to the judgment of motives, which no mere human being can know of another, and to judgment of external forms. Paul says, "Therefore let us not judge one another anymore, but rather determine this—not to put an obstacle or a stumbling block in a brother's way" (Rom. 14:13).

The Bible consistently forbids individual or vigilante justice that assumes for itself the prerogatives of a duly established court of law. It also consistently forbids hasty judgments that do not have full knowledge of the heart or of the facts. "He who gives an answer before he hears, it is folly and shame to him" (Prov. 18:13). Sometimes what appears to be wrong is nothing of the sort.

It is significant that, though God is omniscient, He gives us many examples of the care we ourselves should take before making judgments, especially those that involve serious consequences. Before He judged those who were building the tower of Babel, "The Lord came down to see the city and the tower which the sons of men had built" (Gen. 11:5). Before He destroyed Sodom and Gomorrah He said, "I will go down now, and see if they have done entirely according to its outcry, which has come to Me; and if not, I will know" (Gen. 18:21).

What Jesus here forbids is self-righteous, officious, hasty, unmerciful, prejudiced, and unwarranted condemnation based on human standards and human understanding. He gives three reasons why such judgment is sinful: it reveals an erroneous view of God, an erroneous view of others, and an erroneous view of ourselves.

An Erroneous View of God

Do not judge lest you be judged. (7:1)

Unrighteous and unmerciful judgment is forbidden first of all because it manifests a wrong view of God. With the phrase **lest you be judged,** Jesus reminds the scribes and Pharisees that they are not the final court. To judge another person's motives or to curse to condemnation is to play God. "For not even the Father judges anyone, but He has given all judgment to the Son" (John 5:22). During the millennial kingdom Christ will share some of that judgment with us (Matt. 19:28; 1 Cor. 6:2; etc.), but until that time we blaspheme God whenever we take upon ourselves the role of judge. "Who are you to judge the servant of another?" Paul asks. "To his own master he stands or falls" (Rom. 14:4). Paul was little concerned about how other people judged him, and was not even concerned about how he judged himself. "I am conscious of nothing against myself," he says, "yet I am not by this acquitted; but the one who examines me is the Lord" (1 Cor. 4:3-4).

Except as they may be continually teaching false doctrine or following standards that are clearly unscriptural, we are never to judge a person's ministry, teaching, or life—and certainly not his motives—by a self-styled standard. "Do not speak against one another," James warns us. "He who speaks against a brother, or judges his brother, speaks against the law, and judges the law; but if you judge the law, you are not a doer of the law, but a judge of it. There is only one Lawgiver and Judge, the One who is able to save and to destroy; but who are you who judge your neighbor?" (James 4:11-12). Such evil judgment is blasphemous, because it sets a man up as God—and there is only one true Judge.

Whenever we assign people to condemnation without mercy because they do not do something the way we think it ought to be done or because we believe their motives are wrong, we pass judgment that only God is qualified to make. An unknown poet of past days wrote,

> Judge not the workings of his brain,
> And of his heart thou cannot see.
> What looks to thy dim eyes a stain,
> In God's pure light may only be
> A scar brought from some well-won field
> Where thou wouldst only faint and yield.

The Savior does not call for men to cease to be examining and discerning, but to renounce the presumptuous temptation to try to be God.

An Erroneous View of Others

For in the way you judge, you will be judged; and by your standard of measure, it will be measured to you. (7:2)

Most people feel free to judge others like this because they erroneously think they are somehow superior to others. The Pharisees thought they were exempt from judgment because they believed they perfectly measured up to the divine standards. The problem was that those were mere human standards that they, and others like them, had established far short of God's holy and perfect law.

Jesus says that God will judge us with the same type of judgment with which we judge others. When we assume the role of final, omniscient judge, we imply that we are qualified to judge—that we know and understand all the facts, all the circumstances, and all the motives involved. Therefore, when we assert our right to **judge**, we **will be judged** by the standard of knowledge and wisdom we claim is ours. If we set ourselves up as judge over others, we cannot plead ignorance of the law in reference to ourselves when God judges us.

James has the same principle in mind when he warns, "Let not many of you become teachers, my brethren, knowing that as such we shall incur a stricter judgment" (James 3:1). The person who is qualified to teach is judged on a stricter basis than others because as a teacher he has greater understanding and influence. "From everyone who has been given much shall much be required" (Luke 12:48).

We are especially guilty if we do not practice what we ourselves teach and preach. "Therefore you are without excuse, every man of you who passes judgment, for in that you judge another, you condemn yourself; for you who judge practice the same things. And we know that the judgment of God rightly falls upon those who practice such things" (Rom. 2:1-2).

God has no double standards. In criticizing unjustly or condemning unmercifully, we play God and give the impression that we ourselves are above criticism and judgment. But God sets none of us as final judge above others, and we dare not set ourselves as judge above others. Other people are not under us, and to think so is to have the wrong view of them. To be gossipy, talebearing, critical, and judgmental is to live under the false illusion that those whom we so judge are somehow inferior to us.

Such judgment is a boomerang, Jesus says, and will come back upon the one who judges. Self-righteous judgment will become its own gallows, just as the gallows Haman had erected to execute the innocent Mordecai was used instead to hang Haman (Esther 7:10). Just as the cruel Adoni-bezek had ordered the thumbs and big toes cut off seventy other kings, so his own were eventually cut off (Judg. 1:6-7).

In ancient Persia a certain corrupt judge who accepted a bribe to render a false verdict was ordered executed by king Cambyses. The judge's skin was then used to cover the judgment seat. Subsequent judges were forced to render their judgments while sitting on that chair, as a reminder of the consequences of perverting justice.

To be judgmental is dangerous to the victim because of the bias against him. It is even more dangerous to the judge, because by the **standard of measure** with which he judges others **it will be measured to** him.

AN ERRONEOUS VIEW OF OURSELVES

And why do you look at the speck that is in your brother's eye, but do not notice the log that is in your own eye? Or how can you say to your brother, "Let me take the speck out of your eye," and behold, the log is in your own eye? You hypocrite, (7:3-5a)

When we judge critically we also manifest an erroneous view of ourselves. All three false views are connected. When we have a wrong view of God, we cannot but have a wrong view of others and of ourselves. Putting ourselves in God's place as judge perverts our perspective of others and of ourselves.

A *karphos* (**speck**) is not a tiny piece of dust or soot but a small stalk or twig, or possibly a splinter. Though small in comparison to a **log**, it is not an insignificant object to have in the eye. Jesus' comparison, therefore, is not between a very small sin or fault and one that is large, but between one that is large and one that is gigantic. The primary point, of course, is that the sin of the critic is much greater than the sin of the person he is criticizing.

Some interpreters suggest the **speck** represents a rather minor ceremonial infraction, whereas **log** represents an extremely vulgar and repulsive sin. But people with obviously terrible sins usually spend their time trying to hide or justify their own great sin, not in criticizing the small sins of others.

The wretched and gross sin that is always blind to its own sinfulness is self-righteousness, the sin that Jesus repeatedly condemns in the scribes and Pharisees, not only in the Sermon on the Mount but throughout His ministry. Almost by definition, self-righteousness is a sin of blindness, or of grossly distorted vision, because it looks directly at its own sin and still imagines it sees only righteousness. The **log** in this illustration represents the same foundational sin of self-righteousness that Jesus has been condemning throughout the sermon.

The very nature of self-righteousness is to justify self and condemn others. In so doing people play God, because they judge themselves on the basis of their own standards and wisdom. Self-righteousness is the worst of sins because it is unbelief. It trusts in self rather than God. It trusts in self to determine what is right and wrong and to determine who does what is right or wrong. Self-righteousness claims to be both lawgiver and judge, prerogatives that belong only to the Lord.

Consequently it denies and opposes the gospel, because the gospel proclaims man's sinfulness and lostness even as it proclaims God's mercy and grace. Because the self-righteous person sees no sin in his life, he sees no need for God's grace in his behalf. The term **notice** conveys the idea of serious, continuous meditation. Jesus is saying, in effect, "Will you not stop and think about your own sin? Until you have done that, how can you confront another with his shortcomings?"

Thus, the self-righteous person can never be anything but a **hypocrite**, because he continually puts on a deceitful act of righteous superiority. That is why he feels qualified to say to his **brother, "Let me take the speck out of your eye"**—let me tell you what is wrong in your life and let me straighten you out.

The **hypocrite** "is like a man who looks at his natural face in a mirror; for once he has looked at himself and gone away, he has immediately forgotten what kind of person he was" (James 1:23-24). He sees but he does not see. He is like those to whom Isaiah was sent, a people who would listen but not perceive and look but not understand, because their hearts were insensitive and "their ears dull, and their eyes dim" (Isa. 6:9-10).

The Right Balance

first take the log out of your own eye, and then you will see clearly to take the speck out of your brother's eye.

Do not give what is holy to dogs, and do not throw your pearls before swine, lest they trample them under their feet, and turn and tear you to pieces. (7:5b-6)

The person who has the mind and attitude of the kingdom citizen—the person who is poor in spirit, humble, and who hungers and thirsts for God's righteousness (see Matt. 5:3, 5-6)—will be the person who first of all sees and mourns over his own sin (see 5:4).

Jesus here gives the corrective to the wrong kind of judgment by showing the right balance of humility and conviction, poverty of spirit and power in the Spirit. The Lord's command is, **First take the log out of your own eye, and then you will see clearly to take the speck out of your brother's eye.** First of all we confess our own sin—often the sin of self-righteousness and of a condemning spirit toward others—and ask for God's cleansing. When our own sin is cleansed, when the **log** is taken out of our **own eye**, then we will see our brother's sin clearly and be able to help him. Then we will see *everything* clearly—God, others, and ourselves. We will see God as the only Judge, others as needy sinners who are just like ourselves. We will see our **brother** as a brother, on our own level and with our own frailties and needs.

This right balance of humility and helpfulness is reflected in Psalm 51. David first prays, "Create in me a clean heart, O God, and renew a steadfast spirit within me. . . . Restore to me the joy of Thy salvation, and sustain me with a willing spirit. Then," he is able to say, "I will teach transgressors Thy ways, and sinners will be converted to Thee" (vv. 10, 12-13). Jesus told Peter that after he had recovered from his moral defection, he could then "strengthen [his] brothers" (Luke 22:32). Paul advises us, "Brethren, even if a man is caught in any trespass, you who are spiritual, restore such a one in a spirit of gentleness; each one looking to yourself, lest you too be tempted" (Gal. 6:1). All confrontation of sin in others must be done out of meekness, not pride. We cannot play the role of judge—passing sentence as if we were God. We cannot play the role of superior—as if we were exempt from the same standards we demand of others. We must not play the hypocrite—blaming others while we excuse ourselves.

There is also danger, however, even for the truly humble and repentant believer. The first danger, already mentioned above, is of concluding that we have no right to oppose wrong doctrine or wrong practices in the church, lest we fall into judgmental self-righteousness. We will then not be willing to confront a sinning brother as the Lord clearly calls to do. The second danger is closely related to the first. If we are afraid to confront falsehood and sin in the church, we will be inclined to become undiscriminating and undiscerning. The church, and our own lives, will become more and more in danger of corruption. Realizing the impact of sin in the assembly (1 Pet. 4:15), Peter made a powerful call for a confrontive, critical church when he said, "For it is time for judgment to begin with the household of God" (v. 17). Believers must be discerning and make proper judgment when it is required.

Jesus closes this illustration with a thunderbolt that completely shatters the sentimental interpretation that, in the name of humility and love, we are never to oppose wrong or correct wrongdoers. It is clear that Jesus does not exclude every kind of judgment. In fact, He just as plainly commands a certain kind of right judgment here as He forbids a wrong kind in the preceding verses. **Do not give what is holy to dogs, and do not throw your pearls before swine.** To obey that command it is obviously necessary to be able to determine who are **dogs** and **swine.**

In biblical times **dogs** were seldom kept as household pets in the way they are today. Except for those used as working animals to herd sheep, they were largely half-wild mongrels that acted as scavengers. They were dirty, greedy, snarling, and often vicious and diseased. They were dangerous and despised.

It would have been unthinkable for a Jew to have thrown to those **dogs** a piece of **holy** meat that had been consecrated as a sacrifice in the Temple. Some parts of those offerings were burned up, some parts were eaten by the priests, and some would often be taken home and eaten by the family who made the sacrifice. The part left on the altar was the part which was consecrated exclusively to the Lord, and therefore was **holy** in a very special way. If no man was to eat that part of the sacrifice, how much less should it be thrown to a bunch of wild, filthy **dogs.** Such an act would be the height of desecration.

Swine were considered by Jews to be the epitome of uncleanness. That is the reason Antiochus Epiphanes' sacrifice of a pig on the Jewish altar and forcing the priests to eat it was such an absolute abomination—and touched off the Maccabean revolt against Greece in 168 B.C.

Because a Jew would never have tried to domesticate a pig, most of the **swine** they encountered were, like the dogs, wild animals who foraged for themselves, often in garbage dumps on the edge of town. Like the scavenging dogs, those **swine** were greedy, vicious, and filthy even by ordinary pig standards. If you came between them and their food they would likely **turn and tear you to pieces** with their tusks and sharp hooves.

Jesus' point is that certain truths and blessings of our faith are not to be shared with people who are totally antagonistic to the things of God. Such people are spiritual **dogs** and **swine**, who have no appreciation for that which is holy and righteous. They will take that which is **holy**, the **pearls** (the rarest and most valuable of jewels; see Matt. 13:45-46) of God's Word, as foolishness and as an insult.

A wild animal whose primary concern is scavenging for food will hardly appreciate being thrown a pearl. He will resent its not being something to eat and possibly attack the one who throws it.

Jesus did not give all of His teaching to everyone who happened to be listening. On one occasion He prayed, "I praise Thee, O Father, Lord of heaven and earth, that Thou didst hide these things from the wise and intelligent and didst reveal them to babes" (Matt. 11:25). On another occasion He said to His disciples, in answer to their question about why He spoke to the multitudes in parables: "To you it has been granted to know the mysteries of the kingdom of heaven, but to them it has not been granted. . . . Therefore I speak to them in parables; because while seeing they do not see, and while hearing they do not hear, nor do they understand" (Matt. 13:11, 13). And after Jesus rose from the dead He showed Himself to no one who was not a believer.

Peter warns, "But false prophets also arose among the people, just as there will also be false teachers among you, who will secretly introduce destructive heresies, even denying the Master who bought them, bringing swift destruction upon themselves. And many will follow their sensuality, and because of them the way of the truth will be maligned; and in their greed they will exploit you with false words" (2 Pet. 2:1-3). A few verses later he speaks of such people as being "like unreasoning animals, born as creatures of instinct to be captured and killed, reviling where they have no knowledge" (v. 12). Using as examples the same two animals Jesus mentions in our present text, Peter closes his warning with the words: "It has happened to them according to the true proverb, 'A dog returns to its own vomit,' and, 'A sow, after washing, returns to wallowing in the mire'" (v. 22).

Dogs and **swine** represent those who, because of their great perversity and ungodliness, refuse to have anything to do with the **holy** and precious things of God except to **trample them under their feet, and turn and tear** God's people **to pieces.**

There will be times when the gospel we present is absolutely rejected and ridiculed and we make the judgment to turn away and speak no more, deciding that we should "shake off the dust of [our] feet" (Matt. 10:14) and begin ministering somewhere else. There will be times when those to whom we witness will resist the gospel and blaspheme God, and we may speak words of judgment. Like Paul, we must then say, in effect, "Your blood be upon your own heads! I am clean. From now on I shall go to the Gentiles" (Acts 18:6). When people not only reject the gospel, but insist on mocking and reviling it, we are not to waste God's **holy** Word and the precious **pearls** of His truth in a futile and frustrating attempt to win them. We are to leave them to the Lord, trusting that somehow His Spirit can penetrate their hearts—as He apparently did with some of those who at first rejected the preaching of Paul and the other apostles—or leaving them to the just judgment of God.

A warranted judgment is made when we "reject a factious man [one who belongs to a sect, or a heretic] after the first and second warning, knowing that such a man is perverted and is sinning, being self-condemned" (Titus 3:10-11). That text shows that in such a situation the believer does not condemn, but rather is able to recognize an already self-condemned person.

Matthew 7:6 is one of the "hard sayings" of Jesus. We must take the command seriously and do our best to obey it, because it is the Lord's will. But because it is so serious and because we may also be inclined to be self-righteous and judgmental, we need to depend on the Lord with special care and sincerity. Even when we determine that a person is too rebellious to hear the gospel or is a heretical and false teacher, we go on our way not in self-satisfied judgment but in great disappointment and sorrow—remembering how our Lord, as He approached Jerusalem for the last time, "saw the city and wept over" those who refused to recognize and receive their King (Luke 19:41-42). To avoid wrongful judging and to accomplish right discernment is to be marked as a citizen of the heavenly kingdom.

Start Loving (7:7-12)

41

Ask, and it shall be given to you; seek, and you shall find; knock, and it shall be opened to you. For everyone who asks receives, and he who seeks finds, and to him who knocks it shall be opened. Or what man is there among you, when his son shall ask him for a loaf, will give him a stone? Or if he shall ask for a fish, he will not give him a snake, will he? If you then, being evil, know how to give good gifts to your children, how much more shall your Father who is in heaven give what is good to those who ask Him! Therefore, however you want people to treat you, so treat them, for this is the Law and the Prophets. (7:7-12)

Here is the conclusion of the main theme of the Sermon on the Mount, which is to give the standards for kingdom living. Jesus has given the standards related to self, to morality, to religion, and to money and possessions. Here He concludes giving the standards related to human relationships begun in verses 1-6.

This passage forms the positive side of Jesus' summation of the principles that lead to right human relations. To love others in the way God wants us to love first of all requires that we do not self-righteously and carelessly criticize and unmercifully condemn others. If that attitude is present, it has to be removed. Not to be unjustly critical of a person is not the same as loving them, but it is absolutely necessary before true love can exist. Yet love is much more than something negative; it is immeasurably more than simply not wishing evil on others or doing them any wrong. The mere absence of hatred and ill will does not constitute love.

The positive side of love is the active side, the productive side, the side that is the true measure and test of love. It is not seen in what we refrain from doing but in what we do. (The Greek verb forms in the descriptions of love in 1 Corinthians 13:4-7 all emphasize action.) The key expression of that principle is in verse 12, **however you want people to treat you, so treat them**, to which verses 1-11 point as advance commentary and illustration. That verse, often referred to as the golden rule, has also been called the Mt. Everest of ethics (William Barclay, *The Gospel of Matthew*, 2 vols. [Philadelphia: Westminster, 1975], 1:272). The famous Bible scholar Alfred Edersheim said it was the closest approach to absolute love of which human nature was capable, and Bishop J. C. Ryle wrote, "[This truth] settles a hundred different points, . . . it prevents the necessity of laying down endless little rules for our conduct in specific cases" (*Expository Thoughts on the Gospels: St. Matthew* [London: James Clarke, 1965], p. 66).

Jesus gives three reasons for obeying the command to love others as ourselves: God's promise to His children demands it, His pattern for His children demands it, and His purpose for His children demands it.

GOD'S PROMISE TO HIS CHILDREN DEMANDS IT

Ask, and it shall be given to you; seek, and you shall find; knock, and it shall be opened to you. For everyone who asks receives, and he who seeks finds, and to him who knocks it shall be opened. (7:7-8)

Here is one of the Lord's greatest and most comprehensive promises to those who belong to Him, to those who are His children and citizens of His kingdom. In light of this great promise we can feel free to fully love others and totally sacrifice for others, because our heavenly Father sets the example in His generosity to us and promises that we have access to His eternal and unlimited treasure to meet our own needs as well as theirs. We can do for others what we would want done for ourselves (see v. 12) without fear of depleting the divine resources and having nothing left.

Verses 7-11 make a perfect bridge between the negative teaching about a critical spirit and the positive teaching of the golden rule (v. 12). Even when we have been cleansed of our own sin—had the "log" removed from our eye—we need divine wisdom to know how to help a brother remove the "speck" from his eye (v. 5). And without God's help we cannot be sure of who are "dogs" or "swine"— who are the false prophets and apostates to whom we should not offer the holy and precious things of God's Word (v. 6). These considerations drive us to call on the Lord.

Of the many things for which we should **ask, seek,** and **knock,** God's wisdom is among our greatest needs. We cannot be discerning and discriminating without divine counsel from our heavenly Father; and the primary means for achieving such wisdom is petitioning prayer. "If any of you lacks wisdom, let him ask of God, who gives to all men generously and without reproach, and it will be given to him" (James 1:5).

God gives us many principles in His Word, but He does not give specific methods or rules for every conceivable situation. For one thing, situations keep changing and vary greatly from age to age and person to person. To give specific rules for every circumstance would require a giant library of volumes. But even more important than that is God's desire that we rely on Him directly. He wants us to be in His Word, and without being in His Word we cannot pray wisely or rightly.

But even beyond our being in His Word, He wants us to be in fellowship with Him as our Father. Along with His perfect and infallible Word, we need His Spirit to interpret and illumine, to encourage and to strengthen. He does not want us to have all the answers in our hip pocket. The Bible is a limitless store of divine truth, which a lifetime of the most faithful and diligent study will not exhaust. But apart from God Himself we cannot even start to fathom its depths or mine its riches. In His Word God gives enough truth for us to be responsible, but enough mystery for us to be dependent. He gives us His Word not only to direct our lives but to draw our lives to Him.

Here Jesus says, in effect, "If you want wisdom to know how to help a sinning brother and how to discern falsehood and apostasy, go to your heavenly Father. **Ask, seek,** and **knock** at the doors of heaven, and you will receive, find, and have the door opened."

Contrary to some popular interpretations, verses 7-8 are not a blank check for just anyone to present to God. First of all, the promise is valid only for believers. Throughout the Sermon on the Mount Jesus' promises are addressed only to believers. A large mass of unbelievers, including some scribes and Pharisees, no doubt were in the multitude on the side of the mountain that day. In this sermon, however, Jesus *always* speaks of scribes, Pharisees, hypocrites, false prophets, insincere followers, and all other unbelievers in the third person—as if none of them were the direct target of His words. On other occasions (as in Matt. 23) the Lord addresses such persons directly; but during this message all of His references to them are indirect. He gives this sermon to His disciples (5:1-2), with the crowd listening in.

Everyone refers to those who belong to the heavenly Father. Those who are not God's children cannot come to Him as their Father. The two overriding relationships focused on in the book of Matthew are those of God's kingdom and God's family. The kingdom concept deals with rule, and the family concept deals with relationship. In the Sermon on the Mount the primary focus is on God's family, and we see repeated references to God as heavenly Father (v. 11; cf. 5:16, 45, 48; 6:4, 8-9, 26, 32) and to fellow believers as brothers (5:22-24; 7:3-5).

The two greatest realities of Christian truth are that God is our Father and Christians are our brothers. Believers are the family of God. Paul speaks of the church as the "household of the faith" (Gal. 6:10) and as "God's household" (Eph. 2:19). John repeatedly speaks of God as our Father (1 John 1:2-3; 2:1, 13; 3:1; 4:14; etc.) and of believers as His children (1 John 3:10; 5:2) and as each other's brothers (1 John 2:9-11; 3:10-12; 4:20; etc.).

Second, the one who claims this promise must be living in obedience to his Father. "Whatever we ask we receive from Him," John says, "because we keep His commandments and do the things that are pleasing in His sight" (1 John 3:22).

Third, our motive in asking must be right. "You ask and do not receive," explains James, "because you ask with wrong motives, so that you may spend it on your pleasures" (James 4:3). God does not obligate Himself to answer selfish, carnal requests from His children.

Finally, we must be submissive to His will. If we are trying to serve both God and mammon (Matt. 6:24), we cannot claim this promise. "For let not that man expect that he will receive anything from the Lord, being a double-minded man, unstable in all his ways" (James 1:7-8). As John makes clear, "This is the confidence which we have before Him, that, if we ask anything according to His will, He hears us" (1 John 5:14). To have confidence in answered prayer on any other basis is to have a false and presumptuous confidence that the Lord makes no promise to honor.

Another possible qualification is perseverance, suggested by the present imperative tenses of **ask**, **seek**, and **knock**. The idea is that of continuance and constancy: "Keep on asking; keep on seeking; keep on knocking." We also see a progression of intensity in the three verbs, from simple asking to the more aggressive seeking to the still more aggressive knocking. Yet none of the figures is complicated or obscure. The youngest child knows what it is to ask, seek, and knock.

The progression in intensity also suggests that our sincere requests to the Lord are not to be passive. Whatever of His will we know to do we should be doing. If we are asking the Lord to help us find a job, we should be looking for a job ourselves while we await His guidance and provision. If we are out of food, we should be trying to earn money to buy it if we can. If we want help in confronting a brother about a sin, we should be trying to find out all we can about him and his situation and all we can about what God's Word says on the subject involved. It is not faith but presumption to ask the Lord to provide more when we are not faithfully using what He has already given.

God's Pattern for His Children Demands It

Or what man is there among you, when his son shall ask him for a loaf, will give him a stone? Or if he shall ask for a fish, he will not give him a snake, will he? If you then, being evil, know how to give good gifts to your children, how much more shall your Father who is in heaven give what is good to those who ask Him! (7:9-11)

These verses continue to point to and illustrate the golden rule of verse 12. We are also to love others as we love ourselves because that is a part of God's life pattern for His children and kingdom citizens. "Therefore be imitators of God, as beloved children; and walk in love, just as Christ also loved you, and gave Himself up for us, an offering and a sacrifice to God as a fragrant aroma" (Eph. 5:1-2).

If we claim to be God's children, God's nature should be reflected in our lives, imperfect as they still are. Jesus here proceeds to show us something of what our heavenly Father's love is like. First, He gives several illustrations from human family relationships by asking two rhetorical questions.

What man . . . among you, that is to say, what loving father, **when his son shall ask him for a loaf, will give him a stone?** The obvious answer is no man, no loving father. The cruelest of fathers would hardly deceive his own son by giving him a stone to eat that looked like bread. Even if the son discovered the deception before breaking a tooth, his heart would be broken by his father's cruelty.

Or, Jesus continues, **if** the son **shall ask for a fish,** the father **will not give him a snake, will he?** The idea is not that the snake would be alive and poisonous, and therefore of physical danger to the son. The suggestion is of a snake that is cooked to look like ordinary meat and would, unlike the stone, meet the son's physical need. But because they were among the unclean animals (Lev. 11:12), snakes were not to be eaten by Jews. A loving Jewish father would not deceive and defile his son into dishonoring the Word of God by tricking him into eating ceremonially unclean food. Our Lord is simply showing that it is not natural for a father to ignore either the physical or the spiritual needs of his son.

In the Luke account Jesus gives the added and more dramatic illustration of a scorpion being substituted for an egg (11:12). Certain Near East scorpions were quite large and resembled a bird's egg when they curled up to sleep. In this instance, the deceit could cause great physical danger to the son, even an agonizing death.

If you then, being evil—as sinful human fathers—**know how to give good gifts to your children, how much more shall your Father who is in heaven give what is good to those who ask Him!** Here is one of the many specific scriptural teachings of man's fallen, **evil** nature. Jesus is not speaking of specific fathers who are especially cruel and wicked, but of human fathers in general, all of whom are sinful by nature.

Those who do not know the true God have no divine source to whom they can turn with assurance or trust. Most pagan gods are but larger than life images of the men who made and worship them. Greek mythology tells of Aurora, the goddess of dawn, who fell in love with Tithonus, a mortal youth. When Zeus, the king of gods, promised to grant her any gift she chose for her lover, she asked that Tithonus might live forever. But she had forgotten to ask that he also remain forever young. Therefore when Zeus granted the request, Tithonus was doomed to an eternity of perpetual aging (*Homeric Hymn to Aphrodite* [5.218-38]). Such are the capricious ways of the gods men make.

But not so with the God and Father of our Lord Jesus Christ. As in the previous chapter, Jesus uses the phrase **much more** to describe God's love for His children (cf. 6:30). Our divine, loving, merciful, gracious **Father who is in heaven** has no limit on His treasure and no bounds to the goodness He is willing to bestow on His children **who ask Him**. The most naturally selfless relationship among human beings is that of parents with their children. We are more likely to sacrifice for our children, even to the point of giving up our lives, than for any other persons in the world. Yet the greatest human parental love cannot compare with God's.

There is no limit to what our heavenly Father will give to us when we ask in obedience and according to His will. Again we get additional truth from the parallel passage in Luke, which tells us, "How much more shall your heavenly Father give the Holy Spirit to those who ask Him?" (11:13).

The truth Jesus proclaims here is that, if imperfect and sinful human fathers so willingly and freely give their children the basics of life, God will infinitely outdo them in measure and in benefit. That is why the children of God are "blessed . . . with every spiritual blessing" (Eph. 1:3) offered by "the riches of His grace, which He lavished upon us (vv. 7-8). If we want God to treat us with loving generosity as His children, we should so treat others, because we are those who bear His likeness.

GOD'S PURPOSE FOR HIS CHILDREN DEMANDS IT

Therefore, however you want people to treat you, so treat them, for this is the Law and the Prophets. (7:12)

The implication of verses 7-11 is made explicit in verse 12. The perfect love of the heavenly Father is most reflected in His children when they treat others as they themselves wish to be treated.

There is no capacity within an unbeliever to love in the way that Jesus commands here. Unbelievers can do many ethical things, and every once in a while they might even approach the level of this highest of ethical standards. But they cannot sustain such selflessness, because they do not have the divine resource necessary for regular, habitual living on that plane.

However you want people to treat you sums up the sermon to this point, and **so treat them** is a summary of **the Law and the Prophets**. It is also a paraphrase of the second great commandment, "You shall love your neighbor as yourself" (Matt. 22:39; cf. Lev. 19:18). The golden rule instructs us as to how we are to love other people, "especially," as Paul points out, "those of the household of the faith" (Gal. 6:10). And "he who loves his neighbor has fulfilled the law" (Rom. 13:8; cf. v. 10; Gal. 5:14).

How we **treat** others is not to be determined by how we *expect* them to treat us or by how we think they *should* treat us, but by how we **want** them **to treat** us. Herein is the heart of the principle, an aspect of the general truth that is not found in similar expressions in other religions and philosophies.

For many years the basic instrument of music was the harpsichord. As its keys are depressed, a given string is plucked to create the desired note, much as a guitar string is plucked with a pick. But the tone made in that way is not pure, and the mechanism is relatively slow and limiting. Sometime during the last quarter of the eighteenth century, during Beethoven's lifetime, an unknown musician modified the harpsichord so that the keys activated hammers that struck, rather than plucked, the strings. With that minor change, a major improvement was made that would henceforth radically enhance the entire musical world, giving a grandeur and breadth never before known.

That is the sort of revolutionary change Jesus gives in the golden rule. Every other form of this basic principle had been given in purely negative terms, and is found in the literature of almost every major religion and philosophical system. The Jewish rabbi Hillel said, "What is hateful to yourself do not to someone else." The book of Tobit in the Apocrypha teaches, "What thou thyself hatest, to no man do." The Jewish scholars in Alexandria who translated the Septuagint (Greek Old Testament) advised in a certain piece of correspondence, "As you wish that no evil befall you, but to be a partaker of all good things, so you should act on the same principle toward your subjects and offenders." Confucius taught, "What you do not want done to yourself, do not do to others." An ancient Greek king named Nicocles wrote, "Do not do to others the things which make you angry when you experience them at the hands of other people." The Greek philosopher Epictetus said, "What you avoid suffering yourself, do not afflict on others." The Stoics promoted the principle, "What you do not want to be done to you, do not do to anyone else." In every case the emphasis is negative. The principle is an important part of right human relations, but it falls short—far short—of God's perfect standard.

Those expressions go only as far as sinful man can go, and are essentially expressions not of love but of self-interest. The motivation is basically selfish—refraining from harming others in order that they will not harm us. Those negative forms of the rule are not golden, because they are primarily utilitarian and motivated by fear and self-preservation. As Scripture repeatedly tells us of fallen mankind, "There is none who does good, there is not even one" (Rom. 3:12; cf. Ps. 14:3); "each of us has turned to his own way" (Isa. 53:6).

Man's basic problem is preoccupation with self. He is innately beset with narcissism, a condition named after the Greek mythological character Narcissus, who spent his life admiring his reflection in a pool of water. In the final analysis, every sin results from preoccupation with self. We sin because we are totally selfish, totally devoted to ourselves, rather than to God and to others. Unregenerate man can never come up to the standard of selfless love—the love that loves others as oneself and that treats others in the same way that one wants to be treated.

Only Jesus gives the fullness of the truth, which encompasses both the positive and the negative. And only Jesus can give the power to live by that full truth. The dynamic for living this supreme ethic must come from outside our fallen nature. It can come only from the indwelling Holy Spirit, whose first fruit is love (Gal. 5:22). In Jesus Christ, "the love of God has been poured out within our hearts through the Holy Spirit who was given to us" (Rom. 5:5). Only Christ's own Spirit can empower us to love each other as He loves us (John 13:34). We can only love in a divine way because God Himself has first loved us divinely (1 John 4:19).

Selfless love does not serve in order to prevent its own harm or to insure its own welfare. It serves for the sake of the one being served, and serves in the way it likes being served—whether it ever receives such service or not. That level of love is the divine level, and can be achieved only by divine help. Only God's children can have right relations with others, because they possess the motivation and the resource to refrain from self-righteously condemning others and to love in an utterly selfless way.

Which Way to Heaven? (7:13-14)

42

Enter by the narrow gate; for the gate is wide, and the way is broad that leads to destruction, and many are those who enter by it. For the gate is small, and the way is narrow that leads to life, and few are those who find it. (7:13-14)

Here is the appeal to which Jesus has been moving through the whole sermon. He gives the call to decide now about becoming a citizen of God's kingdom and inheriting eternal life, or remaining a citizen of this fallen world and receiving damnation. The way to life is on God's terms alone; the way to damnation is on any terms a person wants, because every way but God's leads to the same fate.

Jesus has been giving God's standards throughout the sermon, standards that are holy and perfect and that are diametrically opposed to the self-righteous, self-sufficient, and hypocritical standards of man—typified by those of the scribes and Pharisees. He has shown what His kingdom is like and what its people are like—and are not like. Now He presents the choice of entering the kingdom or not. Here the Lord focuses on the inevitable decision that every person must make, the crossroads where he must decide on the **gate** he will enter and the **way** he will go.

Our lives are filled with decisions—what to wear, what to eat, where to go, what to do, what to say, what to buy, whom to marry, what career to follow, and on and on. Many decisions are trivial and insignificant, and some are essential and life-changing. The most critical of all is our decision about Jesus Christ and His kingdom. That is the ultimate choice that determines our eternal destiny. It is that decision that Jesus here calls men to make.

In perfect harmony with His absolute sovereignty, God has always allowed men to choose Him or not, and He has always pleaded with them to decide for Him or face the consequences of a choice against Him. Since mankind turned their backs on Him in the Fall, God has bent every effort and spared no cost in wooing His creatures back to Himself. He has provided and shown the way, leaving nothing to man but the choice. God made His choice by providing the way of redemption. The choice is now man's.

While Israel was in the wilderness the Lord instructed Moses to tell the people, "I call heaven and earth to witness against you today, that I have set before you life and death, the blessing and the curse. So choose life in order that you may live, you and your descendants, by loving the Lord your God, by obeying His voice, and by holding fast to Him" (Deut. 30:19-20).

After Israel came into the Promised Land, Joshua confronted the people again with a choice: of continuing to serve the Egyptian and Canaanite gods they had adopted or of turning to the Lord who had delivered them from Egypt and given them the land promised to Abraham. "Choose for yourselves today whom you will serve," Joshua pleaded (Josh. 24:13-15).

On Mount Carmel the prophet Elijah asked the people of Israel, "How long will you hesitate between two opinions? If the Lord is God, follow Him; but if Baal, follow him" (1 Kings 18:21). The Lord commanded Jeremiah to set the choice again before His people: "Thus says the Lord, 'Behold, I set before you the way of life and the way of death'" (Jer. 21:8).

In John 6:66-69, Jesus called for a choice: "As a result of this many of His disciples withdrew, and were not walking with Him anymore. Jesus said therefore to the twelve, 'You do not want to go away also, do you?' Simon Peter answered Him, 'Lord, to whom shall we go? You have words of eternal life. And we have believed and have come to know that You are the Holy One of God.'"

That is the call that God has been making to men since they turned away from Him, and it is the supreme appeal of His Word.

In his poem *The Ways,* The British poet John Oxenham wrote,

> To every man there openeth
> A Way, and Ways, and a Way,
> And the High Soul climbs the High Way,
> And the Low Soul gropes the Low,
> And in between, on the misty flats,
> The rest drift to and fro.
> But to every man there openeth
> A High Way and a Low,
> And every man decideth
> The Way his soul shall go.

In the Sermon on the Mount Jesus presents still again that great choice of choices. This sermon therefore cannot be simply admired and praised for its ethics. Its truths will bless those who accept the King but will stand in judgment over those who refuse Him. The one who admires God's way but does not accept it is under greater judgment, because he acknowledges that he knows the truth.

Nor does this sermon apply only to the future age of the millennial kingdom. The truths Jesus teaches here are truths whose essence God teaches in the Old Testament and throughout the New Testament. They are truths for God's people of every age, and the decision about the **gate** and the **way** has always been a *now* decision.

The choice is between the one and the many—the one right and the many wrongs, the one true way and the many false ways. As John Stott points out, in Matthew 7:13-14 "Jesus cuts across our easy-going syncretism" (*Christian Counter-Culture* [Downers Grove, Ill.: InterVarsity, 1978], p. 193). There are not many roads to heaven, but one. There are not many good religions, but only one. Man cannot come to God in *any* of the ways that man himself devises, but only in the one way that God Himself has provided.

The contrast Jesus makes is not between religion and irreligion, or between the higher religions and the lower ones. Nor is it a contrast between nice and upright people and vile and degraded ones. It is a contrast between divine righteousness and human righteousness, *all* of which is unrighteousness. It is a contrast between divine revelation and human religion, between divine truth and human falsehood, between trusting in God and trusting in self. It is the contrast between God's grace and man's works.

There have always been but two systems of religion in the world. One is God's system of divine accomplishment, and the other is man's system of human achievement. One is the religion of God's grace, the other the religion of men's works. One is the religion of faith, the other the religion of the flesh. One is the religion of the sincere heart and the internal, the other the religion of hypocrisy and the external. Within man's system are thousands of religious forms and names, but they are all built on the achievements of man and the inspiration of Satan. Christianity, on the other hand, is the religion of divine accomplishment, and it stands alone.

Even the law given through Moses, though divine, was not a means of salvation but rather a means of showing man's need for salvation. "By the works of the Law no flesh will be justified in His sight," Paul explains; "for through the Law comes the knowledge of sin" (Rom. 3:20). The law came to show us our sinfulness and guilt before God, and to show us that we are incapable in ourselves of keeping God's perfect law.

But when self-righteous, ego-centered man saw that he was sinful by the law's standard, he simply set the law aside and devised standards of his own. He invented new religions that accommodated his shortcomings and that were humanly achievable. By meeting his own attainable standards, man therefore considered himself righteous. That is what the rabbis and scribes had done in regard to their traditions. They lowered God's standards, raised their own estimates of themselves, and felt they had achieved a righteous standing with God (Rom. 10:3). And that is exactly the type of self-ascribed righteousness that Jesus declares will never bring a person into the kingdom of God (Matt. 5:20).

From here through the rest of the sermon (vv. 13-27) Jesus repeatedly points out two things: the necessity of choosing whether to follow God or not, and the fact that the choices are two and only two. There are two gates, the narrow and the wide; two ways, the narrow and the broad; two destinations, life and destruction; two groups, the few and the many; two kinds of trees, the good and the bad, which produce two kinds of fruit, the good and the bad; two kinds of people who profess faith in Jesus Christ, the sincere and the false; two kinds of builders, the wise and the foolish; two foundations, the rock and the sand; and two houses, the secure and the insecure. In all preaching there must be the demand for a verdict. Jesus makes the choice crystal clear.

In verses 13-14 Jesus deals with the first four of those contrasts: the two gates, the two ways, the two destinations, and the two groups.

THE TWO GATES

Enter is in the aorist imperative tense, and therefore demands a definite and specific action. The command is not to admire or to ponder the **gate** but to **enter** it. Many people admire the principles of the Sermon on the Mount but never follow those principles. Many people respect and praise Jesus Christ but never receive Him as Lord and Savior. Because they never receive the King and never enter the kingdom, they are as much separated from the King and as much outside His kingdom as is the rankest atheist or most unethical pagan.

Jesus' command is not simply to enter *some* gate but to enter **the narrow gate**. Every person enters one gate or the other; that is unavoidable. Jesus pleads for men to enter the *right* gate, God's gate, the only gate that leads to **life** and to heaven.

Jesus has repeatedly shown the narrowness of God's internal standard of righteousness, in contrast to the broad and external standards of Jewish tradition. The path to that narrow way of kingdom living is through **the narrow gate** of the King Himself. "I am the way, and the truth, and the life; no one comes to the Father, but through Me" (John 14:6).

When we preach, teach, and witness that Christ is the only way to God, we are not proclaiming our own view of right religion but God's revelation of truth. We do not proclaim the narrow way simply because we are already in it, or because it happens to suit our temperament, or because we are bigoted and exclusive. We proclaim the narrow way because it is God's way and God's only way for men to find salvation and eternal life. We proclaim a narrow gospel because Jesus said, "I am the door; if anyone enters through Me, he shall be saved" (John 10:9). We proclaim a narrow gospel because "there is salvation in no one else; for there is no other name under heaven that has been given among men, by which we must be saved" (Acts 4:12), and because "there is one God and one mediator also between God and men, the man Christ Jesus" (1 Tim. 2:5). We proclaim a narrow gospel because that is the only gospel God has given and therefore the only gospel there is.

The person who enters **the narrow gate** must enter alone. We can bring no one else and nothing else with us. Some commentators suggests that a turnstile represents the idea implicit in **narrow gate**. A turnstile allows only one person through at a time, with no baggage. People do not come into the kingdom in groups, but singly. The Jews had the mistaken notion that they were all in God's kingdom together by racial salvation, signified by circumcision.

Furthermore, God's gate is so narrow that we must go through it naked. It is the gate of self-denial, through which one cannot carry the baggage of sin and self-will. When we sing, "Nothing in my hand I bring, simply to Thy cross I cling," we are testifying to the way of the gospel. The way of Christ is the way of the cross, and the way of the cross is the way of self-denial. "If anyone wishes to come after Me, let him deny himself, and take up his cross, and follow Me. For whoever wishes to save his life shall lose it; but whoever loses his life for My sake shall find it" (Matt. 16:24-25).

Jesus confronted the rich young ruler who sought eternal life and presented a test of his willingness to submit to His lordship: "One thing you still lack; sell all that you possess, and distribute it to the poor, and you shall have treasure in heaven; and come, follow Me" (Luke 18:22). As his response proved, that man's desire to rule his own life and to hold on to his earthly wealth prevented his entering the kingdom, because "when he had heard these things, he became very sad; for he was extremely rich" (v. 23). He also gave evidence of self-righteousness and self-deceit in denying his true state of sin (v. 21), because if he had in his heart truly kept all the commandments as he claimed, he would surely have kept the greatest commandment—which is to love God with all one's heart, soul, and might (Deut. 6:5; cf. Matt. 22:37). Thus he would have followed Christ with total commitment. The issue with that young man was very simply a matter of lordship. Jesus confronted him on the matter of life control. One who comes to salvation yields control to Christ whether that means he gives up all or is allowed to keep all and receive more. Salvation turns sovereignty over to Christ.

To love God with everything we have is to jettison self—self-confidence, self-achievement, self-righteousness, and self-satisfaction. "Unless you are converted and become like children," Jesus said, "you shall not enter the kingdom of heaven" (Matt. 18:3). The mark of a child is dependency, utter dependency for everything he has. Saving faith is not merely an act of the mind; it counts the cost (Luke 14:28); it is also a stripping of the self and crying, as did the tax-gatherer in the Temple, "God, be merciful to me, the sinner!" (Luke 18:13). Easy believism is not scriptural believism. The **narrow gate** means that those who enter do so stripped of all they possess, rather than adding Jesus to their accumulated treasures. Salvation is the exchange of all that we are for all that He is (see Matt. 13:44-46). And as He did for Job, the Lord will give back much more.

The **narrow gate** demands repentance. Many Jews believed that simply being a Jew, a physical descendant of Abraham, was sufficient for entrance into heaven. Many people today believe that being in a church qualifies them for heaven. Some even believe that simply being a human being qualifies them, because God is too good and kind to exclude anyone. God does offer the way to all, and His greatest longing is that everyone enter, because He does not desire "for any to perish but for all to come to repentance" (2 Pet. 3:9). Paul preached "repentance toward God" (Acts 20:21) as Jesus had preached it (Mark 1:14-15). John the Baptist readied a people for the Lord by repentance (Luke 3:1-6). The way of repentance, of turning from our own way and our own righteousness to God's, is the only way to enter His kingdom and therefore the only way to keep from perishing.

Charles Spurgeon said, "You and your sins must separate or you and your God will never come together. No one sin may you keep; they must all be given up, they must be brought out like Canaanite kings from the cave and be hanged up in the sun."

The repentant life will be a changed life. The primary message of John's first epistle is that the truly redeemed life will manifest itself in a transformed life, in which confession of sin (1:8-10), obedience to God's will (2:4-6), love of God's other children (2:9-11; 3:16-17), and practice of righteousness (3:4-10) are normal and habitual. "By this is My Father glorified, that you bear much fruit, and so prove to be My disciples" (John 15:8). Anything less is damning demon-faith (James 2:19) that is orthodox but fruitless.

Those who preach a gospel of self-indulgence preach an utterly different gospel than Jesus preached. The gate of pride, of self-righteousness, and self-satisfaction is the **wide gate** of the world, not the **narrow gate** of God.

Most people spend their lives rushing around with the crowds, doing what everyone else does and believing what everyone else believes. But as far as salvation is concerned, there is no security in numbers. If every person in a group is saved it is because each of them individually comes into the kingdom by his own decision, energized by the Holy Spirit, to trust Christ.

Two Ways

The two gates lead to two ways. **The gate** that **is wide** leads to **the way** that **is broad**; and **the narrow gate**, which **is small**, leads to **the way** that **is narrow**. The narrow way is the way of the godly, and the broad way is the way of the ungodly—and those are the only two ways in which men can travel. The godly person delights "in the law of the Lord, and in His law he meditates day and night. And he will be like a tree firmly planted by streams of water, which yields its fruit in its season," whereas the ungodly "are like chaff which the wind drives away" (Ps. 1:2-4).

The way that **is broad** is the easy, attractive, inclusive, indulgent, permissive, and self-oriented way of the world. There are few rules, few restrictions, and few requirements. All you need do is profess Jesus, or at least be religious, and you are readily accepted in that large and diverse group. Sin is tolerated, truth is moderated, and humility is ignored. God's Word is praised but not studied, and His standards are admired but not followed. This way requires no spiritual maturity, no moral character, no commitment, and no sacrifice. It is the easy way of floating downstream, in "the course of this world, according to the prince of the power of the air, of the spirit that is now working in the sons of disobedience" (Eph. 2:2). It is the tragic way "which seems right to a man," but whose "end is the way of death" (Prov. 14:12).

A West Indian who had chosen Islam over Christianity said his reason was that Islam "is a noble, broad path. There is room for a man and his sins on it. The way of Christ is too narrow." It seems that many preachers today do not see that issue as clearly as that unbelieving Muslim.

The way that **is narrow**, however, is the hard way, the demanding way, the way of self-denial and the cross. *Stenos* (**narrow**) comes from a root that means "to groan," as from being under pressure, and is used figuratively to represent a restriction or constriction. It is the word from which we get stenography, writing that is abbreviated or compressed.

The fact that **few are those who find** God's way implies that it is to be sought diligently. "And you will seek Me and find Me, when you search for Me with all your heart" (Jer. 29:13). No one has ever stumbled into the kingdom or wandered through the narrow gate by accident. When someone asked Jesus, "Lord, are there just a few who are being saved?" He replied, "Strive to enter the narrow door; for many, I tell you, will seek to enter and will not be able" (Luke 13:23-24). The term *agōnizomai* ("strive") indicates that entering the door to God's kingdom takes conscious, purposeful, and intense effort. That is the term from which we get agonize, and is the same word Paul uses to describe an athlete who agonizes ("competes") to win a race (1 Cor. 9:25) and the Christian who "fights the good fight of faith" (literally, "struggles the good struggle," 1 Tim. 6:12). The requirements for kingdom citizenship are great, demanding, clearly defined, and allow for no deviation or departure. Luke 16:16 says, "Everyone is forcing his way into [the kingdom]," implying conflict and effort (cf. Acts 14:22).

The kingdom is for those who come to the King in poverty of spirit, mourning over their sin, and hungering and thirsting for His righteousness to replace their own (Matt. 5:3-4, 6). It is for those who want the kingdom at any cost, who will sell all they have to buy that great treasure and that great pearl (Matt. 13:44-46). It is not for those want a cheap and easy way to assure heaven, while continuing to live their own selfish and worldly lives on earth. Jesus only saves those for whom He becomes Lord. Sadly, most people think that heaven can be obtained on much easier terms than those prescribed by Christ.

William Hendriksen comments,

> The Kingdom then is not for weaklings, waverers, and compromisers. . . . It is not for Balaam, the rich young ruler, Pilate and Demas. . . . It is not won by means of deferred prayers, unfulfilled promises, broken resolutions and hesitant testi-

monies. It is for strong and sturdy men, like Joseph, Nathan, Elijah, Daniel, Mordecai and Peter . . . Stephen . . . and Paul. And let us not forget such valiant women as Ruth, Deborah, Esther and Lydia. (*Exposition of the Gospel According to Matthew* [Grand Rapids: Baker, 1973], p. 490)

As Paul expresses it in Romans 7:14-25, it should be the desire of our hearts as Christians to fulfill every command and requirement of our Lord, even though we know that we will fail. But we also know that "if we confess our sins, He is faithful and righteous to forgive us our sins and to cleanse us from all unrighteousness" (1 John 1:9). And the gracious God who saved us because we could not fulfill His law in our own power knows that, even after salvation, we still cannot fulfill His law in our own power. The great difference is that in Christ we not only have a Savior but a burden bearer. He helps us carry all our burdens, including the burden of obedience. "Take My yoke upon you, and learn from Me," Jesus says, "for I am gentle and humble in heart; and you shall find rest for your souls. For My yoke is easy, and My load is light" (Matt. 11:29-30).

God's way of salvation is remarkably simple, but it is not easy. We can give nothing or give up nothing that will earn us entrance into the kingdom, but if we long to hold on to forbidden things it can keep us out of the kingdom. That is another reason why **few are those who find it.**

We can pay nothing for salvation, yet coming to Jesus Christ costs everything we have. "If anyone comes to Me," Jesus says, "and does not hate his own father and mother and wife and children and brothers and sisters, yes, and even his own life, he cannot be My disciple. Whoever does not carry his own cross [a willingness even to die if necessary] and come after Me cannot be My disciple" (Luke 14:26). The Lord goes on to show the seriousness of deciding to follow Christ. "For which one of you, when he wants to build a tower, does not first sit down and calculate the cost, to see if he has enough to complete it? . . . Or what king, when he sets out to meet another king in battle, will not first sit down and take counsel whether he is strong enough with ten thousand men to encounter the one coming against him with twenty thousand?" (vv. 28, 31).

The person who says yes to Christ must say no to the things of the world, because to be in Christ is to rely on His power rather than our own and to be willing to forsake our own way for His. It can cost persecution, ridicule, and tribulation. In His last instructions to His disciples, Jesus several times reminded them of the price they would pay for following Him: "Because you are not of the world, but I chose you out of the world, therefore the world hates you. Remember the word that I said to you, 'A slave is not greater than his master.' If they persecuted Me, they will also persecute you" (John 15:19-20); "They will make you outcasts from the synagogue" (John 16:2); "Therefore you too now have sorrow" (16:22); and "In the world you have tribulation" (16:33).

When we identify ourselves with Jesus Christ we declare war on the devil, and he declares war on us. The one whom we formerly served now becomes our great enemy, and the ideas and ways we once held dear now become our great temptations and pitfalls.

With the warnings about suffering the Lord also gives promises that our hearts will rejoice (John 16:22b) and that we are to take courage because He has overcome the world (16:33b). But He promises to enable us to prevail over those times of suffering, not to escape them.

Two Destinations

Both the **broad** and the **narrow** ways point to the good life, to salvation, heaven, God, the kingdom, and blessing—but only the **narrow** way actually leads to those. There is nothing here to indicate that the **broad way** is marked "Hell." The point our Lord is making is that it is marked "Heaven" but does not lead there. That is the great lie of all the false religions of human achievement. The two very different destinations of the two ways are made clear by the Lord (cf. Jer. 21:8). The **broad . . . leads to destruction**, whereas only the **narrow . . . leads to life**. Every religion except Christianity, the only religion of divine accomplishment, follows the same spiritual way and leads to the same spiritual end, to hell. There are many of those roads, and most of them are attractive, appealing, and crowded with travelers. But not a single one leads where it promises; and not a single one fails to lead where Jesus says it leads—to **destruction**.

Apōleia (**destruction**) does not refer to extinction or annihilation, but to total ruin and loss (cf. Matt. 3:12; 18:8; 25:41, 46; 2 Thess. 1:9; Jude 6-7). It is not the complete loss of being, but the complete loss of well-being. It is the destination of all religions except the way of Jesus Christ, and it is the destiny of all those who follow any way but His. It is the destination and destiny of perdition, hell, and everlasting torment. "The way of the wicked will perish" (Ps. 1:6).

But God's way, the **way** that is **narrow**, leads to eternal **life**, to everlasting heavenly fellowship with God, His angels, and His people. Everlasting **life** is a quality of life, the life of God in the soul of man (see Ps. 17:15). "In My Father's house are many dwelling places; if it were not so, I would have told you; for I go to prepare a place for you. And if I go and prepare a place for you, I will come again, and receive you to Myself; that where I am, there you may be also" (John 14:2-3).

Two Groups

Going into the two gates, traveling down the two ways, and heading for the two destinations we find two groups of people. Those who go in through the **wide gate** and travel the **way that is broad** toward the destination of **destruction** are **many**. The many will include pagans and nominal Christians, atheists and religionists, theists and humanists, Jews and Gentiles—every person from whatever age, background, persuasion, and circumstance who has not come to saving obedience to Jesus Christ.

In the day of judgment many will claim to be followers of Christ, but "many will seek to enter and will not be able," Jesus warns. "Once the head of the house gets up and shuts the door, and you begin to stand outside and knock on the door, saying, 'Lord, open up to us!' then He will answer and say to you, 'I do not know where you are from.' Then you will begin to say, 'We ate and drank in Your presence, and You taught in our streets'; and He will say, 'I tell you, I do not know where you are from; depart from Me, all you evildoers" (Luke 13:24-27). "Many will say to Me on that day, 'Lord, Lord, did we not prophesy in Your name, and in Your name cast out demons, and in Your name perform many miracles?' And then I will declare to them, "I never knew you; depart from Me, you who practice lawlessness" (Matt. 7:22-23). Those particular ones who are excluded will not be atheists or rank pagans, but nominal Christians who professed to know and trust Christ but who refused to come to Him on His terms—through His **gate** and by His **way**.

The group that goes through the **narrow gate** and travels the **narrow way** and is destined for **life** is **few** in number. When Jesus said, "Do not be afraid, little flock" (Luke 12:32), the word He used for "little" was *mikros,* from which we get our prefix *micro,* meaning something small. "Many are called, but few are chosen," He says in another place (Matt. 22:14).

Believers are not **few** in number because the gate is too **narrow** or too **small** to accommodate more. There is no limit to the number who could go through that gate, if they go through in God's way, in repentance for their sins and in trust in Jesus Christ to save them. Nor is the number few because heavenly space is limited. God's grace is boundless, and heaven's dwellings are limitless. Nor is the number few because God desires that most people perish. He earnestly desires "for all to come to repentance" (2 Pet. 3:9).

A letter written to a Melbourne, Australia, daily newspaper expresses clearly the attitude of a person on the broad road to destruction.

> After hearing Dr. Billy Graham on the air, viewing him on television and reading reports and letters concerning him and his mission, I am heartily sick of the type of religion that insists my soul (and everyone else's) needs saving—whatever that means. I have never felt that I was lost. Nor do I feel that I daily wallow in the mire of sin, although repetitive preaching insists that I do.
>
> Give me a practical religion that teaches gentleness and tolerance, that acknowledges no barriers of color or creed, that remembers the aged and teaches children of goodness and not sin.
>
> If in order to save my soul I must accept such a philosophy as I have recently heard preached, I prefer to remain forever damned.

Every person who *will* come to Jesus Christ *can* come to Jesus Christ. "All that the Father gives Me shall come to Me, and the one who comes to Me I will certainly not cast out," Jesus assures us. "For this is the will of My Father, that everyone who beholds the Son and believes in Him, may have eternal life; and I Myself will raise him up on the last day" (John 6:37, 40).

Beware of False Prophets (7:15-20)

43

Beware of the false prophets, who come to you in sheep's clothing, but inwardly are ravenous wolves. You will know them by their fruits. Grapes are not gathered from thorn bushes, nor figs from thistles, are they? Even so, every good tree bears good fruit; but the bad tree bears bad fruit. A good tree cannot produce bad fruit, nor can a bad tree produce good fruit. Every tree that does not bear good fruit is cut down and thrown into the fire. So then, you will know them by their fruits. (7:15-20)

After giving the invitation to "enter by the narrow gate," to come to God by the only way He has provided, Jesus warns that not everyone who claims to belong to God and to speak for Him actually does so. When we stand at the crossroads of decision, we should remember that the true way to God is narrow and that the false way is broad; the true way is difficult and demanding, and the false way is easy and permissive; the true way has relatively few following in it, and the false way has many.

Jesus now says, in effect, "As you strive to enter that narrow gate and walk that narrow way that leads to life, beware of those who would mislead you. Just as there is a misleading gate and a misleading way, there are also misleading preachers and teachers who point to that gate and promote that way." Just like the false gate and way, they will claim to show the way to heaven and life, but they actually show the way to hell and destruction. The false gate has false prophets standing in front of it who seek to lead people into the false way and hinder them from entering the true.

In the present passage Jesus first gives a warning and then calls us to be watchful. Just as He described the true and false ways, He now describes the true and false teachers of those ways.

WARNING

Beware of the false prophets, who come to you in sheep's clothing, but inwardly are ravenous wolves. (7:15)

False prophets were not new to Israel. As long as God has had true prophets, Satan has had false ones. They are seen from the earliest times of redemptive history. Moses warned,

> If a prophet or a dreamer of dreams arises among you and gives you a sign or a wonder, and the sign or the wonder comes true, concerning which he spoke to you, saying, "Let us go after other gods (whom you have not known) and let us serve them," you shall not listen to the words of that prophet or that dreamer of dreams; for the Lord your God is testing you to find out if you love the Lord your God with all your heart and with all your soul. You shall follow the Lord your God and fear Him; and you shall keep His commandments, listen to His voice, serve Him, and cling to Him. But that prophet or that dreamer of dreams shall be put to death, because he has counseled rebellion against the Lord your God. (Deut. 13:1-5)

False prophets always find a hearing and often are encouraged by those who are displeased with God's ways. "For this is a rebellious people," Isaiah said of Israel, "false sons, sons who refuse to listen to the instruction of the Lord; who say to the seers, 'You must not see visions'; and to the prophets, 'You must not prophesy to us what is right, speak to us pleasant words, prophesy illusions'" (Isa. 30:9-10). From chapter 5 through chapter 23 of Jeremiah we see that man of God repeatedly against the false prophets by whom his people were being so terribly misled.

As Jesus sat on the Mount of Olives shortly before the last Passover week, His disciples asked, "Tell us, when will these things be, and what will be the sign of Your coming, and of the end of the age?" He replied, "See to it that no one misleads you. For many will come in My name, saying, 'I am the Christ,' and will mislead many. . . . For false Christs and false prophets will arise and will show great signs and wonders, so as to mislead, if possible, even the elect" (Matt. 24:3-5, 24). John warns against the same problem, pointing out that "many deceivers have gone out into the world" (2 John 7).

Paul warned the Roman believers, "Now I urge you, brethren, keep your eye on those who cause dissensions and hindrances contrary to the teaching which you learned, and turn away from them. For such men are slaves, not of our Lord Christ but of their own appetites; and by their smooth and flattering speech they deceive the hearts of the unsuspecting" (Rom. 16:17-18). In other parts of the New Testament **false prophets** are spoken of as "deceitful spirits" who advocate "doctrines of demons" (1 Tim. 4:1) and as those "who will secretly introduce destructive heresies, even denying the Master who bought them" (2 Pet. 2:1).

They are called false brothers (2 Cor. 11:26), false apostles (2 Cor. 11:13), false teachers (2 Pet. 2:1), false speakers, that is, liars (1 Tim. 4:2), false witnesses (Matt. 26:60), and false Christs (Matt. 24:24). The apostle John tells us, therefore, "Beloved, do not believe every spirit, but test the spirits to see whether they are from God; because many false prophets have gone out into the world" (1 John 4:1).

Paul's last words to the Ephesian elders, when he met with them for a farewell on the beach near Miletus, included a somber warning about inevitable false teachers. "I know that after my departure savage wolves will come in among you, not sparing the flock; and from among your own selves men will arise, speaking perverse things, to draw away the disciples after them. Therefore be on the alert" (Acts 20:29-31).

There has always been a large market for false prophets, because most people do not want to hear the truth. They prefer to hear what is pleasant and flattering, even if it is false and dangerous, over what is unpleasant and unflattering, even if it is true and helpful.

THE DEFINITION OF A FALSE PROPHET

From the beginning of God's redemptive work on behalf of fallen mankind, His true representatives have been marked by two things: they are divinely commissioned, and they present a divine message. They are called by God, and they declare the message of God and only that message. A true prophet is God's voice to men.

When Moses was called he said, "'Please, Lord, I have never been eloquent, neither recently nor in time past, nor since Thou hast spoken to Thy servant; for I am slow of speech and slow of tongue.' And the Lord said to him, 'Who has made man's mouth? Or who makes him dumb or deaf, or seeing or blind? Is it not I, the Lord? Now then go, and I, even I, will be with your mouth, and teach you what you are to say'" (Ex. 4:10-12).

The most dangerous characteristic of false prophets, however, is that they, too, claim to be from God and to speak on His behalf. "An appalling and horrible thing has happened in the land," God told Jeremiah. "The prophets prophesy falsely, and the priests rule on their own authority; and My people love it so!" (Jer.

461

5:30-31). Again He said, "The prophets are prophesying falsehood in My name. I have neither sent them nor commanded them nor spoken to them; they are prophesying to you a false vision, divination, futility and the deception of their own minds" (14:14). And still again He said,

> "Also among the prophets of Jerusalem I have seen a horrible thing: the committing of adultery and walking in falsehood; and they strengthen the hands of evildoers, so that no one has turned back from his wickedness." . . . Thus says the Lord of hosts, "Do not listen to the words of the prophets who are prophesying to you. They are leading you into futility; they speak a vision of their own imagination, not from the mouth of the Lord. . . . I did not send these prophets, but they ran. I did not speak to them, but they prophesied." (23:14, 16, 21)

In a promise of judgment the Lord told Zechariah, "For behold, I am going to raise up a shepherd in the land who will not care for the perishing, seek the scattered, heal the broken, or sustain the one standing, but will devour the flesh of the fat sheep and tear off their hoofs" (Zech. 11:16). Such a shepherd is a greater danger to the flock than wild animals, because he comes among them as their protector. Under the guise of the one who is supposed to feed and care for them, he instead slaughters and eats them himself. That is a picture of the antichrist, who is the prototype of all false prophets.

One of the most frightening discoveries about the People's Temple Christian Church was that a large majority of its members had been raised in Christian homes of one sort or another. Most of those who joined that church did so in the belief that it offered a higher and more genuine experience of Christian fellowship and service. Yet the church dissolved overnight when its leader, Jim Jones, and nearly a thousand of his most loyal followers committed mass suicide at Jonestown, a remote church settlement in the jungles of Guyana, South America.

In his book *Deceived,* Mel White tries to determine why so many people could be so fatally misled. Among the reasons he suggests are:

> He [Jim Jones] knew how to inspire hope. He was committed to people in need; he counseled prisoners and juvenile delinquents. He started a job placement center; he opened rest homes and homes for the retarded; he had a health clinic; he organized a vocational training center; he provided free legal aid; he founded a community center; he preached about God. He even claimed to cast out demons, do miracles and heal.
>
> But on the other hand we find all the marks of a false prophet. He promoted himself through the use of celebrities, a very common vehicle for false prophets to gain credibility. He manipulated the press; he wanted certain favorable stories; he was big on playing the press. . . . And he used the language and the forms of faith to gain his power.

Jim Jones created a warm, purportedly Christian community. But he replaced Jesus Christ as the authority and more and more garnered loyalty to himself. He began demanding money for every service he offered and was preoccupied with sex, in both its normal and deviant forms. He would lie convincingly about anything in order to gain an advantage or make a desired impression. Before his bizarre death he had managed to gain the admiration and praises of countless church leaders, governors, senators, congressmen, and even the president of the United States.

The greatest tragedy of Jonestown was not that nearly a thousand people died, but that they died believing they were serving God. In truth, of course, they were serving Satan, and were on their way to hell if they did not know Christ. Any believers who may have been among them incurred great loss of reward.

"For false Christs and false prophets will arise," Jesus warned, "and will show great signs and wonders, so as to mislead, if possible, even the elect" (Matt. 24:24). Jude declares that "Certain persons have crept in unnoticed, those who were long beforehand marked out for this condemnation, ungodly persons who turn the grace of our God into licentiousness and deny our only Master and Lord, Jesus Christ" (Jude 4).

The scribes and Pharisees were classic examples of false shepherds. In the name of leading and caring for God's people they instead led them further and further from His ways. Posing as God's spokesmen they used the people to feather their own ecclesiastical nests, and cared nothing for the people or for God. They were rapaciously self-seeking and self-serving. When Jesus completely unmasked their deceit and hypocrisy (see Matt. 23) it is no wonder they crucified Him.

The scribes and Pharisees, and those who followed their pernicious teachings, did not accept Jesus' teaching because they were dedicated to falsehood rather than the truth. On one occasion Jesus said to them,

> Why do you not understand what I am saying? It is because you cannot hear My word. You are of your father the devil, and you want to do the desires of your father. He was a murderer from the beginning, and does not stand in the truth, because there is no truth in him. Whenever he speaks a lie, he speaks from his own nature; for he is a liar, and the father of lies. But because I speak the truth, you do not believe Me. . . . He who is of God hears the words of God; for this reason you do not hear them, because you are not of God. (John 8:43-45, 47)

"Let no one deceive you with empty words," Paul warns the Ephesians; "for because of these things the wrath of God comes upon the sons of disobedience. Therefore do not be partakers with them" (Eph. 5:6). To the Colossians he says, "See to it that no one takes you captive through philosophy and empty deception, according to the tradition of men, according to the elementary principles of the world, rather than according to Christ" (Col. 2:8).

THE DANGER OF FALSE PROPHETS

Beware always warns of danger. It is not a call simply to notice or sense something, but to be on guard against it because it is so harmful. The word conveys the idea of holding the mind away. **False prophets** are more than wrong; they are dangerous, and we should not expose our minds to them. They pervert thinking and poison the soul. They are more dangerous than a cobra or a tiger, because those animals can only harm the body. False prophets are spiritual beasts and are immeasurably more deadly than the physical ones. Both Peter and Jude call them "unreasoning animals." Peter goes on to warn that they "deceive unstable souls, luring them into their jaws through the lust of flesh" (2 Pet. 2:12; cf. Jude 10).

In Palestine, **wolves** were the most common natural enemy of sheep. They roamed the hills and valleys, looking for a sheep that strayed away from the flock or lagged behind. When a wolf found such a sheep it quickly attacked and tore it to pieces. Even a grown, healthy sheep was utterly defenseless against a wolf.

Wolves are known for being merciless and ferocious (cf. Ezek. 22:27). *Harpax* (**ravenous**) is also translated "swindler" (Luke 18:11; 1 Cor. 5:10-11; 6:10), referring metaphorically to those who deceitfully and mercilessly ravage a person of his money and possessions. **False prophets** and **wolves** are clever and wily, and are always on the lookout for new victims.

Jude gives a strong warning against false prophets and tells how believers are to respond to them. He writes, "Keep yourselves in the love of God, waiting anxiously for the mercy of our Lord Jesus Christ to eternal life" (v. 21). Our first need is to get ourselves right with the Lord, to make sure we are in the place of divine fellowship, blessing, and power. Then we will be prepared to "have mercy on some, who are doubting; save others, snatching them out of the fire; and on some have mercy with fear, hating even the garment polluted by the flesh" (vv. 22-23).

The first group Jude mentions is composed of believers who have been tempted to doubt their faith, and who need comfort and assurance. The second group is composed of unbelievers who are on their way to hell and who need to be grabbed, as it were, and held back. The third group, however, is composed of those who are confirmed in false religion and who are extremely dangerous, even to the most mature Christian. We must witness to such people with special care and in special dependence on the Lord for wisdom and protection, lest we ourselves become spiritually contaminated by their polluted views and ways.

False prophets and those who follow false prophets are as dangerous to God's people as **ravenous wolves** are to sheep.

THE DECEPTION OF FALSE PROPHETS

The danger of **false prophets** is greatly increased because of their deception. When an enemy is seen for what he is, we are alerted and can be prepared to defend ourselves. But when an enemy poses as a friend, our defenses are down. The dogs and swine of verse 6 are much more easily recognized because of their open sinfulness and rejection of God.

In Old Testament times prophets were often recognizable by what they wore. Like Elijah, they often wore rough, hairy, uncomfortable clothing as a symbol of their foregoing the normal comforts of life for the cause of God. John the Baptist, as the last prophet of the Old Covenant, wore a camel's hair coat and ate locusts and wild honey. There were exceptions, but prophets generally could be identified by their plain, coarse clothing. For that reason, a person who wanted to impersonate a prophet would sometimes wear such clothing. Zechariah speaks of such men who "put on a hairy robe in order to deceive" (Zech. 13:4).

Similarly, shepherds invariably wore woolen clothing, made from the wool of the sheep they tended. That is the **sheep's clothing** of which Jesus here speaks. **False prophets** do not deceive the flock by impersonating sheep but by impersonating the shepherd, who wears **sheep's clothing** in the form of his wool garments. Just as the ancient false prophets often wore the garments of the true prophet, so false shepherds often disguise themselves as true shepherds. Satan's man goes under the guise of God's man, claiming to teach the truth in order to deceive, mislead, and, if possible, destroy God's people.

Scripture speaks of three basic kinds of false teachers: heretics, apostates, and deceivers. Heretics are those who openly reject the word of God and teach that which is contrary to divine truth. Apostate teachers are those who once followed the true faith but have turned away from it, rejected it, and are trying to lead others away. Those two kinds of false teachers at least have the virtue of a certain honesty. They do not claim to represent orthodox, biblical Christianity.

The false shepherd (the deceiver), on the other hand, gives the appearance of orthodoxy, frequently with great declarations and fanfare. He is not a liberal or a cultist but one who speaks favorably of Christ, the cross, the Bible, the Holy Spirit, and so on, and who associates with true believers. He may go out of his way to appear orthodox, fundamental, and evangelical. From his looks, vocabulary, and associations he gives considerable evidence of genuine belief. But he is not genuine; he is a fake and a deceiver. He has the speech of orthodoxy, but is a living lie.

"For such men are false apostles, deceitful workers, disguising themselves as apostles of Christ. And no wonder," Paul goes on to explain, "for even Satan disguises himself as an angel of light. Therefore it is not surprising if his servants also disguise themselves as servants of righteousness" (2 Cor. 11:13-15). These **false prophets** are especially dangerous because they masquerade as true prophets and therefore are able to creep into Christian circles unnoticed (Jude 4; cf. Acts 20:28-32).

False prophets are almost always pleasant and positive. They like to be with Christians, to talk like Christians, and to be identified as Christians. They know and use biblical terminology and often appear highly knowledgeable about Scripture. The doctrines they affirm are seemingly biblical.

Many false prophets also appear to be sincere, and because of that sincerity they can more easily mislead others. Paul warns that "evil men and impostors will proceed from bad to worse, deceiving and being deceived" (2 Tim. 3:13). Being themselves deceived by the ultimate deceiver, such people can be thoroughly convinced in their own minds that their perverted beliefs are true. They have become so deeply devoted to falsehood that darkness seems to be light, and black seems to be white.

If they are so deceptive, how then can they be identified? Most frequently they show their true colors by what they do not affirm. In other words, they are identified not so much by what they say as by what they do not say. They usually do not openly deny Jesus' divinity, His substitutionary atonement, the depravity and lostness of man, the reality and penalty of sin, the destiny of hell for unbelievers, the need for repentance, humility, and submission to God, and other such "negative" and uncomfortable truths. They simply ignore them.

In order to carry out their deceit effectively, these spurious leaders live moral and upright lives on the surface. The great commentator John Broadus wrote that many of the false prophets have come from traditional religious training, and because of the ingraining of early traditional Christian moral values they find it difficult to overtly overcome the restrictions on their minds by their early training. (*Matthew* [Valley Forge, Pa.: Judson, 1886], p. 167). Outward morality helps give the impression of spiritual genuineness and therefore helps perpetuate the deceit. But the truth is they are energized by "deceitful spirits and doctrines of demons" and have become "liars seared in their own conscience as with a branding iron" (1 Tim. 4:1-2). They are motivated by the desire for "sordid gain" (1 Pet. 5:2). Their false faith cannot restrain their unregenerate flesh, so the true sensuality of those "slaves of corruption" (2 Pet. 2:19) often becomes known, and it is evident that "in their greed" they exploit people "with false words" (2:3). They also have "eyes full of adultery" and "never cease from sin," possessing a "heart trained in greed" (2:14).

In *The Didache,* one of the earliest Christian writings after New Testament times, we find a section devoted to dealing with false prophets. The term used to describe them is *Christemporos,* which means "Christ merchants." False prophets use Jesus Christ and His gospel and church as means for serving their own ends. They use the things of God as mere merchandise to promote and dispense to their own advantage.

The Didache gives several means for distinguishing true prophets from false. One was that a true prophet would not remain as a house guest more than two days, because he would need to be up and about his work. A false prophet, however, would willingly stay indefinitely, since he had no real mission to accomplish except serving his own interests. The second test was in regard to asking for money. The true prophet, said *The Didache,* would ask for bread and water, but nothing more—that is, only for necessities to keep himself going. A false prophet, on the other hand, is not the least averse to asking for or even demanding money. A third test was in the area of life-style. A person who does not lead a life that corresponds to the standards he teaches is clearly not a man of God. Still another test was in regard to willingness to work. If a person wanted to live off others and would not work for his own keep, he was a Christ trafficker.

A false prophet is always in church work for himself, to pad his own pockets, to satisfy his own greed, ego, and prestige and to gain power, influence, and recognition for himself.

Our day has more than its share of Christ merchants. Through books, radio, television, recordings, in churches, conferences, seminars, crusades, and by various other means they package and sell the gospel in much the same way that Madison Avenue sells cars and soap. They are insincere peddlers of the Word of God who corrupt it for their own ends (2 Cor. 2:17).

THE DAMNATION OF FALSE PROPHETS

The destiny of **false prophets** is only implied in verse 19, but it is made explicit in both the preceding and following passages. Because they enter by the wide gate and travel the broad way, their end is destruction (v. 13). And when they come before Jesus in the day of judgment and say "Lord, Lord, did we not prophesy in Your name, and in Your name cast out demons, and in Your name perform many miracles?" He will respond, "I never knew you; depart from Me, you who practice lawlessness" (vv. 22-23).

Peter tells us that, along with the heretics and apostate false teachers, "their judgment from long ago is not idle, and their destruction is not asleep," that they will be kept "under punishment for the day of judgment," that like wild beasts they will "also be destroyed," and that "the black darkness has been reserved" for them (2 Pet. 2:3, 9, 12, 17; cf. Jude 13).

WATCHING

You will know them by their fruits. Grapes are not gathered from thorn bushes, nor figs from thistles, are they? Even so, every good tree bears good fruit; but the bad tree bears bad fruit. A good tree cannot produce bad fruit, nor can a bad tree produce good fruit. Every tree that does not bear good fruit is cut down and thrown into the fire. So then, you will know them by their fruits. (7:16-20)

After warning about false prophets, Jesus tells us what to watch for in identifying them. Because they are so extremely deceptive and dangerous—ravenous spiritual and moral wolves in sheep's clothing—the Lord would hardly have left us without means of determining who they are.

Jesus assures us that we **will know them by their fruits.** A fruit tree may be beautiful, decorative, and offer pleasant shade in the summer. But its primary purpose is to bear fruit, and it is therefore judged by what it produces and not by how it looks. (That understanding is the key to interpreting John 15 properly.)

Similarly a prophet—used in this passage in the broadest sense of one who speaks for God—is judged by his life, not simply by his appearance or his words. The kind of person he really is cannot help being revealed. Some false prophets are noticeably spurious and only the most gullible person would be taken in by them. Others conceal their true nature with remarkable skill, and only careful observation will expose them for what they are. But there is a true assurance in the statement **you will know them.** There is no need to be deceived if we look closely.

It is the cleverly deceptive false prophet that Jesus is speaking about here. No one needs help in deciding that a tree is bad if it bears shriveled, discolored, and obviously rotten fruit—or no fruit at all. It is the tree that appears to bear good fruit, but does not, that is deceptive.

It is possible for **grapes** to be stuck on **thorn bushes** and for **figs** to be stuck on **thistles.** From a distance they might appear to be growing on real fruit trees. Because the fruit is genuine, naive persons might conclude that the tree itself also has to be genuine.

It is possible for real Christians to be taken in by false prophets. When believers are careless about study of and obedience to the Word, lazy about prayer, and uncritical about the things of God, it is easy for them to be deceived by someone who pretends to be orthodox—especially if he is pleasant, positive, and permissive. When that happens, they are in danger of becoming **grapes** on **thorn bushes** and **figs** on **thistles.** Satan loves to use God's own people to promote his evil work, seeking, if it were possible, even to snatch them from their heavenly Father (Matt. 24:24).

It is also possible for a tree itself to bear fruit that is colorful, well formed, and attractive, but which is bitter, distasteful, and even poisonous. That kind of **bad tree** with its **bad fruit** is much harder to judge than **thorn bushes** that have **grapes** on them or **thistles** that have **figs** on them. In the second case, both the tree and the fruit appear to be genuine. What it **bears** has to be examined carefully to determine if it is **good fruit** or **bad fruit.** A mature believe who has developed discernment can spot the bad tree and bad fruit (Heb. 5:14).

Judging the fruit of false prophets, of course, is not nearly so easy as judging fruit in an orchard. But from Scripture we discover at least three primary tests we can apply in order to know. They are in the areas of character, creed, and converts.

CHARACTER

A person's basic character—his inner motives, standards, loyalties, attitudes, and ambitions—will eventually show through in what he does and how he acts. John the Baptist told the hypocritical Pharisees and Sadducees who came to be baptized to first "bring forth fruits in keeping with repentance" (Luke 3:8). Their manner of living belied their claim that they loved and served God. When the multitude then asked John what good fruit was, he replied, "Let the man who has two tunics share with him who has none; and let him who has food do likewise" (v. 11). To the tax-gatherers who asked what they should do, John said, "Collect no more than what you have been ordered to" (v. 13). John was saying that the person who is genuinely repentant and who truly trusts and loves God will also love and help his fellow man (cf. James 2:15-17; 1 John 3:17; 4:20).

No person is saved *by* good works, but every believer is saved *for* good works. "For we are His workmanship," Paul tells us, "created in Christ Jesus for good works, which God prepared beforehand, that we should walk in them" (Eph. 2:10). In another place Paul admonishes us to "walk in a manner worthy of the Lord, to please Him in all respects, bearing fruit in every good work and increasing in the knowledge of God" (Col. 1:10). "By this is My Father glorified," Jesus says, "that you bear much fruit, and so prove to be My disciples. . . . If you keep My commandments, you will abide in My love; just as I have kept My Father's commandments, and abide in His love" (John 15:8, 10).

As with everything that is godly and righteous, true fruit-bearing begins on the inside, in the heart. Paul speaks of our "having been filled with the fruit of righteousness which comes through Jesus Christ" (Phil. 1:11) and informs us that "the fruit of the Spirit is love, joy, peace, patience, kindness, goodness, faithfulness, gentleness, self-control" (Gal. 5:22-23).

A person who belongs to Jesus Christ and who is called by God and given God's message will give evidence of **good fruit** both in his attitudes and his actions. A person who does not belong to God, especially a false prophet who claims to be God's messenger, will sooner or later manifest the **bad fruit** that the **bad tree** of his sensual life inevitably produces.

False prophets can disguise and hide their **bad fruit** for a while with ecclesiastical trappings, biblical knowledge, and evangelical vocabulary. They can cover it by belonging to Christian organizations, associating with Christian leaders, and by talking about divine things. But how they talk, act, and react when not in the view of Christians will eventually expose their true loyalty and convictions. What is in the heart will emerge, and corrupt theology will result in a corrupt life. False teaching and perverted living are inseparable, and eventually will become manifest.

Peter tells us that the true and mature believer will be growing in faith, moral excellence, knowledge, self-control, perseverance, godliness, brotherly kindness, and love. "If these qualities are yours and are increasing," he says, "they render you neither useless nor unfruitful in the true knowledge of our Lord Jesus Christ" (2 Pet. 1:5-8). Those, on the other hand, who are false and deceiving prophets, in "speaking out arrogant words of vanity . . . entice by fleshly desires, by sensuality, those who barely escape from the ones who live in error, promising them freedom while they themselves are slaves of corruption" (2:18-19). And their false believers may temporarily escape "the defilements of the world," but they will eventually return to their "vomit" and "to wallowing in the mire" (2 Pet. 2:20-22).

Unless those who claim to be God's spokesmen give evidence that their deepest motives and life patterns are to honor, glorify, and magnify God, and to grow in humility, holiness, and obedience, we can be sure that God has not called or sent them. If they are oriented to money, prestige, recognition, popularity, power, sexual looseness, and selfishness, they do not belong to Jesus Christ. If they are proud, arrogant, resentful, egotistical, and self-indulgent, they clearly are false prophets. The true test, a beatitude attitude of humility, can be summed up in Jesus' words: "He who speaks from himself seeks his own glory; but He who is seeking the glory of the one who sent Him, He is true, and there is no unrighteousness in Him" (John 7:18).

Martyn Lloyd-Jones wisely comments,

> A Christian can generally be known by his very appearance. The man who really believes in the holiness of God, and who knows his own sinfulness and the blackness of his own heart, the man who believes in the judgment of God and the possibility of hell and torment, the man who really believes that he himself is so vile and helpless that nothing but the coming of the Son of God from heaven to earth and His going to the bitter shame and agony and cruelty of the cross could ever save him, and reconcile him to God—this man is going to show all that in his personality. He is a man who is bound to give the impression of meekness, he is bound to be humble. Our Lord reminds us here that if a man is not humble, we are to be very wary of him. He can put on a kind of sheep's clothing, but that is not true humility, that is not true meekness. And if a man's doctrine is wrong, it will generally show itself at this point. He will be affable and pleasant, he will appeal to the natural man, and to the things that are physical and carnal; but he will not give the impression of being a man who has seen himself as a hell-bound sinner, and who has been saved by the grace of God alone. (*Studies in the Sermon on the Mount* vol. 2 [Grand Rapids: Eerdmans, 1977], pp. 258-59)

It is nearly always the case that false prophets will attract avowed unbelievers as well as nominal and carnal believers. He appeals to the natural man and carefully avoids anything that is offensive to man's proud, fallen nature. He makes a point of being attractive, likeable, and of giving no offense.

But no person, no matter how clever and deceitful, can indefinitely hide a character that is rotten and out of tune with God. John Calvin said, "Nothing is more difficult to counterfeit than virtue." It demands too much. It demands more than any person has in himself, and when God's divine provision and power are absent the charade cannot last long.

CREED

A second area in which a false prophet can be judged is that of doctrine. Superficially what he teaches may seem biblical and orthodox, but careful examination will always reveal ideas that are unscriptural and the absence of a strong, clear theology. False ideas will be taught, or at least important truths will be omitted. Frequently there will be a combination of both. Eventually the fruit will show a tree for what it is, because **a good tree cannot produce bad fruit, nor can a bad tree produce good fruit.**

On a later occasion Jesus said to the Pharisees, "You brood of vipers, how can you, being evil, speak what is good? For the mouth speaks out of that which fills the heart. The good man out of his good treasure brings forth what is good; and the evil man out of his evil treasure brings forth what is evil" (Matt. 12:34-35).

When judging whether or not a teaching is from God, Isaiah counsels: "To the law and to the testimony! If they do not speak according to this word, it is because they have no dawn," that is, they have no light (Isa. 8:20). The teaching of a false prophet cannot withstand scrutiny under the divine light of Scripture.

All false prophets will have an incomplete, distorted, or perverted view of Christ. If Satan can confuse and mislead people about the person and work of Christ, he has confused and misled them at the very heart of the gospel.

Jesus has just shown that the way of salvation, the gate to God's kingdom and life, is narrow and demanding, whereas the gate to hell and destruction is broad (Matt. 7:13-14). Immediately He begins the warning about false prophets and how to identify them. The false shepherd's way to heaven will never be God's way, and their way of living will never be according to God's standards.

Arthur Pink says, "False prophets are to be found in the circles of the most orthodox, and they pretend to have a fervent love for souls, yet they fatally delude multitudes concerning the way of salvation. The pulpit, platform, and pamphlet hucksters have wantonly lowered the standard of divine holiness and so adulterated the Gospel in order to make it palatable to the carnal mind."

The creed of false prophets never has a narrow gate or a narrow way. On the surface their message may sound difficult and demanding, but it will always rest on the foundation of man's works and will therefore always be accomplishable by man's own effort. They never reveal the depth or danger of sin and depravity, the need for repentance, forgiveness, and submission to the Lord, or the destiny of judgment, condemnation, and eternal destruction for those apart from God. There is no brokenness over sin and no longing after righteousness. They have easy answers for small problems. "They have healed the brokenness of My people superficially," Jeremiah says, "saying, 'Peace, peace,' but there is no peace" (Jer. 6:14). There is no humility, no warning of judgment, and no call for repentance and a contrite heart of obedience.

They have a ready hearing among most people, because they say only what people like to hear. Just as did ancient Israel in Jeremiah's time, people today like it that way (Jer. 5:31). They want to hear illusions, not truth. They are enamored with pleasure and fantasy and resent being confronted with anything disquieting and condemnatory. They want encouragement but not correction, positive words but not negative truth. They will accept grace as long as it is cheap grace and does not reflect against their own sinfulness, inadequacies, and lostness.

The creed of the false prophet, if he has any at all, will be vague, indefinite, and ethereal. No demanding truth will be absolute or clear-cut, and every principle will be easy and attractive.

Arthur Pink declares, "Any preacher who rejects God's law, who denies repentance to be a condition of salvation, who assures the giddy and godless that they are loved by God, who declares that saving faith is nothing more than an act of the will which every person has the power to perform is a false prophet and should be shunned as a deadly plague" (*An Exposition of the Sermon on the Mount,* p. 362).

False prophets talk much about the love of God but nothing of His holiness, much about people who are deprived but nothing about those who are depraved, much about God's universal fatherhood of every human being but nothing about His unique fatherhood only of those who are His children through faith in His Son, Jesus Christ, much about what God will give to us but nothing about obedience to Him, much about health and happiness but nothing about holiness and sacrifice. Their message is a message of gaps, the greatest gap of which leaves out the truth that saves.

CONVERTS

False prophets can also be identified by their converts and followers. They will attract to themselves people who have the same superficial, self-centered, and unscriptural orientation as they do. "Many will follow their sensuality," Peter tells us, "and because of them the way of the truth will be maligned" (2 Pet. 2:2). They have many followers because they teach and promote what the majority of people want to hear and believe (cf. 2 Tim. 4:3).

Their followers will be like them—egotistical, proud, self-centered, self-indulgent, self-willed, and self-satisfied, while being religious. They will be both self-oriented and group-oriented, but never God-oriented or Scripture-oriented.

God has not ordained false prophets, but He has ordained that they exist. Paul explains to the Corinthian church, "There must also be factions among you, in order that those who are approved may have become evident among you" (1 Cor. 11:19). False factions will act as magnets to attract others who are false. In that indirect way they will help protect true believers by partly separating the chaff from the wheat.

But true believers who are carnal and worldly can also be attracted and corrupted, becoming grapes on thorn bushes and figs on thistles. Generally speaking, however, false prophets attract false believers, and in that way act as a sort of negative protection for the true church.

False prophets and their false followers do "not receive the love of the truth so as to be saved. And for this reason God will send upon them a deluding influence so that they might believe what is false, in order that they all may be judged who did not believe the truth, but took pleasure in wickedness" (2 Thess. 2:10-12). Ultimately, God makes sure that **every tree that does not bear good fruit is cut down and thrown into the fire** (cf. John 15:2, 6). Peter says such shepherds are "bringing swift destruction upon themselves" (2 Pet. 2:1; cf. Jer. 23:30-40).

Our Lord closes this potent section with an affirming repetition of verse 16, **so then, you will know them by their fruits.** Thus we are once again called to be discerning when listening to preachers who call us to the broad way that leads to death and hell.

Empty Words and Empty Hearts (7:21-29) ## 44

Not everyone who says to Me, "Lord, Lord," will enter the kingdom of heaven; but he who does the will of My Father who is in heaven. Many will say to Me on that day, "Lord, Lord, did we not prophesy in Your name, and in Your name cast out demons, and in Your name perform many miracles?" And then I will declare to them, "I never knew you; depart from Me, you who practice lawlessness."

Therefore everyone who hears these words of Mine, and acts upon them, may be compared to a wise man, who built his house upon the rock. And the rain descended, and the floods came, and the winds blew, and burst against that house; and yet it did not fall, for it had been founded upon the rock. And everyone who hears these words of Mine, and does not act upon them, will be like a foolish man, who built his house upon the sand. And the rain descended, and the floods came, and the winds blew, and burst against that house; and it fell, and great was its fall.

The result was that when Jesus had finished these words, the multitudes were amazed at His teaching; for He was teaching them as one having authority, and not as their scribes. (7:21-29)

Jesus is still giving the invitation of his sermon—calling people from false

473

religion to the true kingdom. He has said that few enter the narrow gate of salvation because first of all it must be found (v. 14), implying that it must be sought and searched for. No one stumbles into the kingdom inadvertently. Second, the narrow and demanding way of salvation is the complete opposite of the way of the world, which is broad, easy, and indulgent. Third, the narrow gate into the kingdom requires going through alone and naked, taking no possessions, no works, no pride, no self-righteousness. Fourth, as the Lord mentions in the parallel account in Luke 13:24, we must strive to enter in penitence and brokenness of heart. Fifth, false prophets must be avoided, because they deceive many people by luring them into the broad way that leads to destruction (vv. 15-20).

Now Jesus gives a final reason why so few enter the narrow gate of salvation: self-deception. J. C. Ryle says, "The Lord Jesus winds up the Sermon on the Mount by a passage of heart-piercing application. He turns from false prophets to false professors, from unsound teachers to unsound hearers" (*Expository Thoughts on the Gospel: St. Matthew* [London: James Clarke, 1965], pp. 69-70). Not only can false prophets deceive us about the way of salvation, but we can deceive ourselves. After warning us about false prophets, the Lord now warns men about themselves. Sinful man is biased in his own favor and, because of pride, tends to reject the true gospel.

The two categories of self-deception are those of mere verbal profession and of mere intellectual knowledge. The first, described in verses 21-23, involves those who say but do not do, and the second, described in verses 24-27, involves those who hear but do not do.

The Lord is not speaking to irreligious people, to atheists or agnostics. Nor is he speaking to pagans, heretics, or apostates. He is speaking specifically to people who are devotedly religious—but who are deluded in thinking they are on the road to heaven when they are really on the broad road to hell. They are not unlike those in the last days who Paul says will hold a form of godliness but will deny its power (2 Tim. 3:5).

Various polls in recent years have estimated that perhaps fifty percent of Americans identify themselves as born-again Christians. But on the basis of the Bible's description of true believers and the fact that few (cf. Matt. 7:14) really come on God's terms, those estimates could not be remotely correct. By scriptural standards, it is hard to believe that even half of the church members in the United States are true believers.

The New Testament not only gives extremely high standards for judging the true Christian life, but also gives many warnings about spiritual self-deception in regard to salvation. In Matthew 25 Jesus tells of the five foolish virgins who pretended devotion to the bridegroom but missed meeting him because of their unpreparedness (vv. 1-12), and of those professed believers (symbolized as goats) who are surprised that the Lord rejects them because they never truly served Him (vv. 32-33, 41-46).

What lulls people into such deception? First of all, many professed Christians—and even many true Christians—hold a false doctrine of assurance.

Often it is because the person who witnessed to them told them that all they had to do was make a profession of faith, walk an aisle, raise a hand, say a prayer, and never doubt what the Lord had done in their lives. Perhaps they have been taught that to ever doubt their salvation is to doubt God's Word and integrity. Unfortunately, many evangelists, pastors, and personal workers attempt to certify a person's salvation apart from the convicting work of the Holy Spirit and the evidence of fruit with continuance in obedience to the Word (John 8:31). But we have no right to assure a person of something we cannot be certain is true. God's own Holy Spirit will witness His reality to those who truly belong to Him (Rom. 8:14-16).

Peter makes clear that one's calling and choosing are made secure by increasing qualities of fruitfulness that demonstrate the genuineness of salvation and eliminate stumbling over doubt (2 Pet. 1:3-11). And our Lord teaches that some people appear saved, but are not (see Matt. 13:20-22). Quick and easy assurance can deceive.

A second contributor to self-deception is <u>failure of self-examination</u>. Through a faulty and presumptuous view of God's grace, some professed believers blithely go through life oblivious to and unconcerned about their sins. Yet the Lord tells His people to examine their lives each time they come to His table (1 Cor. 11:28). Paul tells us, "Test yourselves to see if your are in the faith; examine yourselves! Or do you not recognize this about yourselves, that Jesus Christ is in you—unless indeed you fail the test?" (2 Cor. 13:5). Such examination looks at the heart and the inner motives and desires to see if they are set toward God's holiness and glory. Even the weakest Christian has pure longings in his heart for righteousness—even though he lets his flesh hinder their fulfillment (Rom. 7:14-25).

John tells us, "If we say that we have no sin, we are deceiving ourselves, and the truth is not in us. If we confess our sins, He is faithful and righteous to forgive us our sins and to cleanse us from all unrighteousness" (<u>1 John 1:8-9</u>). A person who is not concerned about having his present sins cleansed has good reason to doubt that his past sin has been forgiven. A person who has no desire to come to the Lord for continued cleansing has reason to doubt that he ever came to the Lord to receive salvation.

When a couple lives together without being married, when a person practices homosexuality, is deceptive and dishonest in business, is hateful and vengeful, or habitually practices any sin without remorse or repentance, such persons cannot be Christian—no matter what sort of experience they claim to have had or what sort of testimony they now make. God's Word is explicit: "Do you not know that the unrighteous shall not inherit the kingdom of God? Do not be deceived; neither fornicators, nor idolaters, nor adulterers, nor effeminate, nor homosexuals, nor thieves, nor the covetous, nor drunkards, nor revilers, nor swindlers, shall inherit the kingdom of God" (1 Cor. 6:9-10). Again Paul warns, "For this you know with certainty, that no immoral or impure person or covetous man, who is an idolater, has an inheritance in the kingdom of Christ and God. Let no one deceive you with empty words, for because of these things the wrath of God comes upon the sons of disobedience" (Eph. 5:5-6). In each of those extremely somber warnings Paul pleads with his readers not to be deceived.

The person who professes to be a Christian but who habitually and unrepentantly continues in known sin makes out God to be liar, because His Word expressly denies that any such person belongs to Him (1 John 3:6-10).

A third cause of self-deception is inordinate concentration on religious activity. Attending church, hearing sermons, singing songs of the faith, reading the Bible, attending Bible studies, and many other perfectly good and helpful activities can actually insulate a person from the very God he is supposedly worshiping and serving. Those things can cause a believer to think he is being faithful and obedient, when in reality he may not be; and they can cause an unbeliever to think he is saved, when in reality he is not.

A fourth cause of self-deception is what may be called the fair exchange, or balancing out, approach. Instead of confessing and asking forgiveness for his sins, a person may give himself the benefit of the doubt and rationalize his salvation by thinking that the good things he does balance out the bad, that the positive cancels the negative. But in the first place, apart from God it is impossible to do anything that is truly good, because "there is none who does good, there is not even one," Paul tells us (Rom. 3:12), quoting David (Ps. 14:1-3; 53:1-3). In the second place, it is the sin itself—not an excess or imbalance of it—that separates us from God and brings death and damnation (Rom. 5:12; 6:23). Whatever good we might somehow accomplish would not cancel those consequences of sin, any more than eating right and exercising will save the life of a person infected with a deadly disease. His only hope is in receiving a cure for the disease, not in trying to balance off its deadly effect by keeping his body otherwise healthy. Isaiah said that the best deeds of men before God are as "a filthy garment," that is, a menstrual cloth (Isa. 64:6).

Apart from outright hypocrites and the blatantly disobedient, there are two other common kinds of deceived people who believe they are Christians when they are not. One is the superficial person, the one who has had little or no instruction in the gospel and who thinks that his attending Sunday school as a child, having been baptized, being a church member, or other such things put him in good standing with God.

The other type of person is much more knowledgeable about the Bible and the gospel, and is often heavily involved in church activities of various sorts. But he lives in a constant state of sinfulness, with no thought of confessing and forsaking his sin or of seeking after righteousness. He looks to feelings, experiences, healings, angels, earthly material blessings, promises, and a host of other external things for proof of his salvation. He is not concerned about decreasing sin or increasing righteousness. He is not concerned about God's commands, God's standards, or God's glory, but only what he can get out of God for himself. As Martyn Lloyd-Jones suggests, he is more concerned about the by-products of the faith than the fruit itself (*Studies in the Sermon on the Mount* [Grand Rapids: Eerdmans, 1977], 2:285).

This group includes those who are more committed to a denomination or Christian organization than to the Word of God. It includes those who are academically interested in theology—even orthodox, biblical theology—but not in obedience to the Bible on which that theology is based. It includes those who overemphasize and distort a particular aspect of biblical truth, to the exclusion and sometimes contradiction of other truths. It encompasses those who are overindulgent in the name of grace but lack penitence.

Just as there are many people who are deceived by the broad road that leads to destruction (Matt. 7:13), there are also many ways in which those people are deceived, of which the ones mentioned above are only a sampling. There is almost no limit to the means by which men can be deluded by Satan, by other men, and by themselves. In every case there is failure to come through the narrow gate with repentance, submission to the Lord, humility, and a desire for holiness. It is therefore of immeasurable importance to recognize and be on guard against beguilings of every sort. But the most important objective is not to identify all of the many deceitful ways but to find and follow the one true way.

The many delusions found in the broad way of destruction are evidenced in two basic manifestations, which Jesus focuses on here: empty words and works and empty hearts. Those in the first group make mere verbal profession of faith and works. Those in the second have mere intellectual knowledge of the gospel they hear. Those in the first group *say* but do not do; those in the second *hear* but do not do.

Empty Words

Not everyone who says to Me, "Lord, Lord," will enter the kingdom of heaven; but he who does the will of My Father who is in heaven. Many will say to Me on that day, "Lord, Lord, did we not prophesy in Your name, and in Your name cast out demons, and in Your name perform many miracles?" And then I will declare to them, "I never knew you; depart from Me, you who practice lawlessness." (7:21-23)

A Jew could use the term **lord** simply as a title of respect and honor, given to any political, military, or religious leader, including teachers. But for those people to say, **Lord, Lord,** suggests much more than human respect, as their following comments make clear. That they claimed to have prophesied, cast out demons, and performed miracles in Jesus' **name** indicates they acknowledged Him as **Lord** in a supernatural way. **Lord** was a common Jewish substitute title for Jehovah, or Yahweh, which name they considered too holy to utter. Therefore to address Jesus as **Lord** was to address Him as the one true God. To address Him as **Lord, Lord** was to add a spirit of intense zeal to demonstrate strength of devotion and dedication. In verse 22, the three references to **your name** are emphatic and convey the significance of who He is. Jesus is therefore talking about those who make a profession of faith in Him.

These people claim to be followers of the God of Israel, the Creator and

Lord of all earth. Not only that, but they acknowledge Jesus Himself to be divine, because they **will say to Me** [that is, to Jesus] **on that day,** "**Lord, Lord.**" And the fact that they have claimed so many outstanding works in His **name** tells us they are especially fervent religious workers.

The final judgment, **on that day,** is presented here in general, without reference to the distinction between the separate tribunals for believers (2 Cor. 5:10) and for unbelievers (Rev. 20:11-15). **That day** is a frequently used reference to the era of divine judgment known throughout Scripture as "the day of the Lord" (Isa. 2:12; Joel 2:1; Mal. 4:5; 1 Thess. 5:2; 2 Pet. 3:10; etc.). Matthew uses **that day** here and in 24:36, where it refers to the second coming of the Savior. It is noteworthy that the second coming parable of the ten virgins (Matt. 25:1-13) makes reference to those virgins who are shut out of the kingdom as crying out, "Lord, Lord," to which He also replies, "I do not know you" (vv. 11-12). These few passages together reveal that Matthew has in mind the unspecified season of judgment that will accompany the return of Jesus Christ.

That some of the ones Jesus is talking about here are true believers is shown by His saying, **Not everyone** and **many.** The same **many** who entered the wide gate (v. 13) are now at the end of the broad way facing the Judge. For some people, however, the claim **Lord, Lord** will be legitimate, because Jesus will have indeed been their Lord on earth and they will have served Him genuinely.

If Jesus is speaking about the great white throne judgment, many professing believers who are *not* genuine will already have spent centuries in hell awaiting their final judgment (see Luke 16:23-26; Acts 1:25). Because they were so zealous and active and diligent in religious work—in the Lord's own **name**—they are incredulous that they are even standing before Christ to be judged. Even at that time they will address Christ as **Lord** and speak to Him in desperation with the greatest respect and sincerity. Their words and their works will seem impressive to them, but their lives will not support the claim of their lips. In Luke 6:46 Jesus said, "Why do you call Me, 'Lord, Lord,' and do not do what I say?"

It is not the one who simply claims the Lord, but the one **who does the will of My Father who is in heaven** who is saved. The issue is obedience to the Word of God. "If you abide in My Word, then you are truly disciples of Mine," Jesus said (John 8:31; cf. 6:66-69; Matt. 24:13; Col. 1:22-23; 1 Tim. 4:16; Heb. 3:14; 10:38-39; 1 John 2:19). Salvation and obedience to the will of God are inseparable, as the writer of Hebrews makes clear: "He became to all those who obey Him the source of eternal salvation" (5:9; cf. Rom. 1:5; 6:16; 15:18; 16:19, 26; 1 Pet. 1:2, 22).

Jesus' word to the disobedient claimers will be, **I never knew you; depart from Me, you who practice lawlessness.** All their words of respect and honor and all their works of dedication and devotion will be declared empty and worthless. They may have had God's name in their mouths, but rebellion was in their hearts.

His saying, **I never knew you,** does not, of course, mean that Jesus was unaware of their identity. He knows quite well who these persons are; they are deceived professing Christians whose lives were spent in the **practice** [of] **lawlessness.**

"To know" was a Hebrew idiom that represented intimate relations. It was frequently used of marital intimacy (see Gen. 4:1, 17; etc.; where "had relations" is literally "knew," as in the KJV). It was also used of God's special intimacy with His chosen people Israel and with all of those who trust in Him. In a unique and beautiful way the Lord "knows those who take refuge in Him" (Nah. 1:7). The Good Shepherd knows His sheep intimately (John 10:1-14).

Jesus therefore will say to those who claim Him but never trusted in Him, **I never knew you.** "I have never known you as My disciples, and you have never known Me as your Lord and Savior. We have no intimate part of each other. You chose your kingdom, and it was not My kingdom." **Depart from Me** is the resulting final sentence to hell, and is identical in thought to the judgment of Matthew 25:41 at the Lord's return: "Depart from Me, accursed ones, into the eternal fire which has been prepared for the devil and his angels." The lake of fire awaits all false professors (Rev. 20:15).

Practice lawlessness is a present participle in the Greek, indicating continuous, regular action, and identifies the unforgiven sin and unrighteous life patterns of those claimers of salvation. **You** continually and habitually **practice lawlessness** is the idea. Profession of Christ and **practice** of **lawlessness** are totally incompatible. A good tree *cannot* bear that sort of fruit (Matt. 7:18; John 3:4-10).

A good tree not only can but will bear good fruit, and a life that professes to be Christian, but in no way reflects Christ's righteousness, has no part in Him. That kind of profession comes from the kind of faith that has no works and is dead (James 2:17). It is the demon faith James refers to (James 2:19), which is orthodox and accurate, but unholy. In the ultimate and most tragic sense such a false profession is to take the Lord's name in vain. "The blasphemy of the sanctuary," G. Campbell Morgan observed, "is far more awful than the blasphemy of the slum" (*The Gospel According to Matthew* [New York: Revell, 1929], p. 79). Mere professed devotion to Christ is but another Judas kiss.

The Lord knows well that even His most faithful disciples will fail, stumble, and fall into sin. Otherwise He would not have told us to pray, "Forgive us our debts" (Matt. 6:12). And when "we confess our sins, He is faithful and righteous to forgive us our sins and to cleanse us from all unrighteousness" (1 John 1:9). No Christian is sinless, but the fact that we continually confess our sins, seek the Lord's forgiveness, and long for righteousness (Matt. 5:6) is evidence that we belong to Him. God's will may not be the *perfection* of the true believer's life, but it is the *direction* of it.

Those who continually **practice lawlessness**, however, give evidence that they do *not* belong to Christ. They do not recognize or confess their sins or hunger for righteousness, because they have no part of Christ. All religious activity, no matter how orthodox and fervent, that does not result from obedience to the lordship of Christ and the pursuit of His glory is rebellion against the law of God, which demands heart conformity.

This passage is all the more amazing when one considers the impressive works that those professing believers claim to have accomplished. They tell the Lord, **Did we not prophesy in Your name, and in Your name cast out demons, and in Your name perform many miracles?**

As already mentioned, we know from verse 21 (**not everyone**) that some of these claims will be made by genuine believers. And because Jesus does not question the factualness of the claims, it is possible that actual prophecies were made, demons cast out, and some kind of miracles performed even by those who were not genuine believers.

There are three possible explanations for the claim of the false believers. It may be that they were allowed to do those amazing works by God's power. God put words in Balaam's mouth, even though that prophet was false and wicked (Num. 23:5). King Saul, after he became apostate had the "Spirit of God [come] upon him mightily, so that he prophesied" (1 Sam. 10:10). The wicked high priest Caiaphas unwittingly and unintentionally "prophesied that Jesus was going to die for the nation" (John 11:51).

A second possibility is that those amazing acts were accomplished by Satan's power. Jesus predicted that "false Christs and false prophets will arise and will show great signs and wonders, so as to mislead, if possible, even the elect" (Matt. 24:24). The unbelieving sons of Sceva, for example, were Jewish exorcists, who made their living casting out demons (Acts 19:13-14). Mark 9:38-40 tells of someone outside the apostles casting out demons. Paul promises false signs in the last days, lying wonders of Satan (2 Thess. 2:8-10). Acts 8:11 describes the work of a satanic sorcerer. Today there are miracle workers, healers, and exorcists who claim to work for Jesus Christ but are satanic deceivers.

A third possibility is that some of the claims were simply false. The prophecies, exorcisms, and miracles were fake and contrived. No doubt all three will be represented.

But whether the works themselves were done in God's power or not, the people who did them did not belong to Him and did not truly recognize Him as **Lord,** despite their profession. They had no part in His kingdom or its righteousness, and those works, whether genuine or false, divine or Satanic, would stand them in no good stead before the judgment seat of Christ.

The words of an engraving from the cathedral of Lübeck, Germany, beautifully reflect our Lord's teaching here:

> Thus speaketh Christ our Lord to us, You call Me master and obey Me not, you call Me light and see Me not, you call Me the way and walk Me not, you call Me life and live Me not, you call Me wise and follow Me not, you call Me fair and love Me not, you call Me rich and ask Me not, you call Me eternal and seek Me not, if I condemn thee, blame Me not.

EMPTY HEARTS

Therefore everyone who hears these words of Mine, and acts upon them, may be compared to a wise man, who built his house upon the rock. And the rain descended, and the floods came, and the winds blew, and burst against that house; and yet it did not fall, for it had been founded upon the rock. And everyone who hears these words of Mine, and does not act upon them, will be like a foolish man, who built his house upon the sand. And the rain descended, and the floods came, and the winds blew, and burst against that house; and it fell, and great was its fall. (7:24-27)

The second evidence that the many (vv. 13, 22) who are in the broad way will not enter the kingdom is that their lives are not built on the foundation of Christ and His Word. Again Jesus picks up the theme of man's own righteousness, the righteousness that is totally unacceptable to God and that will in no way qualify a person for His kingdom (Matt. 5:20).

In the first illustration (vv. 21-23) we see a contrast between the true and false verbal professions of faith and good works. Here we see contrasts between obedient and disobedient hearers. Both groups hear God's true Word, but some hear and obey, and some hear and disobey; some turn their trust to God's righteousness, and some continue trusting in their own, though that does not become visible until the judgment.

The implication is that even those who disobey believe that they belong to Christ and make a convincing profession of faith in Him. They hear God's Word and recognize it as God's Word, but wrongly believe that simply knowing and recognizing it are enough to please God and guarantee them a place in His kingdom. Like those who say, "Lord, Lord," and do amazing religious works but really "practice lawlessness," the false hearers build their religious house, but are self-deceived as to its viability.

In the illustration of those who make false professions, the true believers are mentioned only by implication ("not everyone who says to me," v. 21). In the illustration of the hearers and builders, however, both the true and the false believers are clearly described. In these two groups we see many similarities but also some radical differences.

SIMILARITIES

First of all, both builders have heard the gospel. **Everyone who hears these words of Mine** applies both to the **wise man** (v. 24) and to the **foolish man** (v. 26). They both know the way of salvation.

Second, they both proceed to build a **house** after they have heard the way of salvation. The **wise man** builds his house, which represents his life, on **these words of Mine**. The implication is that the **foolish man**, although he **does not act**

upon Christ's **words**, thinks that his **house** is secure simply because he has heard and acknowledged the **words**. He believes the life he lives is Christian and therefore pleasing to God. He does not intentionally build a **house** he thinks is going to **fall**. Both builders have confidence their houses will stand; but one man's confidence is in the Lord and the other man's is in himself.

Third, both builders build their houses in the same general location, evidenced by their apparently being hit by the same storm. In other words, the outward circumstances of their lives were essentially the same. One had no advantage over the other. They lived in the same town and possibly attended the same church, heard the same preaching, went to the same Bible study, and fellowshipped with the same friends.

Fourth, the implication is that they built the same kind of **house**. Outwardly their houses were very much alike. From all appearances the **foolish man** lived much in the same way as the **wise man**. We might say they were both religious, theologically orthodox, moral, served in the church, supported it financially, and were responsible citizens of the community. They seemed to believe alike and live alike.

DIFFERENCES

The differences between the two builders and the two houses they built were not noticeable from the outside. But they were immeasurably more important than the similarities. The key is to understand that one does **act upon** God's Word (obedience) and the other **does not act upon** His Word (disobedience). One builds using the divine specifications, the other uses his own.

By far the greatest difference between the specifications of these builders and the way they build is in the foundations they laid. The **wise man . . . built his house upon the rock**, whereas the **foolish man . . . built his house upon the sand**.

Petra (**rock**) does not mean a stone or even a boulder, but a great outcropping of rock, a large expanse of bedrock. It is solid, stable, and unmovable. **Sand**, by contrast, is loose, unstable, and extremely movable. The land agents selling lots on the sand are the false prophets Jesus has just warned about (vv. 15-20).

The scribes and Pharisees had a complex and involved set of religious traditions which they regarded as having great value before God. But all those traditions were external, superficial, and unstable. They had no spiritual or moral substance or stability. They were shifting **sand**, composed entirely of the opinions, speculations, and standards of men. Those who created and followed them took no account of obedience to God's Word, purity of the heart, spirituality of the soul, or integrity of behavior. Their only concern was for appearance, the compelling desire to be seen and "honored by men" (Matt. 6:2).

As Arthur Pink says of such people,

They bring their bodies to the house of prayer but not their souls; they worship with their mouths, but not "in spirit and in truth." They are sticklers for immersion or early morning communion, yet take no thought about keeping their hearts with all diligence. They boast of their orthodoxy; but disregard the precepts of Christ. Multitudes of professing Christians abstain from external acts of violence, yet hesitate not to rob their neighbors of a good name by spreading evil reports against them. They contribute regularly to the "pastor's salary," but shrink not from misrepresenting their goods and cheating their customers, persuading themselves that "business is business." They have more regard for the laws of man than those of God, for His fear is not before their eyes.

But the **wise man** builds **his house upon a rock**, and I believe the **rock** spoken of here is God's Word—**these words of Mine**. This builder is one who hears Jesus' **words . . . and acts on them**. Building on the **rock** is equivalent to obeying God's Word.

After Peter confessed, "Thou art the Christ, the Son of the living God," Jesus said, "flesh and blood did not reveal this to you, but My Father who is in heaven. And I also say to you that you are Peter, and upon this rock I will build My church" (Matt. 16:16-18). This "rock" (*petra*) is the same **rock** as that in Matthew 7:24-25. It is the bedrock of God's Word, His divine revelation. It is the divine revelation such as was given to Peter by the "Father who is heaven," and is the only **rock** on which the Christian life can be built.

The mark of true discipleship is not simply hearing and believing, but believing and doing. The true disciples of Jesus Christ, the only true converts of the gospel, are those who are "doers of the word, and not merely hearers who delude themselves. For if anyone is a hearer of the word and not a doer, he is like a man who looks at his natural face in a mirror; for once he has looked at himself and gone away, he has immediately forgotten what kind of person he was" (James 1:22-24). In other words, a person who professes to know Christ but does not obey Christ, has no lasting image of what the new life is all about. He glimpses Christ, and glimpses what Christ can do for him, but his image of Christ and of the new life in Christ soon fade. His experience with the gospel is shallow, superficial, and short-lived.

"By this we know that we have come to know Him, if we keep His commandments," John declares. "The one who says, 'I have come to know Him,' and does not keep His commandments, is a liar, and the truth is not in him; but whoever keeps His word, in him the love of God has truly been perfected. By this we know that we are in Him: the one who says he abides in Him ought himself to walk in the same manner as He walked" (1 John 2:3-6). Paul powerfully and convincingly asserts the same thing: "To those who are defiled and unbelieving, nothing is pure, but both their mind and their conscience are defiled. They profess to know God, but by their deeds they deny Him, being detestable and disobedient, and worthless for any good deed" (Titus 1:15-16).

To profess knowledge of God and His truth but not follow God obediently and live His truth is to be deceived. It is to have entered by the wide gate and to be walking on the broad way that leads to destruction. It is to have a **house** built **upon the sand**.

The only validation we can ever have of salvation is a life of obedience. That is the only proof Scripture mentions of our being under the lordship of Jesus Christ. Obedience is the sine qua non of salvation.

The **house** built on the **rock** is the life of obedience, the life Jesus has been explaining throughout the Sermon on the Mount. It is the life that has a scriptural view of itself, as described in the Beatitudes. It is the life that has a scriptural view of the world, and sees itself as God's means for preserving and enlightening the world while not being a part of it. It is the life that has the divine view of Scripture and that determines not to alter God's Word in the slightest degree. It is a life that is concerned about internal righteousness rather than external form. It is a life that has a godly attitude toward what is said and what is done, toward motives, things, money, and other people. It is a life of genuineness rather than hypocrisy, and of God's righteousness rather than self-righteousness.

The **house** built on the **rock** is the life that empties itself of self-righteousness and pride, that is overwhelmed by and mourns over its own sin, that makes the maximum effort to enter the narrow gate and be faithful in the narrow way of Christ and His Word. Such a builder does not build his life or place his hope on ceremony, ritual, visions, experiences, feelings, or miracles but on the Word of God and that alone.

The **sand** is composed of human opinions, attitudes, and wills, which are always shifting and always unstable. To build on **sand** is to build on self-will, self-fulfillment, self-purpose, self-sufficiency, self-satisfaction, and self-righteousness. To build on **sand** is to be unteachable, to be "always learning and never able to come to the knowledge of the truth" (2 Tim. 3:7).

To build the **house** of one's life on the **sand** is to follow the ultimate deception of Satan, which is to make a person believe he is saved when he is not. Because that person is under the delusion that he is safe, he sees no reason either to resist Satan or to seek God.

Besides the great difference in the foundations they lay, the **wise man** builds his **house** the hard way, whereas the **foolish man** builds his the easy way. The one chooses the narrow gate and the other the broad. The one searches carefully for a solid foundation of **rock** on which to build; the other simply finds a section of sand in a desirable location and starts to build.

The easy way is attractive for several reasons, the first of which is that it is quick. The foolish person is always in a hurry. His first desire is to please himself, and he takes the shortest route to that end. In church work he wants the quick, easy solution, the one that causes the least controversy and hassle, with no consideration of how the solution may square with Scripture. He is for easy evangelism, easy believism, and easy discipleship, because they bring quick results that are simple to see and measure. He has no time for searching the Word for the right truth with which to witness, or for soul-searching or sound conviction. He sees a verbal profession, a card signed, or a prayer prayed as sufficient to bring a person to Christ. He is perfectly willing to declare a person saved without his having any awareness that he is lost.

The foolish person also likes the easy way because he is basically superficial. That which is superficial requires little planning, little effort, little care to detail, and little concern for quality or standards. The person who is superficial looks for what is pleasing rather than for what is right, for what is enjoyable rather than for what is true, for what satisfies himself rather than what satisfies God. He looks to Christianity for instant results, instant pleasure, and instant rewards. He cares much about spiritual "highs" but nothing about spiritual "depths."

Of his own day Charles Spurgeon wrote,

> Want of depth, want of sincerity, want of zeal in religion—this is the want of our times. Want of an eye to God in religion, lack of sincere dealing with one's soul, neglect of using the lancet with our hearts, neglect of the search warrant which God gives out against sin, carelessness concerning living upon Christ; much reading about Him, much talking about Him, but too little feeding on His flesh and drinking of His blood—these are the causes of a tottering profession and a baseless hope. (Cited by Pink in *An Exposition of the Sermon on the Mount* [Grand Rapids: Baker, 1974], p. 423)

In His parable of the sower Jesus spoke of the person who "hears the word, and immediately receives it with joy; yet he has no firm root in himself, but is only temporary, and when affliction or persecution arises because of the word, immediately he falls away" (Matt. 13:20-21). He receives quickly and falls away quickly. He likes God's promises but not His requirements.

The **foolish man** always has excuses when Jesus makes demands on his life. When he first hears the gospel he says to the Lord, "I will follow You wherever You go." But when he hears, "The foxes have holes, and the birds of the air have nests, but the Son of Man has nowhere to lay His head," he suddenly remembers that he has to bury his father (that is, await his father's death in order to receive the inheritance) or "say good-bye to those at home." Such a person who puts his hand to the plow and then looks back, Jesus says, is "not fit for the kingdom of God" (Luke 9:57-62).

The rain, the floods, and **the winds** do not represent specific types of physical judgment but simply sum up God's final judgment. The storm is the ultimate test that the **house** of every human life will face. As the angel of death in Egypt passed by the blood-sprinkled homes of Israel's children while slaughtering all the first-born in the rest, so the same judgment that harmlessly passes over the **house** that is **founded upon the rock** of Christ and His Word will utterly destroy the one that is **built . . . upon the sand**—which is anything other than Christ and His Word.

Whether one's religion is true or false, one day it is going to be tried. And that trial will prove with absolute finality what is wheat and what is chaff, who are sheep and who are goats, who have entered by the narrow gate to walk the narrow way and who have entered by the wide gate to walk the broad way.

Those whose houses are on the **rock** of Jesus Christ and His Word will be delivered "from the wrath to come" (1 Thess. 1:10), and will only have praise from God, says Paul (1 Cor. 4:5). That wrath is ultimately poured out at the judgment at the great white throne, which John describes in Revelation 20. "And I saw the dead, the great and the small, standing before the throne, and books were opened; and another book was opened, which is the book of life; and the dead were judged from the things which were written in the books, according to their deeds. . . . And if anyone's name was not found written in the book of life, he was thrown into the lake of fire" (vv. 12, 15).

The only difference about the storm in regard to the **wise** and the **foolish** men is in the way it affects their houses. The **house** of the **wise man** may have been shaken, **yet it did not fall, for it had been founded upon the rock.**

But when the same adversity came upon the **house** of the **foolish man** it disintegrated—**and great was its fall.** It was utterly demolished, leaving its builder with absolutely nothing. That is the destiny of those who build on the **sand** of man's ideas, man's philosophies, and man's religions. It is not that such people will have little left, but nothing left. Their way is not an inferior way to God, but no way to God at all. Always and inevitably it leads to destruction; its absolute destiny is to **fall.**

The greatest problem in evangelism is not follow-up but conversion. Right follow-up is not nearly so difficult as right conversion. Follow-up is the hardest when conversion is the easiest, because easy conversion is frequently no conversion. It results from seed falling on rocky soil, where it springs up quickly and dies just as quickly. The unconverted are indeed hard to follow up, whereas those who have truly come to Christ are eager to learn from His Word and associate with His people.

I heard of a large church that one year claimed 28,000 conversions, 9,600 baptisms, and 123 additions to the church! After reflecting on those figures, one of the church staff members decided that something was terribly wrong and decided to minister elsewhere. It is quite impossible that so many true conversions would produce so few Christians who would want to identify with their new brothers and sisters in the Lord.

The **wise man** builds carefully, because there is substance and great importance to what he is building. In the parallel passage in Luke, Jesus says, he "dug deep and laid a foundation upon the rock" (6:48). He is not satisfied with superficial confessions of faith, with quickie conversions that involve no repentance, no mourning over sin, and no despairing of self.

Knowing that he owes everything to the Lord, this man desires to give Him his maximum effort. After he does everything his Lord commands he declares that he has only done his duty (Luke 17:10). Yet he does not consider his work for the Lord burdensome. For one thing, the work we truly do for the Lord is the work He does through us. For another, the work that is truly done for the Lord is done out of love, not out of compulsion or fear. As the anonymous writer of the hymn "How Firm a Foundation" says, the Lord promises this man:

> The soul that on Jesus hath leaned for repose,
> I will not, I will not desert to his foes;
> That soul, though all hell should endeavor to shake,
> I'll never, no, never, no, never forsake!

The most tragic difference between the builders is in their final destinies. Jesus' unequaled and unparalleled sermon masterpiece ends with a devastating warning of judgment. Its final words are: **and great was its fall.** The bottom line of the gospel for those who reject Christ is not that they forfeit a great deal of blessing or even that they forfeit a life of eternal bliss with God in heaven—though those things are absolutely true. The bottom line for those who reject Christ is that they are destined for everlasting torment, destruction that keeps on destroying forever. To reject Christ is to look forward to being "cast into hell, where their worm does not die, and the fire is not quenched" (Mark 9:47-48). Because of this inevitability every professing Christian needs to hear the words of the Holy Spirit through James: "Prove yourselves doers of the word, and not merely hearers who delude themselves" (James 1:22). As we learn from Proverbs, "There is a kind who is pure in his own eyes, yet is not washed from his filthiness" (30:12).

RESPONSE TO THE SERMON

The result was that when Jesus had finished these words, the multitudes were amazed at His teaching; for He was teaching them as one having authority, and not as their scribes. (7:28-29)

The response to this most magnificent discourse ever given was as astounding in a negative way as the sermon itself was in a positive way. It seems certain that some of those in **the multitudes** who were there that day believed in Jesus. But the number who then entered the narrow gate proved what He had said: "few are those who find it" (7:14).

But any conversions that may have taken place are not reported. We are only told that **the multitudes were amazed at His teaching** (cf. John 7:46). *Ekplēssō* (**were amazed**) literally means to be struck out of oneself, and was used figuratively of being struck in the mind, that is, of being astounded or beside oneself. The crowd was totally dumbfounded by the power of what Jesus said. They had never heard such comprehensive, insightful words of wisdom, depth, insight, and profundity. They had never heard such straightforward and fearless denunciation of the scribes and Pharisees or such a black and white presentation of the way of salvation. They had never heard such a fearful warning about the consequences of turning away from God. They had never heard such a powerful and demanding description of true righteousness or such a relentless description and condemnation of self-righteousness.

But the most remarkable thing that struck the audience that day was that Jesus **was teaching them as one having authority, and not as their scribes.** **Authority** (*exousia*) has to do with power and privilege, and is a key word in Matthew's presentation of Jesus' kingship (9:1-8; 21:23-27; 28:18). In the New Testament it is used for the power that proves and reflects the sovereignty of Jesus. The **scribes** quoted others to lend authority to their teachings, but Jesus quoted only God's Word and spoke as the final **authority** on truth. He spoke eternal truth simply, directly, with love (in contrast to the bitter hatred of the Pharisees), and without hesitation or consultation. That astounded the crowd.

All of those things were important for them to hear, and it was entirely appropriate, in fact unavoidable, that they should be **amazed,** because **His teaching** was indeed amazing. But what they needed was not amazement but belief, not astonishment but obedience. Jesus did not tell them all of those things for their amazement, or even simply for their information, but for their salvation. He did not intend merely to show them the narrow gate and the narrow way, but pleaded with them to *enter* that gate and to follow that way, which He would make accessible by paying the penalty for their sins.

But most of the people only watched and listened, only heard and considered—but did not decide. Even by not deciding, however, they decided. For whatever reasons—possibly for no conscious reason at all—they decided to stay on the broad road.

C. S. Lewis gives a remarkable illustration from his own life of what the attitude is of many who hear the gospel:

> When I was a child I often had toothache, and I knew that if I went to my mother she would give me something which would deaden the pain for that night and let me get to sleep. But I did not go to my mother—at least, not till the pain became very bad. And the reason I did not go was this. I did not doubt she would give me the aspirin: but I knew she would also do something else. I knew she would take me to the dentist next morning. I could not get what I wanted out of her without getting something more, which I did not want. I wanted immediate relief from pain: but I could not get it without having my teeth set permanently right. And I knew those dentists; I knew they started fiddling about with all sorts of other teeth which had not yet begun to ache. They would not let sleeping dogs lie. (*Mere Christianity* [New York: Macmillan, 1977], p. 177)

It is that very sort of thinking that keeps many people out of the kingdom: the price is more than they want to pay. Lewis goes on to say, in the imagined words of Christ, "You have free will, and if you choose, You can push Me away. But if you do not push Me away, understand that I am going to see this job through. . . . I will never rest, nor let you rest, until you are literally perfect—until My Father can say without reservation that He is well pleased with you, as He said He was well pleased with Me" (p. 158).

That is the decision the Lord demands before He can turn empty hearts, with their empty words and empty works, into full hearts that produce the good works for which they are recreated. It is God's great desire that no person perish and that every person "come to repentance" (2 Pet. 3:9), that he might "be filled up to all the fulness of God" (Eph. 3:16-19). That only became possible through the Savior's death and resurrection, which climaxed His work for sinful man and will be the great conclusion to Matthew's good news.

Bibliography

Barclay, William. *The Beatitudes and the Lord's Prayer for Everyman*. New York: Harper & Row, 1964.

_____. *The Gospel of Matthew*, vol. 1. Philadelphia: Westminster, 1958.

Boice, James Montgomery. *The Sermon on the Mount*. Grand Rapids: Zondervan, 1972.

Broadus, John A. *Commentary on the Gospel of Matthew*. Valley Forge: Judson, 1886.

Eerdman, Charles R. *The Gospel of Matthew*. Philadelphia: Westminster, 1966.

Gaebelein, Arno C. *The Gospel of Matthew*. Neptune, N.J.: Loizeaux, 1961.

Hendriksen, William. *New Testament Commentary: Exposition of the Gospel According to Matthew*. Grand Rapids: Baker, 1973.

Lange, John Peter. *Commentary on the Holy Scriptures: Matthew*. Grand Rapids: Zondervan, n.d.

Lenski, R. D. H. *The Interpretation of St. Matthew's Gospel*. Minneapolis: Augsburg, 1964.

Lloyd-Jones, D. Martyn. *Studies in the Sermon on the Mount*. Grand Rapids: Eerdmans, 1977.

Morgan, G. Campbell. *The Gospel According to Matthew*. Old Tappan, N.J.: Revell, 1939.

Pentecost, J. Dwight. *The Sermon on the Mount*. Portland: Multnomah, 1980.

Pink, Arthur W. *An Exposition of the Sermon on the Mount.* Grand Rapids: Baker, 1953.

Plummer, Alfred. *An Exegetical Commentary on the Gospel According to St. Matthew.* Grand Rapids: Eerdmans, 1963.

Sanders, J. Oswald. *Bible Studies in Matthew's Gospel.* Grand Rapids: Zondervan, 1973.

Tasker, R. V. G. *The Gospel According to St. Matthew.* Grand Rapids: Eerdmans, 1977.

Watson, Thomas. *The Beatitudes.* Carlisle, Pa.: The Banner of Truth Trust, 1975.

Indexes

Index of Hebrew/Aramaic Words

Index of Greek Words

Index of Scripture

Index of Subjects